PSYCHOLOGY FOR TEACHING

PSYCHOLOGY

FOR TEACHING

George J. Mouly

Florida International University

Allyn and Bacon, Inc.
Boston/ London/ Sydney/ Toronto

ACKNOWLEDGEMENTS: Photographs on pp. 157, 288, and 307 by Bobbi Carrey; p. 464 by Pat Coffey; pp. 28 and 88 by Rick Friedman; p. 12 by Julie O'Neil; p. 326 by Michael Serino; p.264 ©Frank Siteman MCMLXXX; pp. 75, 144, 357, 372, 426, and 434 by David S. Strickler; p. 31 by Richard Wood; all courtesy of The Picture Cube.

Photographs on pp. 16, 59, 121, 131, 340, 391, and 407 by Joe DiDio, courtesy of The National Education Association.

Photograph on p. 205 by Anthony Taro; p. 230 by Jonathan A. Meyers; p. 487 by F. Jenney.

Portions of this book first appeared in *Psychology for Effective Teaching,* Third Edition, by George J. Mouly, copyright © 1973, 1968, 1960, by Holt, Rinehart and Winston, Inc.

Library of Congress Cataloging in Publication Data

Mouly, George J.
~~Psychology for the classroom teacher~~.

Bibliography: p.
Includes indexes.
1. Learning, Psychology of.   2. Learning—Philosophy.
3. Teaching.   I. Title.
LB1060.M68   370.15′23   81-10933
ISBN 0-205-07697-1 (pbk.)   AACR2

Printed in the United States of America
10 9 8 7 6 5 4 3 2 1   87 86 85 84 83 82

Contents

Part Three   The Teaching-Learning Process   211

8   Nature and Conditions of Learning   213

9   Guiding the Learning Process   237

10 Classroom Management 275

15 Personal and Social Adjustment

16 Mental Health in the Classroom

Preface

A course in educational psychology as part of the teacher-education sequence attempts to provide the student with insights into those psychological principles on which effective classroom practices can be based. To serve its purpose, it must promote a thorough grasp of the basic facts, principles, theories, and viewpoints of psychology that have a bearing on the successful operation of the classroom in all its implications. These, in turn, must have a sound basis in research, logic, and other systematic approaches to dependable knowledge.

The text in such a course must orient the student toward this knowledge while at the same time emphasizing its empirical and theoretical origin as the means of clarifying its validity and the theoretical perspective from which it is to be appraised. It must rest on a firm psychological foundation as the ultimate source of ever-more precise and dependable answers. On the other hand, it must also emphasize the tentativeness of scientific generalizations, particularly those of the social sciences where the complexity of human nature makes for numerous gaps, inconsistencies, and the possibility of alternative interpretations—and especially it must emphasize that even rigorous research findings do not lead directly to unequivocal pedagogical prescriptions.

A certain degree of simplicity is in order in any introductory text. Certainly a deliberate attempt should be made to keep the style of writing clear and direct and to avoid disputes over complex technicalities that have no functional relationship to the work of the classroom. On the other hand, the treatment must not do violence to the natural complexity of human behavior. This is no time for simplistic generalizations about people and recipes for handling them. Rather, it must provide a sound basis for effective operation in the classroom and a firm foundation for more advanced work.

The vast amount of psychological material bearing on the work of classroom teachers makes it imperative that authors be highly selective in the choice of content to be included in an introductory text. The primary criterion in this selectivity undoubtedly should be its functionality from the standpoint of dealing with youngsters in dynamic interaction with their environment. However, functionality is not to be equated with practicality at the level of rules of thumb to be applied mechanically and routinely; neither can it be conceived as a matter of providing a specific answer to each specific problem to be encountered in the classroom. On the contrary, prospective teachers must focus on broad principles and overall theoretical perspectives that will not only educe meaningfulness out of the confusion of otherwise unorganized facts but will also enable them to deal with insight with the myriad situations that inevitably characterize imaginative teaching.

The present edition has undergone a major change from its predecessor. It has, for example, achieved a better balance between humanism and behaviorism. The author still believes that humanism—with its concern for the dignity of the individual child and a need to set him or her on a spiral of self-actualization—has a great deal to contribute to the education of future teachers. The author also continues to favor a cognitive approach, particularly as it relates to the learning of meaningful verbal materials, which must necessarily be of prime interest in the classroom. On the other hand, there is a growing recognition that educational psychology must focus not only on *learning* but also on teaching—not only on what the child must do if he or she is to learn effectively but equally on what teachers must do if effective learning is indeed to take place. This, in turn, emphasizes the obvious merits of the behavioristic position, particularly as it relates to the technology of instruction, a point of obvious relevance in the education of prospective teachers.

In comparison to its predecessors, the present revision reflects a better balance between the humanistic (cognitive) and the behavioristic position, between the psychology of learning and the technology of instruction, between theory and practice, between understandings and insights and their classroom implications. More specifically, it has telescoped the determinants of human behavior and self-actualization (chapters 3 and 4) into a single chapter. It has correspondingly added a chapter on instructional objectives and a major section on instructional strategies, including the views of Ausubel, Bruner, Gagné, and the humanists, as well as an overview of the Montessori school, open education, mastery learning, and "packaged" instruction. It has also telescoped the three chapters on physical, socioemotional, and cognitive development into one and has combined classroom motivation and discipline into a single chapter entitled "Classroom Management." It has also shortened the three chapters on attitudes, adjustment, and mental health and eliminated the last chapter of the previous edition.

Each chapter contains a list of related readings to complement the materials presented, a number of questions, suggested projects, and a short self-test to help students assess their grasp of the chapter's contents. It is hoped that students will use these materials. It is also expected that the textbook materials will be supplemented by classroom visits, films and other direct and indirect contacts with children.

Although the text is the work of a single author, many persons have contributed directly and indirectly to its completion. Many have been cited in the references; to them and their publishers, the author expresses his appreciation. Special thanks go to colleagues, former students, and numerous others whose criticisms of the previous editions and of the present draft have been most helpful.

PART ONE

The Scientific Basis for Educational Practice

Presents the scientific foundation for and the perspective from which the content of educational psychology is to be approached if the latter is indeed to make a meaningful contribution to educational practice.

1 Psychology and the Classroom Teacher

Discusses the contribution of educational psychology to the effectiveness of educational practice. The emphasis is on its dual responsibility to both learning and teaching.

2 Educational Objectives

Emphasizes the importance of clear-cut objectives as a guide to effective teaching but also cautions against the misuse of behavioral objectives and accountability.

3 Theoretical Perspective

Presents a theoretical perspective from which the contents of educational psychology can be interpreted as the basis for understanding and evaluating current classroom practices.

4 The Determinants of Human Behavior

Introduces the important concept of motivation as the basis for understanding behavior in and out of the classroom. The emphasis is on need satisfaction, the self-concept, need for achievement, and self-actualization.

ONE

Psychology and the Classroom Teacher

One aim of education is to make available the wisdom of the past and present so that youth will be equipped to solve the problems of the future.

Gordon W. Allport (1961)

The teacher is fully successful . . . when his student has become as thoroughly emancipated, self-motivated, and self-directed as to be no longer in need of a teacher. . . . The ideal teacher is so successful at making himself unnecessary that he teaches himself out of a job.

Robert B. MacLeod (1965)

It is simply not true that the demands of teaching many people require us to teach badly.

Arthur W. Combs (1962)

— Emphasizes the contribution of psychological insights to
the effectiveness of educational practice.
— Provides an orientation to educational psychology as
a critical component of meaningful teacher education.

PREVIEW: KEY CONCEPTS

1. Although educational practice must rest on a firm psychological foundation, educational psychology is more than the routine application of the principles of general psychology to the school situation.
2. The field of educational psychology is so broad as to require selectivity of coverage.
3. Educational psychology seeks to provide not prescriptions but insights into the various aspects of classroom operation. An understanding of its principles is a necessary, albeit not a sufficient, condition for effective teaching.
4. Educational psychology needs to balance its emphasis on effective learning with a corresponding concern for effective teaching.
5. Teachers do indeed make a difference, but the dimensions of teacher effectiveness are complex and subtle.

PREVIEW QUESTIONS

1. Specifically, what do you expect to learn from this course in educational psychology that will enable you to be a better teacher?
    Identify two specific areas to which educational psychology might be expected to make a significant contribution.
    What are the limitations of general psychology as a foundation for educational practice? Must all education be ''practical''?
2. What is teaching all about? What makes the difference between a good and a poor teacher? (It might help to recall the ''best'' and the ''worst'' teacher you had in school and list, say, five critical ways in which they differed.) Evaluate your own suitability as a prospective teacher in the light of these characteristics. What led you to consider teaching as your life work?
3. The school is forever under attack. Identify one area of especially serious weakness. What might you suggest by way of solution? How might educational psychology help?

The status of any profession is determined in large measure by the quality of the professional services it provides. This quality, in turn, depends on the adequacy of the professional insights and understandings on which professional decisions are made. If the true importance of teaching is to be recognized, teachers must demonstrate a thorough understanding of the principles of educational psychology, for these principles necessarily constitute the major part of the foundation for effective teaching.

PSYCHOLOGICAL BASES OF EDUCATION

Educational psychology: a field in its own right

In a broad sense, educational psychology is concerned with the application of the principles, techniques, and other resources of psychology to the solution of the problems confronting teachers as they attempt to promote maximum pupil growth. Its contribution to education is directly proportional to the degree to which it maintains contact with the broad field of both psychology and educational practice. Educational psychology is much more than the routine application of psychology to education; it is a field in its own right, drawing not only from clinical, social, and experimental psychology but also from sociology, human relations, anthropology, physiology, biology, biochemistry, neurology, and genetics. From these broad areas, educational psychologists select those aspects they consider of greatest value to the classroom teacher.

In practice, it is impossible to cover all that is important, and it becomes necessary for instructors and authors to focus on those areas that they believe will make the greatest contribution to the effective operation of the school. Most authors today concentrate on such topics as the nature of the learner, the nature of the learning process, the role of the teacher, and the evaluation of learning outcomes, but it is inevitable that there should be considerable disparity as to the relative emphasis placed on these topics and even greater variation as to the relative coverage of such subsidiary topics as educational objectives, individual differences, instructional strategies, and testing, which are often covered in other courses in the teacher-education sequence.

SOURCES OF DATA OF EDUCATIONAL PSYCHOLOGY

Educational psychology derives its data from sources that range from the relatively objective and scientific to the highly subjective, if not intuitive. Unfortunately, except for the last category, too little of our knowledge of educational psychology has been discovered by the classroom teacher who is in actual contact with the youngsters to whom these data are to apply. Too frequently, it seems, the classroom teachers solve vital problems on the basis of common sense, while college professors write articles in professional journals that teachers do not read on problems teachers do not have.

Educational Experimentation

Foremost among the sources of the data of educational psychology is experimentation. Many current classroom practices, such as the emphasis on periodic review to promote retention, have a relatively sound empirical basis in scientific experimentation. Experimentation, whether in education or in any other field, rests on the assumption that there exists an invariant relationship between a certain antecedent and a certain consequent so that, provided a given set of conditions prevails, if one does this, that will follow. Thus if an object is thrown out of the window of a tall building, it will fall at an accelerating speed. This would be as true today and tomorrow as it was yesterday, as true in Brooklyn as in Timbuctu. That such invariance in time and space should prevail seems logical since denying its existence would mean subscribing to a view that all is chaotic and unpredictable (see Mouly 1978:12–13).

Science is invariant

No law is universal

Yet exceptions do occur; many a farmer has seen his hat fly upward in a twister and been thankful it was not his barn. In such cases, we must recognize that even though unusual conditions have acted to overcome gravity, the law of gravity still expresses a relationship that is valid, provided we state the conditions to which its validity is restricted. Experimentation in education has also produced a number of generalizations, principles, and laws that are valid *under certain stated conditions.* The beginning student in educational psychology who looks for quick answers is likely to be frustrated at the number of contradictions to be found in regard to a given problem. Thus, one investigator finds method A superior to method B with regard to a given outcome, while a second investigator finds method B superior to method A. The apparent contradiction can be explained in terms of differences in the conditions under which each of the conclusions was reached. Whereas a certain method of study might be superior to another for children in the primary grades, the reverse might well be true for high school seniors (see External Validity, Campbell and Stanley 1963; Mouly 1978). Similarly, one needs to be extremely cautious about applying to the classroom the results of laboratory experimentation and, for that matter, about transplanting any educational results from one situation to another.

Control is essential but difficult in the social sciences

If he is to determine the actual effectiveness of a given treatment or method, the investigator must control the operation of extraneous variables. In practice, this means having a *control* group that is identical to the *experimental* group in all relevant respects except for the one factor under study. Failure to establish equivalence between the two groups would tend to make for erroneous conclusions. If group A is more highly motivated than group B, for example, it might make greater progress even while using an inferior method of study. Particularly difficult to control is the *Hawthorne effect,* the tendency for

1-1 THE HAWTHORNE STUDIES

This well-known study was part of a series of studies on employee productivity conducted at the Hawthorne Plant (Chicago) of Western Electric, the manufacturer of telephone equipment. The major report, published in 1939, covers the first twelve years of the study.

The results of the various substudies revealed a pattern of increased worker productivity attending almost any and all changes in working conditions. In the study of lighting, for example, output increased with an increase in lighting, but it also increased when illumination was brought back to its original level and even when it was reduced to a mere 3 foot-candles. Output increased when the work week was shortened and rest periods were introduced, and it rose again when they were returned to their original status.

The results suggest that social factors connected with the experimental changes rather than the changes themselves were responsible for the increase in output. A major feature of the study was the special status the experimental workers enjoyed. Their advice concerning proposed changes in working conditions was sought, and they were made to feel that management really cared about their welfare. It would seem that increased output resulted not so much from the improved lighting, the rest pauses, and other factors, as from improved morale and feelings of status. Absenteeism and griping dropped off drastically, for example.

Despite certain limitations—for example, their partial reliance on small, volunteer groups—the Hawthorne studies have made a significant contribution to our understanding of the importance of human relations in industrial production. They also have a direct bearing on classroom performance at both the individual and group level. The modern emphasis on classroom motivation, attitudes, counseling, and group dynamics is consistent with their findings. More pertinent to the immediate context is the vitiating influence the "Hawthorne effect" often has on the validity of experimental findings.

COOK, DESMOND L. "The Hawthorne Effect in Educational Research." *Phi Delta Kappan* 44 (1962):116–122.
ROETHLISBERGER, F. J., and WILLIAM I. DICKSON. *Management and the Worker.* Cambridge: Harvard University Press, 1939.

the subjects to react to the novelty and other features of the experiment itself and thus produce positive results, regardless of the actual "effectiveness" of the experimental treatment (see Box 1.1).

Because educational psychology has to deal with material infinitely more complex from the standpoint of interaction than that studied by a chemist, for example, it is often difficult to establish rigorous equivalence of the two groups—hence the correspondingly greater danger of erroneous conclusions and greater likelihood of conflict. For that reason, psychologists sometimes prefer the laboratory, where they can exert greater control on the variables of the situation. To the extent that this greater control represents a departure from regular classroom conditions, however, the results can only provide hypotheses as to what is likely to occur in a nonlaboratory setting. The results would have to be verified under actual classroom conditions before teachers could accept them with confidence.

Treatment interacts with student characteristics

Probably no variable is more troublesome from the standpoint of scientific control than the interaction of teacher characteristics and the "true" effectiveness of a given method. A teacher may find a certain method suited to his personality, his style of teaching, and/or the nature of his classes, even though it may have serious inherent limitations. In other words, the teacher's personality, competencies, and other characteristics, as well as the nature of the students being taught and the objectives being sought, constitute variables that have to be taken into consideration in generalizing as to which of two methods is the more effective. The question is not, "Which is the more effective?" but rather, "Which is more effective for whom and under what conditions?" (see Aptitude Treatment Interaction; ATI; Mouly 1978:262–265). Thus, even though method is subject to scientific law, the choice among methods must often be made on an individual rather than a general basis—and rightly so, for there is no single universally best method of teaching.

Other Sources of Data

Less rigorous methods

Many of the problems teachers face are of such a nature that they cannot, at least for the present, be subjected to rigorous experimental study. As a consequence, much of what goes on in the classroom is based on nothing more substantial than general consensus or even personal experience and opinion that a particular procedure is generally effective. Much of our knowledge of the child, for example, has been derived through methods that are essentially clinical in nature.

One of the most common sources of data in educational psychology, and also one of the most subjective, is observation. Alert teachers are bound to notice that certain techniques are generally effective and that children of a certain age display certain behavioral tendencies. As a result of their experience, teachers often generate a personal frame of reference that they use to understand children and their behavior. A teacher may believe, for example, that acceleration—or retardation, or ability grouping—is detrimental to the maximum growth of the child. Unfortunately observation is subject to considerable error. There is, for instance, the ever-present danger of slanting observations to fit preconceived notions and to note only those instances that agree with one's viewpoint.

Another important source of the data of educational psychology involves questionnaires, inventories, scales, tests, and other instruments by means of which the various aspects of pupil status and pupil growth can be determined. Some of these, such as measures of height and weight used in establishing physical growth, tend to be very accurate. Others, such as questionnaires relating to attitudes or motivation, are less dependable, although still useful in providing insights into human behavior. Somewhere between these two extremes lie tests of intelligence and achievement, which, despite their imperfections, not only yield information useful in dealing with children as individuals but also permit research on a variety of educational and psychological problems, such as experimentation into the relative effectiveness of different teaching methods.

Need for theoretical structure

There are still many gaps in our knowledge. In fact, we lack not only the answers to many of our problems but also the techniques and tools whereby the answers can be obtained. Particularly lacking in the establishment of education as a science is a unifying theory, such as that found in the physical and biological sciences, that would provide both the basis for interpreting the data obtained from research and a framework for guiding our efforts in the discovery of new data. Nevertheless, a number of relatively self-consistent theories of human behavior have been advanced, each attempting to provide a theoretical framework from which the empirical data of educational psychology can be placed into meaningful perspective, but none is completely satisfactory. A brief overview of the major theories is presented in chapter 3.

PURPOSES OF EDUCATIONAL PSYCHOLOGY

The School and Its Critics

The school as an institution is often blamed for whatever goes wrong in society—delinquency, maladjustment, alienation, even failure in the national space program. In times of war, it is accused of having failed to emphasize physical fitness and patriotism; in times of peace, it is accused of indoctrination. It is forever accused of neglecting the sciences and the "hard" subjects or, on the other hand, of not providing youth with adequate vocational skills. These often-conflicting criticisms, whatever their validity, are aimed primarily at educational *philosophy* rather than educational *psychology*, for it is not the function of educational psychology to define the goals for which we ought to strive. Whether the goal of the school is to indoctrinate children into various social ideologies, to turn them into miniature adults, or to let them be carefree youngsters, this is an issue to be resolved on the basis of the philosophical perspective of the social order.

Educational psychology is concerned with the discovery of techniques by means of which we can attain most effectively whatever eductional goals we have selected rather than with their actual selection. It can, of course, lead to a reconsideration of specific objectives by demonstrating that they are impractical or unattainable or that the procedures and techniques by means of which they are supposedly to be attained are based on false premises. Whereas most people agree on academic excellence as a worthy educational objective, for instance, educational psychologists would question whether excellence is to be attained by a return to the classical curriculum of yesteryear or to stiffer grading (with presumably a higher rate of student failure).

Clear-cut goals are essential

There is need for meaningful, clear-cut, and attainable goals. In 1954, for example, B. F. Skinner complained that true academic achievement was being sacrificed in favor of such vague ideals as "education for democracy" and "educating the whole child" and that the resulting ambiguities in the instructional process were subverting the true aims of education. Educators frequently resort to clichés as pat solutions to complex problems, clichés that parry questions but do not give answers. Perhaps as educators, we need to be more concerned with simplistic "answers" that do not get questioned than with questions that do not get answered. Teachers are often unaware of the assumptions underlying their various pedagogical views and practices; to say that Tommy "is not ready for school," for example, implies a considerable belief in the role of the maturational components of readiness. Opposing acceleration for the gifted on the ground that these children should remain with their age-mates is also making crucial assumptions about the relative importance of the factors involved in the optimal grade placement of children.

The school and its critics

More pertinent to educational psychology is the criticism that our schools are relatively ineffective, that children sit by the day working at half-steam, being led under duress toward goals that have been made neither meaningful nor desirable, and being subjected to competition and examinations that serve only to debase their sense of worth. Unfortunately, these criticisms are partly true for a number of our classrooms. As Lindgren (1962) points out, some teachers have a propensity for getting themselves in difficulty, for violating the principles of educational psychology, and for otherwise negating rather than facilitating the process of education.

Actually public education has always been under fire. This is to be expected: education is too important to national welfare for American society to be indifferent to its operation. Typically criticisms of the school come in waves. After a decade of relative quiet since the major attack that followed Sputnik, the alleged inadequacies of our schools were again the target of a number of "neo-humanistic" publications during the period of social unrest of the late 1960s.[1] The theme was invariably the same: inefficiency, mediocrity, bureaucratic inflexibility, impersonality, and irrelevance. Hart (1969), for ex-

---

1. Among the better-known are William Glasser, *Schools without Failure;* Paul Goodman, *Growing Up Absurd; Compulsory Miseducation;* Leslie A. Hart, *Classroom Disaster;* J. Kohl, *36 Children;* and J. Kozol, *Death at an Early Age.* A number of more benign but nevertheless critical accounts of what goes on in the school are: E. Fuchs, *The Teachers Talk: Views from inside City Schools;* John I. Goodlad et al., *Behind the Closed Door;* John Holt, *How Children Fail;* and J. M. Stephens, *The Process of Schooling.*

ample, argues that the schools' educational output is ridiculous in relation to its vast expenditure of time, money, and effort. In fact, he suggests that we can no longer complain that all that stands in the way of our success is the lack of adequate resources; with all the money poured into education by the federal government in the 1960s, one might have expected notable gains to have been achieved, but there was no evidence of spectacular gains. Moynihan (1972) for example, suggests that, with our present state of knowledge, the least promising way to aid education is to spend more money on it. Meanwhile the school has been troubled by delinquency, violence, drug abuse, student unrest, and apathy—problems that are really sociological in nature but that nevertheless bear directly on the school, distracting our efforts, draining our energies, and precluding success.

Demand for
accountability

Recognizing the critical role of education in matters of social welfare, if not survival, Americans are once again taking a hard look at the public school to see if it is truly meeting the needs of today's society. Concern over deficiencies in public education has led to new demands for *accountability* along lines of clearly defined student productivity (see chapter 2) and more recently, for evidence of literacy on the part of students as a condition for graduation from high school.

The Role of Educational Psychology

Educational
psychology provides
insights

The purpose of a course in educational psychology is to promote a greater understanding of the principles underlying the task of guiding children toward maximum self-realization. It is as crucial to teacher education as physics is to engineering or anatomy is to medicine. Specifically, its function is to promote greater understanding of the learning process, the learning situation, and the learner—not singly but rather in dynamic interaction, for they cannot have meaning apart from such interaction. Knowledge of educational psychology will not guarantee good teaching, but, without it, teaching can only be a matter of rules of thumb, routine habits, and trial-and-error procedures, many of which can be detrimental to children. In the area of discipline, for example, a teacher unfamiliar with educational psychology might attempt to prevent pupil misbehavior through such expedients as autocratic disciplinary procedures that would probably worsen the situation by promoting resentment, hostility, apathy, and even personality damage. The role of educational psychology is to provide not prescriptions but rather functional insights into the various aspects of the teaching-learning process.

An understanding of educational psychology will help put teachers in a better position to decide what can be done and how, what will not work and why. It will give them a clearer perspective of what constitutes realistic goals for children in their present state of development and how they can be helped to achieve these goals. It should enable teachers to do a more effective job of gearing the curriculum to the needs, goals, and purposes of individual children in their class. In short, an understanding of educational psychology should in-

crease the effectiveness with which teachers help children toward maximum realization of their capacities and, no less important, should result in a reduction of frustration for teachers and pupils alike.

Unfortunately, procedures that are psychologically sound are sometimes difficult for beginners to use effectively. Just as the person learning to type on his own often settles for the hunt-and-peck approach, so the beginning teacher is often tempted to use threats of detention, failing grades, and other forms of punishment instead of something more constructive from a long-term point of view. What is best for a given situation typically is far from obvious. As a result, new teachers are often so befuddled that they are willing to grasp at any method regardless of its effectiveness. Actually, psychology is better at telling what not to do than it is at identifying what to do. Laymen are often annoyed at what they consider the psychologist's evasiveness when he answers, "It depends," to their questions as to what should be done about a given child. Educational psychology does not provide teachers with a formula to be used to determine what is right for every child; it can only alert them to the principles on the basis of which enlightened decisions can be made.

Contributions of Educational Psychology

The fact that a course in educational psychology invariably is required as part of the professional teacher-education sequence suggests that knowledge of educational psychology is generally considered a necessary, although certainly not a sufficient, precondition for effective teaching. This makes sense. Logically one would expect educational psychology to provide valuable insights into all aspects of the educational enterprise, from the characteristics of developing children and the nature of the teaching-learning process to the conditions that maximize pupil growth. Conversely, it is difficult to imagine how a teacher can be competent without such a background.

Contribution to date has been disappointing

On the other hand, there is a growing feeling that educational psychology is not making the contribution to educational practice one might expect it to make (Herbert and Ausubel 1965). Actually, educational psychology does not and cannot provide direct prescriptions for the myriad problems encountered in the operation of the school. First, psychology just does not have drawer upon drawer of solutions to educational problems neatly indexed and catalogued. Theories of learning, for example, cannot be converted directly into guaranteed answers to specific classroom questions. Wittrock (1967) notes that research in educational psychology has not progressed far enough for the development of an organized body of knowledge relevant to the understanding and the control of classroom instruction.

Ausubel (1969a) attributes our present predicament to the fact that, instead of conducting their own research, educational psychologists have simply extrapolated the findings of psychology—many of them based on animal research—to classroom problems, without conducting the additional research required to bridge the gap between the two levels of generality. In fact, there is a growing belief that the two fields may be relatively discontinuous in that the laws that apply to the learning of animals, with their limited linguistic and conceptual facilities, are different from the laws that apply to human learning—indeed that the laws that relate to the rote learning of paired associates and nonsense syllables have little to do with those that govern meaningful verbal learning as it occurs in the classroom.

Some also believe that educational psychology as taught in the preservice sequence may be too abstract and academic (Aspy 1970). Regardless of its potential contribution to classroom teaching, it seems unrealistic to expect a sophomore-level course, with its emphasis on content as an academic exercise, to transfer in any meaningful and effective way to teaching strategies two or three years later. In the Frey and Ellis study (1966), a number of the teachers thought the course in educational psychology had come too early in their program and that it would have been more effective had they taken it after practice teaching. There is a need to devise a more systematic way to synchronize the learning and the application of the principles of educational psychology into effective teaching. Meanwhile it may also be that educational psychology has grossly overemphasized what the student is supposed to do in *learning* and correspondingly underemphasized what the teacher is supposed to do by way of *teaching*. There is, in fact, a growing belief that the current overconcern of educational psychology with *learning* (as reflected, for instance, in the emphasis on theories of learning) has led to a corresponding neglect of the development of effective *teaching* strategies.

Educational
psychology must be
integrated into
practice

Obviously, teachers must master the concepts and principles of educational psychology, but they must also integrate these concerns and principles into effective teaching strategies designed to promote the efficient attainment of meaningful educational goals. Most current textbooks in educational psychology simply present the principles and theories of learning, leaving students to decipher the implications of these principles for teaching. They tell what *learners* should do. There is now a need for a parallel emphasis on what *teachers* should do—that is, on how they can manipulate the conditions of learning in order to ensure that learning will indeed be effective. The educational psychology course in preservice teacher education is not a methods course, but neither is it simply a course in the psychology of learning. To be of maximum usefulness for prospective teachers, it must not only clarify how students can learn (as if they were the sole participants in the educational process) but, equally important, it must also provide prospective teachers with definite insights into the implications of psychological concepts and principles for effective *teaching*. More specifically, the course in educational psychology must orient itself to all aspects of the educational enterprise from the setting of goals, the understanding of the characteristics of the learner, and the effectiveness of different teaching-learning strategies to the evaluation of teaching-learning outcomes.

Because educational psychology can never provide definitive prescriptions as to educational practice, teaching is and must remain somewhat of an art, much of it depending on the teacher's adaptation of techniques to a variety of situations. On the other hand, it is easy to jump from the fact that we do not have all the answers to educational problems to the conclusion that we do not have any of the answers.[2] A more realistic appraisal is that we are not using anywhere near all the knowledge with which educational psychology has provided us. Certainly educational psychology cannot contribute to educational practice if it is not applied at all or if it is applied incorrectly. There is a need for a more systematic integration of educational psychology with actual practice in the field.

WHAT IS TEACHING?

Emphasis on Growth

Among the more significant changes in educational thought resulting from recent advances in educational psychology is the shift in emphasis from learning as the acquisition of subject matter to learning as a dynamic process of

2. See Turner (1975) for an overview of research on teacher education; see also Ryan (1975).

change in behavior and from techniques of presenting subject matter to strategies for promoting pupil growth. Children must do their own learning; no one can do it for them. But this does not mean that teachers have outlived their usefulness beyond acting as custodians while children learn. On the contrary, teachers have a very definite function to perform; theirs is the task of stimulating, guiding, monitoring, and generally facilitating children's learning so as to ensure their attainment of meaningful goals.

Teaching is more critical than ever

This new concept of teaching has made the work of teachers more challenging but also more difficult. Instead of concerning themselves with only a few patterns of effective presentation of subject matter, modern teachers are responsible for ensuring that everything that goes on in the classroom is of maximum benefit in promoting the total development of each child. With learning now recognized as a dynamic and continuous process involving all aspects of child growth and development, "teaching" calls for a much greater degree of professional insight and expertise in the use of growth-producing strategies.

Recent developments, including the current knowledge explosion, have placed teaching in a new perspective. The original purpose of the school—namely, to transmit stored knowledge—while appropriate one hundred years ago, is neither feasible nor sufficient today. If we are to survive in today's rapidly changing world, the primary goal of education must be the facilitation of change. According to Rogers (1969), the only person who is educated today is one who has learned to adapt to change. Because it is no longer possible for the school to provide children with an adequate command of all the information in each subject necessary to serve them throughout the balance of their lives, the only sensible aim of education is to teach them how to learn—that is, to help them to develop both the skills that they will need to continue to learn after graduation and a deep interest in the continued pursuit of meaningful knowledge. Modern teachers will continue to play a crucial but increasingly different role. Their task as the chief dispensers of knowledge will become progressively less important as they assume more critical responsibilities.

Teacher Effectiveness

The question of who should teach has always been a matter of major concern to school officials and school patrons alike—and rightly so, since the effectiveness of our schools revolves in a critical way on the competence and the dedication of their teachers. Society has the right to expect a certain effectiveness in promoting the purposes for which teachers and schools exist. Certainly some teachers will always be more effective than others. In fact, there are probably teachers whose overall effect on the children placed in their care is essentially negative, or at least the growth they promote in some children or some aspect of the development of certain children appears to be outweighed by the harm they do in other respects.

There is no easy solution to determining who will be an effective teacher: teaching is a composite activity involving teachers, students, and subject matter in a dynamic interaction that is too complex to be defined in terms of a simple set of teacher traits or academic procedures. A half-century of research into the distinctive features and characteristics of good and poor teachers has failed to provide a universal profile of the effective teacher. Although certain teaching patterns undoubtedly are better than others, there is no one kind of good teaching that fits all teaching situations, all teachers, and all pupils.

Teaching is a complex undertaking

Teaching is far too complex an enterprise to be operated at the level of rules of the thumb. On the contrary, it must be based on well-documented principles that a capable teacher can adapt in order to deal with the variety of problems that constantly occur in the classroom. At a higher level of science, these principles must be integrated into comprehensive theories that give insights and perspective. But we must also recognize that principles and theories do not translate into immediate specifications for classroom practice. Rather they set directions within which competent teachers can exercise professional judgment, taking into consideration the complex interaction of pupil characteristics, teaching variables, and situational factors. We must also recognize that although effective practice comes with experience, it is only under the guidance of sound principles and theories that experience leads to professional competence and expertise.

Perhaps teaching is so complex, so intangible, so subjective, and so bound up with the fact that teachers are unique individuals (rather than computerized production machines) that it will never be possible to reduce its components into guaranteed operational patterns. Heil and Washburne (1960), for example, found that different teacher personalities induced different reactions from different students. The "self-controlling" teacher got the most achievement out of all the children combined; the "fearful" teacher got the least. But the "turbulent" teacher, who works on impulse and tends to place low emphasis on structure and order, got almost as much achievement as the "self-controlling" teacher from students identified as "conformers" and "strivers," that is, from students who have inner security and order of their own.

Good and Brophy (1976) present a strong argument against the common claim (Coleman et al. 1966; Jencks 1967) that student achievement is determined almost exclusively by the ability level and other characteristics of the student population, with the school (its budget, the caliber of its teachers, and other factors) relatively inconsequential. They point out that the Coleman study, for example, by focusing on schools, that is, lumping together the results of various classrooms within a given school rather than examining individual teachers, simply covered up the evidence that certain teachers indeed do have an impact on student output that is statistically and practically significant (see Veldman and Brophy 1974; Rosenshine and Furst 1973; Walberg and Rasher 1977). Good and Brophy also reject the claim by Stephens (1967) that, no matter what the school does by way of new curricula or teacher or administrative strategies, the results from the standpoint of student achievement invariably are the same. They point out that educational strategies can be effective only to the extent that they are actually and correctly implemented, a point Stephens presumably did not take into sufficient account in reaching his conclusion. In other words, it seems that teacher effectiveness can be defined only in specific, rather than general, terms.

Obviously teacher effectiveness depends critically on the choice of a criterion. Teacher behaviors that lead to the efficient attainment of one set of goals often seem to impede the attainment of other equally significant objectives. In the Turner and Thompson (1974) study, for example, the teachers rated most favorably by their students were also the teachers whose students performed the most poorly on the tests, and vice versa. Apparently democratic leadership and learner-centered orientation fostered student morale, while a tight organization and authoritarian leadership fostered greater academic productivity. If this is so, we need to order our priorities. On the other hand, as Good and Brophy caution, any statement that a particular teaching behavior is good or bad regardless of the context is almost always an overgeneralization.

Too often the emphasis has been on immediate goals (for example, student progress as revealed by end-of-year standardized tests) at the expense of more global but more personally profitable and psychologically sound long-range goals. What has the student really gained from passing tests on Shakespeare if he never reads Shakespeare again? Or from achieving academic honors if in the process she fails to develop the more personal goal of human-

Teachers do make a difference

The choice of criterion is critical

ness? To the extent that immediate goals are often false goals, they can, by their very tangibility and immediacy, distort the overall educational process. Overemphasis on the demonstration of teacher effectiveness can also lead to such a distortion.

Although it is easy to insist that children deserve good teachers, it is considerably more difficult to pinpoint characteristics that make for effectiveness in teaching. Effectiveness is an aspect of the total personality that characterizes good teachers. Among the contributing factors are emotional stability, a good disposition, democratic and cooperative attitudes, kindliness, empathy, patience, humor, and fairness. There is obviously a need for professional competence, for the ability to make effective use of sound personality patterns and professional insights in relating to children and in promoting their overall growth. Goodwill is not enough. Teachers must be conversant with the principles of educational psychology and proficient in the use of their own assets for the benefit of their students. They also need reasonable facility of expression, a mature sense of trust, and, above all, dedication, professional alertness, and interest in self-improvement.

HIGHLIGHTS OF THE CHAPTER

This chapter serves as an orientation to the field of educational psychology. The major ideas presented can be summarized as follows:

1. Educational psychology provides the foundation for effective educational practice. It is concerned with facilitating the process through which the school's goals can be achieved. As such it is a necessary, although not a sufficient, condition for effective classroom operations.
2. Educational psychology derives its data from various sources, ranging from the relatively scientific to others that are relatively intuitive. Much of our current knowledge has been extrapolated from psychology. There is a need for further development of educational psychology as a semiautonomous discipline.
3. Educational psychology is oriented toward promoting in the prospective teacher a greater understanding of the child, the learning process, and the learning situation as they come together in dynamic interaction within the setting of the educational enterprise.
4. To date, educational psychology has focused on the principles of learning. There is a need for greater emphasis on effective teaching.
5. Although there is agreement as to the need for good teachers, teacher effectiveness has been an elusive concept. To a substantial degree it seems that effective teaching is a function of the interaction of individual teachers with individual students.

SUGGESTIONS FOR FURTHER READING

BEERY, JOHN R. Does professional education make a difference? *J. Teach. Educ.* 13 (1962):385–395. Shows that the professional education sequence (foundations of education, educational psychology, teaching methods, and practice teaching) does indeed contribute to the effectiveness of first-year teachers.

BIJOU, SIDNEY W. What psychology has to offer education: Now. *J. Appl. Beh. Anal.* 3 (1970):65–71. The great majority of psychologists argue that psychology can offer an impressive collection of data about children and their development. A substantial number would point to tentative answers. A small minority would point to principles of development for experimental research and a methodology for implementing research findings.

BROUDY, HARRY S. Criteria for the professional preparation of teachers. *J. Teach. Educ.* 16 (1965):408–415. There is no general formula, no one pattern of effective teaching. Although the primary role a teacher must play is that of a human being, this does not deny the need for professional competence and academic knowledge.

COMBS, ARTHUR W. *The Professional Education of Teachers.* Boston: Allyn & Bacon, 1965. Presents the humanistic view of teacher preparation, emphasizing self-understanding and self-actualization.

GAGE, N. L. *The Scientific Basis for the Art of Teaching.* New York: Teachers College Press, 1978. Covers three major topics: the research on teaching effectiveness, the applications of the research, and the conceptual perspective for research on effective teaching, with a view to improving its scientific basis. See also Berliner, David C., Impediments to the study of teacher effectiveness, *J. Teach. Educ.* 27 (1976):5–13, and Shavelson, R. J., and D. Dempsey. *Generalizability of Measures of Teacher Effectiveness and Teaching Process.* Far West Lab, 1975.

———. The yield of research on teaching. *Phi Delta Kappan* 60 (1978):229–235. Contends that, despite pessimistic reviews, research on teaching has produced important results.

GALLUP, GEORGE H. The 11th Annual Gallup Poll of the Public's Attitudes toward the Public School. *Phi Delta Kappan* 63 (1981):33–47. An annual series of major interest to professional and lay personnel alike, this poll summarizes the views of the American public toward critical issues in public education.

GOOD, THOMAS L., et al. *Teachers Make a Difference.* New York: Holt, Rinehart & Winston, 1975. Argues that, contrary to prevailing opinion, teachers indeed can have an impact on students. See also McDonald, Fred, *Teachers Do Make a Difference* (Princeton: Educational Testing Service, 1976.)

JACKSON, PHILIP W. *Life in Classrooms.* New York: Holt, Rinehart & Winston, 1968. An interesting account of what actually goes on in the classroom, the good and the bad. Presents a number of useful insights.

LEVINE, LOUIS S. The American teacher: A tentative psychological description. *Psychol. Sch.* 6 (1969):245–252. Shows that no single set of characteristics describes the good teacher; teachers, like every other profession, differ widely. Men differ from women, elementary teachers from secondary teachers, teachers from administrators. There are also interesting differences between college students in education and those who pursue other majors.

McLEOD, ROBERT W. The teaching of psychology and the psychology we teach.

Amer. Psychol. 20 (1965):344:–352. Suggests that instead of serving the needs of students, psychology courses are becoming progressively more irrelevant. Increasingly, introductory courses are simply preparation for admission to graduate courses.

MILLMAN, JASON. Teaching effectiveness: New indicators for an old problem. *Educ. Horizons* 51 (1972–1973):68–75. Reviews various indicators of teacher effectiveness—presage, process, and product variables—as they relate to the school of the past, the present, and the future, and discusses their implications for teacher selection, teacher training, and teacher certification.

————, ed. *Handbook of Teacher Evaluation.* Beverly Hills: Sage, 1981. Provides a critical analysis of the issues and practices in teacher evaluation. A teacher evaluation guidebook for practitioners.

PHI DELTA KAPPA. Reform in teacher education. *Phi Delta Kappan,* 62 (1980):81–149. Special issue of the *Kappan.* Leading educators review current problems in teacher education and suggest changes for the 80s.

SCANDURA, JOSEPH M., et al. Current status and future directions of educational psychology as a discipline. *Educ. Psychol.* 13 (1978):43–56. Report of a committee of the American Psychological Association set up to clarify and reassess the role of educational psychology as a discipline. Reviews current goals and status of the field, including its suggested contents. Also identifies promising recent advances and presents tentative recommendations for the future.

TREFFINGER, DONALD J., et al. *Handbook on Teaching Educational Psychology.* New York: Academic Press, 1977. Discussions by a number of leading educational psychologists on various aspects of the teaching of educational psychology, including the role of theories of instruction, behavioral objectives, competency-based teacher education, and individualized programs. An excellent reference.

U.S. NEWS AND WORLD REPORT. Give us better schools. *U.S. News,* Sept. 10, 1979, pp. 31–40. A series of articles on the growing public demand for better schools and some of the changes taking place in response to this demand.

QUESTIONS AND PROJECTS

1. Become acquainted with the library as it relates to educational psychology. You should know how to use the card catalog and be familiar with a number of the better references, including other current texts in educational psychology, child psychology, general psychology, tests, and measurements. Also familiarize yourself with some of the professional journals. Make a practice of consulting some of the sources of related materials listed at the end of each chapter.

2. If you have access to children—perhaps in a recreation center or a camp—observe a couple of youngsters who seem to present problems and follow them through the various topics of educational psychology discussed in this book. Thus, with regard to chapter 4, attempt to un-

derstand the psychodynamics of their behavior; with regard to chapter 5, make a study of their general growth patterns, etc. As you read the various chapters, attempt to relate each bit of information to the child as a whole. You will find the project not only interesting, but also extremely valuable in understanding children and in giving the course continuity and meaning.

3. Each teacher has a philosophy of teaching. What are some of the concepts in which you believe? What are your present views toward the child who loafs in school? Who is rebellious?

So far your perspective has been that of a student. You will soon find yourself on the "other side of the desk." What difference might that make in your thinking?

To what extent are you open to change? Before you start the course, state in three or four sentences your current position on the following issues: (a) accountability, (b) criticism of the school, (c) discipline, (d) compulsory education, (e) grading, (f) examinations, (g) merit pay for teachers, (h) values and character education, (i) violence in the school.

4. What do you see as the major problems confronting American education today?

What changes do you expect to see in the next two or three decades? What role might eductional psychology play in the "improvement" of the school?

Evaluate some of the recent criticisms of the school. Analyze (a) the validity of the criticism and (b) the adequacy of the proposed solutions.

5. Because it is constantly buffeted by various pressures, the school often has difficulty in maintaining a proper balance among its major objectives. Identify some of these forces and appraise the effect they have had on American education. How can the school maintain sensitivity to the demands of the society it serves without losing its focus on the essentials?

SUPPLEMENTARY READINGS

Inasmuch as no single textbook can provide complete coverage of a given course area at the college level, conscientious students will want to consult one or more of the many excellent textbooks in educational psychology. They should also refer systematically to relevant periodicals and other sources of original research. Also of prime interest are the relatively large number of recent handbooks presenting in most cases a thorough treatment of certain topics of direct relevance to educational psychology. The following are pertinent:

BERELSON, BERNARD, and GARY A. STEINER. *Human Behavior: An Inventory of Scientific Findings.* New York: Harcourt, 1964.
BORGATTA, EDGAR F., and WILLIAM LAMBERT, eds. *Handbook of Personality Theory and Research in Child Development.* Chicago: Rand McNally, 1968.
EBEL, ROBERT L., ed. *Encyclopedia of Educational Research.* New York: Macmillan, 1969.
GAGE, N. L., ed. *Handbook of Research on Teaching.* Chicago: Rand McNally, 1963.
HOFFMAN, MARTIN L., and LOIS B. HOFFMAN. *Review of Child Development Research.* 2 vols. New York: Russell Sage, 1964, 1966.
MARX, MELVIN H., ed. *Learning.* 3 vols. New York: Macmillan, 1969, 1970.
MUSSEN, PAUL H., ed. *Handbook of Research Methods in Child Development.* New York: Wiley, 1960.
———. *Carmichael's Manual of Child Psychology.* 2 vols. New York: Wiley, 1970.
TRAVERS, ROBERT M. W., ed. *Second Handbook of Research on Teaching.* Chicago: Rand McNally, 1973.

SELF-TEST

1. Psychology contributes to educational practice primarily by
   a. clarifying the goals toward which education is oriented.
   b. clarifying the nature of the interaction among learner, teacher, and learning process.
   c. determining the relative effectiveness of various teaching methods.
   d. placing human behavior under scientific control.
   e. promoting an understanding of human nature.

2. Experimentation in educational psychology attempts
   a. to define the goals of education.
   b. to determine the cause of human behavior.
   c. to develop a technology of instruction.
   d. to discover functional relationships among educational phenomena.
   e. to explain educational phenomena.

3. In an experimental study of the relative effectiveness of teaching methods, the most difficult factor to control is
   a. the bias due to personal preference.
   b. the extra practice often occurring between learning sessions.
   c. the interaction among teacher, learner, and method.
   d. the operation of chance.
   e. student motivation due to novelty (the Hawthorne effect).

4. A course of educational psychology is designed
   a. to promote an understanding of the nature of the child.
   b. to provide the scientific basis for curriculum development.
   c. to provide rules for effective teaching.
   d. to provide the scientific basis for educational practice.
   e. to serve as the basis for evaluating teaching methods.

5. The major reason for the failure of educational psychology to make a greater contribution to educational practice is probably that
   a. it is not sufficiently developed as a science.
   b. it can only tell the teacher what *not* to do.
   c. it is primarily a science, not a technology.
   d. most of its content is derived from the study of animal learning.
   e. teachers are not sufficiently versed in its principles.

6. Probably the most critical criterion of "who should teach" is
   a. a high level of scholarship and intelligence.
   b. knowledge of subject matter.
   c. personal warmth and a mature liking for children.
   d. a sense of personal integrity and professional commitment.
   e. skill in the use of effective teaching methods.

7. The relative unproductivity of teacher-effectiveness research is mostly due to
   a. the complexity of the teaching process.
   b. the fact that teaching and learning are essentially independent processes.
   c. the nonamenability of teacher behavior to scientific appraisal.
   d. our failure to devise meaningful theories of teaching.
   e. the unwarrantedly global conception of "teacher effectiveness."

TWO

Educational Objectives

"Would you tell me, please, which way I ought to go from here?"
"That depends a good deal on where you want to get to," said the Cat.
"I don't much care where——" said Alice.
"Then it doesn't matter which way you go," said the Cat.
"——so long as I get *somewhere*," Alice added as an explanation.
"Oh, you're sure to do that," said the Cat, "if you only walk long enough."

Lewis Carroll (1865)

— Points to the importance of stating instructional objectives in precise and measurable terms
— Presents arguments for and against stating instructional objectives in behavioral terms
— Explores the concept of accountability in education and points to its potential dangers of abuse
— Introduces the *Taxonomy of Educational Objectives* and outlines its operation in the three major domains: cognitive, affective, and psychomotor

PREVIEW: KEY CONCEPTS

1. If it is to be productive, education must necessarily begin with clarity as to its goals and objectives.
2. To be helpful as a guide, instructional objectives must be stated in precise and measurable terms.
3. The question of whether instructional objectives should be stated in behavioral terms has been the subject of controversy.
4. Current public dissatisfaction with the productivity of the school has led to demands for accountability, also a controversial topic.
5. *The Taxonomy of Educational Objectives* provides a useful classification of objectives in the cognitive, the affective, and the psychomotor domains. The first is probably the most functional as a guide to instruction and evaluation.

PREVIEW QUESTIONS

1. What specific purposes might be served by clear and precise educational and instructional goals?
   Why are teachers so reluctant to identify specific goals?
2. Specifically, what is to be gained from stating instructional goals behaviorally? What objections might be made?
3. How legitmate is it for the public to hold the school accountable for the attainment of prespecified educational objectives?
   How realistic is it for the public not to hold the school accountable for its performance?
   List major arguments pro and con accountability
4. What role might the *Taxonomy of Educational Objectives* play in the identification of meaningful educational and instructional goals?
   How can the affective domain of the taxonomy best be operationalized in the service of a meaningful education?

Any operation must begin with a definition of its purposes and its goals. This is especially true of such a complex and somewhat nebulous enterprise as education, where the clarity and the viability of its underlying goals are major factors in its success or failure.

GOALS AND OBJECTIVES

Sources of Objectives

Selecting the objectives for a given activity is a philosophical question. Whereas there may be certain objectives that are relatively universal—learning to read, to calculate, and to communicate through language—most others are questions of judgment based on personal priorities. That our schools should emphasize Shakespeare, American history, and the sciences rather than the psychology of parenthood, social relations, and vocational skills simply reflects the priorities we have set for ourselves as a nation.[1] Our task, then, is to define long-term educational goals by first clarifying the broad purposes of education in the context of the social goals of a modern democracy. From such broad social and educational goals, we can gradually move toward more specific *course objectives* and finally to precise *instructional objectives:* What do I want my students to gain? or, in the language of Robert Gagné (1977; see chapter 12), What capabilities do I want my students to acquire as a consequence of this particular learning experience?

Educators have always been concerned with goals and objectives. Unfortunately, in the past, these have been stated in such vague and global terms—e.g., "to liberate and perfect the intrinsic power of the human intellect"—that they have been relatively meaningless from the standpoint of curriculum planning, day-to-day instruction, or evaluation. To expect students "to gain a meaningful understanding" or "to have command" of the concepts and principles of educational psychology may be fine as a *general* objective, but the statement says nothing as to specifically what students are to gain from the course, how they are to proceed in its mastery, and how their progress is to be monitored. In the absence of more specific objectives, teachers typically rely on the textbook, assigning one chapter after another as the content students are to cover, assuming that somehow the students' learning will fall in line with the major goals of society and the school.

Clear-cut instructional objectives are essential to both effective learning and effective teaching. Formulation of precise instructional objectives increases teachers' awareness of what students are trying to accomplish; it permits them to identify prerequisites and to assess student readiness and thereby leads to a more systematic planning of productive instructional activities.[2] It enables teachers to exempt certain students from having to repeat what they already know or, in the case of deficiencies, to provide remedial and developmental work. Instructional objectives enable teachers to share with their students what the latter are to achieve, to involve them in planning appropriate learning experiences and thus place teachers and students on the same side as a team rather than as uncoordinated partners in a nebulous venture or even as adversaries bent on outwitting each other.

Precise instructional objectives enable teachers to plan more carefully even to the point of conducting a task analysis (Gagné, 1977) designed, for example, to identify what prerequisite learnings are necessary in order for the student to learn a given principle in science. They even provide the basis for

Our objectives are often vague

Clarity as to objectives is essential

1. For a humorous account of educational priorities, see Harold Benjamin's *The Sabre-Tooth Curriculum.*
2. A detailed study guide listing specific requirements and specific resources for each subunit might help further.

knowing when learning has occurred and instruction should cease. Clear-cut objectives permit students to proceed at their own pace, using their own idiosyncratic approach to the attainment of well-defined goals. Finally, precise objectives serve as the basis for evaluation and remove many of the objectionable features of the typical classroom testing. In short, precise objectives reduce guesswork and more generally serve to coordinate the whole educational enterprise.

Behavioral Objectives

Following through on the notion that instructional objectives should be formulated in precise terms, the past decade or two have provided a strong movement toward what are known as *behaviorial objectives* (or *behaviorally defined objectives*, BDO): an insistence that instructional objectives be stated in terms of actual overt behavior. The argument is that such terms as *to know* and *to understand* are ambiguous. To be of benefit from an instructional point of view, objectives must be specified in such behavioral terms as *the student will be able to define . . . , to identify instances of . . . , to distinguish. . . .* In other words, proponents of behavioral objectives insist that instructional objectives be defined in terms of such action verbs as:

analyze	design	prove
arrange	differentiate	reconstruct
categorize	discriminate	restate
classify	extrapolate	revise
choose	formulate	select
compare	identify	synthesize
compile	interpret	specify
derive	match	systematize
describe	outline	translate

Behavioral objectives
should specify . . .

They insist that the formulation of instructional objectives specify (1) the evidence of achievement (what the student will be able to do when learning is completed); (2) the conditions of performance; and (3) acceptable levels of performance. We might formulate, for example, "Given a list of twenty proper fractions (condition 2), the student will correctly convert them into decimals (condition 1) with 80 percent computational accuracy (condition 3)"; or "Given an outline map of the United States, with dots representing twenty major American cities (condition 2), the student will from memory correctly match (condition 1) sixteen of the twenty cities (condition 3)."

Although appealing at first glance, behaviorally defined instructional objectives are a matter of major controversy. While we all agree that instructional objectives should be stated in clear, measurable terms (such as "Does the student know, or does he not know, what an isosceles triangle is?"), many educators seriously question behavioral objectives on a number of philosophical, logical, and operational grounds.

Arguments against
behavioral objectives

Behavioral objectives stem from reductionistic premises: for example, from the notion that all human phenomena must be approached from the standpoint of dissection into their simplest elements (see association theories in chapter 3). This is objectionable to many psychologists, particularly the Gestalt psychologists, who, for more than fifty years, have been arguing that the whole is more than the sum of the parts. Humanists are also opposed to behavioral objectives, which they consider mechanistic and dehumanizing (see Combs 1972). Objecting on the basis of logic, Ebel (1970) points out that the true objectives of instruction are the knowledge, the understandings, and the attitudes that induced the behavior or made it possible, not the behavior itself. Wight (1962) presents essentially the same argument: that the proponents of behavioral objectives are confusing the objective with the means of determining whether it has been achieved. Objectives are important but, as Ebel sees it, it does not follow that they have to be stated behaviorally. He makes a distinction between *training*, for which behavioral objectives are clearly appropriate, and *education*, for which they are seldom appropriate. Russell (1965) sees this tendency to elevate behavior to the central role in the educational process as the "educational fallacy of the twentieth century."

A number of more specific objections have been raised. It has been argued, for example, that behavioral objectives frequently represent trivial aspects of the true goals of instruction, that they are frequently stilted, mechanical, and meaningless. Ausubel et al. (1978) argue that behavioral objectives are more appropriate for rote learning and that they tend to discourage meaningful verbal learning. Whereas these criticisms have been challenged (see Popham 1972), it seems that the truly important outcomes of meaningful education are not easy to formulate in behavioral terms and that they are often slighted as a consequence. As Ebel points out, as one moves from the psychomotor and the concrete to the more abstract aspects of human learning, the behavioral component of the activity in question becomes progressively more unavailable, nonexistent, irrelevant, or trivial. "Go fetch the stick" is a perfectly appropriate (behavioral) objective in the training of a dog; on the contrary, understanding the meaning of *reinforcement, democracy,* or the role of the computer in modern American society is relatively lacking a correspondingly critical behavioral component. There ought to be more to *understanding* the concept of reinforcement than being able to write a paragraph of unspecified enlightenment on the meaning of the concept.[3]

To the extent that this is true, behavioral objectives probably are more appropriate in the lower grades and for the lower intellectual levels than for the more advanced levels of educational and intellectual functioning. Formulating incisive and critical behavioral objectives tends to be more difficult when dealing with content of a high level of abstractness; it may also be inappropriate to insist on behavioral objectives when dealing with a field that is relatively open-ended.[4] Concerning the verbs presented earlier, the more educationally significant and meaningful these action verbs become—*to analyze, to synthesize, to evaluate*—the more subjective they also become and the more difficult it becomes to establish precise levels of proficiency and competency.

It has also been argued that behavioral objectives tend to stifle teacher and student initiative and that they destroy flexibility, imagination, and a sense of personal pride. They restrict what is to be learned to what is prescribed and generally make classroom learning a mechanical, assembly-line operation that prevents the teacher from capitalizing on the many opportunities for spontaneous learning that occur in the course of the teaching day.

Perhaps more fundamental is the philosophical issue of control. By definition, behavioral objectives tend to define the products of education; if they did not they would be useless. If they are followed too religiously, however, they can become a straitjacket, regimenting education down to the last detail. Although objectionable from a humanistic point of view, this might have compensating features of efficiency if we could only be sure of where we are going. But realizing that we cannot be sure of the specific goals best for each child

Behavioral objectives
imply . . .

---

3. See Mouly (1978) regarding operational definitions as a diminished version of the true construct under study.

4. Mastery learning, competency-based education, and criterion-referenced testing all assume a relatively closed system. The possibilities that boundaries can indeed be set as to what territory is being encompassed in a given educational experience is a most negative and erroneous view of education. See Heath and Nielson (1974) for a review of competency-based teacher education. Gage and Winne (1975) advise against a hasty implementation of competency-based teacher education.

with respect to each academic activity in relation to both the present and the future, it might be better to give children a bit of leeway as to what education befits their individual backgrounds, their special needs, interests, and aspirations. Or must we prescribe the *what, when,* and *how* of their every move? There is a need for a precise formulation of instructional objectives but, as some educators believe, there is also a need for student participation and initiative and some degree of flexibility (see Eisner 1967; Steinberg 1972).[5] In fact, given the lack of consensus in the field of education, it may be premature to overemphasize specific objectives. Perhaps education is far too complex to be encompassed by a few behavioral objectives; to attempt to do so may only serve to rigidify education along debatable lines.

Do behavioral objectives help?
    A strong argument against behavioral objectives is that the achievement of students whose teachers operate from behavioral objectives does not surpass that of students whose teachers rely on more global objectives or even implicit but unstated goals (Duchastel and Merrill 1973:15; Melton 1978). The evidence is equivocal, depending, for example, on the nature of the criterion of performance selected in relation to the objectives in question—that is, whether the criterion measure relates directly to the specific behavioral objec-

5. It should also be noted that much of the impetus for the behavioral objectives movement comes from the demand for accountability, a process that is possible only when the goals are relatively fixed as agreed upon.

tives prescribed or to more global understandings and insights. Behavioral objectives may actually discourage high levels of mastery by causing learning to stop at the level of minimal competency. It may be very tempting to the student who has achieved 80 percent proficiency as required to move on to the next unit rather than spend more time reaching for competence beyond the minimal prescribed level.

Yes, but . . .

The major issue here is how specific and precise we must be in stating instructional objectives. Certainly they should be stated in measurable rather than in global terms; the question is how much further must we go. Tyler (1973), generally acknowledged as the father of the behavioral objectives movement, strongly deplores the current confusion between clarity of objectives (which he sees as essential) and the overspecificity represented by the behavioral objectives approach. Objectives do not have to be stated behaviorally in order to be clear, attainable, and capable of assessment. He sees the specific-

---

2-1   CRITERION-REFERENCED TESTING

The evaluation of student performance relative to behavioral objectives is generally based on what is known as *criterion-referenced testing* (CRT):Can (or cannot) the student perform the task in question? This is in contrast to the better-known *norm-referenced* (NRT) approach, in which the student's score on a test is evaluated in relation to that of his or her peers and recorded as a percentile or letter grade.

In criterion-referenced testing, while the teacher is obviously concerned with the performance of the whole class—for example, 80 percent of the students will have correctly answered 80 percent of the addition combinations—the performance of each child is considered independent of that of his or her peers. All of the children can—indeed are expected to—achieve the specified criterion level on the items covering a given unit. If they do not on the first trial, they simply keep trying until they do. As it relates to instruction, each behavioral objective is considered separately: Can the student define criterion-referenced testing? Can he or she distinguish between criterion- and norm-referenced tests? The understanding is that inadequacies in student performance on any one objective are an automatic indication of a need for reteaching.

Behaviorally defined objectives and CRT are particularly appropriate for use in the context of accountability, mastery learning (see chapter 12), and competency-based education: Did the first-grade class achieve 80 percent accuracy with regard to the 100 addition facts? Can 80 percent (or 85 percent) of Ms. Smith's fifth-grade class convert proper fractions into decimals with 80 (or 85) percent computational accuracy as specified? The topic will be discussed further in chapter 13.

ity error as a transfer from industry, where the task is to train workers in a highly specific skill for specific job performance (such as soldering electronic equipment), to the school, where the task calls for generalized understandings, broad problem-solving capabilities, and the development of cognitive structure.[6]

The concept of behavioral objectives—along with its counterparts, criterion-referenced testing and mastery learning (see box 2.1)—is equally weak from a logical point of view in that it makes a dichotomy out of what, in many cases at least, must necessarily be a continuum. To insist that the student either *can* or *cannot* distinguish between operant and classical conditioning (see chapter 3), either *can* or *cannot* type or drive a car, is to resort to simplistic and arbitrary cutoffs and definitions that have little or no relation to reality.

In summary, behavioral objectives can serve a purpose in clarifying what the teacher and the student are trying to accomplish; it can thereby improve educational practice. It must also be noted that every criticism of behavioral objectives is subject to rebuttal (Popham 1972). On the other hand, we must be careful that overemphasis on actual behavior does not distort the goals of education toward the mechanistic and trivial or that it does not become an educational straitjacket.

ACCOUNTABILITY

Over the past decade, the American public has increasingly sought to hold the school accountable for its performance. In principle, accountability is a sound business practice of long standing; it implies a contract in which the school specifies its intended learning objectives, evaluates the extent of its successes relative to these objectives, and accepts responsibility for shortfalls, if any. Formal accountability was first introduced in education in *performance contracting,* in which private corporations contracted with a given school district to provide a specified instructional package, say, to culturally disadvantaged children, for a fee geared to student performance (Elam 1970; U.S. News & World Report 1972; see also Saretsky 1972). Apparently underlying the current emphasis on accountability is a considerable degree of dissatisfaction on the part of the public over the relative unproductivity of the school, a strong feeling that, despite considerable financial outlay, the schools are simply not producing the student gains society expects. Accountability is intended to assign responsibility for the successes and failures of the school in fulfilling its obligations.

Although the issue of accountability appears logical and legitimate on the

6. Behavioral objectives are largely a product of World War II, during which military psychologists found that traditional methods of instruction did not work well in training combat pilots and other military personnel. They found it worked better when they divided the overall task into specific units, each with specific objectives.

A controversial issue

surface, it is highly controversial, primarily because of difficulties in implementation (Lieberman et al. 1970; Ornstein and Talmage 1973; Combs 1972). As we noted in chapter 1, the school is not the sole determiner of the student's academic progress. It is impossible to isolate the school's contribution from that of the home and the community, which according to Coleman (1966), Jencks et al. (1972), and others is presumably more basic. Is the school to be held responsible for the limited intelligence of some of its students, for the antieducation attitudes of the community, for student absenteeism, for noncooperation on the part of the home, for the antisocial mores of the ghetto—all critically detracting from the school's efforts in achieving its goals? How can the algebra teacher be held responsible for the progress of a student who does not know how to add or subtract, and no longer cares? Who is to blame when, because of inadequate diagnostic and remedial services, learning difficulties have been allowed to grow beyond the point of retrievability?

Another major obstacle to meaningful accountability, one clearly related to difficulties mentioned in connection with behaviorally defined objectives, concerns the identification of the objectives and outcomes in terms of which accountability is defined. The more complex the outcomes, the more difficult they are to define and measure. Whereas we can easily identify such objectives as skill in adding, in spelling, in reading, or even in defining terms, it is often next to impossible to grasp the essence of critical thinking, arithmetic reasoning, and other complex educational processes. It is equally, if not more, difficult to measure values and attitudes of crucial importance to true education and which could easily suffer as the teacher applies pressure in order to achieve its more tangible academic goals.

The point is critical: if accountability is restricted to those learning outcomes that can be readily measured—and this tends to be a common pattern, if not an inherent feature—accountability will distort educational priorities as the more complex and the more significant aspects of true education are sloughed off while the teacher focuses on what is on the accountability list. At best, it might be expected that overemphasis on accountability will encourage teachers to "teach toward the test," to exploit those aspects of the program for which they are held accountable and correspondingly to neglect the other, often more significant, aspects of the educational program.

Equally frustrating problems are connected with the actual evaluation of student growth, however defined: (a) establishing the validity of the instruments used in relation to the specific objectives of the program and (b) determining student progress in the face of the unreliability and invalidity of whatever criterion measures are used, all of which complicate the task of assessing actual student progress as the basis for determining the school's success or failure in fulfilling its contract.

Benefits but also dangers

This is not to say that accountability is all wrong; certainly every enterprise, whether business or education, must be accountable for its performance. Teachers must be accountable for their performance: to themselves, to students and their parents, if to no one else. Nor can society's vital interest in the academic progress of its children be casually dismissed. By defining clear-cut goals, accountability makes for more meaningful motivation and for greater cooperation among teachers, students, and parents.

But many people consider accountability as a simplistic solution to a complicated problem. Not only is it unrealistic to hold the teacher (or the school) responsible for things over which they have no control, but overemphasis on accountability, besides possibly distorting the curriculum toward the trivial, can rob education of its dynamic and spontaneous quality and even encourage teachers to apply undue pressures on children to achieve impossible goals. Whereas accountability may be preferable from a certain point of view to the typical situation in which, as Good et al. (1975) suggest, schools have dozens of amorphous and elusive goals relative to which they are vaguely responsible for everything but held explicitly accountable for nothing in particular,[7] there is undoubtedly need for considerable caution in its use.

THE TAXONOMY OF EDUCATIONAL OBJECTIVES

The taxonomy: Three domains

A useful guide for formulating instructional goals is the *Taxonomy of Educational Objectives,* a detailed classification of objectives arranged hierarchically along the pattern of the classification system used, say, in biology in connection with plants and animals. The taxonomy first divides objectives into three major areas or domains:

1. The *cognitive* domain (Bloom et al. 1956), dealing with verbal knowledge, skills, and abilities.
2. The *affective* domain (Krathwohl et al. 1964), relating to attitudes and values.
3. The *psychomotor* domain (Harrow 1972), covering motor skills.

Each domain is, in turn, divided into levels on a hierarchical basis (table 2.1). The cognitive domain, for example, ranges from simple *knowledge* to *evaluation,* with each of the six levels (except *application*) further divided into subcategories. The affective domain has five levels, from the simple act of *receiving* (being aware) to *characterization.* The psychomotor domain lists six levels with corresponding subcategories.

---

7. This in no way prevents the school from holding the *child* responsible for his or her failures. It is interesting to note that, while our schools systematically fail a number of students, rather than hold this as evidence of our incompetence, we have simply made student failure an index of virtue, an indication that we are indeed "holding up standards." This seems to be a no-lose proposition.

Table 2-1 Taxonomy of Educational Objectives

Cognitive Domain	*Affective Domain*	*Psychomotor Domain*

6.0 Evaluation
  6.1 Internal criterion judgments
  6.2 External criterion judgments
		6.0 Nondiscursive communication
		  6.1 Expressive movements
		  6.2 Interpretive movements

5.0 Synthesis
  5.1 Unique communication
  5.2 Plan of proposed operation
  5.3 Set of abstract relations
	5.0 Characterized by a value
	  5.1 Generalized set
	  5.2 Characterization
		5.0 Skilled movement
		  5.1 Simple adaptive skill
		  5.2 Compound adaptive skill
		  5.3 Complex adaptive skill

4.0 Analysis
  4.1 Analysis of elements
  4.2 Analysis of relationships
	4.0 Organization
	  4.1 Value conceptualization
	  4.2 Organized value system
		4.0 Physical abilities
		  4.1 Endurance
		  4.2 Strength
		  4.3 Flexibility
		  4.4 Agility

3.0 Application	3.0 Valuing
	  3.1 Acceptance of a value
	  3.2 Preference for a value
	  3.3 Commitment
		3.0 Perceptual ability
		  3.1 Kinesthetic discrimination
		  3.2 Visual discrimination
		  3.3 Auditory discrimination
		  3.4 Tactile discrimination
		  3.5 Coordinated abilities

2.0 Comprehension
  2.1 Translation
  2.2 Interpretation
  2.3 Extrapolation
	2.0 Responding
	  2.1 Acquiescence in response
	  2.2 Willingness to respond
	  2.3 Satisfaction in response
		2.0 Basic fundamental movement
		  2.1 Locomotor movement
		  2.2 Nonlocomotor movement
		  2.3 Manipulative movement

1.0 Knowledge
  1.1 Specifics
  1.2 Ways and means of dealing with specifics
  1.3 Universals and abstractions in a field
	1.0 Receiving
	  1.1 Awareness
	  1.2 Willingness to receive
	  1.3 Controlled or selective attention
		1.0 Reflex movement
		  1.1 Segmental reflexes
		  1.2 Intersegmental reflexes
		  1.3 Suprasegmental reflexes

Source: Adapted from the *Taxonomy of Educational Objectives: Handbook I Cognitive Domain* by Benjamin S. Bloom et al. Copyright © 1956 by Longman Inc.; *Taxonomy of Educational Objectives: Handbook II Affective Domain* by David Krathwohl, Benjamin S. Bloom and Bertram B. Masia. Copyright © 1964 by Longman Inc.; and *A Taxonomy of the Psychomotor Domain* by Anita J. Harrow. Copyright © 1972 by Longman Inc. Reprinted by permission of Longman Inc., New York.

Cognitive Domain

The best known and, in a sense, the most functional from the standpoint of implementation is the cognitive domain. It relates most clearly to what many teachers see as the major function of the school: namely, the teaching of academic content.[8] Table 2.2 elaborates on the major categories of the cognitive domain shown in table 2.1 and for each level identifies both action verbs as might be used in formulating behavioral objectives and the typical learning outcomes to be expected.

The same pattern can be extended to the various subcategories within each level, e.g.,

1.10: Knowledge of specifics
1.11: Knowledge of terminology
   Action verbs: *Acquire, compare, contrast, define, distinguish, identify, recall, recognize*
   General learning outcomes: Definitions, meanings, vocabulary
1.12: Knowledge of specific facts
   Action verbs: *Enumerate, identify, list, recall, recite, recognize*
   General learning outcomes: Factual information (names, dates, persons), examples

The cognitive domain has been the subject of numerous publications, beginning with Mager's *Preparing Instructional Objectives* (1962), the bulk of the discussion based on behavioral premises. It lends itself readily to most subject-matter areas, particularly at the high school and college levels where the attainment of abstract reasoning permits adolescents to operate at the level of *synthesis* and *evaluation.* The following are examples formulated in relation to select units of a course in educational psychology:

The taxonomy and behavioral objectives

Upon completion of the unit, the student will be able:

1. Knowledge (nature of learning): To define the following terms: *classical conditioning, reinforcement, incentive,* etc.
2. Comprehension (measurements): To explain how a test can be reliable and yet not necessarily valid.
3. Application (classroom management): To apply operant principles to reduce disruptive behavior in the classroom.
4. Analysis (theories of learning): To identify the theoretical premises of various motivational strategies used in the typical classroom.
5. Synthesis (instructional strategies): To draw common implications of relevant behavioristic and field theories as they relate to effective instructional strategies.
6. Evaluation (objectives): To assess the relative merits of behavioral and nonbehavioral objectives in promoting the school's academic purposes.

8. See Webb (1970) for a parallel hierarchy of intellectual processes.

Table 2.2 Major Categories of the Cognitive Domain

Description	Examples of Action Verbs	General Learning Outcomes
1. Knowledge: Refers to the retention of previously learned materials, as might be involved in the simple recall of factual information.	*Defines, describes, distinguishes, identifies, labels, lists, names, recalls, reproduces, reorganizes, recognizes, states*	Factual materials (names, dates, properties, etc.), categories, concepts, definitions, symbols, vocabulary
2. Comprehension: Refers to the understanding of the meaning of previously learned materials as might be revealed by explaining, restating, interpreting, or summarizing	*Converts, distinguishes, explains, differentiates, extends, generalizes, gives examples, organizes, paraphrases, rewrites, summarizes, transforms, translates*	Meanings, insights, interpretations, understandings, generalizations, predictions, new rules and relationships
3. Applications: Refers to the use of previously learned materials in new situations (e.g., the use of rules and principles in the solution of a problem); typically requires a deeper understanding than comprehension	*Changes, computes, demonstrates, manipulates, modifies, operates, produces, relates, solves, uses*	Applications, generalizations, solutions
4. Analysis: Refers to the breakdown of previously learned materials into their basic elements so as to gain insights into their underlying relationships and organizational structure	*Breaks down, diagrams, contrasts, differentiates, discriminates, distinguishes, identifies, illustrates, infers, outlines, points out, relates, subdivides*	Insights into underlying relationships, recognition of underlying assumptions and premises, recognition of fallacies and gaps, distinctions between facts and inferences, between relevance and irrelevance
5. Synthesis: Refers to the restructuring of basic elements of what has been previously learned into a new pattern (e.g., the formulation of a new perspective or a new strategy)	*Categorizes, classifies, combines, compiles, creates, derives, designs, devises, formulates, generates, plans, rearranges, revises, rewrites, summarizes*	Integration of isolated elements into a solution, a new perspective (e.g., a new pattern, plan, theory, or principle)
6. Evaluation: Refers to a judgment as to the quality, validity, or value of ideas, productions, etc., based on appropriate criteria in relation to a given purpose	*Appraises, compares, contrasts, criticizes, discriminates, interprets, judges, justifies, summarizes, validates*	Judgment as to the quality of a creative production, judgment as to internal logic, or as to external criteria

Source: Adapted by permission of Psychology Press, from Metfessel et al., 1969.

The Affective Domain

Table 2.3 elaborates the brief outline of the affective domain shown in table 2.1 by including a description of the different levels and sublevels, together with learning outcomes and the typical action verbs to be used in formulating behavioral objectives.

The importance of the affective domain as a major component of the educational enterprise is obvious, particularly to the humanists who insist that, in order to be educationally profitable, learning experiences must be personally meaningful. Teachers typically attempt to make the learning climate pleasant and attractive in the hope that such an atmosphere will generate positive affect toward themselves as individuals and as teachers, toward the sub-

Table 2.3 Major Categories of the Affective Domain

Description	Examples of Action Verbs	General Learning Outcomes
1. Receiving: The student simply attends to the particular input	*Attends, follows, listens, perceives*	Reception ranging from simple awareness to deliberate selective perception
2. Responding: The student reacts to the incoming stimulus in some form of active participation	*Answers, complies, conforms, elaborates, performs, practices, participates, presents, repeats*	Participation in discussion, voluntary involvement in special assignments, compliance with rules, active interest in the topic
3. Valuing: Implies concern with the value (worth) the learner attributes to the input, ranging from simple acceptance to total personal commitment	*Clarifies, differentiates, initiates, justifies, selects, studies*	Attitudes and values, appreciations, commitments
4. Organization: Implies a restructuring of different values to resolve conflicts and develop an integrated internally consistent value system	*Adheres, arranges, combines, compares, contrasts, generalizes, integrates, modifies, orders (priorities), relates, resolves (conflicts), synthesizes*	Personal consistency, values clarification, affective clarity, self-understanding
5. Characterization by a value complex: Implies internalization and operationalization of a value system capable of promoting a characteristic lifestyle featuring pervasively consistent, integrated, and predictable behavior	*Acts, exemplifies, discriminates, displays, practices, proposes, questions, revises, resolves*	Behavioral consistency, personality integration, personal integrity, self-acceptance

Source: Adapted by permission of Psychology Press from Metfessel et al. 1969.

ject, toward the school, toward society in general, its values and its mores. Unfortunately, however, the affective domain presents the classroom teacher with a number of difficult problems. First, there are operational problems of just how to promote and how to measure changes in student attitudes and values. It seems, for example, that the more personally and educationally significant values develop slowly, often evolving over a period of years, long after the child has left school. Teachers have no way of knowing if their efforts are paying off, or even if they are on the right track. Complicating the matter is the pervasive notion that teachers have no right to influence the value system of their students—that in a democracy people, including children, have the right to think and feel as they please (see chapter 14). As a consequence, much of our present operation in this area is ambivalent, haphazard, and unproductive.

The Psychomotor Domain

The psychomotor domain was developed only recently (Harrow 1972) and to date has received only limited attention. It is, of course, of central importance in handwriting, typing, sports, and other skills emphasized in both the classroom and the playground.

HIGHLIGHTS OF THE CHAPTER

Society has delegated to the school responsibility for the education of the nation's children. If we are to be successful in accomplishing this all-important mission, we had better first decide where we are going.

1. Education, like any other operation, must necessarily begin with clear-cut precise goals and objectives.
2. Instructional goals must be stated in precise and measurable terms. To date, our goals have been so global that they have been of limited value as the basis for teaching or evaluation.
3. Behavioral objectives call for a statement of the performance to be expected, the conditions under which it is to occur, and the level considered adequate. Whether instructional objectives should be stated behaviorally is a matter of lively debate between those who insist on specificity and those who fear the distortion of the educational process toward the trivial.
4. By contrast to norm-referenced testing, criterion-referenced testing is concerned with the extent to which the class has achieved prespecified objectives or standards rather than how one child's performance compares with that of his peers.
5. The current movement toward behavioral objectives and criterion-referenced

testing is closely related to a parallel trend toward holding the school accountable for meeting its objectives. A major danger of overemphasis on accountability is that it may distort the priorities of a meaningful education.

6. The *Taxonomy of Educational Objectives* provides a logical framework for conceptualizing educational objectives and as such constitutes a significant contribution to the technology of instruction. The cognitive domain appears more amenable to implementation and has received greatest attention to date.

SUGGESTIONS FOR FURTHER READING

BAKER, EVA L. Beyond objectives: Domain-referenced tests for evaluation and instructional improvement. *Educ. Technol.* 14 (June 1974):10–16. A good discussion of the nature of criterion-referenced testing and its role in the improvement of instruction.

BROUDY, HARRY S. *A Critique of Performance-Based Teacher Education.* Washington: Amer. Assn. Coll., Teach. Educ., 1972. Argues that current emphasis on competency-based teacher education creates a learning situation in which the teacher is no longer a professional but simply a didactic machine. Such a training approach concerns itself only with whatever knowledge is instrumental in teacher performance.

COMBS, ARTHUR W. *Educational Accountability: Beyond Behavioral Objectives.* Washington: Assn. Superv. Curr. Devel., 1972. Presents the strong objections of humanistic psychologists to the current emphasis on behavioral objectives, accountability, and related behavioristic concepts.

MacDONALD-ROSS, M. Behavioral objectives: A critical review. *Instr. Sci.* 2 (1974):1–51. Presents a thorough discussion of the issues.

MAGER, ROBERT F. *Preparing Instructional Objectives.* Palo Alto, Calif.: Fearon, 1962. Provides information and practice in preparing instructional objectives. One of the first publications in the field and still one of the most adequate guides to preparing behavioral objectives.

POPHAM, W. JAMES. Must all objectives be behavioral? *Educ. Lead.* 29 (1972):605–608. Reviews how his own stand has moved from that of an unyielding advocate of behavioral objectives to a more moderate view that most educational objectives should be stated behaviorally.

POPHAM, W. JAMES, et al. *Instructional Objectives.* Chicago: Rand McNally, 1969. No. 3 of the Amer. Educ. Res. Assn. Monograph Series on Curriculum Evaluation. Presents an excellent overview of the subject.

ROSNER, BENJAMIN, et al. *The Power of Competency-Based Teacher Education.* Boston: Allyn & Bacon, 1972. Probably the most comprehensive presentation of the competency-based teacher education concept.

VARGAS, J. S. *Writing Worthwhile Behavioral Objectives.* New York: Harper & Row, 1972. A self-instructional booklet giving clear examples of how to write good behavioral objectives.

WRIGHTSTONE, J. WAYNE, et al. *Accountability in Education and Associated Measurement Problems.* Test Service Bull., No. 33. New York: Harcourt, n.d. An excellent presentation of the nature and the purpose of accountability in public education.

QUESTIONS AND PROJECTS

1. List three major arguments for—and three arguments against—the use of *behavioral* objectives.

    What overall statement might you make as to their role in education today?

2. What are the relative roles of criterion-referenced and norm-referenced testing in the operation of the modern classroom?

3. Contrast the views of the teaching profession and of the public concerning accountability in education.

    What might be a fair resolution of their differences?

    How might accountability be implemented?

4. How do the concepts of behavioral objectives, criterion-referenced testing, and accountability fit together?

    Can they operate independently? Explain.

5. Determine the taxonomic level (cognitive domain) of the items of the self-test to this chapter.

6. For any chapter in this book, list specific behavioral objectives to cover each of (a) the levels of the taxonomy for (b) each of the cognitive, the affective, and the psychomotor domains.

7. Specifically, how might the teacher maintain adequate focus on affective goals in the face of the ever-present demands for accountability along the more tangible cognitive dimensions? How might success in the attainment of affective goals be evaluated?

SELF-TEST

1. The primary purpose served by insisting on clear-cut instructional objectives is
    a. to clarify the role of education in democratic society.
    b. to define optimal social goals for national welfare.
    c. to gear the curriculum to what is feasible.

     d. to help plan effective evaluative strategies.

     e. to help plan effective instructional experiences.

2. The strongest argument in favor of stating instructional objectives behaviorally is that

     a. they cause the teacher to engage in more effective teaching.

     b. they focus instruction toward more critical educational goals.

     c. they make for clarity in communication between teacher and student.

     d. they serve as criteria for evaluating student outcomes.

     e. they synchronize instruction with current demands for accountability.

3. The greatest objection to requiring that instructional objectives be stated in behavioral terms is that

     a. their attainment can be measured only through physical performance.

     b. they cannot deal with the affective domain.

     c. they can operate only in the context of criterion-referenced testing.

     d. they do not identify the process through which they can be achieved.

     e. they tend to distort the curriculum to the lowest level of the taxonomy.

4. The greatest danger from overemphasis on accountability in education is that

     a. it can distort the educational process toward the trivial.

     b. it can force teachers to teach toward the instrument of accountability.

     c. it can increase student failure and grade retention.

     d. it can result in unhealthy pressures on certain students.

     e. it can standardize American education to minimal essentials.

5. Criterion-referenced testing is to norm-referenced testing as

     a. formative is to summative.

     b. informal is to standardized.

     c. individual is to group.

     d. objective is to criterion.

     e. short-term objectives are to long-term objectives.

6. The teacher choosing between CRT and NRT for assessing mastery of the present unit would probably fall at the _____ level of the taxonomy.

     a. analysis

     b. application

     c. evaluation

    d. knowledge

    e. response

7. Knowledge is to receiving as
   a. application is to analysis.
   b. comprehension is to response.
   c. concrete is to abstract.
   d. evaluation is to characterization.
   e. facts are to attitudes.

THREE

Theoretical Perspective

In reality, preference for understanding-level over memory-level means belief in the proposition that *the only way to make teaching genuinely practical is to make it basically theoretical.*

Ernest E. Bayles (1960)

Everything a teacher does is colored by the psychological theory he holds. Consequently, the teacher who does not make use of a systematic body of theory in his day-to-day decisions is behaving blindly.

Morris L. Bigge (1964)

The pathway of all sciences is littered with discarded theories, and psychology does not differ in this respect.

Howard Kingsley and Ralph Garry (1957)

— Provides a theoretical perspective from which psychological data can be interpreted as the basis for evaluating current classroom practice
— Presents the basic tenets of the major behavioristic and field theories of learning and their implications for classroom practice

PREVIEW: KEY CONCEPTS

1. Psychology as a science must not only identify functional relationships among behavioral phenomena but must also integrate research findings into theoretical structure.
2. In their pursuit for scientific clarity, scientists invent hypothetical constructs to explain empirical relationships among phenomena.
3. Psychological theories can be classified as behavioristic or cognitive, with variants in each camp. Among the better known are Thorndike's bond theory, Skinner's operant conditioning, Lewin's field theory, and the phenomenological theories.
4. None of the current theories of learning is totally acceptable to all psychologists. They nevertheless provide a useful perspective from which to interpret psychological data and suggest interesting implications for educational practice.
5. Educational psychology must not be interested only in the psychology of *learning* but must also concern itself with the psychology of *teaching*.

PREVIEW QUESTIONS

1. Given that theories of learning do not give prescriptions for teaching, why should teachers be familiar with the major theories of learning?
2. What are the primary goals of psychology as a science?
3. What is the major danger in scientists' postulating hypothetical constructs to explain psychological data? What are some of the more common hypothetical constructs used in psychology?
4. What major differences distinguish between behavioristic and cognitive theories of learning? How are these differences reflected in actual classroom practice?
5. How can a theory of *learning* serve as the basis for effective *teaching?*

Research attempts to
discover functional
relationships

The purpose of research in psychology is to identify the factors that affect behavior and the conditions under which modification of behavior occurs. The first task confronting the researcher is to formulate laws and principles that express functional relationships among psychological phenomena. At a higher level of science, the theorist attempts to synthesize into theoretical structure the various empirical findings derived from research. The ultimate goal is the relatively complete understanding of the learning process and its antecedents so as to permit the prediction, and eventually the control, of the occurrence of the behavioral changes in question.

THE NATURE OF RESEARCH

In an experiment, the investigator seeks to determine what effect a certain variable, e.g., the schedule of reinforcement, has on some aspect of the response, e.g., its resistance to extinction. The latter is called the *dependent* variable since its operation depends on that of the *independent* variable—i.e., in this case, the reinforcement. The experimenter's task is to discover a functional relationship between a certain antecedent and a certain dependent variable or consequent. In order to do this, the experimenter must exercise sufficient control of the situation to ensure that whatever effect is noted in the dependent variable can be clearly attributed to the operation of the independent variable under study rather than to various extraneous factors. This kind of control is difficult to achieve in the natural setting of the classroom, where a multitude of factors interact with the dependent variable and with each other to the point where the unequivocal identification of the "cause" of the phenomenon is difficult, if not impossible, to establish. An experiment, therefore, generally calls for a simplification of the natural situation in order to isolate the influence of the variable under investigation. The choice of a criterion is also crucial. We are primarily concerned with learning, but learning can be inferred only through some aspect of performance such as accuracy of response, resistance to forgetting, or perhaps some combination of criteria. And we may obtain one set of findings if we focus on one criterion and different— even opposite—results if we choose another.

Need for control

The operation of the independent variable with respect to the dependent variable is not a matter of a one-to-one direct-line operation; rather, scientific explanations typically involve postulating *hypothetical constructs* to account for the relationships noted among the variables in the situation. Chemists, for example, postulated the existence of molecules long before their existence was verified under a microscope. They simply found that scientific relationships, e.g., magnetism, were more logically and meaningfully explained when matter was *assumed* to be made of molecules. Chemists also postulated the concept of valence to account for the strength of various chemical reactions. Such hypothetical constructs are used in all sciences—genes in genetics, cell assemblies in physiology, habits and attitudes in psychology. The scientist's task is to discover laws that govern the operation of these hypothetical constructs. Meanwhile it is important to remember that hypothetical constructs are simply *explanatory* terms and not actual entities.

Learning itself is a hypothetical construct. We speak loosely when we say that practice causes learning. Practice is simply related in a functional way to performance, the adequacy of which is affected by numerous other variables operating in the situation. Performance is a measurable empirical concept, but learning as such does not exist; we simply postulate that children have learned as a way of accounting for the fact that they now can do something that they

could not do before. On the other hand, psychology makes learning a central concept and views performance simply as its external manifestation.

Hypothetical constructs can be conceived as *intervening* variables since they are assumed to intervene between the independent and the dependent variables. Motives, for example, are intervening variables whose existence we infer from the learner's persistence in potentially rewarding situations. We see motivation as a set of conditions encompassing a wide range of behaviors, from food seeking to striving for a grade, that predispose the organism to seek certain goals.

Intervening variables, in turn, can be categorized as *experiential* or *background* variables (relating to the extent to which one has the prerequisites for acquiring the behavior in question); *transfer* variables (including motivation, attitudes, and learning sets); and various *process* variables (such as the ability to make associations and discriminations, to generalize). The last, dealing with

Intervening variables

the capacity to perform certain internal processes, are known as *mediating* factors because they mediate between stimulus and response.

Perceptual processes   A special class of mediating factors is the perceptual processes, where *perception* is defined in its broad psychological sense with emphasis on the selectivity with which the individual attends to certain stimuli (and not to others) and emphasizes certain factors and minimizes others in interpreting a situation. Actually we do not respond to a simple stimulus or even the situation as it exists but rather to the phenomenon as we visualize or interpret the totality of the situation against the background of the social and physical setting, our potentialities, our motivational status, our past experiences, etc. It is possible, for example, for an experience to be rewarding and pleasant to some people and unpleasant to others, depending on their perception of the situation. Furthermore, this is an area in which only the individual can give a report; the world of personal experience (labeled the *phenomenal field* by such writers as Combs and Snygg 1959) is not accessible to outsiders except by inference.

All behavior involves mediating factors. In fact, learning refers to changes taking place in the mediating processes, and a major objective of teaching is the development of effective mediating processes. As learning proceeds, many of the mediating processes necessary in the early stages are discarded in the interest of a more efficient operation. The scientist's task is to identify the conditions (e.g., the pattern of teacher behavior) that are likely to be effective in this connection and, of course, the conditions to be avoided.

CONTEMPORARY THEORIES OF LEARNING[1]

Theory adds structure and perspective

Attempts to provide theoretical perspective for the empirical findings of modern psychology have led to the formulation of a number of competing theories, some of which have had an important influence on modern psychological and educational thought and practice. These theories are simply systematic attempts to synthesize empirical results into meaningful structure in order to explain the various aspects of behavior. All fall relatively short of providing a completely convincing framework comparable to those of the physical sciences. Nevertheless, they represent reasonably consistent statements of basic psychological perspective that can be used to advantage in dealing with psychological and pedagogical problems.

For purposes of the present discussion, contemporary theories of learning can be classified into two major systems: *association* theories, and *"field"* or *cognitive* theories, under each of which, in turn, can be categorized several

1. These theories are more appropriately conceived as theories of behavior or theories of psychology; i.e., a perspective from which the empirical data of psychology can be structured.

somewhat different and yet basically similar subsystems. This classification is somewhat arbitrary, with agreements and disagreements among the subsystems frequently running across system lines. Nevertheless there is a relative difference in outlook and orientation, as well as in emphasis, that allows us to group learning theories in these two major categories with contrasting common ground. The following discussion presents a brief overview of the better-known theories.

Association (Behavioristic) Theories[2]

Associationism dates back to Aristotle's concept of the association of ideas based on similarity, contrast, and contiguity. It became the only explanation of learning accepted by early psychologists. The standard approach was *introspection;* the investigator simply observed the working of his own mind. A reaction soon set in, however, as psychologists, realizing the highly subjective nature of introspection, turned to the examination of *overt* behavior on the premise that psychology could be a true science only if it switched its focus to behavioral processes whose occurrence could be verified, and a new version, known as *behaviorism,* developed from the older associationistic position.

Behaviorism focuses on overt behavior

Early behaviorism was overtly mechanistic. Watson (1930), for instance, objected to the concept of *satisfaction* and *annoyance* as factors in learning on the grounds that these were subjective terms that had no place in a truly scientific discipline. He confined his study to those aspects of behavior that were sufficiently overt to permit objective observations. This extreme emphasis on verifiable evidence led psychology to a relatively sterile position inasmuch as many significant psychological phenomena are not amenable to this sort of verification. The position has been somewhat softened (see Patterson 1977; Kitchener 1977), but its influence is still felt in the orientation of some contemporary psychologists.

Two major versions of associationism are currently in vogue: *connectionism* (often referred to as the bond theory) and *conditioning,* with the latter divided further into *classical* and *instrumental* conditioning.

Thorndike's contributions

CONNECTIONISM.   The foundations of modern associationism were established around 1900 by Thorndike, whose work over a period of fifty years constitutes what may be the most significant single contribution to the psychology of learning, especially from the standpoint of its influence on educational practice in America. As a result of his experiments involving a variety of animals, Thorndike came to see learning as a process of developing neural con-

2. Also known as *reinforcement* theories. They are sometimes referred to as *reductionistic* theories, in that they tend to reduce all behavioral phenomena to simple stimulus-response sequences. In the interest of simplicity, these terms, although not entirely synonymous, will be used interchangeably in the present discussion.

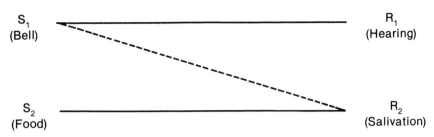

Figure 3.1 Paradigm of Classical Conditioning (Pavlov 1927)

nections (or bonds) between stimuli and responses. He was impressed by the typically trial-and-error nature of the behavior displayed by his experimental animals, and he concluded that learning was largely a matter of stamping in correct responses as a result of their rewarding consequences.

Thorndike postulated the *Law of Effect* as the fundamental principle underlying the formation of bonds between stimulus and response. When the animal was placed in a given situation, it would tend to repeat those responses that on previous occasions had been followed by satisfying aftereffects. Learning was a matter of the animal's trying various approaches to the problem until, perhaps by accident, it hit upon the correct response, which was then stamped in as a consequence of its satisfying aftereffects. Thorndike's contribution to the psychology of learning is of major significance. Although it no longer commands the monopoly it once held and although some of the pedagogical practices to which it lent theoretical support, e.g., overemphasis on drill, are no longer accepted, the influence of connectionism is still felt at both the practical and the theoretical levels.[3]

CLASSICAL CONDITIONING. Classical conditioning is best represented by Pavlov's well-known experiment demonstrating the formation of an association between salivation in a dog (the conditioned response) and the sound of a bell (the conditioned stimulus) through the repeated simultaneous presentation of the bell along with food (the unconditioned stimulus) serving to reinforce the association. (See figure 3.1.) In a way, conditioning represents the simplest form of learning; on the other hand, it accounts for much of the incidental learning that goes on in everyday life, e.g., the development of attitudes.

Guthrie and contiguity

Guthrie's contiguous conditioning. Although based on classical conditioning, Guthrie's contiguous conditioning model (Guthrie 1959) differs from classical conditioning in that it makes *contiguity* of a given stimulus and response the only factor necessary for the two to become associated. It is Guthrie's position that:

3. See Miller (1959) for a more recent connectionist view.

1. The only necessary (and sufficient) condition for conditioning to take place is that the response occur in the presence of (i.e., contiguously with) a particular stimulus.
2. A given association is established at full strength on an all-or-none basis on the first pairing of stimulus and response, and it remains at full strength until displaced by an incompatible association.

Motivation has no formal place in Guthrie's theory. It is important only to the extent that it keeps the organism active until the goal is attained, during the course of which an adequate response can be conditioned to the desired stimulus, and, further, that attainment of the goal removes the organism from the field and thus protects the most recent (presumably the successful) association from becoming displaced. The teacher's task, according to Guthrie, is simply to induce, by whatever means he can contrive, the organism to make the desired response when the stimulus is presented.

Hull and
reinforcement

Hull's behavioristic reinforcement theory. Hull's theory (Hull 1943; Logan 1959; Spence 1960) is probably the most elaborate from the standpoint of scientific development, having as its basis a structure of theorems and postulates from which he attempted to deduce the fundamental laws of learning. In contrast to Guthrie, Hull subscribed to the view that *reinforcement*, in the sense of the reduction of the tension associated with the frustration of a drive, is both necessary and sufficient for associations to be formed. In fact, his drive-reduction theory constitutes a major contribution to the field of motivation (see chapter 10).

INSTRUMENTAL CONDITIONING. Somewhat more recent is *instrumental* conditioning, so-called because here the animal's response is instrumental in accomplishing a given purpose; e.g., it presses the bar in order to get a pellet. Instrumental conditioning differs from classical conditioning in that it is goal directed or purposive in nature.

Whereas in classical conditioning, the behavior to be conditioned is elicited by a known stimulus (e.g., food), behavior in instrumental conditioning is simply emitted by the organism—undoubtedly as the result of some antecedent, but the nature of the stimulus is really irrelevant. All that is necessary is for the response to occur, generally as part of the spontaneous activity of the organism, so that it can be rewarded and brought under the control of its consequence.

In contrast to classical conditioning, where a given response is associated with a new but constant stimulus, the response in instrumental learning undergoes continuous modification as a consequence of feedback from the previous response. Learning is not a matter of forming the association between S and R with greater strength, greater precision, and greater probability of occurrence but rather of shaping a progressively more adequate response through successive approximations geared to a schedule of differential reinforcement.

Instrumental conditioning (Skinner 1959) has come into considerable prominence in recent years as a result of Skinner's success in training animals and in shaping academic behavior through programmed instruction. Skinner uses the term *operant behavior* to refer to the fact that, in order to get a reward, the organism must do something; it must operate on its environment. Although most of Skinner's work has been with animals, he has also been successful with children and even psychotic patients, all of whom, he claims, show amazing similarities in their learning processes. His basic premise is that the subject tends to repeat what it was doing at the time its behavior was reinforced. The instructor's task is a matter of baiting each step of the way and thus gradually leading the subject to the required performance.

Skinner's procedures are designed to shape behavior through selective reinforcement of progressively more adequate approximations to the desired behavior (and, of course, the extinction through nonreinforcement of inadequate behavior). An experimenter who wants the pigeon to peck at a given disk places the pigeon in a relatively restricted area in the presence of the disk. As the pigeon, in its spontaneous activity, moves closer to the disk, it gets a bit of food; it will get its next morsel when it gets still closer. Over time, just being close is no longer good enough: it must get its head next to the disk. Eventually it will get the reward only when it pecks at it. A sophisticated pigeon can learn this in minutes. This differential reinforcement of the subject's successive approximations to the required behavior is both necessary and sufficient for shaping its behavior.

Although he accepts both positive and negative reinforcement, Skinner believes that learning must be based on positive reinforcement, and he strongly opposes any form of aversive control. He has no interest in physiological explanations; that the rat should learn a certain association is all that matters, not how this is accomplished. To look inside the organism is to obscure what lies outside immediately available for observation. Neither does he subscribe to the concept that behavior is under the control of a goal, motive, or purpose; the subject does not respond in a given way because of the consequences that *will* follow behavior but rather simply because of the consequences that have followed similar behavior in the past.[4]

Skinner and the shaping of behavior

Skinner's opposition to "inner states"

Field (Cognitive) Theories

The second major family of contemporary learning theories originated in Germany around 1912 with Wertheimer's presentation of what became the Gestalt theory—which, as suggested by the term *Gestalt* (i.e., "configuration"), focuses on the global aspects of the situation. Gestalt psychology has consis-

---

4. Skinner's position is sometimes referred to by its critics as the *empty-organism theory*.

tently emphasized the study of behavior as a totality and in a sense represents a reaction against the mechanistic reductionistic orientation of behaviorism. Kohler (1927), for example, observed that apes displayed considerable insight, and concluded that Thorndike's emphasis on trial and error as the basis for learning was essentially incorrect.

Gestalt psychology has become known as *field* or *cognitive* theory, within which are a number of subgroups, varying in their emphasis on some of the more peripheral aspects but subscribing to the basic concept that human experiences have certain field properties that make the total phenomenon more than the sum of the separate parts. Field theories operate on the premise that behavior cannot be considered in isolation; to reduce experience to a sequence of elementary associations is, according to field theorists, to lose sight of its true properties. Cognitive theories are based on the principle of relativism; nothing is perceived as a thing-in-itself but rather in relation to other things in the sense of a *figure-and-ground* arrangement. Learning is part of the larger problem of organizing perceptions into a more complex structure exhibiting increasingly adequate field properties.[5]

The "field" concept

Field psychologists interpret the term *field* as the total psychological world in which the person operates at a given moment; the individual does not react to the environment as it is but rather as he or she perceives it at the moment of behavior. What is important from the standpoint of behavior is the meaning the situation has for the individual. Learning involves structuring the cognitive field and formulating cognitive patterns that correspond to the relationships among environmental stimuli. However, cognitive theorists place major emphasis on the selectivity of perception. We are aware of only certain aspects of the total environment; i.e., as we face a given situation, certain aspects come into focus while others remain in the background of a figure-and-ground arrangement. What we see in a given situation depends on our needs, our purposes, our insights, our past experiences, our potentialities, as well as what is really "out there." In other words, things are experienced in terms of the individual's psychological makeup so that reality is psychological (i.e., *phenomenological*) rather than physical and objective.

A second point of emphasis in field psychology is the purposiveness of behavior. We set our goals on the basis of our insights into the meaning of the situation; our behavior will be intelligent or shortsighted depending on the adequacy of our perceptions. Learning involves the development of insight—i.e., the development of a more adequate cognitive structure of the total situation, enabling us to perceive more effective ways of utilizing its elements in order to achieve our purposes. Practice is important in that it provides repeated exposures from which a more adequate cognitive structure can emerge.

5. The current trend is to view cognitive theories as "information-processing" theories (Wittrock 1978). The point will be discussed in chapter 9.

Learning as the
reorganization of
experience

Learning involves the reorganization of experience into systematic and meaningful patterns. According to field theorists, learning is more than the accumulation of simpler elements into a complex and integrated sequence. On the contrary, mental life begins with undifferentiated wholes out of which the parts are gradually differentiated. The whole is primary; the parts are meaningful only in the context of the whole in which they appear. Learning is a matter of proceeding from a complex whole that is only partially understood to a gradual clarification of the totality of the situation. The emphasis is on organization, relationships, meaningfulness, and cognitive clarity.

Lewin's life-space

LEWIN'S THEORY.   A major concept in Lewin's theory is that of the *life-space:* i.e., the psychological world in which the individual lives (see Cartwright 1959). It includes every person, every object, every concept, and idea with which the person has psychological contact. The person occupies a central position in his or her life-space. At first, it is relatively unexplored and the individual has only a superficial understanding of his or her world; in fact, at all times there are within the life-space areas of various degrees of differentiation and organizational clarity. The objective is an ever-greater clarification of the life-space, uncovering layer after layer and pushing its boundaries further and further back, thus attaining ever-greater contact with reality. A problem situation is simply an unstructured region in the life-space so that the individual does not know how to get from point to point. It must also be noted that the individual's life-space is of a moment's duration, even though there tends to be some basic continuity as one experience shades into another. We might compare this to the need for the football player carrying the ball down the field to make continual reappraisal of the situation. In other words, the life-space is continually undergoing reinterpretation as a result of changes in cognitive structure. Learning refers to the process of differentiating one's life-space so as to connect more of its subregions by defined paths as, for example, deriving interrelationships among heretofore isolated aspects.

Valence, a function
of perception

Another important concept in Lewin's theory is that of *valence,* a term borrowed from chemistry to refer to the strength of attraction and repulsion of the elements of a given situation for a given individual at a given time. The outcome of a particular situation is the net result of the various forces of attraction and repulsion of the overall system as experienced by the learner. In other words, valence resides in the meaning the situation has for the individual, not in the situation per se, so that what attracts one person may actually repel another. An important aspect of learning is the change in the valence value of the various goals as a result of the further clarification of the life-space; as we meditate or mature, for example, we may get insights into the shortsightedness of our present goals. Reinforcement is not a central concept in Lewin's vector theory; yet the more motives lead us to explore our environment, the more likely we are to restructure our perceptual field and the more likely we are to see new and more effective approaches to the attainment of our goals.

TOLMAN'S PURPOSIVE BEHAVIORISM.   According to Tolman (1959), behavior is both cognitive and purposive in the sense that the development of cognitive structure is designed to facilitate effective use of the various aspects of the environment as tools or *means-objects* in the attainment of one's goals. Behavior is goal oriented, but there is more than one way to attain a given goal. The rat in the maze is really learning its way about; it is developing a maplike representation of the situation (i.e., *expectancies*), not a sequence of running and turning habits. Once it has attained this cognitive structure, it can use cognitive signs to guide itself to the goal, not necessarily by the route to which it is accustomed but by the route it sees will get it there most effectively under the present circumstances.

Tolman and cognitive structure

PHENOMENOLOGICAL PSYCHOLOGY.   In even greater contrast with the mechanistic orientation of behavioristic theories is the phenomenological version of field psychology (Combs and Snygg 1959; Combs 1962; Maslow 1962; Rogers 1959a), a position whose possibilities, though perhaps most obvious in a clinical setting, are equally relevant in other areas of human endeavor. Educators, for example, are becoming more aware of its implications with regard to the various aspects of classroom operation.

The phenomenological nature of perception

Phenomenological psychology represents a systematic attempt to deal with the world of phenomena in the psychological reality of its essential characteristics. Like other field theories, it views the individual in a state of dynamic equilibrium within the field in which he or she operates, but it places special emphasis on the phenomenological nature of perception. Perception is defined relativistically; what determines behavior is not objective reality but rather psychological—i.e., *phenomenological*—reality. This world of personal experience is accessible to outsiders only through inference, and although this might make such data questionable as scientific evidence, to the phenomenologist the raw data of experience as recorded by the individual are legitimate and meaningful. This is the environment that has psychological significance, since this is what the individual is reacting to. In a real psychological sense, this is "what's out there," without regard to why, when, and wherefore.

Phenomenological psychology relates directly to recent emphasis on humanistic psychology, e.g., the Third Force as postulated by Maslow (1968) and the concept of becoming (see Combs 1962). The phenomenologist accepts as subject matter of inquiry all data of experience, including feelings; meaning is central and inescapable. In a sense, phenomenological psychology attempts to rescue psychology from the narrowness of behaviorism. Rogers (1964), for example, feels that it is unfortunate that, in our attempt to walk in the footsteps

Objections to behaviorism

of Newtonian physics, we have permitted the world of psychological science to be narrowed to behaviors observed, to sounds emitted, to marks scratched on an answer sheet. To limit ourselves to the study of observed behavior, and thus to rule out of consideration the universe of inner meanings and purposes and the inner flow of experience, seems to Rogers to be closing our eyes to the great areas that confront us when we look at the human world. Maslow (1966) voices similar concerns. The humanist sees the human person not as the defenseless victim of reinforcement schedules[6] but rather as a purposeful being geared to the pursuit of self-determination, self-fulfillment, and self-actualization. The role of education is to foster individuality by helping each child actualize his or her potentialities to the fullest—not to turn out identical, interchangeable "pieces" on an assembly-line basis.

Other Theories

Other theories can be mentioned. Functionalism, as introduced years ago by John Dewey, for example, is an eclectic approach that has considerable appeal for classroom teachers and psychologists who cannot subcribe totally to one or the other of the more theoretically consistent viewpoints. It is a relatively free and flexible attempt to draw from various theoretical positions whatever explanation has greatest meaning from the standpoint of the practical situation. The emphasis is on the functionality of relationships rather than on their theoretical origin.

A theory of long standing in the clinical field is (Freudian) psychoanalysis. Freud's emphasis on the influence of early experience on personality development, for example, has found support in such findings as those of Hunt (1941) of the effects of early frustration on adult hoarding in rats and of Wolf (1943) on the effects of early sensory deprivation on the later functioning of rats under stress. The Freudian concepts of anxiety, fixation, and repression have considerable significance for educational practice and will be presented in the various sections of the text without further reference to their psychoanalytic origin.

Also of major interest are the more recent and somewhat incomplete "learning" theories, e.g., Rotter's (1954) social learning model; Bandura's (1969, 1977) modeling theory (see also Miller and Dollard 1951); Hunt's (1960) cumulative learning model with its special reference to cumulative deficit; and Guilford's (1968) information model, best known with respect to the structure of the human intellect. Also of importance is Piaget's cognitive development theory, to be presented in chapter 5. Of special significance to the operation of the classroom are Ausubel's (1968) cognitive theory of meaningful verbal learning and Gagné's (1977) hierarchical model, both of which will be discussed at length in the section on learning.

6. Social learning theorists (e.g., Bandura 1969, 1977) voice a similar conviction.

EVALUATION OF LEARNING THEORIES

Major Issues

Need for theory

The progress of a given discipline depends as much on theoretical advances as on experimental productivity, for, without a theoretical framework, science constitutes a mere accumulation of isolated facts and laws. The result of scientific investigation is the discovery of functional relationships among phenomena, but only through the organization of these relationships into theoretical structure can we attain a broad understanding of their true nature. Although there are those who hold contrary views—Skinner (1950), for example, questions the need for learning theories—most psychologists agree on the value of theoretical perspective in the understanding of psychological phenomena. Certainly theory has been productive in the advancement of the physical sciences.

Differences in interpretation

Principles and laws are invariant under the conditions for which they are defined. It is in trying to place these empirical findings into theoretical structure that we run into different points of view. This is especially true in psychology, where we have a good number of theories, each with its specific orientation. They all agree as to the basic facts but disagree as to their interpretation. Some theories are perhaps more adequate—i.e., more plausible, comprehensive, and parsimonious—than others, but that depends on the perspective from which the data are approached. Actually, the task of reconciling these positions is the concern of psychology rather than education. The primary responsibility of the teaching profession is not to define or to explain learning processes but rather to deal with the practical problems of guiding learning activities. Yet, in order to carry out these duties in a professional and responsible manner, teachers must have an overall understanding of theories that enable them to extrapolate from what is known as the basis for effective teaching practices. This is especially necessary in that our present knowledge does not, and probably never will, cover every possible situation that arises in the course of the school day. Typically, pedagogical situations are so complex that teachers must improvise and extrapolate beyond existing data. Thus they need some overall perspective from which to deal with the myriad of relatively unique situations for which they lack clear-cut guidelines. A theoretical perspective is equally central to the proper evaluation of psychological data. Students need to understand the perspective from which the data are presented and the validity of the theoretical framework superimposed thereon.

Criticisms of current theories

That none of the theories postulated to date is acceptable to all is abundantly clear from the divergent views presented and the many objections raised against any one theory by subscribers to the opposite views. At a general level, many critics object to psychology's over-orientation toward animal subjects. Melton (1956) suggests that to concentrate so much research energy and scientific eloquence on the rat with its limited symbolic capabilities and non-

existent verbal capabilities seems too high an intellectual price to pay for ease of procurement, maintainability, and reproduction of kind. Maier (1960) goes a step further: he suggests that psychologists often use theory to supersede rather than to synthesize the facts. A common strategy is to give the facts a new name. Since it is no longer fashionable to speak of *instincts,* psychologists now talk of *imprinting* or *species-specific behavior,* which apparently means essentially the same thing; they simply make the conflict disappear through word magic. Another common way of dealing with a difficult situation is to give circular answers. Frequently scientific "explanations" simply restate the problem. To say that people enjoy working because they are motivated is saying nothing more than people enjoy working because they enjoy working; it is simply describing at a different level of language the phenomenon it alleges to explain.

Behaviorism: A reductionistic approach

At the more specific level, behaviorism, for example, has been the target of increasing criticism concerning its reductionistic premises, i.e., its tendency to analyze complex human phenomena into the simplest elements of behavior. Whereas this approach may be appropriate for dealing with simple psycho-motor or even verbal skills (as it has been in, say, chemistry), psychologists are beginning to accept the notion of a discontinuity between the learning of simple and complex behavioral patterns and correspondingly between the learning of animals and that of humans. Skinner's behavioristic model has been particularly criticized for its insistence that all that is required for learning to take place is the proper contingencies of reinforcement and its corresponding rejection of inner states, motivation, intent, experiential background, etc., as irrelevant.[7] Gage (1963), for example, sees conditioning as a blind, irrational process which, regardless of how powerful it might be in shaping the behavior of pigeons or of children, is essentially alien to the dignity of man as a thinking animal. He feels that, despite its scientific appeal, conditioning as a theory is too narrow in scope to explain adequately the more significant aspects of behavior, e.g., problem solving and creativity. This is perhaps a point of unavoidable weakness in the behavioristic position, which, in order to be scientific, must sacrifice the more subjective aspects of phenomena. There is always a danger of buying scientific rigor and precision at the expense of psychological significance and meaningfulness. On the other hand, psychoanalytical and phenomenological theories have been criticized as too vague, subjective, and unverifiable to be of serious scientific value.

Current theories differ from the standpoint of the materials to which they apply; habit formation may well call for a different approach to learning than problem solving, for example. In fact, psychologists are seriously questioning whether all learning phenomena can be accounted for by a single global theory encompassing all aspects of the learning process. Gagné (1974, p. 149), for example, argues that "our trouble in the past is that we have tried to subsume many qualitatively different types of learning under a single explanatory model." Deese and Hulse (1967) suggest that, instead of looking for a single theoretical system, we focus on microtheories dealing with a rather specific bit of behavior.[8] It might be argued, for example, that contiguity may indeed represent a significant factor in the learning of habits, attitudes, emotions, and various relatively involuntary reactions. The development of psychomotor skills, on the hand, might be most effectively seen from the S-R position, while the solution of problems, the mastery of concepts, and the acquisition of complicated insights, differentiations, and integrations, requiring mediation through the higher mental processes, might be most adequately viewed from the perspective of cognitive theory.[9]

Minitheories are probably best

We must avoid both the dogmatism of a premature systematization and

7. See Patterson (1977) for a thorough and essentially negative evaluation of the behavioristic approach. Patterson notes that most behaviorists are moving away from this extreme behavioristic position, to incorporate inner states as an essential factor in human learning. Travers (1977) is also highly critical of Skinner's reductionistic views; he even questions the evidence of success of operant conditioning in the shaping of behavior. See also Herrnstein 1977a, 1977b; Skinner 1977.

8. Travers (1966) makes a similar suggestion regarding theories of instruction.

9. It might also be noted that although operant conditioning strategies are ideal for the training of animals, such procedures are hopelessly ineffective by comparison to verbal instruction or perhaps modeling when dealing with human subjects (see Bandura and Walters 1963).

close-minded adherence to a single point of view and a superficial, naive eclecticism with regard to conflicting positions. For the time being, perhaps a broad, flexible position is best. As Deese and Hulse (1967, p. 2) suggest, "Complete devotion to one particular theory is almost certainly dangerous, given our present ignorance about the facts of psychology." Whereas some of the more theoretically oriented psychologists prefer to commit themselves to one theory, others hold that a theory is useful or useless rather than correct or incorrect and that, at the practical level, a fair use of different viewpoints is preferable to adherence to a single theory just for the sake of consistency. Nevertheless, if we are to avoid the confusion likely to result from the contradictory implications of an uncritical combination of different frames of reference, we need to work for an increasingly coherent and systematic core of operational principles, say, as the basis for educational practice.

Curricular Implications

More important in the present context is the extent to which the various theories provide a consistent and dependable foundation for educational practice. First, we must recognize that a principle or a theory of educational psychology cannot be translated directly into a specific method of learning or teaching. More than one method may be consistent with a given theory or principle; one method may be appropriate for certain conditions and quite different techniques equally suitable for different circumstances. All that can be expected is for a theory to provide basic insights as to broad classroom strategies.

A curriculum based on behavioristic premises would . . .

A curriculum based on behavioristic premises would be characterized by simplicity. In its extreme form, it would call for identifying the responses that mark the educated person, identifying appropriate stimuli, and presenting these stimuli in order to promote their association with the desired responses either through contiguous presentation or through reinforcement. These associations could then be sequenced to form whatever behavior pattern is required. At a relatively mechanistic level, behaviorists would emphasize having the learner, in a state of readiness, attack a given problem with variable and multiple response and rely on reinforcement to clinch correct responses. The desired connections would be consolidated through properly motivated practice and generalized to related situations. Behaviorists would caution us to be careful as to what we reinforce. The child who finds that a headache saves him from having to face a difficult assignment is being reinforced into reliance on illness. Skinner would counsel teachers not to dismiss the class while the children are being rowdy; they should insist that they be quiet and then reward them through dismissal.

The curriculum based on operant conditioning is specific and definitive. The key to successful teaching is to analyze the nature of the task to be learned, to design techniques that manipulate the process with persistence and consistency, and to set up definite and specific reinforcing contingencies so that behavior can be brought under the precise control of its consequences. Teaching (as reflected, for instance, in the teaching-machine movement) is a matter of a carefully designed program of gradual changes in the contingencies involved and in the skillful use of reinforcement to maintain behavioral strength.

A curriculum derived from cognitive premises would . . .

The curriculum devised according to cognitive specifications, on the contrary, would stress the structuring of the learner's perceptual and cognitive field. The focus would be on insight, meaningfulness, and organization, and the teacher would emphasize understanding and structure both in the presentation of subject matter and in the learning that the children would do. Classroom procedures would be oriented toward the clarification of issues, the discovery of interrelationships, and the differentiation of relatively unstructured problem situations into situations having greater clarity and focus. The "cognitive" teacher would begin with a broad outline of the material and get to the details only after establishing the basic "scaffolding" onto which the details could be hung. The teacher would rely directly on cognitive feedback to either confirm or redirect learning. Cognitive theorists also recognize that understandings, meanings, and insights once achieved need to be clarified further through practice; they are not opposed to repetition, but they insist that insight precede practice. Lewin, for example, sees repetition as necessary to clarify one's life-space, to structure it more adequately, and to develop new relationships and new differentiations of formerly undifferentiated areas as the basis for more adequate behavior.

Cognitive theorists would stress the dominant role played by the field in which phenomena occur. They would emphasize the development of meaningful relationships within the overall field and would strive to ensure that students grasp clearly what they are attempting to learn in proper figure-and-ground perspective so as to have the phenomenon under discussion properly integrated in the total situation. Cognitive theorists would condemn teaching material out of the context of the total situation in which it occurs or teaching skills in isolation from their use; e.g., the rules of grammar apart from their use in effective communication.

Different views on the role of the learner

More fundamentally, the major difference between the behavioristic and the cognitive position lies in the radically different implications that arise from their opposite premises as to what takes place in the learner while learning is said to occur. Reinforcement theories are geared to external control: the child is systematically controlled through reinforcement made contingent upon suitable behavior. To change behavior, the teacher must change the environment, i.e., change the schedule of reinforcement so that the desired behavior (when it occurs) is properly reinforced. The Skinnerian position, sometimes referred to as the *empty-organism position,* considers what the learner believes or feels as largely irrelevant (see Skinner 1977). By contrast, cognitive psychology brings the whole person into the process of learning. Learning involves first of all a change in the individual's perceptions of the situation—a change at the level of thinking, feeling, interests, values—which then results in a change in behavior. Conversely a change in behavior implies that something has occurred inside the learner.

The behavioristic teacher is in total control, arranging environmental conditions so as to provide systematic reinforcement. According to Lipe and Jung (1971), if the child does not learn, the fault is not with the child but with the environment, i.e., with the schedule of reinforcement that has given him no choice but to behave as he does. A major rule here is to catch the child "being good," i.e., to systematically reinforce every instance of positive behavior and correspondingly to extinguish inappropriate behavior through nonreinforcement. If the child does not do his or her homework, the teacher needs to ensure that any effort in the direction of homework, however minimal, is duly rewarded until "homework" behavior is established on a self-reinforcing schedule.

The cognitive teacher, on the other hand, would attempt to have children incorporate learning (and homework) as part of their life-space. The teacher would operate on the premise that children have an innate need to grow, to learn, to organize the perceptions of their life-space as the basis for behaving more effectively in relation to their environment as perceived. The teacher's task is to get children personally involved, to have them see the need to learn and how homework is relevant to the achievement of their personal goals. More fundamentally, the teacher's task is to provide a learning situation in which children can develop a broader personal perspective to include the truly meaningful features of the world of things and others—i.e., to promote changes in personal meaning consistent with their long-term welfare.

Although primarily oriented toward the development of the individual as a self-actualizing person, the phenomenological approach has important bearings on the curriculum and the operation of the classroom. Only recently have educators begun to appreciate the extent to which the child's self-perception in relation to schoolwork and the totality of the school situation has significance on behavior in the school, both academically and personally. This is particularly emphasized in Rogers's (1969) insistence that to be profitable, education must be personally meaningful. To the humanist, the vital role of education is the discovery of a personal solution to a personally perceived problem. The ultimate purpose is to understand oneself in relation to things that have phenomenological existence. The humanistic teacher, for example, would resist any attempt to mold the learner into the lock-step of the standard curriculum into which everyone must fit, regardless of personal needs and individual differences. The assumption is that children will learn when they see the material as meaningful from the perspective of their goals and purposes.[10]

10. The difficulty with the phenomenological position, as Gagné (1977) points out, is that it is easy enough to encourage the child to get personally involved in problem solving or reasoning, but, in order to get there, he or she must first have worked through many hours of rela-

Behaviorism: The teacher is in charge

Humanism emphasizes personal meaning

The phenomenological position has considerable appeal, particularly to those interested in the personal development of the child in interaction with the totality of the environment. Unfortunately, by contrast to the 1-2-3 precision of behavioristic theory, it is rather vague as to how its various objectives are to be attained. How is the teacher to effect changes in the perceptions of students? Despite its sense of meaningful perspective and its general appeal, its lack of specific means of implementation constitutes a major limitation to its use in the classroom. Its vagueness also raises a question as to its adequacy as a scientific theory (see Wylie 1961, 1968; see also Krasner 1978, for an overview of the behavioristic-humanistic debate).

In summary, the current theoretical position as it underlies classroom teaching is obviously unclear. It certainly does not provide the teacher with a set of prescriptions neatly tabulated to fit each specific situation to be encountered in the classroom. On the other hand, it does provide valuable insights, ideas, and understandings that conscientious teachers should be able to use to advantage. And the more adequately that teachers grasp the various viewpoints, the more adequate the perspective from which they can approach their teaching-learning responsibilities.

THEORIES OF TEACHING

Considerable feeling has been generated in recent years as to the apparent inadequacy of theories of learning as the basis for effective teaching and the consequent demand for theories of *teaching* more closely designed to deal with teacher behavior as it affects pupil learning. As we noted in chapter 1, theories of learning are concerned primarily with what the learner does, but we also need to be concerned with what the teacher does in order to promote desirable behavior changes in the classroom. Whereas teaching and learning are part of the same operation, there are certain aspects of learning that are relatively independent of teaching, and vice versa. The need is for theories of teaching to *complement* current theories of learning. More specifically, a theory of instruction must necessarily differ in function and in content from a theory of learning in that it must move from the descriptive and exploratory to the prescriptive, i.e, to clearly defined procedures to be implemented in practice.

Gage (1964) suggests the need for theories of teaching relatively independent of theories of learning. Ausubel (1968; Ausubel et al. 1978), on the other hand, takes a more conventional stand, pointing out, for example, that whatever is meant by *teaching* has to relate to whatever is meant by *learning* so that

---

tively less exciting prerequisite learning, e.g., the multiplication table. Many children do not have the maturity and the foresight to persevere through the sometimes minimally rewarding foundation work.

theories of learning and theories of teaching must necessarily be interdependent. He argues that it is from theories of learning that we must develop ideas of how crucial factors in the teaching-learning situation can be most profitably manipulated. He contends further that, by contrast to prevailing theories that simply do not deal with the kind of learning that goes on in the classroom, a truly realistic and scientifically viable theory of meaningful classroom learning would indeed give a prominent place to the variables teachers can manipulate in order to influence classroom learning. He believes that inclusive theories of both learning and teaching are needed for a complete theory of pedagogy, with neither a substitute for the other. However, as Atkinson (1972) points out, an all-inclusive theory of learning is not a prerequisite for the development of optimal teaching procedures. On the contrary, theoretical developments in both teaching and learning can be expected to promote corresponding advances in the other.

HIGHLIGHTS OF THE CHAPTER

Chapter 3 presents a broad overview of psychology as a science. It attempts to provide a perspective for understanding psychological phenomena.

1. Science attempts to identify functional relationships among phenomena and to organize these relationships into theoretical structure.
2. In the attempt to account for the relationships noted between dependent variables and the independent variables under study, scientists postulate hypothetical constructs, an important subgroup of which are the perceptual processes. People do not respond to the environment as it actually exists but to the situation as they see it. Learning itself is a hypothetical construct.
3. Theories of learning can be categorized into two broad categories: the association and the cognitive (field) theories, with a number of semi-independent theories under each. Association theories, for example, include connectionism and conditioning, the latter further broken down into classical and instrumental conditioning. Field theories likewise include a number of subtheories.
4. None of the theories of learning as presently constituted is completely acceptable. A number of criticisms of various degrees of validity and of severity have been leveled at each. The major differences among them are essentially a matter of perspective and emphasis. This would be reflected in corresponding differences in pedagogical implications.
5. Teaching from behavioristic principles would be relatively simple and straightforward; the task would be analyzed into subcomponents, appropriate stimuli would be presented, and a systematic schedule of reinforcement would be used to clinch correct responses. A cognitive approach would, by contrast, emphasize structural perspective, meaningfulness, and personal involvement.

6. The major point of distinction between association and cognitive theories is their opposite premises as to the question of internal as against external control of the learning experience.

SUGGESTIONS FOR FURTHER READING

BIGGE, MORRIS L. *Learning Theories for Teachers.* New York: Harper & Row, 1971. One of the most readable presentations of various theoretical positions and their application in the classroom.

GAGE, NATHANIEL L. Can science contribute to the art of teaching? *Phi Delta Kappan* 49 (1968):399–403. Expresses both optimism and concern as to the role of science in the promotion of effective teaching. Suggests ways in which science can contribute to effective teaching.

GORDON, IRA J., ed. *Criteria for Theories of Instruction.* Washington, D.C.: Assn. Superv. Curr. Devel., 1968. Also Atkinson, Richard J. Ingredients for a theory of instruction. *Amer. Psychol.* 27 (1972):921–931. Provide a valuable clarification of the dimensions and structure of theories of teaching.

HERRNSTEIN, R. J. The evolution of behaviorism. *Amer. Psychol.* 32 (1977):593–603. Skinner, B. F. Herrnstein and the evolution of behaviorism. *Amer. Psychol.* 32 (1977):1006–1012. Herrnstein, R. J. Doing what comes naturally: A reply to Professor Skinner. *Amer. Psychol.* 32 (1977):1013–1016. A critical interchange on the alleged shortcomings of the behavioristic position. Provides good insights into some of the basic premises of behaviorism.

HILL, W. F. *Learning: A Survey of Psychological Interpretations.* New York: Crowell, 1977. Presents a broad overview of a wide variety of theories of learning ranging from Watson and Skinner to cybernetics and biofeedback.

MARX, MELVIN H. *Learning. Vol. 3: Theories.* New York: Macmillan, 1970. The third volume of Marx's series on learning. Comprehensive and scholarly.

NUTHALL, G., and I. SNOOK. Contemporary models of teaching. In Robert M. W. Travers, ed., *Second Handbook of Research on Teaching*, pp. 47–76. Chicago: Rand McNally, 1973. Discusses the relative merits of three basic teaching models: the behavior-control model, the discovery-learning model, and the rational model.

PITTENGER, OWEN E., and C. THOMAS GOODING. *Learning Theories in Educational Practice: An Integration of Psychological Theory and Educational Philosophy.* New York: Wiley, 1971. Contrasts associative and cognitive field theories and relates them to the philosophical concepts of idealism and realism. Suggests that the differences are so fundamental that the two cannot be reconciled without doing violence to both.

SCANDURA, JOSEPH N. Teaching—Technology or theory? *Amer. Educ. Res. J.* 3 (1966):139–146. Contrasts teaching as a technology based on a science of learning and as a technology based on a to-be-developed theory of teaching. Suggests that the theories of teaching that will evolve will be relatively independent of current theories of learning.

SKINNER, B. F. *Beyond Freedom and Dignity.* New York: Knopf, 1971. Presents a strong argument against what Skinner sees as a false sense of freedom.

———. *About Behaviorism.* New York: Knopf, 1974. Explains behaviorism and answers many of the criticisms and misunderstandings concerning behaviorism. A clear exposition of the Skinnerian position.

SUPPES, PATRICK. The place of theory in educational research. *Educ. Res.* 3 (1974):3–10. Presents a strong argument for the need for theoretical perspective in education. The alternative is intuition and chaos in practice.

UNGAR, C. Chemical transfer of learning. *Today's Educ.* 58 (February 1969):45–47. Discusses how learning achieved by one rat can be transformed to another through cannibalism. The same process can be used with chickens.

QUESTIONS AND PROJECTS

1. Plan a lesson according to contrasting behavioristic and cognitive specifications. What differences might exist in the objectives that the two approaches would emphasize? How might the relative effectiveness of the two approaches be evaluated?

2. Collect a series of statements expressing various theoretical orientations on key issues, e.g., the definition of learning the role of motivation, etc. Survey the members of the faculty of the departments of education and of psychology as to the position they would take on these matters.

3. Evaluate: To the extent that teaching is an art, theories of learning contribute nothing to the practical job of teaching. What benefits might the classroom teacher derive from a knowledge of learning theories?

4. How does a theory differ from a model? Identify teachers using apparently different teaching styles. What model does each follow? What differences might be expected in student outcomes?

5. Do different teaching styles reflect one's personal philosophy of life? How is this reflected in the neohumanistic view of education as implemented in the free school (see chapter 12)?

SELF-TEST

1. Which of the following *least* qualifies as a hypothetical construct?
   a. behavior
   b. genes
   c. learning
   d. learning sets
   e. motivation

2. Which of the following associations is *incorrect?*
    a. Guthrie (classical conditioning): contiguous association
    b. Hull (classical conditioning): reinforcement
    c. Skinner (operant conditioning): motivation
    d. Thorndike (connectionism): law of effect
    e. Tolman: means-end expectancies

3. All major theories of learning agree on the importance of _____ in the learning process.
    a. motivation
    b. part-whole relationships
    c. previous experience
    d. reinforcement
    e. None of the above has complete acceptance in all theories.

4. Disagreement among theories stems primarily from differences in
    a. the empirical data from which they spring.
    b. the interpretation they give to the empirical evidence.
    c. the kind of learning to which they apply.
    d. the terminology they use to describe empirical events.
    e. their willingness to sacrifice scientific precision to gain pedagogical relevance.

5. Which statement best characterizes the phenomenological frame of reference?
    a. It is based on sound Freudian concepts.
    b. It is a common-sense (rather than scientific) approach to behavior.
    c. It is of clinical rather than academic interest and relevance.
    d. It is the only school of psychology that owes its origin to Aristotle.
    e. It is totally speculative and philosophical.

6. A curriculum derived from cognitive specifications would emphasize
    a. the framework that gives the material meaning.
    b. the motivational bases of all learnings.
    c. the phenomenological nature of perception.
    d. the setting in which learning takes place.
    e. the unity of the parts.

7. The major point of difference between the Skinnerian and the cognitive positions is in relation to
    a. the degree of emphasis on the technology of instruction.
    b. the locus of control (external versus internal).
    c. the role of heredity in determining human behavior.
    d. the role of practice in learning.
    e. the role of research in defining effective educational practices.

FOUR

The Determinants of Human Behavior

People do not work because of their love for me. They work for pay, in the form of money, affection, and belongingness, and the status that permits self-approval. When this pay gets too low they will leave their jobs and seek something else.

A. D. Woodruff (1951)

To summarize, much behavior, both in and outside the classroom, is determined by the child's image and by his attempts to "be himself"—the self that he perceives.

Don C. Charles (1964)

Two essential aspects of living organisms are the need to change, to grow, and differentiate toward greater complexity, and the need to integrate and to maintian equilibrium and wholeness, to consolidate our gains.

Caroline Tryon and W. E. Henry (1950)

The interdependence of pupils and of pupils and teachers for a mutual satisfaction of needs would seem to demand that each group receive training in understanding each other's social needs.

Glenn M. Blair, et al. (1962)

— Presents the all-important concept of motivation from the standpoint of both drive-reduction and stimulation theories
— Introduces the self-concept as the focus of just who and what the individual is and emphasizes the phenomenal nature of perception through which one maintains and protects the self
— Presents openness to experience as the key to self-realization; describes how under conditions of stress, the individual closes off access to experience

PREVIEW: KEY CONCEPTS

1. Behavior does not just happen; it occurs in response to some need.
2. Motives can be classified as physiological and psychological. For the greater part, they are learned and vary in kind and intensity from person to person and even from time to time.
3. The drive-reduction theory (and its counterpart, reinforcement) postulates that behavior occurs in response to the deprivation of a need. Stimulation theories recognize needs in which deprivation is less obvious. An important concept here is the need for achievement, i.e., a generalized level of aspiration.
4. The self-concept is best conceived as a system of attitudes toward the self; as such, it permeates every aspect of one's behavior.
5. Although some level of tension is conducive to effective behavior, anxiety tends to have a detrimental effect on the quality of one's behavior.
6. Of special interest is the concept of self-actualization (becoming) as presented by Combs, Maslow, Rogers, and other phenomenologists.

PREVIEW QUESTIONS

1. Why do people behave as they do? To what extent is human behavior more than simply the inevitable response to external demands?

2. How can we all satisfy our needs without simultaneously depriving others of their share of the satisfiers?
3. What can the school do to ensure that every child develops a positive self-concept?

   What are some of the school-related factors that interfere with positive growth?
4. How can the school protect children from devastating levels of anxiety and still meet social demands for standards of excellence?

Motivation can be considered the key to understanding behavior—ours as well as that of others. It underlies every phase of human relations: at home, in the community, on the job, and, of course, in the classroom. A primary benefit to be derived by prospective teachers from a course in educational psychology is a greater understanding of the dynamics that cause people in general and children in particular to behave as they do.

BASIC CONCEPTS OF MOTIVATION

The drive-reduction
theory

Behavior, desirable or undesirable, does not just occur; it arises in response to some form of stimulation and is generally directed toward the attainment of a goal. Despite the fact that almost all phases of the motivation of behavior are characterized more by controversy than by unanimity, there is a general consensus that behavior is an attempt to satisfy some need. A somewhat restricted version of this position, commonly known as the *drive-reduction* theory (see Chapter 3), is that behavior stems from the tension arising from the frustration of a need and is oriented toward the reduction of this tension. More recently, the concept of motivation has been broadened to include such needs as the need to explore and to manipulate, where the element of tension resulting from frustration is not readily apparent.

The Nature of Motives

The determination of behavior implies not only the energizing of the organism, as might be implied by *need* or *drive*, but also the directing of its behavior toward certain aspects of the environment capable of overcoming the deprivation the need implies. A distinction might, therefore, be made between the inner stimuli, such as the contraction of the stomach walls in the case of hunger (the energizing aspect), and the learned behavior patterns by means of which it strives to satisfy its hunger (the directional aspect). Implied is the existence of a goal, i.e., a state or condition the organism seeks to attain in order to satisfy some need. Goals do not exist apart from the person whose behavior is being directed toward them as a result of some inner need; food is a goal only to someone who is hungry.

The term *motive*, in contrast to *need* and *drive*, is generally used to refer to certain conditions within the organism that, besides arousing and sustaining activity, actually predispose it to behave in ways appropriate from the standpoint of the need in question. In other words, although needs continue to be appropriate antecedent conditions for activity, it is the directing of this activity toward the goal that ties down the definition of a motive. Consequently it is probably more correct to speak of hunger or sex as *motives* rather than simply as *needs* or *drives*. This is especially true of social needs, which are even more obviously affected by learning; the individual does not seek affection or social approval but, because of previous experiences, the affection or approval of certain persons, so that again it is better to think of affection and social approval as they influence behavior as motives rather than simply as needs. On the other hand, as Hall (1961) points out, it would be misleading to suggest consensus on the use of these terms.

The determinants of human behavior—whether called *needs*, *drives*, *motives*, or *purposes*—are generally encompassed under the broad heading of motivation, which has, therefore, at least two fundamental components: a need state and an external goal. We might say that motivation refers to a state of the organism in which its energies are mobilized selectively toward the attainment of a given goal. More specifically, motives serve three important functions:

1. They energize, i.e., activate and sensitize the organism toward certain stimuli.[1]
2. They direct its behavior toward certain goals.
3. They reinforce behavior that is effective in the attainment of desired goals.

Motives as Determinants of Behavior

Motivation is not directly observable; it is a hypothetical construct that psychologists postulate to explain certain behaviors. The strength of the individual's motivation must be inferred from the extent to which he or she exerts himself in order to satisfy an alleged deprivation or to attain a given goal. Whenever learning is characterized by persistence and seems to result in satisfaction upon the attainment of the goal, we assume the presence of motivation. The identification of the particular motive or motives in operation is, of course, precarious since motives are generally complex and often disguised.

Most psychologists subscribe to the concept of motivation, but there is

Motives imply direction

---

1. Modern cognitive psychologists see the organism as a dynamic energy system that does not need to be activated through external stimuli (see Bolles 1979).

Acceptance of
motivation

considerable disagreement as to its origin, its essential nature, and its role as the determinant of behavior.[2] As we saw, theories of learning range from those in which motivation occupies a central position to those in which it is relatively incidental. Tolman (1932) made the purposive nature of behavior the central theme of his theory. Earlier Thorndike (1913) had given a similarly critical role to the law of effect. Field theorists likewise see the individual in dynamic suspension in psychological space, impelled, propelled, as well as repelled by field forces in complex simultaneous interaction.[3]

The relationship between motivation and learning is neither simple nor unequivocal. A high level of motivation (i.e., anxiety) may actually interfere with the learning of a complex task with several alternatives by narrowing the range of cues the individual can utilize effectively (see Weiner 1969). Yet it seems logical to assume some form of motivational control as one of the conditions underlying meaningful learning in the classroom. In fact, that learning results from the goal-seeking behavior of the organism is essentially the central theme of present-day psychology. The view that behavior is purposive rather than accidental, although simply a theory, is supported by considerable data suggesting its adequacy, and it has proven productive in the study of both human and animal behavior.[4]

CLASSIFICATION OF MOTIVES

Classification is an unavoidably arbitrary process governed by such factors as the author's purpose and even personal preferences. The classification of motives is no exception; motives are so complex and interacting that their classification into neat, clear-cut categories is impossible. Not only does the expression of a given motive vary from person to person, but some motives can be expressed through different behaviors and, conversely, similar behavior may represent the expression of different motives. What is more, the behavior displayed by a person at a given time is not the outcome of a single motive but rather the net resultant of the multiplicity of motives operating at the moment in his or her motivational space.

2. Bolles (1978) suggests that motivation as a construct is part of the mechanistic (passive) view of the organism postulated by learning theorists years ago and that, since by contrast the more dynamic (cognitive) theories of today see the organism as intrinsically active in the pursuit of his goals, they no longer need the conventional concept of motivation to account for behavior. They would reject, for example, the role of motives in energizing the organism to activity. Motivation may still be of interest and value in the context of the classroom.

3. Behaviorists, on the other hand, avoid the "mystique" of inner drives and focus instead on the deliberate manipulation of behavior through selective (externally controlled) reinforcement.

4. See Mouly (1973) for a critical analysis of motivation as a scientific construct. Objections have ranged from the use of *word magic* (Marx 1960) to unwarranted extrapolation from animal subjects (Glaser 1962).

Physiological Needs

Physiological needs
are basic to life

A number of the needs that underlie human behavior are organically induced. These needs are sometimes considered primary in the sense that they are basic to the sustenance of life, and, in cases of severe frustration, they tend to take precedence over such nonorganic needs as affection and self-esteem. On the other hand, experience can modify this relationship, and people have starved themselves to death in order to hoard money. On the other hand, to the extent that such needs are satisfied in everyone, they become a common denominator that no longer functions as the basis for different behavior in different people.

At the physiological level, we can cite the need for food, water, sleep and rest, activity, and sex, all of which operate in various degrees of urgency in different situations. It would seem logical that food, for example, would be no problem in an affluent society like ours. Yet as many teachers can testify, children often become restless and irritable just before lunch. The important thing is for teachers to approach the question of behavior from the standpoint of its underlying basis in needs. The young child cannot remain quiet for long periods, for example; the wise teacher will simply build the program around the needs of children and aim for a fair balance among novelty, variety, exercise, and study.

Psychological Needs

Psychological needs are important determinants of behavior primarily because they are incapable of complete satisfaction. A person may eat to the point where he cannot touch another bite, but he can never have all the love, security, or social recognition he would like. No sooner are you elated over having been promoted to branch manager than you are unhappy until you become president of the company. To the extent that the frustration of these needs will inevitably cause children to be restless, inattentive, disruptive, etc.—if for no other reason than that of operational efficiency—the school cannot be indifferent to the plight of some of its students. Unquestionably, of course, the bigger problem is the effect of the frustration of these needs on the student's personality development. Among the major needs in this category, we might mention:

NEED FOR EMOTIONAL SECURITY.   Everyone wants to be loved, to belong, to be an accepted member of a group. This need for emotional security is particularly critical in infancy (see Erikson's concept of trust discussed in chapter 15). Infants have no way of knowing why they are not picked up when they cry; they can only fear the worst. They must be able to depend on their world and to know that the people on whom they depend will not let them down. Security is also crucial in adolescence as teenagers attempt to relate to the peer culture. And children must also find security in the classroom situation. It should be noted in passing that the child can satisfy this need just

as well by belonging to a group of hoodlums as by belonging to the church choir and that it might just behoove the school (and society) to make acceptance by desirable groups within the reach of all children.

NEED FOR ACHIEVEMENT. People like to succeed in what they set out to do and to feel that that their accomplishments are worthwhile. Need for achievement is closely related to such other needs as social recognition and self-esteem and probably derives much of its potency through conditioning as a consequence of the fuss parents make over the child's early achievements. It will receive special consideration in a later section under the heading of "achievement motivation."

Schools make it difficult for certain children to satisfy their need for achievement. For the dull child, the likelihood of solving all the problems, getting good grades, or turning out a masterpiece in English is relatively remote. It is equally true that schools often make it difficult for the gifted child to obtain a sense of accomplishment; ordinary schoolwork is often so infantile that he gets no more sense of success from getting it done than the housewife gets from hanging the family laundry. Our schools need to—and can—be made more vital and dynamic to the bright, the dull, and the average child. Teachers need to pay closer attention to the diversification of assignments so that each child is challenged to his or her level of ability and experience. They need to provide a fair balance between ease that conveys no challenge and difficulty that frustrates.

NEED FOR INDEPENDENCE.   People want to govern their own lives, to set their own purposes without interference or compulsion. This is probably a relatively basic need. A baby stiffens when held too firmly; a young child wants to eat without help; adolescents particularly resent being pushed around.

NEED FOR SOCIAL RECOGNITION.   This need, also called the need for *status* or *approval,* concerns the apparently universal desire to feel that what we are and what we do is looked upon favorably by others. Since so much of their lives centers on the work of the school, the satisfaction of this need in children is largely in the hands of their teachers, who must be aware of their responsibility in this connection. Besides being essentially the sole dispensers of social recognition, teachers also set the pattern for other children to follow. Teachers should especially remember that children persistently denied recognition and acceptance by the "desirable elements" of society are being forced to seek acceptance in less desirable groups.

NEED FOR SELF-ESTEEM.   The need to feel that what we are and what we do comes up to our own standard is closely related not only to the other psychological needs just discussed but also to the *self-concept,* to be mentioned later. What we think of ourselves revolves around our standards of what is adequate and what is inadaquate. Thus, if past experience has led us to prize scholarship, morality, or the social graces, to fail in these respects causes frustration of our need for self-esteem. This need revolves primarily around the values acquired during the process of socialization, by means of which society perpetuates its way of life.

SATISFACTION OF NEEDS

Needs are relatively uniform, but the goals one seeks in order to satisfy these needs vary from person to person and even from time to time. Thus, whether a person seeks steak, oysters, or frog legs depends to as great an extent on the particular tastes he or she has developed as on their availability and adequacy relative to the need for food. Behavior is not a simple matter of satisfying a single need. We are constantly besieged by a multitude of needs, on the one hand, and of goals through which these needs can be satisfied, on the other. Since we cannot attend to all these needs or attempt to reach all goals at once, we must be selective—the child may have to choose between the approval of the peer group and that of the teacher. Moreover, social values often run counter to basic needs, e.g., the ideal of sexual morality in relation to the sex drive. In fact, one's own values may be self-contradictory, e.g., the middle-class disapproval of both fighting and cowardice. Individuals usually resolve these conflicts on the basis of the relative dominance of the values involved and of their ability to rationalize the violation of their other values. They may suffer from guilt in the process.

Maslow's hierarchy of needs

Maslow (1943) has proposed an interesting hierarchy in the prepotency of needs. Starting with the classification of needs into [a] physiological, [b] safety (including routine, consistency, and security), [c] love, [d] esteem, [e] self-actualization, [f] the need to know and to understand, and [g] aesthetic needs (figure 4.1), he suggests that normally one cannot consider a given need unless those lower in the scale are reasonably satisfied. Although certain reversals in the hierarchy may occur as a result of past experiences, people usually will not attend to their love needs until their physiological and safety needs are adequately met. It follows from this arrangement that, whereas the physiological needs may be met nearly 100 percent, each successive level will be satisfied to a lesser degree, and the last three—which have been variously called *Abundancy* (A), *Being* (B), or *Growth* (G) needs in contrast to the other four *Deficiency* (D) or *Survival* (S) needs— may go relatively unsatisfied. The need to know and to understand, for example, the *cognitive* need, as reflected in intellectual curiosity, desire for knowledge, a tendency to systematize, to organize, to analyze, and to look for relationships, is far more evident in some people than in others.

Satisfying one's needs: Sometimes a problem

Satisfying one's needs is bound to involve a certain amount of difficulty; there are simply not enough satisfiers to go around. Not everyone can be president or valedictorian. Reality is such that the satisfaction of one's needs is far from automatic and assured. We are constantly being frustrated by the elements, by personal limitations, by social injustice. Even the taking of food is governed by numerous restrictions ranging from the unavailability of certain foods to regulations dictating what, when, where, and how they are to be eaten.

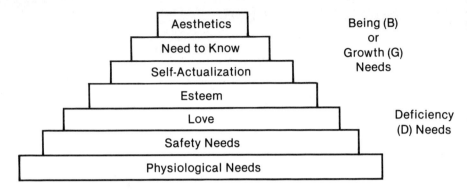

Figure 4.1   Maslow's Hierarchy of Needs (Maslow 1943)

The school has a responsibility to see that every child achieves at least minimum satisfaction for his or her needs. Not only is pupil adjustment a primary objective of modern education, but, if nothing else, failure to provide for need satisfaction soon results in disruption of classroom activities. Furthermore, the school is perpetually bringing into focus the degree to which children are meeting the demands made upon them. John may not know he is dull until he enters first grade but, once he enrolls, the school does not let him forget it. So much of the child's life revolves around the work of the school that serious harm can be done if the school is not conscious of its potentially devastating effects.

The teacher's task

Teachers must provide each child the opportunity to satisfy needs in socially desirable ways. The child who boasts needs to be shown how to achieve social recognition more constructively. Teachers must be alert to opportunities for children with special limitations to gain status; the overage pupil might be made custodian of the baseball equipment, for example. An imaginative teacher should be able to find a dozen ways within the framework of the activities of the school in which this can be done. A well-organized cocurricular program of diversified group activities has tremendous possibilities in providing need satisfaction for children who find this difficult within the more restricted phases of the academic curriculum.

Some children have considerable difficulty in satisfying their needs. Some have limited assets, others have learned ineffective need-satisfaction patterns and are unable to graduate to more effective strategies. Furthermore, needs have to be satisfied within the framework of the local situation, and some children find themselves in an environment that is particularly severe or perhaps incompatible with their makeup. Generally the more people deviate from the average, the more likely they are to have difficulty satisfying their needs. The child who is short, tall, fat, who matures early or late tends to have special problems. The dull child is particularly likely to have difficulty in satisfying his needs. From the day he comes to school, he finds endless frustrations and often, for good measure, rejection at school, disappointment at home, unreasonable pressures all around, shame, and ridicule. We need to be particularly concerned with these special cases, not that their needs are any different from those of other children, not that they deserve special privileges at the expense of their more typical peers but rather that they deserve a share of the satisfactions to which every youngster is entitled as an inalienable right, and without which personality distortion is likely to occur, to the detriment of all.

One thing is sure: frustrated children will not just sit there. Tensions resulting from the frustration of their needs will force them to look for other ways in which they can be satisfied. If they have assets in other areas, e.g., sports, all may yet be well. By thinking of themselves as athletes and rationalizing that academic work is unimportant, they can shrug off failure in schoolwork. But the brutal fact is that dull children are not necessarily endowed with compensating talent. In desperation they may find it "necessary" to resort to counterproductive behavior, e.g., delinquency, to a achieve satisfaction.

It should also be noted in passing that teachers are only human. They too have needs to satisfy, and they are in a position to attempt to satisfy them at the expense of their pupils. Their need for status, for example, may make it rough on children with a similar need. Actually, in view of the mutual interdependence of teachers and pupils, an enlightened attempt at satisfying each other's needs would be advantageous to both. In this, the teacher must set the pattern.

THE DRIVE-REDUCTION THEORY

Until recently, psychologists subscribed almost exclusively to the *drive-reduction* theory of motivation, which postulates that behavior stems from the frustration of a need and is oriented toward attaining relief from the resulting tension. According to this theory (Hull 1943), behavior becomes goal oriented by virtue of the selective reinforcement of certain responses through tension reduction resulting from the attainment of the goal. This selective reinforcement leads to an increase in the probability of occurrence of effective responses so that they develop into an integrated goal-directed behavior pattern. Behavior that does not lead to the goal, on the contrary, does not lead to the removal of tension and is therefore extinguished.

Until recently, the concept of reinforcement through drive reduction was accepted as the sole explanation of motivated behavior. However, organisms learn to attach reinforcement value to objects that cannot possibly have need-reduction properties. Money, for example, can provide reinforcement for a variety of behavior patterns even though it cannot constitute primary reinforcement for basic needs. In order to deal with this problem, reinforcement psychologists introduced the principle of *secondary reinforcement*, which postulates that reinforcement properties can be conditioned to neutral stimuli through their repeated simultaneous presentation with a primary reward. The

Secondary
reinforcement

fact that chimps work for poker chips that they can exchange for a raisin (Wolfe, 1936) can be explained on the basis of secondary reinforcement of the hunger drive. In fact, the response will soon extinguish itself if there is no periodic primary reinforcement.

It is not necessary for reinforcement to occur at every instance of a given response. Research suggests that animal subjects reinforced 100 percent of the trials tend to learn more efficiently than when reinforced only intermittently, but the difference tends to be small and in some cases even negative. On the other hand, *intermittent* (partial) reinforcement has consistently promoted responses more resistant to extinction (Jenkins and Stanley 1950; Lawrence and Festinger 1962). Behavior can be maintained over a long period of time by simply introducing the occasional reinforcement. This has interesting implications for, say, child training; the fact that children who cry are generally reinforced on an intermittent schedule may explain why some children are so persistent in their crying. Partial reinforcement may also explain why bad habits are so hard to break.

Delayed reinforcement seems to produce results similar to partial reinforcement, perhaps because long-delayed reinforcement can be construed as nonreinforcement. With animals, delay in reinforcement tends to retard learning, even to the point that reinforcement has no effect if the delay exceeds some ten seconds (Spence 1947; Grice 1948; see reviews by Markowitz and Renner 1964; Tarpy and Sawabini 1974). With children, on the other hand, the results are inconsistent. In a study by Atkinson (1969), under one set of conditions, learning showed a marked decrement with increased delay, but under other conditions no effect was observed, and under still other conditions, learning improved with increased delay intervals. On balance, the evidence suggests that the learning of school-like materials is facilitated by delay in reinforcement (Sassenrath and Yonge 1968; Sturges 1972).[5] In the Sturges study, for example, reinforcement delays of up to twenty-four hours produced superior performance, particularly with respect to delayed retention. Apparently reinforcement remains effective despite the delay if the subject maintains an orientation toward both the task and the reward or, as in the case of human subjects with language possibilities, if they can reactivate the connection between the response and its consequent when the reinforcement occurs. Human beings can get immediate reinforcement in the knowledge that, since they have made the correct response, they have only to wait and the reward will be forthcoming. Children can get adequate reinforcement from the promise of a candy bar next week. On the other hand, it is characteristic of us all to lose sight of remote goals, and the younger the child, the greater the need for immediate reinforcement through the establishment of short-term as well as intermediate subgoals.

A number of objections have been raised to what appear to be weaknesses

Marginal notes:

Intermittent reinforcement

Delayed reinforcement

---

5. Extrapolating from animal learning, Skinner made immediate reinforcement a major argument for the use of teaching machines in the classroom.

in the drive-reduction theory. (For more complete coverage, see Harlow 1953; Hunt 1960; R. White 1959.)

1. The drive-reduction theory postulates that behavior stems from the tension resulting from the frustration of a need. A basic premise, then, is that the satisfaction of a need will lead to a period of inactivity as far as the need is concerned (although other needs might then become dominant). But the fact is that, when the organism appears to be completely satisfied, it does not generally become inactive; rather, it seeks activity such as manipulation, exploration, or even exercise. Children play without apparent need; monkeys explore, manipulate, and otherwise resort to various activities. Hunt (1960) visualizes living matter not as an inert substance to which motion must be imparted by extrinsic forces but rather as open systems of energy exchange that exhibit activity intrinsically (see also Smith and Smith 1966; Bolles 1978).

2. A second premise of the drive-reduction theory is that the organism is running away from tension, a position not only essentially negative but also contrary to fact. Certainly man is activated by something more fundamental and more constructive than the mere avoidance of pain and discomfort. People are often seeking not a state of equilibrium but rather a state of disequilibrium; much of their behavior is need-producing rather than need-reducing. The fact that boredom is tension-producing was particularly evident in the McGill studies (Hebb 1958; Lilly 1956) in which college students, paid to lie in a stimulus-free environment, soon found the situation intolerable.

3. Behavior frequently occurs in situations where need reduction is clearly not attained. Rats can be made to learn with a reward of saccharine, which, having no food value, cannot reduce hunger. The same is true of experiments involving the injection of a saline solution or the self-administration of electrical shocks, which apparently serve as motives but which cannot be need reducing. Learning also takes place when the food pellets are so infinitesimally small that they can hardly have significant need-reducing properties.

Other objections have been raised. On the other hand, it is generally easier to find fault than it is to devise a criticism-free alternative theory, and the need-reduction theory, with certain reservations, is still held by many and is perhaps essentially true in its main arguments. Recent criticisms simply represent a reluctance to accept the need-reduction theory as the exclusive theory of motivation.

STIMULATION THEORIES OF MOTIVATION

People seek stimulation

A more positive orientation to motivational phenomena is that of the so-called *stimulation* theories, whose basic premise is that the organism seeks not equilibrium but rather disequilibrium. Leuba (1955) and Hebb (1955) speak of an organism seeking an optimal level of stimulation. Glanzer (1958) suggests that the organism requires a certain amount of stimulation per unit of time. If too little stimulation is present in the environment, it will seek stimulation; if there is too much stimulation, it tries to reduce it.

Among the more commonly accepted stimulation theories are those based on curiosity (Berlyne 1950; Butler and Harlow 1957), exploration (Montgomery 1953), activity (Hill 1956), manipulation (Harlow 1953; Terrell 1959), and competence (White 1959). They overlap in their basic premise that novel stimuli function as motivational agents. In other words, these drives are evoked exteroceptively by the presentation of a novel stimulus object and incorporate both the behavior-energizing and the behavior-directing functions of motives. They apparently represent a need for mastering the environment and are perhaps part of the overall need for new experiences. Very early in life young children demonstrate the need to explore; they are attracted by bright objects, they want to see what is on the other side of the street, they have an almost compulsive desire to touch everything, including the stove and the electric socket. This is closely related to the need for achievement; children want to ride a bicycle, to know what makes a watch work.

Exploratory and Other Stimulation Drives

A number of experiments have shown that animals and human beings display behavior that is motivated by no "need" other than to explore the environment. A rat free to make successive choices of the arms of a T-maze displays a marked tendency to choose different arms on different trials (Glanzer 1958) and to select a pathway with the greatest stimulus complexity (Dember et al. 1957; Havelka 1956). In the Butler and Harlow (1957) study, monkeys learned to discriminate between two opaque doors, one of which was unlocked, permitting the animal to look into the laboratory. Not only did the monkeys learn the discrimination problem, but they continued opening the unlocked door by the hour and by the day without extinction with no reward other than a one-minute peek into the laboratory.

Resistance to extinction

It is significant to note that these drives are externally determined and that they are as effective in promoting learning as are those based on primary reinforcement. One of the fundamental features of these drives is that they show continued motivational strength with repeated elicitation, suggesting that they are as basic, innate, and self-sustaining as their internally initiated counterparts. This is particularly significant in that the more readily individuals can take care of their survival requirements, the more energy and attention they can devote to the exploration and extension of their world through maximizing stimulation. These drives are particularly exciting in an affluent society where primary needs are generally fulfilled and people have time to explore the environment and seek new experiences (see figure 4.1). The fact that a desire to learn and to know is as fundamental as any drive based on need reduction is especially important in the light of the quest for self-fulfillment as the ultimate human goal, the quest for self-fulfillment in a realm that knows no limitation and no satiation.

A more elaborate formulation of the stimulation view of motivation is White's concept of *competence* (White 1959), in which he explains exploratory, manipulatory, and general activity behavior as part of the process by which individuals learn to interact effectively with their environment. He uses the word *competence* in the broadest sense of the ability to carry on a successful transaction with the environment and thus grow and flourish rather than simply survive. The concept of competence borders on the *achievement motive* postulated by McClelland et al. (1953) and, perhaps even more significantly, on the *self-concept* as adopted by Combs and Snygg (1959), who see the individual's single drive as that of maintaining and enhancing the self. An elabora-

Self-actualization   tion of self-concept is found in the concept of *self-actualization:* i.e., the need to discover and to develop ever more effective and adequate ways of realizing one's potentialities.

The Achievement Motive

Closely related to competence is the need for achievement (*N Ach*) (McClelland et al. 1953; Atkinson 1958), which may be thought of as a widely generalized level of aspiration. People with a high need for achievement see problems and obstacles as challenges to be met. Achievement is a particular avenue toward self-respect in American society, where some degree of mastery over the environment is particularly characteristic of our middle-class way of life, and, up to now, especially among males (Phillips 1962; Marini and Greenberger 1978), presumably because of the greater social expectations in the past for boys to get ahead.[6]

Actually *N Ach* incorporates two contrasting personality predispositions: the need for success and the fear of failure. Research suggests that individuals high in need to achieve and low in anxiety typically prefer tasks of interme-

Need for success   diate probability of success. They tend to maintain a generally high performance level and are persistent in problem solving. They tend to choose more difficult tasks after success and easier tasks after failure. By contrast, individuals motivated through fear of failure—i.e., individuals low in need to achieve and correspondingly high in anxiety—tend to choose tasks with either unrealistically high or unrealistically low probability of success. They tend to choose easier tasks after success and more difficult tasks after failure. Individuals motivated through need for success are attracted to activities requiring the successful exercise of skill; they are not particularly interested in gambling where

6. Horner (1969) found that girls tend to equate intellectual achievement with loss of femininity. She suggests that the bright woman is caught in a double bind, worrying about both failure and success: if she fails, she feels guilty for not living up to her ability; if she succeeds, she feels guilty for having flouted society's expectations for her to be feminine. Hopefully, the situation is changing.

the outcome depends on chance alone, but they do like activities where they can pit their skills against some standards or the skills of others. By contrast, individuals for whom the need to avoid failure greatly exceeds the need to achieve resist all activities where their competence might be evaluated. When forced into competition, they defend themselves by undertaking activities in which success is virtually guaranteed or activities that offer so little real chance of success that the appearance of trying to do something very difficult more than compensates for repeated but minimally embarrassing failure. They often display what can only be called rugged determination in the pursuit of highly improbable goals, but they are quickly frightened from tasks that the average person would see as a real challenge.

Fear of failure

Locus of control

An important concept here is *locus of control* (Rotter 1966; deCharms 1968; see also Weiner's attribution theory of motivation 1969, 1972, 1979): i.e., the extent to which individuals see their successes (and failures) as caused by their own ability and effort (*internal locus of control*) or, on the contrary, see success and failure as simply the result of luck or environmental conditions over which they have no control (*external locus of control*). Research (e.g., Gilmor 1978; Morris and Messer 1978; Ware 1978; see also Bar-Tal 1978) suggests that people with an internal locus of control tend to be assertive, independent, and effective; they tend to be more successful in meeting the demands of life. People with an external locus of control, by contrast, tend to be passive, apathetic, and unproductive.

Locus of control can be tied in to the concept of achievement motivation. Whereas people motivated through the need for success see their achievements as the more or less direct outcome of their ability and efforts, people motivated through fear of failure attribute both their successes and failures to circumstances over which they have no control (Covington and Omelich 1979; Maracek and Mettee 1972). Students with low self-esteem, for example, tend to blame their failure on their lack of ability, a condition they can do nothing about. More typically, they seek safety by reaching for extremely easy tasks where they cannot possibly fail or impossible tasks in which failure is really not failure. What is interesting is that they should disavow success, but that too is understandable: to accept success as due to ability and effort is to accept responsibility for continued success. It implies a direct obligation for a repeat performance, an obligation they cannot accept. Their need to reject credit for success also makes it impossible for them to accept praise; after all, praise and reproof are generally restricted to success and failure in which ability and effort are involved. Strangely, then, both success and failure have a negative effect on their future performance. They might do better if allowed to attribute their successes to external forces and encouraged to continue "trying their luck." In time, they might conceivably develop a more positive self-concept.

N Ach: Its development

The need for achievement tends to develop in early childhood within the dynamics of mother-child interaction. The parents of children high in *N Ach* tend to insist that they develop on their own rather than remain subordinate parts of the family unit to which they must sacrifice individual interest. Whether this occurs because children are neglected or because they are rewarded for developing independence, achievement motivation is fostered by mothers who set high expectations for their children, do not maintain emotional ties that are too tight, and encourage their children to master their environment, while at the same time providing some degree of protection and support, thus saving the children from undue failure. Once a home base of dependency and security has been established, they encourage as much independence as the child can assume (see Winterbottom 1953). The mothers of sons low in achievement motivation, on the contrary, tend to continue restricting their children beyond the age at which most mothers have relaxed their restrictions. On the other hand, the results of research have not been entirely consistent, particularly with respect to girls, for whom the female sex role, presumably up to now at least, places greater emphasis on social approval than on achievement.

Sensory Deprivation

Of considerable support to the stimulation view of motivation is the substantial evidence concerning the unbearable effects of sensory deprivation noted in the studies by Hebb (1958) and Lilly (1956). Subjects paid to lie in a stimulus-free environment soon found the reduced sensory input so intolerable that they had to be relieved. Also of interest are the parallel McGill studies (Heron 1957; Melzack and Scott 1957; Melzack and Thompson 1956), showing irretrievable deficits, resulting from early sensory deprivation, in the intellectual and personality development of puppies.

Importance of sensory stimulation

These studies have obvious implications not only from the standpoint of adjustment but especially from the standpoint of social, emotional, and intellectual development. They suggest that one of the primary prerequisites for human (and apparently animal) welfare is the impact of a considerable amount of environmental stimulation, especially in the early period of development. They also raise the possibility that an organism accustomed to a high level of stimulation will have a higher stimulation requirement than one from an impoverished environmental situation. This emphasizes the differential effects of early experiences and may well have a significant bearing on the success of children from the lower class and their readiness for school, for example.

OTHER THEORIES OF MOTIVATION

A number of other theories of motivation could be mentioned, some of them offshoots of those previously discussed. Probably the oldest theoretical formulation is that of Freud, whose psychosexual stages of development are based largely on unconscious motives and have greatest application in the clinical interpretation of behavior. Erikson's relatively parallel theory of psychosocial stages will be presented in chapter 15. Another well-known view of motivation is Hebb's theory of dissonance (Hebb 1946, 1949), which explains fear (and anxiety) as the result of the incongruity that arises when something previously familiar suddenly takes on an air of unfamiliarity. In his experiments, infant chimps displayed spontaneous fear of a plaster cast of a monkey's skull and the deflated rubber figure of a monkey being dragged across the floor. Festinger makes the motivational value of the discrepancy between expectations concerning a given situation and actual perceptions of that situation the basis of his *Theory of Cognitive Dissonance* (1957). He postulates that cognitive dissonance is an annoying state of affairs that elicits behavior aimed at reducing the dissonance.[7]

THE SELF-CONCEPT

Nature and Importance

Of major significance to the classroom teacher is the *self-concept*. Originally proposed by Lecky (1911, 1945) and adopted by Rogers (1951) as the keystone of his system of nondirective counseling, the self-concept is of critical importance in education, particularly in the more personal aspects of motivation, attitudes, character formation, and adjustment, all of which, in the final analysis, are the foundations on which school and out-of-school success must ultimately rest. Lecky's basic premise is that all of our values are organized into a single system, the nucleus of which is our valuation of ourselves. The fundamental need of every individual is to develop and maintain a unified mental organization. As we undergo new experiences, we accept or reject them in terms of their compatibility with our present self, we thereby maintain our individuality and avoid conflict.

The self-concept:
Attitudes toward
oneself

The self-concept is best conceived as a system of attitudes toward oneself. Just as people, as a result of experience, form attitudes that they organize into a self-consistent system and defend against attack even if it calls for disregard or falsification of the evidence, so they, also as a result of their experiences, form attitudes toward themselves. All attitudes are important determinants of behavior, but attitudes concerning the self are much more basic than those in which the individual is less ego involved and therefore correspondingly more potent in determining his or her behavior.

7. See Zastrow (1969) for a critical review of cognitive dissonance. See also Greenwald and Ronis (1979) for a case study of its evolution.

The self-concept
develops as a result
of experience

The development of the self-concept involves a slow process of differentiation in which children gradually emerge into focus out of their total world of awareness and define progressively more clearly just who and what they are. It follows that underlying the development of the self-concept are one's assets and liabilities in relation to the various components of one's environment. The body is a major point of reference in the self-concept of many persons; the athlete and the movie star would be different persons were they to have different physiques. Others who are less well endowed physically may minimize the body and emphasize such other personal characteristics as intelligence or musical talent as the foundation for their self-concept. A physical defect may also serve as the focus around which the self-concept is organized.

Early environmental
inputs are crucial

The orientation and adequacy of the self-concept that individuals develop out of their interactions with their environment are, to a large extent, a function of the quality of early parent-child relationships. If the mother is forever angry at the baby, punishes and rejects him, he begins to conceive of himself as bad. As new experiences follow, he tends to evaluate each new situation in the light of his previous generalizations. Children who fail to learn to read and who are berated by their teacher for their stupidity see the school as an unpleasant place and themselves as stupid. They then interpret future school occurrences in this light and reject new material on the prejudgment that, since they are stupid, they cannot learn even if they try. As they become convinced of this, they give the environment less and less of a chance to treat them differently; they simply schedule themselves for a continuation of the failure they have experienced in the past.

Young children are relatively neutral at first as to the kind of self-concept they develop, but they become progressively less free in their choice of the experiences they assimilate or of the interpretation they place on them in order that they may be assimilated without conflict. As children begin to perceive order in their environment, the most important thing they discover is themselves. At first, they discover their nose and the rest of their body; eventually they recognizes their voice. They also recognize that *good, bad, cute,* etc., are attributed to them. Gradually they develop a picture of themselves that they then strive to maintain and protect by ordering their behavior accordingly. Because one's self-image tends to continue developing in the direction in which it started, early childhood is the critical period in the development of the self-structure. Each new experience is important both in itself and as the basis for accepting or rejecting future experiences.

The School and the Self-Concept

The school plays a significant role in determining the quality of the child's self-concept, especially with respect to school-related activities. It provides children with an opportunity to measure themselves against their peers in a variety of situations ranging from intellectual and physical competence to being attractive to members of the opposite sex. The school can also do harm: indiscriminate grading and reporting to parents followed by condemnation at home may be a significant factor in the development of a negative self-concept. Too frequently, the school is instrumental in inflicting upon certain children the view that they are inadequate, undependable, or unworthy. To make matters worse, it often confirms their sense of inadequacy by making their evaluation of themselves a matter of official record. It is a sad truth that many children (adults too) sell themselves on the idea that they are incompetent, thereby cheating themselves of the success that could be theirs under conditions of more positive thinking.

Promoting a positive self-concept

The necessity of helping children build a positive self-concept is obvious from its role in determining what they will be and do. Coopersmith (1967), for example, points to substantial differences in outlook and behavior between children high and low in self-esteem. Children with a high self-concept tend to be energetic, relatively free from anxiety, realistic in their assessment of their abilities, and confident that their efforts will meet with success. By contrast, children who because of systematic failure develop a negative self-concept may well find themselves on a self-perpetuating spiral characterized by feelings of discouragement, isolation, and unworthiness and a consequent need for

punishment that can be self-administered on schedule by simply programming in periodic failure. Such people lead exemplary lives but nevertheless suffer from guilt over imagined sin. Unconsciously, their need for self-punishment often turns to failure; they always try just hard enough to ensure failure in order to suffer the needed punishment.[8]

Self-esteem is obviously related to actual achievement. Not only are children who achieve likely to form a positive view of self but for them to learn, they must see themselves as learners. Besides, their self-concept determines what they will learn, what ideas are relevant and meaningful to them. Continued academic failure, on the other hand, leads to a "I-am-dumb" self-concept. As children change their self-concept from "adequate" to "inadequate," new failure experiences prove less devastating since failure is now consistent with their revised self-image. But now they can no longer assimilate success without conflict.

Since the self-concept children develop depends directly on the way experiences enhance their self-esteem, the reactions of adults in authority toward them are of special importance. Yet, apparently on the assumption that the more vigorously they bat them down the higher they will bounce, adults often go out of their way to destroy children's self-confidence. By constantly nagging and failing them, they succeed in convincing children that they are stupid and worthless and lead them to confirm that self-evaluation on a self-fulfilling basis. With the best of intentions, parents frequently set such high goals for their children that the latter feel inadequate and unacceptable. The peer group also may encourage the formation of a self-concept that interferes with the work of the classroom and, at times, with development of behavior in line with the general code of society. Children from the lower class tend to develop a self-concept relatively antagonistic to the "silly stuff" required in school, for instance.

The curriculum must be meaningful

There is a need to set the curriculum in line with the self-concept of students. Davis and his colleagues (Davis 1948; Eells 1953; Eells et al. 1951), for example, argue that we do children from the lower classes a great deal of harm by systematically assigning to them tasks that are far removed from their experiences and inconsistent with the values of their culture. By failing them when their work does not meet our demands, however unsuitable, we lead these children to believe that they are failures. Once they are convinced of this, a vicious circle sets in, which makes it impossible for them to succeed. It is also likely that poor grades followed by nagging actually reduce rather than increase the academic output of below-average students. This is especially true for children from the lower class for whom underachievement in school often stems from the conflict between being academically competent and yet not being a sissy—a conflict they can resolve rather readily by not trying.

8. See Cowan (1978) for some of the better-known measures of the self-concept.

It is a safe bet that we as teachers can get more out of students, and lead them to get more out of themselves, by encouraging than by destroying them. We need to stress the positive: stress the fact that we expect students to succeed rather than give them the impression we would be surprised if they did. It is particularly important that one's first attempts at a task be successful. Success in learning to read, for example, should be among their early experiences in school. Some degree of failure is inevitable, but it should not be introduced too soon nor too often. Children faced with unrealistic goals or impossible demands will either have to incorporate failure as a part of their self-image or avoid conflict by being "uninterested." This pattern is far too common in our schools. Many students who might not be able to set the world on fire but who could do respectable work if they were encouraged are instead forced by repeated failure to adopt an "I-can-but-I-don't-want-to" attitude. They cannot allow themselves to try because they could be involved in a self-conflict if they failed after having tried.

Rarely do people concede that they are complete failures; they may give in on some front while emphasizing all the more their adequacy in other areas in order to maintain self-respect. A high-school boy having difficulty with his studies may cease trying to be a scholar and concentrate on being an athlete; he may rationalize that only sissies do well in school. What he is doing is building a somewhat different concept of himself to match what he can do. Of course, this is possible only when the self-concept is relatively unformed and the shift is such that it can be assimilated within the current self.

The self-concept
must agree with
reality

The child's self-image does not always agree with reality. Distortion of reality is a potential danger in the case of all attitudes, but the danger is correspondingly greater when the attitudes relate to the self. Thus, in order to defend themselves against conflict, children may blame the teacher for their poor grades and continue thinking of themselves as academically competent. Or they may become chronic, compulsive overachievers in a determined attempt to maintain their self-image. By forcing children into numerous activities by which they can evaluate themselves, the school plays an important part in the formation of their self-image. It ought to make sure their self-concept is realistic, for not only must there be consistency within the self but there must be consistency with external reality. As Combs and Snygg (1959) point out, people who are unable to accept themselves as they are operate under a serious handicap because they must deal with life from false and inadequate premises.

Relation to Perception

Perceptions from the external world are the basic ingredient from which the self is developed and maintained. However, in an attempt to avoid conflict with incompatible ideas, we see only what we want to see and hear only what we want to hear. More specifically, we perceive only what is consistent with our motives and goals and interpret our experiences to make them compatible with our present self-concept. Not only is perception selective; it is often false as a result of the distortions brought about by screening through the existing self-structure. We see our enemies as sneaky connivers when, by objective standards, they are of the highest integrity. Our perception of a student's behavior is colored to a considerable extent by whether we like him or not just as one's views of the Kremlin varies according to whether one was born in Leningrad or in Boston. All of which suggests that the old adage "Seeing is believing" might be closer to the truth stated in reverse: "Believing is seeing."

The self acts as a selective screen, the permeability of which is determined by the nature of the environment relative to the self. Under conditions of stress, this screen becomes a barrier that isolates the individual, who then becomes a prisoner of his or her own defenses, for eventual inadequacy is the inevitable consequence of closing off one's avenues of communication with the outside world. To the extent that extended or intense fear occurs, *tunnel vision* or, in Gestalt terminology, a narrowing of the perceptual field, sets in, which makes a person incapable of seeing or trying anything new. Children whose needs for belonging are severely frustrated, for example, persist in antisocial behavior, which only serves to accentuate their rejection; they are so busy warding off anxiety that they have no time or energy to devote to constructive attempts to solve their problem. But since they cannot stand doing nothing, they continue in a way that, even though it provides temporary and partial satisfaction, is not in their best interest from the standpoint of long-term adjustment. As Jersild (1952) points out, whenever people resist learning that would be beneficial to them, we can suspect they are trying to safeguard their self-image. Their self-picture may be false and unhealthy, but it is the only one they know. Only under conditions of security can they afford to lower the barriers so that access to experience can be reestablished.

The Level of Aspiration

The level of expectation individuals set for themelves determines their relative success not only in the performance of a given task but also as persons and thus determines the kind of self-concept they are likely to develop. In other words, "success" and "failure" are defined not on the basis of actual performance measured on an absolute scale but rather with reference to the target toward which the individual was aiming. For Nancy to get a B when she was shooting for an A is a matter of "failure," while to get a C when all she was looking for was a *pass* is really a form of success. No matter how adequate from an objective point of view, performance on a task that is considered too easy does not yield a feeling of success, while inadequate performance will not result in a feeling of failure if it is in an area in which the individual makes no claim to competence. To have significance from the standpoint of success and failure, performance must be within the narrow range of the individual's aspi-

Setting realistic goals

rations. Although research findings are ambiguous, it would seem that a comfortable level of aspiration is necessary for personal happiness. It also follows that, inasmuch as the level of aspiration depends on past successes and failure, children should be encouraged to set their aspirations in line with reality and, further, that they should be assisted in attaining certain successes in order to develop an adequate level of aspiration.

As we noted earlier in the chapter, inability to set realistic goals is characteristic of the person motivated by fear of failure. People who are secure set their goals in keeping with their potentialities; they expect slight but regular improvement and are willing to take a certain element of risk. Insecure people, on the other hand, because they cannot tolerate failure become either compulsive overstrivers who set impossible goals that they attempt desperately to attain or that they use as an alibi to avoid feelings of inadequacy in the event of failure, or they become underachievers who set such easy goals that they "just can't miss." People who fail continually also develop a reluctance to commit themselves to a specific goal and to make an earnest attempt to attain it. It is common for students who have been systematically disappointed by their performance to refuse to set a goal of a given grade; they simply coast along, hoping for the best and, in the meantime, keeping their perceptual field at a low level of differentiation. It is characteristic of the inadequate person to be lacking in both motivation and achievement.[9]

CHANGING THE SELF-CONCEPT

Stability and change
in self-concept

Despite the tendency of the self-image to perpetuate itself through the selectivity it exercises over the experiences it integrates or rejects, a person's self-concept and the meaning the environment has for him or her are constantly undergoing revision and reorganization. Whereas older views tend to cause the rejection of incompatible ideas, the new gradually erodes and causes a shift in the old. In the adjusted person, this process is harmonious and gradual, but, for the insecure, it may lead to a disorganization of behavior.

People are faced with the dual problems of maintaining harmony both within themselves and with the environment. In order to understand the environment, they must keep their interpretation consistent with the reality of their experiences, but in order to maintain their individuality they must organize these interpretations to form a system that is internally consistent. Learn-

9. The unfortunate part of the situation is that, after a period of nonachievement, cumulative deficiencies set in so that, even when the self-concept changes, achievement is often impossible, as many high school underachievers find out when they enroll in college. In other words, just as achievement is cumulative, so is nonachievement. Which is the cause and which is the effect is not clear; they probably act as complementary parts of a vicious circle.

ers perceive, interpret, and accept or reject events in the light of the self-system they have developed. Experiences that, if assimilated, would force a reorganization of the self tend to be resisted through denial and distortion or, under conditions of threat, through a closing of communication with the threatening conditions.

However, continued stability calls for a gradual evolution through the assimilation and integration of new experiences rather than simply the maintenance of the status quo. Individuals are continually engaged in the process of self-discovery, the insights from which have to be incorporated into a new and more adequate self-image. But this reorganization must be gradual and orderly, consolidating itself as it goes along, and it must occur within the framework of the current self-image. It takes time to change a self-concept that has taken years to develop; the delinquent, for example, cannot be expected to change to socially acceptable behavior overnight. There is also need for reasonable stability in the perceptual field; chaos in the environment can lead to confusion and to a disorganization of the self (see Toffler 1970).

ANXIETY

The Meaning of Anxiety

Bearing directly on the question of change in the self-concept is *anxiety,* a concept fundamental to the understanding of all aspects of human behavior from adjustment-maladjustment to efficiency in learning and flexibility in problem solving. Tension is generated whenever people face a situation where an obstacle prevents the ready satisfaction of their needs. This tension is usually mild and quickly dissipated as equilibrium is restored through the attainment of a suitable goal. In the case of intense or long-continued frustration of important needs, however, the tension may reach such drastic proportions as to interfere with the effective attainment of the goals through which the needs can be satisfied. The term *anxiety* generally is used to refer to disruptive tension of this sort although, to be sure, there is no sharp dividing line separating anxiety from the more normal levels of tension.

Fear and anxiety   As used here, anxiety is a conscious experience of relatively intense dread and foreboding. It differs from fear in that it is conceived as a vague, diffuse, objectless state of tension, while fear is temporary, more directly related to the threatening situation, and conducive to relevant behavior. Fear can be conceived as a state of apprehension with a focus on a recognizable danger; in anxiety, on the other hand, it is the security pattern that the individual has developed to deal with threatening situations that is itself being threatened. Because anxiety attacks the very foundation of personality, the individual cannot stand outside the threat, objectify it, and is therefore powerless to take steps to meet it, especially in the case of neurotic anxiety, where the threat is repressed into the unconscious.

To the extent that anxiety implies a relative lack of perceptual clarity concerning the nature of the threat, reaction to anxiety tends to be more chronic and disproportionate than in the case of fear. The complicated system of defense people develop against such threats to the self is frequently abnormal and harmful from the standpoint of their long-range welfare. Yet we must remember that whatever distress people may be experiencing in an attempt to protect a neurotic self is presumably less, at least for the moment, than they would experience if they behaved in any other way. In therapy, the counselor helps clients explore their feelings until the latter are able to pinpoint the cause of their difficulty, for only when it is differentiated can it be approached constructively, This is a painful process, for the more clearly one perceives the real problem, the greater the threat and, for such a clarification to occur, it is necessary for the client to be convinced that the benefits to be gained by moving ahead are greater than those to be gained by avoiding the problem.

Reactions to Anxiety

The normal reaction to stress is a more determined effort to deal with the situation. Under conditions of inadequate tension (i.e., of inadequate motivation), individuals tend to be apathetic. As tension increases, they become more alert and reach a higher level of efficiency. With further increases in tension to the level at which the term *anxiety* might be applied, however, the stress becomes such that it is disruptive rather than facilitative. It can result in a deterioration of performance, especially in the finer areas of creativity, problem solving, and subtle human relations. Reactions to severe anxiety may take different forms, but they tend to be similar from the standpoint of being ineffectual, stereotyped, and generally compulsive. A common way of dealing with anxiety is to keep threatening experiences at a low level of differentiation, i.e., to prevent them from coming into focus. Rationalization and denial are other ways of distorting a situation to protect the self. The clearest example of denial is amnesia, where threatening experiences are simply blocked out or disguised as a means of eliminating conflict. A more drastic reaction to anxiety is the nervous breakdown.[10]

Need for Anxiety

At normal levels, tension resulting from difficulty in meeting the demands of a situation is highly beneficial from the standpoint of the individual's maximum

10. See Basowitz et al. (1955) for an authoritative statement on the influence of anxiety on behavior.

self-realization. Without this powerful force impelling us to regain equilibrium through the satisfaction of our needs, we would remain forever childish, ignorant, and incompetent. Lynn and Gordon (1961), for example, refer to a golden mean of anxiety for maximal efficiency in performance.

The need for anxiety is fully recognized in the classroom, where a certain level of tension—i.e., of motivation—is considered necessary to effective learning. Tension plays a critical role in socialization. Children learn acceptable behavior only as a result of the frustration that occurs when their behavior fails to earn the approval of the social group. Social sensitivity results from learned anxiety, and, unless their experiences lead to anxiety over the possible frustration of their needs for social acceptance and recognition, children will remain essentially unsocialized, spoiled brats with no concern for the feelings and rights of anyone but themselves. Moral conscience develops out of the anxiety and guilt feelings resulting from a failure to live up to the standards and values one has internalized in the process of socialization. On the other hand, although mild tension exerts a facilitating influence on adjustment, it must not be assumed that all people who are selfish or shortsighted are lacking in anxiety. On the contrary, it is neurotic anxiety, by forcing individuals to close off the avenues to the significant aspects of their environment, that keeps most people from learning the tasks essential to their growth toward maturity and self-actualization.

Research suggests that tension is conducive to increased effort, and it is likely that in routine tasks, especially those involving gross physical exertion, strong tension may result in increased productivity, although excessive tension may just as easily result in perpetual nervous exhaustion, in stupid, erratic, and circular behavior, and in decreased output. It may increase speed of performance, but it is also likely to increase the rate of error (Palermo et al. 1956). When the task calls for sheer persistence or the use of well-learned habits, high-anxiety students tend to work harder and to outperform their less anxious peers (K. Spence 1954; Castaneda et al. 1956).

However, since excessive tension leads to fixation, stereotypy, perceptual rigidity, and closure tendencies, it almost invariably exerts a disruptive effect on the quality of performance in tasks involving complex discrimination in novel material, creativity, innovation, flexibility, originality, and the more subtle aspects of learning as represented by high-level skills and abilities in which there is greater possibility of interference. Sarason et al. (1960), for example, note that on tasks requiring flexible and creative orientation, less-anxious students are more spontaneous, more productive, and show better judgment. High-anxiety students are superior on tasks requiring caution and alertness to error, but they tend to have difficulty when they have to reorganize their thoughts creatively or to improvise, i.e., when they have to leave the psychological safety of the memorized solution, the traditional answer, and the routine performance.

Anxiety can be helpful

Anxiety can lead to fixity

A well-known study of the debilitating effects of anxiety on problem-solving behavior is that of Maier et al. (1940, 1949). A rat was placed on a jumping stand, facing two doors, one locked and the other unlocked; if it jumped against the locked door, it bumped its nose and fell into the net below. If it jumped against the unlocked door, the door opened and it got a reward of food. The rat soon learned to identify which door led to the food, but then the problem was made insoluble by making the assignment of which door was locked and which unlocked a matter of chance. Under these circumstances, most animals, when forced to jump, developed a fixed habit of jumping either to the door at the right or at the left, which, even though a stereotyped reaction, was, under the circumstances, as good as any other. But some animals jumped at the post between the two doors, a stupid compromise. Furthermore, even when the investigators made the problem soluble again by attaching the punishment to the side on which it was fixated, the rat persisted in jumping to the same side even though it was now being punished every time. This behavior lasted through hundreds of trials, even after the door on the other side was entirely removed so that the rat could plainly see on which side the food was to be found.

Anxiety leads to narrowing of the perceptual field so that anxious individuals lose sight of the broader circumstances to which the problem is attached; they focus so completely on the barriers that they are totally blind to alternative pathways and substitute goals. As a result, their behavior is characterized by stereotypy and rigidity (and corresponding ineffectiveness). It is particularly lacking in abstract qualities and flexibility in higher intellectual functions. A compulsive repetition of errors is characteristic of anxious children, for example. The more desperately they need love, the more incapable they become of refraining from obnoxious behavior; they cannot free themselves from tension sufficiently to be able to use their energies constructively. Thus, whereas secure children are curious and adaptable, anxious children are rigid; they stay with their ineffectual adjustments simply because their anxiety does not permit them to perceive and to experiment with more effective ways. It is also possible that individuals may cease to try as a means of ensuring a face-saving alibi in case of failure. Although it is true that some people work best under stress, generally people prosper when they are challenged, but their performance deteriorates when they are overwhelmed.

Implications for Educational Practice

The implications of the concept of anxiety for educational practice are so far-reaching as to warrant careful consideration. To the extent that anxiety implies helplessness in meeting situational demands, the importance of building up emotional security cannot be overemphasized. This can be accomplished through providing an atmosphere of permissiveness and acceptance in which children can experience tension at a level that is educative rather than disruptive and through ensuring reasonable success by making sure that what is expected is consistent with their level of readiness. The situation must provide the security of clearly defined demands and restrictions. The goal of education is self-direction but, until the children can provide their own direction in matters of behavior planning, adult guidance must be supplied if anxiety is to be avoided and learning to take place.

Although considerable individual differences exist in the ability to operate under tension, overemphasis on anxiety tends to be self-defeating, particularly in the case of young children. Only when they are relatively free from undue concern over the defense of the self can they gain the perspective necessary to see themselves and the world constructively and to have time and energy to devote to self-improvement. Even though some students may suffer from insufficient anxiety regarding schoolwork, it seems likely that, for the tasks that are of significance in education, anxiety is a dangerous weapon to use. Classroom learning typically arouses a superabundance of anxiety, much of it teacher created (through competition, grading, threat, etc.). When teachers go beyond the lower levels of anxiety, they are probably making difficulties for themselves and risking harm to children.

THE PHENOMENAL FIELD

An extension of the self-concept that has direct bearing on the work of the classroom is the *phenomenal field*, a position based on field theory and closely related to the life-space postulated by Lewin to describe the effectual environment to which the individual responds. The phenomenal field is based on the concepts of field theory. It postulates, for example, that greater adequacy in behavior goes hand in hand with greater differentiation of one's psychological space. It agrees that the characteristics of the parts are determined by the properties of the field and recognizes the figure-and-ground character of perception and the importance of the ground in determining behavior. Experience has meaning only from the standpoint of the individual's psychological field and relates to the reorganization of that field. More fundamental in the present context is that people behave as they do because they perceive the situation as they do. As they structure the situation differently, their behavior will change in keeping with their new perceptions. Correspondingly, any attempt to change their behavior must proceed indirectly through a restructuring of their perception of the situation.

Perception is selective and phenomenological

Teachers frequently complain that certain children are not motivated; actually, they are annoyed that children do not perceive from the same perspective the goals that the teacher happens to see as important. Children who misbehave are trying to accomplish what they consider best, no matter how misguided they may be from the standpoint of the teacher's perceptual outlook. Teachers who deplore a lack of classroom motivation might profit from perceiving in a new light the effects of their procedures on the children and, while they are at it, getting a new perspective on what constitutes a good education from the perspective of the child whose education it is.

We sometimes find it difficult to understand children because we are looking at them from *our* perceptual framework. There is much needless conflict between adults and teenagers resulting from their differences in perspective. Clinicians rarely see parents who deliberately set out to destroy their child, but frequently they see parents who accomplish just that—parents who do vicious things in the firm conviction that they want the best for their child. People do their best to be adequate according to their perceptions, no matter how futile and misguided their behavior may seem to a person whose phenomenal field is more enlightened. They simply need to develop a more adequate perspective. For the same reason, we cannot superimpose our own perceptions on neurotics and assume that they will obviously want to shed their symptoms; they will not. They will remain neurotic as long as their perceptual field is that of a neurotic.

SELF-ACTUALIZATION

The Concept of Becoming

As noted in chapter 3, the shortcomings of the drive-reduction theory of motivation have led to increased emphasis on the more positive stimulation (or fulfillment) theories. The child is not an inert mass to be prodded into action by an external force. On the contrary, inherent in each individual is an inner force, an urge, a pressure toward growth and development, an overwhelming drive toward *self-actualization.* According to Combs and Snygg (1959), the individual is sparked by one basic drive, namely, to actualize, maintain, and enhance the self. All one's strivings can be conceptualized as basic aspects of this fundamental need.

A particularly adequate discussion of self-actualization is that presented by Combs, Kelly, Maslow, and Rogers in the 1962 ASCD yearbook, *Perceiving, Behaving, Becoming.* Although these authors speak variously of the *adequate person,* the *fully functioning person,* and the *self-actualizing person,* and although some points are more pertinent to one or the other of their separate presentations, they generally agree on the major points of emphasis and on the underlying view of behavior as the direct outgrowth of perception at the time of behavior. The central theme concerns the fundamental human drive to push one's self-realization to the limit—i.e., what the authors have labeled *becoming.* The basic premise is that there is an all-pervasive force impelling people to grow, that children will actualize themselves in the direction of growth in spite of hardship and the loss of certain advantages because it is more satisfying to grow than it is to remain a child. It is only when traumatic experiences occur too systematically that this ongoing process is stopped and the direction of movement is reversed.

The self-actualizing person

The four authors portray the self-actualizing individual as maximally open to experience. By contrast to their defensive counterparts, self-actualizing people are able to accept into awareness any and all aspects of reality. This openness to experience, with its consequent richness and availability of the perceptual field, is the key to their success. Because they have free access to available data, they are likely to behave more intelligently. Such individuals are characterized by psychological freedom to move toward ever-greater adequacy; they make effective use of their potentialities; they are self-actualizing in the sense that they provide their own power to grow and are moving forward in the direction of a self-actualizing spiral of ever-widening scope.

The inadequate person

By contrast, inadequate people are characterized not so much by inability to meet environmental demands—everyone is inadequate in at least a number of dimensions—but by the fact that their pattern of life is oriented toward their becoming progressively *less* adequate. When people are faced with persistent and overwhelming odds against which they have to prove their adequacy, they resort to boasting, rationalizing, and other inadequate ways of meeting life's demands. They soon find themselves in a vicious circle of having to resort to the same inadequate mechanisms with progressively greater vigor and frequency. In time, ever-greater threat is met with ever-greater attempts at self-defense and increasing inability to accept reality and develop the necessary competence.

The constructive way of dealing with threatening perceptions is to incorporate them into a more adequate self-structure, but this neurotic people cannot do. Instead they defend themselves by distorting threatening experiences to fit their present system or by preventing them from coming into their focus of awareness. To the extent that defensiveness leads them to convert their self-concept into an impregnable fortress, access to which is guarded by an impermeable shell, inadequate people cut themselves off from communication and soon find, as did the dinosaurs of old, that it becomes progressively more difficult to fit into a changing world. They are operating from false premises. They may, for example, continually complain about mistreatment without examining the possibility that they are to blame. However, even when suppressed, the threatening perceptions hardly remain inactive; on the contrary, they keep these people in a continuous state of anxiety. Furthermore, since no action can be taken against them as long as they are kept vague and diffuse, their destructive influence continues to undermine their ability to take positive steps (see Jourard 1963). Meanwhile, they consume so much of their energies in protecting their existing self-structure that they have little energy left for constructive remedial and developmental action. The result is inefficient, if not desperate and stupid, behavior.

Educational Implications

The implication of the concept of self-actualization is all-pervasive; it under-lies the adjustment of the individual and, by definition, ensures maximum per-sonal and social success and happiness. It has direct bearing on learning in and out of the classroom. Certainly teachers have no greater responsibility than to set each and every child on a spiral of self-fulfillment. The means of so doing are multiple rather than single, so no recipe can be given. On the other hand, this is really not new; the discussion here has simply emphasized and elabo-rated on the type of sound pedagogical practice that psychologists have advo-cated for years.

Openness to experience is so crucial to self-fulfillment that its cultivation should be of prime concern to the school. No matter what else we do, it is of no avail if the child simply retreats into a shell. We need to pay particular atten-tion to educational practices that cause children to devaluate their self-con-cept, to become defensive, and to close off the supply lines necessary for con-tinued growth. We need to give serious thought to the elimination of the petty rules and arbitrary regulations that serve no purpose, of the lockstep promo-tion of children, the fixed curriculum, impossible standards, overcompetitive grading, grade retention, one-way communication, and, above all, the auto-cratic climate—the threats, the nagging, the punitive and repressive disci-pline—and other forms of rigid bureaucratic nonsense that dehumanize and alienate. There is room for meaningful evaluation, for example, but there is no need for our overcompetitive policy of pitting child against child that causes everyone to feel threatened, insecure, and defensive, never sure that they are good enough except as they capitalize on the deficiencies of others.

Constructive classroom procedures

This is in no way to imply that teachers abdicate; every organization must have its leaders, its coordinators, as well as its followers. But it does not serve any purpose for our schools to continue what Dinkmeyer and Dreikurs (1963) call the slave mentality of viewing children as subordinates to be kept in line through fear and intimidation. It should especially be noted that implement-ing the principles of humanistic psychology in the school is not to deny the im-portance of subject matter but rather to recognize that the fundamental goal of education is to promote personal as well as cognitive growth.

Just as we can think of an adequate person, so we can think of an ade-quate classroom characterized by warmth, acceptance, trust, and encourage-ment (see Dinkmeyer and Dreikurs 1963), and an appropriately challenging and constructive academic program in which children can achieve success in personally meaningful tasks as the basis for developing trust in their own com-petence. A prime determinant of whether children grow toward adequacy as a consequence of classroom experiences is the teacher's handling of the situa-tion, and teachers, like students, need to develop greater adequacy. This is not easy for teachers who, like everyone else, tend to cling to their perceptions as to correct classroom procedures. Many see the child as an enemy to be kept in check or to be coerced; they are convinced that decisions as to what is good for the child must come from the teacher, who knows best. They conceive of the child's task in the classroom as one of listening and learning; there is no time to explore feelings and attitudes.

Self-actualizing teachers

If teachers are to assume responsibility for developing self-actualizing children, they themselves must be self-actualizing. To the extent that teachers' behavior is a direct function of their private world of perceptions, teacher education must help prospective teachers know themselves (as a prerequisite to knowing their students) by providing systematic opportunities for self-encounter and self-development. Perhaps more fundamentally, we need to select for teacher education young people who are personally adequate, people who are open to experience, people who see themselves and others in realistic and essentially positive ways.

HIGHLIGHTS OF THE CHAPTER

Teachers who want to deal effectively with their students, their colleagues, and the school's patrons should be thoroughly familiar with the principles presented in this chapter.

1. Behavior is purposive. It does not just happen; rather it occurs as part of the individual's attempts to reach goals and attain purposes.
2. Children learn to satisfy their needs in a given way. The basic determinants of behavior are not *needs*, which simply energize the organism, but rather *motives*, which direct the energized organism toward the attainment of relevant goals.
3. Although questioned as the sole explanation of motivated behavior, the drive-reduction theory is still useful. The more recent stimulation theories are more positive in outlook.
4. A basic premise of field psychology and a point of special emphasis in the writings of Rogers, Maslow, and Combs is that the adequacy of one's behavior is a direct function of the adequacy of one's perceptions.
5. An individual's self-perceptions are centered in the self-concept, a system of attitudes, ideals, and values developed as the person emerges into clearer focus and defines progressively more clearly just who and what he or she is.
6. Well-adjusted people maintain a small, positive gap between their self-ideal an their self-image. Continued frustration tends to promote an unrealistic or erratic level of aspiration.
7. The self acts as a selective screen, filtering and distorting experiences so as to have them fit in with the existing self, even to the point of closing off from awareness any threatening experience. Under conditions of anxiety, perceptual and behavioral rigidity develops, with the inevitable consequence that

the individual is no longer capable of taking constructive action to deal with the world.

8. The concept of self-realization, as incorporated in such terms as the *self-actualizing* or the *fully functioning* person, has more recently been presented under the concept of *becoming*. The person in the process of becoming is maximally open to experience and therefore capable of maximal utilization of potentialities and environmental opportunities for self-improvement.

9. The fact that the child's behavior will at all times be consistent with his or her system of attitudes and values has far-reaching implications for every aspect of the educative process. Teachers could render the cause of education, democracy, and humanity no greater service than to orient every child toward a spiral of self-fulfillment.

SUGGESTIONS FOR FURTHER READING

ARONFREED, J. Aversive control of socialization. *Nebraska Symposium on Motivation* 16 (1968):271–320. In a thorough review, Aronfreed finds that, contrary to psychology's earlier position, punishment can be highly effective and that unpredictable side-effects (e.g., fixation) do not occur when the subject is able to discriminate what is punished and what is not.

BRONFENBRENNER, U. The changing American child: A speculative analysis. *J. Soc. Issues* 17 (1961):6–18. Notes the changes that have taken place in child-rearing practices in America; analyzes the implications of the current trend toward a bureaucratic society in which "getting along" is prized over "getting ahead."

CARNEGIE, DALE. *How to Win Friends and Influence People.* New York: Simon & Schuster, 1936. The old standby. Should be analyzed against the background of the principles presented in this chapter.

COMBS, ARTHUR W., and DONALD SNYGG. *Individual Behavior: A Perceptual Approach to Behavior.* New York: Harper & Row, 1959. A clear and comprehensive presentation of the phenomenological position.

COMBS, ARTHUR W., et al. *Perceiving, Behaving, Becoming.* 1962 Yrbk. Assn. Superv. Curr. Devel., 1962. Four leading phenomenologists, Combs, Kelley, Maslow, and Rogers, synthesize their relative views on self-actualization under the theme of *becoming*.

DINKMEYER, DON, and RUDOLF DREIKURS. *Encouraging Children to Learn: The Encouragement Process.* Englewood Cliffs, N.J.: Prentice-Hall, 1963. A highly readable and interesting account of how children can be encouraged to grow and to learn. Gives a number of anecdotes, pointing out how discouragement is an important factor in failure and deficiencies.

HECKHAUSEN, H. Achievement motive research: Current problems and some contributions toward a general theory of motivation. *Nebraska Symposium on Motivation* 16 (1968):103–174. A comprehensive treatment of the need for achievement.

KASH, M. M., and G. BORICH. *Teacher Behavior and Pupil Self-Concept.* Reading, Mass.: Addison-Wesley, 1978. Presents a comprehensive look at the research on how teachers influence the self-concept of their students. Each chapter lists a number of practical suggestions for teachers.

MARX, MELVIN H., and TOM N. TOMBAUGH. *Motivation: Psychological Principles and Educational Implications.* San Francisco: Chandler, 1967. A good overview of motivation as it relates to the classroom. A good analysis of research findings.

MASLOW, ABRAHAM H. *Toward a Psychology of Being.* New York: Van Nostrand, 1968. The best presentation of Maslow's theory of motivation, emphasizing the positive aspects of self-actualization, peak experiences, and growth.

ROGERS, CARL R. *Freedom to Learn.* Columbus, Ohio: Merrill, 1969. Questions whether the educational system, the most traditional, conservative, rigid, bureaucratic institution of our time, can come to grips with the real problems of modern life.

WYLIE, RUTH C. The present status of self-theory. In Edgar F. Borgatta and William W. Lambert, eds., *Handbook of Personality Theory and Research*, pp. 728–777. Chicago: Rand McNally, 1968. A thorough analysis of the self-concept. Points to a number of shortcomings as a scientific construct. See also Tannebaum, Mark A. The self-concept: a theoretical synthesis. *Diss. Abstr. Internat.* 39 (1978):205–206; Shavelson, R. J. et al. Self-concept: Validation of construct interpretation. *Rev. Educ. Res.* 46 (1976):407–442.

QUESTIONS AND PROJECTS

1. Discuss the role of needs in the promotion of self-realization. When might the individual's needs lead to self-destruction rather than self-realization? What might be done to ensure proper orientation in this regard?

2. Analyze Dale Carnegie's *How to Win Friends and Influence People* from the standpoint of the psychology of motivation. Does this approach imply a certain degree of manipulation and exploitation of others?

3. Society generally emphasizes normative requirements—e.g., children need to be quiet in school—rather than individual needs. How legitimate are such requirements in a democracy, and to what extent should they be enforced? Discuss specific ways in which the two might be synchronized in practice.

4. Why is it essential for prospective teachers to understand the dynamics underlying the behavior of others? How important is it that teachers be relatively free from unresolved tension?

5. What do you see as the potential benefits in a teacher-education program of emphasis on self-discovery as advocated by Combs? Specifically, what might be the basic components of such a program?

SELF-TEST

1. Drives are to energizing as motives are to
   a. directing.
   b. energizing and reinforcing.
   c. directing and reinforcing.
   d. energizing, directing, and reinforcing.
   e. reinforcing.

2. Research suggests that _____ reinforcement produces responses most resistant to extinction.
   a. delayed
   b. direct
   c. immediate
   d. intermittent
   e. secondary

3. Need of achievement (*N Ach*) tends to be highest in homes in which
   a. the atmosphere is permissive and supportive but not demanding.
   b. the child is pushed into independent behavior from early infancy.
   c. the child is given maximum emotional security and freedom to grow.
   d. the father is friendly, self-confident, and highly successful.
   e. the home is dominated by a strong, supportive, strict, and achievement-oriented mother.

4. The self-concept is best conceived as
   a. the counterpart of Freud's alter ego.
   b. the individual's phenomenological interpretation of reality.
   c. the sum total of one's experiences acting as a guide to future interaction with the environment.
   d. the system of attitudes revolving around one's self-evaluation.
   e. a sytem of values on which the individual bases moral decisions.

5. The primary mechanism by which the individual maintains consistency in her or his self-concept is
   a. avoidance and/or rejection of incompatible evidence.
   b. judicious selection of experiences.
   c. projection of one's shortcomings onto others.
   d. reinterpretation of experience to fit the existing self.
   e. selective perception.

6. The clearest effect of severe anxiety on behavior is
   a. a greater sensitivity to appropriate cues.
   b. increased systematic efforts to achieve a solution.
   c. regression to more primitive modes of behavior.

d. renewed attempts to analyze the problem rationally.
e. rigidity and stereotypy of behavior.

7. The success element of the self-actualizing person is
   a. an enlightened self-interest.
   b. a favorable view of self and others.
   c. a high level of personal integration.
   d. an openness to experience.
   e. a social sensitivity.

PART TWO

Children and Their Development

Presents a brief overview of those aspects of child growth and development that bear most clearly on the classroom. The emphasis is on both theory and practice.

5 Growth and Development

Presents the basic principles of development and the respective role of heredity and environment in relation to readiness and other determinants of student behavior. Reviews the contributions of Piaget.

6 The Child as a Growing Organism

Explores key issues in physical, socioemotional, and intellectual development, with relative emphasis on intellectual development as a critical factor in academic learning.

7 Individual Differences

Reviews the basic dimensions of individual differences and the strategies typically used by teachers in dealing with such differences. Emphasizes sex and socioeconomic differences and their educational implications.

FIVE

Growth and Development

We are quite right in insisting that the demands of the school should not go beyond the child's capacity to perform. We are quite wrong if we do not add that the demands of the school should not be *below* the child's capacity. Since we cannot be perfect, which way shall we err?

Don Robinson (1962)

It appears that an appropriate level of stimulation is necessary not only to provide opportunities for learning but also to maintain normal maturational development.

Karl U. Smith and M. F. Smith (1965)

"Readiness" is a mischievous half-truth. It is a half-truth because it turns out that one *teaches* readiness or provides opportunities for its nurture, one does not simply wait for it. Readiness, in these terms, consists of mastery of those simpler skills that permit one to reach higher skills.

Jerome S. Bruner (1966)

— Presents the basic principles underlying human development
— Discusses the relative contributions of heredity and environment in the development of human potential
— Introduces the work of Piaget
— Emphasizes the importance of readiness as a determinant of the child's ability to benefit from environmental stimuli.

PREVIEW: KEY CONCEPTS

1. Every aspect of one's current status—physiological, socioemotional, intellectual—is a joint function of hereditary and environmental forces impinging on the individual from the time of conception.
2. Not only does heredity set developmental limits but inherited potential cannot develop in the absence of environmental stimulation.
3. Piaget's stage theory of cognitive development constitutes a significant contribution to the literature on growth and development. It highlights a growing tendency toward the rejection of the earlier concept of continuity of developmental phenomena.
4. The question of readiness is critical to the operation of the classroom. Of related interest are questions of developmental tasks, critical periods, and teachable moments.

PREVIEW QUESTIONS

1. To what extent can teaching and other environmentally based influences override inherited limitations and predispositions?
2. Through what mechanism is heredity operationalized? What role do parents play in the transmission of heredity?
3. What are some of the educational implications of the fact, as postulated by Piaget and others, that growth proceeds through a series of qualitatively different stages?
4. What are the implications for educational practice of (a) readiness; (b) developmental tasks, and (c) critical periods?

From a tiny speck at conception, the child multiplies a millionfold until at birth the infant exhibits considerable physical development. Shortly thereafter, the child begins to display motor, emotional, social, and intellectual behavior. Those aspects of growth and development resulting from the interaction of environmental influences on inherited potential are of special interest to teachers, for if environmental influences are to be effective in bringing out the potential of the child, it is necessary that they synchronize with underlying maturational processes.

GENERAL PRINCIPLES

Heredity and environment

The development displayed by an individual at any given time is the result of both the maturation of innate potentialities and whatever modification of these potentialities occurs as a result of environmental influences. Whether a person is tall or short, has a pleasing personality, or achieves a high scholastic standing depends on the interaction of the various hereditary and environmental forces operating in the particular case. Basic to our discussion is *heredity* (or *nature*), which refers to the potentialities with which the individual is conceived. Closely related is *maturation*, i.e., that phase of development that relates to the unfolding of the characteristics incorporated in the genes transmitted to the individual from his ancestors. In contrast, *nurture* and *learning* refer to those changes in behavior resulting from the modification of developmental trends through environmental influences. *Growth* and *development* are more inclusive terms, referring to the result of the interaction of maturation and learning in making the individual what he or she is at a given time.

Maturation and learning are closely interrelated

Maturation and learning are so closely interrelated that their separate influences cannot be isolated. Thus, a person may be short because of an inherited tendency toward shortness or because of inadequate diet. Inherited capacity cannot develop in a vacuum nor can it be measured except through present development, which is the result of both maturational and environmental forces. If a person behaves in an unintelligent fashion, there is no way of knowing to what extent such inadequate behavior is the result of inherited intellectual limitations or the failure of the environment to promote the growth of which he or she was capable. Only when we can rule out lack of opportunity to learn can we consider inadequate behavior suggestive of inherited deficiencies. The relative contributions of heredity and environment to the individual's development have been the subject of considerable speculation and disagreement. Unfortunately the evidence is, and must remain, circumstantial and open to a variety of interpretations. Because of the interaction, interdependence, and functional overlapping of the two sets of factors, any attempt at separating the influence of the one from that of the other is essentially futile.

Instincts

Early in the century McDougal (1908) attempted to explain all behavior in terms of *instincts:* maternal behavior was explained on the basis of a maternal instinct; the behavior of the bully stemmed from a pugnacious instinct. These behavioral patterns were considered innate; they emerged somewhat as a beard appears on a boy's face at the appropriate maturational stage. Psychologists have since rejected the concept of instincts in the sense of complex integrated behavioral patterns emerging naturally and fully as a result of the maturation of innate capacities; certainly maternal behavior includes many components in which learning plays a significant role. The major objection to instincts is that they *describe* rather than *explain* behavior. As the list of instincts grew ever longer, psychologists realized that all they were doing was giving names to certain behavioral syndromes and really not explaining anything.

An essentially similar concept has been introduced by Lorenz (1935), Timbergen (1951), Hess (1964), and other ethologists under the name of *imprinting,* which they define as a process distinct from associative learning or conditioning, occurring during a relatively brief period early in the life of certain birds and having a lasting effect on selected aspects of their behavior. In certain species—ducks, for example—a newly hatched bird will follow the first moving objects to which it is exposed, be it its mother, a wooden bird, a box, or even the experimenter.

Watson: A strong environmental position

Diametrically opposed to the instinctive point of view was that of Watson (1929), who postulated that all babies are alike at birth, having a certain body structure, certain reflexes, three emotions (love, fear, and anger), and certain manipulative tendencies. The fact that they became different was due, according to Watson, entirely to differences in postnatal environment. This seems difficult to accept; certainly infants differ in such obvious things as height and weight and probably also in potentialities in various areas of growth. No one denies the importance of environment in promoting the development of the individual's potentialities, but Watson's position appears to minimize unduly the corresponding role of inherited differences.[1]

Both McDougal's and Watson's views are extreme positions that are difficult to accept. Current opinion would support a more middle-of-the-road stand. Heredity and environment are best seen not as rivals but as cocontributors to development, with the relative contribution of each varying on a continuum with the different aspects of development. Thus heredity is probably a relatively more potent factor in physical growth than in social development. Research evidence is inconclusive; it seems that the earliest prenatal behavior consists of diffuse and generalized mass activity from which more specific responses are differentiated. These are later integrated into complex behavior patterns. But research does not, and cannot, resolve the issue of the relative contribution of hereditary and environmental influences in promoting this differentiation and integration.

---

1. The early 1960s saw a substantial swing back to the Watsonian position. McCullers and Plant (1964), for example, wrote, "The preponderance of current evidence suggest that [Watson's] claim might have been fulfilled. At any rate, it appears that he would have been hampered more by methodological problems than by the nature of his basic assumption. Watson's appeal was made nearly half a century ago; it is indeed lamentable that so much time has been wasted."

PRINCIPLES OF HEREDITY

Mendelian Principles

The exact mechanism through which heredity exerts itself is too complex to permit more than a brief overview here. Heredity is determined at the time of fertilization of one of the egg cells of the female by one of the sperm cells of the male, both of which are unique in that they contain only half the number of chromosomes normally found in other body cells.

The chromosomes contain the *genes,* the real bearers of heredity. The current view is that the genes are complex DNA molecules, the atoms of which serve as a master code governing the formation of the protein molecules for which that particular gene is responsible. In other words, chromosomes consist mainly of molecules of the chemical DNA, which gathers from its chemical environment its own kinds of atom, which it arranges in a perfect replica of itself, which then repeats the process.

The determinant of the individual's inherited characteristics is the particular combination of genes involved in the fertilization of one of the many egg cells of the female by one of the many sperm cells of the male. Since each has twenty-three pairs of chromosomes and each chromosome contains thousands of genes, millions of combinations are possible, thus providing the basis for unlimited differences among the siblings of a given family. That one sibling is taller or brighter than the other does not necessarily call for an explanation in terms of differences in environment, any more than does the fact that one is fair and the other dark, or, for that matter, that one is a boy and the other a girl. The principles of heredity possess within themselves the means of explaining a relatively unlimited range of variations that can occur in the offspring of a given couple. The only exception is identical twins, who are the result of the splitting of a fertilized ovum and thus have identical heredity; whatever differences appear later presumably have to be attributed to differences in environmental influences.

Knowing behaviors   An interesting way of looking at heredity is the concept of *knowing behaviors:* i.e., the organism's preprogrammed capabilities to respond appropriately (adaptively) to stimuli. Knowing behaviors can be relatively simple in the case of the amoeba or the sunflower; they can be correspondingly complex in humans. Lessing (1967), for example, estimates that the genetic information transmitted by human parents to their offspring would fill a thousand books of five hundred pages each. In other words, the organism does not start from zero. On the contrary, it starts with a definite structure of "knowing" accumulated through its evolutionary history. As a consequence of a complex of preprogrammed mechanisms, it simply knows how to respond adaptively to its environment. In the case of the lower organisms, this information is basically instinctive, immediate, and prescriptive; it is considerably less restrictive in the case of humans, for whom inherited tendencies are more subject to modification over a relatively long life span, especially in view of our ability to mobilize various environmental forces under our control to achieve our goals.

Educational implications

As teachers, our views on the heredity-environment issue are important. If we believe that the usual conditions of everyday living are sufficient for children to achieve a large part of their potentialities, there does not seem to be much we need to do beyond helping them acquire certain specific skills. If, on the other hand, children attain only a small fraction of their potentialities unless special efforts are made to provide them with concentrated stimulation—and there is considerable evidence to suggest that this is true—the role of education in promoting effective behavior becomes correspondingly more crucial.[2]

Teachers need to be sold on the important role of the environment in the development of inherited potential. A child is not born a genius but only with the potentialities for becoming a genius, provided certain environmental conditions are met. Furthermore, and this is important, education plays a crucial part in determining the direction in which inherited potential develops and the use to which it is put. At the same time, teachers must also be fully convinced that heredity does indeed set limits and that these limits probably vary from child to child, for harm can be done by setting expectations beyond a particular child's capacities. A realistic view as to what environment can and cannot do in overcoming inherited limitations will serve to save the child from neglect on the grounds that "he'll never make it anyway" and from undue pressure in the belief that "you can do whatever you want to do." We can certainly help the child develop effective study habits or a positive self-concept. But to postulate that equalizing environmental opportunities will make all children equal is probably something else again.

Changes in the Basic Pattern of Development

Changes in developmental patterns

From the moment of conception, environmental forces influence the basic developmental pattern set by the particular combination of genes involved in conception. In fact, drastic changes in this basic and presumably inherited developmental pattern can be brought about by the manipulation of environmental conditions. Siamese twins can be developed in fish through cold, insufficient oxygen, or ultraviolet rays, for example (see Anastasi 1958). It would appear that whereas heredity sets certain developmental patterns, these remain true to form only as long as environmental conditions also remain true to form. What is inherited is not actual characteristics but rather a set of genes that, *under certain conditions*, can give rise to the organism having, at a later date, certain characteristics.

Contrary to previous opinion, the developing fetus is far from immune to environmental influences. X rays in the pelvic region of a pregnant woman and

2. It can be argued that even if environment controlled only, say, 20 percent of one's development, this can still make for vast differences in actual status.

German measles in early pregnancy, for example, can produce physical and mental abnormalities in the offspring. Certain drugs, infections, and other forms of maternal dysfunction also can affect the development of the unborn child. Although there is no neural connection or direct blood exchange between the fetus and the mother, chronic anxiety and hypertension in the mother can activate a constant outpouring of hormones in her bloodstream that can readily cross the placenta and expose the fetus to hormonal imbalance. Deficiency of certain nutrients at certain critical developmental stages can have detrimental effects on fetal development, the specific effect apparently depending on which organ is developing at the time of the deficiency (Cohlan 1954; Asdell 1953; Ingalls 1950). If development is interfered with while the inner ear or the brain is being formed, the result is deafness or mental deficiency in the offspring. It is also known that conditions associated with late or difficult delivery may produce permanent degenerative changes in the brain, ranging from relatively complete brain damage to more subtle brain impairment. Anoxia may be involved in some cases of epilepsy.

Changes in behavioral patterns

Since the living organism is capable of learning, major changes in behavior can be effected through the manipulation of environmental influences. Sparrows raised with canaries in a soundproof cage abandon their own chirps and learn the canary call, just as the wolf-girls of India learned to live like wild beasts. More commonplace, but also more important, are the behavioral changes that result from everyday contacts with the environment as might be incorporated under the term *education*. Of course, it must be remembered that all of these changes are restricted by inherited structure; whereas the wolf-girls learned to walk on all fours like the monkeys in the jungle, they did not learn to fly like the birds. It also seems that certain learnings come more "naturally" to some species than to others. Skinner has been criticized, for example, for overgeneralizing the role of reinforcement as it relates to the behavior of certain species, e.g., rats or pigeons, to other species and to humans, who, in some cases, at least, react differently to reinforcement (see Breland and Breland 1961; Herrnstein 1977a, 1977b; Skinner 1977).

Heredity obviously crucial

The influence of heredity on development must not be minimized. Everyday observation provides ample evidence that tall parents tend to have tall offspring, that bright parents tend to have bright offspring. In studies by Tryon (1940) and Thompson (1954) selective mating of the brightest rats as one group and of the dullest rats as a second group through eight successive generations produced two separate distributions of intelligence, with almost no overlap. Similar studies, also with rats, have produced comparable results in the area of emotionality (Hall 1938) and activity (Rundquist 1933). In the Rundquist study, for example, the spontaneous activity displayed by the active group developed by selective mating was on the average twenty times that displayed by the inactive group.

Regression toward the mean

The problem of heredity is complex. It relates to the concept of survival of the fittest in bringing about an improvement in the species, for example. It is complicated by regression toward the mean, i.e., by the tendency for the offspring of parents superior in a given trait also to be above average in that characteristic but less so than their parents. In fact, some of the offspring would be definitely below average. Conversely, the offspring of parents inferior on a given trait would be less inadequate than their parents and some would be above average. On the other hand, the fact that each generation tends to be taller than its predecessor probably reflects a tendency for succeeding generations to be progressively less stunted; the drastic increase in height of the current generation of Korean and Japanese youth, for example, is apparently the result of dietary improvements connected with the introduction of high-protein American-type foods (see Karpinos 1961).

Principles of Development

The amount of research done in the area of development is so extensive as to preclude adequate treatment of its various aspects. The present discussion is limited to an overview of two major principles of interest to teachers.

Patterns of development are relatively stable

The first is that the rate of development varies from child to child; each child is unique. Thus, in physical growth where the pattern is more obvious, some children grow at a much slower rate than others. However, whereas the short child tends to remain short throughout development, this is not always so, nor is it necessarily so in other aspects of growth. The Harvard Growth Studies (Dearborn and Rothney 1941), for instance, found some children with a fairly consistent rate of development but also others who were highly variable.

Various aspects of development are highly interrelated

The second principle is that the various aspects of development are interrelated and interdependent, and it is only when considered in relation to other aspects that any phase of development becomes meaningful. In fact, growth in any one area can only go so far without parallel development in other areas. Thus, growth consists of a spiral by means of which the individual can climb higher and higher, the gains in one phase of growth contributing to gains in other aspects. Contrariwise, physical limitations—e.g., blindness, deafness, chronic illness, or deformity—can have serious detrimental effects on social, emotional, and intellectual development. As teachers, we need to be particularly concerned with the whole child and resist the temptation to think of any single phase of development as more fundamental or important than the others. The various aspects are so closely interrelated that the child can be approached only as a functioning unit.

Developmental patterns may be discontinous

Of particular interest is the question of the continuity and discontinuity of developmental phenomena. For years, psychologists saw growth as sequential and continuous; the child simply grew progressively bigger, performed progressively better, etc. It was a simple case of bigger and better along the same continuum. In recent years, there has been a growing awareness of discontinuity in the developmental sequence. In 1955, Bayley, faced with the relative lack of consistency of the IQ of a child taken in infancy and again some sixteen years later, postulated that intelligence was best seen as a series of qualitatively different intellectual skills arranged in a hierarchy, with the infant restricted to sensorimotor activities while, in the adult, intelligence is primarily geared to verbal reasoning, much of it an abstract nature. As we shall see later in the chapter, Piaget also sees cognitive development as a series of qualitatively different stages; the "intelligence" of the infant is structurally different from that of the older child. The young child's thinking is idiosyncratic and stimulus-bound. The adult, on the other hand, can deal with concepts, principles, and other abstractions.[3] The difference is no longer one of degree but rather a difference in kind arranged in the form of a hierarchy.

Research Strategies

Growth and development are among the most highly researched areas of psychology.[4] In over a half-century of continuous operation, the Institute of Human Development at Berkeley, for instance, has conducted systematic long-term studies into all areas of child growth. Similar child-growth centers (e.g., Gesell's institute, the Fels Institute, etc.) have also contributed major findings in this area, in widely known studies dating back to the early 1900s. The results have been well-documented and relatively precise norms in all areas, ranging from physical height and weight to self-care and social interaction.

Conclusive research difficult to achieve

The investigation of psychological traits, on the other hand, has been somewhat less definitive. Research in this area is handicapped first by the obvious complexity of the problems it presents, and, equally critical, by the general inadequacies of the survey technique (e.g., the parent interview), on which much of the research has had to depend. Some of the alleged class differences in child-rearing practices, for example, as well as some of the inconsistencies from study to study, may actually reflect in part differences in the parents' sensitivities as to what constitute socially desirable child-rearing strategies (see Robbins 1963). More rigorous research techniques, on the other hand, are not particularly appropriate.

In recent years, psychologists have devoted considerable thought to the

3. The idea recurs throughout educational psychology. Psychologists have postulated discontinuity between the learning of animals and that of humans, between rote and meaningful verbal learning (Ausubel 1968), each governed by a different set of psychological principles. Gagné (1977; see chapter 12) postulates a learning hierarchy of relatively distinct learning levels; Maslow (1943) likewise presents a hierarchy of human needs ranging from basic physiological needs to the more "human" aesthetic needs and the need to know (see chapter 4). Freud and Erikson postulate stages in personality development (see chapter 15; also Cotton 1977).

4. We can point to a number of worthy publications: e.g., *The Handbook of Personality Theory* and *Research in Child Development* (Borgatta and Lambert 1968); *Carmichael's Manual of Child Psychology* (Mussen 1970); *Handbook of Child Development* (Mussen 1960); and *Review of Child Development Research* (Hoffman and Hoffman 1964); as well as a number of periodicals (e.g., *Child Development*), the various monographs of the Society for Research in Child Development, the publications of the Children's Bureau, and a large number of books and articles by various authors.

Early deprivation
can be serious

question of early deprivation. Extrapolating the results of various studies of the ill effects of early sensory deprivation in animals—e.g., the McGill studies—educators postulated that the intellectual deficiencies of lower-class children and their consequent academic difficulties simply represented the cumulative deficit resulting from inadequacies in the stimulation value of their early environment. They also assumed that, if caught early, not only could this deficit be reversed through a suitable preschool compensatory program but, further, that the child's cognitive growth could actually be accelerated to a new and permanent level of intellectual potential. This is still a worthy goal but the solution does not seem to be as simple as we once believed. Enthusiasm for experiential stimulation as the determinant of intellectual development, as reflected in, say, Bruner's (1960) statement that any subject can be taught in some intellectually honest way to any child at any stage of development, if taken literally, seems to have been based more on personal egalitarian conviction than on conclusive evidence, for it now seems that hereditary factors cannot be dismissed so lightly.

PIAGET'S STAGE THEORY OF COGNITIVE DEVELOPMENT

Growth and development have been the subject of a number of relatively thorough theoretical formulations, ranging from maturational theories as championed by, say, Gesell, to highly environmentally oriented positions as presented by, say, Gagné, which account for development largely on the basis of the cumulative effects of learning. In addition, a number of developmental psychologists (e.g., Hunt 1961) have addressed themselves to the opposite end of the continuum, namely, the cumulative deficits that occur as a consequence of failure to learn during the early critical period in life. Such a view was particularly popular during the early 1960s, serving as the theoretical foundation for the Head Start program, for example.

Piaget: Development
as a series of stages

Undoubtedly, the most comprehensive view of development is the cognitive developmental (stage) theory formulated by Piaget (1948, 1950, 1952, 1954), whose basic premise is that the basic mental structure is the result not of hereditary or environmental factors alone but rather of the interaction between organismic tendencies and the structure inherent in the outside world.[5] As a result of this interaction, the child's cognitive development proceeds through a series of steps or stages characteried by relatively distinct qualitative differences in the child's evolving modes of thought. Piaget postulates that:

5. See Braine (1959, 1962); Elkind (1967); Flavell (1963); Kohlberg (1968); Patterson (1977); Rohwer et al. (1974); Sigel and Cocking (1975). See also *Amer. Psychol.* 25 (1970):65–79, for a list of Piaget's publications dating back to 1907.

1. These stages form an invariant sequence in the child's cognitive development, with cultural factors able to slow or accelerate, but not to change, the sequence.
2. At any given stage, the child's behavior does not just represent a specific response to a given task but rather a fundamental thought organization that underlies the child's cognitive functioning at that age.
3. Cognitive stages are hierarchical in nature, forming a series of increasingly differentiated and integrated structures serving a common function.

Although Piaget sees cognitive development as proceeding through a fixed sequence of relatively discontinuous stages, his interactional model differs from the maturational theories in that it assumes that experience is necessary for moving the child from stage to stage. Stages tend to set a relative upper limit as to the nature of the thought processes possible at a given point in the child's developmental sequence, but underlying the orderly progression through the series of developmental stages is the active interaction between new experiences and the child's existing cognitive structure. Piaget's position also differs from that of contemporary learning theorists (e.g., Gagné), who see development as the consequence of the cumulative effects of learning. He agrees that development involves a prolonged cumulative reorganization of existing cognitive structure as developed through prior experience, but rather than a simple linear cumulative process of acquisition, Piaget sees development punctuated by a series of qualitative (i.e., structural) transformations in the child's cognitive organization through which learning is mediated.

The organism necessarily experiences and reacts to the environment in terms of its existing cognitive structure; however, according to Piaget, experiences are not simply recorded as isolated S-R connections impressed on a passive mental field but, rather must be integrated into a constantly changing cognitive structure. Two basic processes are involved: assimilation and accommodation. First, there is a fundamental tendency for the organism to take in experiences for which there already exists an appropriate structural organization. This is *assimilation:* the incorporation of new experiences into a coherent informational or behavioral pattern, i.e., into what Piaget calls a *schema.*[6] For example, 21^2 can be written as $(20 + 1)^2 = 400 + 40 + 1$.

New experiences are assimilated or accommodated

But assimilation in the sense of the capacity to handle new situations within one's current cognitive structure is not enough, since coping with a changing and expanding environment requires more than simple habitual, i.e., previously learned, responses. The child must upgrade his or her thinking and develop new patterns of response. In addition to assimilation, therefore, we have the complementary process of *accommodation:* i.e., the modification of the organism's existing structure in response to the impact of the new environ-

6. Piaget uses the term *operations* to refer to schemata that have become internalized as part of the individual's behavioral organization.

mental content. Cognitive development occurs as a consequence of experiences that clash with the individual's existing cognitive structure and thereby act as a stimulant for internal reorganization, e.g., the extension of the classical Pavlovian conditioning model to cover operant conditioning.

The goal is continuous equilibration

The most fundamental concept in Piaget's developmental theory is *equilibration,* i.e., the process of achieving equilibrium between new environmental inputs and the learner's existing structure of knowledge. Presented with a new sensory input, the child must either distort the information to fit existing categories (i.e., assimilation) or develop a new category for it (i.e., accommodation). Equilibration represents the reorganization of existing cognitive structure to incorporate the new information and achieve a new functional balance. Piaget sees equilibration as a self-regulating mechanism present in all living things, forcing the constant modification of the present structure of knowledge and permitting new information to become part of it and thus maintaining the individual in a dynamic state of adaptation.

On the other hand, people cannot attend to input that they cannot relate to their current cognitive structure. Assimilation and accommodation occur only when incoming stimuli are appropriately matched with the particular level of development attained by the child at a given time. Reading to an infant will not contribute much to its intellectual development simply because it does not have the cognitive structure necessary to respond to verbal meaning. In other words, meaning is not a property that resides in the stimulus being assimilated or accommodated; it is something actually contructed by the learner with an appropriate background (see Ausubel 1968).

Piaget views intellectual growth somewhat as a flight of stairs, with each step in balanced equilibrium. As children mentally mount each stair, they continually interpret stimuli in their environment from the standpoint of their previous experiences. But they are constantly changing their ideas to fit the view from the perspective they have now achieved, with assimilation and accommodation working together to promote successive stages of equilibrium. The goal at the top of the stairs is mature thought, i.e., the ability to perform logical operations. According to Piaget, there is an innate propensity of the mind that continually strives for more comprehensive mastery of the world, although at each stage the individual is concerned only with what lies just beyond his or her intellectual grasp, far enough to present a novelty to be accommodated and yet not so far that accommodation is still possible.

Piaget's Stages of Cognitive Development

According to Piaget, there are three ways in which the individual can cognize the world: motorally, perceptually, and conceptually. The task of cognitive development, then, is a matter of progressive qualitative reorganization from sensorimotor to conceptual operations. We might think of three stages of

mental development or, on the other hand, two major stages: the sensorimotor stage, in which children acquire a knowledge of the objects of their environment through sensorimotor manipulation, and a conceptual stage beginning with a perceptual, then a concrete, and finally a stage of formal operations, e.g., the logical deduction of consequences and other forms of mature thought. More commonly, Piaget speaks of four basic stages.

Piaget's four stages

    1. The *sensorimotor stage* (ages birth through two years): during which the child progresses from a reflex stage in which the world is entirely undifferentiated to a relatively complex level of sensorimotor actions in a world just beginning to be systematically organized. During this stage, the child develops the practical knowledge that constitutes the substructure of later representational knowledge. Meanwhile he or she is bound to immediate reality; absent objects cannot be evoked mentally.

    2. The *preoperational stage* (ages two to approximately seven): basically a transition period in which objects and events begin to take on symbolic (representational) meaning, e.g., the bottle as the source of milk. It is best under-

stood in terms of the child's increasing capacity to acquire and to utilize primary abstractions, i.e., concepts (such as dogs and cats) whose meaning the child originally learns in relation to a series of empirical experiences.

The young child is stimulus-bound

Children in the preoperational stage are still stimulus-bound in the sense that their thought processes are tied to perceptual experiences. Preschool children can walk to the store but cannot draw a map of the route they took. They can understand having six marbles and losing two marbles to leave four marbles but cannot grasp $6 - 2 = 4$ as an abstraction. At this age, a child who asks for two cookies will be perfectly satisfied by being given one cookie that has been broken into two halves.

During the preoperational stage, children are quite inconsistent and even contradictory, saying that one object is bigger than the other and a few minutes later reversing their position, not realizing that the two statements are incompatible. They are egocentric, seeing the world from their own momentary perspective. They do not understand class membership; every bird is simply an instance of "bird." To the young child an object seen from a different perspective is simply a different object.

At this stage, children cannot maintain a single classification. If asked to sort out various geometric forms, they may put all the red triangles in a row, but when they run out of triangles may add red circles, and when they run out of red circles, they may add blue circles. If five coins are placed edge to edge and then are spread out to leave space between the coins, preoperational children will say that there are now more than before. When they are brought back close together again, they will simply indicate that there are now fewer.

Preschool children can grasp only one dimension at a time. They cannot attend to length and width simultaneously. Seeing beads poured from one squat jar into a taller and thinner jar right in front of them, they cannot tell which jar contains the more beads. They are likely to say that the tall jar holds more "because the beads go higher."[7] They cannot simultaneously take into account height and diameter. It is only toward the end of this period, i.e.,

The advent of conservation is a critical milestone

around the age of seven, that they can grasp the important principles of *conservation* and *reversibility*.

On the other hand, there is a marked increase in their ability to extract progressively more complex and elaborate concepts from their experiences, as long as they are provided with concrete exemplars from which they can grasp the criterial attributes that define the given concept.

3. The *concrete operations stage* (ages seven through eleven): during which the child's conceptual schemata begin to be organized into logical operational systems; children now understand, for example, that if $X = Y$, and $Y = Z$, then $X = Z$. They are able to arrange objects in series, e.g., from smallest to

7. The contradiction is easy enough to reconcile: every event, as we have noted, is simply a separate event. Here the two jars are simply separate and independent events. The preschool child does not see the continuity and reversibility between events.

largest (seriation). At this stage, children no longer fall into the perplexing contradictions of their preoperational counterparts. The stage of concrete operations is especially distinguished by the emergence of conservation (and reversibility). Children recognize that if $3 \times 5 = 15$, then 15 divided by 3 equals 5. On the other hand, they still have difficulty with classification on a multiple basis. They are no longer dependent on concrete examplars in order to grasp concepts but cannot understand secondary abstractions, i.e., propositions relating one concept to another, e.g., friction causes heat, or manipulating propositions in problem solving unless they are provided with appropriate exemplars of the concepts involved.

4. The *formal operations stage* (ages eleven on): the distinguishing feature of which is that now children can reason, i.e, they can manipulate the various possibilities of a proposition involving secondary abstractions free from having to refer to relevant exemplars.

Some overlap but yet qualitative differences

These developmental stages overlap to some degree yet are essentially separate and discontinuous in the sense that each is qualitatively discriminable from adjacent stages in the sequential progression of development. The exact age at which this occurs is not very important; it would seem, for example, that American children reach the various stages earlier than the ages listed by Piaget for his Swiss population. It is also inevitable that children will not be completely consistent in the stage of cognitive development at which they operate in different situations.

It should be noted that the formal operations level of thought includes all of the structural features of the previous stages but at a new level of organization. In other words, concrete operational thought does not disappear when formal thought emerges, so that even though it is possible to designate in a general way the child's overall developmental status on the basis of his or her predominant mode of cognitive functioning, children necessarily continue to undergo the transition from sensorimotor to concrete to formal operations with each new subject matter they encounter. Even after they have reached the formal stage of development on an overall basis—for example, when they approach a totally new area of study or a particularly difficult concept—they may revert to a lower stage of cognitive functioning where they can rely on appropriate exemplars to aid in their comprehension. On the other hand, at each stage, the child's mode of response is representative of the underlying thought organization of that particular period in his or her development. At the level of concrete operations, children deal with experiences in a typically concrete way. They are not capable of formal operations and they tend to avoid sensorimotor or preoperational approaches. More generally, except for brief returns to a lower level in order to handle difficult or unfamiliar materials, the child's typical and preferred mode of thought is the highest cognitive level currently available to him or her.

An important question is whether these stages can be accelerated. Although Piaget makes clear that the age at which these stages occur is not fixed, the stages do indeed appear reasonably stable. A number of studies (e.g., Mermelstein et al. 1967) attempting to teach conservation before the age of seven, for example, have met with limited success. Kohlberg (1968) cites comprehensive evidence to support the notion that specific training cannot substitute for the massive general experience that accrues with age. Apparently all that can be achieved through direct teaching is some kind of superficial understanding of conservation that is hardly generalizable and that can be reversed through trick demonstrations.

It seems that, to be successful, the induction of conservation must be oriented toward stimulating the development of the logical prerequisites to conservation as defined by Piaget (Roeper and Sigel 1966; Almy 1966) and further that it is contingent on a *match* in the sense that the child's current cognitive status is relatively near the point where conservation would emerge naturally. Even within this restricted framework, however, a worthwhile degree of acceleration may be possible. After a certain consolidation of a given stage, it is apparently possible to expedite the attainment of the next by introducing exercises under the learning conditions characteristic of the next stage. We might, for example, facilitate the transition from the concrete to the formal operations stage by introducing exercises and learning conditions of an abstract nature, e.g., by requiring the child to deal with abstract propositions—with the aid of empirical props as necessary—as a means of developing his or her ability to manipulate ideas mentally.[8]

Educational Implications

Piaget has been reluctant to address himself to educational issues. In fact, Ausubel, Bruner, Gagné, and others have criticized him for unwarrantedly minimizing the role of instruction in promoting cognitive development. As a consequence, the educational implications ascribed to Piaget's theory are really extrapolations. Nowhere does Piaget's theory tell teachers exactly how to present materials, how to teach so that the learner will indeed assimilate and accommodate the materials into existing structure, nor does he explain how they are to manipulate environmental variables so as to bring about desirable changes in cognitive structure. In fact, Gauda (1974) suggests that, despite all claims to the contrary, Piaget does not really say anything specific about teaching or the curriculum.[9]

Yet, although Piaget does not offer prescriptions for educational practice, his theory does indeed provide certain insights of obvious relevance to the operation of the school. First, Piaget's theory suggests that children do not think

8. Kohlberg (1964) makes a similar suggestion for accelerating the development of moral judgment. See chapter 14.
9. At the theoretical level, MacNamara (1976, 1978) argues that Piaget does nothing more than put new names on the processes of cognitive development.

like adults. It follows that we need to teach children at their own level—or perhaps just slightly above it so as to introduce a conflict and promote learning through the process of equilibration. Any attempt to teach them materials too far beyond their current level will simply force them to gather an odd collection of facts through rote procedures rather than to gain a coherent grasp of the kind that can later be restructured into a more advanced level. Children cannot profit from experiences that do not make meaningful contact with their existing cognitive structure.

Continuous reorganization of cognitive structure

Fundamental to Piaget's cognitive developmental theory is the view that cognitive growth is not an additive process but rather a matter of continuous reorganization of existing cognitive structure. Growth is possible only if the child has the structure necessary for attaining the next step. The child first learns about the nature of objects by seeing how they react when he drops them, bites them, throws them; he learns conservation by seeing how certain objects that are bent can be restored to their original form whereas others simply break. During the preschool period the emphasis is on mastery of prerequisites since, without a firm foundation, cognitive acquisitions can only be shaky and spotty at best. The preschool child, for example, does not have the tools necessary to solve problems intellectually.

Guide to curriculum development

If Piaget's stages can be relied on, they would provide a major timing device for scheduling classroom activities. If it could be demonstrated that successful instruction in a given subject matter area depends on the advent of the concrete operational stage, for example, and that this is not reached until the age of seven, then the school ought to postpone formal instruction until the age of seven. Although the boundaries of the different stages are subject to some variation depending on intellectual endowment, experiential background, and other personality characteristics, we must recognize that the possibilities of accelerating the process are limited and therefore attempt to synchronize the school, its curriculum, and its instructional procedures with Piaget's views. This implies that the teacher must determine both where the child stands in Piaget's developmental sequence and what this means in terms of instructional procedures.

Guide to instructional strategies

The preschool child, for example, must be exposed to a wide variety of objects, pictures, etc., as the basis for the creation of mental schemata that can then be used in dealing with the environment. Actual objects are best, but pictures and films (e.g., TV) are helpful. There is need for parents and teachers to elicit and monitor responses to see whether they really understand. There is also need for practice to promote overlearning and thus provide a firm foundation for learning at a higher level. On the other hand, the preschool child enjoys and can profit from rote verbal learning (e.g., rhymes). To the extent that the mental activities of the child at this stage are pretty much tied to action, the preschool should provide a wide variety of games and other activities, along with accompanying verbal experiences denoting the actions involved (e.g., *Sesame Street*).

With the advent of conservation, a whole new world opens to the primary school child as he realizes that, for every action or operation, there is an opposite operation that cancels it. The stage of concrete operations requires contact with a multitude of concrete objects as the basis for developing the process of grouping and classification. The child's understanding of symbols must always be preceded by an adequate background of direct experiences with the empirical data from which they are abstracted.[10] Only when this meaning has been firmly established as a result of this background of experience can children meaningfully comprehend and use them without reference to concrete empirical props. With regard to complex relational propositions, they are largely restricted to the intuitive level of cognitive functioning, a level that falls far short of the clarity, precision, explicitness, and generality associated with advanced stages of intellectual functioning. On the other hand, it does not follow that all teaching of elementary school children must be on a "discovery" nonabstract basis (see Ausubel 1968, p. 213). Grade school children can deal with abstractions provided we systematically present concrete exemplars of the concepts in question. In fact, failure to provide suitable opportunities for them to acquire an intuitive grasp of scientific concepts not only wastes available readiness for such learnings but also results in the use of valuable time in high school that could be used for more advanced instruction.

With the advent of formal operations at the approximate age of eleven, a qualitatively new capacity gradually emerges, having major implications for teaching-learning strategies in the junior and senior high school. The adolescent is now capable of understanding and manipulating relationships between abstractions without having to refer to their concrete empirical counterparts. As a consequence, the curriculum can now deal with abstractions, and teaching can proceed on a correspondingly abstract (verbal), and more efficient, basis.

In summary, then, although Piaget has not said very much about education, his theory seems to have significant educational implications, at least by extrapolation. Piaget discusses how learners are changed through manipulation of environmental conditions with which they interact, but he does not describe the particular environmental variables that bring about changes in cognitive structure. Nor does he tell the teacher how to manipulate the situation so as to maximize productive interactions between the children and their environment. On the other hand, we need to remember that no theory has ever been able to provide ready-made solutions to teaching problems or provide prescriptions for actual classroom practice. The teaching situation necessarily involves far more variables than any single theory can take into account.

Piaget's theory has special implications for compensatory education. If there is one conclusion to be drawn from Piaget's work, it is that thought grows out of the internalization of sensorimotor and concrete activities. It fol-

10. Piaget's theory for the education of primary school children is probably best implemented in the open classroom (see chapter 12), where children are free to move and to explore a wide variety of constructive activities on their own.

Need for direct experience with concrete objects

lows that educational practice must encourage this process by giving children multiple and varied opportunities in the early years for direct action on concrete objects and, where this is lacking, to provide this experience through preschool education. Children must be able to perform their own operations on objects if these operations are ever to form the basis for their fully developed mental structure. In order to understand classification, for example, they must have had experience in grouping objects in some dimension; to analyze objects, they must have pulled them apart; to understand the properties of the number series, they must have arranged objects in some order. Meanwhile, we might note that there is no cause for optimism concerning marked acceleration of the basic Piaget-type cognitive functions through deliberate intervention of the schooling variety, since such acceleration tends to be limited, specific, and, further, contingent on a narrow gap between the intervention experience and the child's natural readiness.[11]

READINESS

Of critical interest to teachers and the effective operation of the school is the concept of readiness, i.e, the extent to which the learner has the capability to profit from the experiences to which he or she is subjected. More specifically, readiness is a broad concept covering a wide variety of factors, which, for the sake of discussion, may be grouped as follows:

1. Physiological factors: Behavior cannot take place unless there is sufficient maturation of the sense organs, the central nervous system, the muscles, and other physiological equipment.
2. Psychological factors: The individual must have the proper motivation, a positive self-concept, and relative freedom from devastating emotional conflicts and other psychological impediments.
3. Experiential factors: With the exception of the learning that stems from inborn response tendencies, learning can take place only on the basis of previously learned skills and concepts.

To the extent that two of the three components of readiness are, to a degree, amenable to training (e.g., within the limits of Piaget's developmental stages), it is possible to promote readiness for a given learning experience somewhat earlier than it would appear spontaneously. Bruner (1960), for example, sees readiness as a "mischievous half-truth"; with appropriate stimulation, children can be helped to become ready for activities much earlier than if

Readiness: A mischievous half-truth?

11. Kohlberg (1968) makes a distinction between Binet-type and Piaget-type items and suggests that the latter would be more clearly a function of chronological age and less susceptible to short-term intervention. See Fowler (1970), Patterson (1977), and Pinard and Laurendeau (1964) regarding the development of measures to assess the Piaget-type cognitive functions.

left to their own devices. Bruner disagrees with what he considers to be Piaget's overly rigid application of the stage-dependent approach to cognitive development. He sees a logical progression from simple to complex in the structural representation of subject matter that can serve as the basis for a spiral curriculum in which the same concept is introduced at progressively higher levels of insight. Gagné (1970, p. 278) also questions Piaget's stage-dependent views on readiness: "Contrasting with [Piaget's] views is the notion that, beyond a certain early age (perhaps three), developmental readiness for learning is primarily determined by previously acquired intellectual skills." (See Case 1975 for a discussion of Gagné's position on this point.)

In addition, teachers can increase the child's "readiness" by adapting their methods to the particular type of readiness the child has already achieved. As Gates (1937) pointed out,

> Statements concerning the necessary mental age at which a pupil can be entrusted to learn to read are essentially meaningless. The age of learning to read under one program or with one method employed by one teacher is entirely different from that required under other circumstances. (P. 506.)

The fact that children with a mental age of 5.0 can be taught to read at essentially the same proficiency as normally found in the first grade led Gates to conclude that, within limits, there is no mental age that can be set as minimum or even optimum for beginning reading. It would seem that success in reading depends as much on the development of skills in visual and auditory discrimination and on the method used as it does on intellectual maturation per se. We cannot expect to find readiness in precisely the right amount at the moment it is called for in the curriculum, but this need not deter us from attempting to communicate with each and every child; we simply need to incorporate into our curriculum and our instructional strategies sufficient variety and flexibility to permit making the necessary contact.

Readiness for a complex task entails readiness with respect to its different components. It is possible for a child not to be ready despite more than sufficient readiness in some aspects of the task. Negative attitudes can preclude learning, despite adequacy in the other factors; conversely, strong motivation can compensate to some degree for limited ability. Reading readiness, for instance, calls for a certain level of mental development; sufficient eye coordination to permit clear perception; ability to attend to symbols; a fairly large background of experience that allows children to relate what they read to things they have experienced; interest in stories and ability to anticipate what is coming next; favorable attitudes, including a desire to learn to read; social and emotional maturity that permits them to devote their capacities to reading rather than dissipating them in overcoming emotional blocks; and many other developmental aspects, the lack of any one of which can lead to reading difficulty. Teachers devote a great deal of time in kindergarten and in first grade in developing the required readiness through creating interest in stories, expanding experiences, and building gross discriminations, but the reading

Broad background of
experience

readiness program actually begins in the home when children see their parents and siblings read, when parents read to them or relate some of their experiences—in short, when parents help their children develop a desire to read and the experiential background necessary to interpret what they read. It may even go back to the development of perceptual and linguistic skills in the crib and the playpen.

Learning sets   Of particular significance from the standpoint of readiness is Harlow's concept of *learning sets,* i.e., learning how to learn (Harlow 1949, 1959). In his experiment, chimpanzees first learned to discriminate among objects, e.g., a sphere, a cube, a circle, and a rectangle, through reinforcement with, say, a raisin located under one of the objects. Learning at first was largely a matter of trial and error, but in time the chimps caught on; once they had mastered the basic concept of discrimination (e.g., the odd object in a set of three), they were able to solve new discrimination problems with nearly 100 percent accuracy. They had learned not only the solution to specific problems but, more significantly, had developed a *generalized ability to discriminate.* They had become educated monkeys, i.e., adjustable creatures with an increased capacity to react effectively to changing environmental demands. This may be even more crucial at the human level, where a major determinant of the learner's readiness for learning meaningful verbal materials in the classroom, for example, is the availability in cognitive structure of clear and stable relevant concepts and propositions to which the new learnings can be securely anchored (see chapter 8).

Readiness is a matter of the child's being able to bring to bear on a given task capabilities equal to the demands of the situation; as such, it is basic to coordinating the grade placement of subject matter and the pedagogical procedures through which these materials are taught. Successful educational planning requires that we know what pupils are generally ready for at different ages, what elements enter into readiness, how to judge readiness, what can be done to increase it, and how we can adapt teaching methods to capitalize on the child's present level of readiness. Unfortunately, there is no simple and sure way of appraising readiness so that, in the final analysis, there has to be a certain amount of trial and error during which an alert and experienced teacher senses the extent to which the material is consistent with the child's present development.

DEVELOPMENT AND THE CLASSROOM

Developmental Tasks

The general consensus is that training should not be introduced too soon in the maturational sequence. More specifically, it is generally recognized that the child prematurely exposed to a learning task will not only fail to learn the task but, more serious, may develop bad learning habits, fear, and dislike and avoidance of the task and of learning in general; the child may even develop a negative self-concept. But whereas considerable attention has been paid to the problem of ensuring that the task with which the child is presented is *down* to his or her level of readiness, the complementary problem of seeing that the task is *up* to the level of readiness available has been largely overlooked. What if the child is ready for a given task but is denied the opportunity to learn it? It seems that for certain tasks at least, there is an optimal age level for effective learning. Havighurst (1952, 1972), in his treatment of the problems with which individuals must cope at each development level if adjustment is to be maintained, has popularized the term *developmental task,* which he defines as one that

Age of optimal learning

> arises at or about a certain period in the life of the individual, successful achievement of which leads to his happiness and to success with later tasks, while failure leads to unhappiness in the individual, disapproval by society, and difficulty with later tasks. (P. 2.)

As children grow older, they find themselves possessed of new physical and psychological resources. Their legs grow stronger and enable them to walk; their nervous system becomes more complex and permits them to reason more adequately. But they also find themselves facing new demands. They are expected to talk, to read, to spell, and to subtract. A complex of inner and outer forces contrives to set for children a series of developmental tasks that they must master if they are to be successful as human beings. Thus, in the course of development, children reach certain stages that not only make it possible for them to master certain tasks but also make it imperative that they do so in order to be ready to master the other tasks higher in the developmental sequence. The developmental task of infancy, for example, is the establishment of dependency and trust. Childhood is also the ideal time for basic explorations of the world, and failure in this task seriously handicaps the future accomplishment of tasks in the related series (see White 1959). The adolescent, on the other hand, needs to develop personal identity (see Erikson, in chapter 15).

Most teachable moment

A number of examples could be given of the difficulties that arise out of failure to master a given task at its most teachable moment. A child who enters school for the first time at, say, the age of twelve is likely to encounter untold problems in learning to read, ranging from self-consciousness to inability to find materials combining the proper level of difficulty and interest. The teacher's responsibility in this connection is to see that the child masters each task reasonably on schedule and to provide whatever assistance is necessary to keep the process on the move. The teacher also needs to synchronize the curriculum with the student's developmental status.

It may seem quite a problem to provide the right experience at the right time for some thirty youngsters who invariably do not find it convenient to be

ready for the same experience at the same time. However, the task is not impossible. First, children have such a fundamental drive toward growth that they do not have to be pushed over every hurdle. Furthermore, the most appropriate time for mastering a given task is not a matter of minutes or days, and children have remarkable ability to catch up when they have fallen temporarily behind; generally all that is necessary is a bit of guidance and moral support.

The Critical Periods Hypothesis

A more recent thought on the question of the optimal point in the developmental sequence at which to introduce training is the *critical periods hypothesis.* Ethologists, for example, talk of *imprinting,* i.e., a process that apparently involves a brief period of extreme susceptibility to particular types of stimulation in the early development of certain birds during which certain types of behavior are shaped and molded more or less for life. The premise is that certain behavior patterns are evoked by appropriate stimuli presented at a critical time; presumably they are not available before and, if they are not released during this critical period, they can no longer be released at a later date.

A somewhat different version of the critical periods hypothesis concerns

Sensory deprivation

the relative irreversibility of the deficits occasioned by early sensory deprivation.[12] In one of the McGill studies (Melzack and Scott 1957), puppies reared
in isolation from birth to maturity in specially constructed cages that drastically restricted their sensory experiences showed gross inability to make appropriate avoidance responses when tested later as adults. They struck their
heads over and over against a water pipe that ran along the wall just above the
floor in the testing room; they walked into a lighted match, poked their noses
into the flame, withdrew a few inches apparently reflexively, and walked into
it again. The outstanding feature of their behavior was a complete inability to
respond adaptively to noxious stimuli. Apparently, contrary to what one might
expect, responding to pain, which is presumably so important to survival, requires a background of early perceptual experience.

In a similar study (Thompson and Heron 1954), Scotch terriers raised
under conditions of relative isolation displayed significant sensorimotor difficulties; they bumped into objects, they had trouble with stairs, etc. Even after
a year of normal living, the restricted dogs were still quite stupid by comparison with their litter-mates reared under normal conditions. If food was placed
in corner A of the room and then placed in plain sight in corner B, they would
first go to corner A. If a screen was placed in front of the food, they invariably
tried to go through the screen. They were short on attention span and generally did poorly on tasks involving what might be called "intelligence." In social behavior, they were dominated by much younger puppies (Thompson and
Melzack 1956). According to the authors, the experiments clearly indicate the

A stimulating
environment is
essential

importance of a rich and stimulating environment in early life as a condition
for normal development. Restriction of experience during this critical period
results in irretrievable retardation in various psychological dimensions. Sup-
porting this conclusion is the study by Forgus (1956), who found that baby rats
that had been exposed to cutout forms of circles, crosses, triangles, and
squares from the time their eyes opened were superior in discrimination ability to a control group that had been first exposed to the forms at the age of
forty-one days.

The critical periods hypothesis suggests interesting possibilities. If the
characteristics of each period of life could become known, it would be possible
to avoid the dangers and to take advantage of the benefits. To the extent that
there may be a period early in life when primary social relations are established, we might, for example, increase the degree of dependency of the child
by increasing the emotional input during this critical period. It may be that in
the absence of the usual mother-child contact during this sensitive period (as
in the case of institutionalized children), a durable adult-child attachment can
never be established. A lamb isolated from other sheep from birth tends to remain apart from the flock, for example.

Recently, however, a number of questions have been raised as to the basic

---

12. Still another variation of the critical periods concept concerns the dire effects of say,
anoxia, during the fetal period (as presented earlier in the chapter).

validity of the critical periods concept. Imprinting, for example, does not seem to be as irreversible as previously believed (Ambrose 1963). Perhaps more important, it also seems that the sharpness of the limits has been overstated. Rather than short, critical periods during which learning can occur, limited by periods in which it cannot occur, we appear to be dealing with an interval of maximum sensitivity gradually shading into periods of lesser susceptibility. Furthermore, the evidence to date has been restricted largely to rather primitive forms of life.

It is always dangerous to extrapolate from animals to humans, particularly with respect to responses demonstrated to be species specific. We might nevertheless speculate whether such species-specific patterns of behavior do exist in humans, or perhaps to think along the lines of Havighurst's developmental tasks or of certain sensitive periods during which modification of genetic patterns might most readily take place if appropriate stimulus conditions are met. If they are lacking at that time, the modification may be more difficult (or perhaps even impossible) to evoke later.

Sensitive periods? An interesting possibility

Such a concept of *sensitive* (perhaps rather than *critical*) periods is a provocative idea. As we have already suggested, there is a critical period in early infancy for the development of trust. There are also indications of two other critical periods in infancy that could be particularly crucial to later development, especially for learning language and learning to read. First, infants in the first three months of life have a special ability to perceive visual patterns, an ability bound to have significant effect on later perceptive and cognitive development particularly as it relates to learning to read. Second, for a period of about eighteen months beginning at the age of two, preprogrammed genetic (knowing) mechanisms relative to language acquisition apparently make the child especially sensitive to the sounds of speech. From the standpoint of accent, for example, early childhood seems to be the ideal time to learn a language. It may be that the linguistic difficulties that characterize the lower classes likewise stem from the lack of opportunity in infancy to internalize speech as a vehicle of thought. This does not mean that this is the only period in which language can be learned, but it does suggest that complex language patterns are easier to acquire during these periods than at times earlier or later.

On the other hand, it has never been demonstrated that critical periods exist with regard to specified types of intellectual activities such that irretrievable deficits will result unless adequate stimuli are present in that immediate period. On the contrary, according to Piaget, a child who has reached a certain stage finds it easier to retrieve what he or she has missed in earlier stages. The fact that sensitivity to stimulation is contingent on a match between relevant environmental stimuli and the child's current level of development does not mean that stimulation must occur at that particular time of transition. As we have noted, concrete operational thought (or even sensorimotor thought) does not disappear when formal thought emerges but rather continues to be available for situations where efforts at solution by formal thought have failed. Piaget's theory would suggest that specific intellectual skills or meaningful verbal contents not mastered at the earliest appearance of the required readiness can probably be acquired later just as well, if not better.

Ausubel (1969) suggests that the tendency for deficits in cognitive structure to become cumulative and irreversible (as in the case of the disadvantaged) is more parsimoniously explained by the fact that the present and future rates of intellectual growth are always directly limited by the currently attained level of development (see chapter 8). The child who has an existing deficit resulting from past deprivation is simply less able to profit developmentally from advanced levels of environmental stimulation. New growth, in other words, always proceeds from existing structure, i.e., from already acquired and actualized capacity rather than simply from genetically inherent potentialities. Gagné (1977) presents an essentially similar position. In practice, lower-class children find their existing cognitive deficit compounded by the fact that they are less able than their peers to profit from new academic experiences, so that the gap between their current level of cognitive readiness and curricular demands is progressively widened. They soon become demoralized at the school situation and disinvolve themselves from it.

HIGHLIGHTS OF THE CHAPTER

An understanding of the general principles of growth and development is of major importance to teachers whose task it is to coordinate environmental influences with maturational processes. This chapter presented the following concepts:

1. Whatever development an individual displays at a given time is the result of the interaction of environmental influences on the potentialities with which he or she was conceived.
2. Recent research has suggested that genes are best understood as a function of the molecule of the chemical DNA, which has the capacity to generate an exact replica of itself when the environment contains the necessary raw materials. The recent emphasis on knowing behaviors—i.e., the organism's preprogrammed capabilities of responding adaptively to stimuli—presents an interesting perspective.
3. The limits of our capabilities are set in considerable measure by our inherited potentialities. Environmental factors are the prime determinants of both the direction of growth and the degree to which we actualize our potentialities.
4. Readiness for a given activity is the joint function of experiential, motivational, and maturational factors. On the other hand, there is a growing awareness of discontinuity within certain developmental patterns.
5. The interrelatedness of the various aspects of development points to the need for dealing with the whole child. This interrelatedness, along with the fact that development follows a definite sequential pattern, implies that fail-

ure to master a certain developmental task at the appropriate time is likely to impede further progress.

6. Piaget's theory of cognitive development postulates an orderly (hierarchical) progression in the child's cognitive development; his concept of qualitatively (i.e., structurally) different stages in the child's thought processes has major curricular and pedagogical implications. Efforts at accelerating the transition from one stage to the next have met with only limited success.

7. The critical periods hypothesis probably is best seen in the context of periods of maximum sensitivity to certain types of stimulation occurring early in the development, particularly of lower animals. Its validity with respect to cognitive development in humans is open to question.

SUGGESTIONS FOR FURTHER READING

CALDWELL, BETTYE M. The effects of psychological deprivation on human development in infancy. *Merrill-Palmer Quart.* 16 (1970):260–277. A scholarly review of the research on the detrimental effects of deprivation on early development. Points to the difficulties of disentangling one type of deprivation from another, e.g., nutritional deprivation from sensory deprivation.

ELKIND, DAVID. Giant in the nursery—Jean Piaget. *New York Times Mag.*, May 26, 1968, pp. 25–27, 50–54, 62, 77–80. A delightful account of the work of Piaget written at the layman's level.

FLAVELL, JOHN H. *The Developmental Psychology of Jean Piaget.* New York: Van Nostrand, 1963. A good overview of Piaget's theory as it applies to the classroom.

FURTH, H. *Piaget for Teachers.* Englewood Cliffs, N.J.: Prentice-Hall, 1970. One of the most readable accounts of Piaget's position with emphasis on its implication for school-age children.

GAGNÉ, ROBERT M. Contributions of learning to human development. *Psychol. Rev.* 75 (1968):177–191. A good statement of Gagné's emphasis on learning as the determinant of development. Contrast with Piaget's theory.

LIFE MAGAZINE. DNA's code: Key to all life. *Life*, Oct. 4, 1963, pp. 70–90. A well-illustrated and lucid account of the DNA as the determiner of heredity.

MUSSEN, PAUL H., ed. *Carmichael's Manual of Child Psychology.* Vols. 1 and 2. New York: Wiley, 1970. An outstanding collection of major papers on the various aspects of child development. Comprehensive, authoritative, and scholarly. Highly recommended.

QUESTIONS AND PROJECTS

1. To what extent is the problem of heredity and environment one of academic interest rather than one of practical significance? One of sociological interest rather than of educational importance?

Evaluate the statement: All that the individual inherits is a certain body structure which is receptive to stimulation; that is both necessary and sufficient.

2. What position might a teacher take in advising parents concerned about the apparent "slowness" of their child, say, in learning to read?

3. What might be the teacher's position in speaking to parents of preschool children about the possibilities of promoting the maximum readiness for school?

What steps might the government take in optimizing the caliber of its citizens (e.g., prenatal care, preschool education, and parent education regarding child-rearing practices)? What steps have other nations taken (e.g., the Soviet Union or Israel)?

4. Report on a research project designed to promote intellectual and academic readiness on the part of the culturally deprived. Evaluate the results.

5. Specifically, how would you go about enriching the experiential background of city children about to undertake a unit on "The Farm"?

Discuss the role of television as a primary medium for promoting readiness for school.

SELF-TEST

1. Maturation is to learning as
   a. growth is to development.
   b. heredity is to environment.
   c. heredity is to growth and development.
   d. heredity is to nurture.
   e. nurture is to nature.

2. Which statement best characterizes the role of heredity in human development?
   a. It sets developmental predispositions that can be changed through environmental forces.
   b. It probably sets certain maxima that are never approximated.
   c. It sets definite ceilings on every aspect of the developmental process.
   d. It sets the general pattern of development but not its limits.
   e. It sets both the limits and the pattern of human development.

3. The major confounding factor in determining the relative influence of heredity and environment on human growth and development is

    a. the interactive nature of hereditary and environmental influences.

    b. regression toward the mean.

    c. the relative constancy of the environment.

    d. the relatively infinite number of possible combinations of hereditary patterns.

    e. the unavailability of suitable psychometric instruments.

4. Probably the most educationally significant aspect of human growth and development is

    a. the change over age in the organization of developmental components.

    b. the range of individual differences in the rate of growth.

    c. the interdependence of the various components.

    d. the rate of maturation.

    e. uniformity in sequence of development.

5. The most educationally significant feature underlying human development is

    a. the organism's inbuilt sense of direction of growth.

    b. the individual's tendency to revert to earlier modes of behavior.

    c. the individual's natural desire to grow.

    d. the strength of certain abilities, even in the relatively inferior.

    e. the sufficiency of maturation to ensure adequate development of basic abilities.

6. The most effective method of dealing with the readiness problem in school is

    a. to adapt teaching methods to tap the readiness the child has.

    b. to allow the child freedom to choose the activities for which he or she is ready.

    c. to concentrate on formal readiness exercises.

    d. to delay the introduction of certain materials until readiness is achieved.

    e. to provide the child with a rich background of experience.

7. The stages in the development of the child's thought processes, according to Piaget, are (in sequence):

    a. preconceptual—intuitive—formal.

    b. preconceptual—intuitive—causal.

    c. sensorimotor—concrete operation—formal operation.

    d. sensorimotor—formal—inferential.

    e. preconceptual—syncratic—conventional.

SIX

The Child as a Growing Organism

A suit of armor worn by one of the fabled knights of the Middle Ages just will not fit a normal 13-year old boy of today. It is too small.

Phi Delta Kappan 42 (1960): 39

Much of what goes under the name of self-control is a denial, a repudiation, an evasion of life, of genuineness, and of integrity. Control, which means not real control nor realisation nor even self-denial but a form of self-eradication, is not a good rule of health.

Arthur T. Jersild (1952)

Democracy . . . cannot condone development of the individual at the expense of the group. Nor can democracy condone development of the group at the expense of the individual.

Ruth Cunningham et al. (1951)

One thing seems clear: If all students are helped to the full utilization of their intellectual powers, we will have a better chance of surviving as a democracy in an age of enormous technological and social complexity.

Jerome S. Bruner (1960)

— Discusses the nature of physical development and its special implications with respect to the self-concept.
— Explores the relative role of the home, the school, and the peer group in the socialization of the child
— Clarifies the nature of intelligence and highlights some of the issues connected with its definition, its development, and its measurement

PREVIEW: KEY CONCEPTS

1. The individual's physical status has a critical bearing on the development of the self-concept.
2. Probably the most obvious aspect of physical growth is the wide range of individual differences among children of the same age and sex.
3. Socialization proceeds through selective reinforcement of certain acceptable behaviors.
4. The home is the primary agent in the socialization of the child; the school and the peer group also play important roles.
5. Almost all aspects of ''intelligence''—its definition, its nature, its development, and its measurement—are a matter of continued controversy.

PREVIEW QUESTIONS

1. What are the relative roles of heredity and environment in the various aspects of the child's development?
2. What might be done to help youngsters whose physical status deviates drastically from average?
3. Specifically, how does the child manage to internalize social constraints and social values?
4. What role does the home play in the socialization process? The school? The peer group? How can they be better coordinated?
5. What can the school do to optimize the intellectual development of its students?

The school in modern American society bridges practically the whole period from infancy to adulthood. With preschool education extending further down and high school and college enrolling a progressively larger percentage of our youth, the school is second only to the home in its continued contact with children during their formative years. Teachers need to be aware of the many school-based factors that have a psychological impact on children during this extended journey from early childhood to relative maturity.

PHYSICAL DEVELOPMENT

The question of physical development is of primary interest to students of educational psychology, for not only is physical adequacy of great importance in itself, but it is of even greater significance from the standpoint of its psychological implications. Indeed probably no other factor has such obvious bearing on just who and what the individual is.

Physical growth is affected by a number of environmental conditions. Americans have been growing taller and heavier every generation, apparently as a result of dietary and health improvements. A boy of ten today is about the same size as a boy of eleven in the 1930s. Inherited differences may also be postulated, and the general consensus is that physical growth depends more directly on heredity than most other aspects of development. It is generally agreed, for example, that the usual illnesses that befall growing children have only a temporary effect on their growth and do not affect their final status appreciably, if at all. Endocrine imbalance, on the other hand, whether related to heredity or environmental causes, can effect a considerable departure from normality both in the individual's rate of maturing and final status.

Wide range of individual differences

The one outstanding feature of growth is the wide range of individual differences in the physical size of children of any given age. Thus, Falkner's data (1962; see figure 6.1) show 5 percent of the ten-year-old boys to be taller than a sizable percentage of the fourteen-year-olds and 5 percent of the ten-year-old girls to be as tall as the shortest 5 percent of the eighteen-year-olds. In the same way, the tallest seven-year-old boys in both the Simmons (1944) and Baldwin (1921) studies were as tall as the shortest thirteen-year-olds.

The normal curve

When we plot the height of members of any age group, we note they distribute themselves in what is known as the *normal curve*. In any unselected group, we find a few very short and a few very tall individuals, with increasing frequencies as we approach the average. This is typical of the distribution of most other physical and psychological traits, e.g., running speed, strength of grip, intelligence, performance on a test. We do not have separate categories—tall, medium, and short; bright, average, and dull—but rather a continuum ranging from very tall to very short, from very bright to very dull, with an

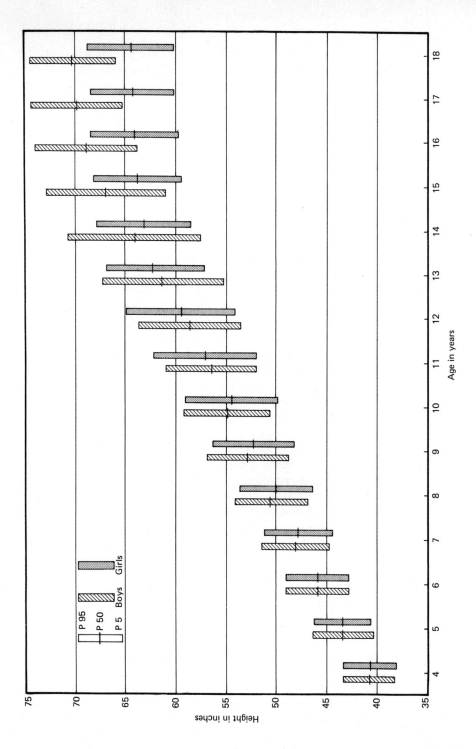

Figure 6.1 Height of Boys and Girls Ages Four through Eighteen (Falkner 1962). Copyright American Academy Pediatrics 1962.

increasing concentration of individuals as we move progressively closer to the average.

Psychological Implications

Physical status and the self-concept

The psychological implications of physical development are probably best understood in terms of its effect on the self-image and on the relative difficulty with which individuals can satisfy their needs. What we think of ourselves and what others think of us, and the demands they make of us as well as those we make of ourselves, depend to a large extent on our physique and the reactions it evokes. Thus, strength and physical size are among the important attributes of the twelve-year-old boy just as an attractive figure and a pretty face are valued attributes of a teenage girl. The individual's whole adjustment revolves in large measure around such ideas as "beautiful," "tall and handsome," "buckteeth," "fatso," or "beanpole."

Physical inadequacies can have serious psychological effects. Being a "runt," a "tub," or "ugly" may easily represent handicaps to adjustment and to success as disastrous as deformities and other deviations from normality. What is even more important, however, is the individual's reaction to physical characteristics. The statuesque teenage girl who feels that she is "too tall," the adolescent with a severe case of acne, and the smaller boy: all must be led toward increased self-acceptance. People who do not accept themselves cannot expect others to do so. Unfortunately, the way others see us often reinforces the attitudes we would like to overcome. A small child may be babied longer and denied the opportunity to assume responsibility. The boy who is tall for his age may, on the other hand, be faced with demands and expectations beyond his overall maturity.

Physical development is directly and vitally related to other aspects of development. Social and emotional development, for example, are greatly facilitated by such physical assets as attractiveness, size, and strength. The physically adequate child has more opportunities to participate in games and to learn vitally important techniques of leadership so that his or her total personality development is enhanced. It is also possible, of course, for a person endowed with abundant physical assets to feel so complacent that he or she neglects the development of other potentialities.

The Advent of Puberty

The preadolescent growth spurt is of particular interest to teachers because of the complications attending the rapid growth that occurs during this period. A boy may add five inches to his height and twenty-five pounds to his weight in a year. Different parts of the body often undergo rapid growth at different times so that the adolescent boy's feet (or perhaps his arms or even his nose) may temporarily grow out of all proportion. This may result in awkwardness at a

time when he is becoming quite self-conscious, and he may trip or knock over a glass as he reaches for it, simply because he is not used to the new length of his limbs. To make matters worse, the glandular changes accompanying this growth spurt are likely to result in adolescent acne at the very time when boys and girls become conscious of the importance of good looks in attracting members of the opposite sex.

None of the physiological changes accompanying the prepubescent growth spurt is any more important than the attainment of sexual maturity and the resulting need for a major reorganization of the self-concept,[1] especially in the area of social relations. Members of the opposite sex suddenly assume an attractiveness not previously apparent, and a new interest in dancing and social sports displaces previous interest in the gang and preadolescent activities. Of major import is the sex drive itself and the conflicts it is likely to introduce because of the sex taboos that are part of our culture.

The drastic changes taking place during the prepubescent growth spurt are bound to have psychological repercussions. This is particularly true in our culture where, in addition to the problem attending bodily changes, teenagers trying to think of themselves as adults willing to assume adult responsibilities

Adolescence in
modern society a
difficult period

1. Probably no better illustration can be found of a major change in the individual's phenomenal field.

are often prevented from doing so. In contrast to adolescence in primitive societies or even in pioneer days in America, where adolescents took their place as full-fledged members of society rather early, adolescence for the modern American youth has become a period of considerable strain and stress. As a result, confusion, insecurity, rebelliousness, and defiance are often as much a part of the adolescent pattern as awkwardness and persistent crazes over teen idols. A number of writers have lamented the current practice of extended dependency imposed on youth by the social system, especially that the school into whose care late teenagers and young adults are placed is not always able to provide them with a meaningful and profitable experience.

Early or late
maturity can be a
problem

    The problems connected with the preadolescent growth spurt and the advent of puberty are complicated when these changes take place early or late. Research has shown that puberty takes place any time from age ten to seventeen for girls and from age eleven to eighteen for boys. The early maturer who suddenly becomes interested in members of the opposite sex while his or her age-mates still "can't see it" is likely to find himself or herself out of joint with the gang. This is somewhat more of a problem for the early-maturing girl who may find herself a year of two out of step with the girls and three or four years out of step with the boys.

    Perhaps the greatest problem lies with the late-maturing boy, who in our culture is likely to encounter a systematically negative sociopsychological environment having potentially adverse effects on his personality development. Being less physically impressive, he is treated as immature by others; he tends to be rejected and dominated, with resulting prolonged dependency and possibly a negative self-concept. There are exceptions, of course, and the boy who is fundamentally secure and has warm, accepting parents may suffer no ill effects from late maturation. Nevertheless, teachers should be ready to provide support in order to prevent developmental delay from turning into lifelong inadequacies. Research studies (e.g., Jones 1957; Jones and Mussen 1958) have shown late-maturing boys to display a significantly less adequate self-concept and somewhat stronger dependency needs at the age of thirty-three than did the early maturers, for example. Conversely, early maturers have been found to be significantly more successful as adults (e.g., Ames 1957) despite relative equality in initial intellectual and social class status.[2]

THE DEVELOPMENT OF SOCIAL BEHAVIOR

The fact that children must live in a social setting makes their social development a matter of prime interest to teachers. Social development involves the

---

2. It is, of course, possible that differences in adequacy as adults are rooted at least in part on such basic factors as glandular balance rather than late maturation per se.

ability to get along with others and implies the ability to get along with one-self. Specifically, it is a matter of integrating one's needs and purposes with those of the social order, for the benefit of both.

The Process of Socialization

Social development is a continuous process by means of which the individual achieves social adequacy. Involved are two complementary phases: *socialization*, which reflects society's attempt to have the child internalize its regulations, values, and mores; and *individualization*, which refers to the child's attempt to retain his or her individuality. In order to maintain itself, society must insist on conformity to its standards; however, although children conform in certain areas, they do so reluctantly and only insofar as they find it to their advantage in satisfying their needs. It is strictly a business deal involving both cooperative and resistant behavior whereby they buy group acceptance at the price of some of their freedom.

Socialization is oriented toward the achievement of social acceptability and social sensitivity. It involves the gradual internalization of social demands as part of the child's reactions to the approval or disapproval of his or her behavior by parents and other significant persons. For this to occur, the young child must first develop dependency as a result of experiencing not only many warm, loving relationships with adults but also their temporary loss when he or she fails to meet expectations. A necessary condition for the development of social control is learning that other people are necessary and that one must take their wishes into consideration in guiding one's behavior.

Social demands From a very early age, children encounter expectations concerning their behavior and must learn to adjust to an increasingly complex set of demands. They learn that they must do what adults want them to do if they are to gain their acceptance. Later they must do what their peers want if they are to be accepted by the group. As a result, their behavior is gradually shaped in the direction of social conformity. They do not have to comply, of course, but then, they must pay a price in terms of social rejection. Unfortunately children often are put in the position of having to comply with conflicting and contradictory demands imposed on them by the different groups to which they belong. Furthermore, many of the outcomes of social learning are intangible and therefore provide inadequate reinforcement. A child may find immediate self-gratification to be more satisfying, as well as more dependably accessible, and may give up attempting to meet the expectations of others. Some of the demands to which the child is subjected are unnecessarily rigid, arbitrary, and repressive. The school, for example, often dictates everything from how children are to behave to how they are to solve problems in arithmetic and what answers they are to accept if they are to do well in social studies. Arbitrary controls of this kind tend to have detrimental effects on overall growth in that they deprive children of the opportunity for spontaneity, autonomy, and experimentation in manipulating their environment.

Wide differences in social development exist even among children of the same family. These differences may have a partial basis in inherited glandular structure. This is particularly obvious in the drastic change in social behavior occurring with the advent of puberty, although to be sure, environmental influences also play a part. Heredity may also be involved indirectly in that many of the physical characteristics that play a determining role in social behavior are largely inherited; a person with such physical assets as beauty, strength, and brains is probably going to achieve social adjustment more easily than one who is unattractive or dull. There is also evidence that certain animals are much more socially oriented than others. The rat has few social needs and can be kept in isolation; the monkey becomes neurotic when denied social contact.

Heredity and environment

The role of learning, on the other hand, must not be minimized, especially since the school has accepted the promotion of socially adequate behavior as one of its primary objectives. This is not contradictory to the position taken in the preceding paragraphs. The problem is one of channeling into socially acceptable behavior whatever predispositions one may have inherited. Behavior is governed not by needs but by motives, and these are learned, so that assuming an inherited predisposition toward aggressiveness does not deny the role of education in channeling this aggression toward constructive behavior any more than accepting the glandular basis of heterosexual attraction implies that there is nothing we can to to help adolescents develop sound boy-girl relationships. It is also true that much of what constitutes socially acceptable behavior is largely a matter of complying with the customs and traditions of one's culture, and this sort of social competence cannot possibly be acquired through heredity, although the capacity to adapt probably is.

Sex Roles

Not only does society demand conformity to its basic values, goals, and mores, but it assigns specific roles to each of its members, expecting them to perform certain functions and generally fit into established behavioral patterns. A good example of this type of social assignment is found in sex roles, i.e., in the socially defined requirement that boys and girls, men and women, behave in ways consistent with the way boys and girls, men and women, are "supposed" to act. Sex roles vary somewhat from culture to culture but, within a given culture, are rather well defined and, what is more, enforced through a rather elaborate schedule of selective reinforcement.

An interesting contribution to the concept of sex roles is that of Lynn (1964), who first differentiates between parental identification, in which children internalize the personality characteristics of their parents, and sex-role identification, in which they internalize the role typical of a given sex in a particular culture. The initial parental identification of both male and female children is with the mother, but the boy must shift his initial mother identification to establish masculine role identification. Here the difference begins: the girl has the same-sex parental model for identification all hours of the day. The boy, on the other hand, sees the father only briefly. Besides, the father participates in many feminine roles, so that the boy must decipher the masculine role from the stereotype spelled out for him by the mother through a system of selective reinforcement, i.e., rewards for typical masculine role behavior and punishment for signs of femininity. As a result, as the boy's identification with the mother role weakens, it is gradually replaced by a learned identification with a culturally defined stereotyped masculine role.

Following through on the Woodworth-Schlossberg (1954) hypothesis, Lynn postulates that the task of achieving the separate kinds of identification—namely, masculine *role* identification for males and *mother* identification for females—entails different methods of learning, i.e., problem solving in boys and lesson learning in girls. The girl learns the mother identification lesson as presented to her, partly through imitation and partly through mother's selective reinforcement of mother-similar behavior. She does not have to abstract principles defining the sex role. The boy has a bigger problem: he must identify with the proper sex role as defined for him largely through negative admonishments (e.g., don't be a sissy) that do not tell him what he should do instead. Since these negative admonishments are typically made in the absence of a male model, the boy must decipher their implications in order to abstract the reverse principles defining the masculine role.

As a consequence of the different processes by which they typically learn sex identification, boys and girls develop different patterns of learning, which they subsequently apply to learning tasks in general. Girls acquire a learning method that primarily involves a personal relationship and identification. By contrast, the learning style acquired by boys involves defining the goals, restructuring the field, and abstracting underlying principles. The result is greater problem-solving skill on the part of boys and greater field dependence on the part of girls, as consistently reported in the literature (see Witkin in chapter 7).

The Home as a Socialization Agent

The home obviously plays a major role in the socialization of the child. First, the parents are the exclusive agents in any social predisposition, if any, that might be inherited, whether through glandular structure or through such mediating factors as intelligence, physical assets, etc. In addition, the environmental influences they provide, besides being persistent and cumulative, are extremely powerful by reason of the critical role the parents play in the parent-infant relation and the high receptivity of the child at that age. Child-rearing practices are crucial in shaping the basic personality; the way the child is handled in early life may well determine whether he or she is spontaneous, imaginative, and curious or, on the other hand, is well behaved, restricted, and resentful (see also Mouly 1973:71–80). Different home situations have different effects on the child's socialization: at one extreme, for example, we might think of the unsocialized delinquent; at the other, we need to recognize the possibility of oversocialization, particularly in the case of girls, with resulting repression, timidity, and oversensitivity to the reactions of others.

The emotional climate of the home

Parents play a critical role in determining the quality of the child's emotional life. A child who, as a result of a warm and accepting relation with the mother, develops basic security can face the world with a positive outlook. The child "damaged" by parental rejection and/or mishandling, on the other hand, often carries an intense feeling of hostility and revenge that leads to behavior that is devious and hard to understand, e.g., unprovoked meanness, cruelty to animals, or unexpected defiance. Some parents train their children in negative emotions, e.g., reinforcing temper tantrums by giving in or by using punitive and counteraggressive procedures in dealing with aggression. In the same way, overprotected children are likely to fear just about everything, including growing up, which will involve them in more complicated situations and deny them the protection of friendly adults.

A major contribution of the home concerns the development of love and affection. Infants are essentially egocentric. Gradually they learn to love their mother as a consequence of her association with feeding and the other comforts she provides. Later they expand their circle to include their father, siblings, and friends, again presumably as they somehow cater to their needs. In fact, it seems that love is always, to some degree at least, self-centered. Friendships are based on the mutual satisfaction of needs and, certainly, mutual need satisfaction is an important component of a happy marriage. What is reprehensible and counterproductive is selfish behavior, i.e., behavior designed to obtain personal satisfaction at the expense of others. We need to help

Enlightened self-interest

children achieve a degree of enlightened self-interest, i.e., we must help them realize that the welfare of others is essential to their own welfare and that selfishness is shortsighted. Our task is to help children perceive their personal realm broadly enough that they can include all those on whom they truly depend for maximum self-realization.

The School as a Socialization Agent

Even though social development has already progressed a considerable distance by the time a child enrolls, the school bears major responsibility here, particularly as it emphasizes social competence by promoting intellectual and academic proficiency and orients this proficiency toward the attainment of socially desirable goals. The school also supplements the work of other socializing agencies. Its role in the socialization of the nation's children has taken an added dimension with the current emphasis on preschool education, especially as it relates to the lower classes.[3] The school has a special responsibility as a remedial and developmental agency for children whose socialization has been hampered by adverse conditions.

The school as a social laboratory

The school makes a particular contribution as a laboratory for social living and self-discovery, for it is here that children gain experience in operating within the limits set by the social order. The school constitutes a miniature society in which children learn social responsiveness. It provides many opportunities for satisfying social needs and for learning techniques of effective group living. In school, children learn differentiated social roles and gradually develop a self-concept in relation to the broader social framework. The school is frequently the first place in which children have a chance to learn the satisfaction of contributing to group goals. It is particularly important in developing attitudes toward a variety of situations with which they have not had previous contact.

The Peer Group as a Socialization Agent

Another powerful socializing agent is the peer group, whose influence as a social testing ground is of special interest particularly as adolescents shift from a passive, infantile dependence on their parents to a more active and assertive dependence on their peers. The peer group offers teenagers supportive companionship and serves as a sounding board from which they learn vital lessons ranging from how to behave in a social situation to what stand to take on various social issues. It obviously has a marked influence on the adolescent's emerging values, attitudes, and standards of conduct and may, at times, countermand the influence of adult society. Coleman (1961), for example, suggests that the adolescent value system in some schools exerts a relatively strong anti-intellectual, antischolarship effect.

The peer culture

The school needs to take a positive attitude toward the peer culture. First, we need to understand the dynamics of the peer group. As adolescents seek emancipation from parental control, as indeed they must, the peer group fills the breech. The problem arises in part from the fact that the adolescent's role in today's adult-centered society is relatively marginal. As a consequence, the adolescent becomes increasingly indifferent to adult approval and disapproval and correspondingly more subject to peer influence. To the extent that, by offering acceptance, social identity, etc., the peer group displaces the parents as a major source of status, it can exact a price; and the more marginal the adolescent's status, the more the peer group can dictate the terms the teenager will have to meet for group acceptance and support. In extreme cases, it can tie adolescents struggling for emancipation from adult control to an even more

3. With an increasing number of mothers working, many children, almost from birth, spend the greater part of their waking hours in infant and toddler care centers, many of them operated and staffed by less than fully qualified personnel.

slavish dependence and conformity to peer group standards, thereby denying them the chance to grow.

On the other hand, we must avoid casting the peer group in the role of a villain luring good kids to their doom. Despite its stranglehold on a few, the peer group can go only so far in enforcing its dictates. Most youngsters go along up to a point where it makes sense to them, participate in some of the ceremonials, but have no intention of forsaking the establishment. They abide by most adult rules, maintain their grades, and expect to graduate from school and eventually take their place in traditional society. We also need to recognize that what we see as overconformity is not necessarily overconformity to youngsters, and really not so terribly damaging at that. We especially need to recognize that the more "available" we are, the more difficult it will be for the peer group to charge exorbitant "membership dues."

The generation gap

The problem stems in large part from the fact that young people, even though physiologically mature, are still held in considerable subservience. At a time when they are eager to exert their freedom, they find themselve subject to all kinds of demands and restrictions, some quite irrational in the sense of being incongruent with their relative maturity and often serving no useful purpose. What is more, they are relatively powerless to do anything about it. A major aspect to the generation gap is the one-way communication system that typically characterizes adult-adolescent interaction. The organization of society (and its various member agencies, e.g., the home, the school, the community, etc.) is best suited to the relaying of orders from those in authority, with teenagers in this case expected to comply. As a result, adult-teenager relations are characterized not only by a considerable degree of tension but also by mutual distrust and misunderstanding. They view each other's behavior and intentions in different and often contradictory terms.

GROUP DYNAMICS

The modern emphasis on the classroom as a functioning and interacting social unit has focused attention on the concept of *group dynamics*. No child operates in a vacuum, and the teacher can no more understand a group of children by studying each separately than a physicist can understand the action of a molecule by studying each atom in isolation. Each group, with its rules, standards, and code of conduct, makes demands on its members, and just as a person has a self-concept, so does the group, when closely knit, have ideals and values it seeks to maintain and perpetuate by rewarding those who further its purposes and invoking sanctions against those who undermine its existence.

Teachers have not taken maximum advantage of the potential of the class as a social group. Presumbaly conceptualizing the classroom on a teacher-versus-pupil basis, they have tried to avoid having to fight a well-organized enemy

Group work in the
classroom

by employing such divide-and-conquer techniques as promoting interpersonal competition, playing one child against the other, and generally fostering group rivalry and preventing the development of group spirit. By its very organization, the traditional classroom tends to keep student interaction to a relative minimum. On the other hand, the children do operate in close proximity, covering the same material for the same reason and subject to the direction of the same leader, and they interact with fellow students and are subject to group approval, acceptance or rejection, interpersonal support, and other aspects of group dynamics. Teachers need to take advantage of the classroom as a group to the point that students develop a sense of belonging, togetherness, and mutual interdependence.

Having the group work toward a common goal makes for more effective motivation and provides a supportive environment within which members are accepted as individuals and as contributors to group success. Under proper guidance, group work might logically be expected to promote the ability to resolve problems democratically, to formulate clearly defined goals, the willingness to assume responsibility as well as consideration of and sensitivity to the views of others without sacrifice of one's integrity—all of which must inevitably be major objectives of education in a democratic society. Group processes are particularly effective in promoting both attitude and behavior changes (see Lewin 1958). Furthermore, the fact that the group expects its members to contribute, or be squeezed out, is a powerful incentive toward pupil growth. Group influences can also be an impediment to wholesome personal and social growth, of course, but in either case—whether as an ally or an enemy in the educative process—they cannot be ignored.[4]

COGNITIVE DEVELOPMENT

Of the many aspects of the child's development with which educators must necessarily be concerned, none has a more direct bearing on the work of the school than the intellectual. This is particularly emphasized in the thinking of those who consider the learning of academic materials to be the primary, if not the sole, justification for having schools at all.

Aspects of Cognitive Development

Although the layman has a fairly clear idea of the meaning of intelligence, no such unanimity of viewpoint exists among experts in the field. There is, however, general consensus that cognitive development involves:

4. See Mouly (1973) for further discussion of group dynamics in the classroom.

1. A widening of intellectual and temporal horizons from those stimuli immediately impinging on the child to those more remote in time and space. As he or she grows older, the child is able to think in terms of yesterday and tomorrow and in terms of what is *there* rather than merely what is *here.*

2. An increase in the ability to deal with symbols, particularly abstract symbols, in manipulating the environment. Probably no other aspect reveals more clearly the child's mental development than this ability to use language as reflected in increased conceptual clarity and in the length and complexity of the sentences used to express ideas.

3. A systematic increase in reasoning ability. According to Piaget (see chapter 3), cognitive development proceeds through a series of structurally different stages ranging from sensorimotor to logical operations. Young children cannot deal with abstractions; they cannot deal with conservation before the approximate age of seven. On the other hand, the reasoning of older children is also often naive, and expectedly so, considering their relative lack of experience, their limited grasp of the concepts and principles necessary for the discovery and evaluation of meaningful and precise hypotheses, and their limited inventory in the area of vocabulary, reasoning strategies, and other tools with which to manipulate ideas. They also tend to be swayed by personal whims and emotional factors that color reasoning. But then, it must be noted that adult reasoning is also often naive and faulty.

The Nature of Intelligence

Probably no other area of psychology has been the subject of so much controversy as intelligence. This is to be expected, considering the importance of intellectual excellence in matters of technological and social advances, if not international survival. To complicate matters, intelligence is an area of deep personal involvement not particularly conducive to objective deliberation.

Intelligence: A matter of controversy

What constitutes intelligence has been the subject of continuous disagreement. The difficulty began with the early psychologists' focusing on reaction time and other measures of neurophysiological functioning as an index of neurological and, therefore, intellectual excellence. This was abandoned in favor of a more operational definition, but even here there has been no agreement as to either its nature or its basic components. Many authors dealing with intelligence accept the layman's use of the term (see Altman 1978; Wechsler 1975), and make no attempt to define it or analyze it. Those who provide a definition display considerable difference in viewpoint, although such global phrases as *a composite of ability to grasp relationships, abstract reasoning, ability to learn, ability to solve problems, effectiveness in dealing with one's environment,* and *ability to manipulate symbols* tend to be used with a certain frequency by authorities in the field. Unfortunately, these definitions are not particularly precise. As Garrett (1946) puts it, these omnibus definitions are in general too broad to be wrong and too vague to be useful.

Beginning with a strong hereditary orientation initiated by Wundt, Galton, and other biologically oriented scientists of the turn of the century, psychologists simply saw intelligence as innate and immutable. As they concentrated on the development of instruments for its measurement, they noted changes in a given person's IQ, some substantial, but it was not until the Iowa studies (see Skeels 1940, 1965) pointed to major IQ gains associated with the placement of orphanage children into more adequate homes that the hereditary and environmental issue was enjoined in debates that lasted through the 1930s. The controversy gave the environmentalists some comfort, but by and large the herditary position prevailed as a consequence of strong attacks on every aspect of the Iowa studies from inadequate sampling to improper use of tests (see McNemar 1940).

The 1950s brought in another decade of criticism from those who charged that current tests focused on the traditional IQ and deliberately discriminated against the creative child to the detriment of human and national welfare. That too came to pass, with Thorndike (1963) and McNemar (1964), among others, pointing to deficiencies in the basic concept of creativity and the corresponding durability of the general intellectual factor, g. The 1960s brought in a strong conviction that the academic and intellectual inadequacies of the disadvantaged could be overcome through early stimulation, and massive programs of preschool education were instituted in the hope of reversing the intellectual deficits of the lower classes and promoting their readiness for formal schooling. Efforts with regard to the former goal appear to be meeting with little success. Meanwhile concern for the disadvantaged was accompanied by charges that current tests were culturally biased and a vigorous effort to devise culture-fair tests.

The first successful attempt to measure intelligence was that of Alfred Binet, who at the turn of the century investigated the causes of academic retardation in the schools of Paris. Conceiving of intelligence as a composite of many abilities, he devised a number of questions dealing with topics with which each child, while lacking in knowledge of the specific questions, would nonetheless be somewhat acquainted. His sampling of many different types of performance in which intelligent behavior might be displayed proved sufficiently successful that in 1905 he published the first intelligence test.

The relatively wide difference in viewpoint as to what constitutes intelligence can be noted from a study of the content of current intelligence tests. Probably the most basic intellectual function involves the ability to perceive relationships such as might be involved in: "A bird flies; a fish _____," and "In what way are an orange and a baseball alike, and how are they different?" (Terman and Merrill 1960). Most tests include at least some items of this nature. Some of the better tests incorporate a variety of items designed to

Heredity? Environment? Both

measure different aspects of intellectual ability, e.g., vocabulary, verbal comprehension, abstract reasoning, memory for words and digits, ingenuity, and spatial relations. Others rely on a simple combination of verbal and numerical items, with emphasis on the former. In fact, some tests measure the verbal factor almost exclusively, much to the chagrin of some psychologists who feel that intelligence tests, supposedly designed to measure "intelligence," do nothing more than duplicate the material encountered in the classroom and, as a result, undermeasure students who do not do well in school work.

Theories of Intelligence

The theoretical picture of the nature of intelligence is no clearer than the practical problem of measuring it. More specifically, the basic controversy is primarily between the proponents of general intelligence (e.g., Spearman, Vernon, Burt, and other British psychologists) who see intelligence as a unitary trait and those who see intelligence as a composite of many factors, e.g., Thurstone (1935) and, more recently, Guilford (1956, 1959, 1967).[5] The issue is further complicated as it gets tied in with behavior development. Gagné (1965, 1977) and Hunt (1961), for example, postulate a learning model, with mental abilities a function of cumulative learning. Piaget, on the other hand, sees cognitive development as a matter of sequential stages of structurally different mental operations (see chapter 5). Meanwhile, the humanists (see Combs 1952) see intelligent behavior as a function of the adequacy of one's perceptions, the primary determinants of which are openness to experience, freedom from anxiety, need for achievement, and any number of what might be called "nonintellective" factors operating in the situation.

The two-factor theory

The *two-factor theory* proposed by Spearman conceptualizes intelligence as composed of a general factor g underlying all mental functions and a multitude of s factors, each specific to a given task. It is also possible to combine the s factors dealing with tasks of the same general nature into a *group* factor. According to Spearman, people differ in the amount of g as well as in the quality of the s or the g factors involved in a given task, so that it is possible for a person who is relatively more intelligent than another by reason of a superior g to be less capable in a given area, e.g., mathematics, because of relatively inferior s factors in that area. On the other hand, since Spearman postulated g as a form of mental energy permeating all mental operations, it would be unlikely for a person who is grossly lacking in general intelligence to be particularly gifted in a specific field.

Primary mental abilities

By contrast, Thurstone's *theory of primary mental abilities* conceives of intelligence as made up of a number of semi-independent mental abilities in the relative amount of any one of which people differ not only from one an-

5. See Bischoff (1954) for a discussion of Thurstone's Primary Mental Abilities, and Burt (1955) for an exposition of the Spearman position. See also Cassel (1969).

other but also within themselves. A person may, for example, have relatively fewer of most of these abilities than another person and so be generally less "bright" but may have considerably more of one ability (e.g., spatial ability), which makes it possible to excel in the tasks where this ability is important (e.g., engineering). Of course, to the extent that many tasks use a combination of these abilities, a person would be restricted in intelligence by a particular weakness in any one area.

Guilford's structure of the intellect

    The most comprehensive conceptualization of the complex structure of the human intellect is that recently presented by Guilford in which he classifies the intellect on three dimensions (figure 6.2):

1. The process or operation performed: cognition, memory, convergent thinking, divergent thinking, and evaluation.
2. The kind of content: figural (e.g., concrete intelligence), symbolic (e.g., vocabulary), semantic (abstract intelligence), and behavioral (e.g., social intelligence).
3. The kind of product resulting from the application of certain operations on certain kinds of content.

These three components of the intellect can be represented by a 5 × 4 × 6 three-dimensional solid model, with each of the 120 cells construed as an intellectual factor. Among the cognitive abilities at the figural level, for example, there is the recognition of familiar picture objects and silhouettes, which can be made as difficult as necessary by blotting out some of the parts. They

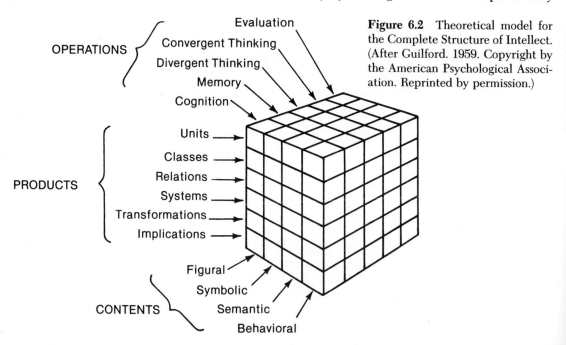

Figure 6.2 Theoretical model for the Complete Structure of Intellect. (After Guilford. 1959. Copyright by the American Psychological Association. Reprinted by permission.)

can also be auditory figures, e.g., melodies and rhymes. At the cognitive-semantic level there is verbal comprehension, as represented by the usual vocabulary test.[6]

Of particular interest is the distinction between *convergent* and *divergent* thinking. The former is oriented toward solving a problem to which there is a known (or, at least, an expected) answer; this is generally known as logical (critical) thinking, or simply *reasoning*. Convergent production dealing with relationships, for example, is generally measured as an aspect of the eduction of correlates through the usual analogies test: "Kitten is to cat as _____ is to dog." Divergent thinking, on the contrary, seeks a new and different solution and might be considered imaginative thinking, or perhaps *creativity*, e.g., ideational fluency: "What are some of the different ways in which a common brick might be used?"

A different view of mental organization is that of Cattell (1963; see also Knox 1976), who classifies mental abilities into two broad categories: (1) those that reflect biological endowment, which he collectively describes as *fluid* intelligence (g_f), and (2) those that reflect experiential influences, which he labels *crystallized* intelligence (g_c). Crystallized intelligence is best seen as a precipitate of experience that results when fluid intelligence interacts with the cul-

Fluid and crystallized intelligence

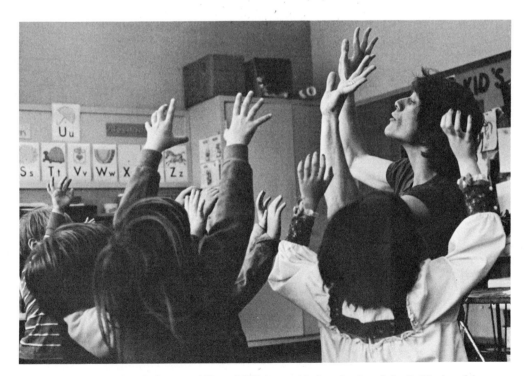

6. See Undheim and Horn (1977) for a critical evaluation of the Guilford model.

ture. It operates in cognitive tasks in which intellectual skills and habits have become "crystallized" as a result of previous experience, including vocabulary, knowledge, and strategies of logical reasoning.

Fluid intelligence, on the other hand, is presumably innate and relatively independent of experience. It might be conceived as a form of energy flowing into a wide variety of intellectual abilities. It would be critical in tasks requiring adaptation to new situations. Fluid intelligence tends to level off around age fourteen or fifteen, whereas crystallized intelligence probably increases to age thirty, forty, or even beyond. Where experience is limited, as in the case of the disadvantaged child, the development of crystallized intelligence tends to suffer, whereas fluid intelligence continues to develop independently of any restriction of experience; almost all children eventually learn conservation, for example.

Still another view of cognitive development is Gagné's cumulative learning model, which conceptualizes mental abilities as a function of cumulative learning (see chapter 12), with differences in intellect presumably a function of differences in prerequisite learnings. Gagné insists that as children acquire a given concept, for example, they are not simply "learning something"; rather they are acquiring new capabilities that enable them to deal effectively with principles and problem solving higher on the learning hierarchy. The child is apparently capable of mastering any intellectual skill for which he or she has achieved the prerequisite capabilities.

Piaget's Theory of Cognitive Development

A major contribution to the field of cognitive development is that of Piaget, whose cognitive-developmental theory we discussed in chapter 5. Of particular interest in the present context are his writings on the growth of logical thought, especially in the area of numbers, time, space, and causation. As previously noted, Piaget views cognitive growth as a matter of sequential steps in the maturation of the child's capacity to perform increasingly difficult logical operations.

Piaget's stages

More specifically, Piaget categorizes the child's thought processes into four main stages of cognitive development: (1) Sensorimotor: which takes the child from a self-centered to an object-centered world. The major task of this period is the *conquest of objects.* (2) Preoperational: here the child acquires language, permitting him or her to deal with the world symbolically instead of directly through motor activities. The major task of this period is the *conquest of the symbol.* (3) Concrete operations: the child can reason but at a very concrete level. The major task of this period is the *conquest of classes, relations, and quantities.* (4) Formal operations: now the child is freed from egocentricism and can conceptualize his or her own thoughts and those of others. The major task of this period is the *conquest of thought.*

An important aspect of Piaget's study of the development of intellectual

Language and mental development

processes concerns the analysis of language from the standpoint of their function in mental life. The language of children of three or four is egocentric; in contrast to the sociocentric speech of older children, preschoolers either talk to themselves or talk for the pleasure of associating others in whatever they happen to be doing. Piaget notes a transition from (1) a syncratic stage in which children make superficial associations among experiences to an intermediate stage in which they are able to reason in the presence of the objects of thought, to a final stage in which they are able to engage in abstract thought; and (2) an animistic and magical mode of thought characteristic of children and primitive people to the logical modes of thought characteristic of adults.

Piaget has devoted considerable attention to the concept of causality, which he views as a matter of relatively uniform stages in the progression of the child's ability to see physical relationships as a matter of physical law. His approach consists of asking children of various ages such questions as "What makes the clouds move?" or "Why does a stone thrown into a pool of water sink to the bottom?" and then classifying their responses into levels of physical causality ranging from the least to the most mature—e.g., from "The stone falls to the bottom because it is white" (phenomenistic), to "The clouds move because they are alive" (animistic), to "The wind pushes the clouds" (mechanistic), to a final stage of logical explanation.

Piaget and the school

Piaget's model has obvious implications for preschool education, particularly as it affects the disadvantaged. A major difficulty of the disadvantaged in our verbally dominated school environment stems from circumstances that interfere with the transfer from the sensorimotor to the later symbolic stages. The fact that Piaget's operations are hierarchically organized means that experiential deprivation at one level can have limiting effects on the attainment of later stages. The lack of objects in the toddler's environment may cause serious retardation in the transition to the preoperational stage, just as the limited and essentially concrete nature of the communication pattern of the lower-class home may well interfere with the easy transfer to formal operations. In the same way, our emphasis on teaching masses of isolated facts rather than the conceptual scheme for ordering these data can result in the underdevelopment of the elementary school child's ability to abstract and to classify. The school needs to take every opportunity to help children gain stage-relevant experiences. In asking kindergarten children to clean up the room, for example, the teacher might ask them to sort out the materials they pick off the floor into various categories. We need to help primary school children develop a multidimensional learning set that this thing on the table is not simply an apple but also a fruit, also something red, and something round, depending on the context. We also need to help children convert concrete experiences into conceptual forms that can be stored in cognitive structure. The school needs to be especially concerned with adapting its instructional strategies to fit the child's current cognitive organization.

THE MEASUREMENT OF INTELLIGENCE

Basic Concepts

Mental age

Mental development is measured in terms of mental age (MA) obtained from performance on an intelligence test. By definition, a mental age of, say, ten is the mental development average for a population of ten-year-olds.[7] The child's answers to the various items of the test are scored and the total converted into a mental age through a table derived from the standardization data. Thus a raw score of 65 might represent an MA of 9 simply because the nine-year-old segment of the standardization population averages a raw score of 65. But *intelligence* is a relative term; a person is not bright or dull in an absolute sense but rather is accelerated or retarded by comparison to other children of the same chronological age. For that reason, psychologists have defined the intelligence quotient as the ratio of the child's mental age to chronological age— or, more specifically, they have defined $IQ = MA/CA \times 100$. Thus, a child of, say, five with a mental age of six would have an IQ of $6/5 \times 100$, or 120.[8] This child's mental development is accelerated by some 20 percent by comparison to that of the children of the same chronological age. The IQ is an index of relative brightness and can be used to estimate the mental level the child is likely to reach at a given age. For example, we might expect this child to reach an MA of (approximately) 12 by the age 10. This assumes that the child's IQ remains constant, an assumption that is only relatively valid, as we shall see.

The Mental Growth Curve

The peak is reached . . .

Mental growth does not continue throughout life; in fact, it begins to taper off during the early teens and reaches its peak somewhere in the twenties.[9] The age at which mental growth ceases is open to question. Wechsler (1958), for example, postulates that most mental functions reach their peak in the mid-twenties.[10]

---

7. This working definition of MA breaks down after the age of around thirteen when mental growth tends to taper off, but it is still useful to understand its basic meaning. The 1972 revision of the Stanford-Binet has abandoned the MA, which Terman had introduced with his first Stanford-Binet in 1916.

8. This method of calculating the IQ as a ratio of MA to CA has been abandoned by modern test makers in favor of the deviation method, in which IQs are simply read off a table. IQ is a matter of the deviation, plus or minus, of the child's performance from the average of the children of the same age in the standardization group.

9. The best representation of the mental growth curve up to age twenty-one (along with a thorough discussion of the problems connected therewith) is undoubtedly that of the Berkeley Growth Study data as presented by Bayley (1955; see McCall et al. 1977 for an update).

10. To the extent that intelligence is a composite of many abilities, each maturing at its own rate, the age at which the peak is reached is a function of the particular composition of the test used. According to Bloom (1964), whereas 80 percent of adult proficiency in perceptual speed is attained by age twelve, for example, this relative level of ability is reached only at fourteen in the case of reasoning and spatial perception, at sixteen in numerical ability and memory, and after twenty for word fluency.

We measure
performance

To the extent that intelligence tests simply measure performance, IQ scores do not cease to increase by age sixteen, but whether to accept or reject these increments in test *performance* as evidence of increased *intelligence* revolves around what we mean by "intelligence." Certainly as people grow older, they gain experience that contributes to their ability to solve problems of the kind included in intelligence tests. But the interpretation of this improved performance is a matter of controversy between (1) those who hold that the concept of intelligence should eliminate at least in large part the improvement in performance that is the direct outcome of experience (who feel that the increase in test performance between the freshman and the senior year, for example, in effect reflects a type of coaching not entirely unlike giving the student the answers to the questions before beginning the test); and (2) those who hold that intelligent behavior is intelligent behavior regardless of its origin *as long as it has relatively wide applicability.* The latter argue that, to the extent that our interest is in the ability to act intelligently, and not in the biological endowment of the species, if these experiential advantages enable college graduates to deal more adequately with complex problems in a wide variety of situations, this is indeed what is meant by being more *intelligent.*

The IQ declines with
age

The converse problem exists at the upper levels of the chronological age scale; the mental growth curve shows a decline in IQ with advancing age, especially after, say, fifty. On the other hand, many people exhibit great mental alertness despite advanced age. It would seem that those engaged in activities calling for the constant exercise of intellectual functions keep themselves at a high level of intellectual fitness. By contrast, the uneducated suffer early and sharp losses in test performance and possibly also corresponding losses in actual intellectual functioning. However, with the common denominator of schooling so far removed, it is virtually impossible to devise test materials that can be considered equivalent across individuals who for years have been living in essentially different experiential worlds.

The amount of decline in IQ registered with age depends in a fundamental way on the material included in the test. Research has shown that performance on the subtests on information, comprehension, vocabulary, object assembly, and picture completion of the *Wechsler Adult Intelligence Scale* hold up well with age, whereas performance on the subtests on digit span, similarities, block design, arithmetic, and digit symbols undergoes considerable decline. It would seem that the "hold" scales are those that tap stored knowledge (i.e., accumulated wisdom, or, to use Cattell's vocabulary, *crystallized* intelligence), whereas the greatest loss in test performance seems to occur in tests emphasizing speed and general flexibility in learning a new task. The general consensus is that the losses in actual intellectual capacity occurring up to the mid-fifties are relatively minor. Furthermore, from the practical point of view of learning ability and effectiveness of behavior, the added store of experience of an older person may well compensate in good part for whatever decline in "intelligence" may have occurred.

Intelligence Tests

A relatively large number of intelligence tests designed for subjects from pre-school to the adult level are available (see Buros: Mental Measurement Year-books). Most of these are of acceptable quality from the standpoint of the purpose to be served by the conventional IQ, and it is up to the school to select the particular instrument that will serve its special needs. Evaluating intelligence tests calls for a considerably greater understanding of the principles of tests and measurements than the present text can provide. The following paragraphs are simply for purposes of orientation, and the reader is referred to the many excellent texts on educational and psychological measurements for a more complete coverage.

Validity of IQ tests

In order to provide meaningful results, a test of intelligence, like any other measuring instrument, must possess certain characteristics, primary among which is *validity* (see chapter 13). To be valid, a test of intelligence must measure intelligence and not some other aspect of the personality. This poses a problem inasmuch as there is no agreement as to what intelligence is or even as to what factors are to be included or excluded. Test makers generally rely on agreement of the scores provided by their tests with such criteria as teachers' judgment of pupil ability, success in school, and results of other tests purporting to measure intelligence. These are relatively inadequate criteria of intelligence, and the lack of more substantial agreement of intelligence test scores with these criteria can be blamed on the test, on the criteria, or on both.

There are certain groups of people for whom the average "intelligence test" cannot give a valid measure of their "intelligence." To the extent that the average test was not designed to measure the intelligence of children with a language handicap, the bilingual child will do poorly, not necessarily because of a lack of mental ability but because of a lack of opportunity to learn the language in which the test is given. In the same way, a child with a reading problem will tend to be underestimated as to intelligence if given a test involving a considerable amount of reading. All that can be said in such a case is that the obtained IQ is probably an underestimate of the examinee's "true" intelligence, although it could be argued that the obtained IQ, no matter how depressed, may actually give a "valid"[11] estimate of *educational potential* since the child's handicap is likely to operate to depress both test and classroom performance. In other words, the validity of a test of intelligence cannot be considered apart from the purpose it is to serve.

A test of intelligence should also be *reliable,* i.e., it must measure consistently whatever it measures. The average intelligence test is fairly reliable, although fluctuations of up to five IQ points can be expected upon retest in two-thirds of the cases and even greater fluctuation in the remainder (see chapter 13).

11. By definition, validity must always be relative to a given purpose. See chapter 13.

Range of Individual Differences in Intelligence

Results of intelligence tests indicate that the distribution of IQs, like the distribution of many other human characteristics, tends to approximate the normal curve. The distribution of IQs has been calibrated at 100 as the average for the general population, with approximately one-third of the IQs ranging from 84 to 100 and another third from 100 to 116. Percentages for other IQ intervals can be estimated from figure 6.3. In a typical unselected group of thirty children, there are likely to be one or two relatively gifted and one or two relatively dull, so that from the standpoint of classroom performance, perhaps one child will have the mental development necessary to do work two or three grades in advance of the present grade placement, while perhaps another child or two will be so lacking as to require placement in a special class.

Relation of IQ to Academic Success

Despite their limitations, intelligence tests have been shown to be of definite value in predicting some aspects of the individual's future behavior. Consequently they are indispensable tools in such fields as psychology, sociology, industry, and especially education; intelligence tests were devised in connection with school problems, and well over 75 percent of the intelligence tests are administered in school-connected situations. Intelligence tests serve their primary function in helping teachers determine the ability of individual children as a prerequisite to gearing the instructional program to the child's ability level and to determine the caliber of the work to be expected from each. Intelligence tests also serve as a partial basis for the classification and assignment of students to special classes for the gifted or the mentally retarded.[12]

Correlation with academic achievement

That imbeciles and idiots cannot succeed in the standard academic pro-

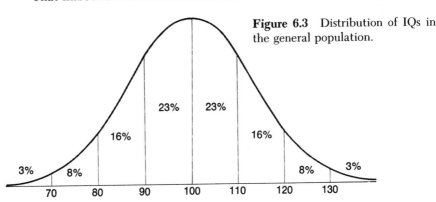

Figure 6.3 Distribution of IQs in the general population.

12. Misused, intelligence tests can lead to illegal de facto segregation. See *APA Monitor*, April 1978, for testimony before a congressional committee concerning the use of IQ tests for the classification of pupils.

gram is generally recognized. At the opposite end of the intelligence scale are the gifted, whose brilliant academic records sometimes border on the incredible; John Stuart Mill studied Greek at the age of three, Ruskin was writing poetry at six. Some 2 percent of Terman's sample of gifted children (Terman 1925) learned to read at three. Even in the more normal range, research repeatedly has shown correlations of .50 between IQ and success in academic subjects. This does not mean that academic success is denied those with a low IQ; it only suggests that their chances of success are somewhat less and that they will have to have special assets or will have to work harder in order to compensate for their intellectual limitations.

It must be realized that intelligence is not the only factor bearing on school success and that there is a wide range of achievement levels among pupils of the same IQ. In fact, all that can be expected from an intelligence test is for it to indicate what particular children might be *expected* to do, not what they *will* do since motivation, work habits, ability to get along with the teacher, etc., have a definite effect on their success in the classroom.

Nevertheless, to the extent that learning ability is accepted as an important aspect of "intelligence," however defined, there must of necessity be a relationship between IQ and success in school, especially since test makers deliberately incorporate into their tests problems closely akin to those common in the classroom. Actually, the principal point of difference between a test of intelligence and a test of academic achievement is one of orientation and purpose. The items of any test, whether achievement or intelligence, are necessarily samples of what a person can do here and now, i.e., of achievement.[13] From these samples an inference is made as to the person's ability to deal with similar situations in the future. An achievement test is concerned with the student's ability to deal with material covered in a given course; it is unquestionably predictive of later success in related activities. Intelligence tests, on the other hand, presumably assay present abilities having applicability in a wider range of activities than those specifically related to a given course, but certainly the courses a student takes can be expected to contribute to intellectual performance.

Intelligence? Aptitude? A matter of purpose

The Cultural Issue

The early 1950s saw a strong reaction against what some people felt was a cultural bias incorporated in existing intelligence tests. Leading the attack were Davis (1948) and Eells (1953), who argued that test designers had accentuated the socioeconomic differential in IQ by choosing items that discriminated on the basis of scholastic success, which, because of the unsuitability of school ma-

---

13. In a scholarly article on this point, Wesman (1968) includes aptitude tests, which also sample achievement but in a more restricted area than intelligence tests and which are, therefore, predictive of likely success in a specialized field for which the items in question are relevant.

terials to the disadvantaged, was the equivalent of deliberately seeking items that discriminate against lower-class children. In other words, they argued that the IQ differential among the social classes reflected primarily a cultural bias *in the test materials* rather than a real socioeconomic difference in ability.

Critics have argued that because the tests incorporate materials that are relatively meaningless in terms of their interests and background, these children are first mislabeled as dull, which leads the teacher to expect relatively little from them and to deny them the benefit of more educationally profitable experiences. Soon everyone, including the children themselves, is convinced of their dullness, and, as a result, they are deprived of the opportunity to achieve the success that could be theirs were new objectives and new approaches stressed (see Loretan 1965). Davis and Eells presented as a solution the Davis-Eells Games (1952), in the construction of which they attempted to abandon the conventional middle-class-oriented emphasis on academic and verbal materials and to emphasize instead practical problems presumably fair to all cultural and socioeconomic groups.

The Davis-Eells controversy centers around confusion as to the purpose intelligence tests are to serve. The function of an intelligence test is to measure current ability (i.e., performance) on certain aspects of intellectual *functioning*, particularly with respect to schoollike activities, not to estimate intellectual *endowment*. The IQ is a measure of current *ability* and almost by definition underestimates the intellectual potential of culturally deprived children to the degree that cultural deprivation has indeed had an adverse effect on their development. But if we are interested in the IQ for what it leads us to expect by way of, say, academic performance, our present tests probably reflect a relatively appropriate socioeconomic differential. No doubt we could devise items on which children from the various socioeconomic levels would perform equally well, but surely many arguments could be advanced to the effect that this would not give a correct picture of the relative "intelligence" of the various groups. What purpose is to be served by measuring the potential of the lower class on a measure artificially contrived to ignore the unfortunate realities of years of deprivation?[14] Russell (1956), for example, found that the Davis-Eells Games did not give as good a prediction of reading progress in first grade as the Stanford-Binet. Rosenblaum et al. (1955) likewise concluded that children from lower socioeconomic levels are lacking not in familiarity with the test materials but rather in ability to make correct associations and discriminations. Apparently the Davis-Eells Games had simply sacrificed predict-

Culture-fair tests? Not really!

14. Current IQ tests have been developed for the purpose of predicting success in our schools as they actually exist. It might, of course, be argued that our schools are too traditional, too verbal, too abstract. Were changes to be made in our academic operations to take these arguments into consideration, different abilities might come to play. Meanwhile there is no point in devising tests that would predict success in these "ideal" but, as of now, nonexisting schools. There may be something wrong with the current orientation of our schools, but it is difficult to find fault with tests that find the disadvantaged indeed disadvantaged from the standpoint of the dominant culture.

ability without any clear-cut gain in the elimination of cultural bias. As Oakland (1977) suggests, one test cannot be universally applicable and fair to persons from all cultures and still assess important psychological characteristics.[15]

The question of the IQ of lower-class children was revived during the 1960s in connection with compensatory education. A basic hope of the proponents of Head Start and other intervention programs was that early stimulation would not only correct accrued deficits but would also place the child on an accelerated schedule of mental growth. This hope has not been fulfilled. It would seem that intelligence is relatively resistant to short-term intervention.

Children of culturally disadvantaged background tend to do poorly on IQ tests; not only do they, as a group, find the content of the typical IQ test much too verbal and middle-class-oriented, but, in addition, their test-taking skills are poor and they see no meaning to the whole exercise and feel no compulsion to do well. This is probably true of their performance on any other formal testing program, but in the case of the IQ—and this is the critical issue—their low scores are potentially harmful in that they serve a self-fulfilling function (see Rosenthal and Jacobson 1968). Having (often incorrectly) labeled them as dull, teachers use the poor performance of these children as a justification for poor teaching and gross complacency over pupil progress (see Loretan 1965). To avoid such abuse, New York City schools, for example, have banned the use of group IQ tests,[16] a move that has, in turn, been subjected to considerable criticism. Wechsler (1966), for example, suggests that eliminating IQ tests does not erase the hard reality that some children are in fact disadvantaged and further that the substitutes (e.g., achievement tests) are not adequate replacements for IQ tests, nor are they culture-fair. In fact, some are probably more culturally biased than the the general IQ tests they replaced.

The problem defies easy resolution. The use of special tests or special norms is hardly the answer as long as the lower classes, whether in school or on the labor market, have to meet the requirements specified by the mainstream culture. A test designed to fit the specific characteristics and background of a particular minority group can have meaning only within that narrow segment of the population. For a minority student to score high in relation to other minority students is not very helpful if he or she has to compete against all other applicants for a given job. On the other hand, in view of the modern emphasis on the whole child, the school needs to abandon its concept of intelligence defined so narrowly as to relate almost exclusively to the ability to do schoolwork in the traditional classroom. In the meantime, caution in the interpretation of the results of testing the intelligence of children of different backgrounds seems in order.

15. See Jensen (1980) for a particularly comprehensive review of the issue of cultural bias.

16. California has taken similar action under court direction. See *APA Monitor*, 1978.

The Jensen Controversy

Probably no other publication has created as much controversy in both professional and lay circles as the 1969 Jensen article (Jensen, 1969, 1970) regarding alleged deficiencies in conceptual abilities among blacks. Jensen postulated a two-level hierarchical model of mental organization going from *associative* to *conceptual* abilities, with the development of the lower-level associative abilities necessary but not sufficient for the development of conceptual abilities.

Level One abilities involve the neuroregistration of stimulus input and the consequent formation of associations. There is relatively little transformation of the input so there is a high correspondence between stimulus input and response output. These abilities are measured mostly by tests of digit memory, serial rote learning, etc. Level Two abilities, on the other hand, involve self-initiated elaborations and transformations of stimulus input before it can eventuate in behavioral responses as might be involved in concept formation and problem solving. These abilities correspond roughly to Spearman's g, the general intellectual factor measured by traditional tests of intelligence involving the more abstract conceptual abilities. Jensen postulates that whereas Level One abilities develop rapidly and are distributed evenly in all socioeconomic classes, Level Two abilities depend on the development of certain neural structures that develop slowly at first and, with age, show increasing differences among socioeconomic groups.

Jensen's Level Two abilities

Whereas Level One processes are basic to survival in most environments, Level Two functions are of major advantage only in a more complex technological culture where there is a premium on abstract and symbolic operations. Culturally disadvantaged children apparently are not lacking in basic learning ability as measured by tests of immediate memory, serial tasks, etc. But they are lacking in the appropriate environmental inputs that promote the development of Level Two abilities. Unfortunately, since it is this kind of acquired intelligence—consisting of a background of transferable knowledge and cognitive skills—that is needed in order to learn through the highly verbal and symbolic medium of the traditional classroom, culturally disadvantaged children are at an educational disavantage, even though they may be average or even superior in raw (basic) learning ability.[17]

Evaluation of Intelligence tests

Despite their shortcomings, intelligence tests serve a definite function, particularly with respect to school work. Although they do not give foolproof an-

17. The work of Bernstein and Cattell is relevant in this context. Also of interest is the evidence presented by Stodolsky and Lesser (1967) of ethnic differences in ability patterns, with social-class variations within each group affecting the level but not the basic organization.

swers to all questions relating to "intelligence," there is considerable empirical evidence of their overall usefulness. They are, on the other hand, subject to a number of limitations that need to be clearly understood if we are to avoid their misuse. They are essentially oriented toward the prediction of scholastic success in the traditional classroom and, in a sense, underestimate the "intelligence" of children, who, because of cultural differences or academic difficulties, do not do well in school or whose talents lie outside the traditional mold of convergent thinking. This can lead to incorrect expectations from such children and can cause them harm. They tell us what a child is likely to be able to do given standard conditions, but our predictions could be in considerable error under a different set of conditions. Also to be noted is that intelligence tests measure only a relatively narrow segment of the many factors typically involved in school performance. There is a need, for example, to incorporate into our measures of academic and vocational potential more of the aptitudes and talents associated with different cultural backgrounds.

Intelligence tests measure . . .

Nevertheless, intelligence tests are indispensable tools to teachers or administrators who use them for the purpose for which they are designed and interpret the results with caution and in relation to other aspects of the whole child. When used in this way, they form the basis for dealing with children at their own level. The school's primary concern is to help children make the most of their capabilities; intelligence tests, despite their shortcomings, are the best indicator of these capabilities currently available (see Hebb 1978).

CONSTANCY OF THE IQ

The question of the constancy of the IQ has received a great deal of attention, for its usefulness rests on the assumption that it will remain relatively constant over the years. This assumption is generally sustained for the majority of individuals. Whereas there is considerable empirical as well as theoretical evidence that such consistency is far from absolute, the dull child typically becomes the dull adult, the gifted child, the gifted adult. This does not imply that considerable change in IQ could not be effected if a determined effort were made.

The IQ is only relatively stable

Sizable IQ changes actually occur over a period of years. Honzig et al. (1948) found that between the ages of six and eighteen, 60 percent of the group changed fifteen or more IQ points and 9 percent actually changed thirty or more IQ points. Bayley (1949, 1955) reports similar IQ changes. Lack of constancy of the IQ over the years is also evident in the correlations obtained in the Harvard Growth Study (Dearborn et al. 1938; see table 6.4). Obviously the longer the time span involved—especially if it extends into Piaget's sensorimotor stage— the greater the possible discrepancy.

Table 6.4 Correlation of IQ's at Different
Ages with Those Obtained at Age 16*

Age	Boys	Girls
7	.58	.54
8	.64	.58
9	.58	.53
10	.74	.70
11	.75	.73
12	.79	.78
13	.78	.81
14	.83	.82
15	.90	.91

* From Dearborn et al. (1938)

That the IQ does not remain exactly constant over the years should come as no surprise; fluctuations can be expected to occur for a number of reasons ranging from the unreliability of the test, the effects of practice, or other factors operating from one test to another, to changes in actual intelligence as might occur in response to an especially enriched or impoverished environment. Probably the most common source of variation concerns differences in the composition of tests in relation to the various abilities of the testee. This can account for sizable differences, especially when the results of early childhood tests with their emphasis on sensorimotor tasks are compared with those of later tests where the emphasis is on abstract reasoning. The correlation between the IQ of infants and their IQ a few years later is typically negative. It is not until the age of four that any degree of stability in the IQ is attained. Certainly, for the first year at least, a better indication of the infant's subsequent IQ can be obtained by testing the mother.

The composition of early childhood tests

Various attempts have been made to supplement or to correct infant test scores to make them more predictive of later IQ, but as Bayley (1955) points out, eventually investigators realized that the infant's behavioral repertoire is pretty well restricted to sensorimotor activities. She suggests that rather than an integrated capacity that grows by steady accumulations, intelligence is better seen as a dynamic succession of developing functions, with the more advanced and complex functions in the hierarchy depending on the prior maturing of the earlier and simpler ones.

No test is completely reliable

Part of the fluctuation occurring in the IQ stems from the fact that no test is completely reliable. Thus, assuming no practice effects, we would expect one-third of the testees to gain on retest from zero to five IQ points (see figure 6.4) and another third to lose from zero to five points. Another 14 percent would lose from five to ten points while 14 percent would gain from five to ten points. The other 2 percent at each end would gain or lose more than ten IQ points. These fluctuations have nothing whatsoever to do with any change occurring as a result of an increased or decreased rate of intellectual growth. They simply reflect fluctuations to be expected as a result of the limitations of the measuring instruments, the carelessness of the psychometrist, and fluctuations within the testee arising from fatigue, loss of motivation, distractibility, and other personal factors. It is also possible that mental growth, like physical growth, goes by spurts and stops, and especially that stages, as postulated by Piaget, may require the child to adjust to qualitatively (structurally) different modes of intellectual functioning.

The problem of the constancy of the IQ is directly related to the relative influence of heredity and environment in intelligence. If heredity were the sole determinant of intelligence, the limits of intelligence would be set at conception, and IQ fluctuations would be restricted to those arising from the unreliability of the tests and the irregularities connected with the spurts and pauses in the mental growth curve. On the other hand, if intelligence is readily susceptible to environmental influences, additional fluctuations can be expected from test to test in keeping with the actual changes in intelligence resulting from changes in the adequacy of the environment.

As we have noted, the relative influence of heredity and environment on intelligence has been the topic of continuous controversy since the turn of the century. Actually, the problem is incapable of resolution because research does not touch on the problem of heredity and environment but simply on the susceptibility of the content of a particular test to environmental influences. The difficulty stems from our inability to measure intelligence except indirectly through performance, which incorporates both an inherited and a learned component so closely intertwined that their relative influence in making this performance possible cannot be separated.

The voluminous evidence on the subject lends itself to conflicting interpretation. It certainly does not permit us to specify the relative contribution of

Figure 6.4 Theoretical Distribution of Changes in IQ upon Retest Due to Test Unreliability

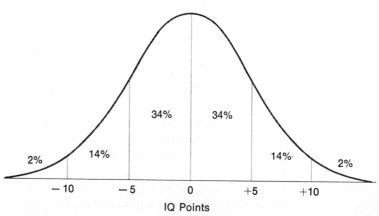

heredity and environment to intellectual status or to approximate the extent of the constancy in the IQ to be expected under various conditions of environmental differences.[18] We must recognize that constancy in IQ is frequently the direct reflection of the constancy of the environment impinging on the average individual. It does not speak to the changes that could take place were the environment to undergo drastic change.

Teachers and especially parents need to concentrate on providing children with a psychologically productive environment within the framework of which they can realize their potentialities in the pursuit of self-actualization. On the other hand, they need to be cautioned against applying pressures to make all children perform like geniuses. The sooner they accept the fact that there are limitations in intelligence as there are in all other areas, the more effective they will be in helping children attain their maximum growth. In the meantime, the amenability of intellectual development to systematic early stimulation is still an exciting possibility deserving of our best research and pedagogical efforts.

HIGHLIGHTS OF THE CHAPTER

If teachers are to deal with the whole child, they must understand the various aspects of development in their dynamic interaction.

1. Probably no aspect of one's natural endowment has a greater impact on the self-concept than one's physical characteristics, especially as they deviate from average. The problems connected with late sexual maturation may be relatively serious.
2. The child is an individualist, becoming socialized only as he or she finds it advantageous to internalize the values of society and to comply with its demands. Ideally, socially adequate behavior is a matter of enlightened self-interest in which one's needs and purposes are integrated with those of the social group for the benefit of both.
3. The home plays the critical role in the socialization of children. This in no way minimizes the importance of the school and the peer group in the socialization process.
4. There is considerable disagreement among psychologists as to the definition of intelligence, its nature, and even its components. The theoretical picture is also characterized by disagreement between those who believe in the general factor *g* and those who favor a multidimensional model.
5. The age at which intellectual growth reaches its peak revolves around the questions of what we mean by intelligence and how it is to be measured.
6. The mental age refers to the *level* and the IQ to the *rate* of one's mental de-

18. Scarr-Salapatek (1975) estimates the influence of environment on the IQ at roughly twenty-five points.

velopment. The IQ tends to follow a normal distribution, with 100 accepted as average and some two-thirds of the general population having IQs within the range 84 to 116.

7. The issue of cultural bias revolves around a confusion of what intelligence tests are supposed to measure.

8. The IQ is relatively constant under the usual environmental conditions facing the average child. So far, attempts to effect substantial increases in intelligence through environmental stimulation have met with relatively little success.

SUGGESTIONS FOR FURTHER READING

BAYLEY, NANCY. Development of mental abilities. In Paul H. Mussen, ed., *Carmichael's Manual of Child Psychology*, 1:1163–1209. New York: Wiley, 1970. A comprehensive treatment of mental development based on decades of experience and research.

ELKIND, DAVID. Piagetian and psychometric conceptions of intelligence. *Harv. Educ. Rev.* 39 (1969):319–337. Presents the Jensen controversy in the context of Piaget's theory of cognitive development.

HEBB, DONALD O. Open letter: To a friend who thinks the IQ is a social evil. *Amer. Psychol.* 33 (1978):1143–1144. Points to the many potential benefits to be derived from the constructive use of the IQ.

LUNZER, E. A. Construction of a standardized battery of Piagetian tests to assess the development of effective intelligence. *Res. Educ.* 3 (1970):53–72. Discusses the construction of a test designed to measure cognitive development as per the Piaget stages.

PHILLIPS, J. L. *The Origins of the Intellect: Piaget's Theory.* San Francisco: Freeman, 1969. This highly readable paperback presents the implications of Piaget's theory of cognitive development for educational practice. Discusses intelligence testing from Piaget's conception of intellectual development.

SCRIVEN, MICHAEL. The values of the academy: Moral issues from the Jensen case. *Rev. Educ. Res.* 40 (1970):541–549. Analyzes the implications of the furor over the Jensen article and raises the question of whether a researcher ought to be able to publish research results even though they might be misused to further unjust causes.

SIGEL, IRVING E., and RODNEY R. COCKING. *Cognitive Development from Childhood to Adolescence: A Constructive Perspective.* New York: Holt, Rinehart & Winston, 1977. This excellent reference provides a thorough exposition of Piaget's position.

WESMAN, ALEXANDER, G. Intelligent testing. *Amer. Psychol.* 23 (1968):367–374. One of the more enlightened discussions of the nature and the measurement of intelligence. Clarifies the distinction among intelligence, aptitude, and achievement.

QUESTIONS AND PROJECTS

1. Evaluate your self-concept as it relates to your physical assets and liabilities. Specifically, what can the school do to help children adjust to physical limitations?

2. A certain amount of information is available as to the early child-rearing practices that lead to adequate socialization. Outline an effective plan for getting the information to parents.

3. (a) To what extent is "socialization" of the child a matter of indoctrination to our American middle-class way of life? Why shouldn't all Americans subscribe to a common set of "American" values? To what extent is "moral development" the core of socialization? How would socialization in a totalitarian society differ from that of a democratic society?

   (b) Can parents overdo the development of social sensitivity? What is the basic ingredient in oversocialization, and what are some of the dangers?

4. Evaluate this statement: The evidence of the constancy of the IQ bears a direct relationship to the constancy of the environment and to the susceptibility of test items to environmental influences and only an indirect relationship to the constancy of the individual's intelligence.

5. How does Piaget-type intelligence differ from the better-known Binet-type intelligence? What differences might be involved in their measurement? What bearing might this have on the differences in ability among cultural groups?

6. To what extent should nonintellective factors (e.g., motivation, background, etc.) be considered part of "intelligence"? How might the school maximize student ability through the development of nonintellective factors?

7. Make a list of some of the better-known tests of intelligence. Check Buros's Mental Measurement Yearbooks and other sources for an evaluation of these instruments.

8. What guidelines and safeguards might the school set in the use of intelligence test data relating to minority groups?

SELF-TEST

1. The most educationally significant aspect of physical growth is
   a. the differences in the generalized curve of various groups, such a boys versus girls.
   b. the relative consistency of the individual's growth pattern.
   c. its susceptibility to environmental inconsistencies.
   d. its unpredictability.
   e. the uniqueness of the individual's growth pattern.

2. Probably the most fundamental component of emotions is
   a. a certain feeling tone.
   b. the directional drive.
   c. the impulse to action.
   d. the neurophysiological basis.
   e. the visceral changes.

3. The ultimate goal of social development is the promotion of
   a. enlightened self-interest.
   b. social adequacy.
   c. social conformity.
   d. social responsibility.
   e. social sensitivity.

4. The major contribution of the peer group to the socialization of the child is that
   a. it defines acceptable social behavior.
   b. it encourages the development of strong loyalties.
   c. it encourages social sensitivities.
   d. it promotes the ability to conform.
   e. it provides security necessary for effective exploration of the world.

5. Spearman is to Thurstone as
   a. a general factor is to group factors.
   b. a general factor is to a multitude of specific independent neural connections.
   c. g is to specific factors.
   d. g is to primary mental abilities.
   e. group factors are to specific factors.

6. Piaget views intellectual growth as
   a. the acquisition of symbolic processes.
   b. the development of the ability to deal with causal relationships.
   c. the develoment of an effective experience-retrieval system.
   d. growth in the effective use of language.

     e. a matter of sequential stages in the ability to deal with logical oper-
       ations.

7. The failure of infant IQ tests to predict the child's IQ at, say, age eighteen is best explained on the basis of
   a. the different content of tests at age one and age eighteen.
   b. the differential effects of intervening environmental influences.
   c. errors arising out of the difficulty of testing young children.
   d. the evolving hierarchical changes in the composition of intelli-
     gence.
   e. the inadequacy of tests, particularly infant tests.

SEVEN

Individual Differences

True education makes for inequality, the inequality of individuality, the inequality of success; the glorious inequality of talent, of genius; for inequality, not mediocrity, individual superiority, not standardization, is the measure of the progress of the world.

Felix E. Schelling

The closer we come to attaining equality of educational opportunity the greater become the inequalities of education, as the capable come closer to reaching their potential and widen the gap between themselves and the less competent.

Don Robinson (1965)

We hold these truths to be self-evident . . . that all men are created equal.

The Declaration of Independence

— Considers some of the basic dimensions of individual differences, particularly as they relate to the work of the classroom
— Gives special consideration to sex and socioeconomic differences
— Considers acceleration, ability grouping, and enrichment as means for dealing with the wide differences in academic adequacy among schoolchildren

PREVIEW: KEY CONCEPTS

1. That individuals differ markedly in every aspect of the human condition—physique, intelligence, cognitive style, personality, etc.—has fundamental implications for all phases of the school's operation.
2. Whereas substantial group differences can be noted, there are typically far greater differences among individuals within a given group than there are between groups. Every individual is unique. Differences in perceptual style present a special challenge to the classroom teacher.
3. The nature of the talents of women and their development has received increasing attention in the past decade.
4. The problems of the lower classes have also been of major concern since the early 1960s, with compensatory education presumably the primary vehicle for the resolution of economic, intellectual, and academic deficiencies.
5. The school's strategies for dealing with individual differences in the classroom generally fall in the categories of grade retention (or promotion), ability grouping, and curriculum modification (e.g., enrichment). None is a panacea.

PREVIEW QUESTIONS

1. What are some of the more obvious differences between boys and girls in the areas of (a) physical development, (b) aptitude, (c) personality, and (d) adjustment to school?
2. What are some of the major characteristics of the culturally disadvantaged?
   What are some of the areas of major deficit as they relate to the requirements of the school?
   How successful has Head Start been in overcoming early deficits?
3. What are some of the major implications of individual differences for the effective operation of the school?

How can the school achieve a common set of objectives in the face of such a wide range of individual differences among its students?
4. How does the school typically deal with individual differences in academic and intellectual ability in the classroom?
5. What purpose is served by identifying differences between groups when in the final analysis we must deal with individual children?

Trying to be all things to all children in the face of the marked differences that exist among them has complicated the task of the school to the point where it has not been particularly effective with a sizable portion of its customers. A number of special programs for exceptional children have been tried with varying degrees of success. What needs to be recognized is that everyone is, in a sense, exceptional and in need of a special program, for, as any classroom teacher will testify, there is no "average" child for whom a standard program can be fitted without alteration.

RANGE OF INDIVIDUAL DIFFERENCES

Everyone recognizes that individuals differ from one another; seldom appreciated, however, is the extent to which people differ, especially with respect to psychological traits where differences are not as obvious as in the physical domain. Although this discussion will be oriented primarily toward differences relating to the learning of academic material, we might review briefly some of the highlights of differences in other areas.

Physical Differences

Individual differences in physical size are particularly evident at the approximate age of puberty when some youngsters are nearly twice as tall and twice as heavy as others of the same age and sex. Vast differences also exist in physical fitness, motor coordination, and motor proficiency.

Sex Differences

PHYSIOLOGICAL DIFFERENCES. Except for a brief period between the ages of eleven through fourteen, boys are generally taller, heavier, and stronger than girls, who, on the other hand, mature earlier. Males appear to be vulnerable to stress and disease. They tend toward baldness. Ten to twenty times as many males have a speech impediment. Colorblindness and hemophilia are male traits. More men die of accidents; the suicide rate for men is three times that of women (although women try unsuccessfully twice as often as men). Garai and Scheinfeld (1968) believe that females are better equipped to cope with most human afflictions because they are genetically better constructed and have a more efficient chemical system.

SCHOOL ADJUSTMENT.   Girls receive higher grades throughout elementary school, with the gap gradually reduced in high school. More boys are nonreaders; more boys fail; more boys are disciplinary cases; and more boys drop out at all educational levels. Underachievement is more prevalent among boys, and it begins in the first grade. It may be that their lack of readiness as they enter school stays with them, accumulating into serious maladjustment to the school situation. For girls, achievement during the first five or six years of school is sometimes followed by a sudden slump in the seventh grade. The major reasons why girls do well in school, particularly at the elementary level, may be the compatibility of the school climate with the female personality and the greater compatibility of the curriculum, e.g., its emphasis on verbal content. The fact that most teachers in the elementary school are females may also help.[1]

Girls tend to do better in grade school; boys in high school

Boys tend to do better in high school, where their greater analytical competencies come into play. They tend to do well on standardized tests but poorly on essay examinations because of their limited verbal facility. The superiority of boys in high school is clearly shown in the National Merit Scholarship Examinations, where it was necessary to establish separate norms for boys and girls. A single standard would have ruled out almost all of the girls, particularly in mathematics and science.

ABILITY PATTERNS.   There is no overall sex difference in IQ since test makers have deliberately eliminated items that favor one sex or the other. From the standpoint of patterning, males do better on tasks requiring judgment and the manipulation of numbers and spatial relations, while females do better on tests involving a quick grasp of details (e.g., perceptual speed and rote memory) or the use of logical reasoning at the concrete level or in accordance with generally approved patterns of linking and classification (e.g., similarities). Females are more verbally fluent from infancy; they display greater facility in the use of rule-bound skills associated with spelling and language. Boys tend to be more proficient in abstract reasoning and are generally better equipped to pursue such fields as mathematics, science, and philosophy. They display consistent superiority in mathematical reasoning; they tend to use broader conceptual categories, focus more effectively on broad relationships and common features, and are better able to ignore irrelevant data. This gives them an edge in problem solving. Girls, on the other hand, tend to focus on the

Girls are more fluent; boys more analytical

_____

1. See L. Weiner (1978) for an attribution approach to sex differences in academic achievement.

more specific details; they tend to be less analytical and more field dependent (Witkin 1962; Witkin et al. 1977; also Lynn in chapter 5). To the extent that they are more socially sensitive, dependent, and conforming, girls are less able to disregard the broad field in which the perceptual patterns they are trying to grasp are imbedded.

It is, of course, possible that some of these differences stem from relatively inherited predispositions, perhaps centering on biochemical differences. On the other hand, it would seem that sex differences arise at least in part from sex role expectations incorporated into the self-concept very early in life.[2] Girls tend to lead more sheltered lives; they are not usually subjected to the same pressures to achieve. To date, girls have shown relatively little need for achievement (*N Ach*). They tend to be bothered by fear of success, the idea that it is not "feminine" to compete, that they are "not supposed to" surpass boys whether in sports, academic achievement, or brain power. Marini and Greenberger (1978), for example, found high school boys to aspire to and expect higher levels of academic attainment than did girls.

Sontag et al. (1958) found twice as many girls as boys in the group of greatest decline in IQ over the early developmental period, a phenomenon he labeled "a descent into femininity," i.e., an adoption of the female role in which the emphasis is on being "feminine." The traits associated with an accelerative IQ pattern, on the contrary, included aggressiveness, self-initiation, competitiveness, and interest in problem solving—all of which are masculine traits. It is also possible that a major reason girls rarely enter the sciences is that until recently, at least, these were considered "male" occupations.

Of interest in this connection is the continued tendency for the school, along with the rest of American society, to cast girls into the passive "female" role and boys into the active "masculine" role. From first grade where beginning readers have Jerry do all the exciting things while Jane looks on, to high school where John is the group leader and Mary the secretary, the stereotype continues on to adult society where even the church sees the ministry as a male occupation (see Sadker and Frazier 1973). Although some progress is being made in the fight against the underdevelopment and underutilization of the talents of one-half of our population, life-styles developed over the centuries linger and progress is necessarily slow (see Van Dusen and Sheldon 1976).

It is interesting to note in this connection that American culture has been traditionally masculine in emphasis, going back to the frontiers, the conquest of the forest, the Indians, the Klondike, the mountains, and now outer space—in all of which "masculine" qualities of initiative, independence, and courage were critical. These are still emphasized in business, sports, and the military. More recently, as a mature society, our greater concerns have been

Girls tend to be low in N Ach

Sex stereotypes continue

2. Recent authors (e.g., Unger 1979) refer to gender differences to emphasize the fact that differences between males and females incorporate a substantial culturally determined component in addition to more basic sex differences.

with the alienation of youth, the education of the masses, racial equality, and other social problems—whose solutions depend primarily on "feminine" qualities of kindness, compassion, forbearance, and nurturance. There is apparently a need to blend the male and female qualities in the solution of the problems of our more mature society, which is no longer concerned with the frontier, survival, and military conquest but rather with human dignity and welfare. In this context, it is interesting to note that the school is still remarkably feminine in its organization but authoritarian in its operation. Boys who are all boys do not fit this system particularly well; the school has passable success with middle-class children, but even there the casualties can be high (e.g., the alienation of middle-class youth in the 1960s).

PERSONALITY.   It is in the area of personality that the clearest sex differences lie. By and large, girls are more emotionally and socially mature than boys of the same age; they display greater social sensitivity and greater skill in interpersonal relations. Even at the age of three months, girls exhibit greater curiosity for faces and people while boys tend to manifest greater interest in objects and patterns. Preschool boys ask more frequently "why?" and "how?" whereas girls are more interested in social roles. There is apparently an early differentiation between the preponderant achievement needs of boys and the predominant affiliation needs of girls, both of which presumably persist throughout life.

Personality
differences appear
early

Girls are more likely to receive affection and to become responsive to affection. The socialization pattern for girls is marked by a disposition toward dependency, anxiety, and sensitivity to social rejection. Girls in elementary school tend to seek more help, more emotional support, and more approval from their parents and their teachers; they tend to work to please the teacher. Boys, on the other hand, become increasingly independent and strive for self-approval; they are more likely to seek mastery as a test of their own personal adequacy.

Boys display greater vitality, independence, initiative, self-sufficiency, and autonomy; in high school, they are likely to do well in subjects they like and poorly in subjects they do not like. Girls, on the other hand, balance their efforts over all their subjects. Girls are more afraid of and more discouraged by failure than are boys. In a sense, girls tend to have greater security inasmuch as their role is much more clearly defined and consistent. Boys, by contrast, are permitted to be active, aggressive, and rebellious in certain situations, but they need to be very accurate and perceptive in their assessment of the particular occasions on which they can and cannot be aggressive and guide their behavior accordingly or face the consequences. A major point of difference here is the self-concept each is allowed to develop as a consequence of sex-role expectations.

PERSONALITY ADJUSTMENT.   Females tend to score higher on measures of neuroticism and emotional instability. Generally, they are less self-sufficient, more introverted, less dominant, less confident, and more socially dependent than males. These differences perhaps stem, at least in part, from sex-role expectations, with males and females simply responding to the "proper" sex stereotype. Boys tend to be more aggressive, perhaps because of the influence of male hormones, but if we include verbal aggression, the difference is considerably less. Boys and girls seem to channel their impulses into different forms of behavior; girls tend to be prosocial, boys are sometimes antisocial. Boys tend to be more impulsive.

INTEREST.   Boys tend to be interested in adventure, mechanics, science, and leadership roles; girls are more interested in artistic, musical, literary, and social service activities. Boys prefer vigorous play involving muscular strength and physical exertion. During the preschool years, they surpass girls in restlessness and general activity; they play more often with blocks, toy cars and trucks, while girls prefer sedentary games. At the adult level, males show greater interest in mechanical, scientific, and active occupations; they lean toward economic, political, and theoretical values. Women tend to choose literary work and clerical occupations and to express stronger social, aesthetic, and religious values.

SOCIOECONOMIC DIFFERENCES

The Culturally Disadvantaged

A major influence in both the extent and the direction of the child's development is social class, particularly as it relates to the stifling effects of poverty in all of its various manifestations. As noted in chapter 5, the 1960s saw increased concern over the plight of the nation's poor, and massive remedial steps ranging from urban renewal to compensatory preschool education were instituted. Some gains have been made, but progress is necessarily slow.

The ghetto syndrome
      The academic difficulties of lower-class youth can only be understood in the context of the ghetto, crowding, stimulus deprivation, hunger, lower-class values and life-style, chronic unemployment, welfare, crime, and other components of the poverty syndrome. In contrast to their middle-class counterparts who are typically born in a friendly, accepting world that systematically provides them built-in positive reinforcement, children from the lower classes are systematically faced with a maximum of irrelevant frustration at home, in the community, as well as in school—not because of what they do or do not do

but simply because of what they are. They have no control over the hunger and poverty at home, the constant failure and rejection at school, the lack of opportunity in the community, etc.

The problem falls in the broad context of *cultural disadvantage,* i.e., the extent to which members of the lower classes are handicapped by a lack of orientation to the middle-class experiences and values to which mainstream American society—and more particularly the school as presently consti-

The lower-class culture

tuted—is geared. It is best understood against the background of the lower-class culture, which, according to Irelan and Besner (1966) is characterized by:

1. A comparative simplification of the experienced world where the alternatives are limited. The poor rarely play a role of leadership or fill any position calling for specialized functioning. Their occupational responsibilities involve few challenges. Their activities are primarily a matter of daily routine.
2. Deprivation: Ours is a society with unlimited goals and high standards, yet the lower classes are drastically limited in the extent to which they can realistically expect to achieve even the most modest goals.
3. Uncertainty: People of the lower classes are at the mercy of life's unpredictabilities: their skills are expendable, they lose their jobs on a moment's notice, they can be arrested on suspicion, their credit is not good, failure to pay the rent means immediate eviction, etc.
4. Helplessness: The position of the poor is one of powerlessness and helplessness based partly on reality and, perhaps more importantly, on a conviction that whatever is going to happen will happen and there is nothing they can do about it. What is unfortunate is that this feeling of a lack of internal control and self-determination becomes the anchor point of their motivational structure. Their mental outlook is not so much a drive for achievement and self-improvement as simply a flight from present discomforts. The life of the lower classes is geared to the present rather than to the future; it is useless to plan for the distant future when "luck" rather than one's initiative and efforts is the basic ingredient in controlling one's destiny. They operate at the deprivation level of Maslow's hierarchy; in a precarious situation, security takes precedence over advancement.

The Lower Classes and the School

Cultural deprivation and the school

The lower-class home is particularly lacking in the assets that make for success in school. Not only are inadequate prenatal care and malnutrition still prevalent among the lower classes, but, more pertinent from a psychological and educational point of view, the lower-class home is especially lacking in the type of stimulation that promotes readiness for school work. There are very little verbal interaction between adults and children and few opportunities for thinking about stimulating issues. After the first year, the lower-class home environment is progressively less able to provide the variety of experience necessary for the proper development of inherited potentialities. Home crowding, chaotic family structure, restricted verbal interaction, a lack of stimulating toys and objects to play with, etc., all act to deprive the child of the kind of environmental encounter required to keep a two-year-old developing at all, let alone developing at an optimal rate and in the direction of adaptation to a highly technical society. The high noise-to-stimulus ratio that typically characterizes the overcrowded living conditions of the lower-class home interferes with the development of auditory discrimination. Children learn to tune out the noises at home. Later they will likewise tune out the teacher.

Lack of academic readiness

That lower-class children typically do poorly in school from the time they enroll to the time they drop out, and that their performance progressively worsens over time, has been known for decades.[3] There are many exceptions, of course, yet too often children from the ghetto come to school so totally unprepared to meet its demands that failure—immediate and continuous—is almost inevitable. They have very few of the kinds of cognitive skills the school requires. Their preschool environment has not provided the necessary experience in dealing with concrete objects; they have not learned to make pertinent discriminations; they have had no practice in the systematic ordering of experiences; they have had no contact with books or other academic tools; they have not developed habits of paying attention. As a consequence, instead of counteracting the deficiencies resulting from an inadequate home background, the school often accentuates the difficulties, producing increasing frustration by the day and by the year to the point that these children equate the school with a place where they experience failure. In time, the school schedules in both itself and children the expectation that the latter will fail.

Irrelevance of the curriculum

The lower-class child's lack of motivation in school probably reflects in large part the "irrelevance" of the competency goals of the school. Living in the present under a philosophy of powerlessness as a way of life is not conducive to the development of habits of delayed gratification essential to both academic success and conventional social behavior. It takes a lot of believing in the future to persist through year after year of the systematic failure and frustration lower-class children typically encounter in school. This is a special problem for blacks who, until recently at least, could see little relationship between schooling and personal advancement. In fact, academic achievement in the setting of the ghetto may well alienate children from their peers and even from their family. The result has been typically a devaluation of academic

---

3. As long as teachers believed in heredity as the relatively exclusive determinant of academic growth, they were effectively protected from having to consider the possibility that the child's difficulties simply reflected the inadequacies of prior learnings due to ineffective or inappropriate instructional efforts. Lack of readiness (presumably due to inherited limitations) became a convenient scapegoat whenever the child failed to learn according to the school's specifications.

7-1   EXCEL

Of special relevance in the present context is EXCEL, the PUSH program for excellence in education. Launched in 1975 by the Reverend Jesse L. Jackson, the former civil-rights activist and disciple of Martin Luther King, Jr., EXCEL is an outgrowth of the PUSH (People United to Save Humanity) movement of the Southern Christian Leadership Conference, which, in turn, was organized in 1971 to push for black economic and political power. More specifically, EXCEL is an outgrowth of the Reverend Jackson's personal conviction that political action will come to naught unless blacks, first and foremost, are willing to help themselves: ''Nobody can save us for us but us.''

EXCEL focuses simultaneously on education, self-discipline, self-sacrifice, and self-help, while condemning what Jackson sees as the diversionary evils of drugs, alcohol, and a lack of discipline that prevent blacks from keeping pressure to have the necessary social changes happen. As the dynamic and charismatic self-styled ''country preacher'' puts it, ''The door of opportunity is open for our people but they are too drunk, too unconscious to walk through the door.'' His primary theme is, ''If we are to survive—and survive we must—we must have the will to greatness and the urge to excel.'' He recognizes, for example, that we need more money for our schools, better teachers, etc. but first there must be a will to learn.

As of now, EXCEL is largely the Rev. Jesse L. Jackson, but he is fully aware of the need to involve an ever-growing number of people in the movement. This is being done. EXCEL is taking root in an increasing number of schools and communities from Los Angeles to Baltimore and Philadelphia as Jackson brings the message to large, enthusiastic crowds in city after city. The strategy is to involve parents, community and church leaders, students, and the media (including disc jockeys) into a partnership so that all forces impinging on the child will do so

goals and a long-standing distrust of teachers, which these children teach each other and confirm on a self-fulfilling basis. It seems that when it comes to school, lower-class children have just as many problems in understanding what the whole thing is about and what they are to get from it all as presumably their middle-class teachers have in relating traditional curriculum and learning procedures to the value system of these children. Unfortunately teachers are more likely to focus on the problems that *the school has* than on the enormous confusion and frustration that children experience as they meet an essentially rigid set of rules and expectations that make no sense to them at all. To make matters worse, these children have no way of expressing their lack of enthusiasm except through apathetic and disruptive behavior.

in a consistent and coordinated manner. A more immediate task is to develop local leadership that can then carry the ball. At the school level, the goal is to develop student leaders who can then help other students develop a sense of order and self-discipline.

The leaders of EXCEL are aware of the need to maintain momentum, but they are also aware of the risk of overextending their resources to the point that they cannot provide each unit with the necessary follow-up. There are other problems. While EXCEL can no longer remain a one-man show, there is a question as to whether local leaders will have the dedication, the wisdom, the status, and the eloquence needed to inspire full community participation.

At the school level, new student dedication alone may not be sufficient. Jackson argues, ''We do best what we do most; and for many of our children that is to play ball. One of the reasons Johnny does not read well is that Johnny does not practice reading.'' Yet unless accompanied by remedial and developmental work, practice may do nothing more than consolidate negative attitudes and bad habits. Perhaps more disquieting is the fact that the school has never been too adept at educating the disadvantaged. It might be that, freed from having to fight unruly, unmotivated, recalcitrant students, the school will have time for one-on-one contacts that will break the long-established pattern of academic deficiency among lower-class children. Maybe at that point the school will undergo a pervasive change in all aspects of its operation. Hopefully, if EXCEL is successful in making it possible for teachers to teach, teachers will rise to the occasion.

COLE, ROBERT W.   Black Moses: Jesse Jackson's PUSH for excellence. *Phi Delta Kappan* 58 (1977):378–382, 388
EUBANKS, EUGENE E., and DANIEL U. LEVINE.   The PUSH program for excellence in big city schools. *Phi Delta Kappan* 58 (1977):383–388.
JACKSON, JESSE L., et al.   In pursuit of equity, ethics, and excellence. *Phi Delta Kappan* 60 (1978):189–229. Also Nov. 1978, and Jan. 1979 issues.

Language Deficiencies

Nowhere are lower-class children as handicapped as in the area of language, particularly as we realize that their ineffective speech patterns frequently reflect correspondingly ineffective thought processes (Deutsch 1963, 1964; Bernstein 1961).[4] Among the more drastic ill effects of an impoverished environment, Deutsch sees an equally impoverished symbolic system, a paucity of concepts and relational propositions, and inadequate discriminative skills.

4. Cole and Bruner (1971) argue that lower-class language is highly functional in the context of the ghetto.

Serious linguistic
deficits, especially in
abstract abilities

By contrast to their middle-class counterparts who come to school fully aware of the power of language and skilled in its use, lower-class children are the product of an environment much less oriented toward language as an instrument for the systematic ordering and manipulation of experience. By the time they enter school, they are already retarded one year in language development. They end up retarded in school achievement an average of two years by grade six and almost three years by grade eight.

Underlying these unfortunate developmental outcomes are a number of basic inadequacies that characterize the lower-class home and its mode of operation. The home is typically lacking in the wide variety of objects that call for labeling and generally serve as referents in language acquisition. Lower-class children are not read to; they are not engaged in extended conversation. There is an almost complete absence of reading materials; adult reading is not part of the family routine. The syntactical models provided by the parents are typically faulty, with short, incomplete sentences and poor enunciation. As a result, they learn to rely on simple or even incomplete sentences. Their memories and attention spans are poorly developed. With the high level of noise and confusion in the lower-class home, they learn not to attend. As a consequence, these children, particularly in the primary grades, are highly distractible and incapable of sustained attention.

Their auditory and visual discrimination, so important in learning to read, is poor. They have had no experience with paint books, toys, various gadgets, and games requiring discrimination that typically are available to middle-class children. Before they can learn to read, they will need to acquire visual and perceptual skills necessary to label, to distinguish, and to discriminate with regard to auditory and visual patterns. They will have to gain experience with objects as a foundation, say, for later movement along the Piaget stages.

It is particularly with respect to the abstract dimensions of verbal functioning that the culturally deprived manifest the greatest degree of intellectual retardation. Deutsch (1964) suggests that because language is a prerequisite to concept formation, the language deficiencies of lower-class children are bound to result in a corresponding deficit in their ability to conceptualize and categorize stimuli. As a result, they have to rely on a perceptual-cognitive style that is relatively inadequate or irrelevant to the demands for academic competence. In fact, probably the most significant aspect of their cognitive growth is their slower and less complete transition from the concrete to the abstract modes of thought as defined by Piaget.[5] Their orientation is more toward the concrete, the tangible, the immediate, and the particularized properties of objects and situations rather than toward their abstract, symbolic, categorical, and relational properties.

---

5. Bauman (1976) estimates that only half of college freshmen have achieved Piaget's formal operation.

BERNSTEIN'S THEORY OF LANGUAGE DEVELOPMENT

An interesting contribution to the psychology of the cognitive development of the disadvantaged is that of Bernstein (1961), who contrasts two basic language patterns, the *restricted* and the *elaborated*, which he finds characteristic of the disadvantaged and the advantaged, respectively. Restricted styles are simple, stereotyped, syntactically poor, and inadequate for the communication of ideas and relationships requiring accurate formulation, and generally lacking in the specificity and exactness required for precise conceptualization and differentiation. Sentences are short, simple, and often unfinished; there is little use of subordinate clauses. In elaborated codes, on the other hand, language is more particularized, more differentiated, and more precise. It is characterized by accurate grammatical order, logical modifications, and emphases mediated through grammatically complex sentence structure. Correspondingly, it permits the expression of wider and more complex arrangements of thought, leading to discrimination among cognitive and affective content. What is more serious, according to Bernstein, is that these linguistic differences between lower and middle classes reflect corresponding differences in cognitive functioning.

Bernstein: Inadequacies in communication pattern

Bernstein argues that the problem is not really one of vocabulary but rather of the strategies available for organizing meaning, with the latter a function of the particular style of mother-child interaction. He postulates that the structure of the family shapes communication and language skills, which, in turn, shape thought and cognitive style. In other words, according to Bernstein, the behavior that leads to social, educational, and economic poverty is learned in early childhood, and the central factor involved in the dire effects of cultural deprivation is the relative lack of cognitive meaning in the mother-child communication system. More specifically, the growth of cognitive processes is fostered under a family control system that offers a wide range of alternatives of action and thought, and conversely it is constricted by a system of control that offers predetermined solutions rather than alternatives for consideration and choice.

Bernstein distinguishes between two types of family control: one oriented toward family status; the other oriented toward persons. In the former, behavior is geared to imperatives: "Do this because I said so." In the person-oriented appeal system, by contrast, behavior is justified in terms of feelings, preferences, personal and unique reactions, and subjective states that not so much permit as they actually demand an elaborated linguistic code and a wide range of linguistic and behavioral alternatives as basic to human interaction.

Restricted and elaborated verbal patterns

In their discussion of the Bernstein position, Hess and Shipman (1965) give the following example: imagine two situations in which a child is playing noisily when the phone rings. One mother says, "Be quiet." The other says, "Be quiet for a minute; I want to talk on the phone." In the first case, the whole range of potential meaning has been cut off by the categoric statement; the child is simply called upon to comply. He has no need to reflect or to make mental discriminations. In the second example, the child is required to consider his or her behavior in relation to its broad range of effects on other people. The child must perform a more complicated task in interpreting situational realities as mediated in part through shared ideas. As a consequence of these two divergent communication styles, repeated in numerous ways and numerous circumstances throughout the preschool years, these two children might be expected to have developed substantially different verbal and cognitive styles by the time they enter school. Restricted verbal patterns of the variety of "shut up" do not provide children with much of a basis for the full development of language and of underlying thought processes.

The person-oriented family, by contrast, encourages children to engage in appropriate behavior by presenting role requirements in a specific context and causing them to weigh the logical consequences of the various behavioral alternatives. Because such an approach blends more easily into a cognitive pattern involving reflective comparison, they are more likely to become reflective and "rational." To the extent that they recognize that behavior calls for a *why*, they are more likely to incorporate *why* as an integral aspect of their behavior. This has obvious implications with regard to socialization, for example. With elaborated language, interpersonal interaction can involve a talking-through of the issues or, in the case of misbehavior, the punishment can take a form of inductive procedures aimed at ensuring guilt and empathy (see Aronfreed 1968).

Status-oriented families, by contrast, tend to present a rule in an arbitrary manner with compliance or defiance as the only alternatives. By restricting the number and kinds of alternatives of action and thought, such a child-control system tends to discourage reflection as the basis for choosing among alternatives. It promotes modes of dealing with problems that are impulsive rather than reflective, that focus on the immediate rather than the future, and that are discontinuous rather than sequential. Restricted language is more compatible with the power-assertive approach and more likely to result in a child who relates to authority rather than to reason, who may be compliant but not reflective, and for whom consequences are defined in terms of immediate punishment or reward rather than long-range goals. It must, of course, be recognized that, despite the interesting generalizations postulated by Bernstein, there is a wide range of individual differences among both the advantaged and the disadvantaged, and that these patterns are not found in all children of a particular background nor are they confined to such children.

Rival hypothesis: Cultural conflict

Also to be noted is the concept of *cultural conflict*, which, in relative contradiction of the notion of cultural deprivation presented above, argues that lower-class language is simply different; that we label it as inferior because we do not grasp its functionality in the setting in which it was devised. It postulates that lower-class children acquire the kinds of competencies they need for adjustment to the conditions of life they are likely to encounter. Many of the skills required for effective living in the lower-class culture are worthwhile in themselves but they are almost totally ignored by the middle-class establishment, especially the school. Cole and Bruner (1971), for example, insist that cultural differences reside more in the situation to which the different cultural groups apply their skills than to differences in the functionality of the skills themselves. They see cultural deprivation as representing a special case of cultural *differences* that arise when an individual is required, say, in school, to perform in a manner inconsistent with his or her cultural background. According to Cole and Bruner, by making middle-class behavior the yardstick of success, we have simply rendered *differences* into *deficits*.[6]

COMPENSATORY EDUCATION

What is a suitable curriculum?

Compensatory educational programs for the culturally disadvantaged have been structured almost exclusively around overcoming deficits so as to enable ghetto children to cope with the basic requirements of the dominant culture. This is necessary and appropriate up to a point. If these children are ever to cope with the demands of American society, there is no denying that all children need to know how to read, write, and manipulate numbers. It is the task of the teacher to help them master these essentials. The danger is that we may be casting the education of the culturally disadvantaged in the mold found effective for the middle-class. By placing our emphasis almost exclusively on verbal ability, a quality that is depressed in lower-class society, we may be guaranteeing the scholastic inadequacy of lower-class children, whose style of life is physical and visual rather than verbal, concrete rather than abstract. These children have talents but these do not fit the middle-class mold. If they are to be successful within the classroom setting, some adaptation to their learning style will have to be made (see Riessman 1966).

On the other hand, there is danger here too. It may well be a totally legitimate purpose of education to expand the receptivity of all children to all avenues of communication. To cater to the disadvantaged child's one-channel reception can result in a narrow, inflexible training as a substitute for a meaningful education, just as the special adaptation of the curriculum to fit his background and talents can result in a watered-down education or a narrow specialization that will effectively bar him from any number of educational

6. See Passow (1974); Kirk and Goon (1975). Also see R. Collins's review of Bernstein's three-volume series, *Class, Codes, and Control,* in *Amer. Educ. Res. J.* 15 (1978):573–581.

goals (see Clark 1965; Kliebard 1967). Whereas education has to capitalize on the child's strengths, there is a question of how far one can go, and should go, in avoiding an abstract verbal approach to certain aspects of education, for example.[7] A contrary point of view is that of Stodolsky and Lesser (1967), who present evidence of ethnic differences in ability patterns, with social class variations within each ethnic group affecting the level but not the basic organization. They found that different ethnic groups tend to display different patterns of ability, with the lower-class members duplicating at a lower level the ability pattern characteristic of the members of their ethnic group of higher socioeconomic status. The ability profile of middle-class Chinese, for example, is duplicated at a lower level by their lower-class counterparts. The authors advocate individualizing instruction so as to capitalize on the strengths of the different ethnic groups rather than to attempt to make all groups fit the mold of the dominant culture.

Teaching the disadvantaged

Teaching the disadvantaged is not easy. There is obviously no special method guaranteed to succeed, nor is there any special kind of "effective" teacher.[8] We might, of course, postulate that it takes greater competence to teach the disadvantaged than it does to teach children who are eager and ready to learn; that it takes greater dedication and internal fortitude to put up with limited progress and maximum frustration. With respect to actual teaching strategies, there is obviously merit in correcting learning deficiencies as a prerequisite to teaching further academic content, in increasing experiential background wherever necessary, in providing frequent and clear-cut reinforcement, etc. It also seems that lower-class children can benefit from a certain degree of structure, presumably to compensate for their failure to develop structure in early childhood. A number of similar suggestions can be extracted from the previous discussion. Piaget would suggest, for example, that we provide lower-class children with a wide variety of experience with objects as the basis for developing clear and stable concepts. Nevertheless, very few rules can be given. Teaching is never a matter of prescription; teaching the disadvantaged is no exception.

We must remember that, despite group generalizations, we are still dealing with individual children and that we must avoid at all cost the tendency to use group labels as the basis for applying across-the board procedures. The fact is that not all lower-class children are lacking in verbal facility; certainly not all of them have a low IQ; certainly not all are, or need be, academically inadequate. We must especially avoid "writing them off."

7. Differentiation of the curriculum to meet the needs of the disadvantaged could mean that a rigorous curriculum becomes the prerogative of the select class, with the school then an agent in social stratification. Whereas adaptation of instruction and course content may be necessary to make education meaningful, we need to be careful that it does not become self-defeating.

8. See E. Gordon et al. (1970) for a thorough discussion of the problems and issues involved.

Compensatory Preschool Education

The past decade saw a massive movement into preschool education designed to overcome the educational disadvantages of lower-class children. As we noted in chapter 5, rejecting their previously unquestioned belief in maturation as the almost exclusive determinant of readiness for school, educators assumed an equally strong environmental position. Operating from the theoretical premise that if cognitive development is the consequence of the cumulative effects of learning as suggested by contemporary learning theorists (e.g., Gagné; see chapter 3 and 12), they argued that the reverse phenomenon of the cumulative learning deficit was simply the consequence of inadequacies in previous learning (see Hunt 1961; Chauncey 1963; Baer 1970).

Extrapolating from a variety of evidence, e.g., the irretrievable stupidity in experimental puppies resulting from early sensory deprivation (see the McGill studies in chapter 5), educators postulated that intellectual and academic deficiencies typically found in ghetto children from first grade on could be prevented by striking at the source, namely, providing such children with the cognitive nourishment presumably lacking in their home. Hunt, for example, talked of raising the intellectual level of the culturally disadvantaged by some thirty IQ points. Chauncey referred to the feasibility of having children achieve a substantially faster rate of intellectual development and a substantially higher adult level of intellectual capacity. The general premise was that the mental processes established very early in life would become a permanent part of the individual's cognitive assets, exerting lifelong effects on mental and educational development.

Ill effects of early sensory deprivation

The ill effects of early sensory deprivation and the corresponding beneficial effects of experiential enrichment have been rather well documented at the animal level (see chapter 5). Support at the human level comes from the dire effects attributed to the sensory deprivation of institutionalized children (see Casler 1961) and the intellectual gains in orphanage children reported in the Iowa studies (e.g., Skeels 1940, 1965). This point of view was further enhanced by the success of New York City's Guidance Demonstration Project (Shaw 1963) and, to a lesser degree, its successor, Higher Horizons (Landers 1963), reinforced by the conviction that whatever shortcomings these programs might have had would have been remedied had the children started earlier. The premise was that the ill effects of experiential deprivation can be reversed by a program begun before irretrievable damage is done. The basic theme was presumably to fill in the gaps in the background of deprived children, as well as to accelerate their intellectual growth so as to enable them to enter first grade on a par with their middle-class peers and thus reverse the pattern of systematic failure so typical of the culturally deprived in our schools. A long-range goal was to break the poverty cycle that has characterized a substantial segment of American society over the years.

Following through on these premises, the federal government sponsored as part of its war on poverty a variety of early childhood compensatory programs, of which Head Start is the best known.[9] These programs are operated through various community agencies and provide health care and social service, as well as preschool activities. Educationally, they vary widely in emphasis, scope, and quality. On the assumption that language deficiencies are among the most obvious difficulties of lower-class children, some programs have emphasized language development. Others have focused on conceptual behavior or on auditory and visual discrimination, and many have concentrated on all of these at once. A few have concentrated on the development of academic skills such as reading and arithmetic.

Limited outcomes of Head Start

The results of Head Start in overcoming the academic deficiencies of the culturally disadvantaged have, by and large, been disappointing. It seems that children served by Head Start have performed better than they probably would have without the program, but the general consensus is that, as far as they can be measured, the gains (see Hunt 1969) are not particularly encouraging.[10] Typically the program has shown short-term gains, e.g., at the end of the Head Start year, but (until recently at least) the general consensus was that these gains did not seem to carry into the primary school.[11] As summarized by Bane and Jencks (1972), for example, the character of the school's output depends largely on a single input, namely the characteristics of the entering children: "Everything else—school budget, its policies, the characteristics of the teachers—is either secondary or completely irrelevant, at least so long as the variation among schools is as narrow as it seems to be in America" (p. 41).

There are more positive reports, however. In contradiction to the negative assessments based on early studies, a more recent NIE study (*Phi Delta Kappan* 1977) suggests a sleeper effect. It appears that Head Start did indeed have a beneficial long-range effect on the IQ, the vocabulary, and the various academic skills of the participating disadvantaged children. Good et al. (1975) argue that children in well-developed and well-implemented preschool programs—i.e., programs featuring a low children-to-teacher ratio, parent involvement, and a structured curriculum with preselected objectives, etc.—do achieve significant gains, and further that these gains are retained over the

9. A somewhat parallel program, Upward Bound, is concerned with preparing disadvantaged high school students for college attendance (see Butler 1968).

10. Unfortunately, most programs were not designed with rigorous evaluation in mind and, with the wide differences as to objectives, content, procedures, and quality, it is difficult to draw compelling conclusions as to the true effectiveness of preschool compensatory education. See Bouchard and Mackler (1967); Brittain (1966); and McDaniels (1975). Head Start has been highly successful in some of its other aspects, e.g., it has provided medical treatment for eye defects, bone and joint disorders, dental problems, and given thousands of shots for polio, measles, etc.

11. A feeling that the failure of Head Start to be reflected in continued superior performance in first grade was due to the lack of articulation between Head Start and the more formal first-grade operation led to the inauguration of Project Follow-Through. Its results have also been limited.

years. Zigler (1978), who has been closely connected with Head Start since its inception, likewise argues that whereas no single study gives unequivocal evidence of success, the overall picture "allows but one conclusion: there are long-lasting positive effects from early intervention programs."

Reorienting compensatory education

The limited productivity of some of the programs can probably be attributed in part to local inadequacies. Many were hastily conceived, many were staffed by personnel relatively inexperienced and untrained in either early childhood or pedagogical strategies, and operated on inadequate funding. Some operated for too brief a period of time. Some of the weaknesses of compensatory education may reside in the inadequate training of teachers in meeting individual and subcultural needs.

Some of the issues, however, are more fundamental. If such a program is to be effective, it must be coordinated with what we know about child development. It is essential, for example, to synchronize the efforts of the preschool program with Piaget's concepts. In a scholarly discussion of the implications of cognitive-developmental theory for preschool education, Kohlberg (1968) argues that the practice of starting the child's formal instruction around the age of seven can be justified on the basis of the shift in cognitive functioning occurring during that period; this is the age at which the child attains concrete operations necessary for much of the elementary school curriculum. Kohlberg points out that these realities are especially limiting for the early education of disadvantaged children.

Synchronizing with Piaget's thinking

The problem is that the types of specific learnings the preschool is able to promote are not those likely to have any long-range developmental effect. We can teach children to discriminate between animals or to count, but all evidence points to the relative difficulty of accelerating the shift in cognitive structure necessary to grasp the concept of conservation, for example. Yet it is conservation that will act as a foundation for later cognitive growth, as well as for arithmetical and classificatory operations. The learnings on which preschool training can be successful are those that require very little structural change but also those that are not likely to have long-range beneficial effects. Other learnings, on the other hand, are not easily amenable to experiential input unless the necessary cognitive structure is also available. Piaget supporters would be skeptical, for example, of any attempt at teaching arithmetic before the age of concrete operations. The rote knowledge of addition and subtraction can be obtained but not the genuine capacity to order quantitative relationships. Children can memorize the names of the numbers, but this is not going to help them very much in understanding the equality or inequality of sets.

No easy solution

It now seems clear that the effects of the interaction of preschool intervention—in all of its complexity as to source, kind, organization, intensity, and timing—on the equally complex phenomenon of cultural deprivation cannot be expected to provide instant solutions. We need to recognize the futility of gimmicks geared to the unrealistic expectation that significant and lasting gains in the cognitive and academic functioning of lower-class children can be achieved through short-term intervention. Perhaps what is needed is for teachers to try a little harder in helping these children gain a feeling of achievement through utilizing in the pursuit of meaningful academic goals the talents that are obviously there to be used. Implied is the need to provide diagnostic, remedial, and developmental services as required and to promote a feeling of belonging, self-esteem, and a positive self-concept in which academic competence plays a significant role.

Sesame Street

An example of an undeniably successful preschool program is "Sesame Street," a televised program for preschool children sponsored by Children's Television Workshop under various grants from Carnegie, Ford, and the U.S. Office of Education. The program has received overwhelming endorsement from both the general public and the more formal study conducted by Educational Testing Service (1971), which found, for example, that children profited more or less in proportion to the amount of their viewing.[12] It is interesting to note that the sponsors relied on the judgment of the producers of the previous program, "Captain Kangaroo," but by and large avoided all conventional classroom techniques and even ignored what previously had been successful in the television teaching of children. It may be said to be an example of an innovative and and imaginative approach to the problem of providing stimulation for preschool children.

AGE DIFFERENCES

Physical height curves extending from birth to maturity follow the expected pattern of progressive (although not smooth) growth, with gradual tapering off in the late teens. Weight curves reach their peak later. The decline with age in physical competence varies from function to function. Agility and fine muscular precision tend to decline sooner than gross muscular strength, for example. There is, of course, a decline in sensory acuity, e.g., vision or hearing. Research suggests that only a minor decline in mental functioning occurs until middle age and further that much of the later decline stems from an increase with age in personal rigidity and a decrease in motivation. Research has also shown that intellectual ability declines differentially from one mental function to another. In areas where knowledge and judgment play an important role, the greater

12. The program is being expanded: it is now bilingual to serve Spanish-American children, and a companion program, "The Electric Company," is now shown for the benefit of the somewhat older elementary school child (MacGregor 1971). There is also a new Latin American version (*"Plaza Sesame"*) being shown in Latin American countries.

experiential background of older subjects more than compensates for the loss, if any, in mental ability. Learning ability in certain areas remains good until late in life, but it falls off rather sharply when the material to be learned conflicts with old habits or evokes motivational resistance.

INTELLECTUAL AND ACADEMIC DIFFERENCES

Student differences in intellectual and academic potential are well known to teachers; indeed each child is unique in the totality of his or her personality, and no two children, even with the same IQ, are intellectual equals, for the child is more than the summation of his or her characteristics. Thus, when for the sake of discussion reference is made to gifted children, no implication is made beyond their relative similarity with respect to intellectual ability, for even among the gifted tremendous differences exist.

To appreciate the range of individual differences among children in the classroom, we might consider the implications of the range of IQ. If, for instance, we consider sixth-grade children (CA = 12) and, for the sake of simplicity, ignore the top 2 percent and the bottom 2 percent of the distribution, we find the MA of the remainder to range from 8 to 16 (see figure 7.1). Thus, there are children in the typical sixth-grade class who intellectually are capable of working at the tenth-grade level while others are fully challenged by second-grade work.

There is considerable overlapping from grade to grade. IQ data suggest that one-sixth of the sixth graders are above the median for grade eight in ability and, conversely, one-sixth of the eighth graders are below the median for grade six (figure 7.2). There is a one-third overlapping between consecutive

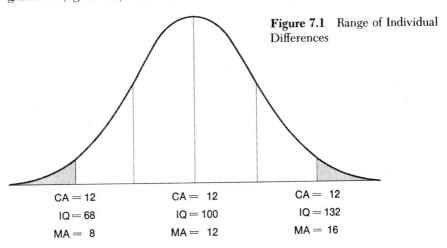

Figure 7.1 Range of Individual Differences

CA = 12	CA = 12	CA = 12
IQ = 68	IQ = 100	IQ = 132
MA = 8	MA = 12	MA = 16

Figure 7.2 Degree of Overlapping in Ability between Grades Six and Eight.

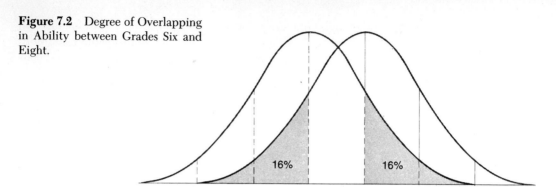

grades. The upper 10 percent of high school seniors are more competent than the median college senior and, conversely, the lower 10 percent of college seniors fall below the median of high school seniors. In Project Talent, 20 percent of the ninth graders surpassed the twelfth-grade average (Flanagan 1964; see also Learned and Wood 1938).

PERCEPTUAL STYLE

Considerable attention has been given in recent years to the matter of style—style of learning, cognitive style, perceptual style, etc. These are too complex for treatment here; the present discussion is simply for purposes of orientation.[13] Witkin (1962, 1977), for example, distinguishes between field dependence and field independence. Field-dependent people rely on environmental support; they are strongly influenced by the situation in which they find themselves. Field-independent persons, on the other hand, are less environment bound. Klein (1951) proposes a *leveling-sharpening* continuum. The levelers characteristically hold tight to the categories of perception and judgment; they tend not to change their mental set even when confronted with new evidence or changing conditions. Sharpeners, by contrast, are alert to change and more able to spot shades of difference. Kagan (1964) distinguishes between *impulsivity* and *reflectivity*, i.e., the degree to which the child reflects on the differential validity of alternative solutions in a situation where different responses are simultaneously possible. Ausubel (1968) talks of *satellizers* and *nonsatellizers:* because they are intrinsically valued, satellizers acquire an indestructible feeling of self-esteem independent of what they accomplish. Nonsatellizing children, on the other hand, are either rejected by their parents or accepted only for what they contribute to the latter's egos. Because they do not have an intrinsic feeling of self-worth, they must forever prove themselves

13. See Messick et al. (1976) for a comprehensive treatment of the topic.

through their own accomplishments. Therefore they tend to be assertive and compulsive.

In general, these styles are fundamental, affecting the individual's perceptions of self and of others and his or her adjustment to various situations, etc. People who feel insecure, inadequate, and self-distrustful, e.g., the levelers and the field dependent, tend to have a perceptual style that is rigid, field bound, and restricted. By contrast, the sharpener or the field independent, by virtue of being more secure and self-confident, is better able to perceive and to think across a broad range of ideas and circumstances. These perceptual frames of reference appear related to early child-rearing practices. Field-dependent children, for example, tend to have mothers who are restrictive, dominative, and inclined to encourage conformity; the mothers of field-independent children, by contrast, tend to encourage individuality, responsibility, exploratory behavior, and independence.

DEALING WITH ACADEMIC DIFFERENCES

Individual differences are all around us, differences between boys and girls, differences between old and young, dull and bright, advantaged and disadvantaged—etc. We find substantial differences among homes with respect to almost any variable. Classrooms also vary in effectiveness, although the specific characteristics that produce results are somewhat elusive. It seems that the important thing is not so much the differences along any one continuum but rather the way the various traits and characteristics are put together.

The important point is that individual differences *between* groups (whether with reference to age, sex, race, or socioeconomic status), while consistent from study to study, are typically quite small by comparison to the wide variability within groups. In Project Talent, for example, high school boys showed greater knowledge of mathematics, science, aeronautics, space, electronics, mechanics, and sports; they outperformed the girls in mechanical reasoning and abstract reasoning, but there was considerable overlap, and the actual differences in test scores between boys and girls were of little practical value. Fairweather (1976), for example, notes that convincing sex differences in the various aspects of cognitive functioning are rare; Macauley (1978) even questions what he calls the myth of female superiority in language, for example.

Between-group differences typically small

Psychology as a science is concerned with the derivation of general laws expressing functional relationships pertaining to the species, but these general laws have only indirect bearing on the individual, who is and must remain unique. And, whereas human uniqueness makes sense only in the context of the regularities that pertain to the subset so that a true understanding of people must involve an understanding of both general laws and uniqueness, yet it is especially important not to be carried away with the quantitative differences as might be reflected in group norms to the point of overlooking qualitative differences. The school needs to be concerned with the characteristics peculiar to each child that distinguish him or her from every other child and to resist all attempts to see children as a series of scores on various continua defined in terms of group norms.

Individual differences pose a difficult problem

Our schools are not well designed to deal with individual differences; children start first grade at the same age, move one grade per year, use the same textbooks, follow the same curriculum, do the same assignments, and face the same standards—all much after the pattern of the industrial assembly line. Our whole operation to date seems to have been geared to a policy of minimizing rather than capitalizing on individual differences. And, to a point, this is understandable in the light of the school's goal of teaching a standard curriculum to a widely different clientele with the objective of having everyone pass standardized examinations. Teachers, forgetting the importance of individual differences to the welfare of society, are frequently as intolerant of those who run ahead as they are of those who lag behind. It is not easy to adjust to the pace of each and every child, and it might be nice (perhaps) if everyone were exactly alike and equally capable of profiting from a standard program, just as it would be nice if everyone wore the same size shoes. But things being what they are, procrustean education is no more comfortable than procrustean shoes would be.

Despite all that is known about individual differences, many teachers still operate on the assumption that grade levels mean definite stages of educational achievement and that all children can do the work "if they will only apply themselves," or that, with large classes, there is nothing teachers can do about children who "can't" or "won't" learn. Both views are bad; the more or less inevitable outcome is that students become frustrated and apathetic, misbehave in the classroom, and even drop out of school. Wolfe (1960) suggests that our sabre-tooth curriculum approach "where all the animals have to take all the subjects" may result in homogeneous mediocrity. Certainly the same education for all is very likely to be an education for no one.

Fortunately changes are taking place as pressure is being applied for the school to capitalize on the assets and the potentialities of each child. We are moving toward greater differentiation through team teaching, flexible grouping, multiage grouping, independent study, resource centers, the open classroom, and, of course, the more elaborate packaged programs (see chapter 9), none of which can be considered a panacea, but nevertheless, on balance, perhaps a step in the right direction.

Promotional Policies

Probably the oldest of the more common schemes for dealing with individual differences within the framework of the traditional school organization involves what might be called strict standards of grade placement. Children are

Grade retention of
limited value

retained in a given grade until they have mastered its content and, conversely, can get a double promotion if they have already mastered enough of the content of the next grade. Acceleration was particularly common in the old one-room school where a gifted child could go through the first eight grades in four or five years. It has been frowned upon in recent years on the argument that it overemphasizes the intellectual and the academic at the expense of the other phases of the child's overall development and that the accelerated child may become a misfit from the standpoint of physical, social, and emotional adjustment.

At the other end of the continuum are those whose work is below par and who, according to the older view on the subject, needed to be retained lest they got hopelessly bogged down and interfered with the progress of students in the next grade. Unfortunately the problem is not that simple. Research evidence dating back over half a century, although far from unequivocal, suggests that grade retention is of limited effectiveness, that it is not a good motivational device, that it does not reduce the range of individual differences in the classroom appreciably, if at all, and that it does not serve to maintain academic standards except as it causes students to drop out (see Mouly 1973; G. Jackson 1975). Despite its current revival as incorporated in the more rigorous monitoring of student proficiency as a prerequisite to high school graduation, probably it should not be seen as any more of a panacea now than it was when it was used extensively years ago.[14] We especially need to remember that, no matter how routinely administrative it may be to the teacher, nonpromotion can be highly devastating to the child, who is gambling pretty heavily against strong odds for social acceptance, personal adjustment, attitudes toward peers, teachers, the school, etc. Grade retention may well result in serious lifelong damage to a child's self-concept.

It does not follow that children should never be retained. A child who is retarded physically, socially, and emotionally and/or mentally and academically may well profit from being put into a somewhat younger age group; each case must be evaluated on its own merits. The decision to promote or to retain should be made only after consideration of all the factors—not just the academic—and generally the teacher should have to show cause why the child should be retained in terms of how he can be helped more through retention than through promotion. The important question is not whether to promote or to retain but what the teacher does after having made this decision, for the element of failure is not eliminated by universal promotion, as attested to by the relatively large number of high school seniors who cannot meet proficiency requirements for graduation.

Optimal grade
placement

Retention should be thought of as a matter of optimal grade placement for maximum growth. The child's instructional needs should take precedence over the teacher's convenience and, if through special help and remedial pro-

---

14. Some proponents of proficiency testing argue that it might eliminate, or at least reduce, the goof-off atmosphere prevalent among some children (and teachers).

cedures the child can be kept with the regular group without taking too much of the teacher's time and energy away from the other children, he or she should be promoted. However, regardless of what decision is reached, it is especially important that definite plans be made to break the pattern of unsatisfactory performance by instituting a program of remediation where indicated, a change of instructional strategies for those whose learning style does not fit the current mold, and a change in curriculum where the current offerings appear unsuitable. Ideally such measures should be instituted before the question of retention becomes an issue.

Instructional Procedures

Restricted objectives

Teachers are in the difficult position of having to get children of widely different ability and background up to grade standards by the end of the year. In other words, they have to extract similar end-of-year performance out of children who are far from being similar. And they manage to do just that through the simple expedient of limiting their objectives. Thus, in spelling, the teacher announces that all the words children need to know for the examination are those on certain lists; in history, the material to be mastered to pass the course is found in certain clearly defined chapters of the prescribed text, etc. Thus, whether it is the one hundred addition facts or the work of grade nine algebra, it makes no difference if the bright child knows it all before he enrolls: he or she can sit and be bored while the teacher prods and pushes the dull past the finish line by the end of the year. For the same reason, teachers emphasize facts and other aspects of the course that can be memorized, since this is an area in which the dull can achieve relatively well if they try hard enough—at least, relatively better than they can in the area of reasoning, dealing with applications and implications, and the other significant aspects of education. Thus, at the end of the year, the class tends to put on a seemingly homogeneous performance.

Putting a ceiling on what students are to cover is one of the surest ways of gearing the educational enterprise to a policy of ineffectiveness. Combined with a strong emphasis on rote learning of facts and details to be covered in the examination, it generally ensures that everyone will achieve the required uniform mediocrity. When the goals are unlimited and related to the higher mental processes, instruction will increase, not reduce, individual differences. To the extent that education should permit everyone to benefit in accordance with one's ability, status after training must diverge in somewhat the same way as differences in mental age between the bright and the dull increase; and the greater the quantity and the quality of instruction, the further apart in achievement students of different ability will be. This is precisely what happens when the goals of education are defined in terms of getting meaning out of a paragraph, solving a problem in mathematics, organizing ideas, using effective English, and other significant educational objectives. Unfortunately these are the things our schools frequently neglect.

Ability Grouping

A solution to the diversity of ability in the classroom that finds some support is *ability grouping*. This approach is not new; it is essentially what schools did years ago when they made promotion conditional upon academic competence. They simply forced those of lesser ability to drop out, which saved the inconvenience of providing separate classes. In a sense, because of the wider range of ability among students enrolled in school today, ability grouping as a means of saving the dull from frustration and the bright from boredom may be more necessary than ever.

Differences within individuals

Before we consider the relative merits of ability grouping, it is necessary to understand that, in addition to the differences that exist from person to person in a given ability (*interindividual* differences or simply *individual differences*), there are differences among the various abilities within a given individual. Further the evidence is that these *intraindividual* differences (i.e., *trait variability*) can be large, particularly in high school and college, for there are indications that trait variability increases with age, presumably as an aspect of the differentiation resulting from the interaction of maturational forces, increased experiences, and diverging interests. As a consequence, it is generally agreed that grouping on the basis of general ability (e.g., IQ), particularly in high school, will not result in appreciable reduction in the variability normally found in any specific subject area when students are simply assigned to groups at random.

Ability grouping may help, but it's no panacea

In summary, ability grouping on the basis of general IQ in grade school and on the basis of relevant abilities in high school can reduce somewhat the range of individual differences within a given class and some school systems are successfully grouping their students. On the other hand, it is not a cure-all. A serious danger in grouping is the very real possibility of a self-fulfilling prophecy in that teachers of the lower-ability groups, expecting less from their students, teach them accordingly. It is also possible that the lower-ability group becomes a dumping gound for students who for a variety of reasons perform poorly in the classroom.[15] This can be highly demoralizing to the teacher who would like to see some progress; after a while, a sense of futility often engulfs the whole operation. Teachers of the gifted, on the other hand, may be tempted to apply unhealthy pressures across the board, to the detriment of some of the students. In their thorough review of the literature, Findley and Bryan (1971), for example, conclude that, whereas ability grouping as currently practiced has mixed effects on the scholastic achievement of superior groups, it almost invariably results in lowered achievement in average and low-ability groups.

The ideal is to place each child in the educational setting that gives him or her the best opportunity to achieve optimal well-rounded growth, but one

---

15. The issue has taken on a new dimension inasmuch as ability grouping often involves illegal de facto segregation of the races. Ability grouping also runs counter to the current trend toward the mainstreaming of exceptional children.

must not assume that ability grouping is the only way of dealing with children at their level. The important thing is that something be done. Teachers who complain that they do not have time to individualize the work of the classroom need to realize that they had better find time before minor troubles become real difficulties; after all, the number of children requiring extended special attention is generally relatively small. A competent teacher can make provisions for differences among individual pupils, whether the class is grouped or not; it is not uncommon to have students in the primary grades, for instance, sectioned into two or three ability levels for a particular activity and reshuffled among the groups for a different activity.

Ability grouping is not an end in itself; it is only a means that, some schools find, facilitates the teacher's task of dealing with children of widely different ability. Wrightstone (1968) for example, suggests that ability grouping is neither a cure nor a calamity. Its value appears to depend on the teacher who uses it. When ability grouping is used, the term *ability* should be interpreted in the broad sense to include such factors as relevant cognitive structure, IQ, special aptitudes, special talents, past scholarship, motivation, social competence, and general maturity. Admission to the various classes should involve an evaluation of each case on its own merits. Even more important, however, all such allocations should be considered tentative and reversible. It should also be emphasized that ability grouping implies a differentiated curriculum fitted to the abilities and needs of the group and of the individual students within the group; presenting the same material at a slower or faster pace just will not work.

GIFTED CHILDREN

Gifted children have always been a problem to the school as they alternately become our most valuable natural resource and forgotten students. Because they are able to take care of themselves academically, they get less attention from the teacher, and because they can get by without effort, they are not encouraged to develop their talents. Hollingsworth (1926) estimated that children with IQ of 140 or above waste half their time in the usual classroom, and those with IQs of 170 or better waste practically all of their time. Terman and Oden (1947) noted that more than half of the children with IQs of 135 or above had already mastered the school's curriculum to a point two full grades—and some, three or four grades—beyond the one in which they were enrolled.

Generally the teacher in the regular classroom cannot take care of the gifted along with the average and the dull. As a result, the gifted are simply neglected. Often their intelligence is not even recognized, partly because many conceal their true ability so as not to appear different. Instead of being encouraged to make a contribution in keeping with their superior ability, they

are often forced into habits of indifference, carelessness, and indolence by
being made to adjust to the pace of the class.

Some common
solutions

Suggestions for dealing with the gifted child generally fall along one of
three lines: acceleration, enrichment, and grouping. All three have merits and
limitations, and the most desirable strategy to follow depends on the particular
situation. Intellectual superiority is a matter of degree, and it is impossible to
devise a standard program that will take care of the needs of the gifted, for,
just like their more average counterparts, gifted children display individual
differences in all areas, including the intellectual.

Acceleration has definite possibilities. In fact, it would seem that a flexible view of acceleration across the board—early admission to first grade, acceleration through the grades, early admission to college, advanced credit by examination, and overload in college—is indicated. Not only can such
acceleration save educational costs but, where warranted and wisely handled,
it can do so without harm and with considerable benefit. It can, for example,
add two or more years to the period of professional productivity.[16]

Enrichment essential

Enrichment or adaptation of the material to the child's level of ability is a
must, regardless of what else is done, for the highly gifted child cannot be accelerated enough without danger of social and emotional harm. Enrichment
can take place in special classes or in a regular classroom where the child is
encouraged to pursue the subject beyond the regular requirements. Unfortunately although ideal in theory, enrichment as the sole means of dealing with

16. Acceleration of the gifted has been recommended by Terman (1954) and more recently by Stanley (1979). See also Passow (1979).

the gifted is too frequently simply an empty promise. Typically, the gifted child ends up doing the same work as the other children—in fact, often more of the same when he or she should be doing less—and the teacher is often too busy with the rest of the class to provide special attention. Some schools allow gifted children to use the study period to work on special projects, but they are entitled to more positive direction from the teacher if they are to make the most of their abilities. Excusing them from routine work and allowing them to take an extra subject is generally to be recommended whenever feasible.

Enrichment is difficult to implement. One possibility (*horizontal* enrichment) is to have the child learn a second language, read the biographies of the great figures of history, or generally learn things outside the regular curriculum. The more common *vertical* enrichment is simply to have the gifted child do assignments normally encountered in the next grade—which then means that the next teacher, often with the same frustration, has to have the child work on materials of the next higher grade (see Herndon 1971).[17] In summary, excusing gifted children from regular work and allowing them to take an extra subject is generally recommended, but probably the best approach combines acceleration, enrichment, and segregation. Most school systems of any size ought to be able to work out some arrangement along these lines.

THE ROLE OF THE TEACHER

Regimentation in the classroom

None of the proposals we have discussed can by itself take care of individual differences. Any administrative plan can only facilitate the work of the classroom teacher, it cannot solve the problem for, in any grade—with liberal or strict promotion, with or without ability grouping—there will always be differences and, even if pupils were to be equated today, by tomorrow some would already have separated themselves from the rest. Unfortunately a number of forces tend to operate to regiment education to the mass-production philosophy of the industrial assembly line where the goal is to have the product emerge capable of meeting the specifications of quality control. These forces range from lockstep grade placement and schoolwide standardized testing beginning in the primary division to standardized curricula punctuated by periodic examinations on prescribed content and complete with prescribed Carnegie-unit patterns and College Boards. Our schools overemphasize conformity. Too frequently the marks of the good student are not resourcefulness, spontaneity, and intellectual curiosity but rather promptness, obedience, dependability, social sensitivity, and orientation toward *the* correct answer.

17. The occasional double promotion, where indicated, might help restore some semblance of common sense to the situation. Some systems have special schools that the gifted attend one or two half-days a week.

In the final analysis it is the teacher who is the key to any plan for dealing with individual differences in the classroom, for it is he or she who has contact with the "customer." We need teachers who are not only familiar with the principles of individual differences and their implications for educational practice but who are also sensitive to individual needs and are sufficiently dedicated to want to adjust requirements and standards to the level of the child. They also have to be ingenious in vitalizing the curriculum and competent in the use of effective teaching techniques.

HIGHLIGHTS OF THE CHAPTER

An understanding and appreciation of the differences among and within individuals are fundamental to implementing the American ideal of providing each child with educative experiences geared to his or her potentialities, interests, and experiential background. The following are among the major points to be considered:

1. Wide differences exist from group to group with respect to almost any trait. On the other hand, to the extent that within-group differences are invariably greater (and of greater significance) than between-group differences, we must avoid gearing classroom operations to stereotypes based on group labels.

2. Substantial sex (or perhaps more correctly, gender) differences have been noted with respect to physiological development, personality, ability patterns, school performance, etc.

3. Even more drastic, particularly as they relate to the work of the classroom, is the wide range of individual differences among socioeconomic classes. To date, attempts to overcome cultural deficits through compensatory education have met with only limited success.

4. Our schools are not too adept at dealing with individual differences. Procrustean practices ranging from uniformity in age at entrance to standardization of curriculum and of textbooks to single standards of evaluation are unfortunately too much part of the present pattern of classroom operation.

5. A number of schemes have been advocated for dealing with individual differences. When used in high school and college, ability grouping should be based on special aptitude as well as past scholarship, general maturity, motivation, social competence, and other aspects of readiness peculiar to the individual case.

6. It is difficult to deal effectively with the gifted within the framework of the regular classroom. Enrichment is essential, regardless of what else is done.

7. None of these schemes is, in itself, an adequate solution to the problem. At best, they can only facilitate the work of the teacher who must necessarily bear primary responsibility for adapting classroom experiences to fit the individual child.

SUGGESTIONS FOR FURTHER READING

BASSETT, G. W., et al. *Individual Differences: Guidelines for Educational Practice.* Sydney: Allen and Unwin, 1978. Thorough and comprehensive evaluation of education in Australia. Much of the evidence cited comes from the United States.

BOUCHARD, RUTH K., and BERNARD MACKLER. *Prekindergarten Programs for Four-Year-Olds: With a Review of the Literature on Preschool Education.* New York: Center for Urban Education, 1967. Reviews the literature on compensatory preschool education and describes some early programs.

BROUDY, HARRY S., et al. *Democracy and Excellence in American Secondary Education.* Chicago: Rand McNally, 1964. Reassesses some of the demands currently made on the secondary school and their implications for instruction.

BUTLER, ANNIE L. From Head Start to Follow Through. *Bull. Sch. Educ., Indiana Univ.* 44 (1968):5–47. Reviews the evidence to 1968 of the effectiveness of Head Start and Follow Through compensatory programs.

COLEMAN, JAMES S., et al. *Equality of Educational Opportunity.* Washington, D.C.: HEW, 1966. The famous report on the education of the culturally disadvantaged. This massive study has been subjected to a number of reanalyses and growing criticism of its findings and conclusions.

DUNN, RITA, and KENNETH DUNN. Learning styles, teaching styles. *N.A.S.S.P. Bull.* 59 (Oct. 1975):37–49. A brief overview of the complexities of teaching occasioned by differences in teaching style as they interact with differences in learning styles.

GARAI, JOSEF, and A. SCHEINFELD. Sex differences in mental and behavioral traits. *Genet. Psychol. Monogr.* 77 (1968):169–229. One of the most comprehensive discussions of all aspects of sex differences. An excellent reference.

GARDNER, JOHN W. *Excellence: Can We Be Equal and Excellent Too?* New York: Harper & Row, 1961. The former secretary of the Department of Health, Education and Welfare (now director of Common Cause) discusses three competing forces in American culture: inherited status, egalitarianism, and meritocracy.

HESS, ROBERT D. Social class and ethnic influences upon socialization. In Paul H. Mussen, ed., *Carmichael's Manual of Child Psychology,* 2:457–557. New York: Wiley, 1970. An excellent and thorough treatment of the topic. A good reference.

KOHLBERG, LAWRENCE. Early education: A cognitive-developmental view. *Child Devel.* 39 (1968):1013–1062. A scholarly review of early compensatory education from the standpoint of Piaget's theory. The skills that compensatory education can promote are not those that accelerate the child's development on the Piaget development sequence.

UNGER, RHODA K. *Female and Male: Psychological Perspectives.* New York: Harper & Row, 1979. A comprehensive, up-to-date treatment of all aspects of sex (gender) differences.

QUESTIONS AND PROJECTS

1. Of what value to the school is the evidence of age, sex, or socioeconomic differences?

2. What might be some of the sociological and pedagogical implications of Bernstein's theory of language development?

Relate Bernstein's basic premises to such concepts as induction in child rearing (chapter 15) and the rational-conscientious character pattern (chapter 14).

3. Make a thorough analysis of the various approaches to teaching the disadvantaged, e.g., Dennison's *First Street School,* Kozol's *Free School,* etc. Identify their mode of operation, their relative success, and the validity of their premises as seen from the standpoint of the principles of educational psychology.

4. Read some of the more interesting accounts of teaching the disadvantaged: Rebecca Segal, *Got No Time to Fool Around;* James Herndon, *How to Survive in Your Native Land* and *The Way It Spozed to Be;* Herbert Kohl, *36 Children;* Edward R. Braithwaite, *To Sir, with Love;* and Bel Kaufman, *Up the Down Staircase.*

5. Outline a meaningful program for the greater development of girls in our society. What is being done now?

6. Comment on the "incompatibility" of providing for individual differences and maintaining academic standards.

Can American public schools, as presently constituted, take care of individual differences? What changes, if any, would you suggest?

Interview parents who have transferred their children to a private school. What are the main reasons for the transfer?

7. How can colleges reconcile the concept of academic excellence with the current demand for open admission?

8. To what extent is it legitimate for the teacher to set aside the curriculum of the school in order to take care of individual differences?

What specific adaptation of the curriculum and of teaching strategies can be made for children of the lower classes while keeping within the framework of the curriculum?

SELF-TEST

1. Probably the widest differences among human beings are differences
   a. among the different aptitudes within any one individual.
   b. between men and women.
   c. connected with age.
   d. from one racial group to another.
   e. within the members of any one group.

2. Which of the following differences is *least?*
   a. Age differences in IQ
   b. Sex differences in IQ
   c. Sex differences in verbal fluency
   d. Socioeconomic differences in attitudes and values
   e. Socioeconomic differences in health and physical size

3. The current emphasis on Head Start is predicated on
   a. empirical evidence of effectiveness in promoting school adjustment.
   b. deductions from accepted theories of learning.
   c. evidence of success in promoting basic security and socialization among lower-class children.
   d. inference from related animal studies of the effects of early sensory deprivation.
   e. substantial empirical evidence of its effectiveness in relation to later academic success.

4. Nonpromotion is best justified as a means of
   a. helping the child catch up.
   b. maintaining standards.
   c. providing for optimal grade placement.
   d. reducing individual differences within a given grade.
   e. reducing unhealthy pressures on the child.

5. Probably the most justifiable means of dealing with individual differences in the classroom is
   a. acceleration or nonpromotion.
   b. ability grouping.
   c. modification of the curriculum.
   d. reduction of curricular requirements to minimal essentials.
   e. reliance on individualized instruction.

6. The key to effective dealing with individual differences in the classroom is
   a. an alert, sensitive, and competent teacher.
   b. a flexible system of ability grouping.
   c. freedom from administrative restrictions and constraints.
   d. a suitable curriculum.
   e. a workable, up-to-date pupil record system.

7. The most convincing argument against reliance on ability grouping as the "solution" to the individual differences problem is that
   a. it is in violation of the democratic framework within which the school exists.
   b. it promotes feelings of inferiority or superiority.
   c. it promotes social isolation along intellectual lines.
   d. the teacher still has to reckon with individual differences within an ability-grouped class.
   e. None of the above; there is no major objection to ability grouping.

PART THREE

The Teaching-Learning Process

Introduces the basic principles underlying the promotion of academic progress; reviews the traditional aspects of the psychology of learning but also emphasizes teaching and evaluation as equally critical components of the educational enterprise.

8 Nature and Conditions of Learning

Presents the various aspects of classroom learning, including the steps of the learning process, the laws of learning, the role of practice, etc.; also introduces Ausubel's assimilation theory of meaningful verbal learning.

9 Guiding the Learning Process

Clarifies basic issues regarding teaching as it relates to effective classroom learning and reviews different teaching strategies.

10 Classroom Management

Discusses the all-important topic of classroom management as an essential prerequisite to effective classroom learning. Builds on the basic concepts presented in chapter 4 to deal with the two components of constructive classroom behavior: motivation and discipline. The organization into two subchapters is necessitated by the fact that motivation and discipline are the two ends of the same continuum, thus precluding separate chapters; yet the amount of crucial material would make a single chapter excessively long.

11 Retention and Transfer of Training

Presents retention and transfer as interrelated phenomena, subject to essentially the same set of factors, and points out a number of educational implications, especially as they relate to meaningful verbal learnings.

12 Major Instructional Systems

Presents the major features of the better-known instructional systems: Ausubel, Bruner, the free school, the open school, the Montessori system, and Gagné. Because it exemplifies a wide range of psychological principles, the latter is covered in considerable detail.

13 Measuring Academic Achievement

Presents an overview of the basic principles of educational measurements as they relate to academic learning and notes the potential psychological hazards of current grading and reporting practices.

EIGHT

Nature and Conditions of Learning

Viewed in its broadest dimensions, learning is the search for meaning.

Henry C. Lindgren (1959)

Probably the most insidious and subtle barrier to formal learning today is the exposure to what is called the sensory overload—the impact of too many different messages and exposure to too much "Noise" beyond the individual's capacity to deal with either adequately.

Lawrence K. Frank (1963)

Most of today's textbooks are pleasant to look upon and easy to read. What they lack, it seems to me, is the rough texture of honesty—the kind of gritty detail that slows up the reading but speeds up the thinking. The slick, effortless prose flows on and on without a ripple, while the student, half-asleep, floats atop the glossy surface. The whole idea, it would seem to me, is not to rock the boat.

Richard J. Margolis (1965)

— Considers the nature of the learning process and some of the factors conducive to effective learning
— Presents the rudiments of Ausubel's assimilation theory of meaningful verbal learning
— Discusses the role of practice as a factor in classroom learning

PREVIEW: KEY CONCEPTS

1. Psychologists see learning as a change in behavior; beyond that there is considerable disagreement, particularly between association and field theorists.
2. The school needs to be concerned with the process as well as the products of learning.
3. Psychologists have identified a number of laws or principles governing the learning process. The Law of Effect (along with its counterpart, reinforcement) is probably the best known.
4. Symbols and concepts serve an essential function in the manipulation and communication of ideas.
5. Ausubel's emphasis on meaningful verbal learning is particularly relevant to the operation of the classroom.
6. Practice is an essential but not a sufficient condition for learning to take place.
7. Psychomotor skills provide good illustrations of the principles of learning.

PREVIEW QUESTIONS

1. What constitutes "learning" as a process? Where would the behaviorist and field theorists disagree on this point?
2. What are some of the major components of the learning act that most psychologists would accept?
3. What is the key determinant of effectiveness in meaningful verbal learning? How can we ensure adequacy of cognitive structure?
4. Why is practice often unproductive? What can be done about the problem?
5. To what extent do the principles of the psychology of learning apply to the learning of psychomotor skills?

Learning has always been of primary interest to teachers as part of their concern for having children master the academic curriculum of the school. It is of even greater concern to the modern teacher interested in the child's all-round growth, for the principles of learning apply just as surely to emotional or personal adjustment as to the multiplication tables. Learning is best conceived as the heart of the larger and more significant process of adjustment to environmental demands. The orientation of this chapter toward the learning of academic materials therefore constitutes an artificial segmentation of behavior justifiable only for purposes of discussion. If they are to fulfill their obligation of guiding pupil growth toward desirable goals, teachers must be familiar with the principles on the basis of which desirable behavioral changes can be achieved.

THE NATURE OF LEARNING

Although a number of theories have attempted to explain the nature of the learning process (see chapter 3), none can be accepted as the final word, and most psychologists subscribe to what might be called an eclectic point of view rather than exclusively to a particular position. In our present state of uncertainty, it is probably best to maintain an open mind and to use theories to the extent that they provide insights into the nature of learning as it applies to the classroom (see Hulse et al. 1975).

Nature of learning: A matter of disagreement

Actually almost all aspects of the nature of learning in its various manifestations are a matter of controversy. Nor is there any consensus as to their neurophysiological basis. Thorndike's original claim that the exercise of an *S-R* bond lowered the synaptic resistance to the passage of a neural impulse was abandoned when research (e.g., Franz and Lashley 1951) showed that learning is more than a simple telephonic-type connection between a given receptor and a given effector. As a consequence, modern psychologists, while recognizing that learning must indeed have a neurophysiological (or neurochemical) basis, have concentrated on a behavioral definition of learning, i.e., they have equated learning with *behavioral changes* resulting from experience.

The word *change* as used here warrants elaboration. Throughout life, the one inevitable thing is change. For purposes of definition, learning refers to those changes taking place as a result of special stimulation; it deliberately excludes the changes directly associated with the maturation of inherited structure and predispositions, as well as such changes in effectiveness of reaction as might be associated with fatigue or drugs. Learning can also be defined as "improvement" in behavior in the sense that the person becomes more proficient at whatever he is doing, i.e., his behavior becomes more efficient, more precise, more probable, and more direct with respect to the goal.

There is general agreement that learning refers to changes in performance arising from experience. Beyond this, the question is one of considerable disagreement, and (as might be surmised from chapter 3) certainly any attempt at definition would make some psychologists happier than others. The controversy is directly related to the basic differences in theoretical perspective between the association and cognitive theorists. The former emphasize the association between stimulus and response under conditions of reinforcement; the latter see learning as a reorganization of cognitive structure.[1] A major part of the problem stems from the fact that certain explanations fit certain learning situations better than others. Operant conditioning appears to fit particularly well the development of specific response patterns in animals (and people) along Skinnerian lines. It would seem less appropriate for the clarification of relationships, discriminations, and problem solving, where a cognitive interpretation would seem more convincing. As we shall see in chapter 12, Gagné (1977), for example, identifies five major categories of learning outcomes: verbal information, attitudes, psychomotor skills, intellectual skills, and cognitive strategies. He further distinguishes among various types of verbal learning tasks arranged in a hierarchy from simple S-R reactions to problem solving, each presumably constituting a different kind of learning and calling for somewhat different learning (and teaching) strategies.

Different kinds of learning

STEPS IN THE LEARNING PROCESS

A well-known formulation of the steps of the learning process, based on reinforcement premises,[2] is that of Dashiell (1949) showing the motivated organism encountering an obstacle that prevents the attainment of its goals and, as a consequence, making exploratory responses until some response gets around the obstacle and is reinforced (figure 8.1). A more detailed analysis of the reinforcement model of learning might include the following steps:

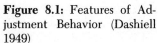

Figure 8.1: Features of Adjustment Behavior (Dashiell 1949)

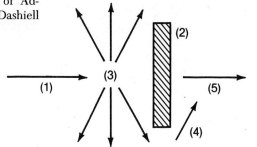

The motivated individual (1)
encounters an obstacle (2)
makes exploratory responses (3)
until some response (4)
gets around the obstacle
to the goal (5)

1. Most lists of the specific steps of the learning process have been devised from associationistic specifications; the more global cognitive viewpoint is not so easily identified by subcomponent.

2. Cognitive psychologists argue against the behaviorists' definition of learning as a change in *behavior*, which they see as simply the *external reflection* of the learning, i.e., of the changes that have taken place *in* the learner. They are less interested in the study of animal behavior and more concerned with explaining how meaningful learning takes place in humans, how different people learn, how they solve problems, how they process information, how they remember.

Motivation. Learning takes place as a result of response to internal or external stimulation. Most psychologists agree that motives play a part of various degrees of directness and cruciality in the organism's learning.

Goal. The motivated organism orients itself toward a goal that past experience leads it to believe, unconsciously perhaps, will be effective from the standpoint of its motives. Behavior does not just happen; it is caused by some need and is oriented toward some goal, i.e., it is purposive. Teachers spend much time and energy in setting up goals of various kinds toward which the children are to strive, but these will be effective only insofar as they become the children's goals. Otherwise the students' behavior will be directed toward goals of their own and toward circumventing those of the teacher.

Readiness. We must assume the organism is basically capable of satisfying its needs. Premature infants whose physiological development has not progressed to the point of their being able to take in food cannot learn to do so.

Obstacle. An obstacle arises between the motivated organism and its goal. If no barrier existed, the goal would be reached according to some previously learned behavior pattern, and the situation would involve no learning. Inability to reach its goal results in tension, which propels the organism toward its attainment. Such tension is beneficial in that it forces it to find a solution, i.e., *it forces it to learn.* The teacher's task is to put realistic obstacles in the path of the child's goals and encourage him or her, with guidance when necessary, to deal effectively with the situation. Changing the requirements of a geometry problem so that it can no longer be handled by the solution given in the text will provide the occasion for learning.

Response. The organism is led to action, the nature of which depends on its interpretation of the situation.

Reinforcement. A response that is successful in attaining the goal will tend to be repeated on subsequent occasions. An unsuccessful response, on the contrary, leads the organism to try other approaches until reinforcement is achieved.

Generalization. The last, and certainly a vital, step in the learning process is the integration of the successful responses with previous learnings so that it becomes part of a new functional whole.

In a more general sense, as seen by cognitive psychologists, for example, learning involves two complementary processes: *differentiation* and *integration,* i.e., a breakdown of the whole into its component parts and a recombining of the parts into a new whole. Differentiation may be considered as the process by which regions of the perceptual field are converted into more highly defined subareas. Integration, on the other hand, is a matter of the reorganization of the individual parts into a new, meaningful whole in which the components fall into place. Some degree of back-and-forth movement between differentiation and integration is involved in most, if not all, aspects of learning. Hence the changes taking place during learning are rarely sudden and complete; rather they are gradual developmental processes that may extend over a considerable period of time. It is also to be noted that the learner must do his or her own differentiating and integrating. Even though the teacher may point out various components and their relationship to each other and to the learner's previous experiences, it is the learner who, in the final analysis, must discover the parts and their interrelationships and fit the individual responses of a complex behavioral pattern into the system in which they belong.

SOME ASPECTS OF THE LEARNING PROCESS

Process versus Product

A distinction must be made between the *products* of learning and the *process* through which they are attained. Teachers are primarily involved in the process of learning, i.e., with implementing effective teaching-learning methods so that both the immediate and long-term goals of education will be attained with maximum efficiency. They need to be more concerned, for example, with helping children develop skills by means of which they can find their own answers rather than giving ready-made answers for them to memorize.

This does not imply that the school can ignore the products of learning, particularly those in the areas of motivation, attitude, and character development, as well as reasoning and problem solving, all of which are often neglected in our overemphasis on facts and skills. Nor is it implied that process and product are separate and independent. The school must be concerned with both; it must not let overconcern with passing examinations or meeting behavioral objectives (i.e., with limited products) divert its attention from the process through which a true education is achieved. The school especially must recognize that different educational products often call for different educational processes and, conversely, that different educational processes often yield different educational products, not all of which are necessarily desirable.

Collateral learnings

Of special interest in the promotion of the child's all-round growth are what Dewey (1938) calls *collateral* learnings, i.e., learnings that invariably accompany, and often overshadow in importance, the primary learnings the teacher deliberately sets out to promote. Whereas the purpose of education is to enable students to deal more effectively with related situations in the future, this will not occur if, while learning arithmetic, for example, they develop a dislike of the subject and a negative self-concept, and generally become less rather than more capable of further growth. The teacher's methods, personality, and classroom atmosphere affect not only the effectiveness with which academic learnings take place but also determine whether the experience will be helpful or harmful from the standpoint of continued growth. Teachers must therefore take care that, in their concern over primary learnings, they do not lose sight of the by-products. Indeed in view of the importance of the latter and the fact that they inevitably occur, teachers must plan for the occurrence of positive learnings in these areas just as deliberately as they do for primary learnings.

Laws of Learning

Over the years, psychologists have derived a number of laws and principles to express empirical relationships between certain conditions and the effectiveness of the learning that results. Thus, Thorndike (1913), as a result of his experiments in animal learning, postulated such laws as the laws of *effect, exercise*, and others. Even though these laws no longer carry the prestige they held earlier in the century, we shall devote a few paragraphs to a brief consideration of their nature in relation to the basic concepts presented in chapter 3.

The Law of Effect

The *Law of Effect*, which states that, other things being equal, those responses followed by satisfying aftereffects tend to be learned, is the most important and the most widely accepted of Thorndike's laws. It is best seen in the context of the broader principle of reinforcement which, as we noted in chapter 3, is fundamental, particularly to association theories. Unless there is some awareness of the consequence of one's behavior—whether called *reinforcement, confirmation,* or *feedback*—it seems unlikely that any significant degree of purposeful learning would occur. Skinner, for example, argues that ineffectiveness in school is related in no small way to its failure to provide systematic reinforcement.[3]

The Law of Effect has been the subject of considerable controversy. At the empirical level, there can be little disagreement that the organism tends to orient itself in the direction of the responses that, on previous occasions, it has found effective in attaining its goals. The theoretical picture, on the other hand, is less clear; as we noted in chapter 4, "stimulation" theorists reject both the notion of reward as necessary for learning and drive reduction as the mechanism through which reinforcement operates. Regardless of its theoretical status, however, the Law of Effect and its underlying concept of motivation is of definite pedagogical value: learning effectiveness is in relative proportion to the extent to which children have identified meaningful goals and their responses are rewarded through the attainment of these goals. The teacher often assumes, for example, that children are committed to certain goals related to school work when, in reality, the goals as seen in the perspective of their overall motivational structure are such that their attainment (or unattainment) is of little concern to them.

3. This is less of a problem in meaningful material where students do not have to rely so exclusively on the teacher to tell them whether their performance is adequate or inadequate, especially when they have formulated clear-cut goals against which to gauge their performance.

The Law of Exercise

Thorndike's *Law of Exercise,* used years ago to justify drill in the classroom, has been more or less abandoned. The present consensus is that, although practice is necessary, it is not a sufficient condition for learning and that the Law of Exercise operates only indirectly through the fact that practice permits reinforcement of correct responses—or, in cognitive language, practice provides an opportunity for cognitive reorganization and the development of insight. In fact, the realization that, without meaning, all that goes on under the guise of education is to no avail has led to a major shift in educational practice from emphasis on drill and memory work to the current emphasis on understanding and meaningfulness. On the other hand, despite the greater recognition of meaningfulness as the cornerstone of education, there is still far too much emphasis in the average classroom on covering a curriculum of half-digested facts. The consequences have been pupil frustration and school inefficiency.

AUSUBEL'S ASSIMILATION THEORY OF MEANINGFUL VERBAL LEARNING

In a significant contribution to the literature on the acquisition, retention, and transfer of learning, Ausubel (1963, 1968; Ausubel et al. 1978) makes a critical distinction between *rote* and *meaningful* learning and points out that, to the extent that the psychology of learning to date has been primarily concerned with simple association learning, it has been essentially irrelevant to the meaningful learning with which the school is concerned. In contrast to learning, say, nonsense syllables, which can only be memorized, meaningful verbal learning takes place as potentially meaningful material is related to what the learner already knows. Conversely, verbal materials are potentially meaningful to the extent that they can be related to existing ideas in the learner's cognitive background or, in Ausubel's terminology, to the extent that they can be *subsumed* under existing cognitive structure. As a consequence, meaningful verbal learning takes place more rapidly and results in greater retention and transfer than a corresponding series of arbitrary associations learned by rote. On the other hand, it also calls for an entirely different set of explanatory principles.

Ausubel's subsumption

Ausubel makes *subsumption* the key underlying the process of the acquisition, organization, retention, and transfer of meaningful verbal materials. Meaningful verbal learning occurs as potentially meaningful material entering the cognitive field interacts with and is adequately subsumed under a relevant and more inclusive conceptual system already existing in cognitive structure. Material is potentially meaningful to the extent that it is subsumable; if it is not subsumable, it can only form arbitrary and isolated associations.

Meaningfulness: A
critical factor

The importance of meaningfulness to the operation of the school, and of civilized society, is obvious. The human brain is extremely limited in its ability to grasp and to retain arbitrary associations. It would seem, for example, that the typical adult can remember approximately seven random items of information presented sequentially (Miller 1956). Since rote materials can be related to cognitive structure only on an arbitrary basis, no direct use can be made of one's existing knowledge in internalizing them. By contrast, because potentially meaningful material can be related in a nonarbitrary fashion to relevant ideas already established in cognitive structure, learners can use their existing knowledge as the basis for assimilating large quantities of new materials and to expand the base of their learning matrix in the process. Furthermore, relating new materials to existing cognitive structure in terms of its general meaning rather than verbatim circumvents the critical verbatim-learning limitations of the human brain. Obviously learners can apprehend and retain more information if they are required only to assimilate the general substance of the passage rather than its exact words.

Meaningful learning must obviously begin with potentially meaningful material, i.e., material having a certain inherent logic. However, whether potentially meaningful material actually results in meaningful learning in the case of a particular learner depends critically on the adequacy of the relevant aspects of his or her cognitive structure. In other words, we must distinguish between *logical* meaning that resides in the material and *psychological* meaning, i.e., the idiosyncratic, personalized meaning the individual gets from the material as it is subsumed in his or her cognitive structure. Conversely, rote learning is inevitable if either the material lacks logical meaningfulness or the learner's cognitive structure is lacking in relevant subsumers.

Crucial role of
subsumers

To the extent that the important variable controlling the learning, as well as the retention and transferability, of potentially meaningful verbal material is the availability in cognitive structure of relevant subsuming concepts, the key to effective learning, retention, and transfer lies in making sure that adequate subsumers are indeed available. It follows that when relevant subsumers are unavailable (or inadequate from the standpoint of relevance, clarity, or stability), suitable organizers will have to be provided if effective learning is to take place. Specifically, Ausubel suggests introducing in advance of the material appropriately relevant general and inclusive *advance organizers*. These are presented at a higher level of generality and inclusiveness so as to provide ideational scaffolding for the acquisition and retention of the more detailed and differentiated material that is to follow. Before introducing operant conditioning, for example, the instructor might review the broad concept of reinforcement and its operation in classical conditioning.

MEANING

The Nature of Meaning

According to Ausubel's cognitive theory of meaningful verbal learning, material is meaningful to the extent that it can be related in a substantive and nonarbitrary fashion to relevant principles and concepts previously established in cognitive structure. Conversely, material that cannot be related in a nonarbitrary and subtantive manner to existing cognitive structure can form only isolated rote associations.

Logical
meaningfulness

Meaning depends on two major factors. First, the material must be *logically* meaningful. On the other hand, our concern in school learning is generally not so much with the *logical* meaning of the material as with its *psychological* meaning, i.e., the actual, phenomenological, idiosyncratic cognitive product that results when a particular learner relates potentially meaningful material to relevant ideas in his or her cognitive structure.

Existing cognitive
structure: The
critical variable

Meaningful material can be learned only in relation to a previously learned background of relevant concepts, principles, and ideas that make possible the emergence of new meanings. More specifically, the adequacy, stability, clarity, and organizational properties of this cognitive structure crucially affect the accuracy and clarity of the emerging new meanings, as well as their immediate and long-term *retrievability* and their *transferability*. If cognitive structure is clear, stable, and suitably organized; if it contains appropriately relevant ideas, then accurate and unambiguous meanings should emerge and should retain their separate identifiability and availability. On the other hand, if cognitive structure is unstable, unclear, disorganized, or if it contains no suitably relevant ideas, then it should tend to inhibit meaningful learning and retention. According to Ausubel, then, it is largely by strengthening the salient aspects of cognitive structure that meaningful learning, retention, and transfer can be facilitated.

Piaget and learning

Also relevant in this connection is Piaget's cognitive developmental theory (see chapters 5 and 6). The central theme of Piaget's formulation is the concept of developmental stages arranged in a hierarchy from sensorimotor to formal logic. During the period of preconceptual thought (ages two through four), children learn symbols or what Piaget calls *preconcepts*. This is followed by a period of intuitive thinking (ages four through seven) during which they are able to counterbalance their perceptions by logic.

During the stage of concrete operations (ages seven through eleven), children develop logical thought. They no longer need to have concrete exemplars at hand in order to grasp primary concepts but still cannot grasp secondary abstractions (i.e., propositions) relating one concept to another. They can reason but only in concrete terms. During this period, they learn about classes, relations, quantities, etc., so that elementary forms of logic and mathematical reasoning are now available. The final period is that of formal operations (ages

eleven on) during which adolescents develop competence in the use of logic
and symbolic processes. By the age of fifteen, most of the additional structure
necessary for logical, mathematical, and scientific reasoning is completed.
They can conceptualize and "think" in terms of, say, causality; in other words,
they can manipulate the various possibilities of a proposition involving secondary abstractions without having to rely on concrete exemplars.

The Development of Concepts

Experience becomes meaningful as it is organized into cognitive structure.
Thus, young children, seeing various animals, cannot determine what to expect from each until they can categorize them as cats and dogs. They now
have formed a couple of *concepts;* i.e., they have assigned a general label not
to a particular cat or dog but to a generalized category of animals having
common cat or dog characteristics, in terms of which other cats, dogs, and
noncats, and nondogs, can be identified. In order to develop adequate concepts, children must first be exposed to a wide variety of situations from which
they can identify the crucial aspects that cause dogs to belong to the dog category and cats to belong to the cat category. In the early stages, they must proceed inductively through the complementary processes of *abstraction* (or *differentiation*), i.e., the identification of critical similarities in otherwise
different things, and *generalization* (or *integration*), the recombining of these
properties into a new meaning.

Concept formation
and concept
assimilation

Ausubel makes an important distinction between concept *formation* and
concept *assimilation*. Young children proceed inductively; presented with an
appropriate series of both positive and negative instances of a given concept,
they identify its criterial attributes by sorting out the relevant from the irrelevant features. This is concept formation. After early childhood, however, concept development is progressively more a matter of concept assimilation, i.e.,
the child no longer derives concepts inductively from a series of exemplars but
rather relies on expository presentation in which the concept is clarified either
by definition or through the context in which it is used.[4]

Concepts are crucial to human life; civilized people particularly live in a
world of ideas rather than simply of things. Concepts telescope experience.
Instead of having to describe a particular animal or object in all of its ramifications, we simply use the generic name, *dog, car, house, mob,* etc. This simplified and generalized representation of reality not only makes for tremendous
mental economy but it also permits the development of language based on
shared meanings among members of a given culture which, in turn, permits
the manipulation of experience, facilitates learning, permits communication,
etc.

Civilized people place heavy reliance on symbols, especially verbal and

4. See Gagné's distinction between concrete and defined concepts (Gagné 1977).

written symbols, for conveying meaning. This is particularly true in the classroom, where language is almost exclusively the medium of instruction. Thus, words—i.e., a specific sequence of letters and sounds—by common agreement have come to mean a particular object or event or to express relationships among experiences. Because they are so easily manipulated, symbols are effective means of classifying as well as communicating experiences, and they are indispensable tools in the process of reasoning, particularly at the higher levels. Symbols facilitate the manipulation of ideas and experiences. They not only permit one to deal more effectively with tangible objects but also go beyond to abstract and hypothetical entities, relationships, and concepts. Modern scientific advances would not have been possible without the use of mathematical and verbal symbolism. In fact, unless concrete experiences are synthesized and generalized through symbolism, they tend to be relatively nonproductive.

On the other hand, we have to postulate that the idiosyncratic nature of psychological meaning does not preclude the possibility of shared meaning, i.e., we have to assume that the logical meaning inherent in the concepts and propositions is potentially meaningful to many persons of relatively similar background. This may cause difficulty, especially when dealing with children whose cognitive structure is bound to differ in adequacy, if nothing else, with corresponding differences in the adequacy of meaning, even to the point of a relatively complete absence of meaning.

Symbols can mean only what they represent in one's cognitive structure. We cannot *convey* meaning. The teacher's logical organization of the curriculum is important as one of the conditions of meaningfulness, but psychological meaningfulness occurs only in relation to a previously learned background of relevant concepts in the *learner's* own cognitive structure. This must remain the learner's contribution; the more the learner carries into the situation in terms of relevant, clear, and stable subsumers, the more he or she can gain. Conversely, if cognitive structure is inadequate, one's understandings will be correspondingly vague. A child born and raised in Florida is likely to have difficulty in getting accurate meaning out of the concept *blizzard*. Many farm children have an inadequate idea of a *skyscraper*; most people have no idea as to how big a sequoia tree really is.

Fuzziness in meaning is not the monopoly of children. In adults as well as in children there are various degrees of clarity of meaning depending on such factors as the difficulty of the concept in relation to the learner's cognitive structure, the logical organization with which it is presented, and the motivation of the learner. Rarely are meanings complete, even in a restricted area. We generally see only one side of an issue; we fail to relate our experiences to all the other experiences to which they could be related. On the other hand, children are even more likely to have inadequate or incorrect meanings, for, in the course of an average day, they are expected to develop a large number of concepts, many of considerable difficulty in relation to their intellectual and experiential background. Elementary school children at the level of concrete operations, for example, who are presented with abstract concepts in the absence of the necessary exemplars find such concepts unrelatable to their current cognitive structure and therefore devoid of meaning. Thus, we have come to expect the occasional boner or the expression of half-baked ideas as normal and unavoidable, when in reality, they reflect nothing more than failure in the educational process.

Since meaning must be related to cognitive structure, effectiveness of communication must be predicated on the supposition that the listener has an experiential background sufficiently similar to that of the speaker that the symbols evoke the proper meaning in the listener.[5] Failure in communication is probably greater in elementary school, especially with children from different cultural or socioeconomic strata. Language is so easy to use that it is dangerous in that it can be used to replace meaning. The use of symbols degenerates into verbalism when the learner has a word or a symbol but does not have the corresponding experience or referent.

Our schools are so highly verbal and bookish that children are often swamped by a flood of words and other symbols concerning which they have no experience. Occasionally the confusion reaches such Babelic proportions that they have no choice but to rely on parrot memory if they are to meet examination requirements. Frequently they do not realize the inadequacy of their understandings or may not be sufficiently interested to clarify meaning through a dictionary or related sources. Teachers need to realize that much of the difficulty children encounter in learning classroom materials stems from a lack of experience that would give meaning to many of the symbols with which the classroom is concerned. In the early grades, it may be necessary to undertake a systematic program of field experiences as a way of building the background necessary for effective communication. In the elementary school, it may also be advisable for the teacher to use systematic questioning to test the adequacy of children's understanding of the basic concepts being used.[6]

Getting meaning from a textbook is not easy. Children must first perceive and recognize each word; any error here is likely to garble the message. Then they must determine the meaning of the words they have read, select from

5. The role of language in meaningfulness is best seen from the standpoint of communications or information theory. A communication system consists of five basic components: a source, a transmitter, a channel, a receiver, and a destination. The operation of converting information into transmittable energy is known as *encoding,* and the messages that pass along the channel are coded signals. The receiver must decode the message to get the intended message. In any communication system there are "noises," or unwanted events which tend to interfere with the communication, e.g., static on the radio. Two kinds of transmittal distortion can occur: one in encoding where the individual does not send the message he or she intends to send; the other in decoding where the listener garbles the message that was actually sent. If they are to be effective, senders must have some form of feedback to tell them whether they are getting through to their audience.

6. See Tennyson and Park (1980) for a review of the research literature on the teaching of concepts.

their experiences the meaning to be associated with each, and organize these experiences into their proper relationships to give meaning to the paragraph. Where words have multiple meanings—and some words have a dozen or more different meanings—the reader must withhold judgment as to which meaning is relevant by relating each possible meaning to the context of the passage. Add to this the fact that the vocabulary load is often excessive, that the vocabulary used is not always the most understandable, and one can get an idea of the difficulty confronting learners when they attempt to develop precise meanings.

To the extent that the clarity of emerging meanings is a function of the ready availability of adequate relevant subsumers, the principal strategy advocated by Ausubel for ensuring the development of clear and stable meaning lies in strengthening the relevant aspects of cognitive structure. Unfortunately teachers often contribute to cognitive confusion by presenting new material without making sure that the child has the necessary cognitive background to which it can be adequately anchored. They sometimes discourage understanding by giving a higher grade to the student who parrots the words of the book than to students whose answers, being in their own words, are not as polished as those of the text. Teachers often teach facts out of context of relationships that would make them meaningful, thereby forcing children to rely on rote learning as a means of passing the inevitable examination.

There can be no objection to teaching facts; reasoning, understandings, and applications would be impossible without facts. What is objectionable is that facts are taught as ends in themselves rather than in relationship to the basic concepts and principles in existing cognitive structure to which children can meaningfully relate the new input. It is easy for the teacher, eager to cover the curriculum, to forget the slow, tedious process through which general meanings develop or even to forget that children are not always helped by glib explanations: "Rainbows are formed as the result of the refraction of the sun's rays by moisture particles."

Experience with concrete objects is essential in the early stages of learning. The school should make a deliberate effort to enrich the experiential background of the children directly through first-hand contact with the environment or vicariously through various aids where personal experience is not possible. But it is imperative that we help children to anchor these experiences to basic concepts and principles in cognitive structure. Concrete experiences that remain isolated and unassimilated are of no greater value than correspondingly isolated symbols. Nor are all concrete experiences necessarily meaningful; laboratory experiences, for example, often provide nothing more than practice in following a manual. They may actually introduce an artificiality that stifles effective dealing with an actual science environment. The lessons in the science lab are often obscured by the commotion and the complexity of the overall operation. Furthermore, such experiences are highly time-consuming, and by the time children have reached the stage of formal

Strengthening existing cognitive structure

Experience with concrete objectives the first step

operations, a given principle might be presented much more efficiently verbally or through a demonstration.

Learning experiences should be preceded by some attempt at mobilizing resources already existing in cognitive structure to serve as ideational scaffolding and, at the end, synthesized and integrated with previous learnings through some form of generalization. As much as possible this synthesis should be in the child's own words, since this is what is meaningful at his or her level of understanding, no matter how inadequate it might sound to the teacher. The child must start at the beginning; generalizations at one level of sophistication help to structure subseqent experiences into more adequate generalizations on a spiral of increasing meaningfulness.

The teacher's role

On the other hand, the fact that children must develop their own meanings does not imply that they must do so without help. A primary purpose of education is to facilitate the development of functional concepts and to sharpen into cognitive clarity children's present fuzzy concepts. By drawing out of the *ground* the significant features, for example, the teacher can focus children's attention on certain aspects of a given phenomenon and thus help them identify its crucial properties. Typically, it is necessary to present the essential elements in a reasonable variety of nonessentials, but it is best not to clutter the presentation with so many details that the essential aspects are obscured. Both too many details and too few are to be avoided. On the other hand, it is rather difficult in view of the differences in ability and background among students to decide the exact point at which the optimal degree of explanation has been reached.

Language enhances understanding

Understanding is facilitated by the clarity and effectiveness of the teacher's use of language. Concepts are sometimes presented in vocabulary that is unnecessarily complicated. We can no more expect children to understand unfamiliar content presented in unfamiliar language than we can expect them to lift themselves up by their own bootstraps. Understanding is also promoted by using a varied approach in presenting the material. Using many exemplars in different settings so that, through the process of contrast, learners can isolate the relevant from the irrelevant and the essential from the incidental is likely to promote clearer understandings than emphasizing a single illustration. There are limits, of course. We must not confuse children with a bewildering array of examples whose relevance to the situation they do not grasp.

One of the more effective ways of promoting mastery is through increasing motivation. Children who are really interested in a subject somehow manage to understand it. On the other hand, we must realize the reciprocal self-reinforcing nature of the relationship; it is too much to expect someone to become interested in something he or she does not understand. The self-concept is also an important factor. Boys may have difficulty understanding literature because of its relative incompatibility with the male image. Girls may have a parallel problem with science.

PRACTICE AS A FACTOR IN MEANINGFUL VERBAL LEARNING

An obvious factor in the effectiveness of one's learning is practice. This is most evident in the learning of psychomotor skills, where the amount and quality of practice is a major determinant of proficiency. Systematic practice is also crucial for the effective learning of meaningful verbal materials. Practice increases one's grasp of the material so that it can be better remembered as an entity. More significantly, each encounter with potentially meaningful material modifies existing cognitive structure in an organizational sense so that, on second encounter, the learner with now a more adequate cognitive structure and more totally sensitized to its import, can see new features that he or she missed the first time. The establishment of gross meaning during the first trial makes it possible for him or her to grasp more refined and more subtle meanings on the second trial. Practice provides an opportunity (1) to acquire meaning whose import the learner was not fully capable of grasping the first time and (2) to correct, clarify, and consolidate the meanings established on first contact.

Practice as a factor in meaningful verbal learnings

Ideally practice gives the learner an opportunity to discard errors, to restructure the situation, to telescope, refine, and integrate its various components into a rapid, smooth, accurate, and effective sequence. But as we noted in connection with the Law of Exercise, although necessary, practice is not a sufficient condition for learning to take place. As a result of practice, performance may improve, remain at a standstill,[7] or even worsen. "Practice makes perfect" only under proper conditions of motivation and effective guidance. Unless the learner cares about the outcome, practice will not improve performance one bit. To be effective, practice should also be meaningful. It is important, for instance, to have the learner develop insight into the nature of the required performance. A basic postulate of the Gestalt position is that practice should come *after* understanding; drill in advance of insight is likely to lead to a consolidation of bad habits.

The most effective type of practice generally is that in which students use their previous learnings in dealing with more advanced work or in the achievement of new goals. They can, for instance, practice correct grammar in writing reports in other subjects. On the other hand, it does not follow that practice must always be in a "natural" context; real-life situations may present an advantage from the standpoint of motivation and meaningfulness, but they are often time-consuming, wasteful, and otherwise impractical. Too much of a given practice session may be spent on nonessentials and far too little on the points to be consolidated. There is definite room for batting and pitching

7. We must distinguish between learning a skill or fact and using it once it has been learned.

practice in baseball, for example. In fact, it is only after separate practice has perfected basic skills that a real-life performance becomes meaningful. There is still room in the modern curriculum for drill, but it need not be of the monotonous variety that so often leads to boredom and apathy.

The fact that we learn by doing has been misinterpreted to imply that the child must be doing something physical or overt. Actually mental practice can be equally, if not more, profitable inasmuch as it often promotes structural organization of the components as the basis for their effective use in actual practice. Even in physical skills, imagining better modes of attack can produce improvements, particularly in complex skills calling for development of strategy where, as in football, thinking of what to do generally leads to more effective performance as well as greater insights for the future than simply "doing something."

A number of suggestions can be given for efficient practice. On the other hand, none can be considered conclusive. Thus, early studies (e.g., Knapp and Dixon 1950) led psychologists to conclude that practice distributed in a series of relatively short periods promotes more efficient learning than the same amount of practice massed into units of longer duration. It now seems that this alleged superiority of distributed practice cannot be applied in any simple way to verbal learnings (Underwood 1961). Spaced practice seems to facilitate learning only under specialized conditions, and, for immediate memory at least, cramming may well result in acceptable performance, as students have always hoped it would. It was believed that spaced practice also facilitated retention, but it now appears that spacing facilitates retention through eliminating interfering associations. Therefore, spacing would be clearly recommended only when forgetting is caused by the interference of *unwanted* associations and not by other school tasks, the retention of which is also at stake.

It is still believed that, under certain circumstances at least, short sessions extended over a period of time tend to produce greater efficiency in learning. Just how short is short, however, depends on many factors in the task, the learner, and the learning situation. Long practice sessions lead to fatigue and tension, which may destroy the rhythm, the flexibility, and the enthusiasm necessary to achieve a good performance. Intermittent practice allows errors and interfering associations, which tend to be less thoroughly learned, to dissipate during the rest period so that it prevents the consolidation of bad habits; it also permits a certain amount of surreptitious practice in the form of rehearsals between sessions. Distributed practice tends to promote more efficient learning when the material is long and not particularly meaningful, when the probability of erroneous response in the early stages is high, or when motivation is low. On the other hand, changing from one activity to another involves waste, particularly when it calls for getting out equipment or for a warm-up period, and this waste has to be balanced against the disadvantages of extending the learning period. The time between practice periods should be

[margin note] Distributed versus massed practice

neither so long that excessive forgetting takes place between sessions nor so short that wrong responses do not have time to drop out. How all of this can be fitted together is something teachers must work out.

Research evidence concerning the relative superiority of learning a given unit by parts or learning it as a whole, while favoring the whole method especially when combined with distributed practice, has also been inconclusive. The answer apparently varies from task to task and from learner to learner. The whole method may be inadvisable with material of uneven difficulty, for example, or with an insecure learner who needs constant reassurance that he or she is making progress.

The problem itself is ambiguous in that it revolves around the question "What is a whole and what is a part?" Any whole is part of a bigger whole and, in the final analysis, all learning has to deal with a part of some larger whole. The question then becomes "What constitutes the optimal unit of study for a given person under given conditions?" It seems the answer to the question must be sought in the concept of meaningfulness. Learning a passage one word at a time obviously would be inefficient from the standpoint of both learning and retention since it would rob the passage of its meaning and therefore would be the equivalent of learning nonsense material. On the other hand, taking too broad a unit would make it difficult to grasp its meaning and would lead to ineffective learning. Thus the learner should probably choose as a unit of study whatever he or she can grasp clearly and meaningfully, whether this be a chapter or a paragraph. It follows that, because of differences in intelligence, experience, organizational ability, attitudes, and motivation, the optimal unit for one person is not necessarily the optimal unit for another.

The parts method when . . .

The parts method tends to be ineffective because it does not provide the structure that would enable the learner to make use of the continuity of the material to relate one part to the other. In addition, putting the parts together after each has been learned may prove troublesome, particularly in a complex passage or skill where fitting the parts into perspective is the crucial part of the learning. In general, a bright person learning meaningful material would find the whole method advantageous, particularly as he or she got accustomed to its use. In fact, whenever one can impose a structure on a unit to the point of perceiving its relationships, one should probably study it as a whole, regardless of its size (within limits, of course). Even in the case of nonsense material, it is usually possible to impose on it some kind of structure to facilitate its acquisition and retention. Furthermore, even when the parts method is used, the learner should first get an overview of the material and structure the field so that the parts fall into place. For the same reason, when the material is too long or complicated to be mastered as a whole, the learner might use the *progressive-parts* method in which—after having gained an overview of the whole—the learner studies the first section, then reviews the first as he or she studies the second, then the first, second, and third, etc. The progressive-parts method might be advisable in the learning of a skill in which the parts are of uneven difficulty.

PSYCHOMOTOR SKILLS

Stages in the learning of psychomotor skills

Although overtly motor, psychomotor skills are governed by the same psychological principles as underlie the more verbally intellectual aspects of behavior. In fact, because of its essentially overt nature, psychomotor learning provides especially good examples of some of the psychological principles of

8-1   PRACTICE AND PROFICIENCY IN PSYCHOMOTOR PERFORMANCE

Practice is a necessary but not a sufficient condition for the learning of psychomotor skills to take place. But to the extent that only meaningful and purposeful practice leads to improvement, learners need a clearly defined goal that they systematically try to achieve. They also need dependable feedback as to the adequacy of their performance. Complicated skills require constant monitoring by a qualified trainer if bad habits are to be avoided. Movies that provide instant replay are especially useful.

In practicing a motor skill, care must be taken to focus on the correct process rather than overemphasize products. The problem is that adequacy of psychomotor performance is immediately obvious—perhaps too obvious: batters know if they have hit a home run or struck out. Because learners are less able to protect their egos in the event of inadequate performance, they may be tempted to emphasize quality of performance at the expense of the adequacy of the process. Beginning typists, for example, may be so concerned with avoiding errors that they adopt an accurate but inadequate style of typing that precludes later proficiency.

It is especially important to focus on the total performance rather than on the separate parts. This may create a problem when the links are of unequal difficulty or when certain subskills, although critical, do not get sufficient attention in the overall sequence, e.g., batting in baseball. In such cases, cognitive psychologists would insist that (1) the learner first gain perspective by going through the whole performance before practicing the separate parts; and (2) after practicing the parts in isolation, he or she reinstate the whole skill from beginning to end as a continuous performance. For the same reason, practice should generally occur in the natural setting, although there may be times when a certain degree of simplification may be advisable in order to permit clarity and a feeling of progress. It also seems that practice periods should be frequent and relatively short so as to maintain concentration and motivation at a high level and to prevent the development of bad habits due to fatigue and resulting loss of concentration and coordination. Not to be overlooked is the fact that mental practice is often much more productive than a mindless or stereotyped repetition of overt activity, particularly in the case of complicated skills where strategy is often the critical element in success or failure.

learning. Psychomotor performance, particularly in complex skills, involves a considerable element of mental activity. Twining (1949), for example, found that even in such simple activities as ring tossing, mental practice results in considerable improvement in performance. It also seems that not only is there a considerable shift in the patterning of abilities required for success in the early and later stages of proficiency but also that advanced competence becomes more and more a function of specific habits acquired in early training (Fleishman and Fruchter 1960).

An essential aspect of the learning of skills is the organization of subskills into successively higher levels of integration and of automation in performance. According to Fitts (1962, 1964), the development of a skill involves first of all a *cognitive* phase during which transfer of training is important, where performance can be helped by training films, demonstrations, etc. But as the learner gets the feel of the situation, the cognitive features drop out as he or she moves into what might be called a *fixation* phase in which various aspects of perceptual motor coordination become more important and during which correct patterns of motor action are refined and fixated. The final or *automation* stage is characterized by rapid automatic performance. A parallel aspect is the elimination of intervening symbolic interpretations and the reduction of the number of cues necessary to clarify the situation as the basis for orienting one's behavior; the batter, for example, must be able to cue his or her performance on very subtle differences in the pitcher's delivery.

Gentile (1972) presents a similar two-stage analysis. In the first stage, the student gets a picture of the activity to be performed. Here the teacher is responsible for structuring the situation so as to give the learner an understanding of what to do. Stage Two is a matter of fixation and diversification in which superficial and unnecessary elements are replaced by more comprehensive and sophisticated components and the performance is changed from a deliberate, labored series of subactivities to a smooth and automatic operation. Here the teacher's task is to provide feedback as the learner engages in both mental and overt practice.

The role of feedback   An important factor particularly noticeable in the learning of a skill is the concept of feedback, i.e., the interpretation and reinterpretation of the situation in the light of the consequences of one's behavior. A person driving a car, for example, does not drive in a straight line but rather continually corrects for drifts from one side of the road to the other. This readjustment is especially evident in mirror drawing where feedback, being reversed, is often misinterpreted. Both experienced and inexperienced performers rely on the continuous correction of error; the skillful performer is simply more sensitive to cues and adjusts more quickly to the results of feedback. There is also a difference in the kind of the feedback by which they operate. Beginning typists must depend on visual feedback; they must actually see the wrong letter just typed. Experienced typists, by contrast, can rely on kinesthetic cues from the stretch of their fingers to tell them when they have gone far enough to avoid making the error. The importance of feedback is shown in a study of Fairbanks and Guttman (1958) in which delayed feedback of speech (through earphones) resulted in a stumbling, disorganized speech pattern very similar to stuttering. A similar deterioration in performance can be obtained in handwriting (Smith and Smith 1966).

HIGHLIGHTS OF THE CHAPTER

The school exists for the purpose of promoting and guiding the child's growth. There is perhaps little that it can do concerning the maturational components of this growth, beyond coordinating its efforts with the various aspects of maturation. The learning component, on the other hand, is not only susceptible to manipulation, but its formal aspects are the primary responsibility of the school.

1. Learning refers to changes in behavior resulting from experience. Beyond this, the explanation of the learning process or even a precise definition is a matter of theoretical dispute.

2. Learning ranges from simple conditioning to the more complex processes of concept formation and problem solving. Complex learning, according to reinforcement theory, generally proceeds through such steps as: motivation, goal, readiness, obstacle, response, reinforcement, and generalization.

3. Teachers should be more concerned with the process whereby learning takes place than with its immediate product. This is not to minimize the importance of the latter.

4. Although incidental learning is often efficient, whatever is worth teaching should be deliberately planned for rather than left to chance. This is particularly true of collateral learnings such as attitudes.

5. The Law of Effect is best seen in the context of reinforcement, drive reduction, and other motivational concepts.

6. According to Ausubel's assimilation theory, the meaningfulness with which potentially meaningful verbal material is learned is primarily a function of the availability in cognitive structure of adequate subsumers to which it can be anchored.

7. Preschool children form concepts out of the concrete experiences they undergo. For older children, on the other hand, concept assimilation is a more efficient method of concept acquisition. The development of precise and functional concepts is crucial for effective classroom operations.

8. Civilized people rely heavily on symbols to help them manipulate and convey ideas. Unfortunately symbols can mean only what they represent in one's experience. When the child is lacking in the required experience, verbalisms and misunderstanding inevitably occur. Clear-cut concepts are not grasped on first contact but rather evolve on a spiral of ever-greater meaningfulness.

9. Practice is a necessary but not a sufficient condition for learning to take place. Learning by wholes tends to promote more efficient learning than learning by parts—when wholes are defined in terms of what the learner can meaningfully grasp. Distributed practice appears to be more efficient than massed practice, but the matter is not simple, nor is the evidence unequivocal.

10. The development of psychomotor skills involves the organization of subskills into successively higher levels of integration and automation. Feedback is essential.

SUGGESTIONS FOR FURTHER READING

BRUNER, JEROME S. *The Process of Education.* Cambridge: Harvard Univ. Press, 1960. Bruner expounds his views on education. Chapter 2 focuses on the importance of structure. He also presents his views on readiness and introduces the concept of the spiral curriculum.

GLASER, ROBERT. Learning. In Robert L. Ebel, ed., *Encyclopedia of Educational Research*, pp. 707–733. New York: Macmillan, 1969. A good overview of the nature of learning and its research foundation. Focuses on the nature of the learning process and the various categories of learning outcomes.

MARX, MELVIN H. *Learning.* Vol. 1: *Processes,* 1969. Vol. 2: *Interactions,* 1970. Vol. 3: *Theories,* 1970. New York: Macmillan. A comprehensive and scholarly treatment of the various aspects of learning.

The Psychology of Learning and Motivation: Advances in Research and Theory. New York: Academic Press. Continuing series. Kenneth W. and Janet T. Spence, eds., 1967; 1968. Gordon H. Bower and Janet T. Spence, eds., 1969. Gordon H. Bower, ed., vols. 4–12, 1970–1978. A comprehensive and up-to-date coverage of the psychology of learning and its underlying empirical and theoretical foundation.

QUESTIONS AND PROJECTS

1. To what extent are "teaching" and "learning" complementary processes? To what extent are they identifiably separate operational processes?
2. How do you account for the wide differences in viewpoint among psychologists as to the nature of learning, retention, and transfer?
3. How do association theorists explain the acquisition, retention, and transfer of meaningful verbal learning?
4. How might the learning processes in the learning of meaningful verbal materials differ from those in learning rote associations? In learning a motor skill? In problem-solving strategies? In the learning of attitudes?
5. What might be done to increase the meaningfulness of the academic aspects of the school curriculum to children of disadvantaged background?

SELF-TEST

1. Learning is best defined as
   a. the accumulation of knowledge and skills.
   b. the change in behavior resulting from experience.
   c. the formation of S-R bonds, learning sets, and other functional operations.

     d. the improvement in performance resulting from deliberate practice.

     e. the modification of behavior over time.

2. The sequence motivation, readiness, obstacle, response, and reinforcement, as part of the learning process, is based on ——————— premises.

     a. associationistic

     b. conditioning

     c. eclectic

     d. Gestalt

     e. phenomenological

3. Probably the most effective learning is ——————— learning.

     a. concomitant

     b. incidental

     c. informal

     d. instrumental

     e. trial-and-error

4. Which of the current theories of learning appear to have the greatest validity and relevance to classroom learning?

     a. Cognitive theories in general

     b. Humanistic theories

     c. Skinnerian conditioning

     d. Thorndike's connectionism

     e. None of the above; no theory has clear-cut superiority over the others.

5. The reason Thorndike's experimental animals relied on trial and error, rather than insight, to solve their problem is related to

     a. their limited "intelligence."

     b. the nature of the problem (and its solution).

     c. their past experiences.

     d. tunnel vision (resulting from anxiety).

     e. the unavailability of adequate reward.

6. Process is to product as

     a. formal is to incidental.

     b. teaching is to learning.

     c. psychology is to philosophy.

     d. skill is to knowledge.

     e. strategy is to competency.

7. Attitudes toward a given subject generally fall within the context of ——————— learnings.

     a. collateral

     b. incidental

     c. formal

     d. instrumental

     e. conditioned

NINE

Guiding the Learning Process

... I have been struck by the fact that when allowed to pace themselves, the slower learners simply take more time doing apparently precisely the same things that a faster learner does. ... Typically, the fas-
test and the slowest learning rates differ by a factor of four or five.

John D. Carroll (1965)

Feedback is a more descriptive term since school situations involve both
informational contingencies and reinforcement contingencies.

Lawrence M. Stolurow (1965)

Altogether, it should be emphasized ... that the belief in the superiority of discovery (Socratic method) over traditional teaching still
rests more on intuitive conviction than on well established
experimental generalizations.

Jan Smedslund (1964)

Frequently a class discussion consists of a campaign of self-defense and self-vindication.

Arthur T. Jersild (1952)

— Presents an overview of the nature of teaching and the complexities involved.
— Emphasizes the role of the teacher in the guidance of pupil learning.
— Discusses the relative merits of the lecture and the discussion, discovery and reception learning, and mastery learning
— Reviews the role of homework, programmed instruction, and similar forms of "independent" study

PREVIEW: KEY CONCEPTS

1. Teaching refers to the strategies used to facilitate student learning.
2. Current emphasis on *teaching* reflects a recent reversal of psychology's traditional focus on *learning*. The impetus for a technology of teaching has come largely from behaviorists.
3. The task is complex and our knowledge limited. It seems clear that no one style of effective teaching applies to all teachers in all teaching situations.
4. The relative merits of the lecture and the discussion have been debated on numerous occasions. The crucial issue seems to be the degree of consensus in the field.
5. The discovery-versus-reception issue is often confused by superimposing parallel continua of "active" versus "passive" and "meaningful" versus "rote."
6. While appealing on the surface, the recent emphasis on mastery learning presents a number of logical as well as operational questions.
7. To be effective, homework and independent study must be carefully integrated within the classroom's regular operation. Programmed instruction, computer-assisted instruction, and other packaged approaches present a more sophisticated way of individualizing instruction.

PREVIEW QUESTIONS

1. Specifically, what is the relationship between learning and teaching? To what extent can we derive effective teaching strategies from the "psychology of learning"?

2. What are some of the major complexities that preclude the development of standardized teaching strategies? What are some of the commonalities underlying all teaching?

3. What are the relative merits of the lecture and the discussion approach to teaching? Of discovery and reception learning? Of mastery learning?

4. Specifically, what purpose is homework to serve in the advancement of the school's program? How might present efforts be improved?

5. To what extent do the recent instructional "packages" constitute a breakthrough in American education?

That schools exist at all testifies to the child's inability to assume sole responsibility for his or her formal education. Growth results from the individual's responses to environmental demands but, although the learner must learn for himself, the learning process can be made more certain and more effective by competent guidance. This chapter considers some aspects of the process by means of which teaching can facilitate learning.

THE ROLE OF INSTRUCTION IN LEARNING

Providing children with a carefully selected sequence of educationally relevant experiences constitutes but part of the school's task; it must further provide the guidance necessary to make these experiences effective in promoting their growth. Common sense suggests that, without guidance, learners will usually stumble on a method that is somewhat short of the best; a person learning to type without instruction, for example, is likely to use the two-finger hunt-and-peck method. Effective methods are generally more difficult to use in the early stages. Thus, in golf, it would seem so much more natural just to go out and club the ball without all the fuss about stance, grip, position of the elbow, of the shoulder—but it would lead to disappointing results. In fact, the more complicated the task, the more important instruction becomes.

Instruction involves . . .

Instruction is a determining factor with respect to both learners' progress and the final status they will attain. Whereas learners must do the learning, instruction can invariably save time and effort and, more important, can prevent the development of ineffective techniques that will preclude any degree of final proficiency. It follows that if they are to provide effective guidance to student learning, teachers need to know specifically what role they are to play and by what techniques effective learning is to be promoted. Their task can be divided into three broad categories:

1. Helping the learner develop insights into the nature of the product to be attained and the process through which this is to be accomplished. Thus, in teaching a motor skill, the teacher needs to direct the learner's attention to adequate techniques and the reason underlying their use,

e.g., the reason for the follow-through in golf. In presenting verbal materials, the teacher should stress the underlying structure of the materials in relation to the learner's existing cognitive background.

2. Anticipating the use of faulty techniques and providing continuous diagnostic and remedial help to prevent the consolidation of bad habits. The instructor must provide a critical evaluation of the learner's performance. Yet he or she must allow for flexibility, for although certain methods tend to be more conducive to success than others, even these must be modified in keeping with individual differences among learners.

3. Giving the learner moral support. The teacher should concentrate on what to do rather than on what to avoid and should refrain from adverse criticism, especially in the early stages.

The relative emphasis to be placed on these aspects of the teacher's role varies; giving moral support would be somewhat less important for a learner who is relatively secure and beyond the novice stage of learning.[1]

In attempting to facilitate student learning, teachers can proceed in a number of ways. They can rely primarily on verbal, or perhaps manual, guidance; they can rely on a visual approach via diagrams, mechanical devices, or other aids or use a combination of these by having a demonstration. The form most effective in a specific case depends on the particular situation. Manual guidance is obviously more appropriate for teaching a skill than for teaching a verbal concept, for example.

Instructional strategies   Verbal guidance can be helpful in the development of meanings and concepts. It can also be effective in improving the skills of a person already familiar with their basic aspects, but it tends to be relatively ineffective for teaching skills to beginners. Films have certain advantages in that they combine visual and verbal clues and, in the case of a skill, can provide a slow-motion demonstration without distorting the performance. But they too have limitations; often a film presents too much material for the beginner to grasp at one time and, as a result, like any other medium improperly used, it causes confusion. Films, charts, and graphs are of definite value in conveying ideas that are difficult to describe by words alone (such as the structure of molecules) and in presenting numerical data. They can be especially helpful when clarity can be enhanced through animation, e.g., the flow of the blood through the body.

---

1. In general, teaching might be expected to benefit the slower students to a greater degree than their more adequate classmates who can more easily learn "on their own." To that extent, instruction tends to lower the correlation between intelligence and achievement, particularly when group instruction sets the pace to that of the slower children geared to the coverage of a minimal preset curriculum.

THE NATURE OF TEACHING

New Focus on Teaching

Although its ultimate concern is to promote learning, particularly as it occurs in the classroom, educational psychology must be equally concerned with what the teacher must do to facilitate student learning. This concern is a relatively new development. As we noted in chapter 1, until recently it was assumed that since teaching can be defined only in terms of learning, theoretical clarity in the area of learning would automatically provide comparable theoretical insights into instructional strategies. The general feeling was that teaching methods made relatively little difference in the overall educational enterprise (Gage 1969; Wallen and Travers 1963), that one teaching method is as good as any other.[2] Stephens (1967), for example, in his theory of spontaneous schooling, relegates teaching methods to a minor role among the factors that determine the attainment of academic objectives. It is only in the past decade that the relative inadequacies of the psychology of learning as a model for developing effective teaching strategies have been openly recognized.

Even now, humanists show little interest in *teaching* in the usual sense of the word. Rogers (1969) sees teaching as a vastly overrated activity; he not only believes that he has rarely taught anyone anything of consequence but further argues that some of our current instructional methods are such as to "almost guarantee that meaningful learning will be at an absolute minimum." Humanists would restructure the role of the teacher into that of a *facilitator* of personal growth. Even more drastic in their downgrading of teaching are the recent neohumanists (e.g., Neill, Goodman, Holt, etc.), who would allow children considerable freedom as to what they choose to learn or even whether they want to learn at all. At Summerhill, for example, students are relatively free to decide whether they want to attend classes.

Bruner, likewise, in his emphasis on discovery, minimizes teaching in the traditional sense.[3] In fact, although certainly interested in teaching—and actually contributing significantly to teaching by their emphasis on the whole, on insight, and on meaningfulness—cognitive psychologists as a group have been somewhat less than precise as to how this is to be achieved.

---

2. Of interest here is the recurring idea that teaching is an art, that it can never be a science. The trouble with seeing teaching as an art is that it more or less obviates the need for developing effective teaching strategies. It seems to suggest that good teaching is something that comes naturally to those who "have it," that teachers are born, not made. This type of thinking must necessarily be wrong; there is indeed something that educational psychology can contribute to effective teaching. See, for example, Good et al. (1975).

3. This much to the chagrin of behaviorists, e.g., Skinner, who sees Bruner's emphasis on discovery as a way of absolving teachers from a sense of failure. Skinner laments the fact that teachers do not teach; they simply hold students responsible for learning and take credit for what the students master on their own.

9-1

COGNITIVE THEORIES AS INFORMATION-PROCESSING MODELS

As we noted in Chapter 3, modern cognitive theories are often referred to as information-processing (IP) theories (see Wittrock, 1978a, 1978b, 1979). In contrast to behaviorists, who see learning as the direct product of externally controlled reinforcement, modern cognitive psychologists see learning as an internally mediated process. The learner is not a passive assimilator of stimuli but rather an active processor of information, responsible for his or her own learning and aware that meaning, for example, cannot be "given" or "received" but rather must be discovered. IP theorists place the learner as an active selector among and processor of stimuli, not simply a passive receptor of or even reactor to stimuli, as postulated by behaviorists. As Ausubel points out, even when the learner is "given" a rule, for example, he or she must still discover its meaning by relating it to rules, principles, and other subsumers in cognitive structure.

In other words, IP theorists attribute a much greater degree of initiative and control to the learner. The emphasis is on the way the learner *constructs* meaning, say, from the interaction between instruction and his or her current cognitive structure. More generally, the focus is on the way the learner receives, reorganizes, retains information; on the way motivation influences attention, or "learning style" influences understandings—which, in turn, influence behavior. Meaning is not the automatic result of selective (externally controlled) reinforcement. On the contrary, it is the product of an active process of building relationships between incoming stimuli and meaningful materials already stored in cognitive structure. The emphasis is on memory, imagery, and other cognitive processes.

A critical factor in IP models is the learner's cognitive (learning) style, i.e., the stable, systematic, and pervasive ways in which a given person perceives, encodes, stores, processes, and retrieves information. As we noted in chapter 7, some learners are analytical and focus on one dimension at a time; others are more global and balance several dimensions at once. It also seems that analytical students are more reflective and field independent. Students who take a more global approach, by contrast, tend to be impulsive and field dependent; they tend to be more aware of surrounding stimuli, to be more socially oriented, and to do better with externally defined goals, external reinforcement, and clearly defined situations. Also critical as determinants of the way the learner processes information are such factors as cognitive style (i.e., the adequacy of one's current background of relevant information), motivation, etc.

The issue in instruction, then, is not so much what the instructor does by way of introducing behavioral objectives, inserted questions, or feedback but rather the way the learner responds to these instructional strategies, e.g., how he or she processes the information presented in the feedback—or, from the instructor's point of view, how the learner's cognitive processes are activated and mobilized by, say, inserted questions. It would seem logical to assume, for example, that behavioral objectives (or advance organizers) as a way of directing the learner's attention would be more useful for the naive learner relatively unfamiliar with the structure of the field than for the more sophisticated scholar. It would also seem logical that people with an analytic style of learning would benefit differently from inserted questions (or programmed instruction) than someone more globally oriented. This would vary further with the kind of question, the type and difficulty of the material, the learner's existing cognitive structure, etc.

More generally, at issue is every aspect of the teaching-learning process in interaction with every aspect of the learner's cognitive, or more broadly, psychological makeup. It is postulated that different instructional stimuli would be processed differently by the bright, the field independent, etc., than by their respective counterparts. It would follow that efficiency in learning would be greatly enhanced by synchronizing instructional strategies with learner characteristic. Conversely, difficulty would arise when children are faced with an instructional or curricular mismatch. Analytic students probably would do better under field-independent teachers, who tend to present curriculum in small, tight, logically structured units, than under field-dependent teachers, who are likely to organize curriculum more globally.

To the extent that a given instructional strategy does not mean the same thing to different categories of learners or different learning situations, IP models revolve critically around the concept of aptitude-treatment interaction (ATI), i.e., on the notion that no method is universally best but rather that teaching effectiveness must be defined in terms of teaching *what to whom*. It seems, for example, "that the lower-class child responds better . . . to didactic teaching with explicit requirements and close-coupled reward. Problem-oriented, ego-motivated, supportive methods of teaching, which educational theorists have long been advocating, seems to benefit only a middle-class cliented" (Cronbach 1975). Unfortunately, as Cronbach points outs, it may be decades before we have adequately established even the more basic interactions.

Motivation is an important variable here, with IP psychologists placing a strong emphasis on *locus of control* (see Rotter 1966; deCharms, 1968): i.e., the degree to which learners accept responsibility for their learning or, on the contrary, see themselves as a pawn at the mercy of their external environment or, according to Weiner's *attribution* theory (Weiner 1969, 1976), the extent to which people attribute their successes and failures to their own efforts or to external agents over which they have no control.

In summary, then, IP models are perhaps not so much a new learning theory as a new, comprehensive, and productive way of looking at the learning process in its many complexities. They see each new art of learning as involving the operation of various internal processes peculiar to a degree to the individual learner and yet modified also to a degree by instruction and other external inputs.

In that sense, then, they combine the thinking incorporated in, say, Ausubel's assimilation theory of meaningful verbal learning, as well as various instructional strategies and other aspects of the instructional program. Unfortunately, as Gagné (1977) points out, whereas IP theories depend critically on the operation of what he calls *executive control* processes, IP theorists to date have not made very explicit how these processes are acquired, developed, or activated by the learner. He also notes that current IP models concern themselves almost exclusively with the acquisition and retention of verbal materials at the level of propositional knowledge, e.g., principles and rules. There is, therefore, a need for other theories, such as modeling theories, with regard to the development of attitudes.

Instructional implications. Like all other theories, IP models offer only general implications for instruction, not prescriptions. In general terms, the teacher's task in an IP context is to stimulate the learner's information-processing strategies, aptitudes, and the store of relevant subsumers already in cognitive structure. More specifically, IP theorists see the purpose of instruction as that of promoting the development of meaningful relationships between incoming information and existing cognitive structure by inducing verbal or visual elaborations by providing the learner with organization, examples, analogies, and diagrams emphasizing the overall structure. The teacher's strategies would take into account such student characteristics as academic background or intellectual status. In the case of the naive learner, there would be greater need for concrete exemplars; with more sophisticated learners who can generate their own structure and devise crucial relationships among elements, the teacher might simply orient attention to key points. See, for example, Mayer (1975), who found different problem-solving outputs to result from the interaction of different instructional strategies and different internal variables.

Operationally, the teacher might address three issues.

1. Attention: There are too many things to perceive for us to see and grasp. Attention must be selective. Furthermore, it must be focused on relevant aspects rather than scattered. The teacher's first task in applying the IP models would be to arouse the child's attention through such factors as intensity, motion, and novelty and otherwise making the critical aspects sufficiently salient for them to emerge from their distracting background. There is also need to develop student interest, i.e., to create a receptive atmosphere by pointing out what to expect. During instruction, it might be necessary to provide further clues to direct student attention.

2. Acquisition: Teachers need to emphasize meaningfulness through advance organizers, mastery of subordinate learnings, etc., taking into account the student's developmental status, current academic background, etc. They might encourage the student to develop appropriate visual and/or verbal images, e.g., in learning an arbitrary association like "cow-ball," to form a mental image of a cow kicking a ball.

3. Retention and transfer: We need to emphasize the quality and the adequacy of the original learning, e.g., meaningfulness, mastery, and overlearning.

Teachers might ensure meaningfulness by making sure of the adequacy of the learner's current background of relevant information, by consolidating crucial relationships between the new learnings and existing subsumers, etc. Focusing on the underlying structure of the discipline, as emphasized by, say, Bruner or Gagné, should enable the learner to process new inputs with maximum efficiency. Teachers might also help the student develop effective study habits and coding strategies for dealing with new information. They might also minimize interference and confusion by reducing the number of irrelevant features in the situation. They would also have to provide confirming or corrective feedback.

Computer simulation. IP theorists have relied heavily on computer simulation as a source of ideas as to how information is processed. Their general premise is that the specific steps the computer goes through in proving a theorem in geometry, for example, is a fairly accurate representation of the steps taken by the human brain in dealing with the same problem and that we can gain insight into human information processing through computer simulation. The General Problem Solver (Newell et al. 1959; see also Newell and Simon 1971), for example, is a computer program capable of solving a variety of problems in a number of fields from an exercise in logic to proving an identity in trigonometry.

Of special interest in this connection, particularly in view of its relevance to educational practice, is R. Atkinson's (1972) simulation of the relative effect of using computer-assisted instruction (CAI) as a supplement to regular classroom instruction under four different instructional goals:

1. Maximizing the average reading performance of the class as a whole, presumably by concentrating on the students most capable of improvement. The results: a 15 percent average gain but also a 15 percent increase in variability within the class.
2. Minimizing within-class differences, presumably by focusing on the slower students. The results: a 15 percent reduction in overall class performance.
3. Maximizing the number of students who scored at grade level by the end of the year, presumably by neglecting those already at grade level. The results: also a loss in overall class performance.
4. Maximizing average class performance without increasing within-class variability, presumably by keeping an eye on all students. The results: an 8 percent overall class gain with no increase in class variability, which would seem to be the most defensible approach although not universally the most effective.

This is not to say that cognitive psychologists are not interested in the mechanics of instruction. As we have noted, Ausubel's theory of subsumption, although primarily a theory of meaningful verbal *learning*, has definite teaching implication (e.g., the use of advance organizers). Nevertheless, it is the behaviorists who have consistently emphasized the need for a technology of instruction.[4] In the mid-1960s, for example, Skinner launched the teaching machine movement; he also introduced behavior modification techniques through which he successfuly demonstrated the shaping of the behavior of pigeons, children, or even psychotic patients. More recently, Gagné (1965, 1970, 1977) has presented a relatively thorough package of instructional strategies to parallel his hierarchical theory of learning (see chapter 12).

Teaching Variables

The total instructional process as it occurs in the classroom involves more than the teacher's presentation of subject-matter content. It involves every aspect of the management of learning in the broad sense of promoting learning, retention, and transfer. As such, it comprises a wide range of variables, primary among which are organization and structure, presentation, feedback and reinforcement, practice, review, and evaluation.

Most teachers want to teach well. Unfortunately, they do not know how, nor can we provide them with easy prescriptions, guidelines, or even usable criteria. Half a century of research has failed to identify characteristics (Barr 1929, 1948; Ryans 1960) or behaviors (Flanders, 1960) that clearly differentiate between good and poor teachers. Nor has research clarified what constitutes effective teaching in the traditional (classroom) sense and how it can be achieved.[5] So far, the magic formula has been quite elusive, leading Stephens (1967) to suggest, for example, that nothing the teacher is, has, or does one way or another is consistently associated with pupil progress.[6] And perhaps this is inherent in the complexity of teaching as an operational variable.

It seems, for example, that contrary to expectations, the teacher's knowledge of the subject matter is not highly correlated with student progress. Apparently beyond a certain minimum—a level that is attained by most teachers and thus becomes a common denominator—additional knowledge gives the teacher no major advantage. This would be especially true in high school and college where the teacher's knowledge is readily supplemented by textbooks and other library sources. There is likewise little relationship between the teacher's use of lesson plans and student progress. It may be that lesson plans in-

4. This is, of course, in keeping with their conviction that the teacher must assume an active role in every aspect of the teaching-learning enterprise. See, for example, the discussion on the difference in viewpoint between behaviorists and humanists regarding control in chapter 3.

5. Some success has been achieved in developing strategies for teaching specific "miniskills" (Borg 1972), e.g., converting fractions into decimals.

6. Good et al. (1975) would disagree.

troduce a certain element of rigidity that precludes on-the-spot adaptability to student needs and student ideas. On the other hand, the evidence is far from conclusive. Teacher vagueness, for example, is associated with lower student achievement, with lack of knowledge a basic element in teacher vagueness.

Critics of the school

Meanwhile, the school has been the target of harsh criticism in a number of highly publicized books by such neohumanists as Holt, Glasser, Goodman, Kohl, and others. Glasser, for example, sees the school as a concentration camp in which children are incarcerated. Illich (1971) advocates deschooling. Meanwhile, standardized test data published widely in local newspapers showing declining academic proficiency on the part of the nation's children— and now the large-scale failure of high school students to meet literacy requirements—are once again being used by critics as direct evidence of the school's ineffectiveness.[7]

Teaching is a complex undertaking

Teaching is unquestionably a complex activity; to date, we simply lack adequate knowledge of its various components. A major problem, for example, concerns the relative emphasis to be placed on the school's multiple objectives in selecting from the many options as to curriculum, teaching methods, classroom activities, etc. open to the teacher. If the school values cognitive development, then one set of experiences and activities is relevant. If, on the other hand, the emphasis is on self-actualization, different teaching strategies are called for. Different teaching methods presumably promote different educational outcomes, but the relationship is rarely simple, nor are the results consistent or universal. Our teaching strategies are necessarily related in some way to the theoretical views we hold as to the nature of the educational process. They also vary with subject-matter content; we do not teach psychomotor skills in the same way we teach psychology or calculus.

The matter is complicated by the fact that regardless of what the teacher does, the final outcome is geared to the highly idiosyncratic internal processes operating within the learner.[8] This idiosyncratic reinterpretation of the teacher's behavior may be especially crucial in the higher mental processes that allow for greater differences in individual approach. Research has shown that major differences exist among learners in style of perceiving, cognizing, and conceptualizing and, further, that these differences are probably as real and as pervasive as the more obvious differences in intellectual ability, motivation, etc. (see chapter 7).

Learners differ widely

Children have characteristic ways in which they approach problems. As we noted in chapter 7, some are analytical; they focus on individual components of the stimulus and solve the problem on that basis. Others are more con-

7. Critics conveniently forget to have society—the breakdown of the family, the stifling effects of the ghetto, society-sponsored violence in the school, etc.—at least share in the unhappy statistics.

8. Loevinger (1959) notes a similar phenomenon in regard to child-rearing practices. What the parent does and the theoretical framework from which the parent operates is one thing; the theoretical framework from which the child interprets the parent's behavior is another.

ceptually oriented; they take a more global and intuitive view, emphasize broad relationships, and pay less attention to the details. Some children need a quick overview rather than a point-by-point explanation; others need a concrete example. Lower-class children, for example, tend to respond better to the visual, the kinesthetic, and the concrete (Riessman 1962; see also Sherman and Schultz 1976). Some students are able to analyze and evaluate information readily in arriving at concepts and principles; others have more difficulty. There are substantial sex differences in thinking processes (Lynn 1966; see chapter 7). Some children are impulsive, others are reflective (Kagan and Kogan 1970). Some students comprehend situations better through discussion than through lecture, reading, or independent study. Some people are field independent; they see objects as discrete and independent of the field in which they occur. Others experience great difficulty in preventing the environmental background from distorting what they perceive (Witkin 1962; see chapter 7).

The problem is further complicated by the fact that teaching involves an interaction between the teacher's operational style and that of the student. In other words, we need to recognize that both teachers and students vary in their cognitive style and that a particular style combination is more appropriate in one teacher-student interchange than in others. Impulsive children, for example, might be taught by a reflective teacher. A phonetic approach might be more suitable for an analytical, reflective beginning reader, whereas the whole-word approach might be superior for impulsive children (Feshbach 1968). However, to the extent that a given class is generally composed of many children, each with an individual cognitive style, there is a limit to the extent to which the teacher can deal with each child on his or her own terms. There is need to help the child broaden his or her ability to profit from different kinds of educational experiences. Catering to a narrow, idiosyncratic style of learning can serve to freeze the child's ability to profit from a variety of educational experiences. On the other hand, despite the child's ability to restructure the teacher's teaching style to fit a particular pattern, we ought not to minimize the effect of teaching style on the child's learning. Taba (1967), for example, found that narrow questioning inhibited the cognitive functioning of students, causing them to adopt irrational, unproductive, and arbitrary modes of thinking in which they depended on memory and authority rather than on judgment and inference.

It would seem that the determinant of student achievement is what the student does—with teacher behavior an indirect influence through what it causes the student to do. The situation is obviously complex, involving student, teacher, and materials in multiple interaction. Interestingly, the one variable that seems to be emerging from this complexity as the critical factor in academic achievement is the student's *time on task*, i.e., the actual time during which he or she is productively engaged in solving arithmetic problems, in reading course assignments, in simply studying (Rosenshine 1971, 1976). More specifically, although not conclusive or even consistent, the evidence suggests

Time on task

that student achievement is positively correlated (r approximately 0.40) with the amount of directed learning (and direct structured teaching) and inversely correlated with such socially oriented classroom activities as games, group work, unsupervised independent study, and other informal student-centered approaches.

Although this would have to be qualified to take into account differences in learner characteristics and differences as to purpose, in general, the stronger the academic emphasis, the greater the academic gains as typically measured. This would imply the need for an orderly, business-like, mission-oriented approach to teaching—complete with systematic monitoring, specific (convergent) questions and immediate feedback, high teacher expectations, remedial work as needed, and a set of organizational and administrative routines that allow pupils to attend to their learning assignments with a minimum of delay and interruption. Such a direct structured approach seems particularly beneficial to students of low socioeconomic status.[9]

There is no one best method of teaching

No one style of teaching applies to all teachers in all teaching situations; conversely, a given type of teacher behavior or teacher characteristic is bound to yield different outcomes for different children, depending on such mediating factors as teacher personality and competence, student background and intellectual status, the nature of the course content, and other aspects of the learning situation.[10] On the other hand, it is clearly illogical to attempt to teach every child according to his or her own idiosyncratic learning style. But if we use group procedures, we need to recognize that the more scientifically precise a given teaching method and the more appropriate it is for one child in one situation, the more obviously inappropriate it is for another child. It would seem that, short of individual tutoring by professionals, which is simply not cost-effective, the only reasonable solution is to help each child develop effective information-processing skills. It may also be as Gage and Unruh (1967) suggest, that the kind of semirandom spraying of ideas, questions, etc., that goes on essentially unplanned in the conventional classroom ends up to be relatively effective as each child processes the instruction according to his or her own cognitive strategies.

It also seems logical that some of the more effective methods are acquired only after long years of experience. It is also likely that good teachers change their teaching style from subject to subject, class to class, and especially from purpose to purpose. Shumsky (1968) suggests that teachers experiment in order to find a style of teaching suitable to their personality and background, as well

9. Bennett's findings (1976) that those who suffered most from informal teaching were the ablest students—with informal classrooms then acting as academic levelers—may actually illustrate the fact that the informal classroom does not keep sufficient pressure on the bright child, who can just coast along. See Gray and Satterly (1976) for a critical review of the Bennett study.

10. For the past twenty years, researchers have emphasized the interaction between teaching methods and student characteristics. See Mouly (1978) for an overview of aptitude-treatment interaction. See Cronbach and Snow (1977) for greater coverage.

as to their students. Teachers, for example, would need to search for a style that is effective in teaching the culturally disadvantaged. The current emphasis on team teaching has advantages in this connection, not only from the standpoint of the learners, who then have access to different teaching styles, but also to the teachers, who can learn from one another.

Theoretical Perspective

If they are to be effective, instructional strategies should probably derive from clear-cut theoretical premises. (On the other hand, we must remember that no matter how enlightened they may be, theories do not generate unique or compelling instructional prescriptions.) As we noted in chapter 3, for example, a technology of instruction along behavioristic lines (as exemplified, say, in programmed learning) would be highly specific. In general, it would not only insist on the precise definition of objectives, preferably in behavioral terms, but would also arrange in sequence the events of instruction, the conditions of reinforcement, etc., that would cause the learner first to attend and then to respond in ways conducive to effective learning.[11]

Teaching must derive from some theoretical model

It would also be necessary for a given theoretical position to deal convincingly with the various components of the educational enterprise. In order to justify the use of the lecture, for example, operant theorists would have to assume that they are indeed interacting with—and reinforcing—each student. They would have to assume that the student does indeed respond, covertly or implicitly, by anticipating the lecturer's next statement. If their predictions are correct, the learner's expectations are reinforced (see Skinner 1968, p. 157). In other words, lecturers would have to assume that as they proceed with the lecture, students are running alongside, predicting the lecturer's next intellectual move and being reinforced for keeping up. By contrast, instructional strategies based on cognitive premises would focus on the organization of the material to be learned and the way it can be logically related to what students already know. The key here is the relationship of the new material to the learner's existing cognitive structure. The implications for instruction would range from the requirement that the new material be potentially meaningful to the need for organizers to ensure the adequacy of the learner's existing cognitive structure in relation to the new material.[12] Modeling theorists would be more concerned with providing an effective performance in areas and in ways the learner would want to imitate.

Unfortunately, with the possible exception of Skinnerian conditioning (in the restricted areas for which it is designed), attempts to marshal research evi-

---

11. Unfortunately, most behavioristic models to date have dealt with the lower end of the learning continuum. Many are based on rote learning and therefore are of limited applicability to the meaningful learning that should characterize the modern classroom.

12. Generally the cognitive position presents a more convincing basis for dealing with material at the higher levels of the taxonomy.

dence in support of these various positions have yielded equivocal results, primarily because of difficulty in securing experimental control. The validation of Ausubel's advance organizers as a fundamental feature of his theory of subsumption, for example, is sometimes frustrated by the fact that the introduction of advance organizers by the teacher may be unnecessary, particularly for the more adequate students who can readily provide their own organizers (see Barnes and Clawson 1975; Novak et al. 1971; Ausubel et al. 1978; Ausubel 1978; Mayer 1979).

Current Interest in the Technology of Instruction

A number of educational psychologists believe that the scientific concepts and principles derived over the past decade or two have reached the point where a relatively adequate technology of instruction may indeed be possible. In contrast to the more limited versions of the past (e.g., programmed instruction), what is now evolving is a much broader scheme of instructional procedures designed to increase teacher effectiveness in performing the many and varied tasks and functions involved in teaching and thus to maximize teacher efficiency and correspondingly optimize student learning (see Glaser 1976).

A technology of instruction is predicated on the assumption that if the instructional process can parallel the conditions of learning, the probability that the child will learn will be correspondingly optimized. To be meaningful, it must deal convincingly with all aspects of the teaching-learning process—objectives, teaching strategies, materials, etc.—each so defined as to ensure that the conditions of optimal learning are indeed met. More precisely, such an instructional package must incorporate such components as:

Components of the teaching act

1. A precise statement of objectives readily available to both teacher and students.
2. A task analysis designed to ensure that learning events are properly sequenced as the basis for learning to take place efficiently and meaningfully.
3. Adequate provisions for ensuring the ready availability of prerequisite learning.
4. A logical arrangement of the events of instruction so as to maximize continuity and ensure optimal learning readiness.
5. An adequate schedule of meaningful practice combined with an equally adequate schedule of reinforcement and corrective feedback.

Gagné's hierarchical model (see chapter 12) is a comprehensive attempt in this direction.

Mathemagenic Strategies

In recent years, there has been a growing emphasis on the need for the teacher to provide systematic guidance to the student's learning efforts. This is particularly critical when students are expected to "learn on their own," as, for example, in preparing for tomorrow's lesson. (This is more critical in the case of the young learner who has not developed effective study skills. More mature scholars can normally provide their own learning strategies.) There is more to teaching than simply telling students, "Study chapter 10." Teachers must not only identify the content to be studied but must also monitor student learning through such strategies as presenting a structural overview through an outline, checking prerequisites, introducing advance organizers as needed, checking comprehension, providing feedback, etc., as is typically done when the teacher is actually "teaching" the class. Such strategies, variously known as *mathemagenic behaviors* (Rothkopf 1967, 1970; Frase 1968, 1970), *cognitive strategies* (Gagné 1977), etc., encompass the identification of meaningful objectives, the introduction of relevant subsumers, the use of prequestions and postquestions, and other features designed to structure and monitor student learning and thus make it more systematic and productive (see Hartley and Davies 1976).

Study questions: Do they help?

The placement of study questions to guide the learner has received considerable attention in recent years (Rothkopf 1967, 1970; Frase 1968, 1970). The evidence (see Bull 1973; Ladas 1973), though far from conclusive, suggests that prequestions focus the learner's attention on specific items to the detriment of the rest of the passage.[13] Postquestions, on the other hand, do not allow students to anticipate what they are to get out of the passage so that they must read all of it with care. If they cannot answer the questions, they must modify their reading accordingly; if they handle the questions well, they get confirmation of the effectiveness of their procedures and may even want to speed up their reading. In other words, postquestions tend to facilitate the grasp of both question-related and incidental materials; prequestions, on the contrary, facilitate the grasp of question-specific materials but presumably limit the range of stimuli with respect to which effective learning takes place and thus depress incidental learnings. A brief synopsis at the beginning of a passage (e.g., a summary preview of a journal article) may, on the other hand, have a beneficial effect in promoting the proper mind-set and providing a meaningful framework from which the passage can be approached.

12. Carver (1972) presents a negative review of mathemagenic research. He sees recent research results as "ungeneralizable to most practical situations wherein questions might be used as aids to study," as well as "invalid with respect to theoretically significant tasks." He even questions the concept of mathemagenic behaviors, suggesting that it contributes more to confusion than to clarity of thought. He suggests that by inserting questions, the textbook developer may be influencing students to use their time inefficiently: "Certainly, it has not been demonstrated that questions are more efficient than the general direction to study long and hard." See Wilson and Koran (1976) for another thorough review of the literature; also Faw and Waller 1976.

COMMON INSTRUCTIONAL STRATEGIES

Lecture versus Discussion

A topic of long-standing controversy concerns the relative merits of the lecture and the discussion approach to classroom instruction. Unfortunately, much of what has been written on the subject to date has been at the level of personal opinion. The discussion, according to advocates, fosters critical thinking in the appraisal of ideas and the ability to support one's opinions; it encourages group participation as a prerequisite to effective citizenship; it develops a willingness to listen; and it promotes the ability to use effective English—all of which are presented as essential to the welfare and the survival of our democratic way of life. The lecture, by contrast, is part of the autocratic syndrome of classroom domination by the teacher.

Lecture or discussion? It depends on . . .

Such arguments are obviously exaggerations. Neither method is universally or even clearly superior to the other apart from any number of considerations. A crucial factor, for example, is the degree of consensus that underlies a given field or topic. Some subjects are highly structured, their major concepts and principles are well established, so that no competent person can raise serious doubts about them. Here there is very little to *discuss*. If discussion occurs, it is largely in the context of clarifying ideas for the slower student or correcting the occasional misunderstanding. A better solution here might be to encourage greater preparation, to have the ideas carefully organized and presented, or to provide tutorial help rather than to take up the whole class's time while tutoring one or two slower students. Perhaps an optional small group session for those who require special help might be in order.

Other fields do not have such a high level of consensus, e.g., the humanities, political science, and sociology. Here people do not always agree as to what is significant, critical, or even relevant. In such fields, a great deal may be gained by batting ideas around. The goal is not to parade facts but rather to generate new viewpoints and new interpretations. Frequently the point is not whether the group arrives at *the* solution (since there may not be a solution) but rather the extent to which the group focuses on the right issues, weighs relevant information, and gains greater insights through the interchange of ideas.

The lecture and the discussion are designed to serve essentially different purposes. In a high consensus field, where the task is to convey a well-established body of knowledge, one-way communication via the lecture (with tutorial facilities as needed) or the textbook may be both efficient and sufficient. In a low consensus field, by contrast, the discussion not only gives a broader perspective from which to deal with a given problem but it also gives students practice in sorting out ideas and in marshaling evidence in the resolution of a complex issue. It is not a question of *which* but rather of *when, where,* and *how.* Our task is not to endorse one or the other as unquestionably superior and to condemn the other but rather to understand the strengths and the limitations of each and to use each where it is the more appropriate.

THE LECTURE.   Despite continued criticism of its alleged shortcomings, the lecture, whether used alone or in conjunction with some form of student participation, continues as probably the primary instructional model in college and even in high school. It has a number of advantages, e.g., efficiency in covering large amounts of material in a short time, particularly when students have reached the stage of formal operations when ideas can be covered abstractly without constant recourse to concrete exemplars. The lecture is highly cost-effective; it can even be taped or videorecorded to cover unlimited audiences. The lecture permits the teacher to control the teaching-learning experience, say, by adjusting the speed of delivery as well as the level of presentation. He or she can structure the field, stressing the highlights through vocal emphasis and repetition, by periodically synthesizing the key ideas so as to facilitate understanding and retention, by increasing motivation through personal humor, dramatics, and the clarification of the expected outcomes of the presentation. The lecture is mutually reinforcing to the instructor and the students. Students get a sense of belonging, security, and even live entertainment; they get satisfaction of the cognitive drive through the new insights the lecture provides. Meanwhile the teacher also finds reinforcement in seeing the class move along.

The lecture survives despite . . .

But it also has weaknesses. Quite frequently it relies too heavily on verbal presentation when it should be at least supplemented by charts, diagrams, demonstrations, etc. The lecture can easily be misused; it often encourages passivity as students just sit at a low level of cognitive involvement, to the point of daydreaming or even falling asleep. If the lecturer simply repeats what is in the text, the lecture becomes wastefully redundant.[14] We would normally have to assume that the lecturer introduces extra materials from a variety of less accessible sources or that he structures the materials so as to bring interrelationships into focus.

A major source of difficulty in the use of the lecture is that the human mind is incapable of processing vast amounts of information as it goes flying by. There is, for example, no easy way of referring back to reconsider a point gone by without losing out on what is currently being presented. This can be serious when the material is complex and relatively unfamiliar; it would be correspondingly less devastating in the case of scholars who can readily sort out the ideas as they are presented. For that reason, the lecture, by and large, should be used only for short explorations involving a brief introduction in

14. Perhaps the popularity of the lecture stems from the fact that students have been conditioned to being told; many have not acquired the ability and the discipline necessary to permit self-instruction. As Ausubel et al. (1978) point out, for example, the common practice of underlining key words in the text is better suited to promoting rote learning than in bringing out the structure and interrelationships of the material.

clarifying the nature of a given topic. The shortness would be especially important in elementary school where children have a shorter attention span but, even in college, teachers ought to break up a solo performance into subunits so as to allow listeners a chance to consolidate as they go along.

Need to maximize
clarity

Care must be taken to maximize clarity. It is generally helpful, for example, for the class to know in advance the general direction the lecture will take and the major points it will cover. This can be done through a class syllabus listing relevant sources to be read prior to class or through providing a quick overview at the beginning of the class. The lecturer should stop periodically to synthesize the main points covered so far. He or she ought to concentrate on developing the structure of the topic—perhaps by using the chalkboard or an overhead projector to present the outline of the lecture—rather than overwhelm the class with endless details. If details, e.g., numerical data, have to be presented, the lecture should be supplemented by hand-outs, charts, and other graphics to which the class can refer both during and after the session. The possibility that other approaches might be more effective should, of course, be considered.

Lecturers should be on the alert for signs that they are losing their audience; they can, for instance, watch faces for frowns suggesting the need to elaborate on some points. They can periodically ask the class whether the material is clear. Where it is not possible to have this feedback, the lecture must be followed by some form of small group work, question-and-answer session, etc. More fundamentally, the lecture must necessarily be predicated on a common background derived from previous preparation as guided by a definite syllabus assignment and monitored, if possible, through a short quiz or small group discussion.

Sensitivity to the
audience

Student participation is essential. If, for example, we accept the Skinnerian view of the student's getting systematic reinforcement through predicting the lecturer's next intellectual move, the latter will have to make sure that the student is indeed "running alongside." Lecturers might pause periodically, ask a question or two, which the student will hopefully answer covertly, then provide the answer as feedback, and move on. Meaningfulness is essential if student involvement is to be maintained. This again means clarity—e.g., the use of precise, short sentences spoken at a reasonable pace, logical organization, clear explanations, etc. Lecturers need to highlight the major points and encourage student comprehension, say, through the use of questions, repetition, and examples. It is especially important to synthesize the main points at the end of the lecture so as to give students a sense of closure. It is also important to help students develop lecture-listening skills, e.g., the ability to structure lecture materials in outline form rather than simply attempting to take notes verbatim.[15]

15. Note taking during the lecture bears a confused relation to student achievement. This needs to be interpreted cautiously. It may be that the low correlation is due in part to the fact that many high-caliber students take only limited notes, simply because they already know the

The effectiveness of the lecture depends critically on the adequacy of the lecturer—voice, style, fluency, ability to organize, etc.—and it may be that some teachers are just not suited to the lecture as a teaching method. The rate of talking may be important. With a rather naive audience, it may be necessary to go slowly, especially over the important parts, repeating as necessary to allow each point to be integrated into cognitive structure. With more sophisticated audiences, the pace might be accelerated in order to discourage daydreaming and other losses of attention. Generally lecturers should be quite dynamic if they are to hold the audience mentally alert. They can, for example, communicate enthusiasm by means of gestures, vocal inflections, the occasional humor, etc.

THE DISCUSSION.   The discussion has a number of strengths, ranging from greater motivation arising from the group atmosphere to actual training in the free exchange of ideas, in weeding truth from trivia, in sharpening one's cognitive, intellectual, and communcation skills, and even in resisting pressures. It can promote a better understanding of the complexity of social issues and the dangers of accepting simplistic answers. It can encourage active involvement in the learning process. The discussion is particularly appropriate for changing attitudes and behavior (see Lewin 1942, 1958), especially when the discussion leads to group commitment to a given position and a given course of action.

But it too has its shortcomings. As Mouly (1973 p. 320) noted:

> Discussion often degenerates into a bull session characterized by a pooling of ignorance, endless arguments over inconsequentials, or worse, the loud expression of unverified opinions and endless verbiage by a few empty-heads and domination by a few demagogues. It can result in a vocal minority imposing its view on the group and monopolizing class time to the point that no one learns very much.

And whereas it is true that in the lecture the teacher does a lot of talking while the students do very little listening, the discussion is often plagued by the same problem: some of the more loquacious members do a lot of talking and the rest sit bored by the whole process—and understandably so, considering the level of discussion.[16]

Group dynamics as a factor in the discussion

A major determinant of the effectiveness of the discussion is *group dynamics:* i.e., the extent to which the group members are capable of complementing each other in arriving at greater clarity. Involved are such critical

---

material, whereas many low-ability students take copious notes. It does not follow that the latter would be as well off if they did not bother taking notes. Logically, notes should be helpful in reviewing, for example. Perhaps more important is the kind of notes the student takes, i.e., the development of skills in taking notes in organized outline form and preventing copious note taking from interfering with listening.

16. It might be noted that the discussion arose out of the criticism of the lecture and other teacher-centered approaches, criticisms going back to the days of Dewey and the progressive education movement (see Ausubel 1968, chapter 14).

factors as group compatibility, cohesiveness, and group spirit as reflected in a sense of personal responsibility and commitment on the part of the members. Conversely, it implies freedom from domination, hostility, animosity, hypersensitivity, and jockeying for status at the expense of group welfare. Particularly important is the network of communication that gradually evolves. There is too often, for example, a tendency toward a *centralized* discussion pattern in which all contributions are addressed to the teacher or group leader. A more adequate arrangement might be the *wheel* pattern or even better, the *all-channel* pattern where everybody reacts to everyone else directly. (See figure 9.1). The latter would be most productive after the group members had learned to work with one another and to tap each other at the point of strength and thus mobilize the total assets of the group for maximum productivity.

Participation of all the members is essential if the discussion is to achieve its purposes. This implies toning down the more loquacious (whose monopolizing of the floor is often more directly a reflection of ego needs than of wisdom), while at the same time drawing out the more insecure members. As group leader the teacher should set certain rules as to sharing class time and perhaps ensure that the group is small enough to permit everyone to participate.

The role of the teacher is crucial. The teacher must avoid dominating the discussion and take every opportunity to keep the "ball in the students' court." He or she must diplomatically discourage students from trying to make "brownie points" by saying what they think he or she would like to hear. There are, on the other hand, times when the teacher will be more or less forced to intervene, e.g., when the discussion has bogged down, where new directions need to be identified, or where serious errors are allowed to go unchallenged. It may take a certain degree of finesse for the instructor to intervene and yet let the students understand that they are still to carry the ball. It is also important for the teacher to appraise the effectiveness of the discussion with regard to a given problem. It may be that a particular topic is not suitable for discussion by students of a given grade and that, in the future, a different approach should be used.

A common background is essential

If the discussion is to be productive, the participants must begin with some common ground, as might be established through a well-defined prior reading assignment or a study guide. As Ausubel (1968) strongly emphasizes, "When this prerequisite condition is lacking, discussion understandably amounts to little more than the sharing of ignorance, prejudice, platitudes, preconceptions, and vague generalities." Before starting the discussion, it might be advisable for the teacher to have each student write down a broad outline of the crucial points the discussion should cover. The teacher might also provide reasonably defined guidelines in order to prevent the discussion from going in all directions at once. In other words, there is need for some degree of structure of the issues, realizing all the while the danger that such

Figure 9.1 Communication Patterns for Classroom Discussion

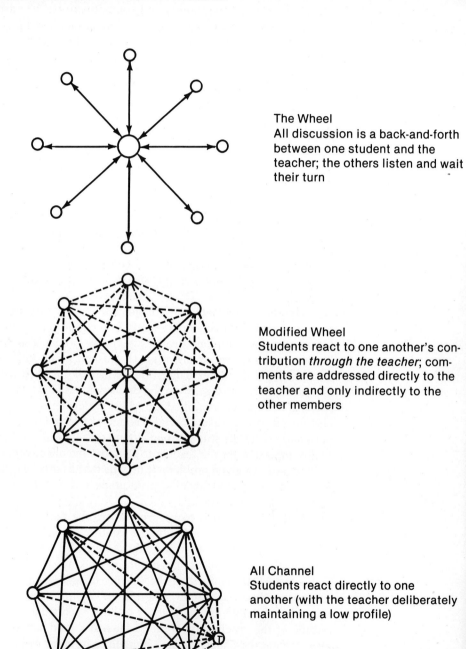

The Wheel
All discussion is a back-and-forth between one student and the teacher; the others listen and wait their turn

Modified Wheel
Students react to one another's contribution *through the teacher*; comments are addressed directly to the teacher and only indirectly to the other members

All Channel
Students react directly to one another (with the teacher deliberately maintaining a low profile)

prestructuring may preclude the critical analysis of important side issues and perhaps lead to predetermined answers.

The teacher's personality and temperament are important as determinants of whether to use the discussion approach. Generally the discussion calls for considerable patience and tolerance for the occasional irrelevant, trivial, or even incorrect contribution, the lack of structure and organization, the slow progress toward closure, etc. The teacher also needs a certain skill in reflecting important ideas that need to be pursued further and, finally, in synthesizing what the discussion has achieved. Equally important is the ability to encourage members to gradually assume the leadership of the group so that he or she can play a progressively less dominant role as consultant rather than director.

In summary, there is no way that the question of the relative effectiveness of the lecture and the discussion as instructional strategies can be resolved. To the extent that they operate in relatively different contexts, serve essentially different purposes, and call into play different skills, the research evidence is necessarily inconclusive, depending, for example, on the appropriateness of the two methods to the materials and the objectives in question, the nature of the criterion, the skill of the instructor in the use of the two methods, and of course, class size. Student preferences also vary depending on a variety of factors, including personality orientation.

That research should show no systematic differences in student performance under lecture or discussion conditions is not surprising in view of the many confounding factors involved.[17] The more profitable question is when to use one or the other and how to maximize its effectiveness. A number of suggestions can be surmised from the previous comments.

1. The lecture and the discussion are not fully interchangeable. By and large:

The former works best in high consensus fields; the discussion is more appropriate for low consensus fields.

The former is more appropriate for large groups, the discussion for small groups where everyone can participate.

The lecture seems best for presenting an overview, where a broad perspective of the area involves diverse viewpoints not readily available in one source, or for getting a broad view of a new area. The discussion is best when background data are readily available and the task is to grasp their meaning and interrelationships.

The lecture would be most effective when the instructor has special lecturing talents, e.g., some degree of eloquence, the ability to structure and organize broad fields of knowledge, sensitivity to student reaction, etc. By contrast, the leader of the discussion

17. Much of the research on the subject has been conducted at the college level (see McKeachie 1963), where mature students can adapt to requirements and compensate for inadequacies in any given method.

should have special skills in group dynamics and be able to tolerate ambiguity and a low level of structure and continuity of dis-
course.

2. Certain strategies enhance the effectiveness of both the lecture and the
    discussion:

    All instructors, whether lecturers or discussion leaders, should see
    themselves on video. They might benefit further by having an
    outside opinion as they watch themselves in action.

    As a lecturer, is he or she dynamic? Does he or she maintain stu-
    dent attention? Speak clearly? At a reasonable pace? Is the lec-
    ture well organized, with periodic questions, recaps, and synthe-
    ses? Does he or she use support materials, slides, and hand-outs
    effectively?

    As a discussion leader, does he or she involve the whole class?
    Draw out the more timid and curb the monopolizers? Keep in the
    background while still guiding the discussion to the consideration
    of critical issues?

    To the extent that the effectiveness of any instructional strategy is
    largely a function of the students' entering status, both lecturers
    and discussion leaders should ensure a high level of student prepa-
    ration. This can be done through advance learnings guided by a
    detailed syllabus supplemented by advance organizers. An occa-
    sional "pop-quiz" might help keep the system functional.

3. A number of suggestions can be made to improve the lecture:

    Prepare. Students quickly sense that you are speaking off the cuff.
    To be effective, the lecture must be structured and planned all the
    way from the identification of instructional objectives to the final
    synthesis. Bring slides and charts to highlight key points.

    Deliver the lecture from an outline. Keep an eye on the class for
    signs of confusion. Use different gestures, inflection of the voice,
    humor, etc., so as to maintain student interest.

    Keep the lecture dynamic and short, especially with young chil-
    dren. Break the monotony by introducing slides or charts; if stu-
    dents can't ask questions, why not ask yourself a question or two?

    Develop lecturing skills. Not everyone can be eloquent, but it
    should be possible for someone to present a few ideas in an en-
    gaging and forceful manner.

    Provide for follow-through with small group question-and-answer
    sessions and periodic quizzes.

4. A number of suggestions can be made to improve the discussion:

    Prepare. The discussion is not something whose success is guaran-
    teed when the topic is selected. Some topics do not lend them-
    selves to discussion by children of a certain stage of development.
    Define your objectives and the means whereby they are to be
    achieved.

Set up ground rules that will ensure maximum student participation. The goal is not only to have students clarify issues but also to develop certain skills, e.g., to distinguish between the important and the trivial.

Establish effective communication patterns. The teacher must get the students to the point where they can make their contribution even if it is not in agreement with the views of the teacher or the "status" members.

Develop group leadership skills, e.g., the ability to guide the discussion to productive ends without undue domination. The teacher and students should take time at the end of each discussion session to evaluate their effectiveness with a view to improving their performance on future topics.

The Recitation

The recitation combines the advantages of both

Most classroom teaching involves not so much the lecture or the discussion alone but rather a combination of lecture, question-and-answer, discussion, etc. At the high school level, for example, we might think in terms of a fifteen- to twenty-minute lecture or basic presentation, interrupted periodically by questions asked by either the teacher or the students, often followed by a brief discussion, questions, and finally seatwork, library work, and homework. During the lecture part, the teacher probably does most of the talking in structuring the field, identifying the issues, suggesting productive approaches, soliciting ideas, and reacting to student input.

This sort of recitation is particularly popular in college where presumably it serves the purposes for which college education is designed: namely, the imparting of large amounts of information while capitalizing on student maturity and student interest. It takes advantage of the lecture, the discussion, and individual study in relative proportion to the students' abilities, the teacher's temperament, as well as the requirements of the subject field. Such an approach is relatively flexible and provides the teacher with important feedback, especially if the class is small enough to allow everyone to participate.

Because of the time element, the recitation is generally restricted to a broad scaffolding of the topic, with the students then responsible for filling in the details in relation to the major principles involved or perhaps for the clarification of key similarities among the various aspects of the subject in relation to one another and to previously learned materials. As with other instructional methods, the effectiveness of the recitation depends critically on the adequacy of self-instruction regarding prerequisites carried out by the students prior to the class session. If prior learnings are indeed achieved, then the back-and-forth interaction has the effect of providing feedback and reinforcement, consolidating previous learnings, and especially fitting the pieces into perspective.

Conversely, the greatest problem with the recitation (as with other forms of instruction) stems from the students' lack of prerequisite learnings. It is often difficult to ensure that college students, for example, have indeed prepared for class so that they can truly contribute and benefit from class interaction. On the other hand, it also behooves the teacher to see that the classroom recitation goes beyond the preparation the students have already made on their own—whether in relating the materials to more general principles, to more specific applications, or to greater depths of insight. Otherwise there is no point in student preparation or in class attendance.

Discovery versus Reception Learning

A variant of the lecture-discussion issue, subject to essentially the same arguments, is the controversy between discovery and reception learning. More specifically, whereas the teacher's primary task is that of guiding the child's learning, a question arises as to the extent, the degree, and the specificity of the guidance that is to be provided for maximum facilitation of pupil learning. Skinner (1954), in his programmed learning approach, insists that learning be so minutely and continuously directed as to require the unfailing guidance of a machine. Bruner (1960), on the other hand, has come out strongly in favor of what he calls the *discovery* method (see chapter 12). The solution, e.g., the underlying principle, is not given; the students discover it. In its more general sense, the teacher's role is that of guide and coordinator, keeping the children's eye on the problem, say, through well-directed questions, prompts, leads, etc. Ideally such an approach might be expected to result in greater motivation, in more penetrating, although perhaps less extensive and continuous, education, in greater understanding and meaningfulness, and in greater proficiency at problem solving. Perhaps more important, assuming the occasional success, it may give children a feeling of confidence in their own ability to think productively about intellectual problems.

Bruner's discovery model: Its premises

On the other hand, the discovery method also has limitations. In a thorough critique, Ausubel (1961, 1968; Ausubel et al. 1978) cautions against overreliance on discovery as a regular instructional procedure. He suggests that discovery be used sparingly in the acknowledged gamble that even its theoretical advantages have not been demonstrated. He sees, for example, a planned discovery unit imbedded in a larger program of expository instruction as well suited for providing students with practice in independent activity without jeopardizing the acquisition of a coherent body of content, but he believes that discovery is far too time-consuming to be used as a standard approach to the curriculum and, further, that there is little need for a discovery approach beyond the concrete stage in the Piaget developmental schedule. Typically, the discovery approach requires a great deal of personal investment and intellectual effort, as well as background, on the part of the learner and is therefore probably best suited to the more intellectually mature students, particularly those fascinated by reflective strategies.

The critical point underlying Bruner's insistence on discovery is his parallel argument that reception learning is typically a passive, semirote pro-

Discovery: A
reaction against
didactic teaching

cess (Bruner 1961). Historically the school's emphasis on student-centered approaches began as a Gestalt reaction to the drill and parrot memory encouraged by (misuses of) the Law of Exercise. It accelerated into a movement toward the *project or activity* method and other forms of progressive education of the 1930s, carrying with it a corresponding repudiation of *reception learning* and *expository (didactic)* teaching on the grounds that they were conducive to the rote learning of isolated and meaningless facts. The current emphasis on discovery is a reflection of the continued dissatisfaction with reception learning, whose critics insist that meaning cannot be *given*, that meaning must be *discovered* if empty verbalisms are to be avoided.

Unfortunately far too much of the learning in school is indeed rote learning. A number of students, for example, memorize the proof of the theorems of geometry. Some teachers encourage this sort of rote learning by penalizing students who do not use the elegant language of the text. Many students resort to rote learning because they lack the necessary background to understand the material. Some lack confidence in their ability to learn meaningfully and, in their anxiety over examinations, rely on rote memory to conceal their lack of genuine understanding.

But while rote learning is generally to be condemned, the repudiation of reception learning as a corollary statement is totally unwarranted. It is true that reception learning can and has resulted in verbalism; it is true that our schools frequently make rote learning more or less "necessary." But then to argue that these are inevitable or even typical outcomes of reception learning is to resort to a straw-man technique designed to make its worst abuse stand out as an inherent characteristic of the method. The solution is to guard against the abuse, not to discard the method. Meanwhile we cannot equate reception learning with inherent meaninglessness and rote learning any more than we can equate its opposite, the discovery or problem-solving method, with inherent meaningfulness.

In the obvious interest of economy and efficiency, the bulk of the learning in our schools must necessarily be reception learning, particularly at the upper levels where it has distinct advantages. While we must recognize the futility of an overly verbal approach with cognitively immature children, we must also recognize that the developmental limitations of early childhood relative to reception learning do not apply in adolescence and adulthood. The fact that the

Expository teaching
best at formal
operations stage

primary school child relies heavily on concrete experiences does not mean that the high school student must also operate from concrete premises. By junior high school, a verbal approach is both necessary and effective. We must especially recognize that reception learning is not necessarily, or even typically, passive. True reception learning, according to Ausubel, calls for learners to relate new ideas to existing principles and concepts in their cognitive structure, to apprehend in what way they are similar and in what way they are different from previously acquired concepts, to translate them into a personal frame of reference consistent with their own idiosyncratic experiences, and often to formulate what for them is a new perspective calling for considerable reorganization of their cognitive structure.

At the empirical level, most studies of the relative merits of discovery and reception learning seem to contrast extreme forms of completely independent discovery against equally extreme rote reception learning (see Ausubel 1968; Wittrock 1966). A more reasonable position might be *guided discovery* in which the learner is given some of the cues. Actually the question is ambiguous. First, we must be sure we are talking about a problem where discovery and reception learning are logical alternatives. Second, they are designed to serve essentially different purposes so that in order to be talking intelligently about their relative advantages, one must state the desired outcome. The teacher might be satisfied with having students memorize rules to apply to the solution of similar problems or, on the other hand, may be interested in having children learn techniques for discovering new rules, i.e., problem-solving skills.

Although the evidence is quite equivocal, it would seem that when the learner lacks the necessary background or motivation, guided discovery is probably most effective; if, on the other hand, the learner has the necessary knowledge and the willingness to assimilate the material, directed (expository) techniques may be both equally effective and more efficient; and where the purpose of the learning experience is to promote effective strategies of problem solving, where the actual subject matter is of secondary importance, then discovery or perhaps guided discovery techniques are most appropriate. On

Guided discovery combines advantages of both

Evidence equivocal

the other hand, we have to assume that the task is not so difficult that the learner actually does not succeed at least occasionally in discovering the underlying relationships. It must also be noted that to be successful, the discovery method must be planned. Nothing is to be gained from simply turning children loose to discover for themselves the solution to an ill-conceived problem. On balance, then, guided discovery seems to offer some of the efficiency of directed learning along with some of the benefits of the discovery process.

Mastery Learning

In recent years, a new emphasis has been placed on mastery as a teaching-learning strategy. The idea is not new: it goes back to the 1920s when Washburne devised the Winnetka Plan (1922) and Morrison (1926) developed a similar program at the University of Chicago laboratory school. Mastery learning was revived in 1963 by Carroll's suggestion that the variable underlying instruction be the time allowed for the students to master a given set of materials rather than the degree to which a given set of materials can be mastered in a fixed unit of time. The idea was picked up by Bloom (1973, 1974; Bloom et al. 1971), who claims that most students (perhaps over 90 percent) can master what we have to teach them if given sufficient time. The task of instruction, then, is to make it possible for every learner to proceed at his or her own pace to the point of mastery.

Operationally mastery learning is generally geared to a modular criterion-referenced model in which the student, working from a self-contained package—complete with study guide, instructional materials, and self-evaluative devices—proceeds independently of one's teacher and peers. Such an approach typically calls for

1. A clear definition of objectives available to both teacher and learner.
2. Diagnostic tools to evaluate the adequacy of prerequisite learnings, followed by remedial and developmental exercises as needed.
3. Self-contained instructional materials, including printed lessons, tapes, slides, references, and self-evaluation devices.[18]

Mastery learning helpful but no panacea

Mastery learning is not a panacea. First, it is not new. It was common in the 1920s and 1930s where adherence to mastery standards resulted in successive grade retention to the point where some students reached the age of twelve while still trying to master the content of grade three. It remains to be seen whether the more adequate definition of objectives, the more adept packaging of curricular content, etc., will somehow make a success out of what had previously been essentially a failure (see Mehrens and Lehmann 1973, p.

18. The idea is best referenced by pointing to such individualized programs as Individually Prescribed Instruction (IPI), Program for Learning in Accordance with Need (PLAN), etc. (See chapter 12.) On the other hand, the idea could also be implemented through the contract system, where a student undertakes a clearly defined project, working at his or her own pace toward a set of well-defined objectives. Provisions would have to be made for systematic reinforcement to keep the student at the task. It may be that such an approach is not suitable for all children or for all units of study.

450). Mastery learning, for example, may soften but does not eliminate competition and invidious comparisons. Some students gallop through the required sequences and have considerable time for the "goodies," while those who simply plod along frequently deal only with the frustrations. (The mastery approach can also be an administrative nightmare. Unless closely monitored, students are likely to pile up at the end of the semester; many end up with an "incomplete," and a number just never achieve the required mastery.)

More fundamentally, as Cronbach pointed out in 1969, the mastery learning model is restricted to subject matter that is *closed*, i.e., to *training*. The task is to have all students master a finite set of learning objectives; it implies that the student can get to the end of what is to be known.[19] The truth is that education is unlimited, that with respect to any meaningful educational goal, far more can be taught (and learned) than can be incorporated reasonably in mastery standards. Operationally, if mastery standards are to be met by all students, they must necessarily be set far short of *complete mastery* (even in a limited sense of the word), perhaps far short of what good students would want to achieve on their own were they not reminded that they had met the prespecified standards and ought to go on to the next unit. As Mueller (1976, p. 50) points out, "By prespecifying a finite number and level of objectives and concentrating efforts on bringing all students to this level, not only does the mastery learning model fail to maximize learning for faster students, it actually precludes it."

Logical and operational difficulties

The mastery learning concept presents serious logical as well as operational problems, the most obvious of which is that both the slower and the faster students have only so many hours in a day to devote to study and presumably only so many years to get an elementary (or high) school education. Countering this reality, Bloom (1969, 1971) makes the highly questionable claim that "as instruction and student use of time become more effective, it is likely that most students will need less time to learn the subject to mastery and the ratio of time for the slow and the faster learners may be reduced from about six to one to perhaps three to one."[20] He postulates that as they proceed through units on a mastery basis, the slower students somehow accelerate their pace of learning relative to that of their faster peers and that initial differences in aptitude or intelligence are not "significant predictors of time and help needed in the later learning units in the series" (Bloom 1974). A number of critics (e.g., Buss 1976; Cronbach and Snow 1977; Nunnally 1976) have strongly challenged this "myth of the vanishing individual differences." Cron-

19. This is again the fallacy of the behavioral objectives. See Russell in chapter 2; also Travers 1973, p. 207.
20. It is not clear how the second half of the sentence follows from the first. A more tenable assumption would seem to be that as both the faster and the slower students develop effective skills (and capitalize on a strong foundation), the faster students will simply outdistance all the more their slower colleagues, as implied in the definition of aptitude (see Ausubel et al. 1978, p. 392). In the Suppes (1965) project in accelerated mathematics, with students free to proceed at their own rate, the pace of the brightest students was five to ten times that of the slower students, even though the participants were all gifted (IQ from 122 to 167).

bach and Snow, for example, note that "the current propaganda for 'mastery learning' appears to make almost precisely the claim that this review has overturned. One simply cannot eliminate individual differences in learning" (p. 214).

It is one thing to accept the view (say, as presented by Ausubel or Gagné) that an adequate cognitive structure of relevant prerequisites is the primary determinant of one's ability to achieve further learnings and to insist on a substantial degree of mastery, particularly in sequential subjects; certainly the student who gets a D in Math 101 is hardly in the best position to undertake Mathematics 102. But it is something else again to claim that mastery learning will somehow virtually eliminate differences in aptitude as a factor in learning. Carroll saw mastery as a trade-off—a matter of covering less material more thoroughly during a given unit of time. Students probably would be better off from the standpoint of establishing a firm base for future learnings to cover less material but to a meaningful level of mastery than to have to cover so much material that they can only get a superficial grasp of what it is all about. It might be advisable, for example, to combine greater mastery of critical sequential subjects such as mathematics, along with some retrenchment of the content of other perhaps less sequentially critical subjects.

INDEPENDENT STUDY

In recent years considerable emphasis has been placed on independent study as an aspect of the school's overall program. The premise is that because of the current knowledge explosion, the only legitimate education for the life children will face is in helping them learn how to learn. In fact, schooling may be viewed as the process by which students are helped to become independent of the school so that they can continue their education after formal schooling has ended. Actually the present impetus toward independent study stems more clearly from the current dissatisfaction with group instruction in the light of the wide range of individual differences in any classroom. More specifically, it can be argued that even with serious efforts to provide for prerequisites through outside preparation, individual differences almost preclude the use of group teaching procedures. The typical outcome is that the bright are bored while the dull are frustrated.

Individualized instruction: The new approach

Operationally, the school has attempted to deal with the problem of individual differences through such strategies as ability grouping, differential promotional policies, enrichment, and other modifications of class load. Independent study and individualized instruction constitute other alternatives. Ideally independent study is designed to develop self-direction, resourcefulness, personal initiative and responsibility, and interest in learning for its own sake. In practice, it would seem that unless considerable direction is provided in such matters as selecting a meaningful area of study, locating information, and developing a work schedule, considerable waste is likely to result, at least at first.

Independent study can be instituted through the use of *contracts* specifying in some detail what is to be learned, the way the students are to demonstrate that they have achieved the objectives, the resources to be used in carrying out the contract, the intermediate checkpoints at which progress is to be evaluated, and other aspects of the enterprise. A critical factor in the effectiveness of such an approach is the student's maturity. Whereas a self-actualizing student can take responsibility and grow to be more self-directive in the absence of compulsory class attendance and teacher monitoring, it does not follow that all children are capable of such independence.

As to the effectiveness of independent study, it is difficult for research to come up with a conclusive answer. To the extent that independent study means striking out on one's own, it automatically precludes the availability of a meaningful comparison group and the identification of a meaningful criterion. If, on the other hand, the question is whether a resourceful student can study independently the content of a course normally offered, say, by lecture, then the whole issue revolves around the caliber of the student, the resources available for independent study, the nature of the content to be covered, the criterion measure, etc. If both the lecture and independent learning are geared to readily available textbook materials, there is no reason to expect differences in outcome.

Evidence equivocal

Also of interest in the context of individualized instruction is tutoring, which in the public school setting typically means teacher aides or peer tutors providing remedial help and practice to slower students. The evidence concerning peer tutoring is inconclusive. Ellson (1976), for example, argues that the widespread belief that tutoring is almost invariably effective is simply unjustified with respect to either the cognitive or the affective domain. Devin-Sheehan et al. (1976) question whether the benefits to tutor or tutee do nothing more than reflect the additional time spent on task (see also Allen 1976). (The record becomes even less favorable if we take into account the fact that a study reporting positive results is more likely to be published than one showing no significant difference.) We have to recognize that tutoring, like all other forms of teaching, differs in quality and appropriateness, but it seems unlikely that the average relatively untrained tutor could provide the insights and the structure that would promote effective verbal learning, for example. Tutoring might be more productive with certain types of one-to-one drill, e.g., helping the child with word recognition or the addition combinations. Peer tutoring can provide on-the-spot developmental and remedial help to the slower child, meanwhile releasing the busy teacher to attend to other responsibilities. This can be profitable, especially since research evidence suggests that the tutor actually benefits more than the tutee, particularly in the area of motivation. Rather than tutoring, Ellson suggests more effective and more systematic teaching, with greater emphasis on diagnostic and remedial help, greater concern for prerequisites, and improvement of teaching materials (e.g., simplifying certain passages in the textbook).

Homework

Homework, as another form of "independent study," can serve a number of purposes, ranging from self-instruction on a prescribed topic to practice on a variety of examples of previously learned rules. It can also involve a special project, e.g., interviewing a city official on some local issue. On the positive side, we might say that high school students who plan to go to college need to discipline themselves to keep up with their studies. Frequently, however, homework is simply routine with no constructive purpose beyond having the slower children finish at home what the faster students do during the class period. Presumably the hope is that whatever difficulty slows children down at school will disappear through sheer exertion. Unfortunately, slow children often come from lower-class homes where the facilities for studying are essentially nonexistent. Their slowness is often indicative of a need for help, which they certainly cannot get at home. As a result, the teacher is generally faced with the need to devote most of the next day's class to a review of the homework assignment, which bores everyone who has done the work the night before, and the whole enterprise becomes a commitment to mediocrity. Unless the school provides supervised study halls, whether during the school day or after school, the usual form of homework is not likely to be too productive.

Homework: Need for clarity

The school needs to clarify its objectives in this area. If homework is to serve a meaningful purpose, it is essential that it be carefully planned and closely integrated with the school's program. It would also seem logical that if children are to engage in self-study at home, they would need to have developed the required self-study skills, e.g., the ability to read with comprehension, the ability to apply underlying rules in solving geometry problems, etc. Homework, including library work, is, of course, essential in college as preparation for class, examinations, term papers, and other assignments. Flexibility in the time element makes it an especially effective means of compensating for individual differences in ability, background, and study skills. The fact that outside help is usually available from other students or graduate assistants frequently means that homework is what spells the difference for many students between academic failure and academic survival.

Programmed Instruction

The programmed instruction movement was launched in the late 1950s as a consequence of the impetus provided by Skinner's (1954) well-known article; it reached a hectic peak in the early 1960s when it was widely acclaimed as the educational discovery of the century. Since then mounting criticism has been leveled at all aspects of programmed instruction, from its theoretical premises to the inadequacies of both programs and hardware. At the theoretical level, for example, Ausubel (1968) argues that the neobehavioristic premises from which the teaching machine operates are more pertinent to learning by rote than to the learning of meaningful verbal materials with which the classroom is concerned.

As to actual results, the research evidence is quite equivocal (see Jamison et al. 1974). Programmed instruction does not seem too effective in promoting outcomes at the higher levels of the taxonomy, for example. The nature of the learner makes a difference; programmed instruction seems to be quite effective when used in industry with more mature individuals motivated toward a definite goal. However, we must recognize that we are not so much evaluating the effectiveness of programmed instruction as we are dealing with the effectiveness of a particular program and that many of them are of definitely inferior quality. As it pertains to the classroom, the issue is not whether a teaching machine is more effective than a live teacher but rather what teaching functions can be delegated to the machine so as to free the teacher to do those things that only a teacher can do.

CAI provides greater flexibility

More promising in this regard is *computer-assisted instruction* (CAI) or *computer-managed instruction* (CMI), which because of its tie-in with the computer, more adequately incorporates the versatility needed for effective programming. Whereas the mechanics have yet to be fully worked out, undoubtedly the potentialities of CAI, whether in the school, business, or general adult education, are relatively unlimited. Its greatest asset is its ability to cater to each student at his or her level of ability as determined from previous performance and current progress and to provide instant feedback. It can also give the teacher an immediate printout of the student's performance. The major drawbacks to date are the relative complexity of the language to which the computer responds and its relatively high cost, the latter now running five to six times that of conventional instruction on a per-student basis.[21] CAI and other computer-based approaches are potentially effective for the transmission of the established contents of most subject-matter fields. They would, on the contrary, be less suitable for dealing with controversial subjects or for promoting originality and independence of thought. Much would depend on the quality of the program, its lucidity, its ability to provide structure, and the logical sequencing of subject matter.

Learning packages

Of special interest here as an implementation of the CAI concept are the various instructional systems developed in the past decade in an attempt at individualization through packaged instruction (see, for example, Gronlund 1974; Hochstein 1971; Hull 1973; Klausmeier and Ripple 1971; Schneider 1972; Sorenson 1970). Individually Prescribed Instruction (IPI), for example, is a comprehensive instructional system geared to a set of educational objectives carefully tailored and sequenced to individual needs, so that instruction is built

21. Cost should be reduced as the expanding market absorbs developmental costs and as advances in the field of minicomputers continue (see Hartmann 1971; Jamison et al. 1974; Koch 1973; Bunderson and Faust 1976). Among the more elaborate systems is PLATO IV (Programmed Logic for Automated Teaching Operations; Smith and Sherwood 1976; see also Bitzer and Skaperdas 1970; Gunderson and Faust 1976), which at fifty to seventy-five cents per student-hour is relatively cost-effective. Another big installation is TICCIT (Time-Shared Interaction Computer-Controlled Information Television; MITRE 1974).

on previous steps and is, in turn, a prerequisite for the next step. Each package consists of teaching materials, including teaching strategies, diagnostic instruments, and a monitoring system carefully synchronized to the attainment of predetermined objectives, so that the student can proceed with minimal teacher intervention. Special features of the program include its emphasis on the diagnosis of current status, carefully prepared prescriptions, and a constant monitoring of pupil progress in the attainment of the objectives.

Program for Learning in Accordance with Needs (PLAN) and Individually Guided Education (IGE) are similarly designed to provide students with an academic program suited to their individual needs, interests, and abilities. PLAN, for example, emphasizes the dual goal of making the program academically relevant to students by giving them a choice in what and how they learn while simultaneously teaching them the skills of appropriate decision making. These programs typically consist of modules incorporating a variety of printed materials, unit exercises, programmed materials, tapes, films, and other audiovisual aids, etc., all specifically selected for individual students on the basis of past achievement and academic goals, and, of course, test feedback.[22]

As to the effectiveness of packaged instruction, again the evidence is equivocal. Good and Brophy (1977), for example, reject the notion that the school can replace teachers with teacher-proof packages, with the curriculum so well selected and the content so well organized and so clear that students can learn completely on their own. They suggest that packaged instruction may work with high-ability students with functional reading ability, independent study habits, and strong motivation: "When these assumptions hold, individualized programmed methods work. Even here, though, it remains questionable whether they are preferable to traditional methods. When these assumptions do not hold, these programs do not work" (p. 207). Travers (1977) presents a similarly negative evaluation of packaged instruction (see also Oettinger and Marks 1968). This is not to suggest that these programs are totally without merit, for indeed they serve a purpose, but it does suggest the need for caution in their use.

HIGHLIGHTS OF THE CHAPTER

Even though children must learn for themselves, their learning can be made more certain and more effective by competent instruction. Schools exist for that very purpose. The present chapter deals with some of the considerations involved in the facilitation of learning.

1. The teacher's main contribution to the child's learning consists of helping develop insight into the nature of the product and the process by which it is to

22. Widely used at the college level is Keller's Personalized System of Instruction (PSI). See Kulik et al. (1979) for a favorable review of PSI.

be attained, preventing the development of faulty techniques, and giving the learner moral support.

2. Educational psychology must be concerned with both how the student learns and what the teacher does to facilitate this learning.

3. The main impetus for a technology of instruction has come from the behaviorists, who have systematically advocated that the teacher assume a relatively directive role in the promotion of learning.

4. Teaching is a complex and complicated proposition, involving the interaction of a number of teacher, pupil, and situational variables. No prescription can be given, and no one style of teaching is effective for all teachers in all teaching situations.

5. A technology of instruction must generally derive from and find support in some established theoretical position.

6. Some progress is being made in the development of instructional methodologies. The evidence concerning the use of mathemagenic strategies is equivocal.

7. Despite considerable attention over the years, the issues concerning the lecture versus discussion, discovery versus reception learning, and, more recently, mastery learning and packaged instruction are still matters of personal preference relative to a given situation rather than of documented superiority of one over the others.

SUGGESTIONS FOR FURTHER READING

Association for Supervision and Curriculum Development. *Learning and the Teacher.* Washington, D.C.: The Assn., 1959. A useful discussion of the role of the teacher in the promotion of learning as seen from a humanistic point of view.

BUNDERSON, C. V., and G. W. FAUST. Programmed and computer-assisted instruction. In N. L. Gage, ed., *The Psychology of Teaching Methods,* pp. 44–90. 75th Yrbk. N.S.S.E., Pt. 1. Chicago: Univ. Chicago Press, 1976. A good discussion of recent development in CAI. Present problems include making CAI cost-effective and producing instructionally effective courseware and developing prescriptive models for the production of such courseware.

GLASER, ROBERT, and LAUREN RESNICK. Instructional psychology. *Annual Rev. of Psychol.* (1972). A scholarly review of current research dealing with instruction and related topics. Appears at irregular intervals; check recent editions.

GORDON, IRA, et al. *Criteria for Theories of Instruction.* Washington, Assn. Superv. Curr. Devel., 1968. Presents guidelines for creating and for evaluating curricular and instructional materials.

HIGHET, GILBERT. *The Art of Teaching.* New York: Knopf, 1950. A good presentation of teaching as seen from the traditional point of view.

McDONALD, JAMES B. Myths about instruction. *Educ. Lead.* 22 (1965):571–576. Points to six myths about instruction that we have uncritically accepted—e.g., that because each discipline has a set of fundamental ideas or principles about which the fabric of knowledge is woven, this is necessarily the way the learner learns and that this is the way to organize knowledge for instructional purposes. A challenging article.

SKINNER, B. F. *The Technology of Teaching.* New York: Appleton, 1968. The clearest presentation of Skinner's point of view concerning the technology of instruction. The emphasis is obviously behavioristic. Should be read.

TOBIAS, SIGMUND. Achievement-treatment interactions. *Rev. Educ. Res.* 46 (1976):61–74. A thorough review of the literature suggesting that adjunct questions are of little help to students with a good background. It seems that the higher the level of prior knowledge, the lower the instructional support required. Conversely, the lower the prior achievement level, the greater and more direct the instructional support required.

WOODWORTH, J. G. Theoretical bases for a psychology of instruction. *Canad. Educ. Res. Dig.* 5 (1965):14–26. A good overview of the various theories of learning as they relate to classroom instruction.

QUESTIONS AND PROJECTS

1. To what extent can learning and teaching be seen as separate and independent activities? To what extent can theories of learning provide the theoretical perspective for teaching?

2. How might teaching a skill, or a fact, or a series of nonsense syllables differ from teaching a concept, or problem solving?

3. Teachers in training often complain that college professors of education operate on a "Do-as-I-say, not as-I-do" basis. Is this a valid criticism?

4. Identify clear-cut situations where discovery methods would be in order. Describe situations in which reception learning would be clearly indicated.

5. College professors often display more interest in increasing their mastery over subject matter than in improving their pedagogical skills. What does this imply about the way they perceive their role? What might be done to improve college teaching?

SELF-TEST

1. Teaching is best defined as the process of
   a. facilitating student learning.
   b. implementing the school's curriculum.
   c. interacting with students.
   d. promoting student growth.
   e. transmitting knowledge and skills.

2. Which of the following is *not* one of the teacher's major tasks in promoting learning?
   a. To forestall the development of faulty techniques
   b. To give the learner moral support
   c. To help students clarify what they are to learn and how
   d. To provide remedial help where indicated
   e. To set the educational goals to be attained

3. What is the major contribution of practice to learning?
   a. It consolidates previously acquired learnings.
   b. It increases precision and smoothness in the learning of skills.
   c. It is a necessary and a sufficient condition for learning to take place.
   d. It promotes insight into the nature of the content to be learned.
   e. It provides the opportunity for learning to take place.

4. The present consensus concerning the parts-versus-whole issue is that the whole method is best when
   a. the learner is relatively mature and knowledgeable.
   b. the material can be divided into logical parts.
   c. the material has an inherent structure.
   d. the material is long and involved.
   e. the material is of uneven difficulty.

5. The lecture-versus-discussion issue revolves primarily around
   a. the characteristics of the students.
   b. the content being presented.
   c. the goals we set for ourselves.
   d. the personal preferences of students and their teachers.
   e. the relative effectiveness of the instructor in the use of each.

6. Which of the following is an *incorrect* statement in the discovery-versus-reception learning controversy?
   a. Discovery is necessarily a slow, time-consuming process.
   b. Guided discovery is a viable compromise between discovery and reception learning.
   c. Not all subject content is amenable to discovery procedures.
   d. Reception learning is a typically passive process.
   e. The relative superiority of reception learning and discovery varies with the educational goals to be achieved.

7. Recently developed instructional packages (e.g., PLAN, IPI, etc.) are most appropriate for
   a. children with learning disabilities.
   b. large classes with inadequate teacher input.
   c. lower-class children in need of remedial help.
   d. mature learners with effective study skills.
   e. the underachiever who does not do well in the typical classroom.

TEN

Classroom Management

In our eagerness to get children to learn the prescribed curriculum, we commonly forget that motivation for learning depends on the needs of the learner, not those of the teacher. As a consequence, we think of motivation as something the teacher does *to* the student.

Henry C. Lindgren (1962)

It has been amazing to me how just one teacher can damage or destroy a child's enthusiasm for a given subject.

William M. Simpson (1963)

One of the fundamental tenets of modern education is that an adequately motivated child disciplines himself, and that the need for extraneous forms of discipline is evidence of failure to provide the kind of motivation needed for adequate performance.

H. Beaumont and F. G. Macomber (1949)

The true measure of the value of "discipline" is in the rapidity with which it renders itself unnecessary.

Morris B. English (1961)

— Discusses motivation and discipline as interrelated phenomena concerned with the effective operation of the classroom
— Contrasts the behavioristic and the humanistic positions regarding motivation and outlines their implications
— Presents an in-depth treatment of classroom discipline

PREVIEW: KEY CONCEPTS

1. Motivation and discipline refer to the two ends of the same problem: how to maximize positive classroom behavior and correspondingly minimize disruptive classroom behavior.
2. Behaviorists and humanists present very different pictures of classroom management. Behaviorists control behavior through selective reinforcement; humanists rely on the child's inherent need to grow.
3. In a sense, effectiveness in classroom management implies effectiveness in the teacher's manipulation of incentives relative to the child's goals.
4. The primary elements in effective classroom motivation and discipline are a positive self-concept and a meaningful academic program. Gimmicks are not enough.
5. Discipline is best seen in the context of a planned program designed to help the child develop self-direction. Excessive classroom misbehavior typically reflects inadequacies in the school's program.
6. Punishment seems more appropriate as a disciplinary than a motivational strategy.

PREVIEW QUESTIONS

1. What do motivation and discipline have in common from the standpoint of the psychology of classroom management?
      To what extent can they be expected to respond to the same "teaching" strategies?
2. What are some of the distinctive features of the behavioristic and the humanistic approaches to classroom management?
      What are the relative merits of the reinforcement and the self-actualization models?
3. What is the classroom teacher's primary defense against undue classroom misbehavior?
4. To what extent are student misbehavior and lack of student motivation indices of teacher incompetence?
5. Just what is the purpose of classroom discipline?
      What role ought punishment play in meaningful classroom discipline?

Classroom management addresses itself to the problem of encouraging children to devote their energies and talents to the fullest in the pursuit of a meaningful education. More specifically, it includes the dual problems commonly referred to as *motivation* and *discipline,* both of which are of critical concern to the classroom teacher and to the effectiveness of the school.[1] It attempts to make explicit with reference to the classroom some of the principles of the dynamics of human behavior presented in chapter 4. It is not intended to provide a bag of tricks for use as a cure-all for the indifference toward school work often encountered among children placed in an unsuitable school environment, nor is it meant as an antidote for an ill-fitting curriculum, pedagogical malpractice, or other inadequacies in our schools. Motivation is more than a rabbit that can be pulled out of the hat at the beginning of a lesson to make the students, individually and collectively, eager to participate in whatever the school has to offer, regardless of suitability.

MOTIVATION IN THE CLASSROOM

The school can achieve its purposes only if it can induce its students individually and collectively to participate wholeheartedly in its activities. Unfortunately this ideal situation seems to be the exception rather than the rule. A casual visit to the average classroom is likely to reveal anywhere from one to several children lackadaisically going through the motions, one or two doing nothing much more than "just sitting here," and another one or two waiting for the first opportunity to disrupt the whole operation. Yet these are often the same youngsters who, on the playground or in their after-school job—where presumably it matters to them—will systematically "give it all they've got." Unfortunately, despite deep concern, most teachers find themselves unable to effect a change in the situation. To date, their major emphasis has been on the relatively unenlightened use of such common incentives as competition for grades, with invariably the major thrust on the aversive side—reproof, condemnation, and other forms of punishment—as the standard item of their motivational arsenal.

The problem is that teachers do not understand what makes children tick. They do not understand that perhaps previous experience has led many children to form a self-image that causes them to reject everything connected with the school, that school work is simply not related to their needs and purposes, that a number of students have never been able to cash in on the school's reward system. The result is typically "a lack of motivation" and a corresponding tendency toward misbehavior. As stated in simple operational terms by

---

1. Discipline is best seen in the context of the failure or the misdirection of motivation.

Problem: Too little
constructive
behavior; too much
disruptive behavior
Kooi and Schutz (1965) in their factor analysis of classroom disruptive behavior, the teacher is faced with too little constructive classroom behavior and/or too much disruptive classroom behavior. The problem is clear and obvious. The solution, unfortunately, cannot be defined so simply. There is no recipe, no prescription. What is called for are broad insights into the dynamics of human behavior as they operate in the context of the classroom.

To put the problem in perspective, we might consider classroom motivation against the background of the two major psychological positions—i.e., cognitive theory and behaviorism—as presented in chapter 3. The first sees motivation as the expression of internal drives that energize and direct the learner's behavior. In the context of McClelland's need for achievement or Maslow's basic drive toward self-actualization, classroom motivation is simply an aspect of the individual's inner need to do, to grow, to *become*. The second emphasizes more direct control of student behavior through selective reinforcement.

The Cognitive Position

The clearest version of the cognitive position on motivation comes from the humanists, e.g., Rogers, Maslow, and Combs. Their basic premise is that every individual has an inherent need to actualize his or her potentialities. Conversely, failure to move in the direction of self-actualization can be explained only in terms of serious environmental obstacles that interfere with this overwhelming need to grow and to become. The teacher's task is to remove these obstacles in order to release the individual's capacity for growth.

Maslow: Deficiency
and growth needs
Fundamental in this context is Maslow's distinction between Deficiency (D) needs and Being (B), or Growth (G), needs in his seven-level hierarchy and the corresponding distinction between safety and growth choice (see chapter 4). Children cannot tend to their needs for self-actualization when their lower needs are seriously frustrated. At the deprivation level, the individual's behavior is necessarily oriented toward self-protection; it is only when the survival needs have been met and the higher needs come into play that he or she has the opportunity to choose lines of behavior that will lead to growth. (See figure 10.1)

Good and bad
choosers
Maslow distinguishes between the bad choosers and the good choosers, with the former so preoccupied with their physiological and safety needs that they typically choose behaviors that are shortsighted, self-defeating, and counterproductive; e.g., rationalizing, boasting, or resorting to defiance or delinquency. They may refuse to participate in the school program because they are afraid of not being able to protect a weak ego in the event they were to be less than totally successful after having tried.

Two sets of forces are active in each of us. One set makes us want to cling to safety; because of fear, anxiety, and uncertainty, we are afraid to take a chance, afraid we might lose the little we have now. The other set of forces

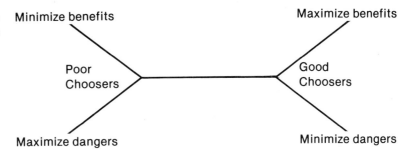

Figure 10.1 Encouraging People to Make Good Choices (Maslow 1968)

impels us toward self-fulfillment of our capabilities. In all choices, we must weigh the two sets of factors in arriving at a line of action. Teachers need to help the child make growth choices by emphasizing the benefits of growth and minimizing the disadvantages.

A major point of emphasis in humanistic (phenomenological) psychology is that behavior, intelligent or stupid, is a direct function of the adequacy of one's perceptions. Predelinquents who see the world as hostile and punitive will act accordingly; they cannot act otherwise. Their perceptions may be false, but to them they are reality, the only reality by which they can guide their behavior.

As long as children see the classroom, its curriculum, and its overall operation as a Mickey Mouse proposition that has very little meaning in relation to their dominant values, goals, and purposes, that the classroom is a dull place where teachers and pupils wage a perpetual war over inconsequentials, their behavior is bound to be inadequate. Their behavior will not change until their perceptions of the situation change. A basic premise as it relates to the classroom, then, is that children will try with all the energy they can muster to achieve goals that are personally meaningful. A lack of motivation, on the contrary, simply reflects the fact that the child does not perceive any relationship between what the school has to offer and the attainment of his or her dominant goals and purposes.

Fundamental as a determinant of children's perceptions (and behavior) is the kind of self-image they have developed as a consequence of their previous experiences. Children with a positive self-concept toward school, toward learning, who see themselves as good students, can be expected to display systematically motivated behavior in school. Children whose self-concept is attuned to seeing school work as "sissy," on the contrary, can be depended upon to put in minimal effort.

The Behaviorist Position

Selective reinforcement

The opposite point of view is that of the behaviorists, whose emphasis is on selective reinforcement: the child's behavior, whether seen from a motivational or disciplinary frame of reference, is the simple outcome of the contingency of reinforcement society has provided in response to previous behavior (see chapter 4). According to Lipe and Jung (1972), children behave in the only way possible for them to behave, considering the system of reinforcement to which they have been subjected. There is no way we can blame them for their inadequate behavior; the fault lies totally within the system. The credit or the blame falls on the external situation. In school, it falls largely on the teacher whose task it is to shape the child's behavior to "specifications." Behaviorists would argue further that the reason teachers have been inadequate in promoting motivated behavior in the pursuit of academic goals is that they have been totally inept in the manipulation of the reinforcement system.

Behaviorists would insist on a systematic schedule of reinforcement as a necessary and a sufficient basis for effective learning in the classroom or anywhere else—for academic learning or anything else. They would go further and suggest that if a teacher has difficulty in encouraging students to learn or to behave, it is because conditions of reinforcement have been improperly arranged or because inadequate or insufficient reinforcement has been supplied. In dealing with an excess of disruptive behavior, for example, the teacher needs to realize that the child is apparently being reinforced in such misbehavior. The task is to shut off the supply of reinforcement. Perhaps the teacher is reinforcing the behavior by making a big hassle over minor incidents of mischief. Or perhaps there is lack of rapport between the teacher and the class so that the child's misbehavior is being sustained through reinforcement from fellow students. According to behaviorists, the child does not have to be motivated; he or she simply has to make responses that the experimenter can reinforce selectively. To Skinner, there is no need to invent innate predispositions, drives, motives, or ego needs; to introduce the mystique of motives is to confuse a simple situation. Our task as teachers is simply to reinforce positive behavior, i.e., to catch the child being good.

Control: A basic issue

The cognitive and behavioristic positions reflect very different philosophies on such basic issues as freedom versus control and correspondingly differ in a number of critical ways. The behaviorists insist on deliberate and systematic manipulation of reinforcement contingencies so as to shape behavior according to a preplanned schedule. They would advocate a technology of reinforcement to cover such questions as, What kind of reinforcement should be used for whom? How much? When and on what schedule? The humanists, on the other hand, would see the role of the teacher as that of ensuring that the child's deficiency needs are adequately met so as to unleash the child's powerful and ever-present drive toward self-actualization.

The cognitive view

In summary, then, the followers of the Maslow point of view would focus on the development of the student as a self-actualizing individual with classroom motivation simply a by-product of personal growth. They would, among other things:

1. Make sure the student's lower-level (deficiency) needs are relatively satisfied and make the classroom situation as nonthreatening as possible.
2. Make every effort to have the learner see the activity as potentially rewarding and self-enhancing.
3. Emphasize the intrinsic appeal of the activity. They would use the occasional external reward to carry essential learnings that are not intrinsically appealing, or to "start" the child who has been "turned off," but avoid substituting gimmicks for a program of personally meaningful learning experiences.
4. Help students develop a realistic level of aspiration and a positive self-concept, leading to the choice of challenging tasks and the beneficial effects of true success. They would maximize the rewards of industry, initiative, self-direction, and positive behavior.

The behavioristic view

By contrast, the behaviorists would focus on the student's behavior and its systematic reinforcement. They would:

1. Clearly identify the behavior to be achieved. Wherever possible, they would break large units into more specific tasks that can be mastered individually and gradually chained into a complete performance.
2. Encourage and reinforce student response, initially reinforcing even low-level approximations to the desired behavior. They would proceed gradually and in small steps toward the final performance by reinforcing closer and closer approximations to the goal, meanwhile extinguishing inadequate behavior through nonreinforcement.
3. When the desired behavior has been achieved, gradually shift to an intermittent reinforcement schedule so as to make the behavior resistant to extinction. They would hope that the self-reinforcement inherent in the activity would gradually take over and make external reinforcement unnecessary.

Humanistic view difficult to implement

Implementing these various points of view presents certain problems. Critics of the humanistic position question the premise that satisfying deficiencies will automatically get the child moving constructively in the direction of self-actualization. They argue that it takes a lot of love and attention to overcome years of insecurity, deprivation, and abuse; that it takes unlimited patience, time, and effort to change the lower-class child's perceptions of the school and what it has to offer, especially that the school's efforts are being constantly and systematically undermined by the reality of the ghetto, the marginal suitability of the curriculum, and the precarious status of the child in school. This is, at best, a long-range proposition, even given continuity from teacher to teacher. But is not always clear how much the teacher can tolerate in the immediate situation while improvement may be slowly taking place. The child who disrupts classroom activities must somehow be restrained; the child who goofs off while he is trying to find himself may well be accumulating relatively irretrievable academic deficiencies. In short, it seems that despite its theoretical appeal, the humanistic position is not readily translated into a guaranteed operational strategy the teacher can use in motivating children to study algebra or history. We have to assume that not only will children overcome their accumulated deficiencies but that they will somehow see subject matter as enhancing in terms of their immediate and long-term purposes.

Behavioristic
position: Its
problems

The behavioristic position is much more direct. Here the teacher is in charge. On the other hand, implementing the behavioristic position also presents a number of problems. We must, for example, recognize that there is no easy way to capitalize on the reinforcement of such primary needs as hunger and thirst. Relying on secondary reinforcement, on the other hand, is considerably less dependable (see chapter 4). There is no guarantee that lower-class children will respond favorably to praise from the teacher or that they will be motivated by the prospect of getting a good report card. Besides, by its very nature, learning is a matter of small, gradual increments that are often hard to detect and therefore are not easily reinforceable Nor can teachers provide constant reinforcement even if they were to detect improvement. On the other hand, this need not necessarily cause undue difficulty, except perhaps in the case of the young child who needs frequent reinforcement. In the case of meaningful material, students do not have to depend on the teacher; they know whether they have solved an equation or substantiated a proof.

A more serious problem in classroom motivation is the teacher's typically ineffective, often self-defeating, use of reinforcement. Even though we know that positive reinforcement is more effective than its negative counterpart, too much of the teacher's motivational repertoire is aversive, e.g., threatening children with failure, berating them for not understanding, punishing them for not completing their work, assigning extra work for misbehavior or even for finishing too soon, etc., all of which are more suited to forcing the child to meet minimal requirements than to generating top-level commitment. Even though a major objective of the school should be the development of positive attitudes and motives toward learning, our schools more commonly train children into some form of passive mediocrity. The secondary school or college should be concerned with promoting personal involvement in lifelong learning. This will not occur unless the student has been curious and inquiring at the elementary school level, and this, in turn, will not occur if the elementary school monitors student behavior through a schedule of aversive control.

External
reinforcement less
critical in
meaningful learning

To the extent that meaningful verbal learning provides its own reward, it is less critically dependent on the usual motivational sequence of motive-goal-external reward than other forms of learning. Furthermore, since reception learning is relatively effortless, Ausubel would suggest that, in dealing with unmotivated students, the teacher simply ignore for the time being their lack of motivation and concentrate on teaching them as effectively as possible. The fact is that, not only will students learn but, because of the satisfaction in having grasped meaning, they will develop intrinsic motivation in the material. In other words, Ausubel suggests that teachers initially focus on the cognitive rather than the motivational aspects of learning and rely on the motivation that is developed retroactively as a consequence of successful learning.

Ausubel sees the cognitive drive as potentially the most important kind of motivation in meaningful verbal learning. On the other hand, he points out that a number of extrinsic considerations predominant in our achievement-oriented culture not only become progressively more significant sources of motivation for school learning but, in the process, mitigate against the potency of the cognitive drive. The fact that in our schools the desire to learn and to understand is almost invariably exercised in the context of competing for grades and other extrinsic rewards is bound to have a detrimental effect on intellectual curiosity as an independent goal. And whereas we cannot deny the importance of relating the school's curriculum to utilitarian goals, Ausubel believes that a greater emphasis must be placed on the value of knowing as a significant goal in its own right quite apart from any utilitarian purpose it may serve.

INCENTIVES

Behaviorists postulate the development of behavior patterns through the systematic reinforcement of positive behavior. This section will be devoted to this aspect of what Skinner calls the *technology of reinforcement,* i.e., the delivery system whereby reinforcement for appropriate behavior is dispensed as best as we can gather from psychological principles gradually developed over the past half-century. It would seem, for example, that reinforcement should follow closely on the response it is to reinforce. As to frequency, the general consensus is that reinforcement should occur just enough to get the job done, more frequently at first and gradually less frequently as the satisfactions inherent in the task assume greater importance. The teacher's role is to integrate these various principles into an instructional package clearly suited to effective delivery. In the past, for example, teachers have attempted to motivate children by promises of future success or status, a particularly weak reinforcer to children who want their reinforcers here and now. When promises have not worked, we have resorted to punishment, causing students to pretend, realizing that they are safe as long as they give the impression of trying.

Effectiveness of incentives depends on . . .

Fundamental here is the concept of *incentives,* i.e., objects or conditions that have possibilities for satisfying needs and therefore for becoming goals toward which behavior is directed. Their effectiveness in orienting behavior is a function of the expectations they hold for the individual from the standpoint of his or her needs. Thus, whereas food may be a powerful incentive to someone who is hungry, it has no incentive value to a person whose hunger is completely satisfied. Furthermore, partly as a result of the specific experiences on the basis of which their motives have evolved, certain foods probably would never be an incentive to certain people, no matter how hungry. An incentive may also derive its effectiveness from being something the learner wants to avoid (e.g., punishment). The picture is complicated by the fact that the organism is always besieged by a multiplicity of unsatisfied needs and that a given incentive may have positive valence with regard to one motive and negative valence with regard to another. Incentives also act in combination: the child may not only be attracted by a good grade but also be pushed in that direction by fear of punishment if his or her grades are low. What behavior results in a given situation is determined by the net force of the various need-goal sequences in the individual's overall motivational structure in relation to situational realities.

Incentives may be: *intrinsic*—i.e., inherent in the activity itself, as in the case of the person playing the violin for the aesthetic pleasure he or she derives from playing—or *extrinsic*—i.e., external to the activity, e.g., the child studying algebra to get a monetary reward or a good grade. In other words, some incentives, e.g., food, derive their appeal from their ability to satisfy a need directly; others, such as money, have appeal of various degrees of indirectness from the standpoint of prestige, self-esteem, etc. Actually, the distinction is not always clear. Most activities involve both extrinsic and intrinsic incentives; a teacher may enjoy working with children but still appreciate being paid.

Incentives derive their effectiveness through their potentiality in tapping the motives the learner already possesses, and the teacher must think not in terms of incentives but in terms of needs and the way they can be satisfied in the course of children's doing what the school considers worthwhile for them to do. If children can be led to find satisfaction for their needs in doing the classwork expected, the desperate jiggling of contrived incentives will be unnecessary, and misbehavior and indifference to school work will cease to be problems.

Intrinsic incentives
preferable

A certain amount of the trouble teachers experience in motivating children stems from too exclusive a reliance on extrinsic incentives. Rather than concentrate on making their subject interesting, challenging, and satisfying from the standpoint of pupil needs and purposes, too many teachers attempt to force learning through rewards that are related only artificially to the activities of the school. This does not imply that extrinsic incentives have no place in the classroom but rather that they have definite limitations that must be recognized. They can be ineffective, and even harmful, for example, when they lead to emotional disturbances. When there is but one prize, it automatically means that all but a few—the winner and those who, convinced that they are not in the running, have ceased to care—are bound to be disappointed.

Overreliance on
extrinsic motivation

Extrinsic incentives are also harmful when they are emphasized to the point of superseding the real goals of education. When rewards, no matter how good, are overemphasized, the significance of a given activity tends to be measured in units of the rewards it brings. Grades are so important to some students that accumulating a good scholastic record or surpassing others becomes the measure of academic and personal worth. Under these circumstances, grades simply serve to teach the child shortcuts such as cramming, cheating, apple-polishing, and other means of circumventing true learning. Furthermore, learning tends to cease the minute the incentives are removed. Sanford (1961) presents a convincing argument that an overemphasis on extrinsic motivation may actually deemphasize the inherent importance of education and the simple enjoyment of learning. An activity that has to be controlled by rewards apparently is not worth doing in its own right.

Overemphasis on extrinsic incentives tends to be self-defeating, especially in that rewards are generally offered on a rationed basis and, furthermore, not always fairly. The gifted child can attain success, praise, etc., without much exertion, whereas the dull child cannot come close, no matter how hard he or she tries. As a result, the latter would often prefer not to try for the reward, except that the threat of punishment is often added to reinforce the goal, which was not particularly attractive in the first place. However, the threat of punishment is conducive only to minimal effort. Eventually, the child decides to look elsewhere for the satisfaction of his or her needs. But in order to do this and still maintain a consistent self-image, he or she may find it necessary to reject many of the values for which the school stands. The result is that the child is no longer subject to the beneficial pressures that the school as a social agency should exert on him or her for the good of all.

Nevertheless there are times when one has no alternatives but to rely on extrinsic incentives. They are acceptable, for example, when they are used to start an activity on a self-sustaining basis or perhaps to reinforce the rewards inherent in the activity. Any new activity can be motivated through intrinsic incentives only after the child has actually tried it at least once under rewarding conditions. It may be necessary to introduce extrinsic rewards—e.g., special privileges, free time, or even token rewards—in order to "motivate" the child who has been "turned off." They can be gradually phased out as the intrinsic satisfaction of the activity takes over. There is nothing wrong with praise added to the natural satisfaction the child gets out of work well done. But what is important is for teachers to realize that, if they could lead children to set realistic goals and deal with meaningful materials, the need for artificial rewards would be correspondingly reduced; it might behoove educators to improve their curriculum and their pedagogical skills rather than continue to rely on gimmicks.

Reward and Punishment

Since every response of the motivated organism is either "rewarded" or "punished" depending on whether it serves to attain its goals, all incentives can be grouped into broad categories of *reward* and *punishment*. In general, the former is more effective in promoting learning than the latter, but that the evidence is far from clear is not surprising in view of the many complicating factors involved. What constitutes reward and punishment for a given person depends on his or her phenomenological appraisal of the situation. We would have to consider, for example, the penalties the lower-class child might have to pay in ridicule and loss of peer status for praise received from the teacher.

Punishment: Pro and con

Likewise, before we consider the effectiveness of punishment, we need to distinguish between punishment in the sense of chastisement, say, for wrongdoing, and punishment in the sense of nonreward. Actual chastisement is obviously more appropriate for disciplinary than for academic reasons. It is difficult to imagine children receiving any more than a reprimand even for gross academic mistakes. If done in a spirit of helpfulness, this type of *punishment* can have positive effects; certainly the child who has made a mistake should be made aware of it. On the other hand, punishment in the sense of, say, constant failing, accompanied by teacher sarcasm and ridicule, can be highly devastating to insecure children especially that—to the extent that anxiety produces tunnel vision—they become progressively less capable of using their resources to get themselves out of their predicament.

The effects of punishment are not all negative. Certainly some punishment is essential if the alternative is a continuous series of success experiences. This does not mean, however, that punishment needs to be introduced deliberately. Children in the process of *becoming* seek challenges and generate their own failures and punishments. Punishment may be effective as a disciplinary measure in stamping out undesirable behavior, but it fails as a motivational device in that it emphasizes what *not* to do but does not tell what needs to be done instead. The loss of a grade for careless errors may make the child more careful but, as anxiety sets in, there is greater focus on routine aspects with correspondingly less openness to subtle cues and less insight into the important things to the point that the child simply becomes more "stupid." Punishment can sometimes be effective in jarring children out of their complacency and leading them to put in the effort required to attain a desirable goal. On the other hand, it needs to be used judiciously with full awareness of its limitations. Applied too frequently, punishment tends to make children progressively less capable of self-direction. It often promotes psychological withdrawal and a closing off of the avenues of improvement. In order to protect themselves from psychological damage, children simply cease to care whether they improve or not. Whereas psychology has taken a more realistic stand as to the potential effects of punishment, it still seems that punishment for academic reasons should be more or less restricted to nonreward and, wherever possible, accompanied by the rewarding of clearly defined positive alternatives.[2]

2. Teachers should probably also take it easy in the use of punishment as a disciplinary measure. Inasmuch as it is impossible to isolate the academic program from the disciplinary aspects of classroom operation, a punitive disciplinary atmosphere is more likely to result in

Success and Failure

Although the effects of failure on personality development vary with such factors as personal security, it seems safe to say that people reach new heights as a result of their success in meeting challenges and that they reach new lows as a result of their continuous failure. Most people like to think of themselves as capable. When first faced with failure, they are likely to redouble their efforts in order to maintain a consistent self-image. But faced with continued failure they are forced to alter their self-image, and having conceived of themselves as inadequate in a given area—or as a complete failure, if their failures cover a number of areas—to live up (or rather down) to this new self-image. They have no alternative: they must either prove to themselves that they cannot do better or suffer conflict.

Early successes essential

The teacher should be particularly careful that children's early contacts with a given activity be successful. Most activities have some degree of inherent appeal once the activity gets underway; failure before students have had a chance to capitalize on this inherent motivation should be kept to a minimum. The teacher can set the stage for success through providing readiness exercises, setting clear-cut short-term goals, pointing to evidence of progress, and not expecting too much too soon. It may even be necessary for the teacher to find areas that matter to children in which they can be successful in order for them to build a positive self-concept. Furthermore, inasmuch as what is success and what is failure is a function of one's level of aspiration, it is important that children be helped to set realistic goals as means of ensuring some measure of reward.

Success and failure have far-reaching consequences. Children whose self-image is one of confidence will do better than those who view each new situation as the occasion that will once again prove them a failure. And to allay the fears of those who might argue that the absence of failure will develop a spoiled, spineless individual unable to meet any form of crisis, it can be said without fear of contradiction that success is a better preparation for both success and failure than is failure. Furthermore, there will always be enough failures to "strengthen moral fiber," especially as success tends to develop secure individuals unafraid of tackling difficult and challenging tasks.

Need for feedback

Knowledge of results (KR), besides reinforcing appropriate behavior, has feedback (informational) value that is essential in redirecting the learner's performance, e.g., in identifying errors and areas in need of further practice. This is especially important in education, where the success or failure of one's efforts is not always clear; the student may not know if his or her composition "is any good" or how it can be improved. Feedback is especially helpful when it is continuous, i.e., *formative* in the sense that the learner is alerted to deficien-

---

pupil-teacher animosity than in effective learning. This does not deny the need to convey to students clearly and forcefully that misbehavior is unacceptable and will not be tolerated.

cies as they occur (e.g., in learning how to drive a car) so that he or she can correct them on the spot. Learning experiences should be so structured as to provide systematic feedback. On the other hand, care must be taken that the learner does not lean on the teacher as the exclusive source of corrective feedback. Some of the better students are sometimes helpful in providing their classmates with feedback at a level the latter can use. Perhaps more important, it is a major goal of education to cultivate in students the ability to gauge the adequacy of their own work and thus free themselves from having to depend on external evaluation.

Praise and Reproof

Effects depend
on . . .

Praise and reproof are also best seen as a dimension of the reward-punishment continuum. And again, their effects are a matter of who is being punished, for what, by whom, and under what circumstances. Considerable research has been conducted on the subject, much of it contaminated by the reinforcement inherent in the activity itself. As a child gets interested in an activity for its own sake or for the status it provides among classmates, praise or reproof by the teacher becomes a progressively more inconsequential aspect of the over-all situation. A distinction must also be made between meaningful criticism given by a friendly teacher in a spirit of helpfulness and the vicious abuse sometimes showered on students by frustrated teachers. Constructive criticism is essential for effective pupil growth, but little good is likely to result from a situation in which the child, because of insecurity, the way the criticism is given, or the person giving the criticism, feels compelled to shut himself off from attack to protect his or her self-image.

Too much reproof,
too little praise

Unfortunately, despite its potential dangers, many of our dealings in the home, the school, and elsewhere emphasize reproof rather than praise. Teachers, in common with people in general, believe in praise but in practice tend to use reproof more often. According to Dreikurs (1957), we know how to discourage; we find it easy to criticize but when faced with the need to encourage, we are clumsy and end up telling the child, for example, that he or she could do so much better if only . . . , thereby implying that the child has not done well up to now (see Gordon 1963). Of course, there is much unspoken praise, but teachers would do well to remember that achievement without recognition is relatively unsatisfying. Praise should be given judiciously and without flattery, but it should be possible to find in the course of the school day numerous occasions deserving of honest praise. It is also important to note that reproof soon loses its effectiveness, and probably nothing could be more senseless from a motivational point of view, and as harmful to mental health, than the constant berating of students.

MOTIVATIONAL STRATEGIES IN THE CLASSROOM

By standards of current achievement, human potential is incredibly unlimited; the gap between human potential and human productivity unquestionably represents the greatest waste of natural resources imaginable. Part of the trouble lies with ineffective techniques, faulty strategies, inadequate tools, etc., but probably the greatest reason for the gap—whether on the industrial production line, in public relations, or courtesy on the nation's highways—lies in the area of motivation. The fact that children seem to have little difficulty in mastering what they consider important suggests that motivation is equally critical in the classroom. Certainly the present situation is far from ideal when considered in the light of what we know. Our goals should be to set youngsters on a schedule of self-actualization through productive contacts with a meaningful curriculum in an atmosphere of challenge and yet security. This is no simple and easy assignment; what is called for is a *systems* approach involving curriculum, methods, teachers, etc. The teacher's task is to manipulate the total classroom situation in such a way that it is personally meaningful and maximally enhancing to students.

Need for Effective Goals

The first prerequisite for productive operation in the classroom is effective goals. When children see a real purpose in school work, there will be no problem in motivating them for they will work with enthusiasm, initiative, and perseverance; coercion and artificial incentives, as well as endless repetitions, will no longer be necessary. Children learn not because they have an innate interest in the intricacies of algebra; they learn because by so doing, they can satisfy their needs for social recognition, self-esteem, and achievement—because it contributes to self-enhancement. Conversely, they may not be "motivated" toward school work simply because they do not see how it contributes to what really matters to them. Much time and effort devoted to improving the students' use of the English language is wasted, for instance, because such improvement has no meaning in their phenomenal field.

The child's inherent
need to grow

According to humanistic principles, children can be expected to strive with all of their potential toward goals that make sense to them. They do not need to be "motivated"; they are always trying to actualize themselves in the best way they know how. Our task is to provide situations that will tap their motivation and make possible the kind of growth of which they are capable. If we really believe the curriculum of the school is best for them, we need to convince them of that point so that we can work together on it. Children must develop a meaningful grasp of the situation in relation to their needs so that they are aware of what the goals are, how they fit in with their purposes, how they can be attained, and how progress toward them can be evaluated. Only then are children in a position to proceed with efficiency on to their destination.

Motivating the
lower-class child

The problem of making school work meaningful to students is particularly acute when dealing with lower-class children whose values are often very different from those incorporated in the curriculum. As a consequence, rarely is the educational program the source of self-enhancement for them that it is for their middle-class counterparts. Teachers subscribe to the typical middle-class view of education as the royal vehicle for improving one's status. They assume that children will want to learn to read, to get good grades, and to please the teacher, when actually for many children these middle-class values are in direct conflict with their present self-structure and that of their peers. Whereas needs do not differ appreciably from person to person, the specific goals one sets and the behavior one displays vary directly with differences in experiential background. If they are to be successful in relating the curriculum to his needs, teachers must know more about each child's background, values, and purposes.

Short-term goals

For goals to be effective, particularly for young children, they must be broken down into smaller, more immediately attainable subgoals. Although reinforcement associated with long-term goals may be sufficient to carry some people through a considerable amount of work, most children need periodic reinforcement. In fact, each phase of the work must provide its own satisfaction if effective learning is to take place. It is unrealistic to expect, "You will need it when you get to college," to be a convincing or motivationally effective answer to the twelve-year-old's question, "What are we doing all this for?" Unfortunately, teachers have a way of deciding the curriculum on the basis of their own adult conception of what the child's motives should be as defined from an adult point of view rather than what they are or ought to be from the child's perspective.

Student and Motivation

The school does not have a monopoly on the student

We need to recognize that many factors conspire to interfere with pupil learning: mental limitations, emotional blocks, environmental distractions, poor teaching, unsuitable curricula, peer pressures, etc. We especially need to realize that with the many other demands made upon children, the school can no longer take for granted that it has a monopoly, or even priority, on its students' time and energies. It must take its turn along with many other activities that compete for their attention. Part of their energies must be devoted to jockeying for peer status, for example; they just cannot afford to ignore or to be ignored by the peer group. Inasmuch as they learn more about the realities of life through peers than through the social studies curriculum, it might behoove the school to take a more tolerant view of what really matters to youngsters or, on the other hand, to become more convincing as to what it has to offer instead.

To be effective, the curriculum not only must relate to the children's needs but also must be made sufficiently dynamic to meet the competition of the other activities bidding for their attention. One might even go so far as to say that generally, although not always, students should not be expected to learn anything that they have not been shown to be meaningful in terms of their goals and purposes. When exceptions to this rule occur, it should be easy enough for the teacher to capitalize on such crutches as the average student's desire to please the teacher—and even on firmness—to carry him or her over such humps, but when used as a steady prop to push over meaningless material, these devices soon lose their effectiveness.

The devastating
effects of cumulative
deficits

A major consideration in this connection is the cumulative nature of academic deficiency. The child who fails to learn to read in grade one, for whatever reason, not only loses interest in reading or even in school but, more importantly, falls behind and compounds the difficulty by developing a negative self-concept, negative attitudes toward the school, toward society, etc. By the time academic problems have been allowed to exist over eight, ten, or more years, the situation is relatively hopeless. There is only so much that can be done for the high school student who cannot read, write, or add. Many drop out at the first opportunity; others remain simply because there is no place to go.

Other Motivational Techniques

Effective education calls for effective coordination with the child's natural growth processes. The education of young children is particularly important in that it sets the pattern of later academic functioning. Preschool children, for example, need to develop and to use their capacities, to exercise their skills, to demonstrate their mastery and their power over the environment, including people. This is the age where they should be encouraged to explore their environment broadly free from a sense of mission that fits everything into a narrow point of focus (see White 1959). We need to make available to them a rich environment of physical objects in keeping with their orientation toward concrete operations and to capitalize on these natural tendencies and help them develop these skills in such a way that they will serve their other purposes. We also need to help them learn to manipulate the world vicariously through TV (e.g., Superman) and later through reading. The elementary school must be particularly careful that with its overregimentation of the curriculum and overreliance on rote learning, together with rigid discipline, costly failure, etc., it does not stamp out the natural curiosity that normal children bring with them to school. As they reach the stage of formal operations, on the other hand, adolescents respond best to a progressively more verbal and abstract approach that can be synchronized with the development of the cognitive drive.

The young child
needs a rich
environment

Whereas a meaningful curriculum and appropriate classroom procedures, once put into motion, are the primary forces in keeping the class on a productive schedule, the more obvious motivational techniques should not be ignored. Generally, for example, effective motivation implies clarity as to the goals and the means whereby they are to be achieved, commitment to these goals, and evidence of progress in their attainment. There is need for frequent reinforcement, at least at first, and especially in the case of the anxious child who needs assurance that he or she is doing well.

Develop positive
attitudes toward
learning

Probably the most important component of effective motivation—and the one overriding concern of true education—is a positive attitude toward the school situation and toward learning itself. For too many children, the school is a failure experience that continually threatens self-esteem. When the school experience provides systematic positive rewards that outweigh the negative, learners soon form desirable attitudes that transfer to future learning situations. They come to expect success. The teacher's task is to set assignments that are within the reach of students so that they learn the pleasure of success and the resulting feeling of self-esteem, confidence, and competence. This does not mean the indiscriminate assignment of easy tasks. On the contrary, since easy tasks offer no challenge and give no feeling of success and achievement, they promote boredom and mischievous behavior. Learners get greatest challenge when they realize that they cannot be right every time, that success is not guaranteed. In an overall atmosphere of success, even mistakes provide a sense of progress.

Motivational Style

Teachers need to be particularly sensitive to the idiosyncrasies of the child's motivational structure. As a consequence of the particular reinforcing experiences they have undergone, different children react differently. The teacher correspondingly needs a wide variety of motivational strategies to be used in dealing with different children. Competent youngsters with a high cognitive drive, for example, want to know for the sake of knowing. They delight at mastery over academic content. Young children, on the other hand, are more likely to be motivated by affiliative needs. They respond best to a warm and supportive teacher with whom they can identify and whose acceptance gives them vicarious status. Later, when they become oriented toward their peers, the affiliative need may actually depress academic achievement if it is negatively valued by the peer group (see Coleman, in chapter 7). There might be a need to counteract this trend or to harness in the service of education whatever values the peer group has.

The ego-enhancement drive in adolescence

The strong need for ego enhancement in adolescents, particularly middle-class boys, can be used to promote learning as a means of attaining prestige and peer status, as well as feelings of adequacy and self-esteem (see Box 10.1). On the other hand, when carried to excess, the ego-enhancement drive can have undesirable consequences, e.g., it can generate anxiety that disrupts learning, leads to unrealistic academic aspirations, sometimes followed by catastrophic failure and collapse in self-esteem, and disinvolvement from academic pursuits. It may also impair children's capacity for perceiving their limitations and predispose them to rationalize their failures and distort their perceptions. In order to make maximum use of the ego-enhancement drive, the learning outcomes by which status can be earned need to be clearly defined and strategies for achieving these objectives clearly drawn up and organized so as to permit the unequivocal recognition of successful performance. It would seem that the teacher best able to create these conditions would have to be task-oriented and reflect a high degree of personal organization.

10.1   HIS TEACHER IMPROVED TOO

Timothy was a talented youth, altho as his English teacher, I must confess that the mark I gave him at the end of each of the first two marking periods did not in any way reflect his inherent ability.

In the comments I penned on his report card, opinions were expressed concerning his indifference, his uncooperative attitude, and his lack of effort. When Tim's second report was returned to me, I noticed that Tim's father had written in the space reserved for parents' reactions the pithy comment, ''I am dissatisfied, too.''

But the situation changed markedly in February. By chance I learned that Tim was interested in tennis. I asked him to stay after school, and in the conversation I mentioned some of the major tournaments I had seen.

Because of his interest, I invited him to my home on a Saturday afternoon to meet my eldest son, who had acquired some prominence as a local netster. When Tim left my home, after a demonstration of tennis strokes, he took with him a half-dozen books on court technics and strategy.

Frequently thereafter he stayed after school to talk to me about his reading. He developed an eagerness to give expository talks to his classmates on his hobby. He wrote several papers on tennis ethics and the lessons taught by the lives of great net stars. His paper on tennis ethics he must have rewritten at least a dozen times before it was accepted by the school literary magazine.

I believe no one in the class read or wrote more than he did during the next six weeks. His classmates obtained a liberal education in the romance of tennis.

When I totaled his grades for the next report card, I was surprised to see the great advances he had made in his knowledge of and skill in English. When I inscribed his mark on the card, I wrote:

''Timothy has made rapid advances recently as a student, and I congratulate him.''

Back came the father's response. ''You give my son too much credit, sir. It is you who should be congratulated, for the rapid advances you have made recently as a teacher.''

Robinson, Thomas E. *NEA J.* 41 (1952):54. (By permission)

DISCIPLINE IN THE CLASSROOM

Discipline: The
number 1 problem

Of the many problems facing classroom teachers, none is more immediate and threatening than that of maintaining classroom discipline. Indeed discipline in today's schools is seen as the greatest single cause of both teacher anxiety and classroom inefficiency. The classroom environment that prevails in too many of our schools is characterized by apathy and passive resistance, goofing off, and various forms of bedlam, defiance, insubordination, vandalism, robbery, and drugs, not to mention violence and assault on students and even teachers. A three-year study by the National Institute of Education (1977), for example, found that teenagers run a substantially greater risk of personal violence in their own school than on the street (see also Bayh 1977; DeCecco and Richards 1975). The public's concern is reflected in recent Gallup polls (see Gallup 1981) in which discipline is systematically listed as the number one problem in American education.[3]

Actually the school is simply the victim of the same set of social ills that produce crime and lawlessness on the streets, apathy and incompetence in the office or in the shop, and a general sense of futility and frustration at all levels of the social enterprise. The disciplinary problems of the school reflect the breakdown of the home and the community, poverty in the ghetto, violence on TV, and other difficulties that plague current American society. On the other hand, the school is unfortunately, and unavoidably, a special target simply because of the way it is constituted. Compulsory attendance laws, for example, keep in school under duress many adolescents who no longer belong there. They are learning nothing, yet they are faced with systematic demands for conformity, if not academic productivity, demands that they cannot ignore and yet that they neither want to nor perhaps can meet. For a substantial number of our students, the curriculum is essentially meaningless and irrelevant, yet it systematically promotes failure and frustration, leading to resistance, defiance, or at best marginal compliance. Meanwhile crowding in our classrooms, with the depersonalized atmosphere that prevails therein, along with the lack of teacher authority, status, and prestige, lack of referral and remedial services, the poor communication between the school, the home and the community, etc., all serve to preclude easy solutions. The school is often forced to operate in a situation and deal with problems over which it has only limited control.

Source of concern

Discipline is a major source of anxiety for beginning teachers. Eighty percent of Vredevoe's 3,000 prospective teachers (1965) listed discipline as the source of their greatest concern. Teachers want specific suggestions, specific rules to deal with what they see as a major problem. Unfortunately we can no more provide prescriptions for maintaining discipline in the classroom than

3. The National Society for the Study of Education devoted one of its 1979 yearbooks to the problem (Duke 1979). Violence in the schools was the subject of a recent CBS "Sixty Minutes" program (Safer 1979).

we can provide a detailed recipe for a happy marriage. Even consistency, for example—which on the surface should be a matter of relative agreement, turns out to be highly complicated. Despite the need for fairness, the teacher simply cannot dispense discipline on a scheduled basis. Democratic discipline means recognizing that each child is different; each offense is an individual matter that must be treated as such. There is, of course, danger of favoritism. But fear of making an exception can only lead the teacher to engage in punitive, irrational discipline simply for the sake of consistency. In other words, although there is certainly room for something more than a simple haphazard approach, discipline is perhaps primarily a feeling of self-confidence, a matter of personal relationships and goodwill that exist in the classroom, of mutual respect, or maybe even more directly a sense of responsibility that the class develops about its behavior.

Discipline as an Aspect of Social Growth

Discipline as socialization

Discipline is best seen in the broad context of socialization, character development, and, of course, motives, needs, the self-concept, and other concepts presented in chapter 4 and reviewed earlier in this chapter. At the lowest level, children learn to balance what they would like to do against what others expect them to do; more significantly, they learn to synchronize their goals and purposes with those of the social order in a manner of enlightened self-interest. The crucial element is the internalization of society's values and standards to the point where the penalty for misbehavior, whether in the classroom or in one's personal life, is no longer external punishment but rather guilt feelings. The ultimate goal is for children to develop a positive valuing of social standards as a dynamic force toward constructive personal and social behavior (see the taxonomy of educational objectives, affective domain, in chapter 2). A crucial aspect of discipline, for example, is a sensitivity to the social consequences of one's actions and a deliberate orientation of one's behavior toward the promotion of the social good. Unfortunately, classroom discipline is frequently pitched at the level of irrational conformity (see chapter 17) in which the child abides by standards not because of consideration for the welfare of others but because of mechanical adherence to a rule.

Focus on development

Discipline is a matter of progressive development in which children need considerable guidance and support as they work out the details of self-direction. Much of their misbehavior is simply the manifestation of normal growth. The teacher needs to realize how natural it is for children to get into trouble as they experiment with better ways of conduct. If personal and social responsibility, rather than conformity and obedience, are to be the true criteria of discipline, children must be given the freedom to make decisions—and occasionally mistakes. That is the only way they can become increasingly capable of self-direction.

Only by being allowed to test the reality of the limits imposed on their behavior by the social order can children arrive at an adequate grasp of the criteria on the basis of which behavior is judged acceptable or unacceptable, adequate or inadequate. Too much guidance deprives children of the opportunity to learn. A laissez-faire approach is equally bad because, although self-direction is the ultimate goal, the development of control and the integration of the ideals and habits on which it is based require the guidance and, at times, the firm hand of the adult. When the limits are nonexistent or movable, children are not only prevented from learning self-discipline but are left anxious and bewildered as to where they stand.

Need for Discipline

Discipline in the sense of self-direction is essential to the efficient operation of any social group. From the beginning of time, parents, both human and animal, have attempted with various degrees of enlightenment and success to shape the behavior of their offspring. Society has likewise devised an elaborate set of laws and regulations as a necessary aspect of constructive and efficient social interaction. Children must be helped to perceive rules and regulations not as limitations or taboos but rather as facilitators of social interaction, enabling people to realize their individual and collective goals with maximum efficiency.

The school's responsibility

The focus of discipline in the school years ago was on the maintenance of order so that learning could proceed without interruption. Misbehavior was seen as a matter of deliberate intent and deserving of appropriate punishment. A major consideration was that the school's primary concern was to teach reading, writing, arithmetic, etc.; the home did the rest. The modern school, by contrast, has assumed responsibility for social and emotional, as well as academic, learning. In this context, discipline is no longer a separate set of procedures designed to protect the academic schedule from interference but an integral part of the school's overall program of fostering maximal pupil growth. Its focus is developmental, e.g., motivational, and, where necessary, diagnostic and remedial, rather than restrictive and retributive. We realize that punitive and repressive discipline is not conducive to the development of positive attitudes toward learning; it is not conducive to the development of self-discipline and other aspects of social maturity; it is simply not conducive to the attainment of the broad objectives of the modern school. We need to see discipline in the light of its contribution to purposeful activity and meaningful growth. Obedience, for example, is not a virtue; it is simply an interim strategy to emphasize until the student has gained sufficient experience and maturity to exercise self-control.

Order is essential

This is not to say that the maintenance of order in the classroom is a relatively inconsequential and secondary consideration. On the contrary; nothing particularly productive from the standpoint of the child's growth can occur under conditions of chaos. Although the approach to discipline should be positive, it must be realistic. Ausubel (1961), for example, presents a strong case against taking an overly apologetic stance against commonsense discipline. Whereas democratic discipline is as rational, nonarbitrary, and bilateral as possible, it does not imply freedom from all external constraints. While it is true that the teacher stands to gain from ignoring minor misdeeds that do not interfere with the primary function of the school, Ausubel suggests that the teacher take a firm stand on misbehavior. He suggests further that no harm will be done to the personality of any child by having him or her given to understand that there is such a thing as properly constituted authority. By and large, pupils enjoy living up to expectations. When they know that mature conduct is expected, they will meet the challenge; when they fail, the situation will be a learning experience essential to continued growth.

The problem of discipline is much more severe in ghetto schools where up to 90 percent of the teacher's energies may be spent in controlling the class. As a group, lower-class children do not identify with the school or the teacher. As a consequence, they are more likely to be motivated by the antischool, antiteacher attitudes of the peer culture than by teacher approval. Ausubel suggests that, under such circumstances, the teacher take a business-like stand and get on with the curriculum at a level the students can understand. He can progressively relax the disciplinary aspects after rapport and control have been established and as an effective work pattern is placed on a routine basis and the void taken up by increases in task-directed motivation resulting from success in initial learnings. In such cases, rather than present discipline as a separate package to be imposed on students, the teacher may be more successful if he wraps discipline within the framework of meaningful learning activities, even if these activities are not those prescribed for that particular grade at that particular time.

MAINTAINING CLASSROOM DISCIPLINE

The Meaning of Discipline

Discipline means . . .

Discipline means different things to different people. To some, it means punishment, i.e., the use of aversive stimuli in retaliation for student misconduct. To others, it means control, i.e., the enforcement of rules and regulations, the demand for orderly conduct. Discipline is probably better seen in the context of training, whose purpose is to promote eventual self-direction, a sort of coaching to help children master the art of self-discipline. Implied is the assumption that children are currently unable to assume full responsibility for their behavior and must be helped to grow into higher levels of personal and social maturity. Unfortunately some teachers seem to think that it is easier to enforce external control than to help children develop self-control. The problem is that children cannot grow in self-direction in an atmosphere of complete external control. If they are to become responsible citizens sensitive to the rights of others and willing to subordinate self-interest for the welfare of the group, they must have freedom to make their own decisions and to be guided by their consequences. The lesson to be learned from rigid external control, on the contrary, is to comply or, in the event of noncompliance, to avoid detection.

Causes of Misbehavior

The causes of misbehavior in the classroom are best seen in the broader setting of motivation and the satisfaction of needs as presented earlier. Any attempt at resolution must therefore approach the problem from the context of the school's overall program rather than as an isolated phenomenon. The Kooi and Schutz (1965) factor analysis of classroom disturbances into too little positive behavior and too much disruptive behavior, for example, provides a valuable framework for thinking not only of the problem but, more importantly, also of solutions. Too much disruptive behavior calls for some attempt at suppression; too little positive behavior, on the other hand, calls for measures of a motivational nature. But it is only as the two are seen in mutual interaction that either can be resolved. Negative behavior is best eliminated through a constructive program of positive behavior; any attempt to deal with misbehavior as a separate issue is bound to be counterproductive.

Misbehavior is caused by

Looking at the causes of misbehavior at a more specific level, we might identify:

... the child

1. Child-related factors: Many children are immature; many are hostile and aggressive, often because of faulty child-rearing practices. Even at best, children are bound to experience occasional difficulty, say, in meeting Erikson's developmental crises (see chapter 15). To the extent that mature behavior is not innate, nor is it learned overnight, we can expect children to be involved in some degree of misbehavior as a relatively normal condition.

... society

2. Society-related factors: Not only is the school affected by the problems of society at large (crime, violence, frustration, etc.), particularly those of the local community, but, in addition, the operation of the school is critically affected by the peer group. Many instances of misbehavior stem from the child's attempt to maintain peer status. If discipline in the school is to be effective, it must take into account the whole environment rather than focus on the child in isolation.

... the curriculum

3. Curriculum-related factors. For many children, the school's curriculum is unrelated to their needs. This is an especially serious problem for adolescents kept in school under compulsory attendance laws or by the fact that there is no other place for them to go. Many children find

the curriculum unchallenging; many find it so overwhelming that unless given massive remedial help, they have no choice but to disengage themselves from it. A meaningful curriculum is unquestionably the best guarantee against classroom misbehavior; wholesale misbehavior, conversely, is a rather dependable signal that something is wrong with the school's program.

... the teacher

4. Teacher-related factors: Many teachers are their own worst enemy. Whether because of personality quirks, indecision, or inconsistency in pupil control or because of academic or teaching incompetence, some teachers are forever "fighting the students." Many, by constant sarcasm, belittling of students, etc., are systematically creating in their students resentment, animosity, and a desire for revenge. Many teachers are unable to establish positive relationships with students based on mutual respect and goodwill. Many reflect punitive attitudes that antagonize students; many are insecure and preoccupied with student control. They are afraid to let students know they are human, lest students take advantage of them. They adopt a cold, aloof, and rigid stance, apparently hoping to awe students into submission. The eventual result is apathy, personal animosity, and often defiance.

Some teachers are incompetent. They do not know their subject and thus lose student respect, especially if they compound the problem by trying to bluff their way out. Others are poor teachers—monotonous, boring, unable to organize, unable to challenge students or to put life into their teaching.

Often the problem is with discipline itself. Some teachers are unfair and/or punitive, thereby creating student resentment and the need to retaliate. Many are inconsistent, punishing today what they overlooked yesterday. They have no game-plan, operating on a catch-as-catch-can basis as situations arise and their temper gets long or short. In many classrooms, the climate is one of frustration, anxiety, hostility, again serving as the basis for attempts at revenge. Some teachers are forever making threats, often threats they cannot actualize. Sooner or later children will take up the challenge. Many teachers do not understand children, nor do they understand the role and strategies of effective discipline in helping children grow.

Types of Student Control

Some forms of control

We might gain insight into discipline by thinking of the various approaches through which student control can be achieved. We can, for instance, distinguish between:

1. Teacher-imposed discipline: Some degree of externally imposed discipline is essential. In our culture, for example, adolescence is a period of

turmoil in which teenagers constantly test limits as a way of finding out who they are and where they stand. Without the support of reasonably firm adult-imposed limits, they become confused and insist on ever-greater freedom and engage in progressively more inappropriate behavior as a way of finding out the line between acceptable and unacceptable behavior. Eventually the teacher will have to respond by becoming more restrictive and punitive, with the class then becoming apathetic and/or rebellious.

2. Group-imposed discipline: Once the teacher has established a positive relationship with the class and a reputation for goodwill and fair play, he or she can expect the latter to act as a very positive force in the behavior control of its members. The teacher needs to help the group develop a group self-concept incorporating maturity of behavior and consideration for others.

3. Self-imposed discipline: Eventually children must learn to internalize and to live by social standards. They need to develop a conscience through which they take into account the consequences of their behavior and their responsibility to others as well as to themselves (see McLaughlin 1976).

4. Task-imposed discipline: Children need to learn to accept responsibility for performing certain tasks and to develop a willingness to forgo other pursuits until the task is completed. They should be encouraged to undertake certain tasks, small tasks at first, and to experience the satisfaction of work accomplished. Teachers and parents might be encouraged, for example, to invoke the Premack principle: Finish your lesson; then you can go and play.

Dealing with Misbehavior

To the extent that all behavior, including misbehavior, is an attempt at satisfying needs, we must assume that children who misbehave apparently have learned from experience that they can gain status among their peers by annoying the teacher or that continuing in mischief and taking the expected punishment is less anxiety-producing than trying something new (see chapter 4). It should especially be emphasized that many of the discipline problems encountered in the classroom stem from a curriculum that is too easy or too hard or that is irrelevant from the standpoint of the child's goals and purposes, so that instead of being a source of satisfaction and self-fulfillment, it makes for frustration—and misbehavior. Certainly the student who is totally overwhelmed because of accumulated academic deficiencies or who sees no point in a subject will have to look elsewhere for the satisfaction of his or her needs.

The school's task   The school's task is not so much to curb misbehavior as it is to promote constructive and positive behavior. Yet as all teachers can testify, instances of misbehavior inevitably occur and they must be prepared for such situations.

What is important is for them to realize that misbehavior is an indication that the child is having difficulty satisfying his or her needs through acceptable channels. The sooner teachers come to view misbehavior from the standpoint of individual development rather than as a violation of classroom decorum, the more successful they will be. Unfortunately, many teachers are so busy dealing with the symptoms that they never get around to dealing with the underlying causes.

What is discipline to accomplish?

In dealing with misbehavior, teachers must first be clear as to what discipline is supposed to accomplish. They need to develop criteria for determining which incidents may be ignored, which may be corrected informally, and which should be of greater concern. It is easy to lose perspective in "the heat of the battle" to the point where immediate goals become all-important while the real goals are lost in the shuffle. Teachers need to be particularly clear as to just how disciplinary measures are to operate in helping children develop new patterns of conduct. Their approach must be positive: berating, scolding, and expounding on pupil shortcomings in a moralizing tone serve only to foster the development of a negative self-concept, with resulting damage to future growth potentialities. Teachers sometimes expect too much too soon in the line of improved behavior. The ultimate goal is self-discipline based on an understanding of the purposes of rules and regulations for, in the final analysis, good behavior must be a matter of good sense and goodwill. Teachers want to get their students there, eventually, but they cannot start there. Progress toward self-control is a gradual process, and it is necessary to start where the children are, giving them only the freedom they can handle.

A diagnostic approach is best

A diagnostic approach generally accomplishes more than repressive and punitive measures. The wise teacher realizes that inattention is more likely to occur when children are tired or preoccupied with some pressing need, that being noisy and mischievous is almost natural; that some children have found that misbehavior will gain them attention they can get in no other way, and that some find the gamble involved in misbehaving interesting—in fact, it may be the only relief from the monotony of an unsuitable curriculum. An understanding of these principles is fundamental for dealing constructively with misbehavior. Each case is different, and the treatment will sometimes be difficult and complicated, but at least the approach is constructive and therefore more likely to be effective in the long run.

Kounin's study

At the operational level, it seems that the best way to deal with misbehavior in the classroom is to prevent it from occurring. An important study here is that of Kounin (1970), who found that teachers with a minimal amount of disciplinary troubles did not differ from their less adequate counterparts in the desist procedures they used to curtail misbehavior once it had occurred. They did differ significantly, however, in their ability to prevent problems from occurring. They were better at maintaining relationships with the class that precluded the need for disciplinary measures, and especially more alert to danger signals. The better disciplinarians displayed:

1. "With-itness": i.e., they knew what was going on in all parts of the room. Poor disciplinarians, on the contrary, got so involved with one child or two that they did not see difficulties arising in other parts of the room.
2. Overlapping: i.e., the ability to attend to several issues simultaneously.
3. Transition smoothness, i.e., the ability to move the class from one activity to another with minimal disruption. They were more adept at avoiding unnecessary flipflop or overkill, such as dwelling forever on directions or on a point of explanation that the class had already grasped.

What this amounts to is that the teachers must cultivate certain managerial skills, such as keeping abreast of the total operation, capitalizing on momentum, etc. Poor disciplinarians, for example, often lost momentum by interrupting themselves or the whole class to repeat some direction or to clarify a point.

Kounin and Gump (1961) found that punitive teachers tended to threaten children; they were overready to punish, leading the children to react with aggressiveness and less of an orientation toward learning.[4] The children of nonpunitive teachers, on the other hand, were more likely to identify with the school.

Disciplinary Strategies

A meaningful curriculum

If we are to be successful at discipline, we need to know what we are doing. Children will misbehave for dozens of reasons of their own; there is no point in adding to our misery through incompetence. First, it cannot be overemphasized that the primary element in constructive classroom discipline is the instructional program: the curriculum and the feeling of satisfaction and progress it promotes, the teacher's personality, the classroom climate, the appropriateness and effectiveness of teaching strategies. The royal road to self-actualization in the classroom, and the consequent curtailment of misbehavior, is through the satisfactions of meaningful challenges, of solving problems, of learning and growing that the instructional program systematically provides. Disciplinary measures make sense only in that context. It cannot be overemphasized that teachers would save themselves a good deal of the time and energy they spend coping with misbehavior if they oriented themselves with a little ingenuity in the direction of good teaching.

Good teachers keep the whole class involved. In asking questions, they pause long enough for every student to generate an answer before calling on someone. Some teachers have a way of running their questions up and down each row, or around the circle, so that the children at the other end can tune

4. The results are difficult to interpret. Perhaps it was the children's hostile behavior that caused the teacher's behavior to be punitive (see Mouly 1978, p. 80).

themselves out until their turn comes, meanwhile possibly finding time for a bit of mischief or at least daydreaming. It is also necessary to keep the lesson moving along. A student who needs extended help should be provided it on an individual basis rather than hold up the whole class. Teachers must also introduce variety and an occasional change of pace. Above all, they need to show a little enthusiasm that might become contagious.

Operational strategies

A number of operational strategies can be mentioned, none totally effective but nevertheless useful to a degree.

1. Support strategies: Most children tend to be reasonably well behaved, but many can use the teacher's support at times. Spotting children who are about to misbehave and just staring at them, shaking your head, or otherwise communicating nonverbally that you are with it is usually sufficient to help them maintain control. Another possibility is *proximity control*: i.e., moving toward the child who is about to misbehave and just standing there while continuing with your work. For the same reason, it is usually best to seat troublesome children near the front of the room. When children are allowed to go to a work center, it should be relatively accessible to the teacher—although if this represents a special privilege that can be withdrawn, it can be used to provide valuable training in self-discipline.

2. Stage setting: It is advisable for teachers to remove avoidable difficulties, whether in the line of unnecessary temptations or frustration over work. They should make clear exactly what students are to do. Teacher planning should also focus on eliminating all unnecessary delays, anticipating problems, and structuring the class into definite routines that can be managed quickly and effectively. It is also essential to provide situational assistance, say during seatwork, in order to allow students to move along with their assignment. In cases of accumulated deficiencies, it may be necessary to provide systematic remedial work or even to restructure the assignments so that the student can once again satisfy his or her needs through academic success rather than through mischief.

3. Classroom climate: Teachers must develop sensitivity as to what constitutes optimal student anxiety, i.e., the extent to which the student is, on the one hand, sufficiently motivated and yet, at the same time, not frustrated to the point that he or she resorts to misbehavior or other forms of counterproductive behavior. It is especially important for teachers to expect positive behavior; to think otherwise is to promote a self-fulfilling prophecy. At the same time, teachers need to keep in mind that some degree of classroom mischief is part of growing up.

Other suggestions

A number of more specific suggestions can be made:

1. Provide each child with systematic opportunities for need satisfaction. Give each a sense of belonging, emphasize progress, be generous with words of praise and encouragement, especially with children with a weak self-concept.

When criticizing, dwell on the behavior, not the child: "Don't push; somebody is going to fall down and get hurt" rather than "You're just a troublemaker." Make clear what you object to and why, and what the child is to do in the future. Above all, show your children that you care.

2. Be alert to danger signals. Give the class that is getting tense and frustrated a short break or a change of pace. Send the child who is getting restless on a brief errand. Give the child who needs attention the occasional recognition—a nod or a brief comment—rather than wait until he or she disrupts the class.

3. Establish a few basic rules of classroom behavior. Developing rules at the beginning of the term in a cool and calm manner usually works better than announcing new rules in the middle of a behavior crisis. Having students participate in the development of these rules tends to increase their acceptance of the rules and their understanding of the need for rules. Rules should be kept to a reasonable minimum (see Lufler 1978); you cannot cover everything, nor should you want to if students are to learn how to make their own judgment as to what is acceptable and what is not.

4. Establish your reputation as a person who is friendly but yet firm, who has a sense of humor but is not willing to be taken advantage of. Be competent and self-confident, be consistent and reasonable. The first few days are crucial; students want to size up their new teacher. If you look scared and unsure, this will be a signal for them to put on the pressure. It is important to give them the impression that you know precisely what you are doing. In fact, it might be best if this were a reality rather than simply an impression.

Consistency is essential

5. Consistency is important. Strictness one day and leniency the next, punishment of one child and not another for the same offense, is a relatively sure way of creating resentment and encouraging misbehavior. On the other hand, consistency is really a matter of differential treatment so that, in the final analysis, you will have to be consistent within the framework of common sense, understanding, and fair play.

6. Helping children understand how their misbehavior interferes with the rights of others might help them internalize social standards. It might also help to have them develop a limited understanding of the dynamics of their own behavior.

7. Establish some degree of routine. Students need the security of knowing what they are to do, when, and how.

Plan your strategies

8. Preplan disciplinary strategies. Have a number of preplanned strategies to be used as emergencies arise rather than have to devise coping procedures in the middle of a crisis. This does not mean rigidity; you can always make adaptations, but at least you have a general game plan and are less likely to sacrifice your major goals. Beginning teachers might be encouraged to think periodically about discipline, the purposes it is to serve, the effectiveness of present strategies and, where necessary, to try new approaches.

9. Concentrate on establishing positive relations with the class, based on

mutual respect and a sense of responsibility. A mature liking for children helps, but it must be operationalized. Emphasize the positive; children will rise to the occasion. Yet be realistic; do not expect miracles overnight. Responsible behavior may imply a major revision of the child's total behavior structure. Avoid careless use of threats: they are easy to make but they can make you look like a fool if somebody calls you on them. Don't nag. Above all, don't take things personally. And keep your cool; somebody is going to have to show some maturity. Also avoid double standards that permit you to be sarcastic toward students but deny students the same prerogative.

PUNISHMENT

The question of punishment invariably comes up in any discussion of discipline for although the emphasis should be on the positive, teachers occasionally have to punish children as a means of helping them toward self-discipline. This is particularly true inasmuch as there is a limit to the extent to which the teacher can allow the misbehavior of one child to disrupt the class. However, punishment is essentially negative in that it is directed primarily toward suppressing misbehavior. It may be appropriate for dealing with continued violation of classroom regulations, bullying, defiance, vandalism, or physical attack, but if it is to contribute to positive behavior, it should be accompanied by constructive guidance with respect to clearly defined alternatives.

Avoid a punitive approach

A punitive approach can be particularly detrimental in the case of the young child who is relatively incapable of making adequate discriminations as to the pertinence of the punishment and of putting things into perspective and who can actually develop neurotic fixity. The punishment of infants by their parents can interfere with the development of identification and dependency; it can promote the development of blind inhibitions reflected in rigid, stereotyped behavior with no integrative basis for learning to deal with the future. Damaged children tend to be children who were punished too early and too frequently and who were thus prevented from achieving proper identification with the social values of the culture. Sears et al. (1957), in their classic study of child-rearing practices, noted that "the unhappy effects of punishment have run like a dismal thread throughout our findings." The mothers who punished dependency had more dependent children; the mothers who punished aggressive behavior severely had more aggressive children. This does not mean that punishment is to be avoided at all costs; on the contrary, Sears found that a completely permissive atmosphere is also bad.

Punishment can be dangerous and counterproductive

In school, punishment can produce immediate conformity. But there is danger here. It is the easy way out, always available, requiring very little thought or intelligence in its use. It seems to accomplish what it is designed to accomplish; namely, to keep the child in submission. But at the same time it

creates resentment and anxiety. It often destroys teacher-pupil relationships to the point where the teacher no longer has the child's confidence necessary to promote the latter's growth. To make matters worse, there is a tendency to build up a long list of annoyances and then crack down as patience wears thin, so that the punishment is frequently triggered by some rather minor misdeed, which places punishment out of proportion to the offense.

Punishment is another instance of the "tyranny of the immediate"; the teacher has to deal with a situation that is here and now, often causing him or her to sacrifice long-range goals in the interest of an instant solution. Teachers who resort to punishment need to make it abundantly clear to all, including themselves, that the purpose is not to exact retribution through revenge or to release hostility but to improve the child's behavior in specifically defined ways. Punishment can have a constructive influence when the offender realizes that he or she has done wrong, perceives the person administering the punishment as fair, and accepts the punishment as a logical consequence of the misbehavior. On the other hand, it is not particularly effective in promoting guilt necessary to internalize social values.

Despite the extensive use of punishment in psychological experiments, psychologists until recently have taken a strongly negative view of punishment. More specifically, taking their cue from a comprehensive review of the literature by Estes in 1944, psychologists for years maintained that punishment is ineffective and cruel, leading to anxiety and stimulus avoidance; that it does not necessarily deter misbehavior but rather that it often produces unpredictable side effects. It may even strengthen the response it is supposed to eliminate.

Research at the animal level seems relatively convincing that punishment does indeed have unpredictable outcomes (e.g., Maier 1949). On the other hand, more recent analyses of the literature (Solomon 1964; Aronfreed 1968) suggest that our previous views of the effectiveness of punishment were unnecessarily negative. Recognizing that under certain circumstances punishment can be ineffective and even damaging does not mean that we must reject the overwhelming evidence of its necessary role in the socialization of the child. Whereas we obviously favor reward to punishment if there is an option, it is doubtful on both empirical and theoretical grounds that the successful socialization of the child can ever dispense with punishment in the sense of intentionally administered aversive stimulation.

Punishment can also be effective

Solomon and Aronfreed question the persistent myths concerning both the ineffectiveness of punishment as an agent of behavioral change and the inevitability of neurotic outcomes resulting from its use.[5] They argue that the abnormal side effects of punishment occur only when the organism is unable to discriminate the circumstances under which punishment is administered. Under conditions of intense threat of punishment in a situation where the subject is unable to read the discriminative cues, he or she has no way of anticipating the probable consequences of the behavioral alternatives and thus avert the punishment, yet is forced by anxiety to seek relief in any activity that will reduce at least momentarily the tension experienced in anticipation of his or her possible transgression, even if that outcome happens to be punishment. Under such conditions of intense threat and inability to process the information provided in the cues—e.g., when the outcomes are inconsistent—the typical reaction is *fixation*. Here the issue is no longer the suppression of the punished behavior but rather the indiscriminate production of any behavior that will temporarily terminate the anticipatory anxiety. In such cases, behavior can only be erratic since it is no longer under the control of relevant external cues.

Fixation is not likely to occur

But an entirely different picture emerges from the results of experiments in which the control of aversive outcomes is within the subject's ability to discriminate from among explicit cues. When the alternatives are clearly specified, the fixating effects of punishment simply do not occur (Aronfreed 1968; Solomon 1964). In fact, to the extent that they have a wide repertoire of response options, human subjects are not likely to fixate under reasonable conditions of aversive feedback, provided that, along with the punishment of undesirable behavior, we introduce clearly identified rewarding alternatives. When these alternatives are incompatible with the punished behavior, reliable re-

5. This represents a good example of the conflict between social values and scientific evidence. It is interesting how our democratic orientation caused us to ignore for years relatively well-documented contrary evidence (as well as common sense). See Macmillan et al. 1973.

sults are indeed obtained. Punishment can facilitate discriminative learning in children when both punishment and reward are used as complementary outcomes of alternative behavioral choices. The aversive effects of punishment tend to suppress the initially predominant behaviors to the point that positive behavioral alternatives can emerge and be reinforced. It would also seem that if the interaction ends on a note of success and reward for desirable behavior, the potential ill effects of punishment on personality development are relatively minimal.

This is not to endorse deliberate punishment. There are undoubtedly more enlightened ways of dealing with most situations, e.g., rewarding positive responses as advocated by Skinner. But there is no alternative to punishment; it is inevitable. It occurs when students are annoyed at a low score, when they are embarrassed by their "dumb" answer in class, or when they fail to get a reward, all of which can have either a negative or a positive effect depending on the circumstances. Deliberate chastisement, on the other hand, is potentially dangerous and should be used with caution. It seems that, if used, punishment should be given immediately and in amounts sufficient to suppress the unacceptable behavior. But there is no way of knowing how severe the punishment must be in order to serve its purpose. To make matters worse, the child tends to develop immunity to punishment to the point that it is no longer effective, especially that there is a very definite limit to the extent to which society will allow the school to escalate punishment into child abuse.

More constructive techniques

It seems advisable, wherever possible, to rely on more positive techniques, e.g., praise for positive behavior, which are more likely to enhance the child's self-concept and to incorporate adequate social behavior into a functional definition of self. On the other hand, we must realize that even positive reinforcement can be overdone to the point that children work for the reward. Artificial rewards must be phased out as the self-rewarding aspects of the academic program take over. For this to happen, there is a need for a meaningful, challenging, and rewarding curriculum, which, in turn, means remedial help for those who need it and even a considerable adaptation of the curriculum to individual needs as indicated.

Before resorting to punishment in the sense of deliberately administered aversive stimuli, teachers should consider all available alternatives, e.g., withhold rewards: the child who does not finish his or her seatwork simply cannot go to the play area. (Note how correcting the situation is placed directly in the child's lap.) The teacher might also systematically reinforce incompatible positive behavior, e.g., calling only on those who hold up their hands as a way of discouraging children from speaking out before being called. It is not always possible, of course, to find a truly meaningful alternative. In all cases, punishment should be reasonable and fair. Above all, punishment should not be substituted for good teaching and a meaningful academic program.

We need to remember that the effectiveness of punishment varies with such factors as

timing. Generally, punishment should be administered immediately
following the offense, or even better, as soon as the unacceptable behavior begins to emerge.[6]

intensity. If it is to be effective, punishment must be sufficient to suppress the unacceptable behavior; you cannot add bit by bit until
"enough" has been reached.

Whenever teachers punish, it is imperative for them to reestablish rapport with the student by showing their willingness to let bygones be bygones,
e.g., by taking the first opportunity to say something positive. The child should
be made to understand that there was no alternative but to punish, but that
the punishment has cleared the docket and "it's a new ball-game."

What is punishment
to accomplish?

The teacher who resorts to punishment should analyze the setting in
which it is to be administered in order to make sure that something positive is
going to occur. If punishment raises the child's status in the eyes of his or her
classmates to the level of a hero, more has been lost than gained. It is especially important that punishment be administered by design and reason rather
than simply as a reaction to losing one's temper.[7] It must also be remembered
that punishment loses its effectiveness through overuse.

In the face of gross or continued misconduct, the teacher may have no alternative but to resort to punishment designed simply to have the culprit pay a
debt to society. Although this sounds very negative and should be used only
when all efforts have failed, retribution does provide a very valuable lesson,
namely, that people cannot violate social rules of conduct with impunity.[8] In
all cases, punishment should be mild and yet firm in its particular message that
such behavior is not to recur.

When the child's disruptions become such that they can no longer be tolerated, the child should probably be sent out of the room. In the case of a minor
offense (e.g., excessive talking), nonpunitive exile such as standing in the hall
for a few minutes may be sufficient. In the case of a serious offense, the child
might be sent to the principal's office. Exile often works in that it is rather dra-

6. On the other hand, in the case of open defiance, it might be wise to wait until the student has had a chance to cool off. Yet punishment should not be postponed to the point that,
by the time it comes, the student has more or less forgotten the whole incident—at which
point you end up looking simply vindictive.

7. It should be noted that the teacher's own behavior is being conditioned in the process.
The teacher who controls the class by staging periodic temper tantrums is actually being reinforced by student submission. Meanwhile, students are being deprived of a valuable lesson in
what constitutes acceptable alternatives. They cannot learn self-management under such circumstances. Instead they refrain from misbehavior in the presence of the teacher but also learn
how to be sneaky, how to avoid getting caught, how to alibi or blame others, and generally to
avoid the teacher—at which point the teacher's effectiveness has been destroyed. For good
measure, they are learning to model the teacher: when angry, strike out at anyone who cannot
retaliate.

8. Duke (1978) notes how modern society is forever "excusing" misbehavior: the child
comes from a broken home, the teacher is insensitive, the curriculum is inappropriate. This
can be overdone. Sooner or later, children must learn to accept responsibility for their own
behavior. Menninger (1975) raises a similar question: "Whatever became of sin?"

matic, but it entails definite dangers. Some children will engineer a commotion so as to be sent out of the room in order to avoid a subject they dislike. Under such conditions, exile reinforces their avoidance behavior. Even at best, they will miss class and may increase their difficulties with the curriculum. The teacher should certainly require the child to make up the lost time and, if indicated, provide remedial help. If the problem persists, it may be necessary to schedule a private conference where differences can be ironed out and a new start made. What is important is for the teacher to explain why the behavior is unacceptable and perhaps to have the child understand in some intuitive way the dynamics of his or her behavior. If a private conference does not work, the teacher should probably bring in a third party, e.g., the counselor or perhaps the parents, in order to resolve the difficulty. On the other hand, calling in the principal or the parents for every problem is likely to be interpreted by the class as a sign of personal weakness—at considerable cost in student respect.

Dealing with open confrontation

Occasionally teachers are faced with an out-and-out confrontation. This is more likely to occur in senior high, especially in inner-city schools. Actually, some teachers have a way of boxing themselves into such a predicament: they use sarcasm, belittle students, or give them orders in front of their peers in such a way that the students can comply only at considerable cost in self-esteem and peer status. In high school, where peer status is critical, such an approach is almost guaranteed to get the teacher at least an under-the-breath "Go to . . . ," at which point the ball is back in the teacher's court to field between two no-win options: either to pretend he or she did not hear or to escalate the incident into open warfare. The teacher may "win," of course, but the fact that he or she instigated the whole thing will not pass unnoticed by students who, indeed, have the right to expect greater maturity from their teachers.

In the case of open defiance, it is essential for the teacher to keep calm. It would also seem unwise for the teacher to escalate the challenge into an open confrontation while the student is still angry, especially if there is a danger that the student's defiance will trigger corresponding anger on the part of the teacher. Although some cases can be handled with diplomacy, it is generally inadvisable to risk getting punched on the nose (and get the student into deeper trouble) by pushing the issue in front of the class where the student's status is at stake. A teacher might be able to suggest simply, "Let's talk this over after class." But for most teachers it might be best to have someone get the principal, meanwhile continuing with business as usual. When the conference is held, it is important for the teacher to be firm and yet respectful of the student's personal integrity. In the long run, a great deal more will be accomplished by showing maturity and understanding than by being punitive. T. Gordon (1974), for example, suggests what he calls the "no-lose" approach designed to prevent either party from losing face, in which each side gives a little and gains a little.

BEHAVIOR MODIFICATION

Teachers need to realize that quite frequently they reinforce the very behavior they are trying to eliminate. Children may work quietly for hours; nobody notices. Only when they misbehave does the teacher realize that they exist. They soon discover that the only way to get attention is to create a commotion. As a consequence, the teacher's reprimand, which is meant to be aversive and deterring of misbehavior, turns out to be quite rewarding, particularly in terms of peer status. In short, the child is being conditioned to misbehave through a systematic schedule of reinforcement of disruptive and self-defeating behavior.

Behavior modification can help

Considerable success in improving classroom behavior has been achieved through what is known as *behavior modification,* a technique designed to provide systematic reinforcement for good behavior, so that misbehavior is gradually eliminated through extinction and displacement by positive alternatives (see Ackerman 1972). In a study by Hall et al. (1968), for example, the introduction of behavior modification techniques resulted in increased study rates and a corresponding reduction in disruptive behavior. A temporary reversal during which the reinforcement contingencies were discontinued produced a return of the original symptoms. A resumption of the reinforcement schedule once again increased study rates and reduced disruption. Similar results have been reported in a number of studies, particularly studies conducted in a laboratory setting.

Behavior modification techniques have obvious possibilities in maintaining discipline in the classroom, where disruptive behavior can be gradually reduced through a systematic schedule of reinforcement, at first for being quiet, and eventually for active participation in the academic program. Cohen (1968), for example, found that the use of reinforcement techniques with adolescent delinquents with a long history of school failure resulted in improved academic performance.

A wide variety of incentives can be used—cookies, M&Ms, toys, free time, praise, and even money. Tokens that can be redeemed for special prizes or privileges are particularly popular because of their flexibility in terms of what they can be exchanged for and even in terms of the rate of exchange. They tend also to be less disruptive since the actual exchange for the reward can be scheduled, say, at the end of the day. It can even be made into an "award ceremony" as a way of capitalizing on group motivation to entice some of the more reluctant students to participate. These incentives would then be gradually phased out as the pattern of adequate work habits becomes established and the intrinsic rewards of meaningful learning come into play.

This is not to say that behavior modification is a miracle cure for any and all motivational and disciplinary problems in the classroom. Unless it is coupled with a meaningful curriculum, effective teaching strategies, and a sound classroom atmosphere of mutual trust, it will soon deteriorate into a meaningless and counterproductive form of bribery. In fact, some psychologists (e.g., Travers 1977) have taken an increasingly conservative position on the effectiveness of behavior modification techniques when used in the classroom. It seems clear, for example, that certain situational realities will make behavior modification somewhat more difficult to operationalize in the classroom than in the laboratory. There is a very definite limit to which the teacher can ignore disruptive behavior. It may also be difficult to prevent classmates from reinforcing the behavior the teacher is trying to extinguish through nonreinforcement.

It has also been argued that behavior modification concentrates on the symptoms and does relatively little about underlying causes. This may not be a totally valid criticism. First, teachers are not clinicians; they have neither the time nor the training to deal with underlying dynamics. Even if they could identify causes, there might be little they could do about them. On the other hand, removing the symptoms can have not only a beneficial effect on the operation of the classroom but may also help resolve underlying problems, at least to a degree, and thus allow the child's capacity for growth a chance to emerge. As children are rewarded for success in the classroom, they find their energies released for more productive purposes. As their behavior improves, they give the teacher and the class more reason to provide them with acceptance and support. Meanwhile, they find more time to tend to their studies and give themselves more opportunity for legitimate need satisfaction.

DEMOCRATIC DISCIPLINE

Despite its allegiance to democracy, the school is still basically authoritarian. This might have had a place in the school years ago when the motto, "Learn or get out," made sense in the light of its objectives. Today this is no longer relevant; the fact is that many youngsters would like to leave school if the law would let them. Since teachers and students have to put up with each other, it might behoove them to get along in a spirit of mutual understanding and respect. In this, the teacher must take the initiative.

A democratic approach

Whereas youngsters respond positively to firmness with regard to reasonable expectations, a dominative and punitive approach is typically self-defeating. As Dreikurs (1968) points out, punishment tends to be effective only for children who do not need it, since they are the ones with whom one can reason, while those the teacher would like to impress with punishment are more likely to shrug it off as part of the fortunes of war, you win one, you lose one. A hard line in the ghetto high school is more likely to create a confrontation than eagerness for school work. Even if it were to maintain order, this sort of intimidation is more likely to create resentment than to serve the democratic purposes of helping these children grow to maturity.

Teachers need to take a broad perspective on the dozens of minor infractions and childish pranks that are not important in terms of the long-range objectives of modern education. Above all, they need to keep an open mind to the very real possibility that misbehavior is almost inevitable, considering how little the school is doing to meet the needs of some of its students. Nothing very positive will happen as long as discipline is used to foist onto children a meaningless curriculum.

Discipline is best seen in the context of self-actualization (see chapter 4). Children who see school work as enhancing from the standpoint of their major goals give very little trouble. On the contrary, children will not develop a strong identification with the school if it is dedicated to the task of making them look stupid and worthless. The achievement of our democratic objectives in their totality demands that the school be fully committed to the inherent worth of every child. This involves, first of all, a feeling of acceptance and emotional security, a sense of progress, and above all, a sincere belief on the part of the teacher that, if given a chance, the child can and will move toward self-actualization.

The humanistic position, for example, is predicated on the child's inherent capacity for self-direction. Unless serious threats suppress this natural urge, children will move constructively toward worthwhile goals; it is only when they feel afraid, unloved, and helpless that they will resort to inappropriate behavior. Humanists would emphasize a permissive and accepting environment in which children can explore better ways of behaving without fear of rejection; their behavior will improve as they increase in self-knowledge, self-awareness, and self-acceptance. Humanists see the teacher as a facilitator and emphasize the need for developing positive relations with students based on mutual trust and respect.

Many teachers have difficulty in accepting humanistic premises as the sole basis for effective classroom discipline. Although it is true that insensitive teachers often make trouble for themselves, it probably does not follow that complete student freedom is the solution to misbehavior in the classroom. Perhaps what is needed is to combine humanistic and Skinnerian principles into a constructive system of classroom management. Teachers must like and respect students. But they can be both firm and friendly; they can enforce rules and standards that students will appreciate, not fear or resent. They can exert leadership without turning students into zombies. They can set requirements and dispense rewards without destroying student initiative. Not only can positive teacher leadership maximize student growth but in so doing it can enhance, not blunt, the student's natural urge toward self-actualization.

CLASSROOM MANAGEMENT: A SUMMARY

Promoting constructive classroom behavior and correspondingly minimizing classroom mischief is more likely to succeed if teachers proceed on an enlightened course based on established principles of educational psychology. Classroom management cannot be reduced to a set of rules. Constructive behavior—in the classroom or anywhere else—is necessarily a function of the whole child in complex interaction with the totality of the classroom situation, its curriculum, the teacher, the classroom atmosphere, etc., as seen from the child's perceptual frame of reference.

Unfortunately too many teachers approach the problem as a separate item to be resolved—through exhortation, threat, grades, punishment, and varied gimmicks of extremely limited motivational quality to the child, whose goals and purposes are primarily personal and only secondarily academic.

It should not be too difficult to maintain reasonable motivation and discipline if we synchronize our strategies with the child's natural desire to explore, to become. It should not be too difficult to encourage the child to engage in meaningful learning if while so doing he or she can satisfy his or her needs for approval, for achievement, for knowing. Meaningful verbal materials, presumably the stock in trade of the classroom, should provide their own rewards—if the teacher will only see that they are coordinated with the child's natural curiosity, need for exploration and mastery, and inherent need to grow.

This is not to say that recipes can be given; each child is unique. Yet fundamentally all behavior is subject to the laws and principles of psychology; it relates to a relatively common causative base and is presumably amenable to some of the same strategies. A lack of motivation and an excess of misbehavior emanate from such "causes" as boredom due to a curriculum that is too easy, too hard, or simply irrelevant; frustration, which can be reduced through adaptation of the curriculum, remedial help where needed, or simply a change of pace; or a need for attention, which can be handled through providing legitimate opportunity for every child to gain attention and recognition, e.g., commendation for achievement.

In the light of these principles, we might make some suggestions.

If we begin with the two major sources of problems as defined earlier by Kooi and Schutz (1965), we can suggest:

1. For too much disruptive behavior:
   a. Do not reinforce by making a big hassle out of every minor incident, yet be careful not to reinforce misbehavior by default.
   b. It is much better to wait to reward positive behavior; catch children being good.
   c. Don't let the misbehavior get reinforcement from other students;

build good rapport with the class; involve the class in exciting activities; reward the class as a whole for good behavior.

2. For too little constructive behavior:
   a. Be more alert to positive behavior and more careful to reward. At first, reinforce even low-level approximations to desirable behavior.
   b. The contract system might work; use small projects at first.
3. Reward and punishment generally should occur as close to the response as possible.
4. Be consistent. Failure to act to prevent misbehavior may mean that misbehavior is being reinforced on an intermittent basis, which will make it extremely resistant to extinction.

To the extent that misbehavior and lack of motivation often reflect boredom and frustration, the teacher needs to deal with the cause. Here again, the best antidote is a constructive academic program adapted to the background, the needs, and the purposes of every child. A sense of humor, a positive image of integrity and goodwill, and competence in the use of effective teaching strategies are essential.

1. Provide a supportive classroom climate in which childen are accepted for what they are. Motivational strategies will not work if the child's deficiency needs are not met; learning will not occur if the child is hungry, insecure, or afraid. The humanists insist that the teacher's task is to remove obstacles so as to unleash the child's natural need to grow. Expect good behavior and you will get it; treat children as immature and they will respond in kind.
2. Above all, there is need for a good academic program; a meaningful curriculum for every child; remedial help as needed; a sensitivity to pupil difficulty and expertise in catering to student need. The program, not the gimmicks, must carry the load.
3. Motivational and disciplinary strategies can be used only to supplement what must of necessity be adequate conditions of learning. Do not expect a quick and easy miracle; unless conditions are conducive to meaningful and productive learning, these strategies can only fail. You will then have no alternative but to resort to punishment and look for another easy miracle.
4. Motivation and discipline are best seen in the context of the child's overall development. An essential prerequisite is a healthy self-concept characterized by positive attitudes, meaningful goals, and a commitment to learning as an aspect of self-fulfillment.
5. An enlightened system of reinforcement (and extinction) is essential. This calls for immediate reinforcement on a continuous basis at first, designed to shape positive behavior and gradually changed to an intermittent schedule and eventually phased out as the natural reinforcement of the activity takes over. You will know when your rein-

forcers are working; behavior will change to specification; if it does not, you are doing it wrong.

It is a misconception to think that all problems in the classroom can be overcome with love and understanding. But it is equally a misconception to think that students can be "straightened out" if only they are punished sufficiently. It is an even greater misconception to think that unmotivated children can be "motivated" through punishment.

1. Punishment should be kept to a minimum. It is generally much better to wait to reward positive behavior that will then displace inadequate behavior. If punishment is used, it should be "adequate"; it cannot be dispensed by successive approximations.
2. The concept of negative reinforcement would suggest that we make the cessation of aversive measures conditional on improved behavior—e.g., letting the child go out for recess when he or she has caught up on yesterday's work.
3. Of interest in any discussion of motivation is the Premack principle[9] in which the student is encouraged to participate in an activity of limited appeal by tying it to another activity of greater appeal: "Do your grammar now. As soon as you finish, you can go to the materials center and work on your project." It may not be a bad idea for all people to program themselves to the Premack principle: I will finish this assignment; then I am going to reward myself with a cup of coffee and a bit of TV.

HIGHLIGHTS OF THE CHAPTER

Of critical concern, particularly to beginning teachers, are the dual problems of maintaining classroom discipline and generating a certain level of student interest in school work. If they are to be successful in this crucial area, teachers need to be familiar with the following concepts:

1. Motivation stems directly from the concepts of needs, the self, and the phenomenal field (see chapter 4). It incorporates both the arousal of behavior and the orientation of this behavior toward the attainment of certain goals as potential satisfier of individual needs.
2. Behaviorists would deal with classroom motivation from the standpoint of selective reinforcement. A major problem here is the typically haphazard use teachers make of reinforcement principles.

9. Sometimes referred to as "Grandma's rule": "Eat your potatoes and you can have your dessert." The rule is simple; there is no hassle, no threat, no anger. Work now, play later; no work, no play!

3. Humanists, on the other hand, approach motivation from the standpoint of the child's inherent need for self-actualization. Maslow presents an interesting distinction between good and poor choosers.

4. The child is always motivated. The teacher's task is to harness these motives in the service of education through the identification of worthwhile goals meaningful in terms of the child's needs and purposes.

5. A variety of incentives are available to the teacher to tap the motives existing in the child. Extrinsic incentives are often emphasized to the point where they supersede the true purposes of education.

6. All incentives are best understood in terms of reward and punishment, i.e., in terms of whether or not they satisfy the purposes of the motivated organism.

7. Because of the relative inappropriateness of primary needs for classroom motivation, the school has had to rely on secondary reinforcements. Unfortunately these are less dependable.

8. Discipline is best seen as an aspect of the school's systematic effort to promote social growth. The emphasis should be on concern for group and individual welfare rather than on the restriction of individual freedom.

9. Although psychologists have taken a more realistic view of the effectiveness of punishment, its use in the classroom should require clarity on the part of the teacher as to the specific purpose it is to achieve in the particular instance.

SUGGESTIONS FOR FURTHER READING

ACKERMAN, J. MARK. *Operant Conditioning Techniques for the Classroom Teacher.* Glenview: Scott, Foresman, 1972. Explains behavior modification techniques for use in the classroom.

CLARIZIO, H. F. *Toward Positive Classroom Discipline.* 3d ed. New York: Wiley, 1980. Offers useful descriptions of the classroom use of reward, punishment, extinction, etc. Interesting and helpful.

DINKMEYER, D., and RUDOLF DREIKURS. *Encouraging Children to Learn: The Encouragement Process.* Englewood Cliffs: Prentice-Hall, 1963. An interesting and readable account of how children can be encouraged to grow and to learn. Gives a number of anecdotes showing how encouragement works and how discouragement is a big factor in chronic failure.

GLASSER, WILLIAM G. *Schools without Failure.* New York: Harper & Row, 1969. Argues that the traditional school causes too many children to fail, that it leads many children to think of themselves as failures. Suggests greater emphasis on having children relate what they learn in school to outside living. Presents a strong argument for humanistic principles in helping youngsters achieve self-management.

GNAGEY, WILLIAM J. *The Psychology of Discipline in the Classroom.* New York: Macmillan, 1968. Discusses the principles of discipline. Designed as a tool for helping classroom teachers deal with misbehavior. Presents a psychological model of classroom discipline and suggests a number of practical control techniques.

HOLT, JOHN. *How Children Learn.* New York: Pitman, 1967. Describes how children can learn to enjoy learning and gives a number of examples of intrinsic motivation. See also *How Children Fail.* Pitman, 1964, a critique of the ways the school destroys young children.

KOLESNIK, WALTER B. *Motivation: Understanding and Influencing Human Behavior.* Boston: Allyn & Bacon, 1978. A brief look at different theories of motivation, including social factors involved in classroom motivation.

MACMILLAN, DONALD L., et al. The role of punishment in the classroom. *Except. Children* 40 (1973):85–96. Presents arguments for and against the use of punishment in the classroom. Reviews the research evidence.

PHI DELTA KAPPA. The problems of discipline and violence in American education. *Phi Delta Kappan* 59 (1978):298–349. The January issue is devoted to violence and disciplinary problems in the schools, with articles by Senator Birch Bayh, James Coleman, William Glasser, and many others.

POSTMAN, N., and C. WEINGARTNER. *Teaching as a Subversive Activity.* New York: Delacorte, 1969. Presents a system the authors claim makes the students unaware they are learning. Interesting reading for teachers of unmotivated students.

SEGAL, REBECCA. *Got No Time to Fool Around: A Motivation Program for Education.* Philadelphia: Westminster, 1973. Describes a number of motivational strategies and their actual application with boys and girls in the Philadelphia schools.

WEINER, BERNARD. *Theories of Motivation: From Mechanism to Cognition.* Chicago: Markham, 1973. Presents a historical overview of four basic theories of motivation: drive theory, field theory, achievement theory, and attribution theory.

WHITMAN, MYRON, and JOAN WHITMAN. Behavior modification in the classroom. *Psychol. Sch.* 8 (1971):177–196. A good exposition and overview of behavior modification as it might be used in the classroom.

QUESTIONS AND PROJECTS

1. Evaluate: To the extent that the school must necssarily look toward the future, whereas the child is invariably interested in the here and now, motivation in the classroom must inevitably be a half-hearted extrinsic proposition. To what extent is allowing the child to do what he or she pleases the answer? What would behavior modification techniques have to contribute in this regard?

2. Teachers are often accused of being stingy with rewards. How can they deal with the fact that when rewards become plentiful, inflation destroys their valence value?

   Appraise the adequacy of grades as academic incentives. What role might we legitimately expect them to play in the motivation of, say, the culturally disadvantaged?

3. Some teachers rationalize: "Why should I break my neck to teach children who 'just do not want to learn'?" Is it possible that some teachers "just do not want to teach"?

   Specifically, what can the school do with its dozens of "unmotivated" students?

   What motivates some students simply turns others off. How did this come about? What can the teacher do now?

4. Evaluate: Teachers throughout elementary and high school have so played up to the current interests of their pupils that colleges are filled with students who have not learned to discipline themselves into mastering what is important if it should happen to be the least bit hard and not immediately exciting. Besides, they have not learned to study.

   What position would you take in answer to the parent of an underachiever who is considering giving him fifty cents for every A or B he earns at school?

5. How can teachers ensure that they reward effort rather than student aptitude? How realistic is it to give different grades for the same quality work?

6. To what extent is the teacher responsible for the misbehavior in his or her class?

   Evaluate: Autocratic discipline is a shortsighted expedient that is neither easy nor effective.

7. Outline a behavior modification program designed gradually to substitute academic work for disruptive behavior in a given classroom.

8. Comment: Instead of trying to "motivate" students and to suppress misbehavior, teachers would do better to concentrate on good teaching. How can teachers capitalize on success when many of the misbehaving children in the classroom find it difficult to "succeed"?

SELF-TEST

1. The teacher's greatest asset in motivating children is probably
   a. the ability to make the subject matter clear and meaningful.
   b. the ability to organize school routine on an efficient basis.
   c. the ability to relate to and inspire children.
   d. the skill in adapting the curriculum to individual needs.
   e. the skill in manipulating incentives, both positive and negative.

2. An incentive is best defined as
   a. a condition or object with need-satisfying properties.
   b. a learned motive.

    c. a potential goal.

    d. a reinforcement-producing object or condition.

    e. a reward.

3. The difficulty in "motivating" lower-class children is that typically
    a. the curriculum is too difficult in relation to their ability.
    b. the curriculum is meaningless in terms of their background.
    c. their middle-class teachers do not understand them.
    d. they are lacking in the necessary experiential background.
    e. they find the classroom climate cold and rejecting.

4. The primary goal of effective discipline is
    a. conformity to social expectations.
    b. effective self-direction.
    c. a sense of personal and social responsibility.
    d. inhibition of misbehavior.
    e. sensitivity to the consequences of one's behavior.

5. Misbehavior is best seen as
    a. an attempt at establishing what is and what is not acceptable.
    b. an attempt to satisfy one's needs.
    c. a manifestation of an inborn tendency toward evil.
    d. a reaction against society's attempt at socialization.
    e. a symptom of deeper personality difficulty.

6. The school's primary task in the area of discipline is
    a. to deter misbehavior.
    b. to prevent misbehavior from becoming habitual.
    c. to prevent misbehavior from interfering with the attainment of the
       school's objectives.
    d. to promote positive behavior.
    e. to provide suitable outlets for the release of tension.

7. The most effective tool against wholesale misbehavior in the classroom is
    a. a considerate and respected teacher.
    b. an effective and challenging curriculum.
    c. an effective student government assuming responsibility for disci-
       pline.
    d. firm, discipline-oriented teachers.
    e. a permissive and supportive classroom climate.

ELEVEN

Retention and Transfer of Training

Nearly everything that is now known was not in any book when most of us went to school. We cannot know it unless we have picked it up since.

Robert J. Oppenheimer (1958)

The key to retrieval is organization or, in simpler terms, knowing where to find information and how to get there.

Jerome S. Bruner (1961)

I am concerned with one additional dimension of educational objectives, namely, with what has been called the "surrender value" value of the curriculum. Five or ten years after the student has successfully attained the immediate objectives of the curriculum, what is he expected to retain? Should we not construct curricula with conscious attention to their surrender value, that is, to their long-term retention benefits?

John B. Carroll (1965)

— Presents forgetting and transfer of training as interrelated phenomena governed by essentially the same principles
— Introduces various theoretical positions and outlines their implications for educational practice
— Discusses the major factors affecting retention and transfer

PREVIEW: KEY CONCEPTS

1. Without retention and transfer, the educational enterprise is an expensive exercise in futility.
2. Rote learnings are subject to rapid and heavy losses due to forgetting; meaningful learnings, by contrast, are far more resistant to memory losses.
3. Effective retention and transfer of meaningful verbal learnings are a direct function of effective learning, which is, in turn, a function of the adequacy of one's existing cognitive structure.
4. Current consensus is that forgetting, particularly the forgetting of rote learnings, results from the interference of prior learnings and, to a lesser extent, subsequent learnings. According to Ausubel's assimilation theory, meaningfully learned verbal materials are forgotten as they are subsumed under broader concepts and principles already established in cognitive structure.
5. The theory of identical components explains transfer in terms of similarities between the new and prior learnings. Meaningful verbal learnings promote transfer by acting as subsumers for the subsequent learning of related materials.

PREVIEW QUESTIONS

1. Why must education necessarily depend on retention and transfer?
   What effect might one's views on the degree of transfer to be expected from school learnings, for example, have on one's approach to curriculum and to teaching strategies?
2. Why is retention better for meaningful than for rote learnings?
   How does the process of forgetting in meaningful verbal learning differ from that in forgetting rote materials?
   How do such factors as mastery, review, motivation, etc., operate in the retention of both rote and meaningful learnings?
3. How does the modern educational psychologist explain forgetting and transfer of training?
   How functional are current theories of forgetting and of transfer of training as guides for effective classroom practice?

4. To what extent is effective learning the key to effective retention and transfer?

Probably no other aspect of the classroom situation is more frustrating to teachers and pupils alike than the extent to which students not only forget by tomorrow what they have learned today but also seem unable to make effective use of the knowledge they have in dealing with new situations. Because they are closely interrelated, these two aspects of the learning process will be considered together in this chapter. In fact, it must be recognized that retention and transfer are integral parts of the learning process itself and can be understood only in the context of the previous chapters.

RETENTION AND FORGETTING

That a good deal of what children learn in school is soon forgotten is obvious, much to the despair of their teachers—and, of course, the children. Estimates as to the rate and the extent of this forgetting vary greatly depending on such factors as the functionality of the material and the interrelatedness of the components, its meaningfulness as a function of the particular learner's background, intelligence, and motivation, the adequacy of its mastery, the nature of the learning process, and the method used in its measurement. With regard to nonsense syllables, for example, Ebbinghaus's (1885) well-known forgetting curve showed an estimated 75 percent loss over a twenty-four-hour period, with more gradual decline thereafter to a more or less complete loss over a matter of days.

The situation is probably not as bad as it appears on the surface. Forgetting is selective and, although in some areas there is an almost complete loss, in others gains may actually occur during a period of disuse. Furthermore, not only can forgetting be minimized, but a great deal of what is forgotten is not overly important in and of itself. One needs facts to use as stepping stones to higher levels of understanding and, although they are often forgotten and although the mere possession of facts does not ensure insights, generalizations, and principles, the latter would not be possible without the facts. Yet it is these higher levels of understanding, and not the facts on which they are based, that are the important outcomes of education—and those, fortunately, are relatively resistant to forgetting.

We must distinguish between rote and meaningful learning

The crucial issue here is the distinction between meaningful and rote learning. The human brain, unlike the computer, has extremely limited facilities for the storage and retrieval of isolated facts and events. Its ability to grasp and remember meaningful material, on the other hand, is relatively unlimited. Any attempt to put a numerical value on the degree of forgetting therefore must also specify the degree of meaningfulness involved. It must also be noted

that the factors that make for effective learning also tend to make for effective retention. Rapid learning typically implies greater intellectual and/or experiential background (leading to greater meaningfulness), efficient study habits, efficient storage and retrieval procedures, etc.—all of which promote retention.

Storage and retrieval　　　Retention implies two basic processes: storage and retrieval. In a sense, storage of data in memory parallels storage of letters and other forms of correspondence. Throwing one's mail pell-mell in a pile anywhere around the house or office greatly complicates the ready availability of any one item should it be needed. An effective filing system, on the other hand, permits the instant retrieval of any one of the thousands of letters, circulars, etc., a corporation might receive in a month or a year. It is also clear that storage space is far from unlimited so that effective storage calls for condensing and, in many cases, actually discarding marginal information. There is need for an effective strategy of coding as well as a functional filing system of broad categories and subcategories into which newly learned specifics can be placed as a prerequisite for effective retrieval.

Explanation of Forgetting

The layman's view that forgetting results from disuse or decay with the passage of time is true in a sense; with the passage of time, omissions, additions, or condensations take place, particularly in points not too clearly understood or interconnected with the main theme of the material. However, mere passage of time does not explain why forgetting is selective; it is especially inadequate in explaining the difference in retention rate between rote and meaningful learning.

A more sophisticated view is that forgetting is the result of the active interference of what is learned by either previous or subsequent learnings. Thus, the child having learned that $7 + 6 = 13$ and later that $8 + 4 = 12$ confuses the two to the point that he or she is no longer sure whether the sum of $7 + 6 = 13$, 12, or what have you. In the same way, the teacher has no trouble remembering the name of one or two new students but, faced with another twenty-five besides, confuses one name with another to the point of not remembering a single one. This interference of *previous* learnings by *subsequent* learnings, first investigated by Müller and Pilzecker in 1900, is generally known as *retroactive inhibition.*

Proactive rather than retroactive

After a half-century of relatively complete acceptance as the primary explanation of forgetting, the concept of retroactive inhibition was challenged in 1957 by Underwood, who suggested that interference came from tasks learned *previously* rather than those learned *subsequently* to the material in question. In his classic study, subjects learned a list of ten paired adjectives to a criterion of eight out of ten correct answers. Forty-eight hours later, they recalled the list. The following day, they learned a new list, which they again recalled forty-eight hours later and likewise for a third and fourth list. The results showed a sharp decrement from 69 percent recall for the first list to 25 percent for the fourth, suggesting that decrement in performance is a function of *proactive* interference, i.e., interference from previous lists.

Retention of Meaningful Verbal Learning

Following through on his critical distinction between rote and meaningful learning (see chapter 9), Ausubel presents the forgetting of meaningfully learned verbal material as a logical extension of the process of subsumption through which potentially meaningful materials are learned. He accepts the view that forgetting in rote learning occurs when, say, the original response R_1 in the paired association S_1-R_1 is now replaced by R_2 as per the theory of proactive or retroactive inhibition. But according to Ausubel, this short-term interference, so crucial to forgetting in rote learning, is a relatively insignificant factor in the forgetting of meaningfully learned verbal material. Verbal materials are potentially meaningful to the extent that they can be subsumed within the concepts and propositions already existing in cognitive structure. Therefore, the fundamental task in promoting effective retention is that of promoting efficient subsumption; conversely, material that cannot be subsumed has to be learned by rote and is subject to all the limitations thereof. The path to effective retention of verbal materials is clearly via good subsumption, i.e., good and effective learning as discussed in chapter 8.

Meaningful learning enhances retention

Since potentially meaningful material is learned in relation to an existing background of relevant concepts and principles providing the framework for its reception and making possible the emergence of new meanings, it is evident that the clarity, stability, and organizational properties of this background crucially affect both the accuracy and the clarity of the emerging new meanings and their immediate and long-term retrievability. If the cognitive structure is stable and suitably organized, accurate and unambiguous meanings will emerge and will tend to remain available. On the other hand, if the structure is unstable, ambiguous, or poorly organized, it tends to inhibit both meaningful learning and retention. It is, therefore, only by strengthening relevant aspects of cognitive structure that new learnings and their retention can be facilitated.

The reductionistic feature of subsumption

The initial effect of the subsumption of potentially meaningful verbal materials into existing cognitive structure is to facilitate retention as well as learning. But then the new material is immediately subjected to the erosive influence of what might be considered a *reductionist* trend in cognitive organization. Since it is more economical to retain a few inclusive concepts and propositions than to remember a large number of separate and individual items, the import of the latter tends to be reduced to the broad and general meaning of the former. As a result of this reductionistic feature of the subsumption process, the specific items become progressively less dissociable as entities separate from their anchoring concepts until they are no longer available and are said to be forgotten. They simply become subsumed under the relevant and more inclusive conceptual system already existing in cognitive structure.

The primary cause of the forgetting of meaningful learning, then, is this progessive reduction of new meaning to that of the basic ideas in cognitive structure under which it has become subsumed. In other words, as newly learned elements are incorporated into the already existing hierarchical organization of meaningfully learned materials in cognitive structure, they are reduced to the least common denominator of relevant established meaning. This process of memory reduction provides for obvious economy in learning and in initial memory, but the advantages are gained at the expense of details and the more specific information.

Derivative versus correlative subsumption

First, we need to distinguish between two basic kinds of subsumption occurring in the course of meaningful learning. *Derivative* subsumption takes place when the new learning material constitutes a specific example of an already established concept in cognitive structure or simply illustrates a previously learned general proposition—in which case the new material is simply *derivable* from already established and more inclusive propositions in cognitive structure.[1] Under these circumstances, meaning emerges quickly as the new material is quickly subsumed (i.e., lost as a separate entity) since its meaning is adequately represented by the more general and inclusive meaning of the established subsumer. If the item is needed, it can be reconstructed readily, so no major loss has occurred. If you have the concept of reinforcement clearly established in cognitive structure, you do not have to remember specifically what effect praise, reward, or grades would individually have on behavior.

More critical is the typical case of *correlative* subsumption in which the subject matter to be learned is an extension, an elaboration, a modification, or a qualification of a previously learned proposition. In this case, the materials are somewhat more difficult to subsume under the more inclusive propositions in existing cognitive structure, since their meaning is less adequately represented by available subsumers. Yet in the interest of economy in cognitive organization and memory, the same trend toward reductionistic subsumption occurs, particularly if available subsumers are unclear or unstable or if the new material is not particularly salient in its own right. Here, the consequences are more serious. When correlative propositions lose their individual identifiability and can no longer be dissociated from their subsumers, a genuine loss of knowledge occurs. The subsumers do not permit the reconstruction of these subsumed components of the material. A major problem in the school's attempt to foster a firm grasp of an academic discipline, then, is that of counteracting this inevitable trend toward the total subsumption of correlative materials.

Initial
discriminability
important to
retention

A major factor in the degree to which meaningful verbal learning remains dissociable from its broad subsuming carriers in cognitive structure is its initial *discriminability*, for unless the newly learned material is originally salient and clearly discriminable from the already established subsuming structure, it can be adequately represented by the latter and has no reason to continue to exist as a separate entity in its own right. Unless discrimination is sharpened so as to make the distinction of the new from its broader subsumers sharp, clear, and unambiguous, there will be a tendency for A' to be remembered simply as A.

Comparative
organizers

Where such confusion is likely to occur (i.e., when the teacher has reason to anticipate negative transfer), the teacher should rely on *comparative organizers* to sharpen the discriminability between the new idea and the essentially different and yet confusably similar ideas already in cognitive structure: "Let's not confuse instrumental conditioning I am presenting now with classical conditioning we studied last week. They are alike in certain ways, but they also differ in that . . . Classical conditioning, you remember . . . ; now instrumental

---

1. Note, for example, how in recalling a past incident (e.g., an accident), we normally retain only the basic substance of the event and then reconstruct (invent) the details to fit the gist of the experience as incorporated in our cognitive structure.

conditioning . . ." The teacher might also want to increase the adequacy (i.e., the clarity and stability) of the subsumers themselves, for inadequate subsumers can provide neither adequate depth of anchorage for incoming potentially meaningful materials nor the required discriminability between themselves and the new material. In the Ausubel and Fitzgerald (1961) study, for example, students who had a greater knowledge of Christianity were able to process and to retain considerably more information concerning Buddhism than were their less-informed controls.

Forgetting involves not only a loss but also a considerable amount of distortion. Vague, diffuse, and ambiguous meanings may emerge from the beginning of the learning phase because of the lack of adequate anchoring ideas in cognitive structure or perhaps because of the lack of discrimination of either the new materials or their anchoring concepts. Distortion also results from the selective emphasis that takes place as a result of the initial interpretation of the newly presented materials; each individual has a relatively unique set of related anchoring ideas, including personal biases, that causes him or her to assimilate materials in an idiosyncratic way. As a consequence, the resulting meaning is a function of the particular assimilation that occurs and the selective distortions, discountings, reversals of intended meanings, etc., as influenced by the individual's particular self-structure. During the retention phase, newly learned materials are reduced further to the established ideas in cognitive space and therefore become more similar in import to the anchoring ideas. This means that the material is progressively more distorted toward the learner's idiosyncratic cognitive structure. Further distortion may occur during the reconstruction period in accordance with the individual's tendencies to exaggerate or to dramatize certain incidents out of context.

Memory as an Aspect of Information Processing

Information-processing theorists have shown systematic interest in memory as an aspect of the way people process information. More specifically, they postulate a four-step approach to learning and retention:

1. Stimuli from the environment are received through appropriate receptors, primarily the eyes and ears.
2. These sensory inputs are registered in a sensory buffer for a fraction of a second, during which a pattern is recognized and the stimulus identified on the basis of some of its attributes of interest. Thus ||∃ is identified as a B or possibly as 13, depending on the context and one's past experience.
3. Once transformed into a pattern, sensory perceptions are transferred from the sensory buffer to short-term memory (STM), where they can be held for some twenty seconds (longer periods if rehearsed while on hold).

4. At this point, sensory inputs must be translated into something more permanent—i.e., they must be moved to long-term memory (LTM). More specifically, they must be coded so as to fit into the learner's current cognitive structure. For verbal materials, this probably means transforming a purely perceptual event into a linguistic event involving cognitive meaning.[2]

The distinction between STM and LTM is fundamental.

STM *vs.* LTM

1. STM consists of purely perceptual traces that can be erased, not only as a function of time, but especially by succeeding perceptual events. It seems that the number of unrelated items that humans can hold in STM at any one time is on the order of seven (Miller 1956), where items can range from separate letters to separate words or ideas. One can grasp the seven digits of a new telephone number but, without rehearsal or transfer to LTM, would tend to have difficulty in remembering two seven-digit numbers.

   If we assume that adequate perception has indeed been registered in the sensory buffers, forgetting can take place in STM when crowding by new sensory inputs overloads the limited STM storage capacity, causing some of the earlier inputs to be pushed out before they can be encoded and transferred to LTM. Forgetting of this type is essential to clear STM storage space so that new inputs can be stored.[3]

2. Long-term memories, by contrast, are relatively permanent (Penfield 1969). But there may be difficulties in retrieval, particularly if inputs have been incorrectly or carelessly coded and thus misplaced in cognitive structure. They would be subject to interference in recall, for example, from previously and subsequently stored memories.

From the standpoint of classroom operation, information-processing theory would suggest that:

1. Sensory perceptions must be accurate and clear. To the extent that nothing can be remembered that has not entered into sensory registers, the teacher's first task is to ensure that learners pay attention. The teacher might whet the child's curiosity by creating suspense, using a variety of sensory inputs, or perhaps using visual and sound effects. He or she might also present a simplified version of a complex situation or otherwise accentuate its relevant features.

2. Since one's perceptions are necessarily mediated by one's prior experiences—it is much easier to register "dog" than its Chinese counter-

2. Shiffrin and Atkinson (1969) compare human memory to the digital computer, which takes in information through sensory registers corresponding to human sense organs, stores this information briefly in a buffer for short-term storage, and then moves it to long-term storage.

3. Support for this short-term and long-term memory position comes from the fact that different drugs can affect one without affecting the other. The same effect can occur as a consequence of brain damage (see McGaugh 1968). The loss of short-term memory may also be involved in retrograde amnesia.

part—teachers must ensure that the learner has an adequate background or related experiences that permits "seeing" the significant features of the incoming stimulus.

3. Typically the critical step is the semantic encoding of the stimulus for transfer from STM to LTM. Again, it should be noted that sensory inputs can be codified only in relation to existing cognitive structure; that the only coding systems available to us for coding sensory inputs are those derived from prior experience. Since the time is often extremely short (especially when further inputs are being constantly added), it becomes crucial that the learner have ready access to adequate subsumers in terms of which the new inputs can be immediately catalogued. This is especially important inasmuch as the encoding must be accurate and precise if effective retrieval is to be achieved.

Factors Affecting Retention

Considerable research has been conducted into the factors that influence forgetting, particularly in rote learning. Before we review the evidence, we might profit from considering the design of such experiments. Using, for example, the retroactive model, we might want to determine the effect of memorizing logical noun-adjective pairs subsequent to the learning of arbitrary noun-adjective pairs on the retention of the earlier learnings. We would have to start with two groups of subjects—one the *experimental*, the other the *control*—equivalent in all respects relevant to retention. They would have to have approximately the same level of motivation, intelligence, sophistication in paired-association tasks, etc. Both groups would learn the arbitrary pairs to the same degree of mastery. Later the experimental group would study a new list of logical noun-adjective pairs, while the control group would avoid this type of activity. Then the two groups would be tested for their retention of the arbitrary pairs. If, for the sake of discussion, the experimental group were to do more poorly on the retest than the control, we might conclude that the memorization of the second list interfered with the retention of the first. Table 11.1 presents the experimental design in schematic form.

Table 11.1   Paradigm for Retention: Retroactive Model

	Original Learning (Learn A)	*Interpolated Learning (Learn B)*	*Test of Original Learning (Test A)*
Group I (Experimental)	Learn: Arbitrary pairs	Learn: Logical pairs	Test: Arbitrary pairs
Group II (Control)	Learn: Arbitrary pairs	Learn: Unrelated task	Test: Arbitrary pairs

The following are among the more obvious factors affecting the retention of materials learned totally or partly by rote:[4]

Similarity as a factor in retention

1. Similarity of original and interpolated learnings: Research suggests that the more similar the interpolated and original learnings, the greater the interference up to a point. As the two become more similar beyond this point, interference decreases, and eventually as the materials become essentially identical, the interpolated learning naturally reinforces the original learning. Where interference reaches a peak and begins to give way to reinforcement depends on such factors as the intelligence and background of the learner and the meaningfulness of the material. Thus, the bright child might find that learning $(a - b)^2$ after just learning $(a + b)^2$ reinforces his or her understanding of $(a + b)^2$ whereas, for duller children, the second example may only serve to confuse their meager understanding of the first. Interference probably would be greatest when the same (or similar) stimuli call for different responses on different occasions, e.g., studying two lists of responses to the same list of stimulus words. It is probably better, for example, to master one language at a time rather than to undertake two at once.

2. Similarity of learning and testing situations: The more associative cues learners can form, the more likely they are to retain what they have learned. Contrariwise, slight differences in certain features of the learning situation tend to present distracting elements that prevent the recall of the learned response. We are more likely to recognize Mr. Jones if we see him in the office where we first met him than if we meet him on the street.

Mastery enhances retention

3. Degree of mastery: All indications are that the crucial variable in retention is the degree of original learning (Underwood 1964). In fact, it seems that although such factors as intralist similarity or student ability can generate enormous differences in the learning of the material, they do not seem to be reflected in appreciable differences in the rate of forgetting when equivalent levels of learning are involved. If slow and fast learners achieve the same degree of learning before the retention interval is introduced, there is no evidence that the rate of forgetting will differ appreciably. What determines the rate and level of forgetting is primarily the degree of learning, regardless of the time and effort required to get the material up to a given level of acquisition. If rote material is learned only to the point of one correct reproduction, retention will tend to drop sharply, almost to zero (figure 11.1), whereas if it is learned considerably beyond the point of bare mastery, it may never drop below the level necessary to permit its reproduction. Americans would never forget the Pledge of Allegiance, for example. The factor of overlearning is also involved in the retention of skills such as riding a bicycle.

Excessive overlearning tends to be uneconomical. As the shape of the learning curve suggests, the law of diminishing returns in the form

4. These factors are also involved in a different way in the retention of meaningfully learned materials, as we shall discuss presently.

Figure 11.1: Theoretical Retention Curves Associated with Different Degrees of Overlearning

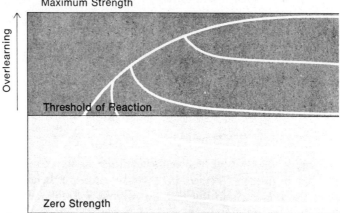

of a ceiling and a decline in motivation sets in so that, after a certain mastery has been attained, relatively little improvement in performance accompanies further efforts to learn. Nevertheless, since good retention revolves around good learning, some overlearning, say 50 percent, is probably a good investment of time and effort from the standpoint of immediate and long-range retention.

4. Review: Review is probably one of the best means of promoting retention in that it overcomes the forgetting that has occurred and brings the material back above the threshold of availability (figure 11.2). As the learner reviews periodically, the loss becomes progressively less, to the point where the material may remain above the memory level almost forever. Periodic reviews are generally more effective than overlearning from the standpoint of economy of time and effort. This is especially true inasmuch as effective review is more than just bringing the material up to the original level. In meaningful material, review involves a reorganization of cognitive structure to bring about deeper understandings and new insights into relationships that are more functional as well as more permanent than the original.

5. Set or intent to remember: Retention is facilitated by having the student learn with full expectation of being tested on the material. Intent to remember is related to motivation, which makes for maximum retention by leading the student to make periodic reviews and, above all, by making for a more intense impression at the time of learning. The more ego-involved the child is, the less likely he or she is to forget. Children do not forget that you (casually) promised them a radio for their birthday but somehow do not remember that you also said, "provided your grades are good."

Figure 11.2:   Theoretical Retention Curve with Periodic Review

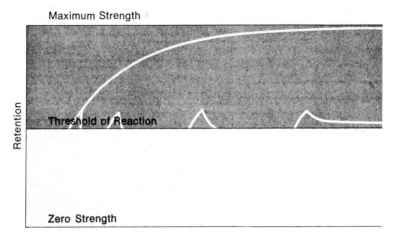

TRANSFER OF TRAINING
TRANSFER OF TRAINING

Throughout life, intelligent people profit from experience in the sense that as a result of experience, they are better prepared to meet new situations of various degrees of relatedness and similarity. This is of special significance in the classroom, where experiences are deliberately planned in sequence so that one serves as a stepping-stone to the next.

Life, and especially the school, is predicated on the assumption that what we learn on one occasion will facilitate our dealing with related situations. Since it is impossible to teach children all that they will need as adults, even if we could foresee such needs, it is necessary to assume that by virtue of what we have led them to learn, they will be able to adapt to new situations. Thus such important decisions as to what and how to teach revolve around our views on transfer, for any curricular offering is justified only to the extent that it serves as the basis for more effective behavior in a later situation. It would follow that the more pessimistic a person is as to the amount of transfer that can be expected from a given educational experience, the more he or she would insist on a practical, utilitarian curriculum.

Measurement of Transfer

The amount of transfer to be gained from prior learnings can be determined through experimentation. If, for example, we are interested in whether experience in playing the piano facilitates the subsequent learning of typing, we might start with two groups—one with experience on the piano, the other without—making sure they are equated with respect to such relevant characteristics as chronological age, coordination, motivation, and relative unfamil-

Table 11.2 Paradigm for Transfer of Training

	Previous Learning (Learn A)	*Present Learning (Learn B)*	*(Test B)*
Group I (Experimental)	Play piano	Learn typing	Test typing
Group II (Control)	Nothing related	Learn typing	Test typing

iarity with the typewriter. The two groups might be subjected to equivalent instruction in typing for a period of, say, two months. If the group having had prior experience on the piano were to make greater typing progress than the other, we could conclude that transfer from the piano to typing has taken place (see table 11.2).[5]

Transfer may be positive or negative

In this case, we are likely to have *positive* transfer, i.e., the previous learning experience is likely to facilitate the subsequent learning. Transfer can also be *negative,* in which case previous learning interferes with the subsequent learning of another activity. Thus, having learned to judge the flight of a softball might at first cause a fielder to misjudge the flight of a baseball. Typically, transfer from one activity to another involves both negative and positive aspects, and the transfer involved is then the net sum of the facilitation and interference of the second learning by the first. Experience in typing on a standard typewriter, for example, would involve both positive and negative transfer to typing on a typewriter with the letters rearranged on the keyboard. The extent to which a person would be "ahead" or "behind" as a result of previous typing skills would depend on the relative balance of the positive and the negative phases of the transfer between the two situations.

Theories of Transfer of Training

Theory of formal discipline

Early psychologists explained transfer of training on the basis of the theory of *formal discipline.* They postulated that the mind was made up of a number of faculties or powers that, like a muscle, could be developed through training and that would be capable of effective performance in all relevant areas. Thus the training of memory through practice with, say, nonsense syllables was supposed to improve one's memory for names, for meaningful material, in fact, for anything involving memory. Accordingly education was largely a matter of *disciplining* the mind by means of rigorous mental exercises in the classics, logic, and mathematics on the assumption that such training would make the person effective in all areas where a given faculty was involved.

5. See Ellis (1965) for a discussion of more elaborate experimental designs.

This view was challenged years ago by James (1890) who found that a month's practice in memorizing poetry did not result in improvement in his general ability to memorize. Following the question raised by James's simple experiment, the theory of mental discipline was challenged by Sleight (1911) in the area of memory; Thorndike and Woodworth (1901) in perception; and Briggs (1913) in reasoning. In these studies, the expected improvement in performance in related tasks did not materialize; in some cases, previous practice actually led to an impairment in performance, i.e., to negative transfer. In a study by Kline (1914), for example, practice in canceling letters interfered with performance in canceling words.

Theory of identical components

The rejection of the concept of general transfer as per the theory of formal discipline led to the almost universal acceptance of the more narrow theory of *identical components* (Thorndike 1916), which postulates that transfer from one situation to another occurs to the extent that the two situations have certain elements in common, e.g., eye-finger coordination in transfer from piano to typing. In other words, transfer occurs to the extent that the learner can carry certain aspects of certain previous learnings to a different situation, which is then only partially novel. The Gestalt concept of transposability, Judd's theory of generalization (Judd 1908), and Bagley's transfer through the formation of generalized attitudes (Bagley 1922) are essentially equivalent positions, provided we define identical components in the broad sense to include not only specific and isolated facts and skills but also broad generalizations, relationships, principles, strategies, and attitudes. We might, for example, distinguish between (1) specific factors involving some identifiable similarity between two situations, such as might occur in the transfer of computational skills to the solution of more advanced mathematical problems, and (2) nonspecific factors such as might be represented by a positive self-concept or warm-ups in physical education, both of which permeate a relatively large spectrum of learning situations. Harlow's learning sets, Gagné's cognitive strategies, and Rothkopf's mathemagenic procedures likewise represent strategies having applicability to a wide range of problems. As Harlow's monkeys figured out the common elements, they were able to deal with related discrimination and even reverse discrimination problems with almost 100 percent accuracy.

Transfer of meaningful verbal learnings

The transfer of meaningful verbal materials is perhaps best conceptualized from the standpoint of the adequacy of one's background as postulated in Ausubel's subsumption theory.[6] Transfer is facilitated to the extent that existing cognitive structure presents a number of well-developed, stable, and inclusive ideas to which new and potentially meaningful material can be anchored. Conversely if adequate subsumers are lacking, potentially meaningful material can be learned only by rote or, at best, inadequately anchored to concepts and propositions that are only partly relevant, so that little or no transfer takes place.

6. Gagné's concept of *prerequisite capabilities* represents an essentially equivalent position.

To the extent that meaningful verbal learning modifies existing cognitive structure, it necessarily affects the incorporability of subsequent learning experiences. In a sense, all meaningful learning necessarily involves transfer for, as Ausubel points out, it is impossible to conceive of any instance of such learning that is not in some way affected by existing cognitive structure and that does not, in turn, promote new transfer by modifying further existing cognitive structure.

It is important to note that, in this context, the critical variable in transfer of meaningful verbal materials is not the similarity between the components of two situations but rather the adequacy of the learner's relevant existing cognitive structure. Transfer is a continuous and sequential process involving the gradual improvement of the cognitive structure—i.e., the increased availability of relevant, stable, and clear subsumers to which new material can be anchored—that has resulted from the continuous process of previous meaningful learning. In this sense, transfer is simply an aspect of learning, subject to the same conditions and operating through the same process.

Transfer can be lateral, vertical, or sequential

We generally think of transfer in terms of the facilitating effects that whatever has been learned in one context has on dealing with a somewhat similar task in a different context, i.e., of *lateral* transfer from situation A to situation B of approximately the same level. The school hopes that what children learn in school will help them meet future situations—whether at school or at home, now or in later life. Children are taught to read, to add and to subtract, to use effective English, to study, to look up information, etc., all with the expectation that these skills will enable them to deal more effectively with the various situations they will subsequently encounter. We might also think of *vertical* transfer, in which learning at one level of, say, the taxonomy (e.g., the comprehension of simple facts) facilitates learning at a higher level in the behavioral hierarchy, e.g., problem solving.

However, as Ausubel points out, the teacher's primary responsibility lies with transfer within the continuity of academic content. Subject matter is typically organized into disciplines with the content arranged sequentially, i.e., with each unit sequentially dependent on prior units. This type of *sequential* transfer points directly to the need to help children develop an adequate system of subsumers so that each successive unit of the subject will find optimal anchorage in cognitive structure. This would be especially important in sequential subjects like mathematics where a loose "anchor" anywhere along the line can jeopardize all subsequent learnings.

Promoting Transfer

Since the transferability, as well as the learning and retention, of potentially meaningful verbal materials is a function of existing cognitive background, the teacher's primary task is to ensure the ready availability of adequate subsumers in cognitive structure to permit the optimal anchoring of new learnings. This implies that when the required subsumers are lacking, the teacher will have to recruit and bolster whatever subsumers might actually exist unrecognized in the learner's background or provide the required system of advance, comparative, and expository organizers to act as ideational scaffolding for the incoming material (see chapter 8). Research evidence (Ausubel 1960; Ausubel and Youssef 1963) suggests that organizers do indeed facilitate transfer. On the other hand, it also shows that the beneficial effects of organizers are greatest in the case of subjects who are low in verbal and analytic ability (Ausubel and Fitzgerald 1962; Schulz 1966) and therefore less able to develop an adequate scheme of their own for organizing the material in relation to existing cognitive structure. Organizers are also most effective in the case of factual materials and correspondingly less critical with materials that have an organization of their own.

A relevant curriculum enhances transfer

If effective transfer is to take place, the curriculum must have relevance to the individual learner. The traditional academic curriculum of the high school is not going to be very effective with culturally disadvantaged teenagers, for example, as long as it deals with a content totally foreign from the standpoint of their backgrounds, goals, and purposes. A high school course in social problems would probably have greater transfer possibilities for a student who plans to go into politics than does a course in trigonometry. This does not imply the outright rejection of the classical subjects or the unconditional endorsement of the social utility approach to curriculum selection. Neither extreme is warranted: we can no more justify a social utility curriculum solely on the basis of its transfer to the attainment of immediate (practical) goals than we can justify the inclusion of the classical subjects strictly on the basis of their alleged disciplinary value.

The "disciplinary" value of classical studies

Three important studies (Thorndike 1924; Broyler et al. 1927; Wesman 1945) have shown that the disciplinary value of the classical subjects has been greatly exaggerated. All in all, the results indicate that the relative contribution of the various academic curricula is not appreciably different; they distinctly refute the alleged monopoly of the classical subjects on the development of intellectual competence. On the other hand, old beliefs tend to hang on. Despite the fact that the theory of formal discipline was discredited half a century ago, there are still people who advocate hard courses to "toughen the mind," who feel that the curriculum has become "soft," that we need a return to Latin, the classics, logic, the great books, and other "hard" courses. They point to the capable people among those who have followed such a curriculum as evidence of the benefits to be derived therefrom. Apparently their tough curriculum did not improve their own reasoning ability enough for them to see that these courses did not make these people capable but simply eliminated those of lesser ability.

The study of Latin is often advocated on the argument that it helps in learning English grammar and vocabulary. As was shown over fifty years ago (Hamblen 1925), it helps when, and almost only when, English derivatives are

stressed. Furthermore, learning Latin is not an economical way of learning English. The question is not whether Latin and the classics are useful—undoubtedly they are—but whether they are more useful than other subjects that also have transfer value, plus a much larger degree of direct value. A course in mathematics has to be evaluated primarily on the basis of what it can contribute to the solution of mathematical and related problems rather than the improvement of reasoning ability, for no subject has a monopoly on that. The curriculum must be closely related to children's experiences and purposes so that they can bring something to the curriculum material and, in turn, see enough benefit to be derived from it for them to generate interest in using it in connection with some other aspects of their purposes.

Probably all subject matter has transfer value, but certain aspects of education have wider application than others and every child should be familiar with such things as common roots of words, suffixes, prefixes, basic numerical concepts, certain rules of grammar, certain principles of science, basic rules of study, and effective modes of problem solving. It is the teacher's responsibility to emphasize those outcomes that have the greatest transfer possibilities; verbalizing the principle underlying a given point, for example, tends to promote transfer to a wider range of related instances. Teachers must capitalize on a variety of procedures promoting insight, meaningfulness, the organization of experience, and the discovery of interrelatedness among ideas and techniques and emphasizing the applicability of knowledge to a variety of situations.

Mastery enhances transfer

A number of other implications for educational practice could be listed. It is particularly important, for example, that relative mastery be achieved; material that is barely learned does not provide an effective foundation for transfer. According to Ausubel, for example, the major benefit of the teaching machine lies not so much in its immediate reinforcement or its structuring of the learning experience as on its promotion of complete mastery and therefore optimal sequential transfer to the next unit. For the same reason, transfer is positively correlated with intelligence. In the Thorndike study, the brighter students gained 20.5 points in reasoning ability while the slower students gained only 1.5 points. This is consistent with the view that greater transfer results from the higher level of learning, meaningfulness, and generalization made possible by greater intellectual and cognitive adequacy.

A positive self-concept enhances transfer

On a different dimension, and undoubtedly one of the most crucial single determinants of transfer, is the personality of the child. If we can develop a person characterized by positive attitudes toward the experiences he or she encounters, by a constructive self-concept, by relative freedom from anxiety and openness to experience (along the lines presented in chapter 4), we will have developed a person who can approach new situations with eagerness and confidence in his or her ability to meet life's demands—and our efforts at education will not have been in vain.

11-1   SYNTHESIS:

Teaching-Learning Strategies Suggested by Various Theories
Concerning Retention and Transfer

A. *General*
  1. Effective retention and transfer stem from effective learning; arranging for retention and transfer is a matter of good teaching
  2. Emphasize meaningfulness wherever possible
      a. Promote readiness; developmental stages (Piaget)
      b. Ensure prerequisites: adequate cognitive structure, subsumers, organizers (Ausubel); prerequisite capabilities (Gagné) mastery (Bloom), etc.
  3. General factors
      a. A positive self-concept, self-confidence, need for achievement, intellectual curiosity, openness to experience, a positive attitude to-

ward learning, toward the subject, etc.—all are critical factors in
promoting learning, retention, and transfer

    b. Language is essential to the manipulation and storage of ideas; help
students synthesize their learnings

    c. Develop effective learning strategies: learning how to learn (Harlow);
mathemagenic strategies (Rothkopf); intellectual skills, cognitive
strategies (Gagné); adequate subsumers (Ausubel); heuristics of discovery (Bruner)

B. *Retention*

  1. General factors

    a. Meaningfulness: Emphasize structure (e.g., seeing the products of a
country in the context of its geographical location)

    b. Retention is really a problem of learning (i.e., storage) for retrieva-
bility; verbalize principles for effective storage

    c. Mastery is crucial; avoid vagueness, cognitive overload, etc.; materi-
als at the lower end of the taxonomy may require more practice

  2. Disuse

    a. Emphasize mastery

    b. Principles are more resistant to forgetting; emphasize meaningful-
ness

    c. Practice: Periodic quizzes provide well-motivated review

  3. Interference (proactive and retroactive)

    a. Emphasize mastery of both prior and subsequent learnings; over-
learning ties the pieces together and prevents the fringes from fray-
ing

    b. Meaningfulness facilitates the consolidation of the materials; move
from isolated facts to principles

    c. Generally avoid putting back-to-back ideas that interfere; use com-
parative organizers, make ideas salient and distinct

  4. Reorganization and distortion

    a. Meaningfulness and mastery ensure that all parts are consolidated
into a solid package with no gaps to fill; periodic review increases
depth of understanding

    b. Emphasize the broad picture through scaffolding, outlines, graphs,
etc.; use language as a tool to synthesize parts into place, to resolve
conflicts and ambiguities, to fill gaps

    c. Be aware of one's biases and preconceptions

  5. Subsumption

    a. Meaningfulness is the best guarantee of retention; emphasize the
structure of knowledge, the sequentiality of subject matter, etc.
(clear subsumers, Ausubel; prerequisite capabilities, Gagné)

    b. Use appropriate organizers, make ideas salient, bring out the struc-
ture, pitch instruction to the developmental level of the child, emphasize mastery, etc.

       c. Make provisions for attention so as to ensure proper registration of sensory inputs, and the availability of subsumers in terms of which sensory inputs can be quickly and correctly coded

C. *Transfer*

  1. General

     a. Teach deliberately for transfer; emphasize applications; make students transfer-conscious; learn in a variety of contexts

     b. Stress meaningfulness; ensure prerequisites; emphasize underlying structure and continuity of subject matter; promote a high degree of mastery for a "top-of-the-hill" perspective; pitch instruction at the child's current level of development

     c. Do not overlook the affective domain; students must want to use what they are learning and be eager to learn more; get the class involved; formulate and communicate clear-cut objectives

  2. Formal discipline

     a. Do not expect too much general transfer.

     b. Yet do not overlook nonspecific transfer, e.g., a positive self-concept, a strong need for achievement, interest in learning, mathemagenic strategies; an extensive and precise vocabulary is a powerful tool usable in many different contexts

  3. Identical components

     a. Emphasize structure; have students synthesize isolated learnings into principles which have greater transferability

     b. Look for applications, for common elements; stress continuity ("in the previous section, we . . . ; we are now . . . ; in the next unit, we will . . ."

     c. Learn and practice in context, but avoid rigidity by practicing in a variety of different contexts

  4. Subsumption

     a. The primary determinant of transfer (particularly sequential transfer) is the adequacy of one's cognitive structure (Ausubel); prerequisite capabilities (Gagné)

     b. Emphasize meaningfulness, ensure ready availability of adequate subsumers through the use of advance organizers, etc. Encourage meaningful practice in order to deepen understanding

D. *Implications*

  1. A broad background of relevant experience meaningfully structured facilitates learning, retention, and transfer: a necessary and essentially sufficient condition.

  2. Meaningfulness based on a well-organized cognitive structure makes for effective learning, retention, and transfer

  3. Focus on good teaching (and good learning); retention and transfer should follow; capitalize on structure inherent in knowledge by sequencing learning experiences in keeping with such structure

4. Emphasize nonspecific factors contributing to learning, retention, and transfer: a positive self-concept, positive attitudes toward learning, cognitive strategies, etc.
5. Clarify and communicate goals; teach to well-defined goals of personal relevance to the learner.
6. Gear instruction to the learner's level of development; ensure prerequisites
7. Shape the child's attention-giving behavior; have the child assume responsibility for learning and gain confidence in his or her ability to learn
8. Get the children involved: they should leave class more confident that they can use what they have learned and eager to learn more; shape their need for achievement through systematic reinforcement geared to meaningful success experiences

HIGHLIGHTS OF THE CHAPTER

The school's effectiveness depends in a fundamental way on the retention and transfer of the material the child has learned. The teacher must, therefore, be familiar with the psychological principles underlying these two functions.

1. Effective retention and transfer as they relate to meaningful verbal materials are a direct function of effective learning. Effective retention, for example, is best promoted through effective storage emphasizing the underlying structure of knowledge.
2. A critical distinction must be made between meaningful and rote learning. Whereas the human capacity for the storage and retrieval of rotely learned materials is extremely limited, the corresponding capacity for meaningful learning is relatively unlimited. A distinction must also be made between short-term and long-term memory.
3. The forgetting of rotely learned material is best explained on the basis of proactive (and to a lesser degree to retroactive) inhibition—i.e., the interference of earlier (or subsequent) learnings with the recall of the material in question. The extent of interference is primarily a function of the degree of mastery. Review is an effective way of ensuring retention.
4. The retention of meaningful verbal learning is best explained on the basis of the obliterative process in which new material is subsumed within the concepts and propositions in existing cognitive structure and is lost as a separate entity. If its separate identifiability is important, efforts must be made to ensure its continued discriminability from these larger carriers.
5. Transfer of training is the cornerstone on which education must ultimately rest; unless children's learnings help them to meet more effectively situations

further along the academic sequence or in later life, they are essentially wasting their time.

6. A long-standing explanation of transfer is Thorndike's theory of identical components where *identical components* can be interpreted to include both specific factors (e.g., specific information, skills, and concepts) and general factors (e.g., a positive self-concept).

7. By providing additional (or more adequate) subsumers to which new materials can be securely anchored, meaningful verbal learnings form the basis for further meaningful learning, i.e., for positive transfer. The teacher's task is to make sure that appropriate subsumers are indeed available.

SUGGESTIONS FOR FURTHER READING

ELLIS, HENRY. *The Transfer of Learning.* New York: Macmillan, 1965. An excellent overview of the theoretical and the practical aspects of transfer of learning. Also includes reprints of well-known articles on transfer. See also Ellis, in Melvin H. Marx, ed. *Learning: Processes*, pp. 205–213. New York: Macmillan, 1969.

GAGNÉ, ROBERT M., and R. T. WHITE. Memory structures and learning outcomes. *Rev. Educ. Res.* 48 (1978):182–223. A thorough review of the research literature and its educational implications.

SHIFFRIN, R. M., and R. C. ATKINSON. Storage and retrieval processes in long-term memory. *Psychol. Rev.* 76 (1969):179–193. Presents the mechanisms involved in storage into and retrieval from long-term memory.

QUESTIONS AND PROJECTS

1. In what order would you rate the following as factors in the promotion of retention: applications and implications; mastery, meaningfulness; practice; readiness, sequential organization of materials; similarity of materials; salience of the material. Distinguish between rote and meaningful learning.

   How would you rank these factors with respect to transfer?

2. Specifically, what can the teacher do to ensure retention and transfer of academic materials on the part of students whose background is relatively limited?

3. What role do examinations play in the promotion of retention and transfer of course content?

4. Specifically, how might a student ensure maximum transfer of the content of this course to teaching a couple of years from now? How might the course be organized to ensure such transfer?

5. Evaluate: If education is to be a lifelong process in which individuals are on their own, the teacher's task is not so much to teach academic content but rather to teach children how to learn.

SELF-TEST

1. Forgetting is best explained on the basis of
   a. the deterioration of neurological processes.
   b. inadequate initial learning.
   c. the interference of prior or subsequent learnings.
   d. the repression of conflicting materials.
   e. the time factor.

2. Which is the *incorrect* association regarding views on forgetting?
   a. Ausubel—subsumption theory
   b. Freud—repression
   c. Müller and Pilzecker—retroactive inhibition
   d. Underwood—proactive inhibition
   e. None of the above; all are correct associations.

3. The primary determinant of the degree of retention in school-connected learnings is
   a. the degree of mastery of the original learning.
   b. the intelligence of the learner.
   c. the logical continuity of the material.
   d. the method of measuring retention.
   e. the time factor.

4. Modern educational psychologists see the school's role in relation to transfer of training to be that of emphasizing
   a. basic concepts, principles, and generalizations.
   b. learning sets.
   c. life-adjustment education.
   d. problem-solving strategies.
   e. vocational and social skills.

5. Forgetting is best viewed as an instance of
   a. failure in positive transfer.
   b. failure in understanding.
   c. negative facilitation.
   d. negative transfer.
   e. nonlearning (or inadequate learning).

6. The degree of transfer from a given educational experience is primarily a function of
   a. the learner's grasp of the relevant fundamentals.

   b. the overall IQ of the learner.
   c. the readiness of the learner for that particular experience.
   d. the teacher's handling of the subject.
   e. the transfer potential inherent in the subject matter.

7. The most crucial factor in ensuring the transfer value of education is
   a. adequacy in basic skills (e.g., reading).
   b. intellectual curiosity and openness to experience.
   c. meaningfulness of the content.
   d. relevance in relation to the learner's goals and purposes.
   e. the use of discovery as a method of teaching.

TWELVE

Major Instructional Systems

It is now becoming quite evident that the development of an educational technology that will benefit the people is far from being the simple matter of applying readily available scientific knowledge.

Robert M. W. Travers (1973)

A description of any educational activity always occurs in the light of the author's biases.

Eva L. Baker (1973)

As a result of experience in studying a given discipline, pupils not only learn *particular* ideas that facilitate the later learning of other particular ideas but also acquire greater *capacity* meaningfully to process more abstract material of *any* nature in *that* particular discipline and *other* disciplines as well.

David P. Ausubel et al. (1978)

We begin with the hypothesis that any subject can be taught effectively in some intellectually honest form to any child at any stage of development. It is a bold hypothesis and an essential one in thinking about the nature of the curriculum. No evidence exists to contradict it; considerable evidence is being amassed that supports it.

Jerome S. Bruner (1960)

— Discusses a number of the better-known instructional systems, their basic features, their premises, and their relative merits
— Expands on the teaching implication of the positions of Ausubel, Bruner, and the humanists as presented in earlier chapters; also surveys the open school
— Presents an overview of Gagné's hierarchical model, with emphasis on the internal and external conditions to be met if learning is to take place

PREVIEW: KEY CONCEPTS

1. A number of instructional systems of varying degrees of comprehensiveness and validity have been devised, each presumably based on its author's interpretation of the important principles of educational psychology.
2. Ausubel makes the adequacy of the student's existing cognitive structure the key to meaningful verbal learning; the teacher's task is to maximize the subsumption of new materials into cognitive structure by providing suitable organizers.
3. Bruner focuses on the structure underlying knowledge as discovered by the learner, with the teacher providing clues and feedback to help the student achieve closure.
4. The humanistic position sees the learning of academic content as a natural by-product of self-actualization; children will learn whatever has personal meaning in terms of their goals as they perceive them. The free school, as an extreme version of the humanistic position, seems to overemphasize children's right to self-determination.
5. The open school emphasizes student initiative, as does the Montessori school, while still maintaining some degree of teacher control.
6. Gagné's hierarchical theory constitutes the most comprehensive teaching-learning model; it is particularly significant in the present context in that it identifies the conditions necessary for learning to take place.

PREVIEW QUESTIONS

1. Can the principles of educational psychology serve as the foundation for an effective teaching-learning model? Or do they, on the contrary, simply serve to legitimize any number of different teaching-learning strategies?
2. What difference in approach to teaching might be based on one's allegiance to a particular theoretical position? Why might you still expect to find differences between systems based on the same theoretical principles?
3. To what extent is it logical to expect the empirical validation of a given position and the corresponding rejection of another?
4. What common features might one expect to find in all teaching-learning models regardless of theoretical affiliation or other considerations?

In the previous chapters we introduced a number of concepts and principles underlying the technology of instruction. We also covered some of the more common instructional strategies, e.g., the lecture and the discussion. This chapter will present a number of the better-known teaching models.[1] As might be expected, there is an obvious lack of agreement among the positions presented. Yet although the various positions begin with different theoretical premises, make different assumptions, place different emphasis on different concepts, relate to different learning outcomes, and often use different vocabulary to say essentially the same thing, they nevertheless converge on certain basic instructional strategies as they relate to response, reinforcement, corrective feedback, practice, and other fundamentals of psychology. The student should strive to note similarities, to demonstrate how ideas of the different models can often be interchanged, and especially to determine how conflicts can be resolved in the context of effective classroom teaching.

AUSUBEL'S COGNITIVE THEORY OF MEANINGFUL VERBAL LEARNING

The essentials of Ausubel's theory of meaningful verbal learning have been presented in chapters 8, 9, and 11. This chapter will focus on its major instructional implications. To review: in Ausubel's cognitive frame of reference, the critical variable affecting the acquisition, retention, and transfer of meaningful verbal material is the availability in cognitive structure of relevant subsumers at an appropriate level of generality to provide optimal anchorage. The teacher's primary strategy for facilitating learning and transfer as well as minimizing forgetting would call for deliberately introducing in advance of the

---

1. Skinner's views on instruction have been discussed repeatedly in different contexts in the previous chapters. They will not be presented again here (see Skinner 1966).

Organizers provide
ideational scaffolding

new materials suitable organizers presented at a higher level of structure so as to provide ideational scaffolding for the more detailed materials that follow. When relatively familiar materials are involved, comparative organizers can be used to delineate the new from essentially different and yet confusably similar subsumers already existing in cognitive structure. When completely unfamiliar material is involved, on the other hand, *expository* organizers can be introduced to provide ideational anchorage in terms that are at least familiar to the learner.

From an instructional point of view, it would follow that adequacy in cognitive structure is probably best achieved through systematic feedback, as provided through classroom discussion, quizzes, etc., designed to rectify vagueness, ambiguity, misinterpretations, and misconceptions before they have a chance to distort later learnings. Teachers might, for example, follow the new material with additional details that are potentially conflicting, thereby forcing the learner to clarify further the relationship between the anchoring ideas and the newly learned material. To the extent that effective learning is essential to both retention and transfer, a certain amount of overlearning is crucial in that it brings about greater cognitive clarity and sharpens the discriminability of new learnings, thereby enhancing their longevity and transferability. It is also important to help children develop effective retrieval strategies by providing an overview of the subject matter at an appropriate level of generality so as to establish a broad framework within which details are correctly classified according to an orderly scheme.

The teacher's task is to bring out the internal logic of the material at a level children can grasp. Here, in order to ensure optimal readiness, Ausubel would recommend, among other things, that the material be programmed from the most general and inclusive principles to the more specific elements in accordance with the principle of *progressive differentiation.* The teacher must especially take into account the children's developmental status. As we have noted, elementary school children at the concrete level on the Piaget scale, for example, depend on concrete exemplars. When presented with abstract propositions in the absence of adequate concrete props, they find them unrelatable to their cognitive structure and therefore devoid of meaning. At best, they can only rely on an intuitive level of cognitive functioning that typically falls far short of the clarity, precision, explicitness, and generality demanded by some of the more complex aspects of the required curriculum. It is only in high school that students become relatively independent of concrete empirical experiences in relating complex abstract propositions to cognitive structure.

The style of presentation should be as simple as is consistent with precise expression. A difficult topic should be presented simply at first, with the level of difficulty progessively raised as the level of the students' sophistication increases. At all times, the emphasis should be on structure rather than on separate details, and the teacher should be careful to make the main ideas as salient as possible. Clarity can be facilitated by the use of various *perceptual* organizers, e.g., topical headings, bold type, italics, or vocal emphasis that brings out the structure of the material and makes the significant parts of the material perceptually salient. We must, of course, be careful, in using chapter and topical headings, not to compartmentalize the material into arbitrary units with artificial barriers between related concepts and thereby obscure common features and interrelationships among ideas that happen to fall under different headings.

BRUNER'S DISCOVERY MODEL

Another important contributor to the technology of instruction is Jerome Bruner, whose position on cognitive development was discussed in relation to that of Piaget in chapter 5. His views on discovery learning were discussed in brief in chapter 9; the section should be reviewed. The present discussion will consider his views on instruction, most of which have been presented in his two major publications, *The Process of Education* (1960) and *Toward a Theory of Instruction* (1966).[2]

Bruner: Focus on internal structure

The key to Bruner's theory is *structure*. The primary purpose of instruction is to help children grasp the inherent structure of the subject—i.e., to help them develop a perspective of the fundamental principles that underlie a given discipline.[3] The child's task is not so much to master subject matter content but rather to grasp the interrelationships that constitute the basic structure of the discipline. Such an emphasis on underlying structure presumably facilitates more advanced learnings, minimizes forgetting, and facilitates transfer.

At the instructional level, Bruner's approach to student learning would focus on the need to specify:

1. The experiences to be learned.
2. The way the body of knowledge is to be structured.
3. The way the experiences of instruction are to be structured.
4. The nature and the pacing of the rewards and the feedbacks.[4]

More specifically, Bruner postulates that learning experiences will be educationally productive to the extent that they are appropriately structured and sequenced and that reinforcement and corrective feedback are provided. To instruct someone in a discipline is not a matter of getting him or her to commit

---

2. See also Bruner, *The Relevance of Education*, 1971.
3. This is reflected, for example, in the rationale of the various post-Sputnik curricula (e.g., PSSC, BSCS, etc.) that emanated from the Woods Hole Conference in 1959 under Bruner's direction.
4. Bruner is not opposed to external reinforcement but argues that the learner should develop the ability for self-correction rather than depend unduly on external evaluation.

facts to memory but rather to promote the development of greater insight into the structure of the field as the basis for gaining a broad perspective of the interrelationships involved. As a cognitive (field) psychologist, Bruner would particularly object to teaching facts and skills in isolation, i.e., apart from the underlying principles that give structure to the subject.

A distinctive feature of Bruner's position on instruction is its emphasis on discovery. Instruction is not a matter of *imparting* structure; on the contrary, the student must *discover* the logical organization that characterizes the interrelationships among phenomena. Learning is a *process* of forming categories (or *coding systems,* as he calls them) as to the similarities and differences that exist among objects and events. The development of such coding systems reduces the complexity of the environment in that it permits recognition of objects and events in terms of class membership, which, in turn, permits learners to go beyond the information given. The point is not what children learn but what they can do with it—or as Bruner puts it, how well they can cross the barrier from *learning* to *thinking.*

According to Bruner, the discovery approach presents the following advantages:

1. Increased transferability, i.e., *intellectual potency,* as he calls it.
2. Increased retention.
3. A shift from extrinsic to intrinsic motivation.
4. Training in the heuristics (strategies) of discovery.

Contrariwise, he sees nondiscovery methods of learning (e.g., expository teaching/reception learning) as relatively passive, meaningless, and nonproductive.

In line with cognitive theory, Bruner emphasizes insight, which he prefers to call *intuition* (or *intuitive thinking*) and which he sees as crucial to the act of discovery. Bruner is highly critical of traditional methods that emphasize analytical ways of thinking at the expense of the intuitive approach. For Bruner intuitive thinking is essential in the early stages of learning as the basis for getting a general picture of the problem; the learner can pursue the matter with analytic methods at a later stage of development.

Although a disciple of Piaget, Bruner disagrees with what he considers to be Piaget's overly rigid application of the stage-dependent concept of cognitive development and the corresponding underplay of the role of teaching.[5] As reflected in his classic statement (Bruner 1960, p. 33), "Any subject can be taught effectively in some intellectually honest way to any child at any stage of development," Bruner sees readiness as a "mischievous half-truth." Children can be taught if we simply fit instruction to the developmental level available to them at a given time. More specifically, Bruner advocates what he calls the

5. Bruner also disagrees with Piaget on the question of language. He gives language an important role in the promotion of cognitive development; Piaget, on the contrary, tends to see language as simply a by-product of cognitive development.

The spiral
curriculum

spiral curriculum, in which the same concepts, carefully organized with regard to underlying principles, are presented on a spiral from simple to progressively more complex on a rotating basis. If children are to study geometry in junior high school, they should have experience with blocks and other geometric figures during the preschool period. Bruner sees this progression in the curriculum as an ideal way of coordinating curricular content with the children's natural development. In other words, he believes that by providing children with a challenging program of instruction geared to a spiral concept, we can accelerate their rate of cognitive growth. Bruner is not denying the reality of developmental stages. He is simply emphasizing the idea that the structure of most learning materials is adaptable to different levels of cognitive functioning; that even young children can get an intuitive feel for a subject that later they will understand at a more complex level.

Bruner and discovery

Implementing Bruner's discovery approach typically calls for the teacher to present a provocative problem within the level of development and interest of the students, individually and collectively, and skillfully to lead them to discover the solution. First, the teacher must structure the problem so as to permit insight into its underlying relationships; his or her responsibility is to provide clues, ask leading questions, and generally structure the situation so that closure—and learning—can be achieved. It is essential, for the teacher to ensure that the group has the required capabilities—i.e., adequate command of prerequisites to arrive at a solution. If learners are to participate effectively in the discovery process, it is important for them to have been exposed to a wide range of experiences designed to encourage the development of organizational codes, i.e., skills in problem-solving strategies. Presumably Bruner's discovery approach would work best in a comfortable and relaxed classroom atmosphere where children feel free to take intuitive leaps. Contrariwise, Bruner deplores the passivity of "knowledge-getting" where the task is the gaining and the mechanical storing of information in the identical form in which it was presented.

In his *Toward a Theory of Instruction* (1966), Bruner presents a number of examples of discovery learning in various subject areas. In a unit on geography, for example, he would encourage students to figure out why Chicago was bound to become a large industrial and trading center. One of the most systematic implementations of the discovery method is Suchman's *Inquiry Training Program* (Suchman 1961), in which, for example, children are encouraged to make educated guesses as to what is happening as a bimetallic knife held over a flame bends one way, then the other. Presumably participation in this type of discovery causes children to become quite adept at the techniques of inquiry. To Bruner, the development of such problem-solving strategies is important in its own right quite apart from any particular content to be learned (see Strike 1975).

A number of psychologists have questioned Bruner's claims as to the alleged superiority of the discovery approach. More specifically, they feel that

Some people disagree

Bruner's claims concerning the alleged effectiveness of discovery have been grossly exaggerated, that his criticisms of reception learning and expository teaching are correspondingly overdone, and that the arguments that support discovery as a method are themselves based on intuitive feelings rather than on well-documented empirical evidence. The fact is that none of Bruner's claims has been conclusively shown. And although a highly planned discovery session may actually produce many of the desirable outcomes claimed, the perhaps more common semihaphazard fumbling-through guess session may lead at best to a hodgepodge of unrelated bits of information (and confusion), lowered rather than increased self-confidence, and even negative attitudes. Most psychologists (and teachers), it seems, would prefer to see instruction proceed along a more systematic basis than through the relatively loose approach suggested by Bruner.

Discovery is not a panacea. Suchman, for example, recognizes that inquiry training cannot totally replace good didactic teaching. Discovery is not suited to certain subject matter contents, nor can all children benefit from discovery procedures, e.g., the young child at the egocentric level of development.[6] Careful choice of a problem and skillful monitoring are essential; nothing will happen if the class is left to flounder without the internal resources or the guidance necessary to achieve closure.

There are a number of practical difficulties in implementing the discovery approach. In a large class, it is often difficult to prevent the bright students from making all the discoveries, often prematurely, with the slower students then restricted to very ordinary reception learning, and meanwhile rarely experiencing the "joys of discovery" that they could have experienced more efficiently with the teacher assuming a more active role. If someone is going to give out the solution, why not the teacher, who can probably spell it out more logically and more clearly? As Gagné (1977) points out, there is no evidence to suggest that children must discover, say, principles, on their own in order to be able to process them into cognitive structure. In fact, it may be that meaning is more likely to emerge as a result of a systematic presentation by someone who is knowledgeable than by having students, whether individually or in a group, fumble through to a solution.

Discovery versus reception learning

As we noted in chapter 9, a particularly strong stand against overemphasis on discovery is taken by Ausubel, who argues that discovery is hopelessly inefficient; that many concepts, for example, can be taught far more quickly and effectively through simple expository teaching, especially when children have reached the stage of formal operations. Ausubel suggests that children do not have to rediscover the wheel in every instance; that each generation must start from what adults already know. He particularly objects to Bruner's attempt to equate discovery with active learning and reception

6. Good and Brophy (1975) suggest that proponents of discovery learning make wildly unrealistic assumptions concerning the nature of learners, namely picturing children as continually thirsting for knowledge and eagerly seeking information at every opportunity.

learning with passive (rote) learning leading only to verbalism. Skinner also feels that discovery is inefficient and impractical; that it is no solution whatsoever to the problems of education. He sees discovery as time-consuming, with learning often proceeding fitfully and at a snail's pace. He particularly objects to the apparent implication that it is below the dignity of students to learn what scholars already know.

Gagné (1977) also takes issue with Bruner's emphasis on learning as a process. For Gagné, the primary objective of education is to have students acquire intellectual capabilities, i.e., *products* (e.g., intellectual skills and competencies). Whether they acquire these by discovery or through reception learning is immaterial. Gagné also points out that "there is little research evidence to indicate that students who have been exposed to (discovery) training actually are better able to solve problems than those who have not."

THE HUMANISTIC (PHENOMENOLOGICAL) POSITION

Another well-known group within the cognitive camp are the humanists, a rather diverse and loose conglomerate joined primarily by a common interest in the individual as a person. At the more established end of the continuum are Rogers, Maslow, Combs, and other members of the "Third Force," a term coined by Maslow to represent the humanistic movement in contrast to the two major systems of psychology: psychoanalysis and behaviorism (see chapters 3 and 4). At the other end are the recent neohumanists, e.g., Holt, Goodman, etc., whose common ground is perhaps better characterized by their highly critical stand against traditional education than by any rigorously defined educational posture of their own.

Humanists: Focus on the learner

The main thrust of the humanistic position is their concern for the individual; the question of cognitive development or the achievement of academic goals is an important but nevertheless secondary consideration.[7] Their primary emphasis is on the worth and dignity of humanity, self-realization, the enhancement of the self, etc. (see chapter 4). The focus is on the *learner* rather than on *learning;* the latter is assumed to occur as a more or less natural output of the person in the process of self-actualization. Humanists are particularly opposed to the Skinnerian concept of control of the individual through the deliberate application of the science of behavior as presented in *Walden Two,* for example.

The humanistic position regarding instruction is perhaps best reconstructed from the basic premises of phenomenological psychology as presented in chapters 4 and 10. Humanists believe in the individual's overriding need to grow, to actualize his or her potentialities, to "become"—an overwhelming need that will cause the person to develop in the direction of healthy growth—unless prevented from so doing by a hostile environment that forces him or her to seek safety rather than growth. The primary concern of the school, then, is to foster children's continued ability to cope with a changing world. Learning experiences must help children become more self-directive, take on more responsibility for themselves, actualize their potentialities. Humanists place only secondary emphasis on the standard curriculum, lesson plans, etc. Teaching in the traditional sense is relatively inconsequential—in the words of Rogers (1969), "a vastly over-rated activity." They want to

Teacher as a facilitator

7. Rogers and Maslow offer few guidelines for teaching. Most of their suggestions are vague and not particularly applicable to the typical classroom. Combs is a bit more specific in describing how teachers might use humanistic principles in education (see Combs 1965).

change the teacher's status from *teacher* to *facilitator* of human growth. Humanists would emphasize self-direction; to a large extent, students—in keeping with their personal needs, goals, and purposes—would decide what they are to learn. The facilitator's role at the academic level would be to help students achieve their purposes.

Phenomenological
nature of perception

A major point of emphasis is the phenomenological nature of perception: behavior is a goal-directed attempt on the part of the individual to achieve his or her purposes *as perceived* in a field *as experienced;* it can be understood only from the individual's idiosyncratic frame of reference. To the extent that children will strive for goals that are personally meaningful to them, they should be given considerable freedom in the choice of learning experiences. More fundamentally, they should be helped to orient their perceptions toward growth as defined in relation to their long-term welfare. Since this can occur only in a nonthreatening atmosphere, the facilitator's task is to establish a classroom climate conducive to security and thus to personally meaningful learning. A major part of the facilitator's responsibility is to help students meet their needs, particularly at the safety level so that their capacity for self-actualization can be mobilized in the service of personal growth.

The Free School

Summerhill

A rather extreme version of the humanistic position is represented by the free school movement launched in America in the mid-1960s by such neohumanists as Dennison, Kozol, Holt, Goodman, Glasser, and Kohl as a negative reaction to some of the more obvious shortcomings of the traditional school. Summerhill in England, the oldest and best-known of the free schools, is based on the philosophy of its originator, A. S. Neill (1960), that "a child is innately wise and realistic. If left to himself without adult suggestion of any kind, he will develop as far as he is capable of developing." The free school operates outside the mainstream of the regular school system. It is less structured and tends to avoid the restrictive and prescriptive aspects of the traditional classroom. In fact, the free school allows children relatively complete freedom. At Summerhill, students choose what they will learn. They can even elect not to attend class.

In general, the free school has had only limited success. Bernstein's evaluation (1968) of the graduates of Summerhill, for example, was essentially negative. A report from the British Ministry of Education sees the results of the Summerhill enterprise as "unimpressive" and the achievements of its students as "rather meager." The inspectors thought that better results would have been obtained had the teachers assumed a more directive role. In the United States, most of the free schools of the 1960s have been discontinued, which is perhaps understandable, considering the nature of their student body and the ever-present problem of financing. On the other hand, some of their problems probably reflect on more fundamental issues. It would seem logical, for exam-

The question of
individual freedom

ple, to attribute some of their shortcomings to their inadequate conception of freedom. Whereas the school should be responsive to student needs—or, as Dewey would have it, student centered—the question of whether students should learn to read or to remain illiterate is hardly a matter of student prerogative. It is patently absurd to think that everything children choose totally on their own has, by definition, deep educational and personal value. Kozol (1972), a leader in the free school movement, for example, strongly recognizes the need for a more realistic definition of freedom than one based exclusively on the alleged need to respect the child's right to self-determination.

Part of the problem undoubtedly stems from the lack of clarity as to goals and operational strategies. Many of the free schools of the past decade seem to have operated on a day-to-day trial-and-error basis. The leaders of the movement seemed to have known what they are against; this came through loud and clear in harsh, often exaggerated, criticisms of the traditional school (see Jackson 1972). But they seemed to have considerably more difficulty articulating what they are for.[8] Many of their criticisms have obvious merit; the adequacy of their solutions is not so obvious. In fact, given certain basic and unavoidable realities under which the school must operate, many of their "solutions" are unrealistic, impractical, and essentially illogical.

Evaluation of the Humanistic Position

Beginning with the premise that children have an inherent need for self-actualization that teachers can capitalize on, humanists insist that the children's safety needs be met. They postulate that, with this kind of freedom, children will want to grow, to learn, to master, to create. They will become spontaneous, responsive, unafraid, realistic about goals, flexible, and progressively more the persons they would like to be.

An antidote for
extreme behaviorism

The humanistic position constitutes an antidote for extreme behaviorism. It suggests that by contrast to the regimented, autocratic classroom of the past, the school should be student centered, with the facilitator displaying consistent respect for children, confidence in their ability and willingness to grow, and sensitivity in understanding their perceptions. There would be correspondingly less emphasis on the academic curriculum or teaching in the sense of the imparting and monitoring of academic learning. The facilitator's task is more in the area of making the classroom as nonthreatening as possible so that the inner forces of children toward self-actualization can be released. Under such ideal conditions, humanists insist that not only will children orient themselves toward growth, but an integral aspect of this growth will be the productive learning of academic content.

---

8. Cremin (1961) feels that the free school movement is reminiscent of the progressive education movement of the 1930s, whose demise he attributes to negativism (they also knew what they were against but not what they were for), in-fighting among factions, teacher incompetence, and overkill (i.e., the tendency to continue to seek reform even after reforms had been effected).

These are obviously important goals in education. But they are difficult to specify in terms that can be measured. Since humanists deemphasize knowledge and skills as a primary goal and concentrate on the more personalized outcomes, growth becomes difficult to evaluate. The question is whether these personal goals can be achieved without undue sacrifice of the more obvious academic objectives.

Humanistic claims
difficult to
substantiate

The humanistic position is obviously "soft-nosed" and not easily documented. Typically the humanists are opposed to the scientific precision of, say, the behaviorists. They are, for example, opposed to various forms of external objective evaluation—examinations, grades, etc.—which they see as potentially threatening to the individual and typically oriented toward aspects of behavior that do not constitute the important things of life. Furthermore, the variables on which the humanistic position rests—self-actualization, self-direction, autonomy, etc.—are extremely nebulous and lacking in the scientific precision necessary for conclusive evaluation of their claims. Up to now much of the evidence in support of their position has come from student testimonials: e.g., "I liked the course," "I appreciated the freedom and trust; I have never been so totally challenged," "I never experienced such a sense of personal growth"—etc.—all of which are of questionable scientific validity.

Behaviorists have accused humanists of refusing to admit they have goals or of stating their goals so globally that they become mere platitudes (see Pittenger and Gooding 1971).[9] Their position has obvious appeal in our current democratic context, but to date there is little or no evidence presented to indicate their claims are capable of fulfillment. To make matters worse, humanists have made themselves vulnerable to criticism by claiming too much. Not only do they propose to teach subject matter but also to create students who are happy, well-adjusted, self-actualizing, with a deep sense of personal identity, etc. Unfortunately the product does not always meet specifications. The *Émile* generated by the humanistic surge of the late 1960s, as Skinner (1973) sees it, does not work very hard, does not learn very much, does not think very clearly, nor does he seem particularly creative, well-disposed toward peers, or even particularly happy. On the other hand, this in no way denies the many benefits that are likely to accrue from a humanistic touch in the operation of the nation's schools (see Weinstein and Fantini 1970; Aspy 1972).

THE OPEN SCHOOL

Among the more recent innovations is the open classroom developed in England in an attempt to individualize instruction. In a way, it resembles the Montessori school in that it places considerable responsibility on the children

9. Humanists have, in return, accused the behaviorists of focusing on the most specifiable and observable objectives, frequently of utmost triviality.

for their own learning. It is an open educational system within a relatively structured learning environment, complete with definite instructional objectives and organized learning experiences and activities preplanned by the teacher. There the traditional ends. Not only is the system individualized but the learner, rather than the teacher, is the primary actor. The teacher's task is to prepare and arrange various learning situations and thus offer various options from which the children can choose. What they choose, when, and how is largely their prerogative.

Features of the open school

Among the more obvious features of the open classroom, we might mention:

1. Activity: Typically, many activities are going on at the same time, with children free to move from one activity to another.
2. Learning areas: The open classroom is usually divided into different learning areas, separated by screens, bookcases, and planters. There is, for example, a reading area, a language arts area, a science area, etc. The open classroom contains many different kinds of learning materials for children of various stages of development. This is in keeping with the Montessori concept that the classroom environment be sufficiently flexible to accommodate children with a wide variety of interests and abilities. The major responsibility for providing materials rests with the teacher, who continually talks with children about their interests and preferences.
3. Cooperative planning: At the beginning of each day, the students engage in a free, self-directed examination of the materials in the various centers. The class is then called together for a planning session where the teacher describes possible activities and calls attention to the additions in the different centers. The students come together again at the end of the day and describe the activities they have found instructive.
4. Teaching: The teacher normally works with a small group or perhaps a given child, then moves to another. Teaching is largely replaced by individual tutoring, involving asking questions, following through on the learner's responses, providing information as needed, and conducting an ongoing evaluation. The teacher rarely presents materials to the class as a whole but must be sensitive to the individual needs of a large number of children and help them select and carry out tasks of individual benefit to them. He or she provides systematic reinforcement, thus helping each child develop responsible freedom of choice and self-direction. The teacher is an observer and guide who does not hesitate to be forceful when necessary but still gives the child considerable freedom in the choice of activities. The premise is that children are capable of individualizing their own instruction.
5. Freedom: The term *open education* implies a free choice by students concerning the activities in which they will participate. There is no

rigid timetable. Children are free to perform the particular activities that interest them at a given time; they may explore certain parts of the room or remain in a familiar work area. They can work alone or in groups. Each child is expected to do some reading, writing, and arithmetic each day, but when and what is a personal choice and responsibility.

Open education presents a number of definite advantages, and early reports (e.g., Silberman 1970; Featherstone 1971) were highly favorable. The Plowden report (1967), dealing with the quality of education in the British infant schools, found that the more successful schools tended to be open in their approach to teaching, with teachers allowing students considerable freedom both in daily classroom activities and in curriculum planning. On the other hand, extended use has revealed a number of weaknesses apparently overlooked in earlier evaluations.[10] Open education can be extremely demanding on the teacher, who has to provide materials for a large number of children of different interests and backgrounds. Unless aided by self-instructional devices, he or she may have difficulty in coping with the demand. Perhaps as students become more capable of independence and self-management, the load might be somewhat reduced.

Some problems

The open school assumes that children can take responsibility for their own behavior (and their own education), that they will display self-discipline, etc. This presupposes that they want to learn and are capable of learning, which may not necessarily be true of all children, particularly those from the lower classes who require considerable monitoring in behavior control and in systematic reinforcement of their learning efforts as they develop responsibility in small, sequential steps. It may not even be the most effective approach for all types of learning. It also needs some getting used to: children who have been accustomed to teacher control may have difficulty in adjusting. So may teachers who are accustomed to traditional strategies and who may worry about the noise level and the apparent chaos as children are forever moving from here to there.[11] There is also the possibility of censure by administrators and parents whose ideas of school may be more traditional.

10. This is a common pattern; innovations at first look promising but then unforeseen difficulties surface and the method is discarded, hopefully leaving some residue that can be fashioned into a better innovation. Bennett (1976) labels the Plowden Report a "subjective, and perhaps hopeful assessment." See also Horwitz (1979).

11. If used, the open classroom approach probably should be introduced gradually, first with certain students who show initiative and self-direction (e.g., a gifted child who needs enrichment), and gradually extended to other members of the class. The teacher should probably have an option of going back to the traditional model for certain units for certain children as the occasion arises.

THE MONTESSORI SYSTEM

The Montessori system (see Montessori 1977) is based on what might be called a planned environment; everything in the classroom from the dimensions of the furniture to the arrangements of the chairs is carefully designed with youngsters in mind. The children are encouraged to use the materials at their disposal in order to teach themselves. The teacher's task is to manipulate and supervise the overall learning environment so as to promote experiences conducive to the total development of the child. The basic aim of the Montessori approach is to free the learner's potentiality for self-instruction and self-development through a specially prepared environment. It is a matter of helping the learner become more self-managing, self-motivated, self-disciplined, and self-taught.

The Montessori approach operates on a number of rules, e.g., children are free to work with any material as long as they use it with respect. They are free to do nothing as long as they do not disturb others. The main sources of reinforcement are the reward of discovery and the satisfaction of success. Punishment involves the withdrawal of rewarding consequences. The program encourages freedom of movement within the room, but this must be orderly. The emphasis is on motor and sensory training as well as on the development of cognitive and social skills.

The Montessori approach is in basic agreement with the teaching of today's educational leaders. It agrees with Bruner on such major points as the use of the spiral curriculum and discovery learning. It agrees with Piaget regarding emphasis on activity and on concrete experiences. So far the method has been used with preschool children; although it could possibly be used on older children, the availability of appropriate materials could be a problem.

GAGNÉ'S HIERARCHICAL THEORY OF LEARNING

Gagné presents not only the most comprehensive and detailed view of the various types of classroom learnings, but also the most explicit as to instructional implications. More specifically, he postulates an eight-level hierarchy of instructional contents, ranging from simple S-R learning to problem solving and further specifies the conditions (internal and external) to be met if effective learning is indeed to take place (see *Conditions of Learning*, 1965, 1970, 1977).

Gagné: Capabilities rather than knowledge

Contrary to Piaget, Gagné views development as the long-term change resulting from learning. More specifically, Gagné sees children learning concepts and rules not as verbalized *knowledge* but rather as an ordered set of *capabilities*, capabilities that they now *have*, that they can *use*—not a matter of knowledge that they can recall from memory but, rather, intellectual skills that enable them to perform tasks requiring special capabilities. He also postulates that the simpler capabilities must be learned before the next higher level capabilities are achieved. Before dealing with Boyle's law (PVT = Constant), for example, children have to know the basic concepts of pressure, volume, temperature, and constant (see White 1973 for a critique of Gagné's hierarchy).

Gagné also disagrees with Piaget on the question of readiness; he suggests that, if stages *à la Piaget* do indeed exist, they are largely irrelevant after, say, the age of three. Presumably children can master any intellectual task for which they have the prerequisite capabilities. Gagné would postulate that, having learned a particular rule, for example, students now have a capability that they can transfer to other higher-order rules.

Operationally the sequential nature of these capabilities provides us with learning hierarchies that can then serve as the foundation for developing effective instructional strategies—permitting us, for example, to work backward to determine what prerequisite capabilities learners must have if they are to achieve a given learning task. Guiding student learning, then, is primarily a matter of clarifying the nature of the task in terms of its prerequisites (task analysis) and then sequencing its various components so that these prerequisite capabilities will be available as needed.

Emphasis on structure

Gagné's primary concern is to organize instructional strategies so as to capitalize on the structure of the content to be learned—in other words, to identify a series of prerequisites in their proper order subordinate to a final objective. Gagné is not alone, of course, in his emphasis on structure. As we have noted, Bruner arranges content so that the relationships become accessible to the learner through the process of discovery. Ausubel also emphasizes the structure of knowledge but relies on expository presentation of materials by the teacher. In all three cases, the intent is to arrange the academic content so as to highlight the relationships so that they can be processed into cognitive structure.

Beginning point: Task description, task analysis

More specifically, Gagné proceeds systematically from:

1. *Task description*—the process of breaking down long-range goals into specific instructional objectives—to
2. *Task analysis*—the process of specifying what learners must be able to do in order to achieve the various objectives in question and the prior capabilities they must have if they are to be successful.

Five learning outcomes

From there, he identifies specific conditions to be met if instruction is to be effective. For example, he postulates five major categories of learning outcomes, each calling for different conditions of effective learning:

1. Verbal information.
2. Attitudes.
3. Motor skills.
4. Intellectual skills, e.g., rules to transfer terms from one side of the

equation to the other in algebra, how to blend sounds in learning to read, how to syllabicate or pronounce new words, etc.; and

5. Cognitive strategies, e.g., mnemonic devices, "learning how to learn" strategies, and various self-instructional devices the learner uses to manage the processes of attending, remembering, and thinking, etc.

Of particular interest from the standpoint of instruction is that prerequisites at any given level of Gagné's hierarchy can be translated into conditions that must be met if learning is to take place. If learners are to master problem solving, they must have at their command principles which, in turn, call for a mastery of underlying concepts, and, in turn, discriminations, etc. These conditions can be classified as:

Conditions of learning, internal, external

1. Internal: i.e., conditions within the learner, primary among which are the availability of subordinate capabilities and the ability and willingness (motivation) to attend.[12]

2. External:[13] i.e., conditions residing in the learning environment, or, more specifically, conditions that must be incorporated as part of the instructional strategies, e.g., the presentation of the stimulus situation, corrective feedback, selective reinforcement, etc.[14]

The Nature of Instruction

Instruction refers to the strategies used in controlling the external events of the learning situation, including the events manipulated by the teacher, the textbook author, the tutor, or even the learner taking over responsibility for learning on his or her own. More generally, instruction calls for:

Steps of the instructional process

1. Gaining and controlling the learner's attention.
2. Clarifying the nature of the desired outcomes.
3. Stimulating the recall of prerequisites.
4. Presenting the stimuli inherent in the learning task.
5. Providing guidance as needed.
6. Providing corrective feedback and reinforcement.
7. Appraising performance.
8. Making provisions for retention and transfer.

12. It might behoove the teacher to shape the learner's attending behavior (receptivity) through a process of systematic reinforcement, i.e., to reward the child for attending to the teacher, for being alert to verbal directions, for being quiet when the bell rings, etc.

13. Ausubel et al. (1978) list parallel conditions under the headings of (1) intrapersonal (i.e., variables in the area of existing cognitive structure, developmental readiness, intellectual ability, motivation, aptitude, and personality traits) and (2) situational factors (e.g., practice, arrangement of instructional materials, classroom climate, and teacher variables).

14. Gagné does not give prescriptions as to specifics. He may, for example, specify the need for reinforcement: the teacher must now translate this into exactly what kind, how much, and for whom, taking into account the nature of the task in relation to the characteristics of the class, etc. Gagné gives us the outline; we must bring to bear on the situation all the psychology we know if we are to convert his model into effective teaching and effective learning at the individual level.

We can add a number of general requirements critical to effective teaching:

1. Analyzing long-range goals in order to specify clearly the instructional objectives.
2. Analyzing the subject matter so as to organize it in sequence from initial to final phases.
3. Evaluating the current status of the learner in relation to what is to be taught.
4. Designing appropriate learning experiences, e.g., teacher overview, demonstration, discussion, etc.
5. Sequencing learning experiences, e.g., providing concrete exemplars in the early stages, especially for younger children.
6. Incorporating into each experience the necessary motivational components, e.g., goal setting, commitment, corrective feedback, and reinforcement.
7. Providing guidance as needed.
8. Evaluating progress on a relatively continuous basis, particularly at first, but then helping the student become his or her own evaluator.

Gagné's Hierarchy of Learning Contents

Hierarchy of verbal information

Gagné postulates the following eight-level hierarchy of verbal contents[15] ranging in order from simplest to highest:

Problem Solving _____

Rules _____

Concept Learnings _____

Discriminations _____

Verbal Chains _____

Motor Chains _____

S-R Learnings _____

Signal Learnings _____

15. In his latest revision of *Conditions of Learning* (1977) Gagné replaces motor chains and verbal chains with *chaining* (in which he emphasizes motor chains, although he also discusses motor learning as one of the five major learning outcomes) and *verbal associations* (in which he discusses verbal sequences and chains). He also distinguishes between *concrete* concepts (to refer to *dog, house,* which are generalized from actual experience) and *defined* concepts (e.g., uncle, calorie, etc., which can be established only by definition). The latter is discussed in the context of *rules* (category seven).

He not only discusses each from the standpoint of its basic nature but further lists for each relatively definite instructional implications. The following discussion, modeled on Gagné, focuses on each level of the hierarchy, with particular emphasis on the internal and external conditions to be met if learning is to take place and their implications from the standpoint of teaching.

SIGNAL LEARNING.   Signal learning represents the lowest level of learning, namely, the acquisition of involuntary behaviors through classical conditioning, e.g., the conditioning of fear in a young child or of attitudes toward a given subject or object as a result of its association with pleasant or unpleasant consequences. Stimulus generalization is important here: the child learns to fear not only the rabbit but also other furry animals, and even a woolen mitt.

Conditions:
1. Internal: All that is required for signal learning to take place is for the child to have the neurophysiological equipment necessary to receive and to respond to the stimulus.
2. External
   a. Presentation: We need to present an appropriate stimulus to elicit the response.
   b. Contiguity: The unconditioned stimulus must be presented in close time proximity with the natural stimulus; the noise must accompany the presentation of the rabbit.
   c. Repetition: The presentation of the unconditioned and the conditioned stimuli generally must be repeated.
   d. Reinforcement: Initially reinforcement must be provided on every presentation of the stimuli. Later reinforcement should be intermittent so as to promote resistance to extinction.

S-R LEARNINGS.   Here the responses are more precise and, of course, voluntary, as in the case of operant conditioning (Skinner) or trial-and-error learning (Thorndike). Despite their relatively low status on the taxonomy, such learnings are of critical importance in reading, in arithmetic, in associating dates and events, etc.

Conditions:
1. Internal: The learner must be capable of receiving the stimulus and of performing certain responses that lead to reinforcement. It is also necessary that he or she attend to the stimulus.
2. External
   a. Presentation: An appropriate stimulus must be presented to elicit a response.[16]

16. Skinner would simply place the animal in the position where he could emit certain behaviors that can be reinforced.

    b. Reinforcement: The terminating response must result in reinforcement—at first on a continuous basis, later on an intermittent schedule.

    c. Contiguity: The response and the reinforcement should follow in relatively close proximity.

    d. Repetition: Practice under guidance generally should be provided primarily to help the learner discriminate the relevant from the irrelevant. How much practice is required depends on the difficulty of the material in relation to the adequacy of the learner.

    e. Selective reinforcement and feedback.

    f. Mediating factors: It would generally be helpful to bring out the underlying structure where such structure exists. Even in dealing with meaningless paired associates, it might be possible to structure the arbitrary association *Cow-Ball* into a mental picture—either verbal or visual—of "The Cow kicked the Ball."

An important consideration here is selectivity of reinforcement. Skinner emphasizes that reinforcement be made contingent on the occurrence of the behavior to be learned or progressive approximation thereto. Wherever possible, the learner should be clearly aware of the goal to be attained.[17] This permits the learner to provide his or her own reinforcement, i.e., confirmation or corrective feedback through knowledge of results (KR) in relation to the goal. It should also be noted that verbal directions play an extremely important role in all forms of human learning.

MOTOR CHAINS.   Chaining is a matter of tying together a number of S-R connections into a complete sequence as might occur both at the motor and the verbal levels. Chaining is of major importance in learning to write or type, throw a baseball, or learn a foreign language.

Conditions:
1. Internal
    a. The learner must have mastered the component S-R units; the teacher should test the adequacy and the availability of the subskills and, if necessary, provide remedial practice.
    b. The learner would have to be able and willing to attend.
2. External
    a. Objectives: The learner must have a clear mental picture of what is to be accomplished and how to go about it, e.g., in holding a baseball in order to throw a curve. He or she must also have made a personal commitment to the achievement of this goal.
    b. Presentation: The units of the chain must be presented in proper sequence at a rate and in a way that the learner can follow. It might

17. It might be said in passing that if Skinner could communicate his objectives to his pigeons, he could save himself a lot of time.

help to have a demonstration emphasizing the points to be noted. In teaching the child to write, models might be provided.

c. Response: The learner must actually go through the motions of carrying out the response in sequence, perhaps at first at slower speed and then gradually at natural speed. There may be need for introductory exercises such as learning the position of the keys on a typewriter before a meaningful response can be attempted.

d. Confirmation (or corrective feedback) and reinforcement: Correct responses should be reinforced systematically and, in general, soon after the response. Corrective feedback geared to the development of proper style is particularly crucial in both the early stages and the development of final proficiency.

e. Repetition: The development of motor proficiency is primarily a matter of intelligent practice. The task is one of integrating the various component links into a smooth, sequential performance.

VERBAL CHAINS (VERBAL ASSOCIATIONS). Verbal associations are especially important in the school where the curriculum tends to be highly verbal, whether in connection with learning to read, learning to speak a foreign language, writing a composition, or in discussing any subject-matter content.

Conditions:
1. Internal: The learner must have mastered and have readily available the necessary verbal links. Again, it might behoove the teacher to make sure that this is indeed the case and, if not, to provide the necessary remedial or developmental exercises. It would also have to be assumed that the learner has the necessary motivation to attend to the task or at least to be reinforced for a suitable response. It is also necessary for the learner to have the necessary mediating connections, whether in the form of visual images, or verbal or even auditory codes as used, for example, in rhymes.

2. External
   a. Objectives: It is important that the learner know precisely what is to be achieved and the purpose thereof. It might help in this connection to carry out a task description and a task analysis in order to identify the conditions necessary to learn various verbal chains. This would be followed by actual testing of the extent to which the learner does indeed have the necessary requisites.

   b. Contiguity: It is necessary that the individual links of the chain be presented in reasonable succession and in proper sequence. Prompts are generally helpful. The use of tutoring, cards, tapes, etc., might be helpful in providing individual instruction.

   c. Reinforcement (confirmation and corrective feedback): Some means must be provided for reinforcing correct responses and correcting those that are inadequate. It might be hoped that the associations are meaningful and the learner is aware of the objectives in question. Verbal chains can carry their own reinforcement, and perhaps the teacher should make every effort to encourage self-reinforcement. If corrective feedback and reinforcement depend on the teacher, problems may arise as to frequency and adequacy of reinforcement.

    d. Repetition and practice: Considerable repetition is required not only to establish such chains but also to counteract interference from prior and subsequent chains. On the other hand, drill should be active, varied, and as enjoyable as possible. Repetition can be incorporated within the context of applying the learnings to related situations.

An important consideration in the learning of verbal chains of a relatively meaningless nature is the extent to which interference sets in, especially if a number of chains are to be mastered at the same time. It might help, for example, to make the individual chains as distinctive as possible and perhaps to provide mediating strategies to minimize such interference. The learning of meaningful verbal chains apparently involves an entirely different learning process and, according to Ausubel, calls for an entirely different set of rules.

DISCRIMINATIONS. An important type of learning involves discriminating between different elements of a given situation. Discrimination is concerned with the distinctive features of phenomena; the child must learn to respond differently to different objects or events in terms of their size, shape, etc., just as he or she learns to discriminate among letters and words in reading, sounds of speech, colors, and people.

Conditions:
1. Internal: The learner must recall and reinstate underlying response chains including mediating links that hold the chains together. Again, the teacher should provide pretesting and remedial work as necessary. The teacher must also capture the attention and interest of the students.
2. External
    a. Objectives: The learner must be aware of the objectives to be achieved and how this is to be done.
    b. Presentation: The elements to be discriminated should be presented in sufficient proximity to highlight the distinction—say, between a rectangle and a rhombus, or between a butterfly and a moth—and to permit the teacher to focus the child's attention on the critical points of difference.[18]

18. Ausubel's comparative organizers may be relevant here.

c. Selective reinforcement, confirmation, and corrective feedback: The learner must be made aware of the correctness of his or her responses, whether this is done by the teacher or a checklist of answers. The problem is much less acute when dealing with meaningful verbal learnings where inherent structure enables students to determine on their own whether they are right or wrong.

In dealing with discrimination, particularly multiple discriminations where the possibility of confusion increases exponentially, the teacher should make the distinction as clear, logical, and meaningful as possible, perhaps even accentuating important differences through verbal or visual means. It might also be advisable to simplify complex situations to the bare bones consistent with some degree of reality; otherwise the neophyte is likely to be so overwhelmed with the details that he or she will overlook the critical point of distinction.

CONCEPT LEARNING.   The major advantage accruing from concepts is generalizability.[19] We are no longer looking at specific differences that set one instance apart from the others: in concept learning, we attend to a general similarity among stimuli in order to group them into a class on the basis of a

19. This discussion will be restricted to *concrete* concepts; *defined* concepts, as introduced in Gagné's 1977 revision, will be presented as part of *rules* in the next section.

common set of attributes. What is significant is that once the learner has mastered a concept, it is no longer necessary for him or her to respond to each stimulus of a given class as if it were unique; but rather now he or she responds to stimuli of a given class on the basis of their common properties rather than on the basis of their individual characteristics.

We cannot possibly present to each student even a fraction of the specific situations and instances each will encounter in regard to a given class of events or objects. Concepts free the individual from the control of specific concrete stimuli in the environment so that thereafter he or she can learn by means of verbal instruction presented either orally or in writing. In fact, once the individual has mastered concepts, his or her ability to learn becomes relatively unlimited.

Concepts are of obvious importance. The world experienced by people is largely organized by means of concepts; we think in terms of concepts, we communicate in terms of concepts. It is difficult to overemphasize the importance of concepts in learning, especially in formal education, where concepts make instruction possible. We can communicate our intentions, our thoughts, our feelings, even abstract ideas, simply because a specific concept evokes in the listener understandings that function for him or her as they do for us. In fact, once the fundamental skills of reading have been acquired, concepts can be introduced in writing, perhaps with accompanying diagrams, as needed, e.g., the fulcrum. On the other hand, there is the ever-present danger that concept learning will outdistance what the student has mastered in basic verbal associations and discriminations on a given topic. Concepts not adequately tied to clear-cut referents in actual experience are mere verbalisms, where the student uses words for which he or she has no meaning.

Conditions:
1. Internal: The learner must have the necessary discriminations and verbal associations readily available in cognitive structure.[20] It is also necessary that he or she attend with sufficient motivation to achieve cognitive clarity.
2. External
    a. Objectives: The learner must be made aware of the task to be performed and the goal to be achieved.
    b. Presentation: There may be a need for the teacher first to reinstate the prerequisite discriminations and verbal chains at an appropriate level of cognitive clarity. This might be done through a teacher-led review, a discussion, or directed readings.

    Whereas verbal instruction is essential in moving toward concepts as abstractions, there is, at least at first, the need for concrete exemplars from which the child can extract the criterial attributes

---

20. We are dealing here with meaningful verbal learning. Ausubel would insist on adequacy of existing cognitive structure as the primary condition for learning concepts.

that make the class. There is also a need to present both positive and negative instances contiguously to bring out the key elements that make certain animals "cats" and not "dogs." It may also be helpful at first to reduce the superabundance of distracting and irrelevant details that would otherwise confuse young children. Verbal instruction should be precise and explicit, and it is probably best to start with exemplars with which the children are already familiar.

c. Response: Learners must be given the opportunity to display their grasp of the concept where it can be either confirmed or corrected. Their response should be in their own words rather than those of the textbook.

d. Reinforcement, confirmation, and corrective feedback: Feedback is essential to help children sharpen their concepts. This is a matter of degree that has to be made consistent with each child's level of cognitive development. It may be necessary to settle for somewhat less than the total truth. Group discussion may be helpful in raising the class's understanding of a given concept, but individual differences will probably ensure a wide range of cognitive clarity.

e. Practice: Practice per se is not necessary if the concept has indeed been meaningfully grasped, i.e., if the other conditions have indeed been met. But as Ausubel points out, meaningfulness is always a matter of degree. At any rate, the learner should be asked to sort out additional exemplars and nonexemplars as a means of verifying his or her grasp of the concept in question. Here practice should not be construed in a sense of drill or simple repetition of the dictionary definition but rather in terms of the expansion of cognitive structure.

It should be noted in passing that whereas behavioristic theory has provided an adequate interpretation of the lower levels of S-R learning, motor and verbal chains, and discriminations, all of which are prerequisite to the acquisition of concepts and other higher forms of learning, these higher-ordered learnings probably are best explained through a cognitive model. When concepts are learned, something happens within the learner beyond what simple association between stimulus and response can explain. The learner now has something to think about, something to apply, to analyze, to synthesize, to evaluate rather than simply to know.

RULE LEARNING (DEFINED CONCEPTS OR PRINCIPLES).
The combining of concrete concepts permits the learner to respond to different situations on the basis of a simple rule or principle, e.g., "Friction causes heat" or "The verb agrees with the subject." A rule is best seen as an inferred

capability that enables the individual to respond to a class of stimulus situations with a class of performances, e.g., the pronunciation of words with a long *a*, as against those with a short *a*.

Concrete and
defined conceptsWe need to distinguish between concrete concepts and defined concepts. Concrete concepts are a generalized version of a physical object or event (e.g., a dog or a house); they are usually achieved during the concrete stage of the Piaget hierarchy, although obviously they become refined over time. It is a matter of responding to various concrete stimuli in terms of some common abstract property. Defined concepts, by contrast, involve a relationship between concepts already known to the learner, e.g., water freezes at 32° F. Defined concepts are strictly abstract; the relationship in question can be described only through a verbal definition (e.g., *cousin, prime number,* or *diagonal*), none of which can be identified by its physical characteristics.

Conditions:

1. Internal: The conditions for learning rules and principles are very similar to those involved in the learning of concrete concepts. Ausubel would suggest that the primary determinant of effectiveness in the learning of rules and principles is the adequacy of the learner's existing cognitive structure (see Ausubel's emphasis on clear stable subsumers and the use of advance organizers), or in Gagné's terminology, the ready availability of prerequisite capabilities in the area of concrete concepts and discriminations. Also important as an internal condition of learning are the learner's intellectual skills, e.g., language skills dealing with subject, verb, and object relationships. It is also essential that the learner be motivated to attend.

2. External
   a. Objectives: The learner must have a clear-cut picture of the objectives to be reached.
   b. Presentation: The rule must be presented whether through verbal exposition or through a Bruner-type attempt at discovery in which the teacher, by means of well-directed questions, prompts, and cues, leads the learner to put the rule together. The presentation generally should include simultaneously and contiguously both positive and negative instances of the rule. It should avoid too many distracting or irrelevant details in the early stages of learning. It would also help for the teacher to use perceptual organizers (e.g., underscoring, headings or verbal instruction of the type, "Remember this," "Look at this") highlighting the key points to be put together into the rule.
   c. Contiguity: It is necessary to have the relevant concepts introduced in close proximity so that they can be seen within the framework of the learner's current cognitive structure.
   d. Response: The learner must actively engage in trying to rearrange

preexisting concepts into a new formulation. By suitable questions, the teacher should help students formulate the rule in their own words.

e. Selective reinforcement, confirmation, and corrective feedback: The teacher (or the group) must be available to react to ideas presented by the student, thereby gradually directing his or her efforts toward closure.

f. Practice: Practice generally is not crucial for either the acquisition or the retention of (meaningful) principles, but it can perhaps overcome interference. Practice could also be expected to sharpen the clarity of the student's grasp of the rule.[21] Generally the teacher might expect the student to state the principle in his or her own words and to give applications and implications.

PROBLEM SOLVING OR HIGHER-ORDER RULES.

Problem solving involves a resolution of an indeterminate situation through the recombination of rules to form new rules. In Maier's two-string problem, for example, (defined) concepts of mass, pendulum, and inertia, etc., are restructured into a new rule (i.e., a solution to the problem): tie a weight on one of the strings and set it swinging. As a consequence of problem solving, the individual's capabilities are more or less permanently changed in the sense that problem-solving strategies underlie the behavior regardless of what he or she is learning; the scientific method, for example, underlies all forms of scientific thinking.

Conditions:
1. Internal: The learner must have mastered and have readily available the prerequisite principles, rules, and concepts and have achieved intellectual skills in the use of such principles and rules in deriving effective problem-solving strategies, i.e., in reorganizing such principles and rules into the solution to a given problem. We have to assume that problem solving is primarily a function of the adequacy, clarity, flexibility, and versatility of the individual's cognitive structure and corresponding freedom from perceptual rigidity (fixity) and stereotyped mind set. We also have to assume an adequate degree of motivation.
2. External
a. Objectives: The learner must be clear as to the nature of the problem and of the solution to be sought.
b. Presentation: The learner, whether individually or in a group, must be helped not only to develop a clear-cut picture of the problem

---

21. When children have difficulty in formulating rules, the solution is not to put more teaching effort into the task but rather to increase the adequacy, i.e., the meaningfulness of the underlying verbal associations, discriminations, and concrete concepts in the learner's existing cognitive structure.

but also to reinstate pertinent rules, principles, and concepts. Advance organizers, prompts, and leading questions would be helpful in keeping thinking on the track and on the move.

c. Response: The learner needs to be encouraged to come up with hypotheses as to the likely solution, followed by critical analyses of these inferences and eventual reformulation into more adequate hypotheses.

d. Reinforcement, confirmation, and corrective feedback: Reinforcement is generally inherent in meaningful problem solving; the student knows when he or she has achieved a solution. On the other hand, it might be helpful for the teacher to reinforce leads and probes in the direction of the final solution even though the student may not recognize them as such. It is, of course, essential that the child (or group) achieve closure.

e. Practice: Practice is not particularly important when the component rules and principles are clear. It might lead to new insight (hindsight) as to interrelationships among rules and concepts pertinent to the problem situation and might thereby promote a more precise and elegant solution, or a more functional (versatile) solution having greater generalizability. In other words, practice may increase the clarity, generalizability, and applicability of the solution.

An important consideration here is the role of personal flexibility and versatility—in Bruner's words, the willingness to take intuitive leaps—as a necessary factor in effective problem solving. The teacher's task is to promote a classroom atmosphere conducive to free inquiry, with the teacher then encouraging production of ideas, setting a good example as an intuitive thinker, and, where appropriate, teaching problem-solving strategies and techniques.[22]

Learning Capabilities versus Knowledge

An interesting point systematically emphasized by Gagné is that learning is defined not by the accumulation of knowledge but by the development of human capabilities. The eight varieties of learning in the Gagné hierarchy—and particularly the higher levels (discrimination, concepts, rules, and problem solving)—establish in the learner identifiable intellectual skills, something the learner is now able to do with reference to the environment. Contrary to the position presented by Piaget, for example, Gagné's cumulative learning model postulates that the attainment of conservation results from the learning

22. What is important is that students restructure and reorganize their perceptions and cognitions—that they perceive the relationships involved. Whether they achieve this change in perception through listening to the teacher, reading it in a book, or deriving it inductively through the discovery approach is not overly important, according to Gagné.

of relatively specific intellectual skills having to do with containers, volume, etc. The implication is that each newly learned intellectual skill increases the individual's intellectual power, allowing him or her to graduate to even more complex rules of increasingly greater applicability and generalizability, i.e., to transfer what has been "learned." The learner is now able to perform not so much a particular response but rather a full class of responses dealing with a given area, e.g., how to convert fractions into decimals, how to pronounce words, how to blend sounds in beginning reading, how to substitute into an equation in algebra, how to transfer terms from one side of the equation to the

Intellectual skills   other. The learner has gained a number of *intellectual skills* relating to discriminations, concepts, rules, and principles forming the fundamental structure of his or her intellectual competence and, coincidentally, of much of the learning that goes on in the classroom. In problem solving, for example, the learner manipulates a combination of previously learned rules into the solution to a novel problem.

Cognitive strategies   But equally important is that, in the process, the learner develops *cognitive strategies:* internally organized skills that modify the process of learning and thinking. As the learner proceeds to learn a given concept or principle, he or she also learns how to learn, how to remember, how to think, i.e., he or she develops cognitive strategies that govern the intellectual processes associated with learning. He or she becomes increasingly capable of self-instruction. Such self-instructional strategies, variously called *cognitive strategies* and *executive control processes* (Gagné 1977), *mathemagenic behaviors* (Rothkopf 1970; Frase 1970), *self-management behaviors* (Skinner 1968), or even *learning how to learn* (Harlow 1949), include how to promote remembering through mnemonic devices (visual images or rhymes), how to direct selective attention to critical points in what one is learning through clear-cut objectives and prequestions, how to organize material for effective storage and retrieval, how to use cues in discrimination problems, how to use mediating strategies in encoding meaningless word pairs for effective acquisition and retrieval, how to ask meaningful questions, how to avoid prejudgment and mind set, how to clarify essential elements in problem solving, etc.

The development of cognitive strategies that can generalize to various learning situations—the promotion of strategies whereby children can become better perceivers, better learners, better rememberers, more creative and productive thinkers, better problem solvers—is obviously a major curricular goal in any educational system. On the other hand, Gagné suggests that we might need to contain our enthusiasm. First, there is a matter of feasibility; we have made only limited progress to date in the improvement and refinement of such strategies. But perhaps more fundamentally, as he points out, the development of cognitive strategies can hardly be education's exclusive goal at the expense of the lower levels of the hierarchy. Besides being crucial to the promotion of cognitive strategies as our ultimate goal, these lower-level objectives are of critical importance in their own rights and cannot be bypassed. The achievement of the higher levels of the hierarchy is predicated on the prior achievement of prerequisites; lower-order skills must be mastered before the learning of related superordinate skills is undertaken.

Evaluation of Gagné's Cumulative Learning Model

Gagné's cumulative learning theory constitutes a major contribution to the field, especially with respect to instruction. Not only does it identify different types of learning, but it lends itself to the development of specific instructional strategies by identifying for each type the conditions essential for successful learning, retention, and transfer. Gagné contends that the reason for the relative unproductivity of current learning theories is that they try to cover very different types of learning outcomes with a single set of rules. Gagné especially emphasizes the need for clarity as to objectives of each learning experience and the prerequisite capabilities for its attainment.

His hierarchical system provides the basis from which the teacher can derive a reasonable answer to the question, "What do I want the learner to achieve?" It is an excellent guide for organizing what the child is to do and lends itself directly to task analysis as the basis for the teacher to decide the sequence in which learning activities should be scheduled. It is also of primary interest to the curriculum builder in planning an orderly program from one achievement to the next for which it is a prerequisite.

Agreement with Piaget

Gagné's position is in relative agreement with those of Piaget, Ausubel, and Bruner. Although differing in terms of formulation and terminology, it agrees with all three with respect to the importance of structure, the role of reinforcement and corrective feedback, etc. (see, for example, Strauss 1972). Of special relevance in the present context is that it is highly specific and therefore particularly suited to the development of instructional strategies. It provides a framework around which a good deal of the data of educational psychology can be fitted into perspective, e.g., the importance of prerequisites, the nature and role of reinforcement, feedback, and practice, etc., in the promotion of learning, retention, and transfer. Its emphasis on the specific conditions to be met if effective learning is to take place should be of particular value to classroom teachers and curriculum developers alike.

HIGHLIGHTS OF THE CHAPTER

A number of teaching models have been devised, each based on somewhat different premises and covering the various dimensions of the instructional process to varying degrees of adequacy. To the extent that they represent the best thinking in the field to date, it behooves the beginning teacher to be familiar with their overall strategies, their premises, and their general applicability.

1. According to Ausubel's assimilation model, the primary determinant of the acquisition, retention, and transfer of meaningful verbal learning is the adequacy of one's existing cognitive structure. The teacher's task is to ensure the ready availability of adequate subsumers, i.e., broad, general concepts and principles under which new materials can be subsumed. The emphasis is on meaningfulness, structure, ideational scaffolding, and advance organizers.

2. The key to Bruner's discovery model is structure; the teacher's task is to help the child discover the fundamental principles that underlie a given discipline. Bruner's concept of the spiral curriculum represents an attempt at helping the child discover underlying structure at progressively higher levels of insight. On the other hand, critics feel that Bruner has overstated the advantages of the discovery method and correspondingly magnified the alleged weaknesses of reception learning by equating it with passive rote learning.

3. Although a disciple of Piaget, Bruner gives language a greater role in child development than does Piaget. He also takes a more liberal view of the concepts of readiness and developmental stages.

4. The humanistic position is based on concern for the individual and belief in each person's overwhelming need and ability to actualize his or her potentialities. The teacher's role is largely that of facilitator of personal growth; students will learn what has personal significance in their world as they see it. This idea is reflected in its extreme in the free school movement. The position is vulnerable to criticism, against which humanists have presented only a weak response.

5. While expecting children to exercise considerable self-discipline and self-direction as to when they learn what, the open school provides some structure through the materials the teacher provides in the various classroom centers. Recent evaluations have been somewhat less favorable than earlier reports. The Montessori school also attempts to promote self-discipline and self-direction through a planned environment of educationally productive materials.

6. The most comprehensive instructional system is that of Gagné, who first distinguishes five different kinds of learning outcomes—verbal information, attitudes, motor skills, intellectual strategies, and cognitive strategies—and further divides verbal information, for example, into eight levels arranged on a hierarchy from signal learning to problem solving. He sees learning not as the acquisition of knowledge but rather as the development of capabilities that enable the learner to deal more effectively with environmental demands.

7. Especially significant in the present context is that Gagné also identifies the conditions (internal and external) that must be met if learning at each of the different levels is to occur.

SUGGESTIONS FOR FURTHER READING

BRUNER, JEROME S. *Toward a Theory of Instruction*. New York: Norton, 1966. Probably the best statement of Bruner's views on instruction, with particular application to the classroom. Examples are primarily from the social studies, English, arithmetic, and elementary school subjects.

HAMACHEK, DON E. Humanistic psychology: Theoretical-philosophical implications for teaching. In Donald J. Treffinger et al., eds., *Handbook on Teaching Educational Psychology*, pp. 139–160. New York: Academic Press, 1977. Presents the humanistic position as it relates to instruction. Sees humanistic psychology more as a viewpoint than as a formalized theory of instruction. Seeks to understand behavior in and out of the classroom within the context of personal meaning.

KOHL, HERBERT. *36 Children*. New York: New American Library, 1967. Describes his experiences as a teacher of a sixth-grade class of disadvantaged children in Harlem.

PATTERSON, C. H. *Foundations for a Theory of Instruction and Educational Psychology*. New York: Harper & Row, 1977. Presents a thorough overview of the teaching implications of various theoretical positions, including Piaget, Skinner, Rogers, and Bruner.

PERRONE, V. *Open Education: Promise and Problems*. Bloomington, Ind.: Phi Delta Kappa, 1972. Presents a first-hand account of the open education movement in operation.

SCHMUCK, RICHARD, et al. *Problem Solving to Improve Classroom Learning*. Chicago: Sci. Res. Assoc., 1966. An excellent booklet on problem solving. Chapter 5, for example, deals with cultural influences on classroom problem solving as they affect children from the lower classes.

SKINNER, B. F. *The Technology of Teaching*. New York: Appleton-Century-Crofts, 1968. The best statement of Skinner's views on the application of science to the development of teaching strategies. Best known is chapter 2, "The Science of Learning and the Art of Teaching."

WEINSTEIN, GERALD, and MARIO D. FANTINI, eds. *Toward Humanistic Education: A Curriculum of Affect*. New York: Praeger, 1970. Present a strong case for implementing humanistic principles at all levels of public education.

WERTHEIMER, MICHAEL. Humanistic psychology and the humane but tough-minded psychologist. *Amer. Psychol.* 33 (1978):739–745. Notes considerable vagueness and confusion as to the meaning of humanistic psychology. It seems that, whereas a humanistic perspective may be defensible, the effectiveness of "humanistic" practices such as the encounter group movement has not been demonstrated, and they should be viewed with great caution.

SELF-TEST

1. Ausubel is to Bruner as
   a. concept formation is to concept assimilation.
   b. passive is to active.

    c. reception learning is to didactic teaching.

    d. subsumption is to structure.

    e. teaching is to learning.

2. Meaningfulness in the classroom is best promoted by
   a. the accumulation and organization of experience.
   b. emphasis on clarity in presentation.
   c. the postponement of difficult materials.
   d. the promotion of intellectual development.
   e. the simplification of vocabulary.

3. The greatest criticism of the humanistic position as it relates to classroom instruction is that
   a. it deals only with the nonacademic aspects of classroom operation.
   b. it cannot deal effectively with the child whose deficiency needs are largely unmet.
   c. it is based strictly on Freudian principles of therapy.
   d. it is opposed to all forms of formal instruction.
   e. it overemphasizes the child's right to self-determination.

4. Which of the following is *not* correctly identified as to the primary determinant of effective learning?
   a. Ausubel: Availability of adequate subsumers
   b. Bruner: Structure of the discipline
   c. Gagné: Prerequisite capabilities
   d. Humanists: Personal meaningfulness
   e. None of the above; all are correct associations.

5. Which of the following are most similar from the standpoint of rationale and operational strategy of classroom learning?
   a. Ausubel and Bruner
   b. Bruner and Gagné
   c. The free school and the open school
   d. The humanists and the Skinnerians
   e. The open school and the Montessori school

6. The distinctive feature of Gagné's hierarchical model from the standpoint of teaching and learning is that
   a. it addresses itself to meaningful verbal learning only.
   b. it deals with verbal information only.
   c. it emphasizes the need for defining instructional goals in precise behavioral terms.
   d. it identifies the conditions that must be met if learning at a given level is to occur.
   e. it identifies specific teaching strategies appropriate for each level of the hierarchy.

7. According to Gagné's hierarchical model, internal conditions are to external conditions as
   a. intellectual skills are to cognitive strategies.
   b. reinforcement is to motivation.
   c. prerequisite capabilities are to presentation.
   d. presentation is to corrective feedback.
   e. verbal chains are to motor chains.

THIRTEEN

Measuring Academic Achievement

Despite their limitations and imperfections, despite the occasional misuse and despite the criticisms, reasonable or unreasonable, educational measurements have established themselves as versatile, indispensable tools of effective education. They are likely to be used more widely and more wisely in the future than they have been in the past.

Robert L. Ebel (1966)

There is little basically wrong with the concept of grading. The notion of measuring achievement and maintaining standards of excellence accords with our ideas of encouraging and rewarding achievement. What is wrong is the limited nature of most testing and grading. Too often tests and grades are equated with pat learning, with convergent thinking and unimaginative regurgitation.

Don Robinson (1967)

Why are schoolmen so insistent upon the importance of tests, measurements, and evaluations and so reluctant to be evaluated themselves? Why are they so gung-ho about having every kind of activity evaluated but their own?

Don Robinson (1966)

— Presents basic concepts of educational measurements as an integral part of the teaching-learning process
— Considers the benefits of academic testing to the student, the teacher, and the administrator
— Emphasizes the psychological implications of current grading practices

PREVIEW: KEY CONCEPTS

1. All operations must conduct systematic evaluation of their effectiveness. Education, with its many-faceted complexities, is certainly no exception.
2. The testing of academic growth must be seen in the context of the total child.
3. All aspects of school measurements have been the subject of relatively continuous criticism.
4. If it is to provide a meaningful appraisal, a test must be reliable, usable, and, especially, valid.
5. The relative merits of essay and objective examinations have been debated since the turn of the century. No simple answer can be given.
6. Most educational and psychological tests are based on an interval scale and can provide only comparative data.
7. Grading must necessarily be a subjective proposition. Unless used with caution, grades can be detrimental to some children. This does not mean they should be abandoned.

PREVIEW QUESTIONS

1. What are some of the shortcomings of the school's evaluation efforts?
   What are some of the factors that mitigate against the school's success in the quality control of its output?
2. Why should the primary beneficiary of the school's testing program always be the student?
   Is this always true?

3. Why is validity generally considered more critical than reliability?
   Why should a test be reliable?
4. How can the teacher judge the validity of a teacher-made test?
5. What are some of the arguments for and against grading?
6. What are your current views regarding grading on the curve?
   What can be done to save the slower child from continuous failure?

MEASUREMENT IN THE CLASSROOM

Since measuring academic achievement is an integral part of the overall teaching-learning process, teachers need to develop in this area the same degree of expertise they display in other aspects of teaching. Specifically, this implies greater competence in defining the goals of education and of particular courses in terms of student needs and in appraising student progress toward these goals. An academic testing program should involve both the measurement of academic progress and its evaluation in relation to meaningful goals (see Shoemaker 1975).

Teachers have always measured the extent to which pupils have mastered the content of their teaching, but not until the 1920s was systematic attention given to the process of measuring educational outcomes. Despite the rapid progress of the past half-century, much remains to be done, particularly in the development of more adequate instruments, the interpretation of test results, and their utilization in promoting the child's overall growth. There is especially a need to integrate the school's evaluation program in the context of its overall efforts in promoting pupil development.[1]

Functions of an Academic Testing Program

Every enterprise, whether business, industry, or education, must make a periodic appraisal of the success of its efforts and the adequacy of its present status in relation to its future goals. This becomes doubly important in education with its multifaceted operation. If the school is to meet the needs of its students, with their wide differences in ability, motivation, and background, as well as those of society, it must evaluate the students' attempts at achieving its objectives and meeting its standards. Evaluation is so crucial to the success of any enterprise that it is hard to imagine the school operating without a well-developed system of quality control (see Kirkland 1971).

1. Since the school is responsible for the child's all-around growth, its pupil-appraisal program cannot be restricted to the measurement of academic status. It must also concern itself with the appraisal of intelligence, special aptitude, interest, personal and social adjustment, etc. On the other hand, these aspects of pupil growth are too complex to be covered adequately in a course in educational psychology. Students should refer to any one of the excellent texts on the subject.

BENEFITS TO THE STUDENT: The primary function of academic testing is to appraise the students' mastery of the various aspects of the curriculum as an indication of their progress in attaining current objectives and as the basis for reorienting their efforts toward the attainment of progressively more advanced goals. More specifically, testing serves a vital information purpose in keeping students on the track, enabling them to set realistic immediate and long-range goals.

Tests are effective
learning tools

Tests promote learning. Not only do they serve as motivational devices by providing short-term goals, but they are in themselves effective learning experiences, forcing students to clarify, to consolidate, and to integrate their learnings. They promote retention and transfer by fostering a mastery of prerequisites that perhaps would be slurred over lightly under less rigorous monitoring. They promote effective feedback that not only tells students where they need to devote their energies but also structures their learning efforts toward the attainment of key instructional goals. Tests constitute a highly motivated way of individualizing instruction. Students study more conscientiously and more systematically when they realize that periodic appraisals will be made.

BENEFITS TO THE TEACHER: Academic achievement tests, along with other instruments (e.g., intelligence scales), serve their main function by helping the classroom teacher (1) determine each child's educational needs (e.g., to identify areas of weakness that need to be rectified before further learning is undertaken), (2) set realistic goals and orient classroom experiences to each child's level of readiness so that these experiences will be conducive to maximum growth, and (3) evaluate progress toward these goals. Tests provide teachers with a perspective of individual students, their strengths and weaknesses, their goals and aspirations, their learning habits, etc. Test feedback constitutes an effective component of the quality control necessary to ensure effectiveness of the educational enterprise, suggesting, for example, what areas need to be reviewed or even retaught. Tests also force teachers to clarify their objectives. They serve as a partial basis for determining optimal grade placement, predicting college and vocational success, and providing diagnostic and remedial work for children who are experiencing difficulty. Tests also enable teachers to appraise the effectiveness of their own teaching and can be as instrumental in promoting teacher growth as in promoting pupil growth.

Tests enable teachers
to evaluate the
quality of their
teaching

BENEFITS TO ADMINISTRATORS: For administrators, tests serve several—perhaps secondary but nonetheless essential—purposes. First, they are useful in orienting the curriculum and in improving instruction by providing a criterion on the basis of which the effectiveness of both curriculum and instruction can be appraised. Tests supply evidence of the status and the progress of pupils, individually and collectively. They help in maintaining standards and serve as the basis for reports to parents, school officials, and the community.[2]

Recent Criticisms

Tests are reasonably valid

On the other hand, testing, in its various aspects, has been subjected to continuous criticism, ranging from general objections concerning invasion of privacy to the inappropriateness of current tests for members of the lower class. In fact, some critics have gone so far as to suggest that all formal testing be abolished; humanists, for example, are opposed to most forms of external evaluation. These criticisms have generated strong rebuttals (e.g., Ebel 1968). Whereas some of the criticisms have an element of merit, many are based on a misunderstanding of the basic function of any testing program. Educators are fully aware of the many shortcomings of current instruments; they realize that tests are subject to misuse and abuse. But it is one thing to see the imperfect nature of our present operation; it is another to conclude that all testing should be banned. The fact is that those who decry the current emphasis on testing have very little to suggest by way of meaningful replacement. Certainly current alternatives, e.g., teacher judgment, informal quizzes, observation, or interviews, have far greater technical weaknesses than present tests, inadequate as the latter might be.

Tests show whether objectives have been achieved

Measurement of the student's current status and progress is essential to the efficient operation of the school. As we have noted, both Ausubel and Gagné insist on the ready availability of prerequisite learnings as a critical condition of effective learning. The adequacy of one's prior learnings is also one of the primary determinants of the effectiveness of both the lecture and the discussion as instructional devices. In fact, testing lies at the root of readiness, corrective feedback, reinforcement, and other well-established psychological concepts of direct relevance to effective learning. Testing is important to helping teachers set meaningful objectives in line with student readiness and in planning appropriate instructional strategies. There is obviously no point, for example, in devising elaborate lists of objectives if no effort is made to determine whether they are achieved. Nor can teachers simply take for granted that prerequisite learnings are indeed available to all students in the class simply because the material has been covered in a previous lesson.

Furthermore, and for the same reason, evaluation cannot be of the casual, off-the-cuff variety—which is invariably subject to unreliability and invalidity due to the halo effect, personal biases, and numerous other vitiating factors. A simple understanding of the dynamics of selective perception clearly suggests that casual day-to-day observation in the classroom is not only ineffective but also misleading and possibly dangerous. It is easy to be misled by the youngster

2. Monitoring student progress is taking on a more immediate meaning as a number of states now require satisfactory performance on literacy tests as a requirement for high school graduation. See Haney and Madaus (1978) for a discussion of the issues.

We need both formal and informal testing

who nods his head "understandingly" or who holds up his hand, really hoping he will not be called. Whatever is worth doing at all is worth doing systematically rather than haphazardly; evaluation is certainly no exception. A formal approach to evaluation is likely to relate more systematically to the school's many objectives and to monitor more closely the true progress of every child in the attainment of these objectives.[3] It is more likely than less compelling approaches to ensure, for example, the thorough mastery of the fundamentals that are necessary as a foundation for later learnings. Without a rigorous formal program of evaluation, it is easy for students (and for the teachers too) to fudge and to convince themselves that they know the materials, at least well enough to get by. Periodic formal evaluation not only provides an opportunity to consolidate as the class goes along but also to monitor the operation before irremediable gaps develop.[4]

Ausubel et al. (1978) likewise argue that for the humanists to insist that genuine learning, independent thinking, creativity, etc., are possible only in a nonevaluative classroom climate greatly overstates the case. Although it is true that testing is used by some teachers as a weapon for controlling and intimidating their students, this constitutes an abuse of evaluation and is not a valid argument for nonevaluative teaching. The solution lies in preventing the abuse, not in abandoning tests. Speaking to the argument that tests induce anxiety that interferes with learning, Ebel (1968) points out that tests neither reward nor punish; they neither praise nor blame. If the results are disappointing to some children, the blame must lie on poor teaching, on unrealistic expectations, or on undue pressure. It is not the gauge that causes the boiler to explode! Instead of worrying about the test, we need to pay more attention to the source.

Tests are not necessarily biased when they show group differences

It is especially in connection with the disadvantaged that tests are being questioned. It is argued that tests depress the self-concept of lower-ability children, eventually discouraging them from putting forth their best effort. Again, we may be blaming the gauge for malfunctioning of the boiler. The test cannot be condemned simply because it registers low performance; the problem lies with the social and educational inequities that have prevented the development of the child's potentialities. No one blames the doctor for finding a high incidence of anemia among lower-class children resulting from dietary deficiencies. If by providing objective data of inadequate status, tests cause the teacher to write off a child, this type of abuse of test results should certainly be corrected. But eliminating the test will serve no purpose; the same teacher will probably misuse whatever instrument is substituted.

A number of criticisms have been leveled against teacher-made tests. Classroom tests, for example, often emphasize the more obvious, easily mea-

---

3. According to Sanders (1966), classroom questions are typically at the lowest level of the taxonomy. See also Gall et al. (1978).
4. The current furor over illiteracy in the senior high school suggests what happens when quality control standards are relaxed.

sured aspects of education rather than the more significant outcomes.[5] Since much testing is simply trivial, students eventually see tests as ends in themselves, displacing in importance the knowledges and competencies they are intended to represent. But again we must recognize this for what it is, namely a reflection on the competence of teachers in the area of testing, coupled with an inadequate perception of the real value of scholarship. If we are truly concerned with the poor quality of teacher-made tests, we need to improve the situation, e.g., putting greater emphasis on tests and measurements in the undergraduate teacher education program.

The Role of Testing in the Learning Process

Academic testing is not a matter of the occasional day of reckoning superimposed upon, but relatively independent of, the teaching-learning process. On the contrary, testing is an integral aspect of this process, and its full value is realized only when it is coordinated with the total educational enterprise. Rather than an end in itself or a means leading only to the report card, testing should lead to the setting of new goals and the planning of effective attempts to reach these goals. Testing and evaluation are not the last steps of the instructional process. Rather, since planning, teaching, and evaluation represent

5. See Anderson (1972) regarding the construction of teacher-made tests to assess comprehension.

a continuous spiral by means of which the child's growth is furthered, what is needed for effective learning is continuous, rather than periodic, appraisal.

There is always a danger of abuse

The testing program is not without danger of abuse. If improperly stressed by administrators, tests can come to dominate the teaching process to the point where teachers feel compelled to ignore all aspects of pupil growth not specifically covered therein. This is often the situation when the end-of-year standardized testing program is allowed to become the sole criterion of pupil growth—or teacher worth.[6] Similarly, if misused, tests can mean to children not an opportunity to measure what they have learned but simply another occasion to fail. Certainly little can be said in favor of the battle of the grades waged periodically in some of our schools in which, by means fair and foul, teachers and pupils attempt to outwit each other.

Tests are harmful when . . .

Tests are generally harmful to students when (1) they become objectives in their own rights, causing students to become so engrossed in getting a grade that learning becomes an insignificant aspect of getting an education; (2) they are given for the purpose of separating the sheep from the goats,[7] of labeling children as "adequate" or "inadequate"; (3) the results are interpreted as final and infallible indications of all we need to know about the child; or (4) they become the only means of communication between the school and the home regarding pupil progress. On the other hand, the fact that the testing done in some of our schools can be criticized on any one of these counts does not imply that tests are bad per se. Working for a grade is not incompatible with getting an education, and it is just not true that, whenever grades are given, students seek the easiest instructor.[8] The testing program does not necessarily lead to distortion of the various objectives of the school, nor does it mean that every student has to be evaluated according to the same standards. When properly used, measurement and evaluation *cannot* have a detrimental effect on the child, for they become an integral part of the process by which his or her growth can be promoted most effectively. It follows that the teacher needs to understand specifically what role tests are to play in the overall teaching-learning process and to be fully aware of their strengths and their limitations.

6. As Brownell (1947) pointed out years ago, when teachers are rated on the basis of the marks their students make on examinations, the prudent teacher will see that, by hook or by crook, his or her pupils pass the examinations regardless of how many other considerations have to be sacrificed.

7. Traditionally, classroom evaluation has been in the narrow framework of grading, classifying, or selecting, i.e., of distinguishing between children who have it and those who don't. The result too often has been discouragement, feelings of inferiority, a negative self-concept, and academic disengagement on the part of children from the lower part of the ability distribution. Actually selective testing may be appropriate if the purpose is to exclude students who do not have the prerequisite to benefit from the experience. This is at the heart of the process of guiding students into appropriate learning experiences.

8. If grades can indeed be adequately geared to mastery of subject matter, then working for a grade actually furthers the cause of education. Who is to complain if a teacher ˙ ˙aches well in order (hopefully) to get a promotion or a raise?

CHARACTERISTICS OF A GOOD MEASURING INSTRUMENT

Whenever we undertake to measure anything—distance, weight, intelligence, or achievement—we must be sure that the measuring instruments we use possess such characteristics as will make for dependability in the results. The characteristics previously mentioned in connection with intelligence tests, e.g., validity and reliability, apply with equal force to academic achievement tests, whether standardized or teacher made.

Validity

First and foremost, a test must be valid, i.e., it must measure what it claims to measure. Thus, a test for a given class in American history must relate to the particular objectives and contents of American history taught in that particular class. It would not necessarily be valid for another class in American history where perhaps a different emphasis was given to the various aspects of the subject. Validity is a specific concept: a test is valid for a specific purpose under specific circumstances.[9] Even within a course in American history, there are many different aspects that can be measured; a teacher may, for instance, emphasize dates and names, or, on the contrary, relationships and understandings, or relative amounts of each.[10]

Validity: Depends on objectives

Many questions arise: "Should the teacher make deductions for misspelled words on the test? . . . for bad grammar? . . . for sloppiness and general illegibility?" "Should the grade reflect the student's attitude toward the course and toward school in general?" These questions can be answered only in terms of the course objectives, and clarifying these objectives is necessarily the first step in constructing a test and in evaluating it from the standpoint of validity. In keeping with the definition of learning, these objectives should be stated in terms of specific changes in student behavior that the course is designed to promote: specifically what behavior patterns is the student to display to give evidence of progress toward these objectives? Although we have to think of the whole child, as we have seen in chapter 2, it is not enough to refer to "all-around growth" when it comes to measurement; the expected changes must be

9. Psychologists think of four kinds of validity (American Psychological Association 1966): curricular validity, predictive validity, concurrent validity, and construct validity. Teachers are generally more concerned with the first two. Curricular validity, sometimes known as content or face validity, is a matter of relating the content of the test to the material of the course: a test has content validity if it correctly covers the content of the course. Predictive validity refers to the ability of the test to forecast subsequent attainment of a given criterion: the College Boards have predictive validity to the extent that performance on the tests is positively correlated with subsequent success in college. (Note: Predictive and concurrent validity are sometimes referred to as criterion validity.)

10. We also need to recognize a wide range of potential threats to validity in academic testing, e.g., cheating, test wiseness, reading or writing skills, penmanship, ability to work under pressure, ability to outguess the teacher, etc.

stated in specific and measurable terms.[11] We also need to communicate these objectives to students so that they know where they are going, what points are important, etc. In fact, we might suggest a study guide outlining not only the objectives but also the contents to be covered, annotated references as to sources, and self-test materials.

The table of specifications

Not all objectives can be measured, and the table of objectives is generally reduced to a table of *specifications*, which contains only those objectives to be covered in the test, together with the emphasis to be placed on each. Thus objectives serve as instructional guides, while specifications are guides to evaluation—and certain objectives, even though pertinent to instruction, would not be listed in the table of specifications. There is generally no point in listing high-sounding objectives that are never measured and probably never attained. Whatever objectives are carried into the table of specifications should be so stated that the teacher can determine whether or not the child has attained them: "Does he or she know a certain fact?" "Can he or she define the technical vocabulary of the course?" This must be done very carefully for, in a very real sense, the test determines the amount and the kind of learning the child does, and objectives that are not stressed on the test tend to be overlooked by the student—and by the teacher too. As Kirkendall pointed out forty years ago (1939, p. 643), "The avidity with which pupils work for marks is equalled only by the assiduity with which teachers teach for marks." Unless all aspects of pupil growth are stressed, those that are measured will be emphasized at the expense of those that are not and testing will distort educational goals.

To be valid, a test must cover all areas of the table of specifications in proportion to the emphasis that has been placed on each. Thus, a test that measures only facts is not valid unless the course is designed to cover only facts. In the same way, whether to deduct for misspelled words depends on whether this is one of the course objectives. One might expect the objectives of a course in American history to include knowing the people who made American history, and, if so, the teacher should probably expect the student to demonstrate the ability to spell their names. On the other hand, a history teacher might not deduct for the misspelling of common words if he or she felt the spelling of ordinary words is only remotely one of the objectives of the course. The question of what to test, therefore, is answered in terms of what learnings the course is intended to promote.

There is often an overemphasis on facts

Most academic achievement tests overemphasize facts simply because they are easy to measure. Correspondingly, they underemphasize the more complicated but usually more significant outcomes of education, such as the ability to organize and integrate raw material into meaningful structure and to use it in situations calling for problem solving, understanding of relationships,

11. See chapter 2 for arguments and counterarguments concerning the advisability of stating instructional objectives in *behavioral* terms.

interpretation of data, application of principles, drawing of inferences, testing of hypotheses, and the other higher mental functions.

In order for a test to provide a valid score, we must assume that reading poses no special problem in a test where reading is not what is being measured, that the child is properly motivated, and that he or she is relatively free from emotional blocking that might impair performance. Inadequacies in vocabulary, for example, may be of considerable importance in an essay examination where, say, the misreading of a question can cause the student to get a score much lower than he or she deserves. The modern emphasis on overall student growth has complicated the task of evaluation by increasing its scope to include phases that are relatively difficult to define in terms of measurable objectives, let alone measure and relate to the child's ability, maturity, and other aspects of his or her background. A major consideration in dealing with validity is the choice of criterion: should the test relate to the ability to understand basic psychological principles as measured by the final examination, or should it relate to the ability to apply these principles in actual practice?

Reliability

An achievement test must also be reliable, i.e., it must measure *consistently* whatever it measures as determined, for example, by correlating the scores on successive administrations of the test to the same students.[12] This correlation can be converted into the *standard error of measurement,* which refers to the size of the fluctuations in the individual's score that might be expected upon retest; the lower the reliability, the greater the fluctuations that are likely to occur. A reliable test is not necessarily a valid test, since it may measure consistently something other than what it purports to measure. On the other hand, a test that is totally unreliable cannot be valid, but if a test is to be valid, it must be reliable.

Students occasionally get a score on a test that is not typical of their performance. This is particularly true in high school and college courses where the content is so extensive that unless a number of tests are given, the final grade will be based on a relatively small sampling of the course, especially with essay examinations. It is also obvious that, as a rule, tests are not sufficiently reliable for a grade to be decided on the basis of a difference of two or three points; student performance should be scattered over a wide range if grades are to be assigned with a certain degree of fairness.

Usability

Usability combines such features as cost, ease of administration, ease of scoring, and other practical considerations. These are secondary in importance,

---

12. Reliability is generally calculated on the basis of equivalent forms, test-retest, or chance-halves. Students are referred to the library for appropriate sources on these techniques.

but, if two tests are of essentially comparable validity and reliability, factors such as cost and labor should be considered. If only a few students are to be tested, for example, the relative ease of constructing an essay examination might outweigh the labor of scoring, whereas if large numbers are involved, a teacher might save time and effort by devising an objective test. It might also be noted in passing that, unless the teacher goes about it in a systematic way, he or she will find the construction of a good teacher-made test expensive in teacher time and energy.

KINDS OF TESTS

Academic tests can be classified according to any number of dimensions depending on the purpose they are to serve and the basis of classification.

Teacher-made and Standardized Tests

A teacher-made (or informal) test is one constructed by the teacher to cover a particular course; logically, therefore, it should be reasonably valid. However, its validity is frequently vitiated by violations of the principles of testing, ranging from failure to relate the items to clearly defined objectives to simple noncompliance with the basic rules of item construction. Its greatest weakness lies in the lack of an external standard of comparison on the basis of which class performance can be evaluated.

Standardized tests, by contrast, are generally constructed by experts, standardized on a representative sample of the population for which the test is intended, and made available commercially. Their greatest advantage is that they provide an outside standard or norm for evaluating pupil performance.[13] Their greatest potential weakness is that they are often oriented toward a set of objectives different from those emphasized in a particular class. They operate on the premise that there are broad general objectives common to all courses of a given title; that despite variations that may occur from instructor to instructor, there are common objectives that apply to all freshman courses in American history, for example. To the extent that this assumption is correct—and it is likely to be reasonably correct in such fields as reading where relative uniformity of objectives can be expected—a standardized test tends to be reasonably valid for a number of situations. But to the extent that local objectives differ from those toward which the test is oriented, the test will be correspondingly invalid and the test norms correspondingly meaningless for that particular class. Standardized tests are available for most elementary and

Question of objectives

13. Norms are neither standards of excellence nor minimal standards; they are simply standards of comparison.

high school subjects, and it is up to the individual teacher to decide whether a given test has sufficient validity for the particular purpose and circumstances to warrant its use.

Objective and Subjective Tests

Tests can be either objective or subjective, depending on the *objectivity of the scoring.* In objective items, such as *multiple-choice, true-false,* and *matching,* the answers are either right or wrong. *Completion* and *simple recall* items also call for a relatively high degree of objectivity in scoring. Essay examinations, on the other hand, require the grader to have a sufficient grasp of the subject to make a subjective appraisal of the adequacy of the answers given.

Each type of item has its purpose

The relative merits of objective and essay tests have been debated on numerous occasions. Most teachers prefer the objective test, especially once accustomed to it, but this view is not universal. Students are also divided as to preference. Obviously much depends on the course content, the way the questions are asked in relation to the way the course is taught, the quality of the items, and the student's experience with the two types of tests. Actually neither is superior to the other; each has its relative advantages. The problem is to use each in the situations for which it is the more appropriate. Each type of item has its purpose, and there are certain aspects of the content of almost any course that lend themselves to the true-false test, others to the multiple-choice, and certain contents and certain objectives call for an essay test. It follows that the school's academic testing program almost of necessity must be varied in order to deal adequately with the different objectives, the different subject-matter contents, and the different psychological processes to be measured. It is probably safe to say that teachers who condemn objective tests as completely inappropriate for their purposes, for example, have not explored their possibilities too closely.

Advantages of objective tests

The major advantages of the objective test are wide sampling, the correspondingly greater likelihood of covering more of the course objectives, and as a result, a tendency toward greater validity and reliability in most situations. Relatively greater reliability also results from objectivity in scoring. Another advantage, ease of scoring, is of particular importance in large classes, where the extra work necessary to construct an objective test is more than compensated for by the saving in scoring time and effort. This is especially so when computer scoring facilities are available, but even a stencil used over separate answer sheets can save the teacher many tedious hours of scoring.[14]

The essay-type test also has its advantages; in fact, it measures certain objectives that are difficult to measure effectively in any other way, e.g., ability to organize and express ideas. Preparing for an essay examination also tends to

---

14. The computer also permits item analysis and hence progressive improvement of the test.

bring into play a higher level of learning, such as getting an overview of the material, organizing the data into meaningful structure, clarifying issues, etc., than its objective counterpart. It may even promote more as well as better learning since the learner has to recall rather than simply recognize the correct answer. The essay test can provide useful diagnostic information in that it reveals the processes used by the student to arrive at the answer.

On the other hand, it must be remembered that none of the various items has a monopoly on the quality and quantity of the mental processes it activates. Contrary to criticisms, for example, objective examinations can be made to measure precise forms of reasoning, interpretation of data, application of principles, etc.; probably the only thing objective examinations cannot do well is to measure the ability to write an essay. Ausubel (1968) rejects the idea that objective tests are superficial, based on guesswork, and that they promote rote memory. Whereas it is true that some objective test items are trivial or faulty, this is not necessarily true, nor is it usually true. In fact, a good objective item forces students to make critical distinctions among alternatives that they have not seen before, so that they cannot rely on rote memory, or at least are less likely to do so than in the case of the essay, where they can choose their own organization—sometimes directly from a rote memory bank. Furthermore, it is not true that objective test items cannot deal with the higher levels of the taxonomy (Kropp et al. 1966). The multiple choice, for example, seems particularly well suited for measuring crucial understandings, discriminations, and evaluations. In short, the choice between objective and subjective items is not based on their alleged structural strengths or weaknesses but rather on the concept of validity (and possibly reliability), i.e., on the purpose the test is to serve. With regard to most educational purposes, each is capable of doing essentially the same job with approximately the same degree of effectiveness (Bracht and Hopkins 1970).

Weakness of the essay   The weakness of the essay examination stems largely from limited sampling and from subjectivity and labor in scoring. Because it requires the writing of many words in order to bring out an idea, the essay is very wasteful of the testing period (courses calling for ability to organize and express ideas excepted), so that only a small segment of the course content can be covered in a one- or two-hour test. Hence it has limited reliability and, in some cases, limited validity, especially since penmanship, verbal fluency, ability to make shrewd guesses as to what will be included in the test, ability to bluff, etc., occasionally play an important part in getting a good score.

For over a half-century, educators have been concerned over the fact that not only is an instructor unable to agree with other graders on the quality of a given essay but is not even likely to agree with himself or herself in rescoring the same paper. In a well-known study years ago, Starch and Elliott (1913) found the grades given a geometry paper by different raters to range from 28 percent to 92 percent. A similar inconsistency in grading is noted in the results of a study by Arny (1953), in which twelve raters grading seven papers disagreed by a minimum of 18 percentage points on one paper to a maximum of 61 points on another. Similar inconsistency in grading is noted in the results of a more recent study in which fifty-three judges graded three hundred essays in college English on a scale from 1 to 9; one-third of the essays received grades ranging the full scale from 1 to 9; 60 percent received 7 or 8 of the 9 possible grades; and no essay received fewer than five different grades (ETS 1961).[15]

The essay examination can be frustrating to both rater and student. It often takes great concentration on the part of the teacher to decipher meaning out of the student's clumsy expression, and it takes infinite wisdom and patience to decide whether he or she is awkward or trying to cover a lack of knowledge. Students often do not know what the instructor is after and how deeply they are to go into the question. The essay test has a number of limitations, some of which are inherent in this type of test. It may even be that the strengths of the essay have been overstated. Many of the examples of critical reasoning the essay is said to promote represent nothing more than parroting from memory the reasoning that has been covered in class. Other weaknesses stem from misuse; many can be minimized by asking clear-cut questions[16] and by devising a system for scoring papers more objectively.

CONSTRUCTION OF TESTS

Space limitations do not permit adequate treatment of techniques of test construction; this discussion is therefore simply for purposes of orientation, and students are referred to the many books on educational tests and measurements for a more thorough coverage.[17] The following suggestions might be given:

1. Sample widely and use a variety of test items; different objectives and different contents call for different testing methods.
2. Keep the difficulty level of the items such that the average student will obtain a raw score approximately 50 percent of the maximum.
3. Make essay questions sufficiently restricted that students can organize their ideas on the subject.

15. More critical (since it relates to validity) is the fact that teachers do not recognize good writing (*Phi Delta Kappan* 1977). Apparently, two-thirds of the teachers assigned a better grade to a complex, wordy essay than to a more concise and brisk version.

16. Teachers sometimes ask questions of the variety of, "Discuss the implications of the Treaty of Versailles." (Why not "Describe the universe and give two examples?") On the other hand, making questions too narrow and specific defeats the very purpose for which essay questions should be used in preference to objective items. "List three characteristics of a good measuring instrument" is not an effective essay item, so that, in a sense, the essay is weakest in the very purpose for which it is supposed to exist.

17. Stated bluntly, if all the reader knows about testing is what is covered in this chapter, he or she does not know enough to be effective in this important area of teaching.

4. Make the questions clear. Avoid trick or controversial questions and avoid giving clues to the answers; and more important,

5. Do not graduate without taking a course in educational tests and measurements.

Probably the most helpful advice that might be given beginning teachers on this subject is for them to organize a file of evaluative material. Keeping such a file of test questions on 3 x 5 or IBM cards will make good testing possible without an undue expenditure of time and effort. Only one item should be put on a card, which can then be coded as to chapter, topic, objective, and level of the taxonomy, together with difficulty and discrimination indexes obtained when the item is used.

Good testing calls for a multiple approach. Each type of test has its particular merits, and it is up to teachers to make effective use of the many testing procedures at their disposal. As situations vary, testing procedures should also vary. In general, the most meaningful way of evaluating learning is to ask students to apply what they have learned to a somewhat different situation, preferably one in real life, but this is not always easy or even possible. Discussion, student reports, and question-and-answer procedures are often effective means of appraising student progress. Such techniques incorporate immediate reinforcement, corrective feedback, and clarification of issues under conditions of high motivation. However, they are ineffective and impractical in a large class, for example. In short, the test must be tailor-made to the particular situation for which it is intended.

INTERPRETATION OF THE RESULTS OF TESTING

Measurement and Evaluation

A testing program involves two interrelated processes: *measurement* and *evaluation*. So far we have considered the first; namely, the construction of a good test from which to derive a valid and reliable score. The more important and, in many ways, the more difficult question of interpreting this score now lies ahead. A score has no meaning in itself; it takes on meaning only as it is interpreted in the light of such other factors as the objectives of the particular course, the caliber of the student, and the nature of the test on which it is based. Thus, sixty items right out of one hundred may represent adequate or inadequate performance, depending on the difficulty of the test.

Implied in the distinction between measurement and evaluation is the fact that performance is not to be interpreted in relation to an absolute standard of perfection but rather in terms of a realistic standard of what level of performance it is reasonable to expect. This is a matter of subjective judgment; as we evaluate a student's performance, we may feel that it leaves much to be desired but that it is satisfactory considering the particular circumstances involved.

The Number System

To interpret the results of testing, we need to be familiar with the nature of the number system underlying measurement. Numerical series can be either *ordinal* (first, second, third), or *cardinal* (1, 2, 3). Cardinal series, in turn, can be on either a *ratio* scale or an *interval* scale, depending on the nature of the zero point. A ratio scale is one that starts from a true zero, e.g., distance or time; an interval scale starts from an arbitrary zero point other than the true zero, e.g., temperature on the Fahrenheit scale. Both then proceed in equal units, e.g., feet, minutes, or degrees of temperature.

The distinction is fundamental to an understanding of educational measurements. In contrast to measurements on a ratio scale, where we can say that John weighs twice as much as Mary, measurements on an interval scale only permit us to refer to "more than" or "less than"; we cannot say that today with a temperature of 40° is twice as hot as it was yesterday with 20°. Except for typing and certain skills in physical education, nearly all of the measurements with which teachers come into contact are on an interval scale. Thus, a score of zero on a test does not mean complete lack of knowledge of the subject but simply zero performance on the test material, the difficulty of which may be well above true zero. A child may miss every word on a spelling test and still be able to spell many words not included in the test. Since the teacher has many choices as to which words to include in a test, it is possible for a student with a given spelling ability to get 95 percent of the words on an "easy" test, only 50 percent on an "average" test, and practically zero if the teacher selected only difficult words. This situation, shown graphically in figure 13.1, demonstrates the fallacy of the common percentage scale in grading student performance; percentage of maximum is completely meaningless apart from the level of difficulty of the questions and the severity of the scoring.

Raw versus Derived Scores

For a student to obtain, say, a score of sixty out of a maximum of one hundred on a spelling test means nothing more than that he or she has a spelling ability greater than zero. Since scores in spelling are based on an interval scale, the only thing that can make them meaningful is to convert them into a *derived* score that relates one student's performance to that of other students who have taken the test.[18] If John's performance, for example, puts him at the twentieth

18. On a criterion-referenced (CRT) basis, we can, of course, say the student knows how to spell eighty-five words of the one hundred presumably selected from the authorized list.

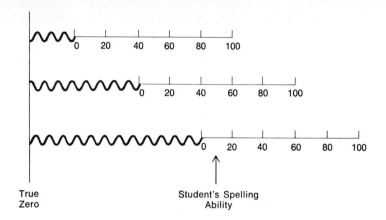

Figure 13.1 Different Numerical Measures of the Same Ability on Three Different Interval Scales

percentile of his class (i.e., his score is exceeded or equaled by 80 percent of the group of which he is a member), we can picture his performance as relatively poor. This is more meaningful than saying he has a raw score of 60 on a test of unknown difficulty, which could represent, for all one knows, the highest or the lowest score on record.

Unfortunately, this can create a problem for children from the lower classes who, as a group, are typically below test norms, which in turn raises the question of the appropriateness of standards often set on a predominantly middle-class population when applied to the disadvantaged. On the one hand, it is clear that any set of norms is valid only to the extent that the background of children being examined is comparable to that of the norm population. But then what constitutes a relevant norm population depends on the purpose for which the results are to be used. There may not be much point in knowing how well a disadvantaged teenager compares with other disadvantaged students if the competition for a job or a scholarship is to be met on the open market.

We also need to remember that the child's final status is not necessarily the answer we are looking for. For certain purposes, the final status would be a meaningful answer, but then we have to recognize that the high-quality output of certain schools is simply a reflection of the caliber of its incoming student population. In the case of the lower-class child, we may well want to consider progress rather than simple status. We may also want to relate pupil progress to ability level.[19]

19. We must recognize that reporting progress relative to ability is notoriously unreliable, even when based on standardized test data, in that it compounds the inaccuracies inherent in both the measures of achievement and of ability.

CRITERION-REFERENCED VERSUS NORM-REFERENCED TESTING

Most testing in our schools to date has been *norm-referenced*, i.e., it has evaluated the performance of a student or a class against that of a relevant norm (comparison) group. It has compared, for example, the performance of one child against that of the other children in the class but it has not indicated how well any of them did with respect to the attainment of instructional objectives. In the past decade or two, we have seen a movement toward *criterion-ref-*

13.1 NATIONAL ASSESSMENT OF EDUCATIONAL PROGRESS (NAEP)

The Number One project in connection with criterion-referenced testing, and obviously a project of national importance, is National Assessment of Educational Progress (NAEP), which involves the continuous study of educational status within the United States through samples of test questions administered to samples of four age groups within the population (Mehrens 1969). The project covers ten basic areas—reading, mathematics, science, music, art, citizenship, literature, social studies, writing, and vocational education—through a series of specially prepared criterion-referenced tests. These are being administered one-third each year (beginning in March 1969) on a three-year cycle to representative groups of some 32,000 children in each of ages nine, thirteen, and seventeen, and 20,000 young adults, with any one participant taking only one forty-five-minute package of a twelve-package battery.

The results, published yearly, have provided interesting information concerning the educational status of American youth. For example, more than one-third of both thirteen- and seventeen-year-olds thought that members of Congress are appointed by the president. Furthermore, nearly one-third of both groups indicated they had no interest in learning more about the government (Phi Delta Kappan 1977). More than half of the seventeen-year-olds and the young adults were unable to handle fractions and decimals as necessary to determine the most economical size of a product to buy (Phi Delta Kappan, 1975). Two especially disturbing points are that girls consistently underperform boys, even in reading and literature, and scores have been declining (*U.S. News & World Report,* 1975a, 1975b).*

JOHNSON, S. S.   *Update on Education: A Digest of National Assessment of Educational Progress.* Denver: Educational Commission of the States, 1975.
   * Another problem for the schools. *U.S. News and World Report.* June 9, 1975, p. 43, Also October 20, 1975, p. 54.

erenced testing (CRT), in which performance is evaluated with respect to preestablished standards of acceptable performance relative to, say, behaviorally stated objectives, e.g., "Can the student multiply two-digit numbers by two-digit numbers?" Nothing is said as to how a given student compares with the other members of the class or how the class compares against, say, regional or national standards.

The relative merits of NRT and CRT have been widely debated, and the reader is urged to consult sources more pertinent to the problem. It is argued, for example, that to say that a given student heads the class on an NRT basis does not tell us very much as to what he or she really knows. From an instructional point of view, it may be more meaningful for the teacher to know whether he or she can convert fractions into decimals and decimals into fractions. But it would also be helpful to know, say, that only 10 percent of children of the same age and grade can make such conversions or, on the contrary, that nationally such skills are generally achieved a full grade earlier (see Hambleton et al. 1978).

Advantages of
criterion-referenced
tests

Criterion-referenced testing has obvious advantages from the point of motivation relative to clear-cut objectives: the student knows exactly what he or she is to achieve. It follows that CRT is particularly adaptable to individualized study. With properly arranged materials students can proceed at their own pace toward the attainment of the prescribed objectives. CRT is often recommended as a way of reducing the failure element connected with NRT, in which each student's "success" is based on someone else's "failure." Informal classroom testing geared to internal norms simply pits every child against every other child; the only way to succeed is to surpass others, so that a child's grade is determined as much by the performance of the class as by his or her own efforts. Slower children invariably find themselves at the bottom no matter how much they work, so they get discouraged and stop trying. By contrast, CRT tends to soften failure (most children master each unit eventually). But it does not totally eliminate either failure or interstudent comparisons. Slower students, having to recycle repeatedly as they fail to meet the required standards on first trial, find themselves getting progressively further behind their brighter peers, who go through the sequence in such a hurry that they have considerable time to engage in interesting activities. CRT can also create king-sized administrative headaches as students of different ability, different background, different motivation, and different degrees of responsibility scatter progressively further apart. (See Davis and Diamond 1971.)

Setting standards: A
precarious
undertaking

Criterion-referenced testing is often used in the context of accountability (see chapter 2), with the teacher expected to set and to have the class meet definite standards, typically stated in behavioral terms—"Eighty percent of the students in the grade will achieve 80 percent proficiency in converting decimals to fractions and fractions to decimals." On the other hand, setting such "absolute" standards is a precarious proposition. How realistic is it to expect 80 percent of a class of ghetto children to achieve 80 percent proficiency in the task above? Who is to set the standards and on what basis (besides general experience and intuition)? (See Meskauskas 1976.) There are obvious dangers in setting standards too low or too high, thereby building in cheap success or inevitable failure. If the standards are set too low, many students are not challenged; not only do they get to see education as "Mickey Mouse," but they also accumulate deficiencies that interfere with later learnings. If the standards are set too high, students give up, teachers then begin to push, and everybody gets frustrated.

Differences between NRT and CRT

CRT and NRT are based on different operational principles and serve essentially different (although related) purposes. In CRT, the task is to get everyone up to standards, i.e., to recycle students as necessary to have everyone reach essentially the same high level of proficiency. The net result is presumably (eventual) homogeneity in performance. NRT, on the contrary, attempts to accentuate differences in performance among students by including in the test only those items that discriminate among students of presumably different caliber.[20] CRT is probably better geared to an instructional sequence designed to have every student achieve key objectives; it would seem more appropriate in a sequential subject where mastery of key objectives is essential for continued progress. It would be especially appropriate in dealing with minimal essentials in a fixed and closed domain, e.g., the driver's test. Here the performance of others is essentially irrelevant.[21] NRT, on the other hand, would seem most effective for measuring progress toward higher-level learning outcomes where development is open-ended and essentially unlimited, e.g., the higher levels of the taxonomy. Operationally we might see NRT in the context of traditional *testing*, e.g., major quizzes, end-of-semester examinations, etc., and CRT in the context of *teaching*, e.g., end-of-lesson or end-of-unit self-study or competency questions as part of an instructional module.[22] It might also be noted that CRT is relatively nonfunctional in the case of high-ability students, for whom the typical CRT represents too low a level of mastery. NRT, on the other hand, tends to leave the poorer students out since most of the questions incorporated in the test have been deliberately selected to be somewhat above their operational level. In fact, NRT may be of limited value to both slow and bright students since discrimination indexes tend to favor items of 50 percent difficulty, leading to the elimination of both easy and hard items.

20. It might be noted in passing that CRT is not particularly amenable to the calculation of validity, reliability, discrimination, and other indexes of classical tests and measurements theory. See Carver's distinction between *edumetric* and *psychometric* (Carver 1974).

21. CRT is best seen in the context of the quality control of an instructional unit where it provides rather definitive evidence of what objectives have been met and what materials need recycling before proceeding to the next unit.

22. A possibility might be to award a grade of C for meeting CRT standards as a minimal requirement and to use norm-referenced tests as the basis for giving Bs and As.

GRADING

Rationale

The grading period is rough on teachers and pupils alike. Many teachers are not too sure of the purpose that pinning a grade on the students' achievement is to serve in the school's function of promoting their all-around growth. To many conscientious teachers, grading has the flavor of a postmortem—in some cases, of retaliation for what is past. Except for the gifted and those who have ceased to care, students also eye the grading period with considerable discomfort.

The obvious question is why grade at all? And it must be made clear that accepting the necessity for evaluation does not mean that evaluation has to eventuate in a grade. All that a grade can do is to provide a synthesis of the various aspects of the evaluation. Thus a good grasp of computational skills, a limited understanding of problem solving, and a relative weakness in the use of formulas might be synthesized into a D. Whether this synthesis is desirable depends on one's purpose.

Examinations seem designed to satisfy the needs of the teacher rather than those of the student. Whereas examinations should have primarily an educational function, their administrative purposes often take precedence to

---

13.2 GRADING: A RATIONALE

When grading is considered from the standpoint of purpose, a distinction can be made between what might be called the *public school* and the *professional school* philosophy. In a professional school, e.g., medicine, grades serve to protect society from professional incompetence. In teacher training, the college sets certain standards of attainment and, for the protection of the children who might be harmed by having an incompetent teacher, fails any prospective teacher unable to meet these standards. Here grades serve as a screening device, and the welfare of society takes precedence over that of the individual aspiring to professional status. In the public school, on the other hand, the primary purpose of measurement and evaluation is to determine the student's status as a prerequisite for planning his or her further growth. Presumably then, a student would be failed only when the teacher is convinced that his or her growth can be promoted more effectively in the present grade than in the next. The teacher who gives a child a low grade on an assignment would likewise have to be reasonably sure that this is the best way of promoting the student's subsequent growth. To deny this would imply that the school is operating at cross-purposes.

the point that grading is essentially a judgmental proposition, with the outcomes a question of pupil success or failure, promotion or retention, classification into grade level, recommendation for college, etc., all according to adult specifications often applied on a wholesale basis. The overall testing program typically is used as the basis for passing judgment on the child rather than on the school's program and its failure to reach its clients. As a result, children learn to fear and to worry about examinations rather than to use them as means of appraising their adequacy and guiding their further growth.

Objections to Grading

Grading is not without danger. When misused, it can easily negate all the school is trying to accomplish through sound teaching and evaluation. Even though, when used wisely, grades are essential to the effectiveness of the school's operation, some people feel that it is a pity that they are so thoroughly entrenched and taken so seriously (see Deutsch 1979 for a discussion of the issues).

From a psychological point of view, the following objections can be raised with some degree of validity against most of the testing done in our schools:

1. Grades are inadequate indicators of the child's total development, and a single letter grade or even two cannot possibly cover all aspects of child growth the school is trying to promote in any one subject area. Some schools give separate grades for citizenship but probably most

teachers, consciously or unconsciously, include as part of the academic grade such things as effort, docility, and attitudes, along with a number of academic considerations.

Grades as motivators

2. Grades exert a strong influence in raising the child's motivational level. This can be desirable for some students, but, for others, grades have detrimental effects ranging from psychosomatic disorders to feelings of resentment, hostility, frustration, and discouragement. Melby (1966) argues that grades are destructive of the self-concept of millions of children, particularly those of the lower class. Children we should be sending home with a greater confidence and pride in themselves end up disappointed in their performance and in themselves. There are more positive and less dangerous means of motivating children.

3. Grades often become ends in themselves so that learning is cast into a secondary role of vehicle toward a grade. Grades represent a sort of academic currency to be exchanged for a diploma, a symbol of academic respectability valued for its own sake, which often detracts from the real purposes of education. Grades tend to orient education toward whatever is emphasized on the test, often at the expense of what would have greater functionality in the lives of students. They sometimes encourage cramming, cheating, and catering to the personal views of the teacher. Often the result is mediocrity on the part of students who are capable of much more, while slower students are discouraged and antagonized by this continuous exposure to, and recording of, their inevitable failure.

4. Teachers often find that giving the student a low grade destroys the student-teacher relationship they have been trying to cultivate. Rather than blame themselves for a low grade, many children project the blame onto the teacher—and, parenthetically, there is enough invalidity and unreliability in the average test to make this entirely plausible to students who need to protect their self-image.

5. A more common criticism of grades is their undependability from the standpoint of validity and unreliability. Students often get lower grades than they deserve because of undue difficulty in the examination or in the grading. Some teachers pride themselves on being tough and proceed to appoint themselves as watchdogs of academic standards. The unfortunate students who are assigned to these teachers are automatically deprived of the recognition for academic performance supposedly available to all and they get to feel, "What's the use?" so that performance goes down, not up. In the meantime, students are being penalized not for lack of effort but simply for the poor choice of an instructor. There ought to be more constructive ways of maintaining standards, and teachers who year after year turn in grades lower than those of their colleagues only show themselves as poor teachers or misguided reformists whose objectives are not in line with reality.

Dangers of easy grading

Easy grading is no better. What does it tell students about teachers, the school, and society, to have their paper given a superior grade when they know it was just "slapped together" in a hurry? What does it do to the values of the student who has devoted thought and effort to the assignment only to have a classmate's sloppy paper also be given a superior grade? Easy graders are simply cowards who let other teachers carry the burden of advising students of their weaknesses, who, rather than helping them to grow, allow them to accumulate deficiencies, bad working habits, sloppy attitudes, and continued immaturity. Students can recognize a free grade. It simply gives them the false idea that the school is a place to goof off; that nobody takes education seriously. It also makes clear that teachers have no pride in their work and that of their students and that there is no reason why students should, either.[23] Whereas each teacher is bound to have a somewhat different point of reference in assigning grades, the school should agree on a common grading policy consistent with its philosophy, its student body, and its faculty, and there should be a reasonable uniformity in the grading standards of the different teachers.

Grades can be discouraging

Perhaps a more fundamental objection to grades awarded on a comparative basis is that high-ability students can get a high grade without really trying, while their low-ability counterparts get low grades, and there is really nothing they can do about it except to minimize the blow by ceasing to care (or pretending not to care). Even above-average students who want desperately to get As find themselves disappointed and discouraged by the ever-recurring B that they too stop trying. If they are to maintain a positive self-concept and continued involvement in school work, students must achieve reasonable success on a relatively continuous basis. This may mean that some children will need extra assistance so that they can succeed at least occasionally and develop confidence in their ability. We must especially provide educational opportunities for children of different patterns of ability, learning style, and interest. One rather effective way of dealing with individual differences, for example, is to have the student negotiate with the teacher a contract specifying just what he or she will do to earn what grade.

No better alternative

The problem with grades is that no clearly better substitute has been found. A teacher returning a student's paper should elaborate on the grade by listing specific strengths and specific ways in which the paper could have been improved, but that need not replace the grade as an index of the overall quality of the assignment. Ebel (1964) presents a strong defense of grades. He first questions the logic of those who claim that learning proceeds best in the absence of a systematic monitoring of achievement; he sees something patently

---

23. A low grade is not necessarily as traumatic for some students as we might suppose, especially when the student knows he or she put no effort into it. Students tend to be realistic about course requirements, both absolute and in relation to their peers. Most students can accept a C without damage and learn from the experience—provided we have not made grades into an infallible index of personal worth.

absurd in the claim that greatest progress is made when no attention is paid to progress. Surely incidental, unsystematic, off-the-cuff procedures cannot in the long run provide more useful information than can a carefully planned, purposeful, painstaking appraisal. Ebel recognizes that the academic program of certain schools offers nothing but a high probability of failure for some students, but what needs to be changed here is the school's program, not the grading. The grade does not create the failure, and the failure will still be there whether we report it or not. He also challenges the claim that a mark cannot be a satisfactory means of reporting the student's level of achievement. It does not tell the whole story, but it provides an excellent starting point. In summary, it would seem that to disparage grades is as wrong as it is to overemphasize grades. We need to eliminate abuse, but eliminating grades is something else again. Improving the quality of the program might be a more logical starting point.

Converting Performance into Grades

The form in which grades are given is perhaps not of major consequence. Yet in view of the strong conviction sometimes encountered relative to the percentage method or "grading on the curve," a word of discussion might be in order. We know whether performance is creditable only by comparing it to that of others. This is particularly true when dealing with scores on an interval scale, which can tell us only that one performance is better or worse than another. But even on a ratio scale, e.g., typing speed, we agree that 80 words per minute is "good" only because we know that few typists type at that rate. To illustrate the point, how would you rate the performance of the thoroughbred that supposedly galloped the mile in two minutes flat?

Converting a student's performance into a grade has to be arbitrary. Preset limits, such as 93–100 = A, are essentially meaningless. The only reason the percentage method works at all is that the teacher can set the severity of the scoring in inverse proportion to the difficulty of the questions so that approximately the "right" number of students get As, Bs, and Cs. Years ago, it took only 50 percent to pass; then the minimum passing mark was raised to 60 percent and then to 70 percent, but the same number of As, Bs, and Cs is given now as before. Teachers simply make whatever adjustment is necessary to have the "proper" percentage of students in each grade interval. On an essay test, the answer to a given question might be worth (by objective standards) no more than perhaps thirteen of the twenty points assigned to the question, but the teacher, realizing that no one is perfect and that this is the best answer he or she is likely to get, scores it eighteen or nineteen; otherwise no one would get 93 percent of the maximum required to get an A. In objective tests, the teacher focuses on limited objectives and emphasizes facts that have been drilled over and over, e.g., "List three types of sedimentary rocks," "Who was president before Mr. Truman?" And so examinations stifle education!

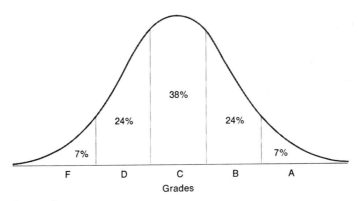

Figure 13.2 Theoretical Distribution of Grades for an Unselected Group

Grading on the curve

Grading on the curve follows directly from the previous discussion. Whenever grading is based on an interval scale, there can be no grading other than grading "on the curve" (although not necessarily on the *normal* curve).[24] Grading on the curve is based on the readily acceptable proposition that if education is to be a matter of helping students make the most of their ability, the distribution of performance on an appropriate evaluative instrument must approximate the distribution of ability among the group members. In an unselected group, the distribution of the factors involved in learning, such as intelligence and motivation, tends to follow the normal curve, and it seems logical, therefore, to expect the distribution of performance also to be relatively normal.

From this distribution of performance, the teacher has to select cutoff scores so as to derive letter grades. This process is entirely and unavoidably arbitrary. Thus, some educators suggest *as a rough guide* for dealing with unselected groups, the percentages of As, Bs, . . . shown in figure 13.2.

Grading on the curve does not imply that a set percentage of the class must fail or that there must be no more and no less than 7 percent As. Depending on its philosophy, a school might set other percentages as points of departure for its teachers in their grading, and certainly a teacher need not give a single F unless some student's performance is so much below acceptable levels as to warrant being labeled unsatisfactory—whatever the basis used in establishing what is to be considered "unsatisfactory." It also follows that with

24. Even in CRT, "typical" performance must be taken into account. The setting of "absolute" standards is necessarily a relative matter, e.g., "80 percent of the class will achieve 80 percent accuracy as measured by items of unknown difficulty." Even passing a driver's test is necessarily geared to a whole range of item difficulty on the written test and a whole range of expertise on the road test from that of the novice to that of the parking lot attendant who can back a car into a parking spot with only inches to spare. Converting the performance to a criterion-referenced pass-fail does not change its nature as a norm-referenced skill; some people can simply drive better than others, and this can be represented as an absolute only if we make an artificial dichotomy out of what is undeniably a continuum.

the proportionally greater incidence of academic mortality among the less able in, say, the sophomore and junior years in college, the distribution of ability gets weighted more heavily toward high ability, and the distribution of grades ought to be correspondingly weighted toward a greater concentration of As and Bs. It must also be noted that there is nothing in the concept of grading on the curve that says a teacher cannot adjust the grade of students whose performance, although below class average, is nevertheless in line with their limited ability.

S-U, pass-fail grading

The point is sometimes made that, in view of the undependability of marks, the only grades we should assign are S for satisfactory and U for unsatisfactory. Actually this solves nothing. When accompanied by verbal or written comments, it may be a way of minimizing the emphasis sometimes placed on grades, but from a tests-and-measurements point of view, it is a step in the wrong direction. Admittedly, marks are subject to error, but lumping all of the As, Bs, Cs, and Ds into a single "pass" category magnifies the distinction between Ds and the Fs, a distinction that is still subject to the same error as ever. As a result, teachers using the S-U system generally give everyone an S, which is equivalent to grading no one. The present letter-grade system is not a particularly effective means of communicating with students and parents, but the S-U system, by itself, is almost completely devoid of meaning. If teachers want to report to students and parents only in cases of unsatisfactory progress, it would be easier to say it that way.

Somewhat the same arguments can be made with regard to the pass-fail option in college, which can serve a number of very legitimate purposes, e.g., allowing students to sample a new field for which they do not have the prerequisites. It is also possible that certain students, relieved of the anxiety of failure, can devote their energies to what they want to get out of the course. Freedom from threat of failure may also increase enjoyment of learning (Reid 1971). Pass-fail may work out well in courses with a certain appeal, assuming that students can be induced to make the initial investment. On the other hand, it is frequently tied to nonattendance at class, particularly in peripheral course, and generally is an easy and quick way of getting a degree, which too frequently seems to be more important to students than learning anything in particular. Perhaps the best that can be said is that there are many questions yet to be answered (see Stallings et al. 1968).[25] The fact that it seems rather susceptible to abuse should not blind us to its potential merits for conscientious students.

25. A major deterrent to the use of the S-U grading system is that many graduate and professional schools give preference (other things being equal) to applicants whose transcripts are free from S-U grades. See Rossman, 1970, for example.

HIGHLIGHTS OF THE CHAPTER

Teachers must develop in the important area of testing the same expertise as they display in other aspects of teaching. This implies a good understanding of the following concepts:

1. Measurement and evaluation are integral parts of the total teaching-learning process. They provide essential information as the basis for promoting student growth.
2. The testing program is of major benefit to the student, the teacher, and the administrator. Too often, the administrative functions take precedence over its academic purposes.
3. Sound evaluation begins with sound measurement derived through valid and reliable instruments, but it goes beyond measurement in that it appraises the results of measurement in the light of the goals of education, the objectives of the course, and the particular circumstances involved.
4. An academic test is valid when it is relatively free from factors that are extraneous to the objectives of the course.
5. A test should also be reliable. The essay examination is notoriously low in reliability.
6. Grading is a matter of synthesizing the evaluation of the various aspects of the student's performance into a single symbol.
7. Considerable criticism, of varying degrees of validity, has been aimed at grading and its abuses. Teachers need to recognize that grading can negate many of the more important things they are trying to do.

SUGGESTIONS FOR FURTHER READING

BLOOM, BENJAMIN S., et al. *Handbook of Formative and Summative Evaluation of Student Learning.* New York: McGraw-Hill, 1971. Encyclopedic coverage of evaluation of learning at both the formative and summative level. Presents a comprehensive list of objectives for different subject areas.

BROMLEY, DAVID G., et al. Grade inflation: Trends, causes, and implications. *Phi Delta Kappan* 59 (1978):694–697. Provides evidence of grade inflation in higher education over the past fifteen years. Suggests that inflation may be leveling off and that a small deflation might even be expected in the immediate future.

GALL, MEREDITH D. The use of questions in teaching. *Rev. Educ. Res.* 40 (1970):707–721. About 60 percent of the teacher's classroom questions require students simply to recall. Only 20 percent require them to think.

SANDERS, NORRIS M. *Classroom Questions: What Kinds?* New York: Harper & Row, 1966. Argues for questions that require students to think rather than simply regurgitate information. Gives numerous examples of questions at different levels of the taxonomy.

SAYLOR, GALEN. National Assessment: Pro and Con. *T. C. Rec.* 71 (1970):588–597. Discusses the history, operation, and potential uses of national assessment. Also points to potential dangers.

WESMAN, ALEXANDER G. Writing the test item. In Robert L. Thorndike, ed., *Educational Measurement.* Washington, D.C.: Amer. Council on Educ., 1971. Probably the most comprehensive discussion of how to write test items and the errors to avoid.

QUESTIONS AND PROJECTS

1. As a class project, develop a test to cover the content of the present course. Be sure to devise clear-cut objectives.

2. Evaluate the pass-fail system as a grading strategy at the college level. Specifically, what does it accomplish? What are the drawbacks?

3. Evaluate the general caliber of the tests you have taken in your recent college courses. What might be done to improve college testing and grading practices?

4. React to this statement: Bright children who do not apply themselves should not be given a top grade even if their performance is superior.

5. Consult Buros, *Mental Measurement Yearbooks,* for an orientation to the instruments suitable for the grade level you are preparing to teach.

SELF-TEST

1. The greatest danger from the misuse of academic tests is that
   a. they create anxiety.
   b. they discourage students from doing their best.
   c. they lead to the neglect of other important aspects of education.
   d. they serve to separate the sheep from the goats.
   e. they supersede the true objectives of education.

2. Probably the most important single benefit of the academic testing program to children accrues from
   a. appraising their progress so as to plan their further growth.
   b. consolidating their learning.
   c. identifying areas of difficulty that could become cumulative.
   d. motivating them to greater (or continued) effort.
   e. satisfying their need for competition as the basis for realistic self-identification.

3. What to include in a given course examination if it is to be valid is primarily a function of
   a. the accuracy with which the various components can be measured.
   b. the emphasis given in class to the various components of the course.
   c. the instructor's judgment as to what is important and measurable.
   d. the objectives of the particular course.
   e. the contents incorporated in the basic text.

4. The most important criterion of a good test is
   a. its difficulty.
   b. its discrimination.
   c. its reliability.
   d. its usability.
   e. its validity.

5. The more reliable a test is,
   a. the greater its predictive accuracy.
   b. the greater its validity.
   c. the greater the homogeneity of the scores it provides.
   d. the more difficult it is to "fake."
   e. the smaller the chance fluctuations in the repeated testing of given individuals.

6. The primary point of distinction between a standardized and a teacher-made test is
   a. the availability of norms.
   b. its commercial availability.
   c. its relative overall quality.
   d. its relative validity.
   e. the standardization of administration procedures.

7. The greatest objection to grades in the public school is that
   a. they can be misleading indicators of pupil growth.
   b. they can create anxieties that interfere with effective learning.
   c. they sometimes distort the school's overall goals.
   d. they sometimes interfere with the development of a healthy self-concept.
   e. they can interfere with the development of effective teaching procedures.

PART FOUR

Children and Their Adjustment

Deals with the development of positive attitudes and values and of effective personality patterns that will enable children to live in wholesome and constructive interaction with their environment. The contributions of Piaget, Kohlberg, Erikson, and others are reviewed.

14 Attitudes and Character Development

Discusses the importance of attitudes and values as determinants of personal and social adequacy; gives special consideration to indoctrination and some of the current theories of character development.

15 Personal and Social Adjustment

Presents personality development within the context of learning theory, need satisfaction, child-rearing practices, etc.; discusses various coping mechanisms and spells out the role of the teacher in promoting pupil adjustment.

16 Mental Health in the Classroom

Introduces mental health as an integral part of the teaching-learning process and emphasizes the mental health implications of certain classroom practices; covers the role of teachers in promoting the mental health of their pupils and in safeguarding their own.

FOURTEEN

Attitudes and Character Development

Our censure should be reserved for those who close all doors but one. The surest way to lose truth is to pretend that one already wholly possesses it.

Gordon W. Allport (1955)

The teacher is constantly and unavoidably moralizing to children about rules and values and about his students' behavior toward each other. Since such moralizing is unavoidable, it seems logical that it be done in terms of consciously formulated goals of moral development.

Lawrence Kohlberg (1966)

— Discusses the importance of attitudes as determinants of personal and social functioning.

— Emphasizes the role of the home and the school in the development of positive attitudes, values, and character patterns; gives special consideration to indoctrination

— Presents Piaget's theory of moral judgment and its extension by Kohlberg; also that of Peck and Havighurst

PREVIEW: KEY CONCEPTS

1. Attitudes underlie all phases of human behavior. Operationally, they involve an affective, a cognitive, and a behavioral component.
2. Attitudes develop through the same psychological processes as other forms of learning, e.g., conditioning, modeling, deliberate cultivation, etc.
3. Although the school has an important responsibility in seeing that children develop positive attitudes toward the dominant values of our society, fear of indoctrination has made its efforts ambivalent and essentially ineffective.
4. Attitudes constitute such a critical component of personality structure that they are extremely resistant to change.
5. Piaget's theory of moral judgment and its extension by Kohlberg see moral judgment as an aspect of cognitive development.
6. The primary responsibility for moral education lies with the home, with the school assuming a secondary but nevertheless essential role. Unfortunately the task does not lend itself to obvious instructional prescriptions.

PREVIEW QUESTIONS

1. What priorities should the school assign to the development of attitudes and values as an educational goal?

    How can the affective domain of the taxonomy be operationalized and monitored?
2. To what extent is indoctrination a violation of democratic principles?

    How is this to be reconciled with society's right to continued existence?
3. What is the meaning of conscience?

    How can society mobilize parents, teachers, and other social agencies in the development of the child's conscience?
4. What is the relationship among values, morality, conscience, and character?

    Why can we not equate character with conformity to social mores and values?

    How can we all contribute to the child's growth toward the higher levels of character development?

Educators are becoming increasingly aware of the crucial role of attitudes in the overall educational enterprise. They recognize, for example, that the attitudes that develop as by-products of the academic program are often of much greater significance than the academic content per se from the standpoint not only of the learner's continued academic progress but also his or her long-term welfare and that of society. This is an area that the school has neglected in recent years, primarily because of the many complicated philosophical and operational problems it presents.

THE NATURE OF ATTITUDES

Attitudes may be thought of as learned patterns of behavior that predispose the individual to act in a specific way toward certain persons, objects, or ideas. Actually attitudes constitute a highly complex system of variables, and any attempt to analyze their nature or operation is likely to be an oversimplification. They are best approached from the standpoint of the individual's motivational structure as presented in chapter 4. More specifically, attitudes can be considered from the standpoint of their three basic components:

1. Affective: A certain feeling tone, sometimes quite irrational, that influences the acceptance or rejection of the attitude-object.
2. Cognitive: Consisting of the intellectualized aspects of one's views regarding the attitude-object.
3. Behavioral: Predisposing the individual toward specific overt action.

These components exist at various levels of intensity and in various degrees of independence of one another. A person may have a rather clear cognitive view of a given issue but have no great feeling about it and have no inclination to take any action concerning its promotion, while another may die for his or her country, for example, without knowing quite what is at stake. On the other hand, attitudes with a strong affective content generally lead to some form of overt action—whether they are correct or incorrect, and whether they are clear or unclear from a cognitive point of view.

Attitudes differ from ideals

Attitudes tend to be definite and specific from the standpoint of the object to which they are attached. They differ from *ideals*, which tend to be more generalized and abstract. Thus tolerance toward a given minority group is an attitude, whereas tolerance as an abstraction is an ideal. Both attitudes and ideals imply generalizations, and individuals who are limited in their ability to generalize, e.g., persons of limited mental ability, may have to rely on habits that are more restricted and hence influence a smaller segment of their lives.

. . . and from values

Attitudes can be differentiated from values in that the latter have reference to social and moral worth; they are also more stable, more general, and, of course, of greater social significance.

Attitudes permeate our very existence. The self-concept, for example, is best viewed as the complex system of attitudes and values people have developed concerning themselves in relation to the external world with which they have psychological contact. Children who see themselves as honest have favorable attitudes toward the class of experiences involving honest behavior; the adolescent who considers himself a "tough," on the contrary, has negative attitudes toward social and moral codes, law enforcement, and other social values. Once incorporated into the self-structure, attitudes force people to react in a way consistent with their self-image. Consequently the cultivation of favorable attitudes toward the values that society treasures is tantamount to promoting behavior in line with the code and the mores of the social order. In the same way, promoting favorable attitudes toward a given school subject is the equivalent of encouraging the student to pursue the subject with eagerness and persistence.

DEVELOPMENT OF ATTITUDES

If it is to fulfill its responsibility to society, the school cannot escape from its responsibility of embarking on a deliberate campaign to influence for the good the attitudes of children. Children will form attitudes anyway—good or bad—and society cannot be indifferent to the outcome. Educators do not tolerate haphazard learning in academic areas, and it does not make sense to let this important phase of education be a matter of accident. It follows that teachers need to be familiar with the general nature of attitudes and the process by which they develop.

The laws of learning

The formation and maintenance of attitudes is subject to the principles and laws that govern other forms of learning. To the extent that attitudes are learned in the process of attaining one's purpose, differences in attitudes can be expected with differences in age, sex, socioeconomic status, and cultural and experiential background. Attitudes tend to develop incidentally, gradually, and generally unconsciously. They often arise as by-products of one's day-to-day experiences and, conversely, everything that goes on in the classroom as it affects the child leads to the formation of certain attitudes. If teachers are pleasant, enthused about their subject, and sensitive to the needs of their students, the latter are likely to develop favorable attitudes toward the school. Furthermore, these attitudes will tend to spread from the situation to which they are attached to related situations in ever-wider circles. If the teacher is punitive, children will tend to develop negative attitudes toward the teacher and toward the subject. This will prevent them from doing well and will serve to reinforce their dislike for the subject and may spread to include a dislike for the whole school and all that it stands for. As a result, the school experience, rather than serving as the basis for self-realization, may well have highly detrimental repercussions on the child's whole life. Furthermore, these attitudes will remain long after the subject matter has been forgotten.

The development of attitudes is probably best explained on the basis of a combination of psychological principles. Attitude formation may be a matter of imitation (see modeling theory discussed in chapter 3). Children accept the views of their parents and other significant persons. Later, as they identify with their peers, with sports and TV stars, with older siblings as well as with teachers, they incorporate the attitudes and general outlook of these other people. What the teacher is as a person is generally more important in fostering desirable attitudes on the part of students than what he or she teaches. Positive attitudes cannot be developed as a result of a fifteen-minute period set aside for attitude formation if the procedures of the rest of the day constitute a negative of the principles involved; children cannot develop attitudes of fairness when they are continually victims of unfairness. To the extent that teachers are often used as models by children, it is imperative that they meet definite standards of suitability from this all-important standpoint. It seems essential, for example, that they have a positive outlook on life and that they be stable people whose integrity and sincerity are unquestioned and who can use their prestige to inspire children in the development of wholesome attitudes that will serve as a foundation for wholesome behavior.

Some attitudes are learned as a result of conditioning through emotionally toned experiences. A student may develop a strong dislike for a certain subject whose teacher habitually ridicules him or her in front of his peers, for example. Attitudes also develop as a result of deliberate cultivation. On the other hand, you cannot teach attitudes like you teach history. Formal instruction can help crystallize attitudes that are already forming, but attitudes are better absorbed gradually as they permeate the whole atmosphere of the school. The school needs to capitalize on the many opportunities for value development presented by the constant interaction of pupils with teachers and classmates and also with its academic content. Shakespearean plays are typically studied as literature; rarely do students grasp their many life lessons. Attitudes are also established as a result of living. Desirable attitudes are formed and gradually adjusted over the years as the children's interpretations are confirmed or denied as they meet or fail to meet social expectations. Attitude development cannot be rushed; it is not possible to build at the last minute a crash program capable of effecting wholesale changes in the attitudes of delinquents or the salvage of dropouts, for example.

Need for success experiences

It is particularly important that children experience success, both as students and as persons. The failure of the school to influence the attitudes of children from the lower classes stems in large part, no doubt, from their inability to achieve success within the framework of the school's program. Desirable attitudes are probably best developed as by-products of meaningful participation in worthwhile activities designed to promote self-enhancement. Attitudes underlying moral behavior are not developed by preaching but by providing children with systematic practice in integrating moral concepts into their total behavior and, whereas part of this integration must involve a verbalization of the basis for one's behavior, sermons are of limited benefit.

ATTITUDES TOWARD THE SCHOOL

An important set of attitudes from the standpoint of the basic purpose of education concerns those attitudes children hold with regard to the school itself and the values for which it stands. Unfortunately we have not been too successful in this area. Ten to twelve years or more of attendance in our schools has led a sizable number of our students to have anything but favorable attitudes toward literature, teachers, education, schools, or desirable behavior.

Many children do not like school

Whereas their education should be just beginning when they leave school, many youngsters, on the contrary, are finished with education the day they graduate or drop out. They take with them a few facts and skills, but all too often their dislike for any kind of learning is by far the most significant aspect of the total situation.

The reasons underlying such negative attitudes should be of primary concern to teachers. The excitement of going to school makes most beginning children highly susceptible to the development of favorable attitudes toward school. But in a few short years, a large number of youngsters do not like school, do not like teachers, do not like what they are studying. They attend only reluctantly for want of a choice in the matter. The school needs to evaluate its offerings and its procedures to see if perhaps it is not responsible, at least in part, for this state of affairs. Unfavorable attitudes presumably develop out of unsatisfying experiences geared to an unsuitable curriculum, rigid, frustrated teachers, or other aspects of the school situation for which the primary responsibility rests with the school.

. . . especially lower-class children

Antischool attitudes are particularly prevalent among children from the lower classes. Not only do many harbor these negative attitudes even before they come to school, but they also get continuous reinforcement from their parents and siblings, who hold similar views; in fact, they are likely to feel disloyal if they like school. On the other hand, the school very often deserves full credit for an "assist" in the development and maintenance of these negative attitudes. Children who are pushed to the limit day by day, often under conditions of threat, to learn things that are meaningless in terms of their goals and purposes and often incompatible with the orientation of their home and community, are bound to develop negative attitudes. These attitudes not only will preclude success but also will set into motion a vicious cycle, a major component of which is the rejection of the school and the development of counterattitudes, which are detrimental to all from both an immediate and a long-term view. The teacher working with the culturally disadvantaged needs to be particularly understanding as well as adept at relating the curriculum and his or her procedures to their needs and backgrounds.

CHANGING ATTITUDES

In order to maintain internal consistency, the individual must necessarily interpret experiences in relation to his or her present self-concept. This implies not only the screening of experiences for compatibility with their present self but also distortion and even rejection of conflicting experiences. Yet despite their resistance to change, attitudes are constantly being modified (see chapter 4). Although this occurs more readily and more smoothly in people open to experience, every individual is constantly being forced by interaction with the environment to reappraise his or her attitudes. Parents play a crucial role here, particularly in shaping the basic personality and thereby controlling later personality development; the child who suffers from insecurity as a result of parental rejection, for example, is susceptible to the development of rigid moralistic attitudes. Parents also have continuous contact with the child through his or her formative years and tend to serve as both authority figures and models.

The school also plays an important role. The interaction of the attitudes developed as a result of home and peer contacts with those of the school causes children to clarify, reappraise, and readjust their views. It also helps them generalize their attitudes in order to extend the scope of their applicability. Its contribution is especially important inasmuch as it relates to areas in which they are, up to then, relatively free from personal conviction.

The difficulty in changing attitudes stems from the fact that they are so thoroughly integrated in the total personality. People can rather easily change their views toward a certain make of car, but it is not so easy for them to change their attitudes toward race, religion, or other issues in which they are deeply ego-involved. This would vary from person to person, depending on the extent to which these attitudes are anchor-pins in their value system. Identical attitudes may have different motivational bases and may have to be approached differently. A possibility in dealing with a person whose attitudes are at the level of personal conviction based on adequate information might be to attack the cognitive object in the frame of reference in which it is perceived through a rational, matter-of-fact approach. Social rewards might be more effective in the case of the conformer who values social approval. Another possibility is through exploiting the system of dominant values to which the person subscribes; one might point out that racial intolerance is incompatible with a belief in fair play.

The effectiveness of any approach to changing attitudes depends on the congruity between what is presented and the current self-concept. A factual approach would be most effective in modifying attitudes when it clarifies an

unstructured situation that the individual is approaching with an open mind. Facts form a good starting point for thinking about issues, but the mere presentation of facts generally has limited effect on a person with definite feelings on a given subject. A gradual and subtle approach generally brings about greater and more permanent changes in attitudes than does a head-on attack, whether based on a well-documented argument of the superiority of the position advocated, the untenability of the listener's present position, or simply an emotional hardsell approach. People are less likely to generate resistance if they are led to believe that their position is basically sound and that the change is simply a minor adjustment of the original attitude.

It is also necessary that the change be undertaken in a permissive atmosphere in which people can admit their errors without fear of losing status. The more insecure they are, the less flexible their attitudes, and the more likely they are to have attitudes in need of change. It follows that any program designed to reduce prejudices, for example, would do well to consider first how necessary these prejudices are to support the self-structure of the people toward whom it is directed. A direct attack that causes the individual to feel threatened will serve only to intensify and consolidate such attitudes as he or she sets up defenses to ward off the attack and thus maintain self-consistency.

Use a deliberate approach   Attitude changes are best effected through a relatively deliberate and systematic approach. An incidental approach, on the other hand, is essentially ineffective because, in an unconscious attempt to safeguard their self-image, people simply find evidence to support their present system of values and reject or reinterpret conflicting data. A general factual approach would be more effective when a person has no information on the subject and no vested interest to protect. Dictators, for example, have been more successful in cultivating certain attitudes through a relentless campaign directed at children than through propaganda directed at adults.

Presenting both sides of an argument is generally more effective than presenting only one side, especially with the better educated (Hovland et al. 1949; Lumsdaine and Janis 1953). Presumably it increases the listener's confidence in the integrity and competence of the speaker to see that the arguments with which he or she is already familiar have been taken into account. Furthermore, it tends to discount the arguments the listener may hear later that otherwise might lead him to believe he or she had been misled.

The prestige of the speaker

Generally the speaker should be a person acceptable to the listeners so that identification can take place. In the study by Scollon (1957), a veteran was more effective in influencing army trainees to use army field rations than was a food specialist.[1] Of significance in this connection is the question of whether teachers have the prestige and credibility necessary for them to be effective in promoting attitude changes in their students. This bears on the type of person we should sponsor as future teachers and also the effect that public criticism may have in undermining the usefulness of teachers in this important area of attitude development. It also suggests that a course toward which favorable attitudes are to be developed, e.g., the tenets of democracy, might be assigned to the most popular and prestigious teacher on the staff. Having a popular student who has gone to college visit the former high school may influence some students as to the desirability of a college education.

A change of attitude, like any other learning, is predicated on motivation. To the extent that our current attitudes serve a need, we are not likely to want to discard them unless we are assured that the new attitudes provide greater satisfaction. Furthermore, we must be given the opportunity to experience reinforcement in connection with these new attitudes. When adequate motivation is present, attitudes can be changed; just note, for example, the rather drastic change in the adolescent's attitude toward members of the opposite sex resulting from the intensification of the sex drive and the accompanying social pressures to join the crowd.

VALUES

Because of their subjective nature, values have not been granted a high level of scientific respectability. Yet values, along with attitudes, ideals, and other motivational concepts, constitute an important component of the individual's

---

1. This would probably be more important in the case of children with strong affiliative needs. See Della-Piana and Gage (1955).

self-concept and as such permeate every aspect of behavior. More specifically, people live by a hierarchy of values incorporated in their self-structure as a result of previous experience. This hierarchy is phenomenological and may at times be quite inconsistent with the true significance of the values involved. A person might be most sanctimonious about petty things while violating basic values or might subscribe to a given value in one situation and violate it in another.

Helping children clarify their values   Society in general and teachers in particular have a responsibility to help children clarify their values and incorporate them into a meaningful self-concept capable of generating consistently desirable conduct. If we are to be successful in this area, we need teachers who themselves have fairly well defined values that they display in consistent and significant ways. Unfortunately society often undermines the child's development of meaningful values by presenting a relatively inconsistent pattern of moral practices at almost all levels of family, local, and political life. The same pattern of inconsistency too often prevails in school where teachers preach honesty, for example, and yet continually provide a situation that makes cheating almost necessary and almost always profitable.

Helping children develop a functional set of values is obviously a complex task. We need to be clear just how we are to proceed. If we believe in modeling, for instance, then we need to provide suitable models. Generally we know more as to what will not work than we know about what will work. Lecturing rarely works. Moralizing or even formal instruction in the values of honesty and integrity typically remains at the abstract level. Unless skillfully woven into the child's value structure, they have relatively little effect on behavior. Sunday school instruction, for example, like much of the teaching in our schools, is too frequently at the verbal level, essentially divorced from the basic concepts of socialization, enlightened self-interest, attitudes, the self, and other aspects of human motivation. As a consequence, it does not seem to be particularly effective in helping children develop an integrated system of values capable of meeting the moral demands of modern life. The curriculum ought to provide an ideal vehicle for value development; literature, history, and the social studies in general are full of examples involving ethical and moral values. Unfortunately, whereas ideally they can inspire students vicariously, rarely are these examples readily transferable to children's day-to-day behavior. Too often, literature presents its heroes so successful and circumstances so artificial (or at least different) that identification cannot occur and often would be of no particular value even if it did.

INDOCTRINATION

The development of positive values on the part of school children cannot be left to chance. Indeed, implied in the very concept of the school as the major agent for the transmission of the culture is a mandate for orienting their attitudes and values in the direction of the dominant values of the social order. If we are to be successful in influencing children's attitudes, we need to give the matter the deliberate and systematic attention that we devote to the attainment of other significant educational goals.

This brings us to the question of *indoctrination* which, in turn, introduces a number of philosophical issues. First, that indoctrination can be relatively effective when used with young children whose minds are pliable and whose background of information on the basis of which to evaluate evidence is relatively limited was amply shown in Nazi Germany. And there are people in our country who argue that if the democratic way of life is to survive, we need to "sell" democracy with some of the same fervor that the Nazis and Communists use in spreading their ideologies. Others object on the grounds that indoctrination is part of the totalitarian pattern of operations and that it has no place in the schools of a democracy.

Supporters of indoctrination argue that . . .

The issue is characterized by long-standing controversy and continuing confusion. Supporters of indoctrination point to the obvious need for adults to guide the child. The preschooler certainly has no basis for favoring honesty over stealing or truthfulness over lying. Since the beginning of times, parents have "indoctrinated" their children in such basic values as honesty, integrity, and courtesy. Education is fundamentally involved in teaching values. Any curriculum that touches life—as indeed it must—has inevitable value implications that need to be exploited. In fact, that schools exist at all is itself a value commitment to truth, knowledge, and human dignity.[2]

If it is to serve the purposes for which it was constituted, the school needs to promote favorable attitudes toward learning, specific subject matter, honesty, integrity, fair play, consideration for others, and respect for law and order. To the extent that these are basic objectives of the "charter" under which we operate, negligence in the fulfillment of these responsibilities constitutes gross neglect of duty in an area of maximum sensitivity (see Christenson 1977). The development of favorable attitudes toward society, toward learning, toward people, etc., is not something that can be left to chance. We cannot be indifferent to the fact that because of our ineptness or carelessness, some children leave school with strongly negative attitudes toward a number of the basic values of our society, including education.

2. The school in early America had a strong moral orientation, as reflected, for instance, in the popularity of the McGuffey readers and their emphasis on religious and patriotic exercises. The importance of attitudes and values in the educational enterprise is also implied in the development of the affective domain of the taxonomy of educational objectives. Currently, there seems to be a revival of interest in moral and character education; the *Phi Delta Kappan* devoted its June 1975 (vol. 57, no. 10) issue to the subject. A survey of Phi Delta Kappans (Ryan and Thompson 1975), for example, revealed almost unanimous support for an active program of moral education in the school. In an earlier poll (Spears 1973), they had placed moral education third among the school's priorities (after "learning how to read and write" and "pride in work and a feeling of self-respect"). A commitment to the moral education and character development of its students almost invariably is incorporated in the formal statement of philosophy of every school in the nation.

The issue becomes more complicated when it deals with values less clearly within the domain of the school's immediate functioning. Should we indoctrinate with respect to democracy? With respect to religion? With respect to moral values? Advocates of indoctrination would argue that we cannot let children, with their limited perspective, limited background of relevant information, and immaturity of judgment, make their own choices; that, for adults to allow children to chart their own course in such a complex area is to court disaster. They argue further that the teacher will have to take sides on these issues, either standing up to be counted or by default. This is inevitable. What is more critical is that despite all the reluctance he or she may have against indoctrinating children, the teacher is perpetually pushed into the position of having to preach morality with respect to trivial violations of classroom decorum. To the extent that the teacher's greatest efforts on behalf of morality are then spent in directions which, according to Kohlberg (1966), can only be termed "Mickey Mouse" by any right-thinking student, the latter must eventually begin to wonder what, if anything, the teacher really believes in and how petty the whole business can be. If teachers have to be involved in moral training, they owe it to themselves to choose dimensions more morally significant than simple matters of rudeness, inattention, and horseplay.

The case against indoctrination

The case against indoctrination, as presented by such authors as Carbone (1970), Paske (1969), Raths et al. (1966), and Wilson et al. (1967), is equally compelling. To begin with, it is a basic tenet of democratic society that people should have the freedom to make apparently wrong decisions, unless these decisions have decidedly disastrous consequences in matters of life or death or perhaps the safety and welfare of others. This point of view pervades all forms of democratic thinking. But the fact is that young children certainly cannot make their own choices, at least not wisely. Nor can we wait for them to reach the point at which they are capable of sufficiently clear abstract reasoning that they can decide on their own. Since, according to Piaget, children of elementary school age are incapable of grasping the rationale underlying moral principles, we have little choice at this stage but to present the rule as if it were part of the natural order of things. At this age some degree of inculcation is inevitable. But the argument for indoctrination goes a little further: since children have to acquire value commitments before they fully understand the import of these commitments, let us see to it that they acquire the right ones—namely ours!

Two basic issues are involved. First, there is an implication that indoctrination with regard to what is true is legitimate, since after all no one has the right to reject truth or even to avoid it. The trouble is that moral truth cannot be shown in the way physical truth is shown; the superiority of democracy or of sexual morality is not "true" in the same sense as the principles of physics or the periodic table are true. Even teaching some values as facts and others simply as hypotheses would result in a dilemma inasmuch as one cannot always tell which is which. More fundamentally, we need to distinguish between *primary* and *secondary* values, where secondary values derive from primary values or from other secondary values. Cleanliness, for example, is derived from the value of health, where the value of health is derived from the value of life, which is primary. Primary values are basic; secondary values, on the other hand, change so that talking of values in terms of truth presupposes we know what will be appropriate in the future. This is not possible, since conditions that make them appropriate will themselves change.

Indoctrination causes children to internalize certain values before they can understand the full impact of the commitments they have made. The danger is that once they have become emotionally committed to a proposition, they will be unable to evaluate it rationally. As a result, they will discount the impact of change and continue to hold secondary values that now frustrate the primary value from which they were derived. The more dynamic the society, the more frequently this will occur. Paske considers indoctrination (i.e., influencing the child to make emotional commitments before he or she can understand their full impact) as educationally bankrupt in that it presupposes nonexisting knowledge and morally corrupting in that it prevents the objective evaluation of one's values.

Even if we were correct in the assumption that our basic value commitments are the best available, it does not follow that we ought to indoctrinate with regard to these commitments. It is not a question of the validity of our commitments but rather of the very nature of education. Every educational system worthy of the name has as one of its primary goals the eventual intellectual freedom of those placed in its care—which, in turn, means that people must be free to examine objectively any and all aspects of their own culture. For this to happen, they must have minimal commitment to those values that are unique to that particular culture.

This refusal to indoctrinate with respect to democracy, religion, etc., does not imply a lack of belief in those values. On the contrary, it represents a deep conviction that these values can withstand the light of rational examination. Underlying the concept of indoctrination, i.e., the need to cause children to internalize certain values before they understand their meaning, by contrast is the apparent fear that, unless this is done before children understand, they will not accept the values of their elders when they are able to make their own choice. The basic premise is that only after children have adequately internalized the basic values of society may they be left safely to themselves. Actually, since genuine education recognizes that particular values cannot be transferred intact from one generation to another, there can be no guarantee that the young will accept the values of their elders. Instead there can only be a conviction that the question of values will be settled rationally—a faith that human beings left free to discover objectively the value needs of their society will be able to arrive at the most adequate values. If children reject the values of the old generation, then the inadequacy of the older values must be ac-

Our values can
withstand scrutiny

cepted. It is not the prerogative of one generation to fix the value structure of the next generation.

Paske sees indoctrination as morally corrupting in that it strives to achieve value commitments independently of reason. Since presumably as children become adults they ought not to believe anything that they do not have good reason to believe, nor disbelieve anything unless they have good reason to disbelieve it, it follows that, as far as possible, we ought to save people from having to acquire any belief or any value until it is either absolutely necessary or until they are capable of understanding the reason and the evidence behind the belief. Paske suggests that the only values to be indoctrinated are those that are more or less transcultural, e.g., affection and respect for people within one's immediate experience, and rationality itself.

Carbone conceives of moral education as involving two relatively well defined levels. The first is concerned with contributing to the socialization of younger children by inducing them to accept values and standards of behavior that prevail in the social order. This unavoidably involves a certain amount of imposition; however, Carbone suggests that we present on a nonrational basis only those norms we are convinced will stand the test of reflective evaluation later on, meanwhile taking every opportunity to cultivate critical thinking. The second phase attempts to advance children to the point of critical and independent judgment as to the validity of their values. The idea is to confront students with moral issues that force them to reexamine their moral commitments and thereby help them develop a solid base of principles from which to evaluate moral convictions.

Raths et al., Wilson et al., and Broudy all take a similar position regarding the need for a systematic program of values clarification (see Raths et al. 1966; Simon and deSherbinin 1975) designed to help adolescents clarify specifically what values they are accepting (or rejecting).[3] This type of moral reflection may, of course, prove embarrassing as there is always a potential danger to conventional morality. A notorious example here is sexual morality; parents certainly do not see the question of sexual morality as one for debate. But this is precisely the kind of reflective morality, the sort of question that needs to be raised and that may not be answered at all or answered in ways different from what the parents would like. There is always risk in inquiry, in reflection, and in knowledge. But according to Broudy, there is no way of avoiding the risk if we intend to be people rather than trained animals. (See Lockwood 1978 for a critical review of recent research on values clarification.)

No standard strategy can be prescribed for encouraging youngsters to examine and clarify their values. According to Raths et al. (1966), the traditional

Indoctrination attempts to instill values independently of reason

Values clarification essential but no teaching prescription

3. The school also influences attitudes toward democracy, toward itself, and toward its dominant values by the emotional climate it provides. This is an insidious form of indoctrination; the child finds the school so pleasant that he or she does not question too seriously the possibility that the school can be wrong about anything. It can work the other way around as well, where some children are conditioned against everything connected with the school.

approaches to teaching values—e.g., setting an example, persuading and convincing, inspiring, appealing to conscience, etc.—have not been particularly effective in helping youngsters form a deep commitment to any meaningful set of values. They suggest that we avoid moralizing about anything if we can help it; it does not have much of an effect, if experience is any guide, except to encourage people not to think for themselves. Underlying each of these approaches is the idea of persuasion; the "right" values are predetermined and, through one method or another of telling, pushing, or urging, these values are passed on to others. They all involve indoctrination, some more subtle than others, but the idea of free inquiry, thoughtfulness, and reason seems to be lost. The approach is not a matter of helping children develop a valuing process but rather to persuade them to adopt the right values ready-made—ours! As Peck and Havighurst (1960) point out:

> It is temptingly easier and assiduously gratifying to "mold" children, or to "whip them into line" by exercising one's superior status and authority as an adult. It is often personally inconvenient to allow children time to debate alternatives, and it may be personally frustrating if their choice contradicts one's own preferences. . . . Then, too, like any dictatorship, it looks "more efficient"—to the dictator, at least. However, the effect on character is to arrest the development of rational judgment. . . .

Even discussion may be inappropriate for value lessons. It would be inadvisable when the participants are motivated by the desire to please the teacher or when it moves toward argumentation. Valuing may be difficult in a room where there is a lot of talking and arguing. Discussion may also create pressures for individuals to accept group consensus, whereas values cannot come from pressure to accept anything.

Broudy goes one step further and points out that freedom implies responsibility. Children have a moral obligation to examine their values in the light of what is known of the good life. In other words, the school's responsibility to refrain from unnecessary indoctrination[4] is paralleled by a corresponding responsibility on individuals to examine the evidence for their beliefs. The argument is that students will accept nothing or reject nothing without making an effort to evaluate what they are accepting or rejecting. The school would have the further responsibility of helping children arrive at the necessary evidence.

4. In sharp contrast to our reluctance to indoctrinate school children is the total acceptance by the Soviets of indoctrination as a necessary component of state-controlled education, as it operates not only in the school, but also in the preschool, the commune, the media, etc. The emphasis is not on moral virtues but rather on Soviet morality as reflected in such slogans as, "One for all, all for one." Their relative success in promoting total commitment to communistic values is evidence of the effectiveness of an all-out program of indoctrination aimed at the young. See Bronfenbrenner (1962); Malkova (1964); Schlessinger (1964).

MORAL DEVELOPMENT

Moral education in the school years ago was oriented to the development of sound moral habits; it emphasized moral knowledge and strict conformity to rules of moral conduct. Unfortunately habits formed under adult supervision rarely carry over into situations in which children are on their own. Character must be based on something more substantial, e.g., well-defined attitudes and values. Children must also have contact with a variety of examples of a given standard of moral behavior in different settings so that they can visualize morality in its different manifestations. Because moral behavior tends to revolve around unconscious motivation, it must be generalized through the verbalization of underlying principles acting as a tool, not only for considering the present but also for reconstructing the past and planning for the future.

Instructional Strategies

Teaching in the sense of promoting behavioral changes is never easy. It is doubly difficult in the area of values, attitudes, and other aspects of the affective domain, which, by and large, has been neglected in the past partly because it presents especially difficult problems of implementation. Attitudes cannot be taught in isolation and, although they do develop incidentally, this type of

haphazard operation cannot be tolerated in an area of high priority. On the contrary, the development of attitudes calls for a well-defined effort designed to mobilize the total resources of the school (in cooperation with the home and community, if possible) in the service of a major goal.

A meaningful curriculum

The first prerequisite to helping youngsters develop wholesome and positive attitudes toward self, the school, and life in general is a meaningful curriculum in which they can experience success in significant areas. We need to vitalize and individualize the academic program so as to provide each child with a systematic schedule of challenging and personally profitable and rewarding experiences, a long-range outcome of which is the generation of increased academic motivation and, more broadly, a positive self-concept.

Equally critical is the parallel need for effective teaching-learning strategies as the basis for ensuring systematic success experiences and the development of a sense of achievement and self-esteem. Implied is the need for diagnostic and remedial help as needed, for attention to the sequential nature of the curriculum (say, along the lines defined by Ausubel and Gagné), and for general compliance with the various principles and strategies developed throughout the text.

A permissive and cohesive classroom climate is essential. In accordance with Maslow's theory, the school must see to it that children's deficiency needs are satisfied so that they can become maximally open to experience and capable of making growth choices.

A deliberate program

Finally there is the need to develop a deliberate program of attitude and character development as a major and legitimate component of the educational enterprise. The school needs to focus on well-defined attitudes and values. More specifically, it needs to clarify what attitudes and values will be promoted, for whom, and through what specific strategies, e.g., the promotion of positive attitudes toward arithmetic in underachieving fifth graders through a systematic schedule of graded exercises, geared to diagnostic and remedial tutoring and immediate reinforcement.

We especially need to develop greater expertise and more effective strategies, based on a clear-cut rationale and coordinated with the child's developmental level. If a modeling approach is to be used, for example, we need to identify adequate models. If teachers are to be used as models, they need to generate—through the systematic display of maturity, understanding, integrity, and wisdom—sufficient credibility and rapport to serve in this important capacity. We especially need to replace our current methods of moralizing, berating, or pressuring with more psychologically sound approaches, e.g., values clarification, inductive methods,[5] etc.

5. Gagné lists attitudes as one of the five major categories of learning outcomes and, as with the learning of verbal information, identifies both internal and external conditions that need to be met if learning is to take place. At the internal level, for example, the learner must have some prerequisite cognitive knowledge of the attitude object. Before one can generate an attitude toward Estonians, we must have some knowledge of who they are so that we can place

Moral standards
develop according to
standard learning
principles

Moral standards develop according to the same principles as govern other forms of learning: reinforcement, imitation, reflective thinking, etc. A significant aspect of a successful character education program, for example, lies in making ethically and socially acceptable behavior more satisfying than undesirable behavior. Children need to realize that honesty *is* the best policy; that greater satisfaction can be obtained from being considerate than from being inconsiderate, and reinforcement might be necessary at first to make sure that certain responses are satisfying. On the other hand, external rewards are beneficial only to the extent that they become progressively more unnecessary as the child gets inner satisfaction from compliance with the standards he or she has internalized.

Social forces often
conflicting

Unfortunately the various social forces playing on children are not only often in conflict with each other, but many are self-contradictory. Thus both desirable and undesirable behavior are at times punished and rewarded as the child is intermittently (if not indiscriminately) ignored and praised for honesty while the cheater is both punished and allowed to profit from cheating. The result is confusion and ambivalent attitudes, the net vector strength of which as it leads to moral behavior is generally weak and easily overcome by conflicting motives operative in the situation. V. Jones (1960) believes that parents and teachers are often so lackadaisical in enforcing basic rules that the child sees good behavior as optional. After a period of such inconsistency, it becomes difficult to reorient the child to the internalization of more adequate standards, especially since our relatively inconsistent and only partially moral society is likely to provide intermittent reinforcement of violations.

Major influences in
moral development

Parents and teachers affect the character of children through all of the principles of learning. They provide models for the stimulation of the growth of the self and the development of feelings of personal worth that is at the very core of character formation. Teachers often exert their strongest influence on the character development of their students just by being the kind of people they are. Subject matter can serve as a potential contributor to the value systems of boys and girls; the school offers many opportunities to discuss problems of conduct and to arrive at a better understanding of what constitutes moral behavior. Literature is full of people worthy of emulation and of episodes having definite character-building possibilities. Inspiring thought along these lines without moralizing is likely to be more profitable than simply hammering away at facts. We need to think of a subject not only as an end in itself but also as an instrument for developing important life lessons. The school is in a good position from the standpoint of character development: not only are children still in their formative years when they come to school but the years of their

---

them in a category in relation to our value system. External conditions, on the other hand, vary with the learning model in question. If a reinforcement model is used, the child would indeed have to be reinforced for displaying the desired behavior. If modeling is involved, a model of adequate credibility would have to display the behavior in question under a reinforcing state of affairs.

attendance are characterized by increasing capacity for understanding the reasons underlying desirable behavior.

The Role of the Home

The home is the
major factor

The home is undoubtedly the greatest single factor in character formation. Peck and Havighurst (1960) suggest that the peer group appears to be less of an originator than simply a reinforcer of the moral values and behavior patterns developed in the home; the school likewise seems to crystallize character rather than to shape it. More specifically, character develops out of the socialization process in which the parents impose demands and conditions on their love, thus forcing the child to realize the need for acceptable behavior. For this to occur, the child must have developed strong dependency needs as a result of the warmth and acceptance of the parents. In fact, the internalization of moral standards and the development of guilt and anxiety over transgressions are best promoted when the young child's feelings of acceptance and personal worth are maintained at a high level where he or she can maintain optimal openness to experience.

Children are constantly finding that their behavior meets or does not meet with the approval of the significant people in their environment. As they grow older, they grasp the common elements in the different situations in which their behavior was approved or disapproved and form a generalized concept of what is good and what is bad. Conscience develops (or fails to develop) in large measure as a function of the nature of the socialization process. Research suggests that the greatest internalization of control occurs when the parents rely on what Hoffman and Saltzstein (1967) call *inductive love-oriented* child-rearing practices, calling not only for love withdrawal in cases of wrongdoing, with reinstatement of affection contingent on the child's expression of regret and a promise of more constructive behavior; but also some explanation (i.e., induction) designed to make children realize the harmful consequences of their behavior on others (Hoffman 1974, 1979; see also Mouly, 1973, pp. 76–78). This arousal of emphatic distress over misbehavior intensifies guilt feelings, leading to reparative action toward the victim or at least a prolongation of guilt, self-examination, and hopefully a reordering of values and a resolution to act less selfishly in the future. In other words, inductive strategies not only activate to an optimal degree children's existing motivational tendencies but also, by emphasizing the human consequences of their transgressions, help them to integrate their cognitive resources with their capacity for empathy in the control of their impulses. By mobilizing the cognitive component necessary to increase children's awareness of the nature of their transgression, inductive strategies facilitate its generalization to other situations and the development of guilt and moral judgment, both of which are essential aspects of a fully developed conscience.

Another advantage of inductive techniques is that they lead children to examine and reexamine their views on rules in keeping with their increasing cognitive development, with the result that they gradually shift from a morality that is external, arbitrary, and constraining to an inner control based on compelling rational considerations (see Bernstein, chapter 7). They then become their own keeper and are guided not so much by the punishment of others as by a meaningful inner code of right and wrong. This internal code is much more severe than that imposed by external authority since, with an internalized code of values, the watchdog is always on the alert, always ready to generate anxiety for any transgression or even for thoughts and desires in this direction.

CHARACTER DEVELOPMENT

Conscience grows out of the parent-child relationship in which the child gradually takes over and exercises the same control over the ego that the parents would have exercised. If children learn to depend on their parents, they have something to work for in meeting parental expectations; they also have something to lose if they fail. If, in addition, parents encourage their children to evaluate their behavior in terms of its effects on others, the children gradually learn that acceptable behavior is a matter of rationality in which goodwill, concern for others, and enlightened self-interest are major considerations. If, on the other hand, the child-rearing practices to which children are subjected are punitive, then parents and other adults are simply perceived as the dispensers of punishment. Under these conditions, why should children become socialized if the only reward for so doing is the privilege of punishing themselves? They then have no reason to internalize parental standards and, therefore, remain oriented toward direct self-gratification, with their only concern that of avoiding punishment.

Conscience refers to values that have been internalized

Conscience consists of the moral values children have internalized. Unless they establish these standards of right and wrong their only basis for acting properly is external control. Difficulty arises when discipline is so inconsistent that children cannot decipher which behaviors are "good" and which are "bad." Problems also occur when discipline is so severe that they develop a fear of authority and ambivalent attitudes of hostility and resentment toward adults. As a result, they become unmanageable except through external punishment, or, on the contrary, develop rigidity of conduct based on severe guilt feelings that tend to be repressed, thus preventing the behavior from coming out in the open where its acceptability can be appraised. The result is a blind allegiance to rules for rules' sake.

The child's behavior at first is neither good nor bad in a moral sense; he or she simply tests various responses to situations and learns from experience to identify those that are encouraged and those that are condemned. This requires a good deal of trial and error under conditions of permissiveness and consistency in an atmosphere of love and acceptance in which the child learns to gauge the acceptability of his or her behavior and gradually shifts from behavior geared to external rewards and punishments to behavior that is based progressively more on internal constraints.

Character refers to behavioral consistency as it relates to moral and ethical behavior. It tends to be reflected in conduct that is in conformity with social values and relates to the degree of internalization of the constraints of the social order. On the other hand, conformity to the standards of society is not, in itself, the criterion of character. The person who conforms simply to get social approval, even if it means sacrificing his or her own values, is a chameleon entirely devoid of character. Character also implies conformity in matters in which the individual *chooses* to act in a way consistent with the welfare of others; the child who does not cheat solely because he or she is afraid of detection is nothing more than a coward.

Character is not the equivalent of conformity to social standards

Character is not the equivalent of morality; it implies a willingness to stand and be counted in the advancement of morality beyond the accepted norms of the present social order. History identifies a number of persons who were willing to fight for an improvement in the standards and practices of the day. Underlying character is an internal compulsion to live by one's system of values rather than by mere rules and sanctions geared to external standards. True character also implies a rational choice based on an understanding of the consequences of the behavior at issue and a consideration of the welfare of all concerned in line with the concept of enlightened self-interest. The individual who has a blind allegiance to honesty as an abstract concept and who tells his hostess that, frankly, he is bored is displaying more rigidity than character, morality, or integrity.

Piaget's Concept of Moral Development

An important component of Piaget's theory of cognitive development (see chapters 5 and 6) concerns its parallel development in the area of moral judgment. In keeping with his hierarchical view of development, Piaget postulates two main stages in the development of the child's conception of rules and sense of justice, the two components he sees as the essence of morality.

Moral realism and moral relativism

The first stage, which may be labeled moral *realism*, is one of blind obedience in which children's concept of right and wrong is based on what their parents permit or forbid. Their interpretation of a rule is literal; a rule is a rule; it is sacred and inviolable. Children expect absolute regularity in their world, whether physical or moral. When they are told a story a second time, they insist on hearing it with exactly the same details as the first time. In the case of damage, it is the absolute extent of damage, rather than the intent, that counts; breaking three cups accidentally is a more serious offense than breaking one cup on purpose. They believe in imminent justice; they expect violations in the moral realm to bring about automatic retribution in exactly the same way as in the physical realm. e.g., if you touch the stove. Children's moral limitations represented in moral realism stem directly from corresponding cognitive limitations, e.g., their egocentrism (i.e., the assumption that others view events the same way as they do) and their realism (i.e., confusion of subjective and objective aspects of experience). Young children assume that there is only one view that is shared by all: an act is either right or wrong.

By contrast, older children judge behavior in terms of its intent rather than of its material consequences and, at the approximate age of twelve, their concept of justice passes from a rigid inflexible notion of right and wrong to *moral relativism* involving a sense of equity that takes into account the subtleties of situational circumstances. As they develop a better understanding of social roles, they see that rules are not inherently sacred but rather the product of agreement based on mutual goals and therefore amenable to change through mutual consent. Correspondingly their views on justice shift from expiation through punishment by the authority whose rule has been violated to compensation for the misdeed through restitution or through retaliation by the victim.

Kohlberg's Theory of Moral Judgment

Kohlberg (1964, 1966, 1970, 1975; see also Adkins 1973; Reimor 1977) presents what might be considered an extension and refinement of Piaget's position, with emphasis on the quality of moral *judgment*. Specifically, on the basis of a study of the responses of youngsters to hypothetical moral dilemmas, Kohlberg devised the following three-stage (six-level) scheme for the classification of moral judgment:

Preconventional: Obey rules to avoid punishment.
1. Punishment and obedience orientation.
2. Instrumental relativist orientation. The child realizes that proper behavior pays off; trade-off emerges.

Conventional: Conform to obtain reward, to have favors returned.
3. Interpersonal concordance (good-boy, nice-girl orientation); conform to get approval of others and avoid their disapproval.
4. Law and order orientation; respect for authority; conform to avoid censure from legitimate authority and resulting guilt.

Postconventional, autonomous, or principled level, i.e., morality of self-accepted moral principles.
5. The social contract, legalistic orientation; conform to maintain the respect of the impartial spectator judging in terms of community welfare (morality of contract, of individual rights, and democratically accepted law).
6. The universal ethical (conscience) orientation; act to avoid self-condemnation (morality of individual principles of justice).

At the preconceptual level (ages four through ten), children may be well behaved but they interpret behavior in terms of its physical consequences. At the conventional level, children are conformists; they abide by the expectations and the rules of adults. At the postconventional level, their behavior is characterized by a thrust toward the autonomous moral principles that have validity and application apart from the authority of the group or the person who holds them. At level 6, for example, conduct is controlled by an internalized ideal that promotes actions that seem right even in the face of social disapproval; here personal conscience often takes priority over social convention of what is right and what is wrong.[6]

Cognitive factors in moral development

Cognitive factors clearly dominate Kohlberg's system. Movement from one moral level to the next is largely the natural outgrowth of cognitive development, with the environment providing the raw materials on which cognitive processes operate. Participation in peer groups, for instance, provides children with direct experience in taking alternative roles from which they gain first-hand experience in the workings of the actual sociomoral world, including its role system, its rules, and an appreciation of its essential functioning rationality. Kohlberg found substantial uniformity in the development of values among youngsters in various countries of the world. The rate at which individuals progressed through the sequence varied, but the sequence was not significantly affected by widely different social, cultural, and/or religious conditions. On the other hand, both Piaget and Kohlberg suggest that we can help children move from one moral level to the next by exposing them to moral conflicts for which their current principles provide no solution, e.g., having students at, say, level 2 interact with those of level 3, with the teacher clarifying level 3 arguments. Kohlberg presents evidence of relative success in the use of such an approach.

Character (Personality) Patterns

Also of major interest is the study of character formation by Peck and Havighurst (1960), who define five basic character patterns on the basis of the relative strength of the individual's moral stability, ego and superego strength, and other components of mature character.

1. The amoral (low in moral stability, ego strength, superego strength, and hostility-guilt): These people have not internalized moral values and disregard the moral connotations of their behavior and its effects on others. They are at the center of the universe, and others are simply means to self-gratification. This is the picture of the one-year-old child. Adults who exhibit such a pattern are said to be fixated at the infantile level and, in extreme cases, are known as psychopathic deviates.

6. Loevinger (1966) presents a somewhat similar seven-stage hierarchy of what she calls *ego development*, ranging from self-identification to an integrated level. See Kincaid (1978) and Trainer (1977) for a critical analysis of the Kohlberg position. See also Maschette (1977).

2. The expedient (below average in ego strength, superego strength, moral stability, and friendliness; high in spontaneity and hostility-guilt): These people are primarily self-centered; they consider other people's welfare only in order to gain their personal ends. They behave in ways society defines as moral only as long as it suits their purposes. They are the only person who really counts but they are aware of the advantages of conforming to social requirements in order to reap long-term benefits.

   The key to their low level of morality is their me-first attitude. Such a motivational pattern is characteristic of many young children who have learned to respect the reward-punishment power of adults and to behave correctly whenever adults are present. External sanctions are always necessary to guide and control their behavior, for in the absence of such control they immediately revert to doing what they please.

3. The conforming (moderate in ego and superego strength and friendliness; low in moral stability, spontaneity, and hostility-guilt): These people have one general internalized principle: they conform to the rules, they do what others do; their only anxiety centers on possible disapproval. They have no generalized or abstract principle of honesty, integrity, or loyalty. They follow a system of literal rules specific to each occasion, with no overall consistency. If the rules by which they live call for kindness to some people and cruelty to others, that is all right. They differ from the expedient in that social conformity is accepted as good for its own sake. They have a crude conscience that does not allow them to depart from the rules, but they do not follow the rules for a moral purpose.

4. The irrational-conscientious (weak to moderate ego strength; low in friendliness; high in hostility-guilt, superego strength, and moral stability): These individuals typically judge a given act according to their own standards of what is right and wrong. The issue is not conformity to group rules but rather conformity to a code that they have internalized. If they approve of an act, they are so honest that they carry it out whether or not others approve. They appeal to an abstract principle of honesty and apply it as they interpret it to any situation, whether or not it is relevant or right. If they fail to live up to their own standards, they suffer anxiety-guilt, i.e., a feeling of having violated their own integrity. The irrational component is visible in their rigidity in applying a preconceived principle; an act is good or bad because they define it as such, not necessarily because it has positive or negative effects on others. This is a blind, rigid morality best represented by Javert in Victor Hugo's *Les Misérables*. It is characteristic of children who have not learned that rules are man-made and intended to serve a functional human purpose.

5. The rational-altruistic (high in ego and superego strength, moral stability, spontaneity, and friendliness; low in hostility-guilt): This represents the highest level of moral maturity. Such people not only have a stable set of moral principles by which they guide their actions, but they also assess the results of their behavior objectively against the criterion of whether it serves others as well as themselves. In the ideal case, they are dependably honest and responsible; they do what is morally right because they want to, because they see such behavior as contributing to human well-being.

Peck and Havighurst point to the need for society to agree on the character structure children should be helped to achieve. We must recognize, for example, that even though the school is vitally concerned with the moral development of children, its emphasis on the promotion of conformity is too often an orientation toward the irrational-conscientious character pattern. Effective morality demands the understanding of the nature, meaning, and purposes of the rules and principles by which one guides one's behavior. The rigid inculcation of cultural standards without explanation of why conformity is expected coupled with inconsistency in discipline leads to behavioral inflexibility by its discouragement of cognitive clarity; it forces children to develop a behavioral pattern that is rigid and unchangeable because it is not clear. This lack of clarity concerning the basic rules of society would present no major problem in a stable culture in which the standards and expectations remain constant from generation to generation, but it would be unfortunate should the child ever have to improvise either because society or his or her role has changed. The school needs to clarify how it can best cultivate rational-altruistic character in children as an aspect of the process of *becoming*.

HIGHLIGHTS OF THE CHAPTER

The school can make no greater contribution to the cause of the nation and of humanity than to promote in its children positive attitudes that will direct their behavior along constructive lines. The prospective teacher needs to be conversant with the fundamentals of this all-important subject.

1. Attitudes permeate our very existence. Operationally, they incorporate an affective, a cognitive, and a behavior component.
2. Attitudes are learned as a result of conditioning, modeling, deliberate teaching, etc. To the extent that children develop attitudes through identification with significant persons, teachers need to be solid citizens who can inspire children and with whom children can identify in the formation of sound values.

3. Once developed, attitudes tend to resist change, especially when they are part of the anchor system of the individual's personality structure. Generally a relentless and systematic but subtle campaign is more effective than an incidental approach or a head-on attack.

4. The school cannot make the development of attitudes on the part of the children entrusted to its care a matter of chance. Special efforts should be devoted to making the curriculum more meaningful, the demands more realistic, and the classroom atmosphere more conducive to self-enhancement.

5. The question of indoctrination continues to be controversial. A strong case can be made either for or against. There is agreement on the need for values clarification, particularly once the child has reached the stage of formal operations.

6. Character development is a major component of the socialization of the child. Inductive, love-oriented child-rearing practices appear to be most conducive to the development of a truly rational-conscientious morality.

7. The development of a sound pattern of values is frequently undermined by conflicting standards existing among and within the various social agencies and forces with which the child comes into contact. Meanwhile truly effective strategies for promoting positive attitudes and values have proved quite elusive.

8. Important contributors to the literature in the field include Piaget, Kohlberg, Peck and Havighurst, Paske, Carbone, Raths, Wilson, and Broudy.

SUGGESTIONS FOR FURTHER READING

ARONFREED, J. *Conduct and Conscience: The Socialization and Internalized Control of Behavior.* New York: Academic Press, 1968. An authoritative discussion of the process of socialization. See also, Aronfreed, Aversive control of socialization. In *Nebraska Symposium on Motivation* 16 (1968):271–320.

BRONFENBRENNER, U. Soviet methods of character education: Some implications for research. *Amer. Psychol.* 17 (1962):550–564. Examines the Soviet system of moral training of its youth. Sees Soviet methods of character training as the direct reflection of the teachings of Makarenko, the Soviet Dr. Spock in moral upbringing.

HERSCH, RICHARD H., et al. Moral development. *Theory into Practice* 16 (1977):51–128. Whole issue devoted to moral development. Articles by Kohlberg, Reimer, and others. Paolitto discusses the role of the teacher.

HOFFMAN, MARTIN L. Moral development. In Paul H. Mussen, ed., *Carmichael's Manual of Child Psychology,* Vol. 2, pp. 261–359. New York: Wiley, 1970. An exceptionally thorough treatment of the subject.

KOHLBERG, LAWRENCE. Moral education in the school: A developmental view *Sch. Rev.* 74 (1966):1–30. Kohlberg's six-level stage theory, presented here, is really an extension of the Piaget concept of moral judgment. See also Kohlberg, The cognitive-developmental approach to moral education. *Phi Delta Kappan* 56 (1975):670–677.

LOCKWOOD, A. The effects of values clarification and moral development curricula on school-age subjects. A critical review of recent research. *Rev. Educ. Res.* 48 (1978):325–364. A critical review of the effects of values clarification programs in the school situation.

REST, J. Developmental psychology as a guide to values education. *Rev. Educ. Res.* 44 (1974):241–259. Presents a review of elementary and secondary teaching strategies and the curricula developed or inspired by Kohlberg.

QUESTIONS AND PROJECTS

1. It would seem that the school invariably gives the cognitive domain priority over the affective. What are the implications of this tendency? Specifically, what can the school do to increase its impact on the attitudes of students?

   Comment: The school can never be truly neutral, and let us hope it never is.

   What steps might the school take to encourage lower-class children to develop positive attitudes toward the school and the values for which it stands (see James E. Heald, In defense of middle-class values, *Phi Delta Kappan* 46 [1964]:81–83)?

2. Why does the peer group have such an impact on student values, despite a relatively haphazard approach, while parents and teachers, operating on a supposedly systematic basis, appear to be so inept? How might the teaching profession get itself more closely attuned to the values of children from the lower classes?

3. Specifically, how might the school fulfill its responsibility of helping students clarify their values? Is the student's choice of acceptable or unacceptable values a matter of indifference to the school? What guidelines might the school use in deciding when intervention might be in order?

   Having agreed on a position, how can the teaching profession translate its views into an operational program? What guidelines as to dos and don'ts might be listed?

4. What are some of the classroom implications of Kohlberg's stages?

SELF-TESTS

1. Attitudes are best conceived as a form of
   a. conditioned response.
   b. emotion.
   c. ideal.
   d. motivational predisposition.
   e. perceptual framework.

2. Attitudes are of special importance in that
   a. Once formed, they are highly resistant to change.
   b. they form the very substance of the self-concept.
   c. they have a direct bearing on personal and social adjustment.
   d. they permeate all aspects of emotional behavior.
   e. they screen the flow of experience feeding the individual's growth.

3. The most significant determinant of the attitudes the child develops toward the school is
   a. the adequacy of the cocurricular program.
   b. the attitudes of the home.
   c. the emotional climate of the classroom.
   d. the suitability of the curriculum.
   e. the teacher's personality.

4. The first consideration in dealing with children of the lower classes is for the teacher
   a. to adapt the curriculum to their background and their needs.
   b. to help them achieve peer acceptance.
   c. to inculcate middle-class values necessary for success in school.
   d. to minimize the emphasis on formal standards of achievement and conduct.
   e. to understand them as individuals.

5. The resistance of attitudes to change is primarily explained on the basis of
   a. functional autonomy.
   b. intermittent reinforcement.
   c. the pivotal position they hold in the total personality.
   d. their longstanding history.
   e. spontaneous recovery.

6. Values are best conceived as
   a. a broad spectrum of ideas and motives subscribed to by the social order.
   b. an orientation toward theological matters.
   c. generalized attitudes toward matters of ethical and moral concern.

     d. internalized concepts of right and wrong.

     e. the code of behavior through which the self is expressed.

7. Morality is defined in terms of

     a. behavior deliberately selected with full awareness of its social implications.

     b. behavior guided toward the social welfare.

     c. behavior in compliance with the moral code, e.g., law abidance.

     d. conscience development.

     e. social sensitivity and social adequacy.

FIFTEEN

Personal and Social Adjustment

No person has an unlimited amount of energy available and the anxious child invests so much of his energy in his problems that there is little left over to conduct the ordinary affairs of life.

Robert F. Peck and James V. Mitchell (1962)

. . . personality change appears to be very difficult for those who think it is difficult, if not impossible, and much easier for those who think it can be done.

David C. McClelland (1965)

There is a general rule about parents: The less mother knows what to do with a child, the better she knows what the father should do. This applies equally for the relationship between teacher and parents. If the teacher were able to deal effectively with her pupils, she would not need to complain about the lack of cooperation on the part of the parents.

Rudolf Dreikurs (1968)

— Presents personality development within the context of learning theory, need satisfaction, and child-rearing practices
— Spells out the teacher's role in promoting pupil adjustment, with special emphasis on the underachiever and the dropout

PREVIEW: KEY CONCEPTS

1. The personal and social adjustment of its students must necessarily be of prime concern to the school.
2. Adjustment is best approached from the standpoint of learning; the individual learns to cope with internal and external demands.
3. The major contributor to personality development is the home; the school plays a secondary but nevertheless crucial role.
4. A number of personality theories have been formulated. Erikson's psychosocial stage theory identifies eight stages in the human cycle, each dealing with a particular developmental crisis.
5. Adjustment-maladjustment constitutes a relatively ill-defined continuum.
6. The coping mechanisms used by the adjusted and by the maladjusted typically differ in degree rather than in kind.
7. The dropout and the underachiever reflect a serious failure in adjustment to the school.

PREVIEW QUESTIONS

1. Why should the personal and social adjustment of its students be "any of the school's business"?
    What is the school's responsibility in this area?
2. How would behaviorists differ from, say, humanists in explaining how adjustment patterns develop?
    What is the teacher to do when experts apparently disagree on fundamentals?
3. What distinguishes between effective and ineffective coping mechanisms?
    How can the school help the child who boasts, who rationalizes, who develops neurotic symptoms?
4. What purpose is served by personality theories?
5. What constructive steps can the school take to deal with the underachiever and the potential dropout?
    Is a high-school education for all American youth a realistic national goal?

The primary responsibility for the child's personal and social adjustment lies with the parents, who set the basic personality pattern through the security they provide, particularly in the early years. The influence of teachers is only slightly less important, for they hold the key to whether the experiences the child undergoes in the extended journey through formal schooling will lead to satisfaction and self-fulfillment—or to frustration and self-defeat.

THE NATURE OF ADJUSTMENT

The Concept of Adjustment

Throughout life we adjust to environmental as well as internal demands. Thus, we are continually eating, drinking, striving for status and approval, seeking excitement. The adjustments we make in response to these demands are not always wise from the standpoint of our long-term welfare, but they are nevertheless attempts to cope with environmental requirements.

Adjustment implies physiological and psychological equilibrium

Adjustment may be defined as the process by means of which people seek to maintain physiological and psychological equilibrium and propel themselves toward self-enhancement. Implied is a state of harmonious relationship between the individual and his or her environment. Adjustment is specific to a given individual under specific conditions; it is meaningful only in terms of "adjusted to what?" It is also relative and temporary. A person can never be *adjusted*, for no matter how contented we may be over the fine meal we have just had, we will be out of harmony with the environment in a matter of hours if our next meal is not forthcoming. When we speak of promoting children's adjustment, we really mean we are trying to develop their capacity for *adjusting* on the premise that, if they can cope with the problems confronting them today they will be able to deal with the problems of tomorrow.

Adequacy of one's behavior patterns

Adjustment refers to the adequacy of the behavior patterns people habitually use to satisfy their needs. Since everyone has, at all times, multiple needs to satisfy, everyone is perpetually faced with adjustment problems and therefore potentially capable of being "adjusted" or "maladjusted," depending on the adequacy of his or her coping behavior. People may be considered maladjusted if, for instance, while they concentrate on satisfying their immediate needs, they actually increase the severity of the problem of satisfying their more basic or future needs, e.g., the child who daydreams instead of developing the skills necessary to convert fantasies into actualities or who resorts to antisocial behaviors that aggravate rather than alleviate problems.

Conflict, Frustration, and Anxiety

The question of adjustment revolves around such concepts as conflict, frustration, and anxiety. If all conflicts were to be resolved automatically, the individual would have no adjustment problem and, of course, no cause for learning. The fact that difficulties arise is the basis for both self-realization and self-destruction. Frustration and anxiety are inevitable and generally desirable components of any conflict situation, for they lead individuals to redouble as well as redirect their efforts to resolve their problems.

As we noted in chapter 4, anxiety is an unpleasant emotional state involving an ill-defined feeling of apprehension occurring in situations in which the self is threatened. Anxious individuals are afraid something terrible is going to happen, but they do not know what or when. As a result they are tense, fearful, disturbed, and driven to do something to reduce the unpleasant state of affairs. Anxiety is normal when there is a reason for apprehension and the response is constructive and proportional to the danger involved. The difficulty arises when anxiety becomes so severe that ineffectiveness or even disintegration of behavior sets in. Marshall (1947) estimated, for example, that fewer than one-third of the soldiers under orders to fire actually fired their rifles, and then not always in the direction of the enemy.

The classic study of the consequences of experimentally induced anxiety is that conducted by Maier et al. (1940), in which rats developed behavioral fixity (see chapter 4). What is interesting is the amazing strength of the fixation: strong punishment persistently administered did not seem to break the stereotyped reaction. Marquart (1946) found similar nonadaptive behavior in people; when confronted with a difficult (but not insoluble) problem, many just kept repeating a solution that had been adequate at one time but that they knew was no longer appropriate. Fixation is probably involved in many forms of inadequate behavior. For the very young child, temper tantrums, thumb-sucking, and aggression are reasonable patterns of adjustment, but they become a problem if continued beyond the developmental stage to which they belong. Too vigorous an attempt to have children shed these inadequate behavioral patterns may simply fixate them; severe punishment for temper tantrums may cause fixation by creating anxiety that so restricts their perceptual field that they are blinded to more adequate alternatives.

Learning and Adjustment

Adjustment has to be approached from the standpoint of learning, for adjustment reactions—whether constructive or detrimental to the individual's welfare—are learned according to the same principles as govern the learning of any other material. Adjustment patterns may develop unconsciously and outside of deliberate intent; they may have a partial basis in heredity, but they nevertheless are learned. Thus, according to reinforcement theory, as a consequence of the confirmation or denial of the adjustment made in a given situation, the individual learns not only a certain response to a specific situation but also certain response patterns for coping with situations in general. Some response patterns are adequate and effective from the standpoint of self-fulfillment; others are unhealthy, yet people persist in their use despite their short-comings. Perhaps they do not know of other approaches; more likely, they are afraid of the risk involved in leaving the safety of their present (albeit inadequate) position to strike out in a more constructive direction. They can withdraw, for example; this is sometimes the wisest thing to do, but, more commonly, they had better develop competence if they are not to become progressively more inadequate in relation to the situation. And again we need to remember that unwise approaches are sometimes reinforced often enough to be learned and also to make them particularly resistant to extinction.

We need to consider the development of adjustment patterns from the standpoint of the various theories of learning presented in chapter 3. Probably the best way of dealing with nonadjustive reactions, for example, is to ignore them; spanking the screaming child is often rewarding because of the attention it brings with it. From a cognitive point of view, maladjustment reflects lack of perceptual insight. All behavior has a purpose according to the individual's interpretation of the situation; his or her interpretation may be shortsighted when overconcern with the immediate situation blinds the person to goals more compatible with his or her long-range welfare. Of obvious relevance here is Maslow's distinction between deficiency (D) needs and growth (G) needs and its extension to "good choosers" and "bad choosers." Once learned, behavior patterns tend to maintain themselves through the satisfaction they provide, and they develop into habit motives, thus giving stability to behavior. As a result, ineffective behavior may become such an integral part of the total personality that it is highly resistant to change, especially in the case of the insecure person who cannot afford to experiment with more adequate modes of adjustment.

It may also be that the individual reaches a goal which, although satisfying in terms of his or her motivation, may involve violations of social standards. If the person is not sold on the standards in question, his or her only concern lies in not getting caught. On the other hand, to the extent that society is successful in having people internalize its rules and regulations, they will not be able to violate social constraints without automatically upsetting some personal value of importance to their continued adjustment. There may also be times when people cannot attain their goals without outside help. This may entail coaching in a special skill or perhaps psychological counseling, which will allow them to achieve reasonable adjustment. On the other hand, the obstacle may be of such resistance in relation to their potentialities that they may be completely overwhelmed. They are then likely to become desperate and aggravate rather than solve their problems. Their only salvation may lie in being removed from the situation or in being provided with considerable support. If this is not possible, their only escape may be an emotional breakdown, with possible eventual recovery with psychiatric help and improvement in the conditions that caused the difficulty.

PERSONALITY

At a superficial level, *personality* refers to the unique and distinctive characteristics that set one person apart from another and, as such, relates to the reaction one evokes from others. Personality is more than that; it represents the whole person—his or her physical, mental, social, and emotional assets and liabilities and the way these are put together into a pattern that is characteristic of and peculiar to a particular individual. It has special reference to the concept of the total organism interacting dynamically with the environment, i.e., affecting as well as being affected by the field forces of the psychological world as he or she attempts to attain his or her multiple purposes. What is important, however, is the integration of the personality acting as a totality and, of course, the direction in which the totality is oriented.

Children maintain themselves in precarious equilibrium between their external world, to whose expectations they must conform at least to a degree in order to be accepted, and their private idiosyncratic world, which they must protect and maintain, often at considerable psychological cost. They are continually reorienting themselves to the present, rehearsing the past, and modi-

fying their perspective. As a result, they are continually discovering themselves anew, revising their self-image with each revision of their world. When experiences are traumatic, however, this reorganization may be too difficult to manage and, as the emotional concomitants persist, their personality may become progressively more incongruous and jeopardize their capacity for further growth.

Personality is rather
consistent

Yet behavioral consistency is fundamental to the concept of personality, for only then can individuals remain who they are. Because personality is derived in part through identification with a variety of people, children may at first display inconsistencies in their personality. They gradually find themselves as they experiment with various roles and finally achieve personal identity, at least in connection with their dominant values. Personality orientation is relatively consistent over the years. Kagan and Moss (1960) found that girls who were highly dependent on their mothers at ages six through ten were still highly dependent on their families as adults. Dependent behavior was not as stable for males, presumably because it conflicts with the male self-concept and is extinguished through nonreinforcement (see Kagan 1964; Bloom 1964). It should also be noted that once people get known, others expect certain kinds of behavior from them and reinforce the role they have selected or that has been selected for them. Personality stability then becomes a function of environmental stability.

Parental Influence

Personality is the result of a wide array of interacting forces, the relative contribution and effect of which vary in the individual case in keeping with the uniqueness and yet the basic continuity of one's personality makeup. Heredity plays a fundamental role through determining the basic assets and liabilities individuals bring to a given situation. On the other hand, environmental factors are the final determinant, especially in shaping the specific ways in which inherited potential is actualized. The school, for example, plays an important role in providing a relatively objective basis from which children get their bearings and assess their potentialities for growth. It exerts a definite influence on the direction in which the personality is oriented—e.g., in determining whether a person dominated by aggressiveness and high energy is motivated toward social service or toward selfish or even antisocial behavior. The peer group also exerts a powerful influence, particularly in adolescence in connection with role identification. However, unquestionably the home plays the major role through establishing the basic personality, which can be modified and shaped as to direction but presumably little as to basic substance. It would seem that the strongest influence on a healthy personality development is a close satisfying relationship with the mother in infancy and early childhood.

The climate of the
home is critical

The climate of the home is of primary importance. Some parents, for example, overprotect their children and insist on prolonging their infancy by rendering service far beyond what is customary for their age. Others rule their children with an iron grip and drive them toward the achievement of goals often far beyond their capabilities in the belief that it is in their best interest that high standards be set for them. Some children submit meekly; if they can meet their parents' expectations, they may internalize parental pressures and themselves become drivers. They often achieve considerable academic and professional success—and occasionally peptic ulcers. Those with less ability may lie, cheat, and otherwise give the impression that they are fulfilling parental expectations and thus stave off unpleasantness. Others simply rebel, especially in adolescence, when psychological forces normally reduce parental influence over their children.

A number of studies have shown that dominant parents create submissive children. Symonds (1936) notes, however, that this apparent submissiveness simply represents a fearfulness of assuming a dominant role in a situation governed by authority. As these children become adults their pent-up aggression causes them to create the same family pattern all over again, and they become the dominant parents of another generation of submissive children. Children need freedom from excessive pressure, whether with respect to eating habits, toilet training, or other aspects of socialization. Discipline, for example, must provide adequate ethical guidelines without unduly restricting natural exploratory behavior. Parents must strike a balance between complete permissiveness, which leads to the development of a weak conscience, and excessive prohibition, which produces unrealistically severe moral constraints.

Personality Theories

A number of theories of personality have been developed, none of which is universally accepted. Each represents a meaningful, though possibly incomplete, way of looking at the complex phenomenon referred to as *personality*. The various theories vary in their emphasis; Hall and Lindzey (1957), for example, found heredity to have high priority in seven theories, moderate emphasis in six theories, and little emphasis in four theories. The self-concept was given high emphasis in eight theories, moderate emphasis in six, and little emphasis in three. For purposes of discussion, these various theories can be grouped into a number of relatively overlapping categories as follows:

1. *Type* theories, most recently represented by Sheldon's attempt to relate body build to temperament (Sheldon and Stevens 1942). Sheldon's theory, like the other type theories before his, is now essentially discredited.
2. *Trait* theories (e.g., Allport's theory of functionally autonomous traits, 1937; Cattell's surface and source traits, 1950), in which personality is described in terms of a number of basic traits generally identified through factor analysis. Hilgard (1962), for example, suggests that the most hopeful basis for characterizing individuals seems to be the con-

cept of personality syndromes—i.e., overall patterns of coping strategies—even if at present clear-cut syndromes can be specified only for certain individuals, e.g., the neurotic personality or the psychopathic personality.

3. *Developmental* theories, all of which emphasize the influence of early experiences and the continuity of development. Psychoanalysts, for example, postulate that overrigorous toilet training in infancy leads to the development of a compulsive personality structure characterized by excessive cleanliness, orderliness, obstinacy, and stinginess. Erikson's psychosocial theory (1968) is a relatively parallel view. Piaget's theory of cognitive development is among the better known.

4. *Learning* theories (e.g., Skinner, Gagné, and Hunt; see chapters 4, 5, and 12), which emphasize the cumulative nature of learning experiences.

5. *Role* theories, which emphasize the way individuals typically meet the demands society makes on them in their roles as parent, child, worker, citizen. These are essentially learning or developmental theories, but they stress the restrictions on people's freedom imposed by their role in life and the extent to which many of the decisions have already been made for them perhaps even before they were born.

6. *Phenomenological* theories, a loosely organized system (e.g., Rogers, Maslow, and Combs), which, in common with other field theories, places the emphasis on the present relationship of the individual with the environment as perceived by him or her at the time of behavior and which further focuses on the individual's basic need for self-actualization as an adequate guarantee of an integrated and functional personality (see chapter 4).

A number of other theories could be mentioned, e.g., Lewin's theory of personality dynamics (which focuses on the constant interaction of personality with the physical and social environment), social learning theories (Bandura and Walters 1963), and cognitive theories. Kelly's (1955) cognitive theory, for example, emphasizes the way in which individuals perceive and interpret stimuli in relation to their already existing cognitive structure (see also Ausubel 1968).

ERIKSON'S PSYCHOSOCIAL STAGE THEORY
OF PERSONALITY DEVELOPMENT

Of major interest in this context is Erikson's psychosocial theory of personality development (1968) in which he identifies eight ages in the human cycle from birth to old age (see figure 15.1). Each stage revolves around a central developmental crisis, with later development facilitated or jeopardized depending on

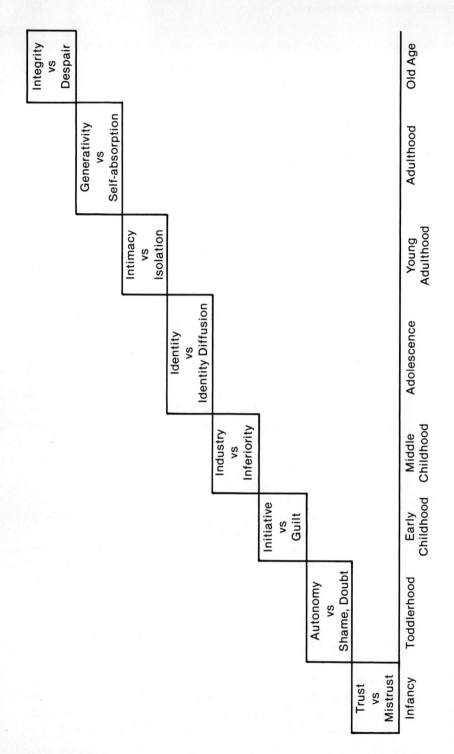

Figure 15.1 Erikson's Eight Stages of Man

the individual's relative success in coping with the crises of the previous stages.

1. Trust vs. mistrust (ages birth through one; Freud's oral stage): Infants are totally dependent on others for the satisfaction of their many needs, in fact, for their very survival. The development of trust and security is best fostered by consistency and continuity of experience in the satisfaction of their needs by the mother. If the mother conveys genuine affection, infants learn to see their world as friendly, predictable, and supportive. If, on the contrary, child care is inadequate, undependable, inconsistent, and otherwise inappropriate, the infant learns mistrust, fearfulness, and insecurity.

2. Autonomy vs. doubt (ages two through three; Freud's anal period): At this stage, parents begin to make demands on the child and to impose rules and regulations. If socialization demands are reasonable and made under conditions of love and encouragement, if children are encouraged to exercise their increasing potentialities to do what they are capable of doing, then they will develop a sense of autonomy. If, on the other hand, the parents are overdemanding, impatient, and critical of his or her efforts, the toddler will develop a sense of shame and doubt in his or her ability.

3. Initiative vs. guilt (ages four through five; Freud's phallic period): Depending on whether the parents respond to the child's increasing capabilities for self-initiated exploration and manipulation of the environment with encouragement, reinforcement, warmth, and acceptance—or, on the contrary, with overcontrol, rejection, impatience at the endless questions, and punitive measures—the young child develops a sense of either industry and personal self-reliance or a sense of inadequacy, inhibition, fear of failure, and guilt.

4. Industry vs. inferiority (ages six through eleven; Freud's latency period): A sense of industry and accomplishment emerges as the efforts of grade-school children at manipulating, organizing, and ordering the environment meet with success, praise, recognition of progress, and encouragement. If their efforts meet with systematic failure or are typically rebuffed, criticized, or ridiculed, they develop a sense of failure and inferiority.

5. Identity vs. role confusion (ages twelve through eighteen; Freud's genital period): As the advent of formal operations enables them to synthesize their various experiences and to sort out their values, adolescents, (1) under conditions of consistency in their personal life together with success, personal satisfaction, and social acceptance, develop a sense of identity and personal direction, i.e., an integration of various roles to the point of experiencing continuity in their perceptions of self, or (2) under conditions of inconsistency, contradiction,

and chaos under which they cannot decipher who they are and where they are going, may experience role confusion or may resort to "negative identity" in which they take on a socially unacceptable role, e.g., a "hippie" copout pattern.

6. Intimacy vs. isolation (young adulthood): The young adult, having established personal identity, now wants to establish intimate personal relationships with others, particularly with a person of the opposite sex, based on mutual affection and trust. People who have had difficulty with previous crises, who mistrust others, who have a low self-esteem, who are afraid to take the initiative, or who are still searching for personal identity are often unable to develop such intimate contacts and suffer isolation.

7. Generativity vs. self-absorption (middle age): The achievement of a successful and rewarding personal life permits adults to extend their concerns beyond themselves to their family, to society, and other aspects of human welfare. Failure to achieve personal success, satisfaction, and self-acceptance may, on the contrary, lead to a narrow Scrooge-like preoccupation with one's own welfare.

8. Integrity vs. despair (old age): Integrity refers to the feeling of satisfaction of having lived a full and rewarding life and acceptance of the future, including eventual death. Despair characterizes those who feel that they have failed, that they never amounted to anything, and that there is no longer time to start afresh.

ADJUSTMENT-MALADJUSTMENT: NORMALITY-ABNORMALITY

Although of prime interest, *adjustment* has never been a particularly satisfactory concept from the standpoint of either scientific or operational clarity. Just what should ideally adjusted persons be like? What should they do? Is the well-adjusted person the equivalent of the "normal" person, and is maladjustment the equivalent of abnormality? The concept of adjustment can be approached from a number of points of view, none particularly acceptable. The statistical view, for example, makes adjustment a matter of conformity to the majority. The pathological version of the statistical position is even more objectionable in that it is oriented toward the negative end of the continuum: to identify a normal person as one who is relatively free from abnormal symptoms is dealing with the dimension of pathology—the idea that everybody is a little queer except thee and me. Shoben (1957) objects to thinking of normality in relativistic terms; delinquency is bad not because it is infrequent but because it *is* bad. He sees normality as a matter of integrative behavior rather than a condition of minimal pathology. M. Smith (1961), in a similar vein, feels that mental health inherently contains an evaluative dimension and that psychology as a science cannot divorce itself from values.

Adjustment can be considered from a number of basic dimensions:

1. The perceptual and cognitive domain: Ideal adjustment is characterized by efficiency in dealing with situational demands. Involved is the concept of competence, which permits individuals to adapt to situations calling for a shift in role, to distinguish between the important and the trivial, the relevant and the irrelevant, etc., but especially it relates to contact with reality based on openness to experience and relative freedom from perceptual distortion.
2. The personal domain: Well-adjusted individuals accept themselves and have confidence in their adequacy.
3. The social domain: Adjusted individuals display social sensitivity; they conform to social expectations not because it is the thing to do, but because it promotes their self-realization and that of others.
4. The affective domain: While happiness is neither a criterion nor a primary goal of adjustment, it is generally a by-product of positive personality orientation characterized by spontaneity, zest, a sense of humor, and openness to experience. Adjusted people live in harmony with their world and derive pleasure from life.
5. The self-actualization domain: Orientation toward self-actualization is an important criterion of personal and social adjustment.

Adjustment results from two sets of forces in dynamic interaction: forces within the individual and forces from the environment. Individuals must maintain their equilibrium while, at the same time, growing toward greater adequacy and greater complexity. Adjustment is not a simple matter of satisfying one's needs but rather of integrating one's purposes and needs with those of the social order. Mature people either conform to social standards because their acceptance eventually leads to greater human welfare or, if they rebel, do so on considered grounds and are willing to pay the price for behaving according to their own values. It is not a question of their fitting into a preconceived behavioral mold that can be considered adjusted or normal but rather a matter of operational functionality. It follows that we need to emphasize the positive—i.e., the promotion of mental health—with the prevention of pathology as a vital but secondary aspect.

On the other hand, we cannot define the normal person as one possessing all the desirable traits, nor can we assume that well-adjusted individuals are free from conflict, happy, successful, etc. It might be expected that mentally healthy people would be characterized by spontaneity, productivity, zest, freedom from severe conflicts, a positive outlook, freedom to use their ability to the fullest, etc., but we must recognize that these traits exist on a continuum and that no one is completely adjusted. Perhaps no one is completely maladjusted. Some degree of "maladjustment" in children is characteristic of development, i.e., "normal"; the preadolescent, for example, is typically quarrelsome. Many signs of maladjustment among children may well represent nothing more than the very normal immaturity of youth.

A multidimensional criterion best

Since it relates to every aspect of the individual's functioning, the concept of normality is perhaps best defined in terms of a multidimensional criterion, such as presented by Jahoda (1958), M. Smith (1961), and W. Scott (1968), to include openness to experience, personal integration, self-respect and self-actualization, adaptability and competence, autonomy, self-reliance, and personal efficiency. We might, for instance, think of the individual's ability to face the stresses of life without caving in or striking out against society. We might also think of resiliency, i.e., the individual's ability to recover, to rejuvenate, to bounce back from the buffeting of the day. This neurotics cannot do; they are constantly overwhelmed by previous setbacks. The sting of a chance remark is never forgotten; they never recover from misfortunes, defeats, and personal blunders.

Adjustment: Accurate perception of reality

Adjustment implies adequate feedback and a relatively accurate perception of reality. Phenomenologists, for example, postulate that one's behavior can be no more adequate than one's perceptions. Because they distort their perceptions and therefore base their behavior on false perceptions of the world, neurotics are necessarily "stupid" (see Dollard and Miller 1950). According to Bower (1969), they are not only emotionally sick; they are also cognitively wrong. Adjusted individuals have a positive self-concept; they know themselves, they have confidence in themselves, and above all they set realistic goals. Maladjusted individuals who, by contrast, set goals beyond their capacities automatically assign themselves to a lifetime of failure and self-inflicted unhappiness.

Adjustment and self-actualization

Adjustment also implies choosing one's coping strategies, not simply to meet obligations, but rather to gain the highest return from one's investment in terms of long-term self-actualization. Direct action, for instance, is preferable to withdrawal, which offers no chance of real success. Maladjusted people are forever dissipating their energies in protecting a weak ego so they have no energy left to deal with the problems of life. Typically, they engage in self-defeating behaviors, e.g., jealousy, fantasy, etc., with cumulative inadequacy the inevitable consequence. In fact, unhealthy people are characterized not so much by negative traits as they are afflicted by a kind of creeping paralysis that spreads across their whole personality.

Adjustment: A matter of degree

On the other hand, adjustment differs from maladjustment in degree rather than in kind and, despite objections, normal adjustment simply entails behavior within the range of tolerated differences, where the limits of such a range are uncertain and flexible. More specifically, adjusted people show a relatively high degree of personal integration; they display behavior that is effective in attaining their goals; they face problems realistically, and devote their energies to attaining their purposes. On the other hand, individuals caught between a resistant obstacle and a persistent motivation find their frustration mounting to the point of causing excessive interference and even disorganization of behavior. Internal conflict may cause them to be at cross-purposes with themselves, with resulting indecision and inability to coordinate their efforts in the pursuit of meaningful goals. When this pattern becomes typical of their behavior, they may be said to be maladjusted, although there is no sharp line separating the maladjusted from the adjusted.

Symptoms of maladjustment

Maladjustment is revealed through any number of symptoms, many of which, at least in their milder forms, are also characteristic of normal adjustment. Among the more common are explosive behavior, general restlessness, preoccupation (daydreaming, absentmindedness, worry), withdrawal (excessive reading for vicarious excitement, shyness, and general avoidance of social situations), and physical dysfunctions. Another set of symptoms such as crying, temper tantrums, fixations, dependence on others, lack of motivation, inability to assume responsibility, attempts to win sympathy, and selfishness are often signs of immaturity rather than maladjustment, i.e., they reflect failure to learn more mature ways of behaving rather than the learning of undesirable behavior patterns. Regardless of differences in antecedents, however, both immaturity and maladjustment are difficult to deal with. To the extent that they are incorporated into the self-image, changing them calls for major reorganization of the total personality.

ADJUSTMENT (COPING) MECHANISMS

People gradually learn certain behavior patterns through which they attempt to cope with situational demands. Thus, the boy who is frustrated by his inability to gain social recognition and self-esteem by getting on the honor roll *rationalizes* that only sissies are interested in grades, or perhaps develops *neurotic symptoms*, e.g., headaches, that make his failure to get on the honor roll "understandable." These strategies, known as *adjustment* or *coping mechanisms*, are neither disorders nor symptoms of maladjustment; they are simply the adjustments individuals make when confronted with certain needs, on the one hand, and certain situational realities, on the other.

Compensation

Compensation is a common form of adjustment. The adolescent whose athletic abilities are limited *compensates* by achieving academic honors or vicariously through *identifying* with some baseball or football hero. Parents compensate through their children, often to the detriment of the latter; the father who harbors a sense of inadequacy over his inability to get past junior high may insist that his son meet unrealistic standards of academic excellence. Compensation is also involved in such attention-getting devices as boasting and exhibitionism. People can also resolve feelings of inadequacy through *rationalization*, i.e., giving plausible but untrue reasons for one's behavior as a

defense against having to admit that, by objective standards, it is irresponsible or otherwise inadequate. Again, rationalization may take on any number of forms from "sour grapes" or "sweet lemons" to blaming the incidental "cause." A more serious form of rationalization is *projection,* in which individuals perceive in others the traits and motives for which they themselves feel inferior; they not only repress the feelings that they find intolerable in themselves but unconsciously attribute them to others so that they feel justified in directing their aggression toward others rather than toward themselves. Selfish people see selfishness in others and convince themselves that their own self-centeredness is made necessary by the selfishness of others. Another common coping mechanism is *withdrawal,* e.g., procrastination, bashfulness, timidity, etc., in which individuals avoid difficult situations; in *fantasy* (daydreaming), for example, they become the conquering hero for whom success and revenge are unlimited, or the suffering hero whose misfortune causes even their enemies great sorrow.

Neuroses   More serious are the *neuroses,* a term used to describe a wide variety of relatively ineffective behavioral patterns involving fear, anxiety, guilt, and repression. Whereas fear is a basic component of all coping mechanisms, abnormal fears (*phobias*) develop as a consequence of the repressing of guilt. Repressed guilt can also lead to *obsessive-compulsive reactions* (e.g., Lady

Macbeth's hand washing) or to various psychosomatic ailments (i.e., *hysteria*) from migraine headaches and backaches to more serious forms of physical dysfunction.

The list of specific coping mechanisms is long, ranging from the simple to the complex, and especially from the constructive aspects of some forms of compensation to the total breakdown in adjustment involved in the psychoses. All people have needs; therefore all have to rely on coping mechanisms. The adjusted as well as the maladjusted use most of these mechanisms; even adjusted people daydream, rationalize, and develop migraine headaches. On the other hand, some of these mechanisms are potentially dangerous when they detract from rather than contribute to personal adequacy. They tend to develop into rigid behavior patterns to the point that people become victims of their own defenses. Insecure children who rationalize their shortcomings, for instance, deny themselves the opportunity of developing greater adequacy and thereby close off avenues of experience. Generally adjustment mechanisms are undesirable when they displace more constructive modes of behavior, when they are relatively ineffective in satisfying basic needs, or when they introduce greater problems than they resolve.

On the other hand, the question is not the use of any one of these adjustment mechanisms by itself but rather the overall pattern of adjustment. Neuroses, for example, are better seen as behavioral syndromes that permeate the whole personality rather than simply a set of specific nonadjustive reactions, for the essence of the neurotic personality is this underlying psychological makeup that makes one's behavior chronically inadequate. Neurotics, for example, are characterized by immaturity, indecision, irresponsibility, self-centeredness, emotional self-pity, and emotional instability, presumably arising out of an inadequate parent-child relation that stood in the way of a healthy ego development and personality integration. They are so busy contriving new defenses and new excuses and indulging in self-pity that they have no energy left for more constructive living. A central feature is neurotic anxiety, i.e., a state of fear completely out of proportion to any discernible cause. These anxiety attacks typically are accompanied by a variety of body symptoms that may involve perspiration, dizziness, heart flutter, and even paralysis. Neurotics are disturbed by these symptoms, but since the latter serve a protective purpose, they cannot relinquish them. What is most devastating is the self-compounding spiral of neurotic involvement that the neurotic person systematically gets into.

THE DROPOUT

School dropout continues to be a major problem confronting American education. Half the ghetto youth drop out before completing high school, for example—this despite the fact that no other country in the world has placed so much emphasis on high school graduation as a minimum educational goal. It is not easy for youngsters to leave school; not only does society insist on the "necessity" for teenagers to complete their education but further makes sure that they have no other place to go except school.[1] The unfortunate thing is that in many cases we have very little to offer these youngsters, who are then maintained in school without gaining anything therefrom. Many of them have been psychologically absent for years; the curriculum has overwhelmed them long ago; the whole operation has turned them off.

Reasons for dropping out from school

The reasons teenagers give for leaving school are varied and, in many cases, quite superficial. It seems that when youngsters feel that they are getting nowhere and that further efforts to succeed are useless, they just drop out. Generally dissatisfaction with school is part of a larger picture of psychological discontent, embracing these students' overall view of themselves in relation to the rest of the world. Lower-class children, for example, often find themselves "incompatible" with almost all aspects of school from the curriculum to the teacher and the dominant middle-class peer group. Except for a few who succeed in athletics, most lower-class children feel unwanted and generally left out. If all of this is to be avoided, the school must emphasize a feeling of belonging, a sense of pride and meaningfulness in what is going on. It is extremely important to provide success within the framework of the school's program. There is no excuse, for example, for failing to provide remedial help for children with serious reading disabilities; they certainly cannot achieve satisfactory academic and peer status if they cannot read.

Parents often contribute to children's difficulties by insisting that they could do better if they only tried; the youngsters on the other hand, remember that trying leads only to greater disappointment. They cannot afford to risk further downgrading of their self-concept or peer status. Overwhelmed by the immediate situation, they may see dropping out as the only way to get relief from unbearable conditions. It also seems that, once it has occurred, dropout is relatively irreversible. Questions of loss of face before peers, making up for lost work, repudiating the "reasons" given for dropping out, and restructuring a new self-concept make returning to the same school quite precarious. Even when dropouts are persuaded to return to school, the same old curriculum presented in the same old way is bound to have essentially the same results and wear down rather quickly any renewed motivation. A technical program related to a clear-cut vocational goal might have a better chance of success.

1. The dropout problem is critical by virtue of a number of factors largely extraneous to the school and peculiar to our times, e.g., unemployment, elimination of certain unskilled jobs through automation, an increase in welfare rolls, increased use of technology on the farm and migration to the cities, delinquency among unemployed youth, etc. Society has marshaled an imposing but highly questionable array of "facts" to convince teenagers that they are doing themselves a catastrophic disservice by dropping out of school. See Berg (1970); Bettelheim (1970); Combs and Cooley (1964); Goodman (1960); and Lammers (1967).

THE UNDERACHIEVER

Related to school dropout and in some ways even more serious is the problem of underachievement, particularly on the part of many high school students who, although still physically in school, have, in all meaningful senses of the word, dropped out. Unquestionably underachievement represents a serious waste of academic talent. As in the case of the dropout, the causes vary widely. Apparently a number of students are not finding in school work the satisfaction they seek. Some have different values; past experience has led them to see sports and other activities as so much more productive of status, popularity, feelings of accomplishment and self-worth that school requirements are, by comparison, rather unattractive.

Many gifted children have so many other interests that make demands on their time and talents in a much more critical way that education simply assumes a secondary role, especially since they are likely to find the standard curriculum rather boring. Underachievement is also prevalent among the disadvantaged, many of whom have simply given up. Some never got going; they began with a deficit and it got worse as day after day they were expected to anchor progressively more advanced material, layer upon layer, on a progressively more inadequate cognitive base. Meanwhile motivation had to falter for lack of nourishment, for underachievement feeds on itself. Children who fall behind in their work accumulate deficiencies that are bound to cause both cognitive and motivational difficulties.

Reasons students lose interest in school

Many underachievers have lost interest in school work, often because the school's failure to provide the necessary diagnostic and remedial work in time has cut them off from meaningful and rewarding participation in the academic program.[2] Some may have had unrealistic expectations and ended up systematically defeated. They gave up in order to stop disappointing themselves and thereby locked in relatively permanent underperformance by changing their self-concept accordingly. Parents and teachers often contribute to the problem by applying pressures, by making the child feel guilty for not trying, when frequently such lack of motivation is "necessary" to protect the self against damage. Research has shown underachievers to be more hostile, to have more negative attitudes toward the school, to have a relatively negative self-concept, and to be lacking in responsibility, seriousness of purpose, self-confidence, and persistence. But such research does not tell us whether these are the cause of underachievement or simply the effect of the continued failure and frustration that precipitated the underachievement (see Asbury 1974).

No easy cure

There is no easy cure. Once the pattern of chronic underachievement has been set, its many problems go deep and defy instant remediation. There is

---

2. The unfortunate aspect of the situation is that by giving up, the student automatically relieves the teacher of any guilt over failure to teach him or her.

obvious need for drastic modification of the educational program to take into account the underachiever's low ego strength and limited aspiration and, especially, to remedy accumulated deficiencies. It is imperative to reverse the long-standing pattern of maladjustment to the school that characterizes chronic underachievers. We just cannot tell them to work harder; that is fine for students who already have a high self-concept and a high need for achievement as well as effective skills but why should children with a poor performance record try when trying brings only further failure? Their self-concept must be bolstered through meaningful reinforcement connected with a systematic schedule of small successes in areas of importance to them. They especially need to be helped to see schooling as a meaningful activity in terms of what really matters to them (see Schaefer 1977; Baker 1975). There lies a real challenge to any teacher who wants to do something for another human being.

HIGHLIGHTS OF THE CHAPTER

To the extent that the school has accepted responsibility for the all-around growth of children, it must make their personal and social adjustment an integral part of its concern.

1. Adjustment refers to the adequacy of the behavior patterns individuals habitually use to satisfy their needs and achieve their purposes. It implies a state of harmony between the individual and his or her environment.
2. Adjustment is best seen as a continuous process of adjusting. Complete adjustment cannot be achieved, nor would it be desirable for people to be "adjusted" to some of the conditions in their environment.
3. Adjustment involves five basic dimensions: cognitive, personal, social, affective, and self-actualizing. It implies integrating one's purposes with those of the social order for the welfare of all.
4. Adjustment is learned according to the same principles as govern other forms of learning. Behaviorists would rely on selective reinforcement. Cognitive psychologists, on the other hand, attribute shortsighted behavior to a lack of cognitive clarity as to the nature of the situation and the means for attaining one's purposes.
5. The home plays a major role in personality development through providing inherited potential, setting up the basic personality through early child-rearing practices, and further influencing the direction in which the personality is oriented.
6. A number of personality theories have been devised, each focusing on a different aspect. Erikson's psychosocial stages provide an interesting perspective.

7. The coping mechanisms used by adjusted and maladjusted persons differ in degree rather than in kind. Maladjustment is defined not so much by negative traits as by the self-aggravating spiral of inadequate and ineffective behaviors that permeate the whole personality.

8. Teachers with their middle-class orientation have difficulty in understanding children of lower-class background. If we are concerned with problems of dropout and underachievement that typically plague our schools, we need to shut off production at the source with a meaningful program of prevention.

SUGGESTIONS FOR FURTHER READING

GINOTT, HAIM. *Teacher and Child.* New York: Macmillan, 1971 This booklet, together with Ginott's other publications, *Parent and Child* (1965) and *Between Parent and Teenager* (1969), emphasizes techniques whereby adults can communicate with children and help them explore and air out their feelings. Suggests a balance among permissiveness, self-control, and personal responsibility.

JAHODA, MARIE. *Current Concepts of Positive Mental Health.* New York: Basic Books, 1958. Presents a multidimensional view of personal and social adjustment and normality.

MILLER, JOHN P. Piaget, Kohlberg, and Erikson: Developmental implications for secondary education. *Adolescence* 13 (1978):237–250. Integrates the developmental works of Piaget, Kohlberg, and Erikson and points to their curricular implications for adolescence.

QUESTIONS AND PROJECTS

1. Evaluate: Much of the problem behavior among boys is nothing more than a healthy nonconformity to impossible standards and demands.
   Evaluate: Far too much of the school's effort has been directed toward the maladjusted, the dull, the unfit, to the neglect of the adequate and the gifted.

2. To what extent is conformity to current social values and mores an aspect of adjustment? Evaluate the "adjustment" of the delinquent, the underachiever, the drug user, etc.

3. What priorities might be given personal and social adjustment among the school's objectives? How might personal and academic goals be integrated?

4. How do you account for the high incidence of maladjustment—immaturity, neuroses, delinquency, strife, etc.—among young and old, pre-

sumably the world over? What role might the school play in the promotion of peace and goodwill in the world of tomorrow?

5. List in order of importance six suggestions for promoting personality development in school—e.g., provide for self-enhancement by helping students set and achieve meaningful goals.

6. Evaluate: Compulsory school attendance is an unrealistic and self-defeating policy. It even saves the school from having to improve its curriculum and its method of operation.

SELF-TEST

1. Adjustment refers to
   a. the adequacy of the behavior patterns through which individuals typically satisfy their needs.
   b. freedom from overreliance on the usual "adjustment mechanisms."
   c. the relative absence of conflict and self-defeating behavior.
   d. the relative absence of tension and anxieties.
   e. the relative success of the individual in coping with situational demands.

2. The most common outcome of anxiety is
   a. experimental neurosis.
   b. functional fixity.
   c. personal maladjustment.
   d. phobia.
   e. restriction of the perceptual field.

3. The adjustment patterns most likely to lead to maladjustment are those that
   a. are highly effective.
   b. are only partially effective.
   c. are totally ineffective.
   d. operate at the subconscious level.
   e. produce definitely noxious results.

4. The crucial feature of personality is
   a. the balance of one's assets and liabilities.
   b. the dependability of one's reactions.
   c. the integration of one's assets and liabilities into a functional unit.
   d. the special characteristics that set one apart as an individual.
   e. one's adjustment-maladjustment balance.

5. Which of Erikson's crises is incorrectly allocated as to age period?
   a. Identity/role confusion: young adulthood
   b. Industry/inferiority: grade school
   c. Initiative/guilt: preschool
   d. Integrity/despair: old age
   e. Trust/mistrust: infancy

6. The primary factor involved in school dropout is
   a. the gap between pupil ability and academic demands.
   b. incompatibility between the student and the peer culture.
   c. the lack of orientation of the home and community to the value of education.
   d. the negative view of the school characteristic of the lower-class child.
   e. the unsuitability of the school's curriculum.

7. The well-adjusted person is characterized primarily by
   a. drive, leadership, and effectiveness.
   b. freedom from conflict.
   c. personal integration and openness to experience.
   d. sensitivity to social pressures and conformity to social constraints.
   e. spontaneity, decisiveness, and zest.

SIXTEEN

Mental Health in the Classroom

I have a strong belief that every learner should feel better, more able to cope with unknown vicissitudes more courageously at the end of a class than he did at the opening. If he feels worse, less able and less courageous, then the class has damaged him, rather than helped him. If this is oft repeated, then he is on his way to the human scrapheap.

Earl C. Kelley (1965)

For the majority of children the most effective mental health benefits they can derive from school is through the intrinsic quality of educational experience rather than by some sort of therapeutic regime that is grafted onto school life.

Viola W. Bernard (1958)

All discussions of mental health in the schools lead back to the personality and competence of the teacher.

Ruth Strang (1960)

A teacher is, by the very nature of his work, denied clear-cut, indisputable proof of his effectiveness.

Robert H. Snow (1963)

— Presents mental hygiene as an integral part of the teaching-learning process
— Points out the mental health implications of common school practices
— Emphasizes the role of teachers in promoting the mental health of their students and in safeguarding their own

PREVIEW: KEY CONCEPTS

1. Mental illness continues to be the nation's Number One health problem; statistics, on the other hand, are difficult to interpret.
2. Despite the many other demands on its services, the school is probably in a better position than any other social agency to deal with the problem.
3. Mental hygiene in the school is necessarily oriented toward the developmental and the preventive rather than the remedial and the therapeutic.
4. The teacher is necessarily the key to the school's mental health program.
5. The classroom operation entails a number of hazards to the mental health of many of its students—standards, grading, discipline, etc. The suitability of the academic program is a critical factor.
6. The mental health of the teacher is of equally critical importance. We can list a number of hazards which, unfortunately, take their toll.

PREVIEW QUESTIONS

1. What is the extent of mental illness in modern society?
    How dependable are available statistics?
2. Why should student mental health be of any concern to the school?
    Can the school afford to take on any responsibility neglected by other social agencies?
3. What are some of the major school-connected hazards to the mental health of school children?
    Is this more or less unavoidable?
4. Why is the teacher's mental health of equal concern?
    Specifically, how can teachers safeguard their own mental health?

EXTENT OF THE PROBLEM

Problems of mental health have always been with us. These range from the mild difficulties that occasionally bother the most serene to the violent disturbances that characterize psychotics. It is only recently, however, that mental health problems have been understood for what they are, namely, a state of ill health in the emotional field comparable to similar conditions in physical health. Mental health is our Number One health problem. No matter from what angle it is approached, the conclusion is unavoidable: there is something seriously wrong with the emotional functioning of a significant percentage of the American people. The cause and, of course, the cure are more elusive.

Except for cases actually hospitalized as psychotics in state institutions, statistics on the prevalence of mental disorders are difficult to get and to interpret.[1] Estimates on the number of persons treated in private clinics or cared for at home vary with the severity of illness used as criterion. Undoubtedly some of the institutionalized patients are less disturbed than some who do not become part of the statistics. All we can do is arrive at educated guesses. It is estimated, for example, that from 10 to 15 percent of the American population suffers from "serious" mental illness (R. Menninger 1978); it also seems that half of the patients in U.S. hospitals on any given day are mental patients. On the positive side, the length of institutionalization in the average case has been drastically shortened. There are also indications of a slight decline in admissions, although this may simply reflect the greater availability of private clinics and perhaps the greater effectiveness of modern drugs and outpatient clinics in keeping potential patients functioning on a day-to-day basis.

It is estimated that some 5 percent of the adult population is sufficiently neurotic to be relatively handicapped in social adjustment. A number of others are making a reasonable adjustment in a sheltered environment but would not be able to withstand more severe conditions. Half the clientele of the average medical practitioner suffers from illness resulting at least in part from psychogenic factors. It is also estimated that more than half of the accidents in which nearly half a million Americans are disabled each year can be traced partly to personality problems. In addition, a million Americans have criminal records, some very long records. Corruption and graft in high office is common.[2] Our streets are no longer safe by night.[3] Anywhere from 10 to 18 billion Americans are heavy drinkers or chronic alcoholics (*U.S. News & World Report* 1978). We have yet to determine the seriousness of the current drug crisis.

Statistics difficult to get and to interpret

1. See Robert D. Allen and Marsha Cartier, *The Mental Health Almanac, 1978–79* (Garland S. T. M. Press, 1978), for current statistics on mental illness, alcoholism, drug abuse, etc.
2. *U.S. News & World Report* (1978) reports that Americans cheat or steal some $25 billion a year from the government. What they rip off from employers, merchants, and fellow citizens is beyond calculation.
3. Some of our schools are hardly safe by day. According to a recent NIE study (see *Phi Delta Kappan*, 59 [1978]: 499), the most dangerous place for a city teenager to be is inside his or her own school.

MENTAL HYGIENE IN THE CLASSROOM

The Nature of Mental Hygiene

The extent to which the school should assume responsibility for the mental health of its pupils is a matter of controversy. Some have questioned the wisdom of trying to be all things to all people by assuming responsibility for tasks not within its sphere of function and competence, perhaps even to the neglect of its primary responsibilities. On the other hand, not only does the school have close contact with children early in life when the damage is not beyond repair, but it cannot ignore adjustment difficulties since they will interfere with the attainment of academic goals, no matter how narrowly these are conceived. Children who are overwhelmed by insecurity, frustration, worry, and resentment cannot be expected to give their full attention to school work. We certainly cannot expect children to operate at the higher levels of Maslow's hierarchy until they have alleviated their tensions, anxieties, and other aspects of personal malfunctioning.

The school is in the best position

The home, and not the school, has primary responsibility for the mental health of the child. However, the school with its greater perspective has a definite contribution to make here. There is a limit to what it can do, yet the task is not impossible inasmuch as perfection is not required. There is no right way of handling a given situation, and generally a certain amount of professional knowledge and technical know-how coupled with good intentions, a wholesome acceptance of children, and a consistency of application tend to produce good results. Children are resilient creatures whose natural desire to grow enables them to adjust to the difference.

The school is in favorable position to promote the positive aspects of personal development. By working with children day by day, it can help them to develop wholesome attitudes, values, and habits and to consolidate these into an effective pattern of life. It provides a variety of opportunities for them to learn satisfying ways of working and playing together; it also provides knowledge and skills that enable them to develop into competent, self-sufficient individuals, capable of meeting social and vocational demands. It has an even greater effect on personality adjustment through the influence it exerts over the parents of the next generation. The school has a more direct responsibility in saving children from undue frustration and relieving undue pressures so that their natural growth potentialities can take over.

Mental hygiene in the classroom attempts to . . .

As an organized program, mental hygiene has three main purposes: the prevention of mental disorders, the preservation and development of mental health, and the alleviation of maladjustment. As it applies to the classroom, mental hygiene is not a matter of the teacher engaging in a desperate struggle to keep children from going insane or to cure those already in difficulty; it is not a body of specialized procedures as might be used in a clinical setting. Rather it is an integral part of the teaching-learning process. In other words, whereas it must necessarily be an important consideration in all aspects of the development of the curriculum, the training of teachers and administrators, and the operation of the whole plant, to be effective, mental health must be an integral part of the school's child development program, not something that is grafted on as a separate activity.

Teachers and Mental Health

The introduction of mental hygiene in the school has been a slow and reluctant process. Schools are always pressured into adding new programs, and the first impulse is to resist such additions, particularly when they involve extra costs in teacher time and energy. However, as teachers began to realize that the frustrated, anxious child is not a "teachable" child, they also began to see concern for the child's mental health as a wise investment from the standpoint of pupil growth as well as teacher satisfaction, and mental hygiene became progressively more accepted—although even now many teachers are operating in more or less direct defiance of its principles.

What the school can do

If the school is to be effective in fostering mental health, it must define clearly what it can and what it cannot do. Teachers must recognize that their training does not allow them to deal with the therapeutic or corrective aspects of mental hygiene. This is one area where love and good intentions are not enough. In advanced cases teachers must restrict themselves to detection of problems, referral to competent authorities, and cooperation with recommendations for treatment as they apply to the classroom. It is in the area of personality development that the school can make its greatest contribution, especially because it has at its disposal the curriculum, social interaction, and other facilities through which the child's natural need to grow and to *become* can operate. The teacher's greatest contribution to mental health lies in providing individual children with meaningful experiences and opportunities for satisfying needs and in creating an atmosphere of acceptance for all children no matter what they do or who they are. On a less positive note, the school can, at least, refrain from contributing to the child's difficulties by adding frustrations of its own.

Recognizing danger signs

Teachers need to acquaint themselves with the symptoms of maladjustment so that they can recognize its existence early and refer the child to a competent clinician. Unfortunately teachers are not well trained in recognizing danger signals; they are likely to consider the quiet, retiring child who never causes trouble as a model student and consider the troublemaker as ready to be institutionalized, whereas actually the former may be in greater danger from a mental health point of view than is the latter, a fact, Margolin (1953) feels, teachers have been slow to grasp, despite years of exhortation by mental hygienists. In the well-known Wickman study (1928), for example, teachers rated fifty behavior problems in somewhat the reverse order of the ratings of clinicians. Although more recent and better studies have shown much closer agreement between teachers and clinicians in their ratings of behavior problems as abstract concepts (Rapkin and Suchoski 1964; Ishee 1969), it seems that even today teachers are still not able to correctly diagnose their behavioral counterparts for possible referral of actual cases (Goldfarb 1963).

Mental Health Factors in the Classroom

Since a large part of children's experiences during their formative years are connected with the school, the latter necessarily bears a responsibility for their adjustment second only to that of the home. The school especially must recognize that by its very nature it incorporates many features that may constitute definite hazards to the mental health of children. The fact that the school has primary responsibility for promoting academic learning, for example, may mean frustration, perhaps even continuous and severe frustration, for some children. Americans tend to get entangled in the concept of precocity; we want to do things earlier and better than the person next door. Parents want their children to walk early; teachers want their children to surpass the norms. This can result in unhealthy pressures being applied on certain children for whom pressures can do nothing but harm.

On the premise that prevention is a more constructive approach than correction after the harm has been done, teachers need to evaluate every classroom procedure for its mental health implications. The following is a partial list of the more obvious factors having a direct bearing on the mental health of the school child.

Individual differences as a mental health hazard

1. The wide range of individual differences in the classroom makes it difficult for teachers to provide meaningful experiences for each child and to have each achieve the satisfaction the school program must necessarily provide if it is to be a positive factor in the child's mental health.[4] The problem is aggravated by the emphasis on grading, with grades referenced to group rather than to personal standards. As a result, the school's whole operation becomes geared to competition, competition not freely chosen by the students but forced on them regardless of their relative chance of success. More specifically, the school delegates some children to relatively continuous failure and frustration on a predetermined basis.

Competition is often unfair

Conflict is introduced when emphasis on good grades by teachers and parents is neutralized by pressures for mediocrity exerted by the peer culture (see Coleman 1961). With the problem complicated further by the necessity for good grades for college admission, the school is systematically putting students in a position of having to meet common standards relative to a common curriculum, with discouragement, cheating, a lowering of ethical standards, etc.,

---

4. For every child frustrated because the material is too difficult, there is likely to be another frustrated because the work is obnoxiously easy; and any number who are bored because the material bears no relation to their goals and purposes. The new orientation toward individualized instruction (see chapter 9) may be of partial help here.

likely, if not inevitable. Perhaps more critical from the standpoint of the reinforcement children must get from their learning if they are to succeed is the
fact that children who should be proud of themselves for having learned something, who need the reinforcement, find themselves robbed of the satisfaction
that should accompany mastery by having their "success" interpreted as a failure by virtue of the fact that other students did better. They end up systematically disappointed and eventually discouraged. Many of our students are so
continually exposed to not-so-subtle conditioning to the unpleasant aspects of
education that they lose forever the joy of learning. Few children actually possess the necessary security and ego strength to tolerate such adverse experiences without suffering personality distortion.

The teacher is in a key role

2. By and large, whatever the school does for the mental health of its
pupils rests with what teachers can do. Their role as classroom leader makes
them the unquestioned captain of the school's mental health enterprise. They
are first of all the manager of learning activities through which children can
gain a sense of achievement, of personal worth, of status, a positive self-concept, or, on the other hand, a sense of disappointment, frustration, and futility.
As trusted and available adults—which they should be if they are to be teachers at all—they not only act as models but they are also the Number One
counselor for most, if not all, of their students, for the classroom operation unavoidably calls for a merging of the emotional and cognitive aspects of growth.
This continuous interaction with pupils is bound to have a cumulative effect in
shaping their growth. Teachers are probably the most significant adults outside the child's immediate family; in fact, being an outsider may actually give
them an advantage in certain situations.

Above all, teachers are responsible for the emotional tone of the classroom and for translating the principles of mental health into effective group
living. More specifically, just as early emotional security is probably the most
important mental health factor associated with the home, so the most important single factor in the mental health of the classroom is the teacher's ability
to generate warm pupil-teacher and pupil-pupil relationships based on mutual
acceptance and respect. Teachers are not qualified to treat severe adjustment
problems, but they can at least listen and show they care. They can show a little friendliness to the child who is left out or who has a trying home situation
and they can make it possible for the slower child to taste occasional success
and recognition. Teachers need to be sympathetic to the child who suffers
from headaches and dizziness when faced with a difficult situation. They need
to recognize problem behavior as the result of severe and persistent frustration
of needs, and especially to understand that the child who needs acceptance
most desperately is frequently the one who "deserves" it least.

Discipline can also present problems

3. Closely related to school climate is the nature of the disciplinary procedures used to promote constructive classroom behavior (see chapter 10).
Discipline in the sense of setting limits or guidelines is essential for promoting
the security necessary for optimal development. When we say teachers should

be permissive we do not mean that they should resign their leadership for a policy of vacillation or abdication; they must remain the leader, not only because of their maturity, experience, training, and position as representatives of the culture to be transmitted to the student but also because children need the security of knowing where they stand. But teachers need to control the class through understanding in an atmosphere of psychological safety in which children allow their drive for growth to propel them forward without undue risk. Discipline must be constructive; nothing is to be gained from cataloging in a rigid, moralizing manner the child's failure to meet adult standards.

Disciplinary problems frequently undermine the emotional climate of the classroom. More is to be lost than to be gained, for example, by the teacher who engages in a power struggle with students. The teacher who brings himself or herself down to the level of the students, who is sarcastic, who ridicules, and is generally punitive induces resentment and hostility to the point that pupils react in kind, thereby generating a never-ending spiral of conflict. More crucially, to the extent that children working at interesting activities do not misbehave, efforts at introducing meaningful activities might be more productive than the same energy spent in keeping discipline.

The academic program must be meaningful

4. The academic work of the classroom should be meaningful in terms of children's abilities, purposes, and interests. When they find they can satisfy their needs through school work, they will work as hard as their abilities permit and there will be no need for the teacher to appoint himself inspector of pupil shortcomings. A meaningful curriculum can do more for the child's mental health and overall growth than can any program of guidance or special help superimposed upon a rigid instructional program supervised by inflexible and authoritarian teachers.

In summary, everything we as teachers do as it relates to the child has implications, for better or for worse, from the standpoint of the latter's mental health. We need to be fully aware of the grave responsibility this places on our shoulders. On the other hand, we are not fighting an enemy; we are working with an ally whose primary motivation is self-enhancement. The fact is that children will grow. They have an inherent need to grow and to move forward, if at all possible. Somebody must give them direction when they need it, but they will "adjust" with our guidance or without it, with our intervention when the situation gets complicated or without, with our concern and support or without. We also need to remember that even though teachers may not be as trained as they might be in clinical matters, yet the cumulative effect they will have over the years for good or for evil is unlimited. We also need to recognize that frequently it is one person in the life of a youngster who was there at the right time to counterbalance a number of negative factors. Most problems are minor, at least at first. In many cases, the situation calls for some supportive hand that will steady the child and prevent him from falling off the wrong end. The basic issue here is faith in children, a conviction that they can indeed exercise freedom in the pursuit of self-actualization.

THE MENTAL HEALTH OF THE TEACHER

Importance of the Teacher's Mental Health

Whereas the focus of the modern school should be on the child, the mental health of teachers is no less important, especially when we consider their influence on both the adjustment and achievement of hundreds of children over the years. Unfortunately, whereas statistics vary, depending on the severity of the criteria used, the fact is that there is a substantial incidence of maladjustment among teachers. Perhaps the strain and stress of the classroom create an adjustment problem too severe for all but the most stable. Or, it may be that teaching attracts a certain number of individuals with personality problems, ranging from a need to boss people around to a desperate need to be loved.

Different teachers present different personality patterns

A number of teacher personality patterns can be identified. Cronbach (1963), for example, contrasts impersonal and supportive teachers. Impersonal teachers may like their pupils but see themselves as work directors; the classroom is a work laboratory, not a place for social interaction. They may operate a very efficient classroom. Too frequently, however, this atmosphere degenerates into a critical attitude and somewhat of a conflict between teachers and pupils who do not understand each other. Supportive teachers, on the other hand, are interested in children and frequently have a need for loyalty, affection, and trust. Often they give children more help than they require. They want them to learn but enjoy having children lean on them. Since they tend to like their students and to be liked by them, they may have a strong influence in their development of attitudes. The classroom atmosphere is likely to be cohesive and warm and particularly suited to children with strong affiliative needs. Achievement-oriented children, on the other hand, may be less happy.

Relevant in this context is the study by Heil et al. (1960) in which pupil achievement was found to be a function of the interaction between teacher and pupil personality. The *strivers* did about as well under all kinds of teachers, but the *conformers* did badly under the *spontaneous* teachers who were less democratic and supportive, while the *opposers* did best under the firm hand of *orderly* teachers but badly under the *spontaneous* and the *fearful* teachers.

Research is not conclusive

Maladjusted teachers might be expected to have a detrimental effect on the adjustment of the children in their classroom. The average person can recall instances of frustrated teachers who had negative effects on students who, in turn, vented their annoyance by making things miserable for them, thereby compounding their adjustment problems. Although the research evidence is not conclusive, it would seem that teachers who have too many troubles of their own can hardly be expected to work effectively in guiding their pupils' growth. It takes only one or two on any faculty to scuttle, in effect, the mental hygiene program of the school. The harm done by a few teachers who are better suited to be recipients than givers of guidance is often as irreparable as it is inexcusable. Teachers whose maladjustment is reflected in their being bossy, often cross, always fussing, and given to nagging and antagonizing children cannot inspire them to do their best; they should be discouraged from further teaching.

Factors Affecting the Mental Health of the Teacher

Much of the material in this book has direct bearing on the mental health of teachers, who should be able to apply the principles we have discussed to their own situation as well as to that of their pupils. For example, they must realize that they must derive certain satisfactions from their job if they are to remain contented and integrated and that they are not promoting their own adjustment nor that of their students when they attempt to satisfy their own needs at the latter's expense.

Teaching, like any other occupation, incorporates both favorable and unfavorable mental health factors. Among the former are the following:

The positive side of teaching

1. Teaching presents ample opportunities for self-actualization. Good teachers have the satisfaction of seeing children grow, feeling their respect and affection, and obtaining the recognition of parents and the community. Teachers who are sensitive to the needs of children and make the classroom pleasant and profitable soon find that the students in turn help satisfy their needs so that teaching becomes rewarding. This is probably the greatest satisfaction to be derived from teaching. It tends to be restricted, however, to those who enjoy teaching sufficiently to be good teachers; poor teachers very often reap nothing but pupil and parental hostility, if not contempt.

Teaching involves a variety of work and a constant challenge for those interested in children. Every child presents unique problems calling for the highest level of professional competence. For imaginative teachers, each day is a new adventure. They will probably not solve all their problems, but there will be no lack of opportunity for them to use their skills, initiative, and ingenuity for the benefit of children and their own self-fulfillment.

2. Teaching offers steady employment with reasonable pay, steady increases, a rather short day, and numerous vacations. This advantage, is, of course, lost when teachers become saddled with heavy cocurricular responsibilities, when they have to attend university classes, or when they feel compelled to take an extra job to supplement their income.

3. Among other advantages are association with educated people of like interest, clean work, and contact with youth whose enthusiasm and vitality will never let teachers grow old—unless they grow sour, in which case it will be remarkably effective in hastening the process.

But there is a negative side

There is also an unfavorable side, reflected in the fact that teaching has the highest dropout rate of all the professions: nearly one-third of beginning teachers quit in the first three years. One of the most obvious causes, particularly in the ghetto areas, is discouragement over student hostility and defiance.

It is also true that many go into teaching without any major commitment to the cause of education, and it might be that a certain weeding out of the unfit is desirable. Unfortunately the dropout is not restricted to the incompetent; every year the teaching profession suffers irreplaceable losses among its most conscientious teachers, who entered teaching with high aspirations and leave totally disillusioned at their inability to break through pupil resistance, parental disinterest, and administrative red tape.[5]

Monotony

For some teachers, the major hazard in teaching is monotony: using the same methods, the same outlines, the same illustrations, the same audiovisual aids, eating the same meals in the same cafeteria. They are in a rut. Presenting the same material year after year, and repeating it for the benefit of the slower children for good measure, is bound to get boring. Actually, good teaching can never be routine; it calls for improvement in method, for changes in content depending on the interests, needs, and purposes of the children, and, above all, it calls for orientation toward children rather than subject matter.

Lack of feedback and reinforcement

On the other hand, teaching can be frustrating in that the results of one's efforts are not clearly or immediately observable. This is especially true in pupil adjustment, where a teacher may not know for years, if ever, that his or her efforts were not in vain. For teachers who need constant reassurance in order to maintain a personal sense of accomplishment and self-esteem, this lack of positive feedback can be devastating to the point that they then seek the more immediate and tangible, but less significant, goals of education, e.g., mastery of facts and skills. It is also true that some teachers try too hard and expect too much too soon and, as a result, end up disappointed and discouraged. Teachers need to develop a sense of balance as to what it is reasonable to expect and a certain tolerance of human frailty. Equally important, they need to develop the expertise necessary to guarantee a relatively steady diet of meaningful successes.

Nervous strain

Teaching can involve a great deal of nervous strain. Not only are numerous emotionally charged situations likely to occur in the course of the day, but, even at best, children are full of pep and vinegar and can be irritating to even the calmest teacher. Teaching has never been easy; students tend to be restless, inattentive, defiant, mischievous, and uncooperative. Teachers frequently react negatively to this kind of immaturity and complicate the issue by resorting to nagging, regimentation, and other self-aggravating behaviors. Teachers also play a number of roles in and out of the classroom, some of which are conflicting—e.g., friend and guide of youth but also disciplinarian, mental hygienist but also guardian of academic standards—often with considerable internal conflict. When the teacher is unstable to begin with, the strain on teacher and pupil alike can become unbearable.

Teachers need time to collect their wits and energy. A free period when

5. See Coates and Thoreson (1976), also Keavney and Sinclair (1978), for a thorough review of research on teacher anxiety.

they can relax without having children underfoot, perhaps time for a cup of coffee, can do wonders in setting the ship back on an even keel. Teaching may cause considerable fatigue depending on the size of the classes, the nature of the students and the subject taught, and, of course, the physical stamina of the teacher. Heavy teaching loads, overcrowded classrooms, university work, and clerical duties were among the major health hazards of classroom teachers in the Kaplan and O'Dea study (1953). Yet generally it is the frustration resulting from things undone and problems unsolved as well as from boredom—rather than hard work—that leads to fatigue. Once the strain starts to accumulate, tension piles up and teachers begin to nag, overemphasize the trivial, and become unable to organize their work on an efficient basis. The result is general annoyance and shortness of temper, which soon leads to animosity on the part of students and thus to a vicious circle.

Frequent conflicts

Closely connected with nervous strain as an unfavorable aspect of teaching are the frequent conflicts that arise during the school day. The atmosphere of student defiance and hostility that characterizes some of our schools is hardly conducive to teacher satisfaction. Maintaining discipline also poses a problem for teachers who want to be liked and yet do not know how to be permissive without having students take advantage. This often leads teachers to compromise their values, with resulting feelings of guilt and anxiety.

Student defiance and hostility are more common in some communities and at certain grade levels than others, but some teachers seem to be perpetually running into one conflict after another while others rarely have serious trouble. When such conflicts occur too frequently, teachers might well ask themselves whether they are bringing these problems on themselves, perhaps by personal rigidity, insensitivity, or incompetence. When a relationship of mutual understanding and respect exists between teacher and pupils, such conflicts are likely to be rare and minor, especially when the teacher is proficient in adapting the curriculum to student needs and purposes. Teachers must give students a feeling of status and recognition and thus make it unnecessary for them to become a behavior problem in order to get attention. They should also provide outlets for draining emotional tension before it reaches explosive proportions.

Need for a sense of concern and understanding

Teachers need to understand not only what causes children to behave as they do, but they also need to understand their own behavior. Secure teachers should be able to tolerate irritations without being unduly upset, and certainly teachers who enjoy children can understand that their buoyancy is bound to get them into trouble once in a while. Teachers who get unduly provoked at a child's behavior might well ask themselves what in their own background causes them to be so disturbed. Teachers need to stop once in a while and ask themselves, "Why is my class noisier?" "Am I pushing John too hard?" It is easy to lose perspective and develop obsessive concern over the routine, mechanical, and often trivial aspects of teaching. It is easy to become hypercritical. Teachers who constantly criticize students, colleagues, and the system may need to ask themselves, "Am I contributing to the solution—or have I become part of the problem?" When tensions become chronic, when teachers can no longer tolerate horseplay and are disturbed over small matters, perhaps they should be oriented out of the profession, for the child must be allowed to be a child on the way to becoming an adult.

Room to be different

Yet teachers must be allowed to be different. Compulsive teachers do not necessarily have a detrimental effect on their pupils. Many teachers are pushers; they move students along as rapidly as possible, they tolerate a minimum of nonsense, and yet many are well liked. Many are warm and are appreciated by their students for their effectiveness in getting them to do their best work. There is no tension, no resentment, and the achievement-oriented child may well find in such a teacher a model with whom he or she can generate strong personal identification. The fact is that there is no ideal teacher. Teachers need not worry that they do not fit the typical teacher pattern; they are not going to have a disastrous effect simply because they are different, nor does the teacher necessarily have to be a paragon of virtue. Although this does not condone teachers who are consistently disgruntled or who berate and belittle students, there are nevertheless wide variations among teacher personality and teaching methods among successful teachers. The fact is that children want to grow, they are resilient to misuse, and will make up the difference, if at all possible. It is, nevertheless, important that teachers be sufficiently secure that they can be open to experience as the basis for self-improvement.

Suggestions for Promoting the Mental Health of the Teacher

Teacher selection and training important

Teaching is not without mental health hazards which take their toll. The fact that some teachers thrive on the challenges of teaching, while others fall by the wayside, suggests differences in the stability and leadership qualities of the teachers entering the profession or in the conditions they encounter after they become teachers. Undoubtedly the most effective way of improving the mental health of the teaching profession (and succeeding generations of youngsters) is to select as prospective teachers emotionally stable individuals who go into teaching because of a mature liking for children. This places a great responsibility on the shoulders of teacher-training institutions, especially since the factors involved in teacher success are not only relatively unknown but also difficult to measure, particularly in the setting of the usual lecture-type college class. More fundamental perhaps is the fact that teachers are *made* as well as selected. Student teachers need to be helped to develop a commitment to the education of youth and a positive self-concept through which this dedication can be effected. Rather than simply the cut-and-dried "intellectualization" promoted by the usual lecture-discussion class, professional education calls for personal involvement with children in supervised teaching and other helping situations, for seminars, counseling, and self-confrontation designed to promote personal discovery and personal development (see Combs 1965; Wilhelms 1960; also chapter 4).

The principal has a particular responsibility not only for choosing good teachers but also for promoting and maintaining high morale and efficiency, for just as the teacher sets the tone of the classroom, so in a more general way the principal sets the tone of the school. Implied are:

1. a democratic organization and operation of the school, including open channels of communication, discussion rather than dictation of policies, constructive supervision, and group action on school problems;
2. adequate salary, equipment, and other facilities that befit the dignity of the teaching profession; and
3. cordial relations among administrators, teachers, pupils, and parents, each aware of their responsibilities and the need for cooperation.

Teachers themselves have the primary responsibility for their own mental health. It is up to them to make their job meaningful and rewarding; if they cannot do that, what can they do for their students? Granted a liking for children, they still must acquaint themselves with the principles of psychology so that they can understand children better. They must be fully convinced that teaching is an opportunity for service and that whatever promotes pupil adjustment is also conducive to their own well-being. They should concentrate on developing positive relationships with students, fellow teachers, parents, and administrators through developing sensitivity and resourcefulness in dealing with people. They also need to understand and accept themselves, for only as they accept their own shortcomings can they accept those of others.

Teachers need to recognize that their mental health as well as their effectiveness revolves crucially around their continued professional growth. Inasmuch as nothing gives teachers so much of a lift as pride and confidence in their ability to do the job, they should strive for competence in both their subject area and pedagogical skills. Above all, they need a positive self-concept based on solid evidence of personal adequacy and professional competence. They cannot view others positively unless they have a positive view of themselves. Nor can they inspire self-confidence in students if they lack confidence in themselves.

As teachers grow in their ability to consolidate children into a functional and cohesive group bent on the pursuit of common goals, they find that troubles disappear; as they grow in security, they find it easier to be tolerant, to look on annoying behavior as something to analyze from the standpoint of causation rather than as a personal affront. Pupil misbehavior then becomes a challenge, just as the principal's criticisms serve as a basis for improvement rather than as a cause for resentment. They can then see things in perspective;

they can distinguish the important from the trivial and no longer need to be defensive. As they become free from having to worry about their own security, they find more time to plan, to devise challenging activities, to organize each working day on an efficient operational basis and to routinize what should be routine. Thus they save their energies for devising more meaningful classroom experiences, for developing greater sensitivity to pupil needs, and generally for increasing their effectiveness as teachers and thus ensuring greater satisfaction from teaching. In fact, one might even suggest that if teachers were simply to concentrate on good teaching, in all that this implies—checking on prerequisites, providing reinforcement, adapting curricular demands, individualizing instruction, etc.—everything else might well fall into place.

Yet despite all the constructive planning of which the teacher is capable, there will be days when everything will go wrong. If this occurs too frequently, he or she may well be in the wrong field and, despite all the glory that attends perseverance, there is even greater virtue in knowing when to quit. Yet teachers must not waste every ounce of the energy they should be spending in teaching worrying about their effectiveness. Instead they should do the best job they can, and they might do well to remember the words of Wattenberg and Redl (1950, p. 743):

> There are too few saints to fill all teaching positions, so imperfect human beings must do the bulk of the instruction of youth. What counts is not your virtues or your vices but what you do to children with them.

HIGHLIGHTS OF THE CHAPTER

Although the primary responsibility for the mental health of children rests with the home, the school is obviously a major factor for good or evil in their mental health. Not only does the school have close contact with all the children throughout their formative years but, since so much of their life centers around the school, their experiences there are bound to have a profound influence on their mental well-being.

1. Mental hygiene is necessarily an integral part of the teaching-learning process through which the child's self-realization is promoted. It is through good teaching that teachers can make their greatest contribution to the child's mental health.
2. Mental hygiene in the classroom has three main purposes: to prevent mental illness, to promote mental health, and to correct mental disorders. The teacher's efforts in the therapeutic aspects of mental hygiene should be restricted to the early detection of danger signs, referral to a competent clinician, and cooperation with the latter's recommendations.
3. A number of factors in the classroom constitute potential mental health hazards—e.g., the demands of the curriculum regardless of student ability, discipline, the emotional climate of the classroom, examinations, grading, etc.
4. The teacher is necessarily the key to the effects of the school experience on the child's mental health. A meaningful curriculum probably constitutes his or her best ally in promoting pupil self-enhancement.
5. The teacher's mental health is of primary importance, considering the effects of his or her personality on a large number of children.
6. Teaching, like other occupations, has both favorable and unfavorable features, and it attracts certain people who can find happiness in such a framework. The best way of improving the mental health of the teaching profession is to select as prospective teachers individuals who are well adjusted and have a mature liking for children.
7. In the final analysis, the teachers must assume responsibility for their own mental health; they need to understand and accept themselves, to develop competence in dealing with children, and to cultivate a sense of perspective that will prevent them from becoming unduly upset at minor irritations.

SUGGESTIONS FOR FURTHER READING

BOWER, ELI. Mental health. In Robert L. Ebel, ed., *Encyclopedia of Educational Research*, pp. 811–828. New York: Macmillan, 1969. Reviews the present status of mental health and the related research literature.

DUKE, DANIEL L. The etiology of student misbehavior and the depersonalization of blame. *Rev. Educ. Res.* 48 (1978):415–437. Notes that recent psychology has systematically shifted the blame for misbehavior from the individual to some environmental force and wonders whether society can continue to prosper when no one is held accountable for his or her own behavior.

DURHAM, KATHERINE. Attitudes and opinions of high school teachers toward mental health. *Diss. Abstr. Inertnat.* (1977) (9–A), 4752–4753.

SOLOMON, JOSEPH C., et al. Neuroses of school teachers: A colloquy. *Ment. Hyg.* 44 (1960):79–90. A number of educational psychologists and clinicians discuss the issue of the mental health of teachers.

YAMAMOTO, K. The healthy person: A review. *Pers. Guid. J.* 44 (1966):596–603. Reviews the characteristics and other personality dimensions of the mentally healthy individual.

QUESTIONS AND PROJECTS

1. Evaluate: A teacher objects to having to concern himself with the mental health of 150 children whom he barely knows. He contends that it detracts from the primary function of the school—to teach. Anyway, he is trained as a teacher, not as a psychologist.

2. Assuming that the school should be involved in the mental health "business" how would you define the relative role of the teacher, the counselor, the school psychologist, the principal, and the parents in the promotion of the school's mental health objectives?

3. Ted is frequently in trouble at school. The fact that he is rejected by his father seems to be a major factor in his difficulty. His teacher argues that there is no way he can help Ted since the problem is in the home. Do you agree?

4. Some parents complain that they sacrifice so much for their children. Analyze the nature of this "sacrifice" from the standpoint of its underlying motivation and its effect on the children.

5. What are the particular satisfactions you anticipated that caused you to select teaching as a career?

6. Interview teachers who leave the profession. What factors were involved? Interview teachers who "love to teach." What satisfactions do they find? What does it all mean in terms of your intentions to become a teacher?

7. Debate: Until the teaching profession implements effective means of eliminating from its ranks the misfit and the maladjusted, it should not be given security of tenure. Is teacher welfare compatible with the best interest of the child and the community?

SELF-TEST

1. Mental hygiene in the school operates primarily through
   a. the classroom and its teacher.
   b. the guidance department.
   c. the principal and his or her leadership.
   d. its referral system.
   e. its special programs of pupil development.

2. Mental hygiene as it operates in the classroom is best conceived as
   a. a body of knowledge and skill.
   b. a point of view relating to a wholesome classroom climate permeating every aspect of its operation.
   c. a program of cocurricular activities designed to promote self-realization.
   d. a systematic program dedicated to the self-realization of each student.
   e. a systematic program of positive character development.

3. The primary purpose of mental hygiene in the school is
   a. to facilitate learning through the elimination of disruptions.
   b. to preserve present student mental health.
   c. to prevent mental disorders.
   d. to promote positive mental health.
   e. to remediate common symptoms of maladjustment.

4. The teacher's major contribution to pupil mental health lies in the area of
   a. academic competence.
   b. alertness to symptoms of maladjustment.
   c. expertise in adapting the curriculum to student needs.
   d. good teaching.
   e. sensitivity to individual differences in personality.

5. The most serious mental health hazard in the school is probably
   a. its inability to cope with individual differences in ability.
   b. its emphasis on discipline geared to the maintenance of classroom decorum.
   c. the lack of a cohesive peer structure.
   d. the teacher's inability to relate effectively to each pupil.
   e. the unsuitability of the curriculum for a sizable number of students.

6. Probably the greatest hazard to the teacher's mental health is
   a. the burden of heavy teaching load, low pay, etc.
   b. the limited need-satisfying climate of the typical classroom.
   c. monotony and loss of enthusiasm.

    d. the petty recurring conflict between teacher and pupils/parents/administrators.

    e. unavailability of feedback as to the success of his or her efforts.

7. Primary responsibility for the mental health of the teaching profession lies with

    a. the individual teacher.

    b. the principal of the local school.

    c. the school administrator.

    d. society in general.

    e. the teacher-training institution.

Bibliography

ACKERMAN, J. MARK. 1972. *Operant Conditioning Techniques for the Classroom Teacher*. Glenview: Scott, Foresman.

ADKINS, DOROTHY C., et al. 1974. Moral Development. In Fred N. Kerlinger, ed., *Review of Research in Education*, 2:108–144. Itasca, Ill.: Peacock.

ALLEN, ROBERT D., and MARSHA CARTIER. 1978. *The Mental Health Almanac, 1978–79*. New York: Garland.

ALLEN, VERNON L., ed. 1976. *Children as Teachers: Theory and Research on Tutoring*. New York: Academic Press.

ALLPORT, GORDON W. 1935. Attitudes. In C. Murchison, ed., *A Handbook of Social Psychology*. Worcester: Clark Univ. Press.

———. 1937. *Personality : A Psychological Interpretation*. New York: Holt, Rinehart & Winston.

———. 1966. Traits revisited. *Amer. Psychol.* 21:1–10.

ALMY, MILLIE. 1961. Wishful thinking about children's thinking. *T.C. Rec.* 62:396–406.

———. 1966. *Young Children's Thinking*. New York: Teachers College Press.

ALTMAN, IRA. 1978. The concept of intelligence in ordinary language. *Diss. Abstr. Internat.* 38 (12–A):7372.

AMBROSE, J. 1963. The concept of a critical period in the development of social responses in early infancy. In B. M. Foss, ed., *Determinants of Infant Behaviour*, no. 2, pp. 201–225. London: Methuen.

American Psychological Association. 1974. *Standards for Educational and Psychological Tests*. Washington, D.C.: APA.

AMES, R. 1957. Physical maturing among boys as related to adult social behavior: A longitudinal study. *Calif. J. Educ. Res.* 8:69–75.

ANASTASI, ANNE. 1958a. *Differential Psychology.* New York: Macmillan.

———. 1958b. Heredity, environment, and the question "how." *Psychol. Rev.* 65:197–208.

ANDERSON, RICHARD C. 1972. How to construct achievement tests to assess comprehension. *Rev. Educ. Res.* 42:145–170.

ARNY, C. B. 1953. *Evaluation in Home Economics.* New York: Appleton-Century-Crofts.

ARONFREED, JUSTIN. 1968. Aversive control of socialization. *Nebraska Symposium on Motivation* 16:271–320.

ASBURY, CHARLES A. 1974. Selected factors influencing over- and under-achievement in young school-age children. *Rev. Educ. Res.* 44:409–428.

ASDELL, S. A. 1953. The effect of controlled ovulation upon the fertility of the mammalian egg. In J. E. Wolstenholme, ed., *Mammalian Germ Cells,* pp. 170–179. New York: Little.

ASPY, DAVID M. 1970. Educational psychology: Challenge or challenging? *J. Teach. Educ.* 21:5–13.

———. 1972. *Toward a Technology for Humanizing Education.* Champaign: Research Press.

ATKINSON, JOHN W., ed. 1958. *Motives in Fantasy, Action, and Society.* New York: Van Nostrand.

ATKINSON, JOHN W. 1964. *An Introduction to Motivation.* New York: Van Nostrand.

———. 1972. Ingredients for theory of instruction. *Amer. Psychol.* 27:921–931.

ATKINSON, RICHARD C. 1969. Information delay in human learning. *J. Verb. Learn. & Verb. Beh.,* 8:507–511.

AUSUBEL, DAVID P. 1960. The use of advance organizers in the learning and retention of meaningful verbal material. *J. Educ. Psychol.* 51:267–27.

———. 1961. Learning by discovery: Rationale and mystique. *Bull., NASSP* 45 (December): 18–58.

———. 1962. A subsumption theory of meaningful verbal learning and retention. *J. Gen. Psychol.* 66:312–324.

———. 1963. *The Psychology of Meaningful Verbal Learning.* New York: Grune & Stratton.

———. 1967. Stages of intellectual development and their implications for early childhood education. In David P. Ausubel, ed., *Readings in School Learning.* New York: Holt, Rinehart & Winston.

———. 1968. *Educational Psychology: A Cognitive View.* New York: Holt, Rinehart & Winston.

———. 1978. In defense of advance organizers: A reply to critics. *Rev. Educ. Res.* 48:251–257.

———. 1969a. Is there a discipline of educational psychology? *Psychol. Sch.,* 6:232–244.

———. 1969b. A cognitive theory of school learning. *Psychol. Sch.* 6:331–335.

———, and DONALD FITZGERALD. 1961. The role of discriminability in meaningful verbal learning and retention. *J. Educ. Psychol.* 52:266–274.

————, and DONALD FITZGERALD. 1963. Organizers, general background, and antecedent learning variables in sequential verbal learning. *J. Educ. Psychol.* 53:243–249.

————, and M. YOUSSEF. 1963. The role of discriminability in meaningful parallel learning. *J. Educ. Psychol.* 54:331–336.

————, et al. 1978. *Educational Psychology: A Cognitive View.* New York: Holt, Rinehart & Winston.

BAER, DONALD M. 1970. An age-irrelevant concept of development. *Merrill-Palmer Q.* 16:233–245.

BAGLEY, W. C. 1922. *The Educative Process.* New York: Macmillan.

BAIN, PHILIP T., et al. 1973. An investigation of some assumptions and characteristics of the pass-fail system. *J. Educ. Res.* 67:134–136.

BAKER, EVA L. 1970. Project for research on objectively-based evaluation. *Educ. Technol.* 10 (August):56–59.

BAKER, HOWARD S. 1975. The treatment of academic underachievement. *J. Amer. Coll. Health Assn.* 24:4–7.

BAKER, ROBERT L. 1969. Curriculum evaluation. *Rev. Educ. Res.* 39:339–358.

BALDWIN, ALFRED L., et al. 1945. *Patterns of Parental Behavior.* Psychol. Monogr. 58, no. 3.

BALDWIN, BIRD T. 1921. *Physical Growth in Children from Birth to Maturity.* Univ. Iowa Studies in Child Welfare, 1921, 1 (1).

BANDURA, ALBERT. 1977. *Social Learning Theory.* Englewood Cliffs: Prentice-Hall.

————, and FREDERICK J. McDONALD. 1963. Influence of social reinforcement and the behavior of models in shaping children's moral judgment. *J. Abn. Soc. Psychol.* 67:274–281.

————, and RICHARD H. WALTERS. 1963. *Social Learning and Personality Development.* New York: Holt, Rinehart & Winston.

BANE, MARY JO, and CHRISTOPHER JENCKS. 1972. The schools and equal opportunity. *Sat. Rev.*, October 16.

BARNES, BUCKLEY R., and ELMER U. CLAWSON. 1975. Do advance organizers facilitate learning? Recommendations for further research based on an analysis of 32 studies. *Rev. Educ. Res.* 45:637–659.

BARR, ARVIL S. 1929. *Characteristic Differences in the Teaching Performance of Good and Poor Teachers in the Social Studies.* Bloomington, Ind.: Public School Publ. Co.

————. 1948. The measurement and prediction of teaching efficiency: A summary of investigations. *J. Exper. Educ.* 16:203–283.

————. 1961. Wisconsin studies of the measurement and prediction of teaching efficiency: A summary of investigations. *J. Exper. Educ.* 30:1–155.

BAR-TAL, DANIEL. 1978. Attributional analysis of achievement-related behavior. *Rev. Educ. Res.* 48:259–271.

BASOWITZ, HAROLD, et al. 1955. *Anxiety and Stress: An Interdisciplinary Study.* New York: McGraw-Hill.

BASSETT, G. W., et al. 1978. *Individual Differences: Guidelines for Educational Practice.* Sydney: Allen & Unwin.

BAUMAN, ROBERT P. 1976. *Teaching for Cognitive Development: A Status Report.* Birmingham: Project on Teaching and Learning in University College, Univ. Alabama.

BAYH, BIRCH (chairman). 1977. *Challenge for the Third Century.* Washington, D.C.: HEW.

BAYLES, ERNEST E. 1952. The idea of learning as development of insight. *Educ. Theory* 2:65–71.

———. 1960. *Democratic Educational Theory.* New York: Harper & Row.

BAYLEY, NANCY. 1949. Consistency and variability in the growth of intelligence from birth to eighteen years. *J. Genet. Psychol.* 75:165–196.

———. 1955. On the growth of intelligence. *Amer. J. Psychol.* 10:805–818.

———. 1970. Development of mental abilities. In Paul H. Mussen, ed., *Carmichael's Manual of Child Psychology,* vol. 1, pp. 1163–1209. New York: Wiley.

BEAUMONT, H., and F. G. MACOMBER. 1949. *Psychological Factors in Education.* New York: McGraw-Hill.

BENJAMIN, HAROLD. 1939. *The Sabre-Tooth Curriculum.* New York: McGraw-Hill.

BENNETT, NEVILLE. 1976. *Teaching Styles and Pupil Progress.* Cambridge: Harv. Univ. Press.

BERG, I. 1970. *Education and Jobs: The Great Training Robbery.* New York: Praeger.

BERLYNE, D. E. 1950. Novelty and curiosity as determinants of exploratory behavior. *Brit. J. Psychol.* 41:68–80.

BERNARD, VIOLA W. 1958. Teacher education in mental health. In Morris Krugman, ed., *Orthopsychiatry in the Schools,* pp. 184–203. New York: Orthopsychiatric Assn.

BERNSTEIN, BASIL. 1960. Language and social class. *Brit. J. Sociol.* 11:271–276.

———. 1961. Social structure, language, and learning. *Educ. Res.* 3:163–176.

BERNSTEIN, E. 1968. What does a Summerhill old school tie look like? *Psychol. Today* 2 (5):37–70.

BETTELHEIM, BRUNO. 1970. The perils of overexposing youth to college. *Educ. Dig.* 35 (April):35–38.

BIEHLER, ROBERT F. 1974. *Psychology of Teaching.* Boston: Houghton Mifflin.

———. 1978. *Psychology Applied to Teaching.* Boston: Houghton Mifflin.

BIGGE, MORRIS L. 1971. *Learning Theories for Teachers.* New York: Harper & Row.

BILODEAU, E. A., ed. 1966. *Acquisition of Skill.* New York: Academic Press.

BINET, ALFRED, and T. SIMON. 1905. Méthodes nouvelles pour le diagnostic du niveau intellectuel des abnormaux. *Ann. Psychol.* 11:191–244.

BISCHOFF, L. J. 1954. *Intelligence: Statistical Conceptions of Its Nature.* Garden City: Doubleday.

BITZER, DONALD, and D. SKAPERDAS. 1970. The economics of a large-scale computer-based educational system: PLATO IV. In Wayne H. Holzman, ed., *Computer-Assisted Instruction, Testing, and Guidance.* New York: Harper & Row.

BLAIR, GLENN M., et al. 1962. *Educational Psychology.* New York: Macmillan.

BLOOM, BENJAMIN S. 1964. *Stability and Change in Human Characteristics.* New York: Wiley.

———. 1971. Mastery learning and its implications for curriculum development. In E. W. Eisner, ed., *Confronting Curriculum Reform.* Boston: Little, Brown.

———. 1973. Recent developments in mastery learning. *Educ. Psychol.* 10:53–57.

———. 1974. Time and learning. *Amer. Psychol.* 29:682–688.

———, et al. 1956. *Taxonomy of Educational Objectives.* Handbook I: *Cognitive Domain.* New York: McKay.

———, et al. 1971. *Handbook of Formative and Summative Evaluation of Student Learning.* New York: McGraw-Hill.

BOEHM, LEONORE. 1957. The development of independence: A comparative study. *Child Devel.* 28:85–102.

———, and MARTIN L. NASS. 1962. Social class differences in conscience development. *Child Devel.* 33:565–574.

BOLLES, ROBERT C. 1978. Whatever happened to motivation? *Educ. Psychol.* 13:1–13.

BORG, WALTER R. 1972. Minicourses: Individualized learning packages for teacher education. *Educ. Technol.* 12:57–64.

BORGATTA, EDGAR F., and W. W. LAMBERT, eds. 1968. *Handbook of Personality Theory and Research in Child Development.* Chicago: Rand McNally.

BOUCHARD, RUTH K., and BERNARD MACKLER. 1967. *Prekindergarten Program for Four-Year-Olds: With a Review of the Literature on Preschool Education.* New York: Center for Urban Education.

BOWER, ELI M. 1969. Mental health. In Robert L. Ebel, ed., *Encyclopedia of Educational Research,* pp. 811–828. New York: Macmillan.

BOWER, GORDON H., ed. 1978. *The Psychology of Learning and Motivation: Advances in Research and Theory.* New York: Academic Press.

BRACHT, GLENN H., and KENNETH HOPKINS. 1970. The commonality of essay and objective tests of academic achievement. *Educ. Psychol. Meas.* 30:359–364.

BRAINE, MARTIN D. S. 1959. The ontogeny of certain logical operations: Piaget's formulation examined by non-verbal methods. *Psychol. Monogr.* 73.

———. 1962. Piaget on reasoning: A methodological critique and alternative proposal. *Monogr. Soc. Res. Child Devel.* 27:41–61.

BRELAND, K., and M. BRELAND. 1961. The misbehavior of organisms. *Amer. Psychol.,* 16:681–684.

BRIGGS, T. H. 1913. Formal English grammar as a discipline. *T.C. Rec.* 14:251–343.

BRITTAIN, CLAY V. 1966. A summary of research on preschool programs for culturally deprived children. *Children,* 13:130–134.

BRONFENBRENNER, U. 1962. Soviet methods of character education: Some implications for research. *Amer. Psychol.* 17:550–564.

BROPHY, JERE E., and C. EVERTSON. 1974. *The Texas Teacher Effectiveness Project: Presentation of Nonlinear Relationships and Summary Discussion.* Austin: Research and Development Center for Teacher Education, Univ. of Texas, 1974.

———. 1974. *Teacher-Student Relationships: Causes and Consequences.* New York: Holt, Rinehart & Winston.

———, and THOMAS L. GOOD. 1972. Teacher expectations: Beyond the Pygmalion controversy. *Phi Delta Kappan* 54:276–278.

BROUDY, HARRY S. 1961. *Building a Philosophy of Education.* Englewood Cliffs: Prentice-Hall.

———. 1970. Can research escape the dogma of behavioral objectives? *Sch. Rev.* 79:43–56.

BROWNELL, S. M. 1947. A workable plan for recognition of merit. *Nation's Sch.* 40:20–22.

BROYLER, C. R., et al. 1927. A second study of mental discipline in high school studies. *J. Educ. Psychol.* 18:377–404.

BRUNER, JEROME S. 1959. Learning and thinking. *Harv. Educ. Rev.* 29:184–192.

————. 1960. *The Process of Education.* Cambridge: Harv. Univ. Press.

————. 1961. The act of discovery. *Harv. Educ. Rev.* 31:21–32.

————. 1963. A theory of instruction. *Educ. Lead.* 20:523–532.

————. 1964. The course of cognitive growth. *Amer. Psychol.* 19:1–15.

————. 1966. *Toward a Theory of Instruction.* Cambridge: Harv. Univ. Press.

————. 1971. *The Relevance of Education.* New York: Norton.

———— et al. 1956. *A Study of Thinking.* New York: Wiley.

BULL, S. G. 1973. The role of questions in maintaining attention to textual material. *Rev. Educ. Res.* 43:83–87.

BUNDERSON, C. V., and GERALD W. FAUST. 1976. Programed and computer-assisted instruction. In N. L. Gage, ed., *The Psychology of Teaching Methods,* pp. 44–90, 75th Yrbk., NSSE, Pt. 1. Chicago: Univ. Chicago Press.

BURT, CYRIL. 1955. The evidence for the concept of intelligence. *Brit. J. Educ. Psychol.* 25:158–177.

BUSS, ALLAN R. 1976. The myth of vanishing individual differences in Bloom's mastery learning. *J. Instructional Psychol.* 3 (spec. ed.):4–14.

BUTLER, ANNIE L. 1968. From Head Start to Follow Through. *Bull. Sch. Educ., Indiana Univ.* 44:5–47.

BUTLER, ROBERT A., and HARRY F. HARLOW. 1957. Discrimination learning and learning sets to visual exploratory incentives. *J. Gen. Psychol.* 57:257–264.

CAMPBELL, DONALD T., and JULIAN C. STANLEY. 1963. Experimental and quasi-experimental designs for research in teaching. In N. L. Gage, ed., *Handbook of Research on Teaching,* pp. 171–246. Chicago: Rand McNally.

CARBONE, PETER F. 1970. Reflections on moral education. *T.C. Rec.* 71:598–606.

CARROLL, JOHN B. 1963. A model of school learning. *T.C. Rec.* 64:723–733.

CARROLL, LEWIS. 1865. *Alice's Adventures in Wonderland.* Many reprints.

CARTWRIGHT, D. 1959. Lewinian theory as a systematic framework. In S. Koch, ed., *Psychology: A Study of a Science,* 2:7–91. New York: McGraw-Hill.

CARVER, RONALD P. 1972. A critical review of mathemagenic behaviors and the effect of questions upon the retention of prose materials. *J. Read. Beh.* 4:93–119.

CASE, ROBBIE. 1973. Piaget's theory of child development and its implications. *Phi Delta Kappan,* 55:20–26.

————. 1975. Gearing the demands of instruction to the developmental capacities of the learner. *Rev. Educ. Res.* 45:59–87.

CASLER, LAWRENCE. 1961. Maternal deprivation: A critical review of the literature. *Monogr. Soc. Res. Child Devel.* 26, No. 2.

CASSEL, RUSSELL N. 1969. Historical review of theories on nature of intelligence. *Psychol.* 6:39–46.

————. 1974. Critical contributions of Piaget to humanistic psychology. *Psychol.* 11 (May):3–9.

CASTENADA, ALFRED, et al. 1956. Complex learning and performance as a function of anxiety in children and task difficulty. *Child Devel.* 27:327–332.

CATTELL, RAYMOND B. 1950. *Personality.* New York: McGraw-Hill.

————. 1963. Theory of fluid and crystallized intelligence: A critical experiment. *J. Educ. Psychol.* 54:1–22.

CHAPANIS, M. P., and A. CHAPANIS. 1964. Cognitive dissonance: Five years later. *Psychol. Bull.* 61:1–22.

CHARLES, DON C. 1964. *Psychology in the Classroom.* New York: Macmillan.

———., et al. 1971. Symposium: Psychology in teacher education today. *J. Teach. Educ.* 22:391–417.

———. A historical overview of educational psychology. *Contemp. Educ. Psychol.,* Jan. 1976, 1: 76–88.

CHAUNCEY, HENRY. 1963. *Annual Report, 1962–63.* Princeton: Educ. Testing Service.

CHRISTENSON, R. M. 1977. McGuffey's ghosts and moral education today. *Phi Delta Kappan* 58:737–742.

CLARK, KENNETH B. 1963. Educational stimulation of racially disadvantaged children. In A. H. Passow, ed., *Education in Depressed Areas,* pp. 142–162. New York: Teachers College, Columbia Univ.

CLAWSON, ELMER U., and B. R. BARNES. 1973. The effects of organizers on the learning of structured anthropology materials in the elementary grades. *J. Exper. Educ.* 42 (Fall):11–15.

COATES, BRIAN, et al. 1976. The influence of "Sesame Street," and "Mister Rogers' Neighborhood" on children's social behavior in the preschool. *Child Devel.* 47:138–144.

COATES, THOMAS J., and CARL E. THORESEN. 1976. Teacher anxiety: A review with recommendations. *Rev. Educ. Res.* 46:159–184.

COHEN, H. L., 1968. Model: Motivationally oriented designs for an ecology of learning. In H. L. Cohen, et al. eds., *Training Professions in Procedures for the Establishment of Educational Environments.* Silver Springs, Md.: Educ. Facilities Press.

COHEN, S., and R. HERSH. 1972. Behaviorism and humanism: A synthesis for teacher education. *J. Teach. Educ.* 23:172–176.

COHLAN, SIDNEY Q. 1954. Congenital anomalies in the rat produced by excessive intakes of vitamin A during pregnancy. *Pediatrics* 13:556–567.

COLE, MICHAEL, and JEROME S. BRUNER. 1971. Cultural differences and inferences about psychological processes. *Amer. Psychol.* 26:867–876.

COLE, ROBERT W. 1977. Black Moses: Jessie Jackson's PUSH for excellence. *Phi Delta Kappan* 58:378–382.

COLEMAN, JAMES S. 1961a. *Adolescent and Society.* New York: Free Press.

———. 1961b. The competition for adolescent energies. *Phi Delta Kappan,* 42:231–236.

———. 1966. *Equality of Educational Opportunity.* Washington, Dept. of HEW.

COLES, GERALD S. 1978. The Learning-Disabilities Test Battery: Empirical and social issues. *Harv. Educ. Rev.* 48:313–340.

COMBS, ARTHUR W. 1952. Intelligence from a perceptual point of view. *J. Abn. Soc. Psychol.* 47:662–673.

———. 1962. *Perceiving, Behaving, Becoming.* 1962 Yrbk. Washington, D.C.: Assn. Superv. Curr. Devel.

———. 1965. *The Professional Education of Teachers.* Boston: Allyn & Bacon.

———. 1971. New concepts of human potentialities: New challenges for teachers. *Childh. Educ.* 47:349–355.

———. 1972. *Educational Accountability: Beyond Behavioral Objectives.* Washington, D.C.: Assn. Superv. Curr. Devel.

———. 1973. Educational accountability from a humanistic perspective. *Educ. Res.* 2 (September): 19–21.

————, and DONALD SNYGG. 1959. *Individual Behavior.* New York: Harper & Row.

————, et al. 1971. *Helping Relationships: Basic Concepts for the Helping Professions.* Boston: Allyn & Bacon.

COMBS, JANET, and WILLIAM W. COOLEY. 1968. Drop-outs in high school and after school. *Amer. Educ. Res. J.* 5:343–364.

COOK, DESMOND L. 1962. The Hawthorne effect in educational research. *Phi Delta Kappan* 44:116–122.

COOPERSMITH, STANLEY. 1967. *The Antecedents of Self-Esteem.* San Francisco: Freeman.

COTTON, JOHN W., et al. 1977. The identification of hierarchical tasks. *Amer. Educ. Res. J.* 14:189–212.

COVINGTON, M. V., and C. L. OMELICH. 1979. It's best to be able and virtuous too: Student and teacher evaluative reactions to successful effort. *J. Educ. Psychol.* 71:169–182.

COWAN, ROBERT, et al. 1978. A validity study of selected self-concept instruments. *Meas. & Eval. Guid.* 10:211–221.

COX, WILLIAM F., and THOMAS G. DUNN. 1979. Mastery learning: A psychological trap? *Educ. Psychol.* 14:24–29.

CREMIN, LAWRENCE A. 1961. *The Transformation of the School: Progressivism in American Education, 1876–1957.* New York: Knopf.

————. 1974. The free school movement: A perspective. *Today's Educ.* 63 (September–October): 71–74.

CRONBACH, LEE J. 1963. *Educational Psychology.* New York: Harcourt.

————. 1967. How can instruction be adapted to individual differences? In Robert M. Gagné, ed., *Learning and Individual Differences.* Columbus: Merrill.

————. 1971. Comments on mastery learning and its implications for curriculum development. In E. W. Eisner, ed., *Confronting Curriculum Reform,* pp. 49–55. Boston: Little, Brown.

————. 1975. Beyond the two disciplines of scientific psychology. *Amer. Psychol.* 30:116–127.

————, and RICHARD E. SNOW. 1977. *Aptitudes and Instructional Methods: A Handbook for Research on Interactions.* New York: Irvington.

CUNNINGHAM, RUTH, et al. 1951. *Understanding Group Behavior of Boys and Girls.* New York: Teachers College, Columbia Univ.

DASHIELL, J. F. 1949. *Fundamentals of General Psychology.* Boston: Houghton Mifflin.

DAVIS, FREDERICK B., and J. J. DIAMOND. 1971. Criterion-referenced tests: A critique. Paper presented at AERA convention, New York, February.

DAVIS, W. ALLISON. 1948. *Social Class Influence upon Learning.* Cambridge: Harv. Univ. Press.

————, and KENNETH EELLS. 1952. *Davis-Eells Games.* New York: Harcourt.

DEARBORN, W. F., and J. W. M. ROTHNEY. 1941. *Predicting the Child's Development.* Cambridge: Sci-Art.

————, et al. 1938. Data on the growth of public school children from the materials of the Harvard Growth Study. *Monogr. Soc. Res. Child Devel.,* 3, No. 1.

DeCecco, John P., and Arlene K. Richards. 1975. Civil war in the high schools. *Psychol. Today.* 9 (November):120.

deCharms, R. 1968. *Personal Causation.* New York: Academic Press.

———. 1976. *Enhancing Motivation: Change in the Classroom.* New York: Irvington.

Deese, James, and Stewart H. Hulse. 1967. *The Psychology of Learning.* New York: McGraw-Hill.

Della-Piana, Gabriel, and N. L. Gage. 1955. Pupils' values and the validity of the MTAI. *J. Educ. Psychol.* 46:167–178.

Dember, D. N., et al. 1957. Response by rats to differential stimulus complexity. *J. Comp. Phys. Psychol.*, 50:514–518.

Dennison, George. 1969. *The Lives of Children.* New York: Vintage.

Deutsch, Martin P. 1963. The disadvantaged child and the learning process. In A. H. Passow, ed., *Education in Depressed Areas*, pp. 163–179. New York: Teachers College, Columbia Univ.

———. 1964. Facilitating development in the preschool child: Social and psychological perspectives. *Merrill-Palmer Q.* 10:249–264.

Deutsch, Morton. 1979. Education and distributive justice: Some reflections on grading systems. *Amer. Psychol.* 60:391–401.

Devin-Sheehan, Linda, et al. 1976. Research on children tutoring children: A critical review. *Rev. Educ. Res.* 46:355–385.

Dewey, John. 1933. *How We Think.* Boston: Heath.

———. 1938. *Logic.* New York: Holt, Rinehart & Winston.

Dinkmeyer, Don, and Rudolf Dreikurs. 1963. *Encouraging Children to Learn: The Encouragement Process.* Englewood Cliffs: Prentice-Hall.

Dollard, John, and Neal E. Miller. 1950. *Personality and Psychotherapy.* New York: McGraw-Hill.

Dreikurs, Rudolf. *Psychology in the Classroom.* New York: Harper & Row. 1957, 1968.

Duchastel, Philippe C., and Paul F. Merrill. The effects of behavioral objectives on learning: A review of empirical studies. CAI Tech. Memo, 1972, 45; *Rev. Educ. Res.*, 1973, 43:53–69.

Duke, Daniel L. 1977. A systematic management plan for school discipline. *Bull. NASSP* 61 (January):1–10.

———. 1978. The etiology of student misbehavior and the depersonalization of blame. *Rev. Educ. Res.* 48:415–438.

———, ed. 1979. *Classroom Management.* 78th Yrbk., NSSE, Pt. II. Chicago: Univ. Chicago Press.

Dunn, Rita, and Kenneth Dunn. 1975. Learning styles, teaching styles. *Bull. NASSP* 59 (October):37–49.

Durkin, Dolores. 1959. Children's concept of justice: A further comparison with the Piaget data. *J. Educ. Res.* 52:252–257.

———. 1961. The specificity of children's moral judgment. *J. Genet. Psychol.* 98:3–13.

Dyer, Henry L. 1961. Is testing a menace to education? *N.Y. State Educ.* 49:16–19.

Ebbinghaus, H. 1913. *Memory: A Contribution to Experimental Psychology.* Translated by H. A. Ruger and C. E. Bussenius. New York: Teachers College. Columbia Univ.

EBEL, ROBERT L. 1962. Measurement and the teacher. *Educ. Lead.* October 20, pp. 20–24.

————. 1964. Should school marks be abolished? *Mich. J. Sec. Educ.* 6:12–15.

————. 1968. The prospect for evaluation of learning. *Bull. NASSP* 52 (December):32–42.

————. 1969. Measurement in education. In Robert L. Ebel, ed., *Encyclopedia of Educational Research*, pp. 777–785. New York: Macmillan.

————. 1970. Behavioral objectives: A close look. *Phi Delta Kappan* 52:171–173.

————. 1978. The case for norm-referenced measurements. *Educ. Res.*, 7 (11) (Dec.): 3–5.

————. 1980. The failure of schools without failure. *Phi Delta Kappan,* 61:386–388.

Educational Testing Service. 1961. *Judges disagree on qualities that characterize good writing. ETS Devel.* 9 (February).

————. 1971. Sesame Street evaluation breaks new ground. *ETS Devel.* 18 (February).

EELLS, KENNETH. 1953. Some implications for school practice of the Chicago studies of cultural bias in intelligence tests. *Harv. Educ. Rev.* 23:284–297.

————, et al. 1951. *Intelligence and Cultural Differences.* Chicago: Univ. Chicago Press.

EGGEN, P. D., et al. 1979. *Strategies for Teachers: Information-Processing the Classroom.* Englewood Cliffs: Prentice-Hall

EISNER, E. W. 1967. Educational objectives: Help or hindrance? *Sch. Rev.* 75:250–260.

————, ed. 1971. *Confronting Curriculum Reform.* Boston: Little, Brown.

ELAM, STANLEY. 1970. Texarkana: Rapid Learning Centers. *Phi Delta Kappan* 51:1–19.

ELKIND, DAVID. 1967. Egocentricism in adolescence. *Child Devel.* 38:1025–1034.

ELLIS, H. C. 1965. *The Transfer of Learning.* New York: Collier-Macmillan.

————. 1969. Retention and transfer. In Melvin H. Marx, ed., *Learning: 1. Process*, pp. 378–478. New York: Macmillan.

ELLSON, DOUGLAS G. 1976. Tutoring. In N. L. Gage, ed., *The Psychology of Teaching Methods*, pp. 130–165. 75th Yrbk., NSSE, Pt. I. Chicago: Univ. Chicago Press.

ENGLISH, MORRIS B. 1961. *Dynamics of Child Development.* New York: Holt, Rinehart & Winston.

ERIKSON, ERIK H. 1963. *Childhood and Society.* Rev. ed. New York: Norton.

————. 1968. *Identity: Youth and Crisis.* New York: Norton.

ESTES, WILLIAM K. 1944. An experimental study of punishment. *Psychol. Monogr.* (57).

FAIRWEATHER, H. 1976. Sex differences in cognition. *Cognition* 4:231–280.

FALKNER, FRANK. 1962. The physical development of children. *Pediatrics* 29:448–466.

FANTINI, MARIO D., and GERALD WEINSTEIN. 1968. *The Disadvantaged: Challenge to Education.* New York: Harper & Row.

FAW, HAROLD W., and T. GARY WALLER. 1976. Mathemagenic behaviours and efficiency in learning from prose materials: Review, critique, and recommendations. *Rev. Educ. Res.* 46:691–720.

FEATHERSTONE, JOSEPH. 1971. *Schools Where Children Learn.* New York: Liveright.

FESHBACH, NORMA D. 1968. *Manual of Individual Variables and Measures.* Los Angeles: UCLA Grad. Sch. of Educ.

FESTINGER, LEON. 1957. *A Theory of Cognitive Dissonance.* Evanston, Ill.: Row, Peterson.

FINDLEY, WARREN G., and MIRIAM M. BRYAN. 1971. *Ability Grouping 1970: Status, Impact, and Alternatives.* Athens: Univ. Georgia.

FITTS, PAUL M. 1962. Factors in complex skill training. In Robert Glasser, ed., *Training Research and Education,* pp. 177–197. Pittsburgh: Univ. Pittsburgh Press.

———. 1964. Perceptual motor skill learning. In A. W. Melton, ed., *Categories of Human Learning.* Pp. 243–285. New York: Academic Press.

FLANAGAN, JOHN C. 1964. *The American High-School Student: The Identification and Utilization of Human Talent.* Pittsburgh: Univ. Pittsburgh Press.

FLANDERS, NED A. 1960. *Interaction Analysis in the Classroom.* Minneapolis: Coll. Educ., Univ. Minnesota.

FLAVELL, JOHN H. 1963. *The Developmental Psychology of Jean Piaget.* New York: Van Nostrand Reinhold.

FLEISHMAN, EDWIN A., and BENJAMIN FRUCHTER. 1960. Factor structure and predictability of successive stages of learning Morse code. *J. Appl. Psychol.* 44:97–101.

FONTANA, G. L. J. 1971. An investigation into the dynamics of achievement motivation in women. *Diss. Abstr. Internat.* (32-B), p. 1821.

FORGUS, RONALD H. 1956. Advantage of early over late perceptual experience in improving form discrimination. *Canad. J. Psychol.* 10:147–155.

FOWLER, WILLIAM. 1970. Problems of deprivation and developmental learning. *Merrill-Palmer Q.* 16:141–161.

FRANK, LAWRENCE K. 1963. Four ways to look at potentialities. In Alexander Frazier, ed., *New Insights and the Curriculum,* pp. 11–37. 1963 Yrbk. Washington, D.C.: ASCD.

FRANZ, S. I., and K. S. LASHLEY. 1951. Studies in the role of the brain in learning. In H. E. Garrett, ed., *Great Experiments in Psychology,* pp. 19–39. New York: Appleton.

FRASE, LAWRENCE T. 1968a. Effect of question location, pacing, and mode upon retention of prose materials. *J. Educ. Psychol. 59:244–249.*

———. 1968b. Questions as aids to reading: Some research and theory. *Amer. Educ. Res. J.* 4:319–332.

———. 1968c. Some data concerning the mathemagenic hypothesis. *Amer. Educ. Res. J.* 5:181–190

———. 1970. Boundary conditions for mathemagenic behavior. *Rev. Educ. Res.* 40:337–347.

FREY, SHERMAN, and JOSEPH ELLIS. 1970. Educational psychology and teaching: Opinions of experienced teachers. *Contemp. Educ.* 21:5–13.

FUCHS, E. 1967. *Teachers Talk: Views from inside City Schools.* Garden City: Anchor Books.

GAGE, N. L., ed. 1963. *Handbook of Research on Teaching.* Chicago: Rand McNally.

GAGE, N. L. 1964. Toward a cognitive theory of teaching. *T.C. Rec.* 65:408–412.

———. 1969. Teaching methods. In Robert L. Ebel, ed., *Encyclopedia of Educational Research,* pp. 1446–1458. New York: Macmillan.

————. 1972. *Teacher Effectiveness and Teacher Education: The Search for a Scientific Basis.* Palo Alto: Pacific Books.

————, and W. R. UNRUH. 1967. Theoretical formulations for research on teaching. *Rev. Educ. Res.* 37:358–370.

————, and P. H. WINNE. 1975. Performance-based teacher education. In Kevin A. Ryan, ed., *Teacher Education,* pp. 146–172. 74th Yrbk., NSSE, Pt. II. Chicago: Univ. of Chicago Press.

————, ed. 1976. *The Psychology of Teaching Methods.* 75th Yrbk., NSSE, Pt I. Chicago: Univ. Chicago Press.

GAGNÉ, ROBERT M. 1967a. Instruction and the conditions of learning. In L. Siegel, ed., *Instruction: Some Contemporary Viewpoints,* pp. 291–313. San Francisco: Chandler.

————, ed. 1967b. *Learning and Individual Differences.* Columbus: Merrill.

————. 1968a. Contributions of learning to human development. *Psychol. Rev.* 75:177–191.

————. 1968b. Learning hierarchies. *Educ. Psychol.* 6 (November):1.

————. 1976. The learning basis of teaching methods. In N. L. Gage, ed., *The Psychology of Teaching Methods,* pp. 21–43. 75th Yrbk., NSSE, Pt. I. Chicago: Univ. Chicago Press.

————. 1965, 1970, 1977. *Conditions of Learning.* New York: Holt Rinehart & Winston.

————, and LESLIE J. BRIGGS. 1974. *Principles of Instructional Design.* New York: Holt, Rinehart & Winston.

————, and R. T. WHITE. 1978. Memory structures and learning outcomes. *Rev. Educ. Res.* 48:187–223.

GALL, MEREDITH D. 1970. The use of questions in teaching. *Rev. Educ. Res.* 40:707–721.

————, et al. 1978. Effects of questioning techniques and recitation on student learning. *Amer. Educ. Res. J.* 15:175–199.

GALLUP, GEORGE H. 1981. The thirteenth Gallup poll of the public's attitudes toward the public schools. *Phi Delta Kappan* 63:33–47.

GARAI, JOSEF E., and AMRAM SCHEINFELD. 1968. Sex differences in mental and behavioral traits. *Genet. Psychol. Mongr.* 77:169–229.

GARDNER, JOHN W. 1961. *Excellence.* New York: Harper & Row.

GARRETT, HENRY E. 1946. A developmental theory of intelligence. *Amer. Psychol.* 1:372–378.

GATES, ARTHUR I. 1937. The necessary mental age for beginning reading. *Elem. Sch. J.* 37:497–508.

GAUDA, GILL. 1974. The Piagetian dilemma: What does Piaget really have to say to teachers? *Elem. Sch. J.* 74:481–492.

GENTILE, A. M. 1972. A working model of skill acquisition with application to teaching. *Quest.* 17:1–23.

GILMOR, TIMOTHY M. 1978. Locus of control as mediator of adaptive behaviour in children and adolescents. *Canad. Psychol. Rev.* 19:1–26.

GLANZER, MURRAY. 1958. Curiosity, exploratory drive, and stimulus satiation. *Psychol. Bull.* 55:302–315.

GLASER, ROBERT. 1963. Instructional technology and the measurement of learning outcomes. *Amer. Psychol.* 18:519–521.

———. 1976. Components of a psychology of instruction: Toward a science of design. *Rev. Educ. Res.* 46:1–24.

———, ed. 1962. *Training Research and Education.* Pittsburgh: Univ. Pittsburgh Press.

———, and LAUREN D. RESNICK. 1972. Instructional psychology. *Ann. Rev. Psychol.* 23.

GLASER-KIRSCHENBAUM, HOWARD. 1976. C. R. Rogers: The study of a psychologist and educator. *Diss. Abstr. Internat.* 37 (1-A):193.

GLASSER, WILLIAM. 1969. *Schools without Failure.* New York: Harper & Row.

GOLDFARB, ALLAN. 1963. Teacher ratings in psychiatric case-finding: Methodological considerations. *Amer. J. Publ. Health* 53:1919–1927.

GOOD, THOMAS L., and JERE E. BROPHY. 1977. *Educational Psychology: A Realistic Approach.* New York: Holt, Rinehart & Winston.

———, et al. 1975. *Teachers Make a Difference.* New York: Holt, Rinehart & Winston.

GOODLAD, JOHN I., et al. 1970. *Behind the Classroom Door.* Worthington: Jones.

GOODMAN, PAUL. 1960. *Growing Up Absurd: Problems of Youth and the Organized System.* New York: Random House.

———. 1966. *Compulsory Mis-Education and the Community of Scholars.* New York: Random House.

GORDON, EDMUND V., et al. 1970. Education for socially disadvantaged children. *Rev. Educ. Res.* 40:1–179.

GORDON, IRA J., et al. 1968. *Criteria for Theories of Instruction.* Washington, D.C.: Assn. Superv. Curr. Devel.

———. 1969. *Early Child Stimulation through Parent Education.* Gainesville: Inst. Devel. Human Resources, Univ. Florida.

GORDON, JESSIE E. 1963. *Personality and Behavior.* New York: Macmillan.

GORDON, T. 1974. *T.E.T.: Teacher-Effectiveness Training.* New York: Wyden.

GRAY, JOHN, and DAVID SATTERLY. 1976. A chapter of errors: Teaching styles and pupil progress in retrospect. *Educ. Res.* 19:45–56.

GREEN, ROBERT L., and THOMAS STACHNIK. 1968. Money, motivation, and academic achievement. *Phi Delta Kappan,* 50:228–230.

GREENWALD, ANTHONY G., and DAVID L. RONIS. 1979. Twenty years of cognitive dissonance: Case study of the evolution of a theory. *Psychol. Rev.* 85: 53–57.

GRICE, G. R. 1948. The relation of secondary reinforcement to delayed reward on visual discrimination learning. *J. Exper. Psychol.* 38:1–16.

GRONLUND, NORMAN E. 1974a. *Improving Marking and Reporting in Classroom Instruction.* New York: Macmillan.

———. 1974b. *Determining Accountability for Classroom Instruction.* New York: Macmillan.

———. 1977. *Constructing Achievement Tests.* Englewood Cliffs: Prentice-Hall.

GUILFORD, J. P. 1950. Creativity. *Amer. Psychol.* 5:444–454.

———. 1956. The structure of the intellect. *Psychol. Bull.* 53:267–293.

———. 1957. *A Revised Structure of the Intellect.* Psychol. Lab., Report No. 19. Los Angeles: Univ. S. Calif.

———. 1959. Three faces of intellect. *Amer. Psychol.* 14:469–479.

———. 1967. *The Nature of Human Intelligence.* New York: McGraw-Hill.

———. 1968. *Intelligence, Creativity, and Their Educational Implications.* San Diego: Knapp.

GUTHRIE, EDWIN R. 1959. Association by contiguity. In S. Koch, ed., *Psychology: A Study of a Science,* 2:158–197. New York: McGraw-Hill.

HALES, L. W., et al. 1973. The pass-fail option. *J. Educ. Res.* 66:295–298.

HALL, C. S. 1938. The inheritance of emotionality. *Sigma Xi Q.* 26:17–27.

———, and GARDNER LINDZEY. 1978. *Theories of Personality.* New York: Wiley.

HALL, JOHN F. 1961. *Psychology and Motivation.* Philadelphia: Lippincott.

HALL, R. V., et al. 1968. Instructing beginning teachers in reinforcing procedures which improve classroom control. *J. Appl. Beh. Anal.* 1:15–22.

HAMACHEK, DON E. 1975. *Behavior Dynamics in Teaching, Learning, and Growth.* Boston: Allyn & Bacon.

HAMBLEN, A. A. 1925. "An investigation to determine the extent to which the effect of study of Latin upon a knowledge of English derivations can be measured by conscious adaptation of content and methods to the attainment of this objective." Ph.D. dissertation, Univ. Pennsylvania.

HAMBLETON, RONALD K., et al. 1978. Criterion-referenced testing and measurement: A review of technical issues and developments. *Rev. Educ. Res.* 48:1–47.

HANEY, WALT, and GEORGE F. MADAUS. 1978. Making sense of the competency tests. *Harv. Educ. Rev.* 48:462–484.

HARLOW, HARRY F. 1949. The formation of learning sets. *Psychol. Rev.* 56:51–65.

———. 1953. Mice, monkeys, men, and motives. *Psychol. Rev.* 60:23–32.

———. 1959. Learning set and error factor theory. In S. Koch, ed., *Psychology: A Study of a Science,* 2:492–537. New York: McGraw-Hill.

HARRIS, FLORENCE R., et al. 1964. Effects of adult social reinforcement on child behavior. *Young Child* 20 (October):1.

HARROW, ANITA J. 1972. *A Taxonomy of the Psychomotor Domain: A Guide for Developing Behavioral Objectives.* New York: McKay.

HART, BETTY M., et al. 1968. Effect of contingent and non-contingent social reinforcement on the cooperative play of a preschool child. *J. Appl. Beh. Anal.* 1:73–76.

HART, LESLIE A. 1969. *The Classroom Disaster.* New York: Teachers College, Columbia Univ. Press.

HARTLEY, JAMES, and I. K. DAVIES. 1976. Preinstructional strategies: The role of pretests, behavioral objectives, overviews, and advance organizers. *Rev. Educ. Res.* 46:239–265.

HARTMANN, EDWARD. 1967. The cost of computer-assisted instruction. *Educ. Technol.* 11 (December):6–7.

HARTMANN, GEORGE W. 1942. The field theory of learning and its educational consequences. In N. B. Henry, ed., *Psychology of Learning,* pp. 165–214. 41st Yrbk., NSSE, Pt. II. Chicago: Univ. Chicago Press.

HAVELKA, J. 1956. Problem-solving behavior in rats. *Canad. J. Psychol.* 10:91–97.

HAVIGHURST, ROBERT J. 1972. *Developmental Tasks and Education.* 3d ed. New York: Longmans, Green.

———, and HILDA TABA. 1949. *Adolescent Character and Personality.* New York: Wiley.

HEATH, ROBERT W., and M. A. NIELSON. 1974. The research basis for performance-based teacher education. *Rev. Educ. Res.* 44:463–484.

HEBB, DONALD O. 1946. On the nature of fear. *Psychol. Rev.* 53:259–276.

———. 1949. *The Organization of Behavior.* New York: Wiley.

———. 1955. The mammal and his environment. *Amer. J. Psychol.,* 91:826–831.

———. 1958. The motivating effects of exteroceptive stimulation. *Amer. Psychol.* 13:109–113.

———. 1978. Open letter to a friend who thinks the IQ is a social evil. *Amer. Psychol.* 33:1143–1144.

HECKHAUSEN, H. 1968. Achievement motive research: Current problems and some contributions toward a general theory of motivation. *Nebraska Symposium on Motivation* 16:103–174.

HEIL, LOUIS M., et al. 1960. *Characteristics of Teacher Behavior and Competency Related to the Achievement of Different Kinds of Children in Several Elementary Grades.* Washington: HEW. (See also Sch. Rev., 1960, 37, 420–428.)

HERBERT, JOHN, and DAVID P. AUSUBEL. 1965. *Psychology in Teacher Preparation.* Monogr. Series, No. 5. Toronto: Ontario Inst. Studies Educ.

HERNDON, JAMES. 1968. *The Way It Spozed to Be.* New York: Simon & Schuster.

———. 1971. *How to Survive in Your Native Land.* New York: Simon & Schuster.

HERON, W. 1957. The pathology of boredom. *Sci. Amer.* 196:52–56.

HERRNSTEIN, R. J. 1977a. The evolution of behaviorism. *Amer. Psychol.* 32:593–603.

———. 1977b. Doing what comes naturally: A reply to Professor Skinner. *Amer. Psychol.* 32:1013–1016.

HERSH, RICHARD. 1972. Behaviorism and Humanism: A synthesis for teacher education. *J. Teach. Educ.* 23:172–176.

HESS E. H. 1964. Imprinting in birds. *Sci.* 146:1128–1139.

HESS, ROBERT D., and VIRGINIA C. SHIPMAN. 1965. Early experience and the socialization of cognitive modes in children. *Child Devel.* 36:869–886.

HILGARD, ERNEST R. 1962. *Introduction to Psychology.* New York: Harcourt, Brace & World.

HILL, WINFRED. 1956. Activity as an autonomous drive. *J. Comp. Physiol. Psychol.* 49:15–19.

———. 1977. *Learning: A Survey of Psychological Interpretation.* New York: Crowell.

HIRSCH, RICHARD H., et al. 1977. Moral development. *Theory into Practice* 16:51–128.

HOCHSTEIN, ROBERT. 1971. The payoff from educational R & D. *Phi Delta Kappan* 52:376–378.

HOFFMAN, MARTIN L., and LOIS W. HOFFMAN. 1964, 1966. *Review of Child Development Research.* New York: Russell Sage. 2 vols.

———, and HERBERT D. SALTZSTEIN. 1967. Parent discipline and the child's moral development. *J. Pers. Soc. Psychol.* 5:45–57.

HOLLINGWORTH, LETA S. 1926. *Gifted Children: Their Nature and Nurture.* New York: Macmillan.

HOLT, JOHN C. 1964. *How Children Fail.* New York: Pitman.

———. 1967. *How Children Learn.* New York: Pitman.

HONZIG, M. P., et al. 1948. The stability of mental test performance between two and eighteen years. *J. Exper. Educ.* 17:309–324.

HORN, ERNEST. 1942. Language and meaning. In N. B. Henry, ed., *Psychology of Learning*, pp. 377–413. 41st Yrbk., NSSE, Pt. II. Bloomington: Public Sch. Publ.

HORST, PAUL. 1976. Comments on The Myth of Vanishing Individual Differences in Bloom's Mastery Learning by Allan R. Buss. *J. Instr. Psychol.* 3 (spec. ed.):17–19.

HORWITZ, ROBERT A. 1979. Psychological effects of the "open classroom." *Rev. Educ. Res.* 49:71–86.

HOVLAND, CARL I., et al. 1949. *Experiments on Mass Communication: The American Soldier.* Vol. 3. Princeton: Princeton Univ. Press.

HOYT, KENNETH B. 1955. A study of the effects of teacher knowledge of pupil characteristics on pupil achievement and attitudes toward classwork. *J. Educ. Psychol.* 46:302–310.

HULL, CLARK L. 1943. *Principles of Behavior.* New York: Appleton-Century-Crofts.

HULL, RONALD E. 1973. Selecting an approach to individualized education. *Phi Delta Kappan* 55:169–173.

HULSE, STEWART H., et al. 1975. *The Psychology of Learning.* New York: McGraw-Hill.

HUNT, DAVID E., and EDMUND V. SULLIVAN. 1974. *Between Psychology and Education.* Hinsdale, Ill.: Dryden.

HUNT, J. McV. 1941. The effects of infant feeding upon adult hoarding in the albino rat. *J. Abn. Soc. Psychol.* 36:338–360.

———. 1960. Experience and the development of motivation: Some reinterpretations. *Child Devel.* 31:489–504.

———. 1961. *Intelligence and Experience.* New York: Ronald Press.

———. 1969. Has compensatory education failed? *Harv. Educ. Rev.* 39:278–300.

INGALLS, T. H. 1950. Dr. T. H. Ingalls describes tests on mice indicating heredity and environment overlap as determining factors. *New York Times,* December 20.

ILLICH, IVAN. 1971. *Deschooling Society.* New York: Harper & Row.

IRELAN, LOLA M., and ARTHUR BESNER. 1966. *Low Income Life Styles.* Welfare Adm. Publ. No. 14. Washington, HEW.

ISHEE, C. 1969. A study of variance of attitudes between teachers and mental hygienists toward problems of emotional disturbances of young adolescents. *Diss. Abstr. Internat.* 29 (12-A):4229–4230.

JACKSON, GREGG B. 1975. The research evidence on grade retention. *Rev. Educ. Res.* 45:613–635.

JACKSON, JESSE L., et al. 1978. In pursuit of equity, ethics, and excellence: The challenge to close the gap. *Phi Delta Kappan* 60:189–229.

JACKSON, PHILIP W. 1972. Deschooling? No. *Today's Education* 61:18–22.

JAHODA, MARIE. 1958. *Current Concepts of Positive Mental Health.* New York: Basic Books.

JAMES, WILLIAM. 1890. *Principles of Psychology.* Vol. 1. New York: Holt, Rinehart & Winston.

JAMISON, DEAN, et al. 1974. The effectiveness of alternative instructional media: A survey. *Rev. Educ. Res.* 44:1–67.

JANIS, IRVING L., and BERT T. KING. 1954. The influence of role playing on opinion change. *J. Abn. Soc. Psychol.* 49:211–218.

JENCKS, CHRISTOPHER, et al. 1972. *Inequality: A Reassessment of the Effect of Family and Schooling in America.* New York: Basic Books.

JENKINS, WILLIAM O., and JULIAN C. STANLEY. 1950. Partial reinforcement: A review and critique. *Psychol. Bull.* 47:193–234.

JENSEN, ARTHUR R. 1969. How much can we boost IQ and scholastic achievement? *Harv. Educ. Rev.* 39:1–123.

———. 1979. *Bias in Mental Testing.* New York: Free Press.

JERSILD, ARTHUR T. 1951. Self-understanding in childhood and adolescence. *Amer. Psychol.* 6:122–126.

———. 1952. *In Search of Self.* New York: Teachers College, Columbia Univ.

JOHNSON, SIMON S. 1975. *Update on Education: A Digest of the National Assessment of Educational Progress.* Denver: Educ. Comm. of the States.

JOHNSON, WENDELL. 1946. *People in Quandaries.* New York: Harper & Row.

JONES, MARY C., and PAUL H. MUSSEN. 1957. The later careers of boys who were early- or late-maturing. *Child Devel.* 28:113–128.

———. 1958. Self-conceptions, motivation, and interpersonal attitudes of early- and late-maturing girls. *Child Devel.* 29:491–501.

JONES, VERNON. 1960. Character education. In C. W. Harris, ed., *Encyclopedia of Educational Research,* pp. 84–91. New York: Macmillan.

JOURARD, SIDNEY M. 1963. *Personality Adjustment.* New York: Macmillan.

JUDD, C. H. 1908. The relation of special training to intelligence. *Educ. Rev.* 36:28–42.

JUNELL, JOSEPH S. 1969. Do teachers have the right to indoctrinate? *Phi Delta Kappan* 51:182–185.

KAGAN, JEROME. 1964. American longitudinal research on psychological development. *Child Devel.* 35:1–32.

———. 1966. Reflection-impulsivity; The generality and dynamics of conceptual tempo. *J. Abn. Soc. Psychol.* 71:17–22.

———. 1971. *Understanding Children: Behavior, Motives, and Thoughts.* New York: Harcourt, Brace & World.

———, and NATHAN KOGAN. 1970. Individual variation in cognitive processes. In Paul H. Mussen, ed., *Carmichael's Manual of Child Psychology,* 1:1273–1365. New York: Wiley.

———, and HOWARD A. MOSS. 1960. The stability of passive and dependent behavior from childhood through adulthood. *Child Devel.* 31:577–591.

KAPLAN, LOUIS, and J. D. O'DEA. 1953. Mental health hazards in the school. *Educ. Lead.* 10:351–354.

KARPINOS, BERNARD D. 1961. Current height and weight of youth of military age. *Hum. Biol.* 33:335–354.

KARRAKER, R. J. 1971. *Token Reinforcement Systems in Regular Public School Classrooms: Readings.* New York: Crowell.

KEAVNEY, G., and K. E. SINCLAIR. 1978. Teacher concerns and teacher anxiety: A neglected topic of classroom research. *Rev. Educ. Res.* 48:273–290.

KEHILER, ALICE V. 1941. *Life and Growth.* New York: Appleton-Century-Crofts.

KELLEY, EARL C. 1965. The place of affective learning. *Educ. Lead.* 22:455–457.

KELLY, G. A. 1955. *The Psychology of Personal Constructs.* Vol. 2: *Clinical Diagnosis and Psychotherapy.* New York: Norton.

KERLINGER, FRED N., ed. 1974. *Review of Research in Education.* Vol. 2. Itasca, Ill.: Peacock.

KERSH, BERT Y., and MERLE C. WITTROCK. 1962. Learning by discovery: An interpretation of recent research. *J. Teach. Educ.* 13:461–468.

KINCAID, M. EVELYN. 1978. A philosophical analysis of Lawrence Kohlberg's developmental stages of moral reasoning. *Diss. Abstr. Internat.* 38 (7-A):4016–4017.

KINGSLEY, H. L., and RALPH GARRY. 1957. *The Nature and Conditions of Learning.* Englewood Cliffs: Prentice-Hall.

KIRK, DIANA H., and SUSAN GOON. 1975. Desegregation and the cultural deficit model: An examination of the literature. *Rev. Educ. Res.* 45:599–611.

KIRKENDALL, LESTER A. 1939. Teaching for marks. *Sch. & Soc.* 49:642–644.

KIRKLAND, MARJORIE C. 1971. The effects of tests on students and schools. *Rev. Educ. Res.* 41:303–350.

KIRSCHENBAUM, HOWARD, et al. 1971. *Wad-Ja-Get? The Grading Game in American Education.* New York: Hart.

KITCHENER, RICHARD F. 1977. Behavior and behaviorism. *Behaviorism* 5 (2):11–71.

KLAUSMEIER, HERBERT J., and RICHARD E. RIPPLE. 1971. *Learning and Human Abilities.* New York: Harper & Row.

KLEIN, GEORGE 1951. The personal world through perception. In R. R. Blake and G. V. Ramsey, eds. *Perception: An Approach to Personality*, pp. 328–335. New York: Ronald Press.

KLIEBARD, HERBERT M. 1967. Curriculum differentiation for the disadvantaged. *Educ. Forum*, 32:47–56.

KLINE, L. W. 1914. Some experimental evidence in regard to formal discipline. *J. Educ. Psychol.* 5:259–266.

KNAPP, C. G., and W. R. DIXON. 1950. Learning to juggle: 1. A study to determine the effects of two different distributions of practice on learning efficiency. *Res. Q.* 21:331–336.

KNOX, J. O. 1976. Ability structure of 10-11-year-old children and the theory of fluid and crystallized intelligence. *J. Educ. Psychol.* 68:411–423.

KOCH, WARREN J. 1973. Basic facts about using the computer in instruction. *Educ. Dig.* 38 (March):28–31.

KOHL, HERBERT R. 1967. *36 Children.* New York: New American Library.

———. 1969. *The Open Classroom: A Practical Guide to a New Way of Teaching.* New York: Random House.

KOHLBERG, LAWRENCE. 1964. Development of moral character and moral ideology. In M. L. Hoffman and L. W. Hoffman, eds., *Review of Child Development Research* 63:383–431.

———. 1966. Moral education in the schools: A developmental view. *Sch. Rev.* 74:1–30.

———. 1968. Early education: A cognitive-developmental view. *Child Devel.* 39:1013–1062.

———. 1975. The cognitive-developmental approach to moral education. *Phi Delta Kappan* 56:670–677.

———. 1977. Moral development: A review of the theory. *Theory into Practice* 16:53–72.

———, and R. MAYER. 1972. Development as the aim of education. *Harv. Educ. Rev.* 42:449–496.

KOHLER, W. 1927. *The Mentality of Apes.* New York: Harcourt, Brace, & World.

———. 1929. *Gestalt Psychology.* New York: Liveright.

KOOI, B. Y., and R. E. SCHUTZ. 1965. A factor analysis of classroom disturbance in-
tercorrelations. *Amer. Educ. Res. J.* 2:37–40, 600–601.

KOUNIN, J. 1970. *Discipline and Group Management in the Classroom.* New York:
Holt, Rinehart & Winston.

———, and P. V. GUMP. 1962. The ripple effect in discipline. *Elem. Sch. J.*
59:158–162.

KOZOL, JONATHAN. 1967. *Death at an Early Age.* Boston: Houghton Mifflin.

———. 1972. *Free Schools.* Boston: Houghton Mifflin.

KRASNER, LEONARD. 1978. The future and the past in the behaviorism-humanism di-
alogue. *Amer. Psychol.* 33:799–814.

KRATHWOHL, DAVID R., et al. 1964. *Taxonomy of Educational Objectives. Handbook
II: Affective Domain.* New York: McKay.

KROPP, RUSSELL P., and HOWARD W. STOKER. 1966. *The Construction and Validation of Tests of Cognitive Processes Described in the Taxonomy of Educational
Objectives.* C.R.P., No. 2117. Washington, D.C.: USOE.

———, et al. 1966. The validation of the Taxonomy of Educational Objectives. *J.
Exper. Educ.* 34:69–76.

KULIK, JAMES A., et al. 1979. A meta-analysis of outcome studies of Keller's
Personalized System of Instruction. *Amer. Psychol.* 34:307–318.

LABOV, W. 1970. The logical non-standard English. In F. Williams, ed., *Language
and Poverty.* Chicago: Markham Press.

LADAS, HAROLD. 1973. The mathemagenic effects of factual review questions on the
learning of incidental information: A critical review. *Rev. Educ. Res.* 43:71–82.

LAMMERS, CLAUDE C. 1967. Automation, drop-outs, and educational dogma. *Bull.
NASSP* 51 (December):31–39.

LANDERS, J. 1963. *Higher Horizons: Progress Report.* New York: Board of Education,
New York City Schools.

LAWRENCE, D. H., and LEON FESTINGER. 1962. *Deterrents and Reinforcement: The
Psychology of Insufficient Rewards.* Stanford: Stanford Univ. Press.

LEARNED, W. S., and BEN D. WOOD. 1938. *The Student and His Knowledge.* Bull.
No. 29. New York: Carnegie Foundation for the Advancement of Teaching.

LECKY, P. 1945. *Self-Consistency: A Theory of Personality.* New York: Island Press.

LEHMANN, IRVING J., and WILLIAM A. MEHRENS. 1979. *Educational Research:
Readings in Focus.* New York: Holt, Rinehart & Winston.

LESSING, L. 1967. *DNA: The Core of Life Itself.* New York: Macmillan.

LEUBA, C. 1955. Toward some integration of learning theories: The concept of optimal stimulation. *Psychol. Rev.* 1:27–33.

LEWIN, KURT. 1958. Group decision and social change. In E. E. Maccoby et al., eds.
Readings in Social Psychology. 3d ed. New York: Holt, Rinehart & Winston.

———, et al. 1939. Patterns of aggressive behavior in experimentally created social
climates. *J. Soc. Psychol.* 10:271–299.

LIEBERMAN, MYRON, et al. 1970. Accountability. *Phi Delta Kappan* 52:193–239.

Life Magazine. 1963. DNA's code: Key to all life. *Life Magazine,* October 4, pp.
70–90.

LILLY, JOHN C. 1956. Mental effects of reduction of ordinary levels of physical stimulus on intact healthy persons. *Psychiatric Res. Rep.* 5:1–28.

LINDGREN, HENRY C. 1959. The teacher helps the learner interpret his experiences.

In D. H. Russell and S. K. Richardson, eds., *Learning and the Teacher*, pp. 81–104. 1959 Yrbk. Washington: ASCD.

―――. 1962. *Educational Psychology in the Classroom.* New York: Wiley.

LINDZEY, GARDNER, et al. eds. 1973. *Theories of Personality: Primary Sources and Research.* New York: Wiley.

LIPE, DEWEY, and STEVEN M. JUNG. 1971. Manipulating incentives to enhance school learning. *Rev. Educ. Res.* 41:249–280.

LOCKWOOD, ALAN L. 1978. The effects of values clarification and moral development curriculum on school-age subjects: A critical review of recent research. *Rev. Educ. Res.* 48:325–364.

LOEVINGER, JANE. 1959. Patterns of parenthood as theories of learning. *J. Abn. Soc. Psychol.* 59:148–150.

―――. 1966. The meaning and measurement of ego-development. *Amer. Psychol.* 21:195–206.

―――. 1976. Origins of conscience. *Psychol. Issues* 9:265–297.

LOGAN, FRANK A. 1959. The Hull-Spence approach. In S. Koch, ed., *Psychology: A Study of a Science*, 2:293–358. New York: McGraw-Hill.

LORENZ, K. 1935. Der Kumpan in der Unwelt des Vogels. *J. Ornithologie* 83:137–213, 289–413.

LORETAN, J. G. 1965. Decline and fall of group intelligence testing. *T.C. Rec.* 67:10–17.

LUFLER, HENRY S. 1978. Discipline: A new look at an old problem. *Phi Delta Kappan* 59:424–426.

LUMSDAINE, A. A. 1962. Experimental research on instructional devices and materials. In Robert Glaser, ed., *Training Research in Education*, pp. 247–294. Pittsburgh: Univ. Pittsburgh.

―――. 1964. Educational technology, programmed learning, and instructional science. In E. R. Hilgard, ed., *Theories of Learning and Instruction*, pp. 371–401. 63d Yrbk., NSSE, Pt. 1. Chicago: Univ. Chicago Press.

―――, and I. L. JANIS. 1953. Resistance and counterpropaganda produced by one-sided propaganda presentation. *Publ. Opinion Q.* 17:311–318.

LYND, ALBERT. 1953. *Quackery in the Public School.* Boston: Little, Brown.

LYNN, DAVID B. 1962. Sex role and parental identification. *Child Devel.* 33:555–564.

―――. 1964. Divergent feedback and sex-role identification in boys and men. *Merrill-Palmer Q.*, 10:17–23.

―――. 1966. The process of learning parental and sex-role identification. *J. Marr. Fam.* 28:466–470.

―――, and I. GORDON. 1961. The relation of neuroticism and extraversion to intelligence and educational attainment. *Brit. J. Educ. Psychol.* 31:194–203.

MACAULAY, RONALD K. 1978. The myth of female superiority in language. *J. Child Lang.* 5:353–363.

McCALL, ROBERT B., et al. 1977. Transitions in early mental development. *Monogr. Soc. Res. Child Devel.* 42, No. 3.

McCLELLAND, DAVID C. 1961. *The Achieving Society.* New York: Van Nostrand Reinhold.

―――. 1965. Toward a theory of motive acquisition. *Amer. Psychol.* 20:21–33.

―――, et al. 1953. *The Achievement Motive.* New York: Appleton-Century-Crofts.

McCULLERS, JOHN C., and WALTER T. PLANT. 1964. Personality and social development: Cultural influences. *Rev. Educ. Res.* 34:599–610.

McDaniels, Garry L. 1975. The evaluation of Follow Through. *Educ. Res.* 4 (December):7–11.

McDonald, R. J., and D. Ross. 1974. Behavioral objectives: A critical review. *Instruct. Sci.* 2:151.

McDougal, William. 1908. *An Introduction to Social Psychology.* London: Methuen.

McGaugh, James L. 1968. Some changing concepts about learning and memory. *Today's Educ.* 57 (February):8–9, 51–54.

McGregor, James. 1971. Sesame Street's worthy sibling. *Wall Str. J.,* November 12, p. 178.

McKeachie, W. J. 1963. Research on teaching at the college and university level. In N. L. Gage, ed., *Handbook of Research on Teaching,* pp. 1118–1172. Chicago: Rand McNally.

McLaughlin, T. F. 1976. Self-control in the classroom. *Rev. Educ. Res.* 46:631–663.

MacLeod, Robert B. 1965. The teaching of psychology and the psychology we teach. *Amer. Psychol.* 20:344–352.

Macmillan, Donald L., et al. 1973. The role of punishment in the classroom. *Except. Child.* 40:85–96.

MacNamara, John. 1978. Another unaccommodating look at Piaget. *Canad. Psychol. Rev.* 19:78–81.

McNemar, Q. 1940. A critical examination of the University of Iowa studies of environmental influences upon the IQ. *Psychol. Bull.* 37:63–92.

———. 1964. Lost: Our Intelligence. Why? *Amer. Psychol.* 19:871–882.

Maddi, Salvatore. 1968. *Personality Theory: A Comparative Analysis.* Homewood, Ill.: Dorsey.

Mager, Robert F. 1962. *Preparing Instructional Objectives.* Palo Alto: Fearon.

Maier, Norman R. F. 1931. Reasoning in humans: 2. The solution of a problem and its appearance in consciousness. *J. Comp. Psychol.* 12:184–191.

———. 1949. *Frustration: The Study of Behavior without a Goal.* New York: McGraw-Hill.

———. 1960. Maier's law. *Amer. Psychol.* 15:208–212.

———, et al. 1940. Studies of abnormal behavior in the rat: 3. The development of behavior fixations through frustration. *J. Exper. Psychol.* 26:521–546.

Malkova, Zoya. 1964. Moral education in the Soviet schools. *Phi Delta Kappan* 46:134–138.

Maracek, J., and K. K. Mettee. 1972. Avoidance of continued success as a function of self-esteem, level of esteem certainty, and responsibility for success. *J. Pers. Soc. Psychol.* 22:98–107.

Margolin, R. J. 1953. New perspectives for teachers: An evaluation of a mental health institute. *Ment. Hyg.* 37:394–424.

Margulis, Stephen P., and Elaine Songer. 1969. Cognitive dissonance: Bibliography of its first decade. *Psychol. Rep.* 24:923–935.

Marini, Margaret M., and Ellen Greenberger. 1978. Sex differences in educational aspirations and expectations. *Amer. Educ. Res. J.* 15:67–79.

Markowitz, N., and K. E. Renner. 1966. Feedback and the delay-retention effect. *J. Exper. Psychol.* 72:452–455.

Marquart, Dorothy I. 1946. The pattern of punishment in its relation to abnormal fixation in adult human subjects. Ph.D. dissertation, Univ. of Michigan.

MARSHALL, S. L. A. 1947. *Men against Fire.* New York: Morrow.

MARX, MELVIN H. 1960. Motivation. In C. W. Harris, ed., *Encyclopedia of Educational Research,* pp. 888–901. New York: Macmillan.

———. 1969, 1970. *Learning.* Vol. 1: *Processes.* Vol. 2: *Interactions.* Vol. 3: *Theories.* New York: Macmillan.

MASLOW, ABRAHAM H. 1943. A theory of human motivation. *Psychol. Rev.* 50:370–396.

———. 1959. Cognition of being in the peak experiences. *J. Genet. Psychol.* 94:43–66.

———. 1966. *The Psychology of Science.* New York: Harper & Row.

———. 1968a. *Toward a Psychology of Being.* New York: Van Nostrand.

———. 1968b. Some educational implications of the humanistic psychologies. *Harv. Educ. Rev.* 38:685–696.

MASCHETTE, DIANE. 1977. Moral reasoning in the real world. *Theory into Practice* 16:124–128.

MASSARI, DAVID J., and JACQUELINE A. MASSARI. 1973. Sex differences in the relationship of cognitive style and intellectual functioning in disadvantaged preschool children. *J. Genet. Psychol.* 122:175–181.

MAYER, RICHARD E. 1975. Information-processing variables in learning to solve problems. *Rev. Educ. Res.* 45:525–541.

———. 1979. Can advance organizers influence meaningful learning? *Rev. Educ. Res.* 49:371–383.

MEHRENS, WILLIAM A. 1969. National Assessment through September 1969. *Phi Delta Kappan* 51:215–217.

———, and IRVIN J. LEHMANN. *Measurement and Evaluation in Education and Psychology.* New York: Holt, Rinehart & Winston, 1973, 1978.

MELBY, ERNEST A. 1966. It is time for schools to abolish the marking system. *Nation's Sch.* 77:104.

MELTON, R. F. 1978. Resolution of conflicting claims concerning the effects of behavioral objectives on student learning. *Rev. Educ. Res.* 48:291–302.

MELZACK, RONALD, and T. H. SCOTT. 1957. The effects of early experience on the response to pain. *J. Comp. Physiol. Psychol.* 50:155–161.

———, and WILLIAM R. THOMPSON. 1956. Effects of early experience on social behavior. *Canad. J. Psychol.* 10:87–91.

MENNINGER, KARL. 1975. Whatever became of sin? *Philippine J. Mental Health* 6 (1):35–40.

MENNINGER, ROY W. 1978. Coping with life's strains. *U.S. News & World Report,* May 1, pp. 80–82.

MERMELSTEIN, E., et al. 1967. Training techniques for the concept of conservation. *Alta. J. Educ. Res.* 13:185–200.

MESKAUSKAS, JOHN A. 1976. Evaluation models for criterion-referenced testing: Views regarding mastery and standard setting. *Rev. Educ. Res.* 46:133–158.

MESSICK, SAMUEL, et al. 1976. *Individuality in Learning.* San Francisco: Jossey-Bass.

METFESSEL, N. S., et al. 1969. Instrumentation of Bloom's and Krathwohl's taxonomies for the writing of behavioral objectives. *Psych. Sch.* 6:227–231.

MILLER, G. A. 1956. The magical number seven plus or minus two: Some limits in our ability for processing information. *Psychol. Rev.* 63:81–97.

MILLER, NEAL E. 1959. Liberation of the basic S-R concepts: Extensions to conflict behavior, motivation, and social learning. In S. Koch, ed., *Psychology: A Study of a Science,* 2:196–292. New York: McGraw-Hill.

———, and J. DOLLARD. 1941. *Social Learning and Imitation.* New Haven: Yale Univ. Press.

MINISTRY OF EDUCATION (England). 1949. *Report by H. M. Inspectors on the Summerhill School.* Leicester (England). (Included in A. S. Neill, Summerhill, 1960.)

MITRE CORPORATION. 1974. An overview of the TICCIT program. Technical Rept., M 74-1. McLean, Va.: MITRE Corp.

MONTGOMERY, K. C. 1953. Exploratory behavior as a function of "similarity" of stimulus situation. *J. Comp. Physiol. Psychol.* 46:129–133.

———, and MARSHALL SEGALL. 1955. Discrimination learning based on the exploratory drive. *J. Comp. Physiol. Psychol.* 48:225–228.

MORPHETT, MABEL V., and CARLETON WASHBURNE. 1931. When should children begin to read? *Elem. Sch. J.* 31:496–503.

MORRIS, SUSAN, and STANLEY B. MESSER. 1978. The effect of locus of control and locus of reinforcement on academic task persistence. *J. Genet. Psychol.* 132:3–9.

MORRISON, H. C. 1926. *The Practice of Teaching in the Secondary School.* Chicago: Univ. Chicago Press.

MOULY, GEORGE J. 1973. *Psychology for Effective Teaching.* New York: Holt, Rinehart & Winston.

———. 1971. *Readings in Educational Psychology.* New York: Holt, Rinehart & Winston.

———. 1978. *Educational Research: The Art and Science of Investigation.* Boston: Allyn & Bacon.

MUELLER, DANIEL J. 1976. Mastery learning: Partly boon, partly boondoggle. *T.C. Rec.* 78:41–52.

MULLER, G. E., and A. PILZECKER. 1900. Experimentelle Beiträge zur Lehre von Gedächtniss. *Erg* 1:1–300.

MURRAY, HENRY A. 1938. *Explorations in Personality.* New York: Oxford Univ. Press.

MUSSEN, PAUL H., and MARY C. JONES. 1957. Self-conceptions, motivation, and interpersonal attitudes of late- and early-maturing boys. *Child Devel.* 28:243–256.

———, ed. 1960. *Handbook of Research Methods in Child Development.* New York: Wiley.

———. 1970. *Carmichael's Manual of Child Psychology.* 2 vols. New York: Wiley.

MUUSS, ROLF E. 1976. Kohlberg's cognitive-developmental approach to adolescent morality. *Adolescence* 11:39–59.

NANCE, DOUGLAS W. 1976. Bloom's mastery learning in college math limits critical and essential coverage. *J. Instr. Psychol.* 3:23–27.

NATIONAL INSTITUTE OF EDUCATION. 1977. *Violent Schools—Safe Schools.* Washington, D.C.: Govt. Printing Office.

NATIONAL INSTITUTE OF MENTAL HEALTH. 1962. *Facts on Mental Health and Mental Illness.* Washington, D.C.: HEW.

———. 1962. *The Teacher and Mental Health.* Washington, D.C.: HEW.

NEILL, A. 1960. *Summerhill.* New York: Hart.

NEILL, GEORGE. 1979. NAEP at age 10 says: Schools are in trouble. *Phi Delta Kappan* 61 (November):157.

NEWELL, ALLEN, and H. A. SIMON. 1972. *Human Problem-Solving.* Englewood Cliffs: Prentice-Hall.

———, et al. 1962. The processes of creative thinking. In H. E. Gruber (ed.) *Contemporary Approaches to Creative Thinking.* New York: Atherton, pp. 63–119.

NEW YORK TIMES. 1968. Giant in the nursery—Jean Piaget. *New York Times Magazine,* May 26, pp. 25–27, 50–54, 62, 77–80.

NOVAK, JOSEPH D., et al. 1971. Interpretation of research findings in terms of Ausubel's theory and implications for science education *Sci. Educ.* 55:483–526.

NUNNALLY, JUM C. 1967. *Psychometric Theory.* New York: McGraw-Hill.

———. 1976. Vanishing individual differences: Just stick your head in the sand and they will go away. *J. Instr. Psychol.* 3 (spec. ed.):28–40.

OAKLAND, THOMAS, ed. 1977 *Psychological and Educational Assessment of Minority Children.* New York: Brunner/Mazel.

OETTINGER, ANTHONY, and S. MARKS. 1968. Educational technology: New myths and old reality. *Harv. Educ. Rev.* 38:697–755.

OJEMANN, RALPH H. Should educational objectives be stated in behavioral terms? *Elem. Sch. J.,* 1968, 68, 223–231; 1969, 69, 229–235; 1970, 271–278; 1974, 74, 291–298.

OPPENHEIMER, ROBERT J. 1958. The tree of knowledge. *Harper's Mag.* 217:55–60.

ORNSTEIN, ALLAN C., and HARRIETT TALMAGE. 1973. The rhetoric and the realities of accountability. *Today's Educ.* 62 (September–October):70–80.

PALERMO, DAVID S., et al. 1956. The relationship of anxiety in children to performance in a complex learning task. *Child Devel.* 27:333–337.

PAOLITTO, DIANA P. 1976. The effect of cross-age tutoring in adolescence: An inquiry into theoretical assumptions. *Rev. Educ. Res.* 46:215–237.

———. 1977. The role of the teacher in moral education. *Theory into Practice.* 16:73–80.

PASCUAL-LEONE, JUAN. 1976. On learning and development, Piagetian style: A reply to Lefebre-Pinard. *Canad. Psychol. Rev.* 17:270–288.

PASKE, GERALD H. 1969. Violence, values, and education. *T.C. Rec.* 71:51–63.

PASSOW, A. HARRY. 1974. Compensatory instructional intervention. In Fred N. Kerlinger, ed. *Review of Research in Education.* 2:145–175. Itasca: Peacock.

———, ed. 1963. *Education in Depressed Areas.* New York: Teachers College, Columbia Univ.

———. 1979. *The Gifted and Talented: Their Education and Development.* 78th Yrbk., NSSE, Pt. I. Chicago: Univ. Chicago Press.

PATTERSON, C. H. 1977. *Foundations for a Theory of Instruction and Educational Psychology.* New York: Harper & Row.

PAVLOV, IVAN P. 1927. *Conditioned Reflexes.* London: Oxford Univ. Press.

PECK, ROBERT F., and ROBERT J. HAVIGHURST. 1960. *The Psychology of Character Development.* New York: Wiley.

PECK, ROBERT F., and JAMES V. MITCHELL. 1962. *What Research Says to the Teacher.* No. 24. Washington, D.C.: AERA.

PERRONE, V. 1972. *Open Education: Promise and Problems.* Bloomington: Phi Delta Kappa.

PHI DELTA KAPPAN. News items. Teachers don't recognize good writing, P.D.K., March, 1976, 57, 46; N.A.E.P., P.D.K., Jan. 1977, 58; also P.D.K., 1978, 59, 573; Head Start, P.D.K., 1977, 59, 69; Violence, P.D.K., 1978, 59, 69.

————. 1973. The father of behavioral objectives criticizes them: An interview with Ralph Tyler. *Phi Delta Kappan* 55:55–57.

————. 1976. Teachers do not recognize good writing. *Phi Delta Kappan* 57:46.

PHILLIPS, BEEMAN N. 1962. Sex, social class, and anxiety as sources of valuation in school achievement. *J. Educ. Psychol.* 53:316–322.

PHILLIPS, J. L. 1969. *Origins of the Intellect: Piaget's Theory.* San Francisco: Freeman.

PIAGET, JEAN. 1932. *The Moral Judgment of the Child.* New York: Harcourt, Brace, and World.

————. 1950. *Psychology of Intelligence.* London: Routledge & Kegan Paul.

————. 1952. *Judgment and Reasoning in the Child.* New York: Harcourt, Brace and World.

————. 1954. *The Construction of Reality in the Child.* New York: Basic Books.

PINARD, A., and M. LAURENDEAU. 1964. A scale of mental development based on the theory of Piaget: Description of a project. *J. Res. Sci. Teaching* 2:253–260.

PITTENGER, OWEN E., and C. THOMAS GOODING. 1971. *Learning Theories in Educational Practice: An Integration of Psychological Theory and Educational Philosophy.* New York: Wiley.

PLANTE, PATRICIA R. 1967. Morality and the mod student. *Lib. Educ.* 53:466–475.

PLOWDEN, LADY B., et al. 1967. *Children and Their Primary Schools: A Report of The Control Advisory Council for Education.* London: H.M. Stationary Office.

POPHAM, W. JAMES. 1968. Probing the validity of the arguments against behavioral objectives. *Convention, Amer. Educ. Res. Assn.* Chicago.

————. 1969. *Instructional Objectives.* Chicago: Rand McNally.

————. 1970. The Instructional Objectives Exchange: New support for criterion-referenced instruction. *Phi Delta Kappan* 52:174–175.

————. 1972a. Must all objectives be behavioral? *Educ. Lead.* 29:605–608.

————. 1972b. The new world of accountability in the classroom. *Bull. NASSP* 56 (May):5–31.

————. 1975. *Educational Evaluation.* Englewood Cliffs: Prentice-Hall.

————. 1978. The case for criterion-referenced measurements. *Educ. Res.* 7 (December):6–10.

POSTMAN, NEIL, and CHARLES WEINGARTNER. 1969. *Teaching as a Subversive Activity.* New York: Delacorte.

POTEET, JAMES A. 1973. *Behavior Modification: A Practical Guide for Teachers.* Minneapolis: Burgess.

PREMACK, DAVID. 1965. Reinforcement theory. In D. Levine, ed., *Nebraska Symposium on Motivation.* Vol. 13. Lincoln: Univ. Nebraska Press.

PULLIAM, LLOYD. 1963. The lecture—Are we reviving discredited teaching methods? *Phi Delta Kappan,* 44:382–385.

PURPEL, DAVID, and KEVIN RYAN. 1975. Moral education: Where sages fear to tread. *Phi Delta Kappan* 56:659–662.

RAPKIN, LESLIE Y., and JOSEPH F. SUCHOSKI. 1967. Teacher's view of mental illness: A study of attitudes and information. *J. Teach. Educ.* 18:36–41.

RASMUSSEN, G. R. 1956. An evaluation of a student-centered and instructor-centered method of conducting a graduate course in education. *J. Educ. Psychol.* 47:449–461.

RATHBONE, CHARLES H. 1972. Examining the open education classroom. *Sch. Rev.* 80:521–549.

RATHS, LOUIS E., et al. 1966. *Values and Teaching: Working with Values in the Classroom.* Columbus: Merrill.

RAYWID, MARY A. 1962. *The Ax-Grinders: Critics of Our Public Schools.* New York: Crowell-Collier.

REIMER, JOSEPH. 1977. A structural theory of moral development. *Theory into Practice.* 16:60–66.

RICKOVER, HYMAN G. 1963. *American Education: A National Failure.* New York: Dutton.

RIESSMAN, FRANK. 1962. *The Culturally Deprived Child.* New York: Harper & Row.

———. 1966. Styles of learning. *NEA J.* 55 (March):15–17.

ROBBINS, LILLIAN C. 1963. The accuracy of parental recall of aspects of child development and of child-rearing practices. *J. Abn. Soc. Psychol.* 66:297–312.

ROBINSON, DON. Scraps from a teacher's notebook. *Phi Delta Kappan,* 1962, 43, 344; 1965, 47, 157; 1967, 48, 248.

ROBINSON, THOMAS E. 1952. His teacher improved too. *NEA J.* 41 (January):54.

ROEPER, ANNEMARIE, and IRVING SIGEL. 1966. Finding the clue to children's thought processes. *Young Children* 21:335–349.

ROETHLISBERGER, F. J., and WILLIAM J. DICKSON. 1939. *Management and the Worker.* Cambridge: Harv. Univ. Press.

ROGERS, CARL R. 1947. Some observations on the organization of personality. *Amer. Psychol.* 2:359–368.

———. 1951. *Client-Centered Therapy.* Boston: Houghton Mifflin.

———. 1954. Toward a theory of creativity. *ETC: Rev. Gen. Sem.* 11:249–260.

———. 1956. Implications of recent advances in prediction and control of behavior. *T.C. Rec.* 57:316–322.

———. 1959a. Theory of therapy, personality, and inter-personal relationships as developed in the client-centered framework. In S. Koch, ed., *Psychology: A Study of a Science,* 2:184–256. New York: McGraw-Hill.

———. 1959b. Some observations on the organization of personality. In A. E. Kuenzli, ed., *The Phenomenological Problem,* pp. 49–75. New York: Harper & Row.

———. 1961. *On Becoming a Person.* Boston: Houghton Mifflin.

———. 1962. Toward becoming a fully functioning person. In A. W. Combs, ed., *Perceiving, Behaving, Becoming,* pp. 21–33. 1962 Yrbk. Washington, D.C.: ASCD.

———. 1963. Learning to be free. *NEA J.* 52 (March):28–31.

———. 1964. Towards a science of the person. In T. W. Wann, ed., *Behaviorism and Phenomenology,* pp. 109–140. Chicago: Univ. Chicago Press, 1964.

———. 1969. *Freedom to Learn.* Columbus: Merrill.

———. 1971. Forget you are a teacher. *Instructor* (August–September).

———. 1974. In retrospect: Forty-six years. *Amer. Psychol.* 29:115–123.

ROSENBLAUM, S., et al. 1955. Davis-Eells (culture-fair) test performance of lower-class children. *J. Consult. Psychol.* 19:51–54.

ROSENSHINE, BARAK. 1971. *Teaching Behaviours and Student Achievement.* London: National Foundation for Educational Research in England and Wales.

————. 1976. Classroom instruction. In. N. L. Gage, ed., *The Psychology of Teaching Methods,* pp. 335–371. 75th Yrbk., NSSE, Pt. I. Chicago: Univ. Chicago Press.

————, and NORMA FURST. 1973. The use of direct observation to student teaching. In Robert M. W. Travers, ed., *Second Handbook of Research on Teaching,* pp. 122–183. Chicago: Rand McNally.

ROSENTHAL, ROBERT, and LENORE JACOBSON. 1968. *Pygmalion in the Classroom: Teacher Expectation and Pupils' Intellectual Development.* New York: Holt, Rinehart & Winston.

ROSSMAN, JACK E. 1970. Graduate school attitudes toward S-U grades. Educ. Rec. 51:310–313.

ROTHKOPF, ERNST Z. 1970. The concept of mathemagenic activities. *Rev. Educ. Res.* 40:325–336.

————. 1973. Course content and supportive environments for learning. *Educ. Psychol.* 10:121–128.

ROTTER, JULIAN B. 1954. *Social Learning and Clinical Psychology.* Englewood Cliffs: Prentice-Hall.

————. 1966. Generalized expectancies for internal versus external control of reinforcement. Psychol. Monogr., 80, No. 609.

ROWHER, WILLIAM D., et al. 1974. *Understanding Intellectual Development.* Hinsdale, Ill.: Dryden.

RUNDQUIST, E. A. 1933. Inheritance of spontaneous activity in rats. *J. Comp. Psychol.* 16:415–538.

RUSSELL, DAVID H. 1956. *Children's Thinking.* Boston: Ginn.

RUSSELL, JAMES E. 1965. *Change and Challenge in American Education.* Boston: Houghton Mifflin.

RYAN, KEVIN A., ed. 1975. *Teacher Education.* 74th Yrbk., NSSE, Pt. II. Chicago: Univ. Chicago Press.

————, and MICHAEL C. THOMPSON. 1975. Moral education's muddled mandate: Comments on a survey of Phi Delta Kappans. *Phi Delta Kappan* 56:663–666.

RYANS, DAVID G. 1960. *Characteristics of Teachers: Their Description, Comparison, and Appraisal.* Washington, D.C.: Amer. Council Educ.

SADKER, MYRA, and NANCY FRAZIER. 1973. *Sexism in School and Society.* New York: Harper & Row.

SAFER, MORLEY. 1979. Violence in the Schools. CBS: 60 Minutes. September 1.

SANDERS, NORRIS M. 1966. *Classroom Questions: What Kinds?* New York: Harper & Row.

SARASON, SEYMOUR B., et al. 1960. *Anxiety in Elementary School Children.* New York: Wiley.

SARETSKY, GARY. 1972. The OEO P.C. experiment and the John Henry effect. *Phi Delta Kappan* 53:579–581.

SASSENRATH, J. M., and G. D. YONGE. 1968. Delayed information-feedback, feedback cues, retention set, and delayed retention. *J. Educ. Psychol.* 59:69–73.

SCANDURA, JOSEPH M., et al. 1978. Current status and future directions of educational psychology as a discipline. *Educ. Psychol.* 13:43–56.

SCARR-SALAPATEK, S. 1975. Genetics and the development of intelligence. In

F. Horowitz, ed., *Review of Research in Child Development*, vol. 4. Chicago: Univ. Chicago Press. pp 1–57.

SCHLESSINGER, INA. 1964. Moral education in the Soviet Union. *Phi Delta Kappan* 46:72–75.

SCHMUCK, RICHARD, et al. 1966. *Problem Solving to Improve Classroom Learning.* Chicago: SRA.

SCHNEIDER, E. JOSEPH. 1972. R & D helps kids. *Today's Educ.* 61 (October):64–66.

SCHULTZ, CHARLES B., and ROGER A. SHERMAN. 1976. Social class, development, and differences in reinforcer effectiveness. *Rev. Educ. Res.* 46:25–59.

SCHULZ, R. W. 1966. The role of cognitive organizers in the facilitation of concept learning in elementary school science. Ph.D. dissertation, Purdue Univ.

SCOLLON, ROBERT W. 1957. A study of some communicator variables related to attitude restructuring through motion picture films. *Diss. Abstr. Internat.* 17:400.

SCOTT, J. P. 1962. Critical periods in behavior development. *Sci.* 138:949–958.

SCOTT, WILLIAM A. 1968. Conception of normality. In Edgar F. Borgatta and William W. Lambert, eds., *Handbook of Personality Theory and Research in Child Development*, pp. 974–1008. Chicago: Rand McNally.

SEARS, PAULINE S. 1940. Levels of aspiration in academically successful and unsuccessful children. *J. Abn. Soc. Psychol.* 35:498–536.

SEARS, ROBERT R., et al. 1957. *Patterns of Child-Rearing.* Evanston, Ill.: Row, Peterson.

SEDDON, G. M. 1978. The properties of Bloom's Taxonomy of Educational Objectives for the cognitive domain. *Rev. Educ. Res.* 48:303–323.

SEXTON, PATRICIA. 1970. How the American boy is feminized. *Psychol. Today.* 3:66–67.

SHAPIRO, KAREN R. 1975. An overview of problems encountered in aptitude-interaction (ATI) research for instruction. *AV Comm. Rev.* 23:227–241.

SHAW, FREDERICK. 1963. Educating culturally deprived youth in urban centers. *Phi Delta Kappan* 45:91–97.

SHOEMAKER, DAVID M. 1975. Toward a framework for achievement testing. *Rev. Educ. Res.* 45:127–147.

SHUMSKY, A. 1968. In Search of Teaching Style. New York: Appleton.

SIMON, H. A., and A. NEWELL. 1971. Human problem solving: The state of the theory in 1970. *Amer. Psychol.* 26:145–159.

SIMPSON, WILLIAM M. 1963. A parent looks at teaching. *J. Sec. Educ.* 38:175–181.

SKEELS, HAROLD M. 1940. Some Iowa studies of the mental growth of children in relation to differentials of the environment: A summary. In N. B. Henry, ed., *Intelligence: Its Nature and Nurture*, pp. 281–308. 39th Yrbk., Pt. 2. Chicago: Univ. Chicago Press.

———. 1965. Effects of adoption on children from institutions. *Children* 12:33–34.

———. 1966. *Adult Status of Children with Contrasting Early Life Experience.* Monogr. Soc. Res. Child Devel., 31, No. 3.

SKINNER, B. F. 1948. *Walden Two.* New York: Macmillan.

———. 1950. Are theories of learning necessary? *Psychol. Rev.* 57:193–217.

———. 1954. The science of learning and the art of teaching. *Harv. Educ. Rev.* 24:86–97.

———. 1958. Reinforcement today. *Amer. Psychol.* 13:94–99.

———. 1959. A case history in scientific method. In S. Koch, ed., *Psychology: A Study of a Science*, 2:359–379. New York: McGraw-Hill.

———. 1966. An operant analysis of problem solving. In B. Kleinmuntz, ed., *Problem Solving: Research Methods and Theory*, pp. 225–257. New York: Wiley.

———. 1968. *The Technology of Teaching*. New York: Appleton-Century-Crofts.

———. 1971. *Beyond Freedom and Dignity*. New York: Knopf.

———. 1973. The free and happy student. *Phi Delta Kappan* 55:13–16.

———. 1977a. Herrnstein and the evolution of behaviorism. *Amer. Psychol.* 32:1006–1012.

———. 1977b. Why I am not a cognitive psychologist. *Behaviorism* 5:1–10.

SLEIGHT, W. 1911. Memory and formal training. *Brit. J. Psychol.* 4:386–457.

SMEDSLUND, JAN. 1964. Educational psychology. *Ann. Rev. Psychol.* 15:251–276.

SMITH, KARL U., and MARGARET F. SMITH. 1966. *Cybernetic Principles of Learning and Educational Design*. New York: Holt, Rinehart & Winston.

SMITH, M. BREWSTER. 1961. Mental health reconsidered. *Amer. Psychol.* 16:299–306.

SMITH, S. G., and B. A. SHERWOOD. 1976. Educational uses of the PLATO computer system. *Sci.* 192:344–352.

SNOW, ROBERT H. 1963. Anxieties and discontents in teaching. *Phi Delta Kappan* 44:318–321.

SOLOMON, RICHARD L. 1964. Punishment. *Amer. Psychol.* 19:239–253.

SONTAG, LESTER W. 1941. The significance of fetal environmental differences. *Amer. J. Obstr. Gynec.* 42:996–1003.

———. 1957. *Maternal Anxieties in Pregnancy and Fetal Behavior*. Report, 26th Pediatric Res. Conf. San Francisco: Univ. Calif. Sch. Med.

———, et al. 1958. *Mental Growth and Personality Development: A Longitudinal Study*. Monogr. Soc. Res. Child Devel., 23, No. 68.

SORENSON, PHILLIP. 1970. Program for Learning in Accordance with Needs. *Phi Delta Kappan* 52:180–181.

SPEARMAN, CHARLES E. 1904. General intelligence objectively determined and measured. *Amer. J. Psychol.* 15:201–293.

———. 1927. *The Abilities of Man: Their Nature and Measurement*. New York: Macmillan.

SPEARS, HAROLD. 1973. Kappans ponder the goals of education. *Phi Delta Kappan* 55:29–32.

SPENCE, KENNETH W. 1947. The role of secondary reinforcement in delayed reward learning. *Psychol. Rev.* 54:1–8.

———. 1951. Theoretical interpretations of learning. In S. S. Stevens, ed., *Handbook of Experimental Psychology*, pp. 609–729. New York: Wiley.

———. 1954. Current interpretations of learning data and some recent developments in stimulus-response theory. In *Kentucky Symposium, Personality Theory, and Clinical Research*, pp. 1–21. New York: Wiley.

———. 1960. *Behavior Theory and Learning*. Englewood Cliffs: Prentice-Hall.

SPENCE, RALPH B. 1928. Lecture and class discussion in teaching educational psychology. *J. Educ. Psychol.* 19:454–462.

STAKE, ROBERT E., et al. 1970. Educational evaluation. *Rev. Educ. Res.* 40:181–320.

STALLINGS, JANE. 1980. Allocated academic learning time revisited, or beyond time on task. *Educ. Res.*, 9 (11) (December):11–16.

STALLINGS, WILLIAM M., et al. 1968. The pass-fail grading option. *Sch. & Soc.* 96:179–180.

STANLEY, JULIAN C. 1979. The study and facilitation of talent for mathematics. In A. Harry Passow, ed., *The Gifted and Talented: Their Education and Development*, pp. 169–185. 78th Yrbk., NSSE, Pt. I. Chicago: Univ. Chicago Press.

STARCH, DANIEL, and EDWARD C. ELLIOTT. 1913. Reliability of grading work in mathematics. *Sch. Rev.* 21:254–259.

STEINBERG, IRA. 1972. Behavioral definition of educational objectives: A critique. In Lawrence G. Thomas, ed., *Philosophical Redirection of Educational Research.* 71st Yrbk., NSSE, Pt. I. Chicago: Univ. Chicago Press.

STEPHENS, JAMES M. 1967. *The Process of Schooling: A Psychological Examination.* New York: Holt, Rinehart & Winston.

STERNBERG, ROBERT J. 1979. The nature of mental abilities. *Amer. Psychol.* 34:214–230.

———, and DOUGLAS K. DETTERMAN, eds. 1979. *Human Intelligence: Perspectives on Its Theory and Measurement.* Norwood, New Jersey: Ablex.

STODOLSKY, SUSAN S., and GERALD LESSER. 1967. Learning patterns in the disadvantaged. *Harv. Educ. Rev.* 37:546–593.

STOKER, HOWARD W., and RUSSELL P. KROPP. 1964. Measurement of cognitive processes. *J. Educ. Meas.* 1:39–42.

STOLUROW, LAWRENCE M. 1965. Model the master teacher and master the teaching model. In John D. Krumboltz, ed., *Learning and the Educational Process*, pp. 223–247. Chicago: Rand McNally.

STRANG, RUTH. 1960. Mental health. In Chester W. Harris, ed., *Encyclopedia of Educational Research*, pp. 823–835. New York: Macmillan.

STRAUSS, SIDNEY. 1972. Learning theories of Gagné and Piaget: Implications for curriculum development. *T.C. Rec.* 74:81–98.

STRIKE, KENNETH A. 1975. The logic of learning by discovery. *Rev. Educ. Res.* 45:461–483.

STRUENING, ELMER, and MARCIA GUTTENTAG, eds. 1975. *Handbook of Evaluation Research.* 2 vols. Beverley Hills: Sage Publ.

STURGES, P. T. 1972. Information delay and retention effect of information in feedback and tests. *J. Educ. Psychol.* 63:32–43.

SUCHMAN, J. RICHARD. 1961. Inquiry training: Building skills for autonomous discovery. *Merrill-Palmer Q.* 7:147–171.

SUPPES, PATRICK. 1964. Predicted in 15 years: A teletype that also talks. *Phi Delta Kappan* 51:103.

———, et al. 1968. *Computer-Assisted Instruction: Stanford's 1965–66 Arithmetic Program.* New York: Academic Press.

———, and MONA MORNINGSTAR. 1972. *Computer-Assisted Instruction at Stanford: 1966–8, Data Models and Evaluation of Arithmetic Programs.* New York: Academic Press.

SYMONDS, PERCIVAL M. 1936. *The Psychology of Parent-Child Relationships.* New York: Appleton-Century-Crofts.

TABA, HILDA. 1967. Teaching strategies for cognitive growth. In E. M. Bower and W. C. Holister, eds., *Behavioral Science Frontiers in Education.* New York: Wiley.

————, and DEBORAH ELKINS. 1966. *Teaching Strategies for the Culturally Deprived.* Chicago: Rand McNally.

TANNENBAUM, MARK A. 1978. The self-concept: A theoretical synthesis. *Diss. Abstr. Internat.* 39 (1-A):205–206.

TARPY, R. M., and F. L. SAWABINI. 1974. Reinforcement delay: A selective review of the last decade. *Psychol. Bull.* 81:984–997.

TELLER, GERALD. 1974. The myths of accountability. *Educ. Lead.* 31:455–456.

TENNYSON, ROBERT D., and OK-CHOON PARK. 1980. The teaching of concepts: A review of instructional design research literature. *Rev. Educ. Res.* 50:55–70.

TERMAN, LEWIS M. 1916. *The Measurement of Intelligence.* Boston: Houghton Mifflin.

————. 1954. The discovery and encouragement of exceptional talent. *Amer. Psychol.* 9:221–230.

————, et al. 1925. *Genetic Studies of Genuis. I. Mental and Physical Traits of a Thousand Gifted Children.* Stanford: Stanford Univ. Press.

————, and MAUD A. MERRILL. 1937. *Measuring Intelligence.* Boston: Houghton Mifflin.

————, and M. H. ODEN. 1947. *The Gifted Grow Up.* Vol. 4, *Genetic Studies of Genius.* Stanford: Stanford Univ. Press.

————, and M. H. ODEN. 1951. The Stanford studies of gifted children. In P. Witty, ed., *The Gifted Child.* Boston: Heath.

TERRELL, GLENN. 1959. Manipulation motivation in children. *J. Comp. Physiol. Psychol.* 52:705–709.

THELEN, HERBERT A. 1967a. *Classroom Grouping for Teachability.* New York: Wiley.

————. 1967b. Matching teachers and pupils. *NEA J.* 56 (April):18–20.

————. 1969. Tutoring by students. *Sch. Rev.* 77:229–244.

THOMAS, DON R., et al. 1968. Production and elimination of disruptive classroom behavior by systematically varying teacher's behavior. *J. Appl. Beh. Anal.* 1:35–45.

THOMPSON, W. R. 1954. The inheritance and development of intelligence. *Proc. Assn. Res. Nerv. Ment. Dis.* 33:209–231.

————, and W. HERON. 1954. The effects of restricting early experience on the problem-solving capacity of dogs. *Canad. J. Psychol.* 8:17–31.

THOMPSON, WILLIAM R., and R. MELZACK. 1956. Early environment. *Sci. Amer.* 194:38–52.

THORNDIKE, EDWARD L. 1913a. *Educational Psychology.* Vol. 1: *The Original Nature of Man.* New York: Teachers College, Columbia Univ.

————. 1913b. *The Psychology of Learning: Educational Psychology.* Vol. 2. New York: Teachers College, Columbia Univ.

————. 1916. *Educational Psychology: Briefer Course.* New York: Teachers College, Columbia Univ.

————. 1924. Mental discipline in high school studies. *J. Educ. Psychol.* 15:1–22, 83–98.

————. 1931. *Human Learning.* New York: Appleton-Century-Crofts.

————. 1932. *Fundamentals of Learning.* New York: Teachers College, Columbia Univ.

————, and ROBERT S. WOODWORTH. 1901. The influence of improvement in one mental function upon efficiency of other functions. *Psychol. Rev.* 8:247–261, 384–395.

THORNDIKE, ROBERT L. 1963. The measurement of creativity. *T.C. Rec.* 64:422–424.

———. 1968. Review of R. Rosenthal and L. Jacobson. Pygmalion in the Classroom. *Amer. Educ. Res. J.* 5:709–711.

THURSTONE, LOUIS L. 1935. *Vectors of the Mind.* Chicago: Univ. Chicago Press.

TIMBERGEN, N. 1951. *The Study of Instinct.* London: Oxford Univ. Press.

TOBIAS, SIGMUND. 1976. Achievement Treatment Interactions. *Rev. Educ. Res.* 46:61–74.

TOFFLER, ALVIN. 1970. *Future Shock.* New York: Random House.

TOLMAN, EDWARD C. 1932. *Purposive Behavior in Animals and Men.* New York: Appleton.

———. 1948. Cognitive maps in rats and men. *Psychol. Rev.* 55:189–218.

———. 1959. Principles of purposive behavior. In S. Koch, ed., *Psychology: A Study of a Science,* 2:92–157. New York: McGraw-Hill.

TRAINER, F. E. 1977. A critical analysis of Kohlberg's contribution to the study of moral thought. *J. Theory Soc. Beh.* 7:41–63.

TRAVERS, ROBERT M. W. 1966. Toward taking the fun out of building a theory of instruction. *T.C. Rec.* 68:49–60.

———. 1973. *Educational Psychology: The Scientific Foundation for Educational Practice.* New York, Macmillan.

———. 1977. *Essentials of Learning.* New York: Macmillan.

———, ed. 1973. *Second Handbook of Research on Teaching.* Chicago: Rand McNally.

TREFFINGER, DONALD J., et al., eds. 1977. *Handbook on Teaching Educational Psychology.* New York: Academic Press.

TRYON, R. C. 1940. Genetic differences in maze learning ability in rats. In G. M. Whipple, ed., *Intelligence: Its Nature and Nurture,* pp. 111–119. 39th Yrbk., NSSE, Pt. I. Chicago: Univ. Chicago Press.

———, and W. E. HENRY. 1950. How children learn personal and social adjustment. In N. B. Henry, ed., 1950. *Learning and Instruction,* pp. 156–182. 49th Yrbk., NSSE, Pt. I. Chicago: Chicago Univ. Press.

TURNER, RICHARD L. 1975. An overview of research on teacher education. In Kevin A. Ryan, ed., *Teacher Education,* pp. 87–110. 74th Yrbk., NSSE, Pt. II. Chicago: Univ. Chicago Press.

———, and R. THOMPSON. 1974. Relationships between college student ratings of instructors and residual learning. Paper presented at Annual Meeting, Amer. Educ. Res. Assn., Chicago.

TWINING, WILBUR E. 1949. Mental practice and physical practice in learning a motor skill. *Res. Quart.* 20:432–435.

TYLER, RALPH W. 1973. Ralph Tyler discusses behavioral objectives. *Today's Educ.* 62 (October):41–46.

UNDHEIM, JOHAN Q., and JOHN L. HORN. 1977. Critical evaluation of Guilford's structure-of-intellect theory. *Intelligence* 1:65–81.

UNDERWOOD, BENTON J. 1957. Interference and forgetting. *Psychol. Rev.* 64:49–60.

———. 1961. Ten years of massed practice on distributed practice. *Psychol. Rev.* 68:229–247.

———. 1964. Laboratory studies of verbal learning. In E. R. Hilgard, ed., *Theories of Learning and Instruction,* pp. 133–152. 63d Yrbk., NSSE, Pt. I. Chicago: Univ. Chicago Press.

UNGER, RHODA K. 1979a. *Female and Male: Psychological Perspectives.* New York: Harper & Row.

———. 1979b. Toward a redefinition of sex and gender. *Amer. Psychol.* 34:1085–1094.

U.S. NEWS & WORLD REPORT. 1972. A novel plan for teaching gets low grade in new report. *U.S. News,* February 14, p. 5.

———. 1975a. Another problem for the schools. *U.S. News,* June 9, p. 43.

———. 1975b. Another problem for the schools: Declining test scores. *U.S. News,* June 9.

———. 1975c. Girls lag in tests: Unequal education. *U.S. News,* October 20.

———. 1978. The great national rip-off. *U.S. News,* July 3, pp. 27–31.

VAN DUSEN, ROXANNE A., and ELEANOR B. SHELDON. 1976. The changing status of American women. *Amer. Psychol.* 31:106–116.

VELDMAN, DONALD J., and JERE E. BROPHY. 1974. Measuring teacher effects on pupils' achievement. *J. Educ. Psychol.* 66:319–324.

VERNON, PHILIP. 1961. *The Structure of Human Abilities.* New York: Wiley.

VOEKS, VIRGINIA. 1970. *On Becoming an Educated Person.* Philadelphia: Saunders.

VON SENDEN, M. V. 1932. *Raum-und Gestaltauffassung bei Operierten Blindgeborenen vor und nach Operation.* Leipzig: Barth.

VON WITTICH, BARBARA. 1972. The impact of the pass-fail system upon achievement of college students. *J. Higher Educ.* 43:499–508.

VREDEVOE, LAWRENCE E. 1965. School discipline. *NASSP Bull.* 49:215–226.

WALBERG, HERBERT J., and SUE D. RASHER. 1977. The ways schooling makes a difference. *Phi Delta Kappan* 58:703–707.

———, and S. C. THOMAS. 1971. *Characteristics of Open Education: Toward an Operational Definition.* Newton: TDR Assoc.

WALLACH, MICHAEL A., and NATHAN KOGAN. 1965. *Modes of Thinking in Young Children.* New York: Holt, Rinehart & Winston.

WALLEN, NORMAN E., and ROBERT M. W. TRAVERS. 1963. Analysis and investigation of teaching methods. In N. L. Gage, ed., *Handbook of Research on Teaching,* pp. 448–505. Chicago: Rand McNally.

WARE, JAMES P. 1978. Student perception of causality in the academic environment: The causal maps of successful and unsuccessful college freshmen. *Diss. Abstr. Internat.* 39 (1-A):206–207.

WASHBURNE, CARLETON W. 1922. Educational measurement as a key to individualizing instruction and promotion. *J. Educ. Res.* 5:195–206.

———, and LOUIS M. HEIL. 1960. What characteristics of teachers affect children's growth. *Sch. Rev.* 37:420–428.

WATSON, JOHN B. 1930. *Behaviorism.* New York: Norton.

———. 1929. *Psychology from the Standpoint of a Behaviorist.* Philadelphia: Lippincott.

WATTENBERG, W. W., and F. REDL. 1950. Mental hygiene. In W. S. Monroe, ed., *Encyclopedia of Educational Research,* pp. 733–745. New York: Macmillan.

WEBB, JEANNINE N. 1970. Taxonomy of cognitive behavior: A system for the analysis of intellectual processes. *J. Res. & Devel. Educ.* 4:23–33.

WECHSLER, DAVID. 1958. *The Measurement and Appraisal of Adult Intelligence.* Baltimore: Williams & Wilkins.

———. 1975. Intelligence defined and undefined: A relativistic appraisal. *Amer. Psychol.* 30:135–139.

———. 1966. The IQ as an intelligence test. *New York Times Mag.,* June 26, p. 12.

WEINER, BERNARD. 1969. Motivation. In Robert L. Ebel, ed., *Encyclopedia of Educational Research,* pp. 878–880. New York: Macmillan.

———. 1972. Attribution theory, achievement motivation, and the educational process. *Rev. Educ. Res.* 42:203–216.

———. 1973. *Theories of Motivation: From Mechanism to Cognition.* Chicago: Markham.

———. 1976. An attributional approach for educational psychology. In Lee Shulman, ed., *Review of Research in Education.* Vol. 4. Itasca, Ill.: Peacock.

———. 1979. A theory of motivation for some classroom experiences. *J. Educ. Psychol.* 71:3–25.

WEINER, LUCY G. 1978. Sex differences in achievement: An attribution approach. *Diss. Abstr. Internat.* 38 (7-A):4065–4066.

WEINSTEIN, GERALD, and MARIO D. FANTINI, eds. 1970. *Toward Humanistic Education: A Curriculum of Affect.* New York: Praeger.

WERTHEIMER, MICHAEL. 1978. Humanistic psychology and the humane but tough-minded psychologist. *Amer. Psychol.* 33:739–745.

WESMAN, ALEXANDER G. 1945. A study of transfer of training from high school subjects to intelligence. *J. Educ. Res.* 39:254–264.

———. 1956. *Aptitude, Intelligence, and Achievement.* Test Service Bull., no. 51.

———. 1968. Intelligent testing. *Amer. Psychol.* 23:367–374.

WHITE, BURTON. 1975. *The First Three Years of Life.* Englewood Cliffs: Prentice-Hall.

WHITE, EDWARD M. 1970. Writing for nobody. *Educ. Dig.* 35 (March):32–33.

WHITE, RICHARD T. 1973. Research and learning hierarchies. *Rev. Educ. Res.* 43:361–375.

WHITE, ROBERT W. 1959. Motivation reconsidered: The concept of competence. *Psychol. Rev.* 66:297–333.

WICKMAN, E. K. 1928. *Children's Behavior and Teachers' Attitudes.* New York: Commonwealth Fund.

WIGHT, ALBERT E. 1962. Beyond behavioral objectives. *Educ. Technol.* (July):9–14.

WILHELMS, FRED T. 1960. *The Professional Education Period as a Time of Self-Discovery and Personal Development.* San Francisco: San Francisco State College.

WILLIAMS, ROBERT L. 1973. Black IQ test a BITCH. *Phi Delta Kappan* 55:86.

WILSON, JOHN, et al. 1967. *Introduction to Moral Education.* Baltimore: Penguin.

WILSON, JOHN T., and JOHN J. KORAN. 1976. Review of research on mathemagenic behavior: Implications for teaching and learning science. *Sci. Educ.* 60:391–400.

WINTERBOTTOM, MARIAN R. 1958. The relation of need for achievement to learning experiences in independence and mastery. In J. W. Atkinson, ed., *Motives in Fantasy, Action, and Society.* Princeton: Van Nostrand.

WITKIN, A. H. 1962. Origins of cognitive styles. In C. Scheerer, ed., *Cognition: Theory, Research, and Promise,* pp. 127–205. New York: Harper & Row.

———. 1964. *Personality through Perception.* New York: Harper & Row.

————, et al. 1977. Field-dependent and field-independent cognitive styles and their educational implications. *Rev. Educ. Res.* 47:1–64.

WITTROCK, MERL C. 1978a. The cognitive movement in instruction. *Educ. Psychol.* 13:15–29. (also Educ. Res., Feb. 1979, 8 (2), 5–11).

————. 1978b. Developmental processes in learning from instruction. *J. Genet. Psychol.* 132:37–54.

WOLF, A. 1943. The dynamics of the selective inhibition of specific functions in neurotics. *Psychomat. Med.* 5:27–38.

WOLFE, JOHN B. 1936. Effectiveness of token rewards for chimpanzees. *Comp. Psychol. Monogr.* 12, no. 5.

WOODRUFF, A. D. 1951. *The Psychology of Teaching.* New York: Longmans.

ZELLNECKER, T., and W. E. JEFFREY. 1978. Attention and cognitive style. In G. Hale and M. Lewis, eds., *Attention and the Development of Attentional Skills.* New York: Plenum.

ZIGLER, EDWARD. 1978. The effectiveness of Head Start: Another look. *Educ. Psychol.* 13:71–77.

Author Index

Subject Index